CHRISTIAN MEDITATION

INSPIRED BY YOGA

AND

A Course in Miracles

CHRISTIAN MEDITATION

INSPIRED BY YOGA

AND

A Course in Miracles

~ . ~

OPENING TO DIVINE LOVE
IN CONTEMPLATION

Donald James Giacobbe

Miracle Yoga Services

Published by Miracle Yoga Services
— miracleyoga@gmail.com —
Cottonwood, Arizona

Printed in the United States of America

BISAC Subject Codes and Headings:

OCC010000 Body, Mind, and Spirit: Meditation

OCC027510 Body, Mind, and Spirit: Spirituality—*A Course in Miracles*

REL012080 Religion: Christian Life—Prayer

Library of Congress Control Number: 2011904984

Giacobbe, Donald James
Christian Meditation Inspired by Yoga and *A Course in Miracles*:
Opening to Divine Love in Contemplation

ISBN 978-0-9843790-1-9

CONTENTS

~ o ~

PREFACE

~ ∘ ~

If you are a beginner, in your first attempts at meditation, you may wonder if you will be able to calm the many thoughts of the mind and find peace within. Before choosing the current title of this meditation manual, one alternative I considered was *How to Get Wet in an Ocean of Love*. I felt this alternative conveyed the comforting idea that learning cannot be difficult when it is in accord with your own nature. Does a saltwater fish in the ocean have to learn how to get wet? A saltwater fish is born and lives in the ocean and being wet is its natural condition. Similarly, you live in an ocean of divine love, and so you are already wet with the love in which you live and breathe.

If this is true, why does this divine love seem so far away? Although love is your natural condition, you have become so involved with *doing* that you have forgotten how to be aware of your natural condition of *being*. You cannot really learn how to get wet with love, but you can learn to realize you are already wet with love. This meditation manual is designed to show you how to quiet your mind and find peace by setting aside the distractions that have limited your awareness. Through finding peace, you can learn to first understand, then appreciate, and finally realize your oneness with divine love that is your true nature.

Hopefully the Spirit within you has guided you to read this meditation manual and that same Spirit will continue to guide you to apply the information, techniques, and disciplines that would be most beneficial for your spiritual growth and to set aside that which would not benefit your growth. You need only to pray to God for His help and remain sensitive and open to His spiritual promptings to further your spiritual journey.

ACKNOWLEDGMENTS

I am grateful for the support, suggestions, and encouragement of my sister Lillian Blackburn and my friend Stuart Dean. I appreciate the copy editing assistance of Marla Markman, and the additional copy editing contributions from Gayle Rodcay, Tina Hardy, Kelly Lydick, Ron Nelson, Charlene Gier, and Christopher Gibbons. My thanks go to Jerry Paul, Nancy Bonfield, and Lillian Blackburn for their service as proofreaders.

ABOUT THE AUTHOR

Donald James Giacobbe recorded his life story in his autobiography *Memory Walk in the Light*. He was employed for sixteen years as a case manager serving developmentally disabled clients. The professional nature of his work limited his ability to express his spiritual motivations overtly, so out of necessity he served as an "undercover agent" for God.

A more direct approach to spirituality was facilitated by living with Zen Buddhist seekers and then being part of a yoga community. Later he was the director of the Aquarian Age Yoga Center in Virginia Beach, VA. He served as an instructor of meditation and yoga, teaching college courses and appearing on television. He specialized in providing yoga teacher training certification courses and leading meditation workshops and retreats. Don has attempted in his teaching of meditation to strip away the rituals of Zen Buddhism and yoga practices and transpose only the bare essence into a Christian context. Techniques of meditation inspired by Eastern sources enhance the use of traditional Christian practices, such as the "Jesus Prayer," and lead to the overshadowing of the Holy Spirit that occurs in Christian contemplation.

Don encourages the doing of God's Will, being receptive to the Holy Spirit, and finding Christ within the temple of one's own heart. While respecting all spiritual expressions, he became a monk by making his vow directly to God, without the stamp of approval from any religious organization. For many years Don used the term "Christian yoga" to describe his spiritual path, which combined following Christ with yoga disciplines. But in recent years he has adopted the term "Miracle Yoga" to describe the specific path of Christian yoga he has chosen. This form of spirituality is a synthesis of yoga and the philosophy of "A Course in Miracles," encouraging the seeker to see with "forgiving eyes" and to perceive Christ in everyone. Don's goal is to maintain a balance between opening to divine love inwardly and allowing that love to be extended outwardly to others.

INTRODUCTION

≈ ∘ ≈

Since this meditation manual is titled *Christian Meditation Inspired by Yoga and "A Course in Miracles": Opening to Divine Love in Contemplation*, a good starting point would be to define the terms in the title. The word "meditation" may be considered the directing of the mind continuously toward one thought. This focusing brings about receptivity to the Holy Spirit and allows you to let go of distracting thoughts. The purpose of your focusing depends upon your spiritual aspirations.

The spiritual aspirations for a Christian would be directly or at least indirectly related to Christ. For many Christians the word "Christ" is exclusively related to Jesus, Who perfectly embodied Christ, so He is known as Jesus Christ. Yet this book takes the broad view that you, too, can identify yourself with your true nature in the one universal Christ that *every* seeker shares. The word "Christian" can be defined as referring to anyone who is a follower of Christ as a spiritual ideal. A follower of Christ may belong to a group, such as a traditional church of a particular denomination or a less structured nontraditional group. Of course, Christians who participate in group worship usually also recognize the importance of a private daily prayer life. In addition, there are followers of Christ who do not choose to belong to any group form of worship, but are concerned solely with developing a personal relationship with God based on inner attunement. The primary purpose of this book is to encourage individual worship by asking you (whether you belong to a religious group or not) to set up an altar within your own personal church, the body, which is the temple of the Holy Spirit, and to offer prayer and meditation at that altar.

This meditation manual encourages both personal and universal devotion, although one may be more important to you than the other. One kind of personal devotion is the opening of your mind and heart to Jesus, for example, by repeating the Divine Name of Jesus, if you are attracted to that form of worship. However, hopefully your personal devotion is not limited to only an acknowledgment of the divine nature of Jesus. Ideally your personal devotion to Jesus can be practiced as an affirmation of your own divine life in the universal Christ that you share with Jesus. In order to affirm the divine within, you may not be drawn to focusing on Jesus, but you may prefer to focus primarily or exclusively on the universal Christ within. There is also the possibility you may want to express a universal devotion directed toward the Oneness of God. Whether your devotion is mostly personal or mostly universal, the key element in your inward practice will be your receptivity to the Holy Spirit.

Jesus is the one who became perfectly identified with the universal Christ. But the universal Christ takes many forms, and you are one of them, yet unaware of your own true nature. Jesus, in becoming aware of His own true nature, is rightly called the "Christ." Following Christ means following the example of Jesus who became the Christ. The long-term aspect of you following Christ is to ultimately become fully identified with your true divine nature in the universal Christ, one with God and one with the Holy Spirit. The short-term aspect of following Christ is to increasingly allow the love of God to flow through you. The love that exists between the universal Christ, the Father, and the Holy Spirit is the ocean of love that is your natural condition of being that you have forgotten. Even though your natural condition is hidden from your conscious awareness, your true nature remains with you, eternally unchanged, having been created by God.

In the yoga philosophy of Vedanta, a term that would be roughly equivalent to the universal Christ is the "Self" (or *Atman*). Since this meditation manual is about a joining of the East and West, this book will at times refer to the universal Christ that you share with Jesus Christ as your true Self or your "Christ Self." However, you may prefer to use the terms "spirit," "the body of Christ," "Christ Consciousness," or some other terminology. Followers of Christ will never have a theology that is universally accepted. Consequently, it is a given that you will have your own terminology and ideas about the meaning of Christ within.

Although there will never be a common Christian theology, there is a *common experience* of the divine within. Fortunately the focus in this manual is on this common experience, rather than theology, which can be divisive. Although there are no dogmas in this book, a fundamental premise of this manual is that the universal Christ is within and can be experienced. This experience that occurs during inward seeking can be called a "remembering" or "recognizing" because these terms imply that your experience of the universal Christ is a "re-knowing"—a regaining of your true nature that has never left you, but has merely been hidden from your conscious awareness. This meditation manual is designed to help you learn how to become increasingly receptive to the Holy Spirit and to experience the universal Christ within. Hopefully you will not allow your theology, whatever it may be, to become a stumbling block to your experience of the universal Christ within.

Speaking of stumbling blocks to the experience of Christ, it needs to be noted that in our society today there are many "alienated Christians." These are individuals who had been raised as Christian church goers, but who for one reason or another have left organized religion. In some cases the reason for leaving was that their church seemed only to make them feel increasingly guilty. In other cases, they could not accept a particular dogma that was integral to their church's teachings. Sometimes this dogma was a zealous and narrow-minded viewpoint that taught that if you do not worship God in a particular way, there would be no salvation for you.

Often these alienated Christians have linked their image of Jesus Christ with the dogma of their former church, so they feel a need to reject Jesus along with rejecting their former church. If you are one of these alienated Christians, you may not realize that Jesus Christ is not a judgmental figure that requires His followers to hold certain set beliefs about Him. Jesus loves you unconditionally, regardless of your beliefs or shortcomings. Your relationship with Jesus is entirely based on His love for you and your openness to loving Him.

On the other hand, there are many alienated Christians who are not alienated with Christ Himself. Often these individuals still would like to follow Christ and are receptive to finding a closer connection with Christ within. If you are one of these alienated Christians, you are, of course, encouraged to use the techniques you will find herein to deepen your inner life with Christ. Also, if you do not currently consider yourself a follower of Christ, but if you at least have an openness to exploring that possibility through learning to meditate, hopefully this manual will be helpful for you.

Some Christian seekers have turned to yoga for answers. The word "yoga" literally means "yoking together" or "union" related to the union of the soul with God. Of course, divine union is the ultimate aim of Christian spiritual seeking. What does yoga have to offer you in this process of spiritual seeking? Yoga has much to offer, although this depends upon your openness to choosing a "road less traveled." Many Christians view yoga with skepticism, yet yoga has become increasingly acceptable when it is presented in the form of yoga body postures and breathing practices, which are seen as a way to reduce stress and improve health. However, most Christians generally do not recognize the value of meditation and specifically do not understand how yoga influences can improve their ability to contact the Spirit within.

Two extreme views regarding yoga need to be avoided. One extreme is that yoga has nothing to offer the Christian seeker. The other extreme is that yoga has all the answers. Those who are open to pursuing a moderate course between these two extremes find that there are not many options available for learning about the benefits of using yoga practices within a Christian context. There are some Christian ashrams in India, notably ones started by two pioneers of East/West understanding, the monastic J.M. Déchanet and Father Bede Griffiths. But I do not know of any Christian-based yoga communities or centers in America that could provide a Christian context for learning about yoga methods. Sometimes Christian seekers who cannot find a Christian context for learning Eastern practices will feel that their only option is to go to yoga communities that focus on the teachings of specific Hindu gurus. Nevertheless, through joining such communities, there is the very real possibility of the seeker losing his focus on Christ.

This book has been written as a blueprint for how to incorporate Eastern influences into the Christian spiritual life. In particular, this book presents a systematic series of meditation practices that are a blending of Christian and yoga disciplines. These practices, as a synthesis of Christian and yoga techniques, can serve as a *secondary means* for your spiritual growth. The *primary means* for your spiritual growth is receptivity to the Holy Spirit, which will allow these methods to actually lead you toward your goal. The need for receptivity is emphasized in this meditation manual by repeatedly using the words "open," "openness," and "opening." All spiritual growth is directly related to your degree of openness, which is required both for inner attunement and outer extension. The ultimate goal of this openness is divine union with God. You grow toward this goal by increasingly revealing your true Self in Christ and by extending love to your brothers and sisters. Focusing in particular on Christ in a personal and/or universal manner helps you to grow toward your goal. The yoga influences presented in this book are integrated into a Christian context that will help you stay focused on Christ.

Prior experience with hatha yoga postures and breathing techniques, especially daily practice of these methods, helps to prepare the body and mind for learning to meditate. If you want to learn how to do yoga postures and breathing practices, you are encouraged to receive personal instruction from a hatha yoga teacher who is not affiliated with any religious organization. Yoga postures and breathing practices are very helpful preparations for meditation, but are not an absolute requirement for benefitting from this manual, which focuses mainly on ways in which meditation can be enhanced by yoga influences. The meditation techniques are explained with a Christian emphasis so that the yoga influences do not become a distraction from focusing on Christ.

One of the specific ways in which this book is influenced by Eastern sources is that the meditation techniques incorporate body awareness as part of the practice. For example, some techniques coordinate the breathing with the repeating of a Christian sacred word or phrase. Most traditional Christian meditation techniques avoid focusing on body awareness. The importance of body awareness in meditation methods is addressed in Chapter 5. The approach that is taken in this book is not to eliminate traditional methods that do not use body awareness, but rather to combine these with nontraditional techniques that incorporate the positive use of body awareness inspired by Eastern influences.

Your goal in meditation is to open to "divine love" and allowing that love to flow through you to others. This experience of divine love may also be called the *divine embrace*, which is another way of describing the goal of yoga, meaning the goal of union. The words "divine embrace" specifically convey the connotation that you want a personal encounter with the divine within. Accomplishing this goal of the divine embrace involves inviting the Holy Spirit not only into the mind, but into all aspects of yourself. This includes inviting the Holy Spirit into every part of the body in order to remove inner obstacles to the divine embrace. The divine presence is embracing you even now, but you can only become consciously aware of the divine love within you by removing inner obstacles that are blocking your awareness. Some of the meditation techniques in this manual include focusing on a specific part of the body to help center the mind, to invite the Holy Spirit into that part of the body, and to release inner blocks related to that part of the body. Removing inner blocks replaces tension with positive energy and creates an openness to the divine within. The removal of inner obstacles also facilitates the natural and beneficial rising of the kundalini, which is part of the purification process of meditation. This slow and natural rising of the kundalini in the practice of meditation is in stark contrast to the sudden and traumatic rising of the kundalini that can sometimes occur due to certain yoga disciplines, such as very extreme breathing practices.

How the body can become a vehicle for spiritual transformation is not well understood in the West, but is very much a part of Eastern understanding and spiritual practices. The systematic process of how to allow the body to become an effective vehicle for Christian spiritual transformation is described in Chapter 8 and elaborated on in Chapter 11. For Christians in the West, meditation methods that include coordinating the breathing and focusing on different parts of the body represent a new and unique way to approach inward seeking. However, adopting these practices does not mean incorporating Hindu words or foreign rituals that would be inappropriate for Christians. These meditation techniques are integrated into an entirely Christian context in which the number one priority is reliance on the action and grace of the Holy Spirit.

Although the word "yoga" is usually translated as "union," it can also be interpreted as "integration." The purpose of joining Christianity and yoga, which can be called "Christian yoga," is integration. However, this joining of East and West in Christian yoga is not an example of syncretism in which Christianity loses its distinctive focus on Christ and faith in Christ. In fact, the Christian yoga of meditation that is presented in this manual is a way of using yoga techniques to intensify the focus on Christ in order to bring about the goal of integration. The word "integration" can be defined as the coordination of all aspects of yourself working together to bring about wholeness, which in a spiritual sense could refer to the ultimate goal of union with God.

The overall effect of the combining traditional and nontraditional meditation methods advocated in this manual is to bring about an integration and unification of the various levels of your being and to deepen your meditation experience. However, these techniques are only the beginning of this integration and unification process. The purpose of the meditation techniques is to prepare you for entering *contemplation*. Contemplation is an overshadowing of the Holy Spirit in which the mind becomes still without needing a focusing object. Through contemplation the Holy Spirit can lead you to a greater degree of integration and unification that will transform you. The transformation process that begins with techniques and that is taken to a deeper level with contemplation is essentially a process of letting go of darkness and accepting the light. You will need to be willing to allow your hidden shadow side to be uncovered and surrendered to the light. This takes pure faith, requiring receptivity and courage. Through facing your dark side and letting go of selfish attachments, you are able to increasingly reveal and accept your true Self in Christ.

Meditation is sometimes mistakenly thought of as a nebulous and airy endeavor, when it is actually both a science and an art, which can be learned only through determined daily application and growth over time. Meditation, as it is presented in this manual, is a doorway leading to contemplation, which brings you into *His World*, an inner world with its own laws and way of being. There are doors within you that are closed. Meditation in coordination with the Holy Spirit helps to open these inner doors, creating a doorway to His World. This sacred inner world needs to be approached with earnestness, respectfulness, and consistency. This book provides a step-by-step approach to entering His World and going to deeper levels of His World. Coming into His World is a journey of discovery and transformation. The meditation methods provided here will help build a solid foundation for making this journey of transformation.

However, these meditation techniques leading to contemplation only represent a part of your transformation. Your transformation will involve changes in your inner meditative life as you become immersed in His World, but your transformation will also involve changes in your outer life manifested in the everyday world. Your goal will be to find balance between living in His World and living in your everyday world. Here again, the word "integration" can be helpful to describe the wholeness you are seeking by reconciling your inner meditative experience and your outer experience of the world. In addition to the general definition provided above, the word "integration" can be defined with a more specific psychological meaning. Therefore, integration can be identified as the coordination of perception, behavior, and personality to bring about harmony with others and with the environment. In this sense, integration can refer to not only the universal goal of divine union, but also simultaneously to the more specific goal of harmony in everyday living in the world. Thus integrated spiritual living is the manifestation of a harmonious interrelation between His World and your everyday world. This is the hope of the prayer, "Thy Will be done on earth as it is in Heaven,"—letting the outer expression in the world come forth from His World as a reflection of inner divine peace.

This book consists of three distinct parts, described as follows:

PART ONE: THE PRACTICE OF CHRISTIAN MEDITATION

This part describes how to make a commitment to deepen your spiritual growth and learn meditation through practical experience. This includes a Twenty-eight Day Demonstration for a beginning meditator, although intermediate meditators would also benefit from this four-week meditation program. You are exposed to five basic meditation techniques that use affirmations and body awareness, and also a sixth method, called "Inner Silence Meditation," in which you let go of body awareness. These six meditation techniques, used in a particular sequence, are steps that lead to higher awareness. These simple steps are like the rungs of Jacob's ladder. Jacob's dream image in the Old Testament of a ladder stretching from earth to Heaven symbolizes various levels of consciousness. These six techniques form the specific portion of Jacob's ladder that leads in a step-by-step manner from lower levels of attunement to contemplation. This combination of techniques is called "Christian Yoga Meditation" because it is a synthesis of the best of what the East and West have to offer. Combining these techniques in this particular six-stage sequence provides a very solid foundation for leading you toward experiencing contemplation.

PART TWO: GUIDELINES FOR DEEPENING MEDITATION

This part offers practical guidelines to show you how to prepare for the gift of contemplation in a systematic manner. This section includes a One Year Program to help you deepen your meditation experience. The six meditation techniques used in Christian Yoga Meditation are experienced separately for one month at a time. For example, one month you use a method that focuses on establishing physical receptivity to the Spirit. On other months you use methods that focus on emotional receptivity and mental receptivity. There are also specific techniques for developing your intuitions and for integrating various levels of your being. In addition, there is an emphasis on learning to practice Inner Silence Meditation, which produces a unifying effect that prepares you to enter contemplation.

After experiencing each of the individual techniques of Christian Yoga Meditation separately for a month at a time, they are then experienced in combination. The result of your practice will be a greater integration and unification of the physical, emotional, mental, and intuitive levels of your being. In turn, this increased integration and unification opens you to contemplation in which you are overshadowed by the Holy Spirit. Through practicing Christian Yoga Meditation on a daily basis and experiencing contemplation, you increasingly become aware of your true spiritual nature.

The primary method of meditation recommended in this manual is Christian Yoga Meditation because all by itself it is sufficient to prepare you for contemplation. However, additional techniques beyond those included in Christian Yoga Meditation are described in this part of the manual to address areas of special interest. There is an emphasis on releasing emotional patterns and refining your feeling nature in order to become sensitive to your intuitive feelings. If you have an interest in the awareness of divine love and light, this section includes methods that expand your ability to experience love and light consciously during meditation.

All of the techniques of meditation are a means of helping you to make progress toward being drawn into contemplation. There are two paths of contemplation that are described for your consideration. One contemplative path is the *path of darkness*—seeking God in pure faith, as was exemplified by St. John of the Cross. The other contemplative path is the *path of light*—also seeking God through faith but with an emphasis on opening to divine light, as was demonstrated by St. Symeon the New Theologian.

PART THREE: MEDITATION AND OVERALL SPIRITUAL GROWTH

This part extends beyond the "how to" aspects of meditation and explores a variety of ways in which meditation plays a part in your spiritual growth as a whole. Chapter 17 highlights the use of prayer and meditation as expressions of doing God's Will in your experience of everyday living. Chapter 18 addresses how to seek guidance and the importance of developing nonattachment.

Chapter 19 deals with relationships in relation to meditation. The practice of meditation is often thought of as an inner—and what might be called a "vertical"—form of seeking that only involves deepening your personal relationship with God. However, a Christian approach to spirituality must incorporate both inner and outer—both vertical and horizontal—forms of seeking that together express the two directions of the cross of Christ. This chapter on relationships focuses on horizontal types of seeking, which involve finding God's presence in your brothers and sisters through manifesting loving relationships. Resolving problems in relation to others is emphasized because in order for inner wholeness to be authentic, it must be expressed outwardly as well as inwardly.

PART FOUR: MEDITATION IN *A COURSE IN MIRACLES*

The fourth and concluding part of this meditation manual addresses meditation and some other aspects of spiritual growth that are related to the spiritual philosophy of *A Course in Miracles*. The first drafts of this meditation manual were written prior to my study of this particular philosophy. But later in my spiritual development, I became a student and advocate of *A Course in Miracles*, which for simplicity will be referred to as the "Course." There are no direct quotations from the Course in the first nineteen chapters of this book, but the ideas expressed in these pages are in most cases identical to or at least very similar to the spiritual principles of the Course. One notable exception can be found in Chapter 19, which describes a method of problem solving that involves a careful analysis of your problems. Analyzing your problems in detail is not compatible with the philosophy of the Course, as will be explained in Chapter 21.

One part of the Course is the *Text*, which explains the philosophical foundation for living a life of extending forgiveness and love to others. Another part of the Course is the *Workbook for Students*, which offers lessons in how to put the philosophy into practical application in your life. For instance, there are lessons provided in how to practice various kinds of meditation. Some general spiritual principles from the Course are included in Chapters 20 through 24 of this meditation manual, but the primary focus in these chapters is on how to understand and apply the approach to meditation recommended by the Course. The objective is to help you open yourself to divine love inwardly in your attunement practices and then to allow that love to extend outwardly to bring blessings to your brothers and sisters. Chapters 23 and 24, the final two chapters, address the importance of moving from an ego-based thought system to a thought system guided by the Holy Spirit. This involves the process of systematically changing false perceptions into true perceptions. Filling the mind with only true perceptions is a preparation for finally awakening to your true nature in God.

This book has been written with an eye toward providing new information to those who are not familiar with the Course and offering helpful insights to those who are already Course students. Those who are familiar with the Course may ask, "Why is such a great emphasis placed on body awareness in this manual in contrast to the Course that does not emphasize the body?" The answer is that the Course states that the purpose of the body is to be a "communication device." The Course is silent about all the specific, different ways the body can be used for divine communication because its philosophy is focused on content rather than form. This meditation manual does not contradict the Course, but merely elaborates upon the many ways in which the form of the body can lead to the content of opening the mind to divine communication. For example, hatha yoga is suggested not for the perfection of the body, but rather as a means of preparing the body to serve as a communication device in meditation.

A more important example of utilizing the body appropriately and effectively is the use of Eastern body awareness techniques with the guidance of the Holy Spirit. These techniques help to release inner blocks and allow the rising of creative energy within the body to make the body the most effective communication device to facilitate divine communion. A prominent theme throughout this meditation manual is the importance of love. This theme is directly related to the aim of the Course, which is described in its introduction as, "...removing the blocks to the awareness of love's presence, which is your natural inheritance."[1] Just as the Course strongly recommends relying on the guidance of the Holy Spirit, this meditation manual encourages you to open your mind to this guidance that comes from within. The fundamental premise is that your spiritual seeking is not about acquiring the truth and indeed the divine presence from outside yourself. Rather, it is about becoming fully aware of the truth and the divine presence of love that is already within you, but which has been hidden yet not lost.

The Holy Spirit...merely teaches you how to remove the blocks that stand between you and what you know. His memory is yours.... Remembrance of reality is in Him, and therefore in you.[2]

The words on the back cover of this meditation manual summarize both the contents and the purpose for reading it. Eastern and Western meditation methods are identified as the means for inner attunement presented here. On the back cover there is a one-sentence quotation from the Course that identifies the goal. Below is the two-paragraph context of that sentence:

All that is needful is to train our minds to overlook all little senseless aims, and to remember that our goal is God. His memory is hidden in our minds, obscured but by our pointless little goals, which offer nothing, and do not exist. Shall we continue to allow God's grace to shine in unawareness, while the toys and trinkets of the world are sought instead? God is our only goal, our only Love. We have no aim but to remember Him.

Our goal is but to follow in the way that leads to You. We have no goal but this. What could we want but to remember You? What could we seek but our Identity?[3]

---

1. T-in.1:7, p. 1
2. T-14.IV.9:5,6,8, p. 281. For those who may not be familiar with references to *A Course in Miracles*, T-14 is the chapter number of the Text, and IV means the fourth section of that chapter. The 9 is the ninth paragraph of that section. The 5, 6, and 8 refer to the fifth, sixth, and eighth sentences in that ninth paragraph. All the page numbers, such as page 281, are for the second and third editions, in paperback or hard cover, of *A Course in Miracles*, Copyright © 1975, 1985, 1992, 2008 by the Foundation for Inner Peace, Inc. P.O. Box 598, Mill Valley, CA 94942-0598.
3. W-258.1:1-5, 2:1-4, p. 423. W-258 is Workbook Lesson 258. The 1 is the first paragraph. The 1-5 refers to the five sentences in the first paragraph. The 2 is the second paragraph. The 1-4 refers to the four sentences in the second paragraph. All page numbers, such as page 423, are for the second and third editions, in paperback or hard cover, of *A Course in Miracles*.

PART ONE

≈ • ≈

THE PRACTICE
OF
CHRISTIAN
MEDITATION

1

WHY MEDITATE?

≈ • ≈

A. Your Motivation for Meditation

The first question you may want to ask yourself is, "Why do I want to meditate?" You may not be satisfied with your prayer life and seek to - good about your communication with God through prayer, but would like to enhance your spiritual life with meditation. Perhaps you may already practice meditation and would like to deepen your meditation experience in order to lead you to contemplation.

Regardless of your background or your experience, the most basic answer to the question "Why meditate?" is that you wish to deepen your relationship with God. This desire for a deeper relationship with God usually originates from a realization that there is a "void" in your life. You can fill your life with activities to fill this void, but you will only be able to temporarily *avoid the void*.

This void is a feeling of incompleteness. You may seek satisfaction and completeness in accumulating money and possessions, in sexual activity, in finding the right partner, perhaps in raising children, in your vocation, in travel, in recreation, and in creative outlets. You understand that all these activities of your life are important, but they are like pieces in a puzzle that do not quite fit together to make a complete picture. It appears to you that there is a major piece of the puzzle that is missing. You may even go to church and adopt all the concepts of your church and not find the missing piece there, either. Because you feel incomplete, you also feel alone and isolated. Perhaps you feel no one loves you, or even if you feel loved by others, you may still feel incomplete.

All these ways of seeking to fill the void in your life are attempts to find the missing piece to the puzzle by looking outside of yourself. All such attempts will ultimately fail. But in that failure comes a grace. There is a Voice inside you that is unlike the many voices, the many desires within you, shouting for your attention. This is a quiet Voice that is whispering, "I love you. Look inside, and you will find Me?" When you give up seeking completion outside of yourself, you can begin to listen to this Voice, not with your ears, but with your heart. This is where seeking to deepen your relationship with God begins. You may try to pray by speaking to God, or if you wish to go deeper within, you may want to enhance your ability to listen to God.

Meditation can help you to listen to God, but needs to be viewed properly. Meditation can be defined as *receptive communication with God*, which may be facilitated by the repeating of one thought in order to quiet the mind and increase your awareness of the divine presence. The holding of one thought in the mind, such as the repeating of the Name of Jesus Christ, is merely a technique. It is not a magic formula that creates an awareness of God. What makes it work is your faith, your intentions, your commitment, and, most of all, God's grace.

There are two elements that may be considered the keys to spiritual growth. The first is *desire* and the second is *application*. You can have spiritual growth to the degree that you both *want* it and are willing to put that wanting into *practical application*. You have been told in scripture that if you seek, you will find, if you knock, the door will open, and if you ask, it will be given. God, for His part, is always willing to give you more blessings than you are willing to receive. Consequently, it is your responsibility to open yourself to receive those graces, which He would so willingly give to you.

Your receptivity begins with your desire for God and the desire to deepen your relationship with Him is already in your heart, planted there by His grace. Your desire for God is like a seed within you, and, as with any seed, you cannot force it to grow. What you can do is simply allow yourself to become aware of the presence of that seed of your desire for Him and water it by paying careful attention to it. You may think of meditation as this act of "paying careful attention" to the desire for God within you that increases your receptivity to Him. If you put your desire for God into practical application by taking the small amount of time needed each day to contact this desire, your meditation will be effective in opening your heart and mind to Him. But if you do not take the time to find within yourself this true wanting, then your meditation will tend to become just another temporary self-improvement activity.

B. Entering His World

Those who meditate from a real desire to be closer to God have found that drawing closer to Him involves leaving your own world and entering His World. Your world revolves around you. If you want an outer symbol of your world, you can pull out your driver's license and look at it. You will see a picture of your face, your birthday, your height, your weight, your sex, your address and your driver's license number.

Your driver's license is a symbol of your world in two ways. First, it shows that you are the driver of your world. Your world is a world of "doing," and you are the doer. Second, if you look at your driver's license, whose image do you see on it? It is not the image and likeness of God that you see there, but only an image of your body. Your world of doing centers around your "doing self," which is your thoughts about your body and your mind. The single thought that you are only your body and only your mind contained in your body may be called the "ego." All the other thoughts you have built around the ego can be called the "doing self," your "self-image," or just the "self." All your daily activities, thoughts, feelings, and relationships center around this self, which is the focus of your doing world. You are so attached to this self that you consider this self to be your personal identity that tells you who you are.

To want a closer relationship with God means you must be willing to leave your doing world, which revolves around you, and enter a "being world" that revolves around God, the source of all being. In His World, you can find your "being Self," which may be called your "true Self," or simply your "Self," made in His image and likeness. What is this image and likeness of God? It is none other than the Christ, the Son of God. There is only one universal Christ, but every seeker is part of this one universal Christ. All the parts of the one universal Christ may be called the "body of Christ," for lack of better terminology. Your Self can be thought of as your "part," "place," or "participation" in the body of Christ, yet these words are inadequate to define your role in the body of Christ. The overall concept is that the universal Christ is a shared identity in which all seekers participate in divine oneness with God as well as with each other as parts of the one universal Christ.

This Christian concept of the Self is different from the nondualistic Hindu concept of the Self, called the *Atman*. In yoga form of nondualistic philosophy the Atman, the concept of God immanent, and Brahman, the concept of God transcendent, are the same. Generally speaking, in Hindu nondualism, when the seeker's ego is released, the seeker dissolves into God and indeed becomes God like a drop of water dissolving into the ocean. The seeker who realizes his true nature as the Self, the Atman, becomes so absolutely one with God that there is no individual identity remaining. Consequently, the *Self is God* in Hindu nondualism, which is incompatible with the Christian concept that the created seeker can never become the Creator, the First Cause.

The Christian viewpoint is that in divine union the individual identity based on the ego is released similar to the loss of the ego in Hindu nondualism. Nevertheless, from the Christian perspective the seeker does not lose all of his individual identity. A transformation in consciousness occurs in which the ego identity is replaced by a divine individual Identity that is centered in perfect oneness with Christ, joined with God and with the Holy Spirit. It is the seeker's part, place, or participation in the body of Christ that provides the seeker with an individual identity. In this manual your true identity will be called your "Self," but to distinguish this Christian concept of the Self from the Hindu concept of the Self it will be important to understand that this means your *Self in Christ.* For greater clarity sometimes this manual will refer to your Self as your "Christ Self," meaning your identity in Christ. Your true identity, your Christ Self, is already established in His World. Your Christ Self has been created by God the Father and therefore is unchangeable. However, you can choose to be aware of your true identity, your Christ Self, or you can choose to allow your true identity to remain hidden from your awareness.

Jesus became fully aware of His true identity and is the example for others to do likewise. Jesus became so identified with His true identity that He became perfectly one with the universal Christ and thus is rightly acknowledged as the "Christ." Following Jesus means more than just acknowledging and celebrating His accomplishment of perfect oneness with the universal Christ. Truly following Jesus means at least attempting to reveal the Christ Self that is already within you in His World. Whereas your world of doing is based upon the idea of separation, His World of being is based upon oneness that reveals to you your Christ Self united with God.

You will probably have your own way of describing your true identity and participation in the universal Christ, which may be quite different from the above description. There is no need for you to adopt the above description or terminology in order to benefit from this book. You are encouraged to retain whatever concepts you feel will help you to draw closer to the divine within. If you have conceptual differences with the above ideas regarding your identity in Christ, perhaps a more basic premise will be easier to accept. This simplified premise is that your being is within the Being of God. To discover your being as an experience rather than as an intellectual idea requires that you proceed by a way of being. To proceed by a way of being requires letting go of reliance upon doing. This includes not only setting aside physical doing, but also setting aside intellectual doing in order to enter into a way of being. Normally, you cannot immediately stop doing and just be. Your world contains habit patterns and belief systems which you have been building for years and which are not easy to leave behind. Making the transition from doing to being is the purpose of meditation. If you truly desire a closer relationship with God, then meditation will allow you to make this transition in a gentle and graceful way.

You may think of the transition from your world of doing to His World of being in the same way that you think of the transition from loud noise to quieter sounds and then finally to silence. If you wish to experience the silence of His World, all you need to do is empty yourself of the sounds of your world. The sounds of your world are your thoughts that revolve around you. Your thoughts clutter up your mind, creating noise that prevents you from dwelling in the silence that is at the core of your being. Meditation is a way of growing toward silence through an emptying of your noisy thoughts that make you a captive of your world. Specific methods of meditation that allow you to empty yourself are described in the upcoming chapters.

Chapter 3 describes a specific series of procedures for meditation. In addition, this chapter will provide information to help you to choose a spiritual ideal, such as Christ, and a mental attitude, such as doing God's Will, in order to focus your spiritual and mental intention to grow toward God. The Twenty-eight Day Demonstration of daily meditation is recommended to increase your awareness of God's presence within you and to serve as a solid foundation for future growth. Chapters 2 through 7 will provide all the information necessary to conduct this Twenty-eight Day Demonstration of your desire to draw closer to God and begin the process of entering His World.

The fact is that God is already calling you to enter His World and leave your own world; otherwise you would not have been prompted by His grace to open this book and seek to deepen your relationship with Him. And your response to His call of love will in itself draw you closer to Him, because your response will be a union of your will and His Will. In your Christian practice of meditation you are not seeking an object or end result that you can possess. Rather, your meditation experience is an ongoing process of uniting your will with God's Will. In that union of wills, you are opening yourself to recognizing the being state of your Christ Self in God. Thus, in meditation, your intention is not to possess something or achieve something or make something happen, as it would be if you were in your world. During meditation, you are still doing something, but it is a doing that is an "undoing"—an emptying of the self. You are letting go of the self to become aware of what is already truly at the core of your being.

The general process of letting go of the self is the same for a beginner and an experienced meditator, but each one's challenge is quite different. If you are a beginner, your challenge is to begin the process of inwardly letting go of the self. If you are an experienced meditator, your challenge is to let go of the self at a deeper level and to increasingly reveal God as the source of your being. In either case, as you read the next six chapters and put them into practice, your act of faithfully seeking God will in itself increase your awareness of His presence within you, or, more accurately stated, of your being within His Being.

However, it is best not to approach meditation with any judgments or preconceived ideas about what you want or expect to get out of the meditation experience. To do so would be to retreat back into your world of self-seeking, rather than to proceed to His World. You can be sure that your loving Father will demonstrate His Love for you, but what you cannot know is just how He will show forth His love. By letting go of these preconceptions, you can be fully open to His Will and know that whatever response He gives to you will be for your own highest good and will meet your deepest needs at the time and in the way that is most appropriate for your growth.

Meditation has been described as a way of leaving your world and entering His World. But it would be an unfortunate error if you assumed that the purpose of meditation is to escape from your everyday world and from your responsibilities in your world. With experience, you will discover that the leaving of your world that occurs in meditation will help you to come back to your world of doing and perceive and experience your world in a new way.

Your world will remain a world of doing, and you will still be the doer of your world. However, your perception of yourself will change so that you will see yourself as one who is being guided. You will recognize that your world of doing does not have to be controlled solely by you in order to insure that your needs are met. You will understand that you can let go of some of that control and allow your decisions and actions to be guided by God because your meditation experience has shown you that God is at the center of your being.

Just as you have learned to become aware of His presence in His World during meditation, you will also learn to sense the influence of His presence in your world. You will allow your doing to flow forth from your being in Him, rather than from self-will. Instead of denying the everyday world or seeking to escape from its responsibilities, you will gradually learn to allow your doing world to be an outer expression of your being in His World. As you allow your world of doing to be a divine reflection of His World, you will discover that your investment in your meditation practice bears fruit both inwardly and outwardly, providing consistency and integration to your life.

2

DIVINE COMMUNICATION

≈ • ≈

A. Three Ways of Seeking God

Generally speaking, there are three ways of seeking God. The most common way of seeking God is through a selection process of concepts. In this process, you add concepts that seem right to you or that are acceptable to a religious group to which you belong. This selection process also involves discarding concepts that are incompatible with your thought system or incompatible with the dogmas of your religious group.

These concepts relate to form, space, and time. In selecting forms, you choose images, rites, and rituals that are symbols of your relationship with God. In considering spatial factors, you select places of worship or take pilgrimages to holy places. In relationship to time, you select times of worship, but also think about concepts related to the past and the future. You consider past religious events, such as the life of Jesus, or consider your own past deeds, which may bring up issues of guilt, atonement, and forgiveness. You consider concepts of the future, perhaps including concepts of a future in hell, purgatory, or Heaven.

Eventually, you may establish a very stable concept of God and may be part of a religious group that shares your conceptual picture of God. Your commitment to God may rest in a solid belief in this conceptual picture. When you seek God in prayer, you express your ideas, petitions, and feelings to God with your conceptual framework in mind. Christians, Hindus, and Buddhists have this basic approach to their spiritual ideal in concepts, and even those who do not belong to a religious group also approach God in this way.

Seeking God with concepts is necessary and helpful, and most people spend their whole lives holding on to this mental framework. Although there are many benefits to a conceptual picture of God, there are some limitations to holding on to a conceptual picture of God. In order to consider the limitations of concepts in regard to seeking God, you can imagine that you are in a bookstore and come across a book with the title *If You See Jesus on the Path, Kill Him*. Obviously, "judging a book by its cover" is not usually a good idea, but if you were to do so, what would you think of this book? Perhaps this book would appear to you to be a heretical mockery of the crucifixion. However, if you were familiar with Eastern philosophy, you would probably remember a similar Buddhist saying, "If you meet the Buddha on the path, kill him." You would understand that both statements are made out of respect, not disrespect.

Both these statements are made for shock value in order to divert your attention away from illusions and to focus your attention on what is real. Any Jesus or Buddha that you meet in your path will merely be an expression of your concepts of the divine. Your concepts, your picture of the divine in form, can only be a false idol, not the reality of the divine. The respectful premise behind these challenging statements is that Jesus and Buddha have attained a universal consciousness beyond form, space, and time. Of course, you cannot kill the real Jesus or the real Buddha. Any Jesus or Buddha that you could kill could not possibly be the real Jesus or the real Buddha. But you *can* "kill," meaning discard, your false idols, your concepts of the divine. Your perceptions in concepts that are within form, space, and time can only be a barrier to direct divine contact.

If you are a Christian, the barrier to divine contact that concepts present to you is that your concepts show you that you live in a world of separation that appears very real to you. In your apparent world of separation you look out and see Christ as separate from yourself, yet this is an illusion created by your concepts. You may believe that you will be united with Christ in the future. However, it is difficult to understand and accept that in reality you are already united to Christ and live in Christ right now. Unfortunately you are not yet consciously awakened to the divine life that is within you in the present moment.

Christ, the Holy Spirit, and God the Father are joined as one, and you are one with Them. *His World* encompasses your world of apparent separation. God is like the air that you breathe. You do not see or notice the air and yet the air allows you to live and if you were deprived of air, you would die in minutes. Similarly, God gives you life and keeps you in existence, but you still do not see or notice Him or His love, just like you do not see or notice the air.

Although the divine embrace in which you exist goes unnoticed, Christ, in His oneness with God, stands at the door to your conscious awareness. Through the Holy Spirit, He would bring His loving embrace into your conscious awareness to reveal your own as yet unrecognized oneness with God. But the door to your conscious awareness is locked. It is locked by your concepts of separation.

You have asked yourself many questions, such as *Who is Christ really? Who is God really? Who am I really?* Your concepts have attempted to answer these questions. However, have your conceptual answers, whatever they may be, really satisfied you and given you inner peace? Would you rather have your conceptual answers or Christ's embrace?

You can unlock the door and bring Christ's embrace to your conscious awareness, if you want to do so. Meditation and contemplation are ways of helping you unlock this door of separation presented by your concepts. These practices may result in a change in your concepts, yet the practices themselves do not require you to give up your concepts altogether. You only need to set aside your concepts temporarily during the actual time spent in meditation and contemplation. In addition to setting aside your concepts temporarily, meditation and contemplation provide opportunities to welcome the divine assistance that would help you to uncover in an experiential way God's Love for you and indeed your love for Him.

Of course, using concepts has its proper place in spiritual growth, and there is no attempt here toward anti-intellectualization. In particular, concepts help you to bring needed understanding to your spiritual seeking. For example, it is helpful for you, as a follower of Christ, to have a conceptual picture of Christ, as long as you know that it is only a picture and not the reality of Christ. Consequently, you can use your concepts to understand conceptually that your concepts themselves are limited. With this understanding of the limitations of concepts, you will be able to use concepts when it is appropriate to do so and to temporarily set aside your concepts at those times when you wish to find God beyond concepts.

You can only find God by *experiencing* God. The experience of God can be defined as firsthand knowledge of Reality that occurs in the present moment and is not based on concepts. In this experience of the divine that occurs in the present moment, there is a higher intelligence at work than conceptual intelligence. This higher intelligence instantaneously infuses the divine experience into the consciousness of the soul, before the experience is registered in the rational mind. The experience itself then filters down into the rational mind and is converted into concepts, bringing this perceptual awareness into the conscious personality.

Concepts enter into the intellect only as an aftereffect of the experience of God. Concepts are mental reflections to identify, understand, evaluate, and explain the divine experience after the experience itself has left the present moment. Obviously, you can have concepts about an experience of God after a few seconds, minutes, days, or even years have passed. Some concepts may appear to be occurring simultaneously along with a divine experience. Nevertheless, even these concepts actually come to your conceptual awareness a tiny fraction of a second after the present moment in which the experience occurs. This tiny fraction of a second is enough to separate concepts from the experience of God.

The experience of God can only be found in the *eternal now*, which is the indivisible present of limitless duration. Concepts being only mental reflections cannot enter this eternal now where God is, and therefore concepts cannot provide an experience of God. Concepts provide helpful reflections about God, but if you wish to find God, you must go beyond concepts in order to experience God in the instantaneous present moment.

Your experience of God can perhaps be a "felt experience" of God. There is a mild and rather common form of felt experience of God that is a state of increased awareness of the divine. This awareness consists of a consciousness of inner feelings, which may include the feelings of love, oneness, heightened awareness, light, the divine presence, peace, and/or bliss. One or more of these inner feelings may possibly occur occasionally or even regularly during meditation or contemplation, or may occur spontaneously in everyday life. A more in depth explanation of these inner feeling and meditation techniques related to these inner feelings can be found in Chapter 14.

There is a less common form of felt experience that is a sudden and surprising encounter with the divine. This unusual spiritual event produces an altered consciousness, which may range from a mild to an extreme experience. If this is a mild divine encounter, it may be a profound experience of connectedness with all others and all of creation. If it is a moderate divine encounter, it may be a flooding of your entire being with an all-consuming divine love. If it is an extreme altering of consciousness, it may manifest in any one of a variety of shocking and strange ways. There may be an inner explosion of light within the body or transcending body awareness. Other manifestations may include a tremendous electrical shock bursting through the body, a thunderous sound heard within the head that is more powerful than any earthly sound, or an awe-inspiring and dynamic force of energy that overwhelms the body and the mind.

An individual seeker who has one of these kinds of extreme experiences is temporarily lifted out of his normal consciousness and elevated to a higher consciousness, which is both totally unfamiliar and at the same time oddly familiar. These unusual kinds of divine encounters may be pleasant or unpleasant. They may be disorienting and/or fulfilling. A very significant factor involved is how prepared the seeker is to receive the powerful forces that are unleashed in these kinds of extreme divine encounters.

The seeker who has gone through a long process of perhaps many years of purifying his heart and mind prior to having an unusual divine encounter is more likely to have a blissful or at least peaceful experience, rather than a distressing experience. Beginners sometimes want to pursue having a spiritual experience by practicing extreme disciplines, which may include extreme breathing practices. These beginners often have the naive idea that a divine encounter will automatically be a blissful experience. The unprepared seeker who has not been purifying himself may not have a blissful or even peaceful divine encounter. In fact, the unprepared seeker could possibly experience an extreme divine encounter that is painful and possibly even physically, emotionally, and mentally traumatic.

Yoga philosophy describes these extreme experiences, both the blissful and painful ones, as the expression of the "kundalini" being awakened. Sometimes kundalini experiences that are painful or traumatic can occur because the seeker has engaged in a self-willed and foolish effort to force a spiritual experience to happen. On the other hand, some kundalini experiences that have a negative effect can occur without the seeker apparently doing anything to precipitate such an experience. Even though extreme spiritual experiences are rightly associated with the raising of the kundalini, the kundalini can be awakened in a less extreme, much more gentle and stable way, as will be described in Chapter 11. Indeed, the techniques that will be described in this manual are intended to facilitate this gentle rising of the kundalini in coordination with the action of the Holy Spirit that brings inner balance rather than distressing symptoms.

Extreme felt experiences that are pleasant or blissful may also occur spontaneously without any apparent overt spiritual seeking. Whether you have been seeking God consciously or not, it may be difficult to understand the nature of your experience intellectually. The deeper your experience of God is, the less likely you will be able to use concepts to immediately understand the meaning of the experience. The first conceptual aftereffect may possibly be a feeling of astonishment and awe, followed by wonder and puzzlement. If the meaning of the experience is not immediately apparent, insights will generally come later. In some cases, it may be necessary to ask in prayer for the Spirit to explain the unexplainable and reveal the significance of what has been experienced.

There are many different kinds of felt experiences of God, ranging from mild to extreme, in addition to the specific examples provided here. These felt experiences of God are given to you as gifts in your lifelong journey of self-discovery, and you will receive the kinds of gifts that will most help you personally. Sometimes these gifts come at the very beginning of your journey as a "mystical initiation" in order to demonstrate that God loves you personally and to inspire you to continue to seek Him out. In other cases, these gifts come only after a time, possibly even many years, of spiritual seeking as an encouragement and blessing. If any of these kinds of felt experiences occur in your spiritual seeking, you can accept them as God's grace for you. But these felt experiences need to be considered as "spiritual accessories" and not really essential for your spiritual growth. These felt experiences of the divine are not your goal because they are not valuable as an end in themselves. However, felt experiences are valuable if they lead you in the direction of your true goal—God Himself.

Many, and probably most individuals, rely solely on the gift of faith that God has given them and do not need the supplemental gift of spiritual experiences. Others are given the gift of certain spiritual experiences in order to strengthen their faith. If you do have spiritual experiences, you may look upon these experiences as clues given to you in order for you to unravel the mystery of who you are and who God is. These experiences are sacred and intimate contacts with your Creator. Hopefully these encounters will not become prideful spiritual possessions to which your ego would want to cling. You need to be willing to let go of these kinds of experiences of God, leaving them in the past, and yet allow the aftereffect of these experiences to motivate you in the present moment to continue to seek God.

A preoccupation with felt experiences can divert you away from what is really essential, which is your faith. Much more important than a felt experience of God is your "faith experience" of God. Your faith experience of being aware of God's presence is the most common, fundamental, and indeed necessary experience of God. Your faith experience of God takes you from your known world of concepts to an unknown world, His World that lies beyond concepts. Faith is your means of knowing God that transcends your normal way of knowing with concepts. Actually your faith experience of God is *your experience of God knowing you.* Your faith, if you invest in it, is your access to a deep and very real personal contact with God. In this contact you realize that God knows you as His Beloved. Your faith is your way of knowing that God loves you. Faith is your greatest need if you want to seek God, especially if you want to seek God through the practice of meditation and contemplation.

Your concepts can assist you if your faith comes first and your concepts take a secondary role in your awareness. Ideally your concepts will arise as an outgrowth of your experience of investing in your faith. But your concepts alone without faith can only give you a conceptual picture of God—only an *idea* about God; it cannot give you an *experience* of God.

Furthermore, your concepts can actually *prevent* you from experiencing God if you are holding on to them too strongly. Your concepts can become an idol if you forget that your ideas are only symbols for a reality that cannot be contained by concepts. Would you be willing to temporarily let go of your concepts of God in order to experience God more intimately? The second and third ways of seeking God that will be described below do not require you to change your conceptual picture of God, but do require you to set aside your concepts at least temporarily while you are seeking to deepen your relationship with God. Most people form their conceptual picture before actually experiencing God. Therefore, you may find that you will want to change your conceptual picture of God *after* your experience of God deepens.

For the sake of clarity it should be mentioned that although your rational thinking mind has limitations, you can potentially become aware of a higher capacity of the mind that is a better reflection of the divine. Yoga philosophy makes a distinction between a lower knowledge, which is called *vijana*, and a higher knowledge, called *jnana*.[1] The lower knowledge is related to the part of the mind, called the *manas*, that is dependent upon the physical brain as the processing center for receiving and sending sensory information.[2] The higher knowledge is related to the part of the mind, called the *buddhi,* which is the highest faculty of the mind.[3]

The buddhi is the portion of the mind that represents divine wisdom. This mental faculty of truly inspired cognition can receive divine light like a physical crystal that can receive light but has no light of its own. Thus this higher wisdom is a much better means of drawing closer to God than the reliance upon the rational thinking of concepts about God. The buddhi of yoga philosophy corresponds with what St. Symeon the New Theologian calls the *nous*, the faculty of mystical cognition.[4] More about the nous and how to grow toward awakening this higher knowledge of the mind is described in Chapter 15. Seekers who rely almost exclusively upon the conceptual thinking of the rational mind in order to approach God will find that their access to God is limited. Although conceptual thinking has its proper place in spiritual seeking, the focus in this meditation manual is on learning how to reduce the reliance upon discursive thinking in order to draw closer to the divine within.

The second way of seeking God is through a selection of just one concept of God and then focusing on that one concept. By focusing on one concept of God, you set aside all the other concepts of God and rely on this one concept as a symbol of all that God is. *Meditation* may be thought of as this process of going from many concepts to focusing on one concept of God. An example of this narrowing of concepts is the repeating of the *Divine Name* of God. For a Christian, this repeating of the Divine Name would be accomplished by repeating the Divine Name of Jesus Christ in the practice of the *Jesus Prayer.* Every major religion has this component of repeating the Divine Name, as will be explained in Chapter 4.

Focusing on one concept is a means of using this one symbol of God to awaken a more direct contact with God, Who is beyond symbols. Although going from seeking God in many concepts to seeking God in one concept is a more direct approach to God, this approach still has the limitation of relying on a concept.

The third and final way of seeking God is the letting go of all concepts and entering into God's silence in order to increase your awareness of the divine presence. Form, space, and time are experienced through the filter of concepts. When you let go of all concepts, you also let go of your usual awareness of form, space, and time, and enter an *objectless awareness*. This process of letting go of concepts is the path of *contemplation* that can be found in Christianity. Likewise, this giving up of concepts as a spiritual path can be found in all the major religions, especially in Hinduism in the practice of yoga and in Buddhism in the practice of Zen disciplines.

Imagine that a Christian, a Hindu, and a Buddhist own three identical bottles, which are placed together. The bottle owned by the Christian has a tiny statue of Christ inside. The bottle owned by the Hindu has a tiny statue of Krishna inside. The bottle owned by the Buddhist has a tiny statue of Buddha inside. Now imagine that someone comes and steals the statues and leaves the three bottles behind. When the Christian, Hindu, and Buddhist find the bottles, they will not be able to distinguish who owns which bottle, because they will each have the same exact experience of each bottle that has been emptied. Similarly, when the Christian, Hindu, and Buddhist empty their minds, they will have a common experience of the divine.

In contrast to the seeking of God with concepts that produces differences in picturing God, the seeking of God in the giving up of concepts produces objectless awareness. This kind of awareness without an object, like the analogy of the bottles without objects, is the same for a Christian, a Hindu, or a Buddhist. This is a good thing because it means that through the emptying of concepts the One God can be sought and found in a more direct way that produces a similar experience in each seeker. This similar experience is a confirmation that each seeker is coming closer to Reality Itself that is changeless and that exists beyond form, space, and time, and indeed beyond concepts. Of course, after the Christian, Hindu, and Buddhist seekers leave the state of objectless awareness, they will return to concepts and describe the significance of their experience in the different terms of their own individual theological understandings.

The analogy of the empty bottles illustrates the importance of being empty of concepts in order to experience contemplation, but you may be left with the mistaken impression that emptiness equals contemplation. In fact, contemplation, as the practice of objectless awareness, is not a vacuum of consciousness. It is a state of being filled with the Spirit. Contemplation requires two gifts: your gift to God and God's gift to you. Your gift to God is your "calm faithful desire and consent." The calm aspect to your gift is your calm mind that is produced by emptying your mind of concepts. The faithful aspect of your gift is the implementation of your trust in God manifested as your investment of time and energy into seeking God. The desire aspect is your intention and willingness to invite the Holy Spirit into your consciousness. The consent aspect is to say "Yes" to God's presence right there within you. God's gift to you is the Holy Spirit overshadowing you. God is always willing to give this gift, but the peace of the Holy Spirit can only come to a mind that is uncluttered and willing to receive it.

If you practice the second way of seeking God by narrowing your concepts to one concept in meditation or if you practice the third way of seeking God by letting go of all concepts in contemplation, you may find that your concepts of God have changed because of your experience. If you are a Christian, when you go back to the first way of seeking God with concepts, you will, of course, still be a Christian, but you will probably need to make adjustments in your thinking about God. Your experience of meditation and to a greater degree your experience of contemplation may affect your outlook on form, space, and time in relation to your spiritual seeking. You may find that you can see God in all forms rather than just some selected forms. You may find God in all places, yet most intimately within yourself. You may be less concerned about the past and future, and instead be more focused on the divine in the present moment, which is the only time in which God can be experienced.

It is natural to seek God with concepts, to adjust those concepts as you grow spiritually, and to express your prayers to God within the framework of your conceptual thought system. However, for a well-rounded spiritual life it is equally important to be open to seeking God with one concept in meditation and without concepts in contemplation. Since contemplation without concepts is a closer contact with Spirit than meditation, which uses one concept, you may think you can just skip meditation and move right on to contemplation. In fact, some seekers are blessed with the ability to do just that. But most seekers find that the transition from going to a mind filled with concepts to the simplicity of a mind without concepts is just too great of a gap to manage in one leap.

Like the Israelites led by Moses into the desert, the mind that is stripped of its familiar ideas wants to revolt and build golden calves of concepts. These concepts function as idols that block the awareness of the divine presence. Relying on such familiar mental idols distracts the mind and prevents it from facing the silence of the unknown, unseen God in faith. The mind is addicted to concepts and needs to learn to first limit concepts before being able or willing to let go of all concepts. The mind is also addicted to desires other than the desire for God, and it takes time to let go of these blocks. A series of specific meditation techniques are offered in this manual to serve as a step-by-step transition that allows you to gradually learn how to let go of concepts and inner blocks so you are better prepared to enter into the silence and simplicity of contemplation.

B. Your Willingness to Change

The three previously described ways of seeking God are as follows: with concepts, with one concept, which is *meditation*, and with no concepts, which is *contemplation*. Everyone seeks God with concepts, even though He cannot truly be found experientially in concepts. Not everyone seeks God in meditation and contemplation, although He can to a certain degree be found in meditation and contemplation. Not everyone wants to find God because not everyone wants to pay the price of finding God. What is the price of finding God? The price that you will pay is that *you will change*. Are you willing to change?

Whether you have a felt or faithful experience of God, it will change you to the degree that you are willing to allow yourself to be changed. So before you decide if you want to learn more about seeking God through the practice of meditation and contemplation, you may want to look at your willingness to change.

Seeking to change spiritually is similar to the process of seeking to change psychologically. Typically a person encounters difficulties in his life and then goes to a psychotherapist for counseling and asks for help. In his first sessions, the person spends a good deal of time talking about outside circumstances that it appears he cannot control. After more time in therapy, the therapist helps this person to understand that instead of focusing on outside circumstances, it would be better to focus on how he could take responsibility for changing himself. This person may sense that he has denied and repressed parts of himself into his subconscious mind. He may also sense that if he stays in therapy he will have to face what he has repressed and as a result he will have to change. At this point, the person decides that he is not willing to change, and he leaves the therapy, or he decides that he is willing to change, and he stays with the therapy.

Meditation and contemplation are forms of *divine healing* that include spiritually guided psychotherapy. These kinds of attunement experiences reveal what is hidden within you of both a positive and negative nature. Just like regular therapy, eventually you will come to a crossroads where you will need to decide whether you really want to change or not. In regular therapy, you have a therapist to help you. In this spiritual therapy, you have the Holy Spirit as your divine therapist. You can be assured that the Holy Spirit is up to the task of assisting you in your process of changing, but you have to be willing to change.

There are many ways in which encountering God will produce changes in your life, and one of these is that it will change your first way of seeking God—your concepts. It will change not only your concepts themselves, but also your attachment to your concepts. If you decide to pursue meditation and contemplation, you will find that based upon your experience of God, your concepts will change and evolve, and you will be less attached to your concepts.

Yet meditation and contemplation are not for everyone because not everyone wants to change and specifically not everyone wants to make conceptual changes. If a person's only way of seeking God is through concepts, it forces him to give a great deal of weight to having the "right" concepts. Also, he will measure the strength of his faith in terms of how firmly he holds on to his concepts of God. Thus he will view the changing of his concepts as a weakening of his faith, and he would not want to do that. If his God is a God of concepts, his God will live or die depending on the rightness of his concepts and the firmness of his holding on to his concepts.

His mission may become to convert others so they will have God in the same way that he has God. It is natural to have concepts of God. However, can you really "have" God with concepts? Having implies containing, grasping, and possessing. Can God be the intellectual property of those who have the right concepts? Who can even define God? Any definition would be too inadequate and too small to contain Him. The very best that can be done is to define God by what He is *not*. Consequently, it is fair to say that God is not a concept and cannot be contained by concepts. Therefore, no one can have God with concepts.

But you can find and have God *by letting Him have you*. In order to let God have you, you need to give yourself to Him. The way to give yourself to God is by letting go of yourself. In this letting go of yourself, you join with God by surrendering to Him in an act of love. Surrendering to Him means surrendering all that you are, which includes letting go of your concepts. In fact, your concepts themselves are what separate you from God. So your concepts must be set aside for you to open your awareness to God's loving embrace. In your openness to divine love you learn that letting God possess you in His loving embrace is the fulfillment of your every desire. God can only be found in this loving embrace by letting go of yourself and letting God be Himself in you— beyond concepts.

This kind of surrendering of yourself requires faith. Your faith in God can and usually does start with concepts. At this initial stage, your faith is invested in your beliefs. For a period of time, your faith in your beliefs gives you a sense of security about spiritual matters. You may form a "religious identity" base upon your beliefs, which can also become your "personal identity" of how you define yourself.

However, for faith to be authentic, it must lead you beyond this initial stage of your faith, resting only in your beliefs. Your faith, in order to truly be faith in God and not just faith in concepts of God, must lead you beyond a religious identity and beyond a personal identity based on concepts. Your faith must lead you to a direct encounter with God so you can begin to find your personal identity in your experience of Him, rather than your concepts of Him. Your faith in God requires you to surrender your sense of security based upon concepts so that you can actually enter His World.

At first, because you are led solely by pure faith, you may feel adrift in a sea of conceptual uncertainty that will feel unfamiliar and uncomfortable. For this reason, it may be difficult for you initially to set aside your concepts in order to focus on one concept in meditation and even more difficult to empty your mind of all concepts in contemplation. Your faith will sustain you beyond this temporary stage in which you may feel insecure and uncertain as you are first entering the unknown territory of His World. But in your willingness to enter the unknown lies the opportunity to encounter Reality, rather than only ideas about Reality.

One of the uncomfortable aspects of meditation and contemplation can be that there will be changes in your personal identity. After all, it is the purpose of meditation and contemplation to change the personal identity of anyone who uses these practices. God's Plan for your life is not for you to stay as you are now, but for you to change. If you are willing to cooperate with His plan, you will change and grow toward increasingly reflecting the image and likeness of God that is your true nature. If you want to practice meditation or contemplation, you will need to be willing to change your personal identity. Your ultimate Identity does not change because God created you as part of Himself, making you eternal and as changeless as He is. Nevertheless, your personal identity in this world *must* change for you to eventually wake up to your true nature in God.

Your personal identity is either centered in the ego, which is the idea of separation, or centered in God. As you change and grow spiritually, you will let go of ego tendencies and will be attracted to divine influences. One of the ways in which meditation and contemplation will change you is that you will learn to withdraw the tendency of the ego to indulge in *projection*. As is the case with all seekers, you have within yourself a "shadow," which is the portion of your consciousness that is closed off from your conscious awareness. The shadow contains all the parts of yourself that you consider to be unacceptable. These unacceptable parts of yourself may be negative aspects of yourself that you have hidden. There may also be positive attributes and potentials that you have hidden from your awareness. If there is an unwillingness to look at the inner shadow, that inner shadow will be seen outwardly. Projection is the psychological defense mechanism of denying the negative aspects of the shadow within yourself and seeing those negative qualities outside of yourself. The use of projection is a very human tendency that every person has, but you can learn to let go of this tendency by looking within and taking responsibility for what you find within. Learning to look at and accept the unacceptable parts of yourself produces an integration that is needed in order to go even deeper within and reveal the divine within yourself.

Letting go of projection does involve a certain amount of conceptual understanding that allows you to see into the psychological nature of this defense mechanism and to understand how counterproductive projection really is. However, it is your letting go of concepts during meditation and contemplation that will provide a way of finding intimacy with God. It is this intimacy with God that is your real food for transformation. Of course, the effectiveness of meditation and contemplation does not rely on your practice as a technique, but rather on your faith in God. Faith is God's gift to you that makes it possible for you to find Him. Since God is beyond concepts and since God wants you to be able to find Him, He has given you the gift of faith to enable you to reach beyond concepts so that you can find Him. It is your faith too that will assist you in making inner changes. Your faith is a gift you receive from God, but is also a gift you give to God. Your faith becomes a gift to God when you invest in your faith by taking steps to increase your awareness of God.

Focusing on outer negativity that is a condition for projection to take place is a serious barrier to seeking God within. If you wish to seek God within, you will need to be concerned with removing any barriers within yourself that would prevent you from being aware of God's presence. Therefore, you would need to look within and face the positive and negative within yourself.

Good and bad, loving desires and unloving desires can be found in every individual human heart, regardless of the correctness or incorrectness of that individual's conceptual beliefs of God. Indulging in projection allows you to look only outwardly for negativity and unloving desires and to be blind to perceiving those negative attributes within your own heart. If you sincerely wish to root out negativity and unloving desires, you must start where they are most deeply hidden within your own heart.

If your ultimate goal is God, your immediate goal needs to be *purity of heart*, which can only be found by examining your heart. With your willingness to change and to go within to examine your own heart, your spiritual therapy begins. Searching your own heart must not be done superficially. Your challenge is to find out just how deeply you can go within your own heart. If you go deeply enough within your heart, you can hear the voices of every character, good and bad, in the New Testament.

You can hear voices of the Apostle John loving Jesus and of Judas betraying Jesus. You can hear the voice of Thomas doubting Jesus and of Peter denying Jesus. You can hear the voice of the Pharisee in the temple in the act of projection, saying, "O God, I thank thee that I am not like the rest of men, robbers, dishonest, adulterers, or even like this publican. I fast twice a week; I pay tithes of all that I possess."[5] And you can hear the voice of the publican saying, "O God, be merciful to me the sinner!"[6]

All these voices are in your own heart, crying out for your attention, and you may want to pretend that these voices are not there. However, if you become deaf to hearing these voices within, you will begin to project and hear these voices outside of yourself in other people. Also, at times you will find yourself expressing these voices outwardly in your everyday life experiences.

Obviously you do not literally hear these voices. This is an analogy of all the human impulses in your heart that cry out for expression and affect you whether you realize this or not. All the very human characters in the New Testament with their virtues and flaws tell the story of what goes on within your heart. If you do not go deeply enough within, you will not realize this, and you will deny and repress both the loving and unloving impulses that are in your own heart. But denial and repression do not bring peace to your heart. You will still be affected by what you have repressed, causing an uneasy anxiety about the denied parts of yourself.

To continue with this analogy, there are so many different voices, good and bad, within your heart that your heart becomes restless and unsettled. To bring peace back into your heart, what if you could silence all these voices of different characters, different impulses? What if you could condense these voices into one voice? Imagine that you can identify with one voice and that you can express that one voice. Imagine that you identify with and express the one voice of a blind man, like the blind man at Jericho.[7] Imagine that you are told that Jesus is passing by. You call out, "Jesus!" The other voices in your heart are the voices in the crowd angrily trying to silence your voice. But you cry out even louder and more persistently, "Jesus, Jesus, Jesus!"

This part of the analogy represents meditation based upon the practice of the *Jesus Prayer*, which is also called the *Prayer of the Heart*. All the voices in your heart, all those impulses, are the thoughts that are in your subconscious mind and that at times float by in your conscious mind. These many thoughts are represented by the voices and impulses of the crowd that angrily try to silence your voice. In order to still these thoughts, you take up one thought with which you can identify. You speak with one voice, "Jesus," to calm all the other voices and thoughts clamoring for your attention. This is the crying out of your heart for Jesus that silences the other impulses of the heart.

But in this analogy, what happens after you, as the blind man, cry for "Jesus," and He actually presents Himself to you? He is right there in your presence. It does not make sense for you to call out for "Jesus," when He is right there in your presence. Consequently, you can then silence your own voice. You can fully open your heart to Him without words. This part of the analogy represents contemplation, in which you are aware of the divine presence without needing words or concepts. Without concepts, how are you able to be aware of the divine presence? The answer can be found in the words of Jesus when He healed the blind man with the words, "Receive thy sight, thy faith has saved thee."[8] Your faith placed in your heart by divine grace takes away your blindness and lets you experience the divine presence beyond concepts.

You can find this faith by uncovering the purity of heart that is within you. Your purity of heart can be uncovered only by stilling the mind and placing the mind in a state of receptivity. Your mind becomes at peace by being emptied of distracting thoughts, and your receptivity is an exercise of your free-will invitation for the incoming of the Holy Spirit.

What has been said so far about meditation and contemplation can be summarized as follows: Meditation and contemplation will produce a change of your concepts and a change of heart. Thus, if you want to experience meditation and contemplation, you will need to be willing to go through an ongoing process of change. This process at first may seem like a movement into uncharted and unfamiliar territory where you may feel lost at times. But if you are willing to take the risk of going into the Great Unknown, you will discover that your journey is to the center of your very own heart, where you will enter His World—and find that you have come Home.

C. Techniques and Receptivity

The first way of seeking God described previously, which is with concepts, includes not only your beliefs about God, but also your forms of worship and in particular all forms of *prayer*. The words "prayer and meditation" are often used as terms that indicate communication with God, yet may have a wide variety of meanings for different people. For the purpose of this meditation manual, prayer may be defined as *expressive communication* with God. In prayer, you use the expressive nature of the mind and consciously direct your thoughts and feelings toward God.

In the early centuries of Christianity, spiritual seekers pondered sacred scripture and referred to this practice of discursive mental reflection as *meditatio*, from which the word "meditation" is derived. Consequently, this meaning has survived so that meditation for some people means the activity of thinking about a topic in order to mentally consider its meaning in a reflective and prayerful manner. However, for this manual, the word "meditation" will have an entirely different meaning. In contrast to prayer in which you express many different thoughts and feelings to communicate with God, meditation may be defined as *receptive communication* with God. For meditation you focus on one thought in order to assume a receptive state of mind that allows you to let go of distracting thoughts.

Actively relating to God in an expressive manner in prayer is very helpful for your spiritual growth but is only a secondary purpose of this book. A more important aim of this book is to provide a step-by-step approach of how to produce the inner receptivity of meditation. Since this is a how-to manual, it is designed and presented in a systematic way that includes many specific techniques. The word "technique" can be defined as a detailed procedure or method containing the directions for becoming skillful in the accomplishment of a particular activity.

How are techniques related to communication with God? This can be compared with the task of an archer. He has the intention of hitting the center of the target, just as your intention is to communicate with God. But he must take into consideration how he holds the bow, how he pulls back the arrow, how he breathes, how he holds himself steady, and how he directs his gaze. If he is an expert archer, he does not even have to think about any of these things because through practice everything has become natural for him. But if he is a beginner, he will have to practice his "technique," his way of carrying out his intention of hitting the center of the target until it all becomes natural for him. In the same way, a beginning meditator can benefit by practicing his technique of sitting with a calm mind, a steady body, and relaxed breathing. Eventually the time will come when he becomes an experienced meditator and everything is natural for him.

Are techniques necessary for everyone in order to learn how to meditate? No, not for everyone. Some individuals can spontaneously feel the divine presence by simply allowing God's grace to bring the mind into a passive and receptive state in which scattered thoughts are set aside. When the Holy Spirit overshadows the seeker and stills the mind, this may be called *contemplation*, which is similar to meditation in that it is a form of receptive communication with God. However, this spontaneous and unstructured divine communion rarely occurs without first having been preceded by a preparatory time of sincere seeking, which requires a pure intention. As long as this pure intention of desiring God above all else is maintained, then specific structured meditation methods can be used as a way of focusing and intensifying that intention as a preparation for contemplation.

Of course, prayer is one way of helping you to express your intention of deepening your relationship with God. However, prayer alone may not be sufficient to produce a deep and intimate personal relationship with God. Perhaps you have met someone who is very expressive of his thoughts and feelings but is lacking in his ability to listen to others. You can have a superficial conversation with such a person, but not real in-depth sharing because that person is not really open to receiving what you may have to express. By this analogy, prayer may be thought of as "speaking," and meditation may be considered "listening." Expressing oneself only by speaking to God becomes a one-sided communication. Therefore, listening to God is necessary for a balanced communication with God.

Listening here, of course, does not mean listening with the ears. It means emptying of your thoughts to produce inner receptivity to the Spirit. Your everyday living experience relies so heavily upon the expression of your rational thinking process that emptying of your mind will seem unnatural at first. When you attempt to stop your normal thinking process, you will find that your thoughts continue to arise. Since you cannot stop your thoughts altogether from occurring, you can at least reduce your thoughts in order to calm the mind. The best way to reduce thoughts is to give the mind something to focus on. Some examples of focusing the mind are looking at a candle flame, observing one's thoughts, or listening to the sounds of nature. However, the primary kind of meditation that will be described in this book is the holding of one thought in the mind, such as a sacred word or brief combination of words, called an "affirmation."

The affirmation of the Jesus Prayer, repeating the Divine Name of Jesus Christ, will be emphasized in particular. Since this is a Christian meditation manual, it is reasonable to assume that you want to follow Christ or at least explore that possibility. Consequently, you are being asked to simply enter the closet of your own heart, close the door to the outside world, and with humility, invoke the Name of Jesus. Repeating the Name of Jesus opens you to the inner workings of the Holy Spirit so that you can find Christ within and learn to trust wholeheartedly and intuitively in divine grace and divine guidance.

The Name of Jesus is not a magic formula that you repeat to get specific results. This affirmation like all other affirmations does reduce thoughts and calm the mind, but it is so much more. In addition to being an affirmation, your repeating of the Name of Jesus is also an "invocation," a calling upon Him who is no farther away than your own heart. Jesus will take you by the hand and, through the action of the Holy Spirit, lead you to the Father.

When the affirmation of the Name of Jesus is successful in calming your mind and opening you to the Holy Spirit, you may also find yourself experiencing the divine presence in contemplation. If this happens, it is important to let go of repeating the affirmation in order to rest in the experience of the divine presence beyond words. The process of meditation in which you hold an affirmation to calm the mind and then let go of the affirmation when you experience the divine presence is called "Inner Silence Meditation." In this book, all of the meditation techniques that use affirmations are designed to lead toward Inner Silence Meditation, as a direct preparation for experiencing the divine presence in contemplation.

Does this mean you must have a consciously felt experience of the divine presence in order for your meditation practice to be effective? Some meditators experience a state of heightened receptivity to the divine within as a conscious experience. It may, for example, be a condition of keen awareness, but not rational thinking awareness. Yet many meditators, and beginners in particular, do not have a conscious experience that confirms an increase of inner receptivity. Nevertheless, your sincere intention of drawing closer to God through Christ insures that you are inviting the Holy Spirit into your life and deep into your subconscious mind, even though you have no conscious experience of this. Therefore, you need to know by faith that your meditation practice is in fact producing increased receptivity to the Spirit even when your meditation experience may not seem to be very focused or effective to your conscious awareness.

The techniques that are described in this manual are designed to meet the varying needs of both beginners and experienced meditators, and to serve as a secure foundation for future growth toward contemplation. Contemplation itself is a gift of the Spirit and essentially not a technique. In fact, contemplation may be thought of as a way of letting go of techniques. Nevertheless, it is often helpful to learn how to use techniques first before learning how to let go of techniques. An artist who becomes proficient at spontaneous abstract painting does not start out by specializing in abstract painting. Invariably, such an artist first learns the techniques of realistic drawing, and then learns the techniques of realistic painting involving elements of color, texture, and design. Even though the techniques of realism will be discarded in his future, these realistic techniques focused on objects will serve as an underlying foundation for his abstract painting.

Similarly, a beginning meditator holds on to a focusing object in the form of a concrete affirmation in order to calm the mind. This calming of the mind is a necessary preparation for learning how to let go of the focusing object and then enter the abstract state of contemplation. Your preparation period of meditation provides a future foundation for the objectless awareness of contemplation. What is required for this preparation is the willingness to grow toward integrating and then unifying the various levels of your being. These levels that need to be integrated and unified are the physical, emotional, mental, intuitive, and spiritual levels of your being. The techniques in this manual will help you to integrate and unify these levels of your being by increasing your openness to the Holy Spirit's ability to bring about an inner transformation.

Meditation methods are the beginning of your transformation process and contemplation takes you to an even deeper level of this same transformation process. This transformation process involves both your effort and divine grace. Meditation techniques imply a greater degree of effort on your part in cooperation with divine grace, while contemplation involves a letting go of self-effort in order to let divine grace take over more fully. Hopefully your meditation experience will lead you to the experience of contemplation in which you present no obstacle to God working within you to bring about your inner transformation.

D. Your Calling

You have a great spiritual potential lying within you. The greatness of your potential is not due to your personal skills, but rather due to the reality of God's presence within you waiting to be awakened into your conscious awareness. Your awakening only requires your willingness to calm your mind and to give your faithful consent to the presence of the Holy Spirit. The techniques in this manual show you a means of how to put your willingness and your faith into practical application.

Besides your willingness, you will need persistence to learn techniques of meditation and gain the benefits. Additional persistence will be needed by you to go beyond meditation techniques and into a deep conscious experience of the divine presence in contemplation. This experience of contemplation is a divine calling that goes out to all Christian seekers, but not everyone answers this call. Luckily, you do not have to be an extraordinarily gifted mystic or saint to be lead from meditation to contemplation. God is accessible to anyone who hears His call and is willing to respond to that call.

In addition to God calling you inwardly, He is simultaneously calling you outwardly. Each and every Christian seeker is called to do God's Will and allow the love of Christ to flow through him to touch the minds and hearts of every person he meets. What does the inward seeking of meditation have to do with this outward expression of love? You may practice meditation without other people being in close physical proximity to you, but you can never practice meditation alone. Yes, meditation has an inward focus, but it has nothing to do with isolation or separation. Meditation is a means of coming to the inner place of joining with all your brothers and sisters and with God. Meditation will not only bear fruit inwardly by revealing inner oneness with everyone and with God, but it will also bear fruit outwardly. It is important that you remember that the primary purpose for you in practicing meditation is that it will make you a better instrument to manifest Christian love and service in the earth.

With a commitment to following Christ, you will increasingly be guided from within by the Holy Spirit and will be shown ways of inwardly and outwardly living a life patterned after Jesus. As you mature spiritually and seek a closer relationship with God, the forms of communication that you use will change from time to time. Therefore, many different techniques are offered in this manual for your consideration.

In regard to using these techniques, it is recommended that you test these methods of meditation through practical application and maintain an attitude of purity of purpose and openness to the divine influence. There is no right way of meditating that is suitable for everyone. But you can be guided to discover the way that is right for you. As your meditation experience deepens, you will gain greater responsiveness to the inner promptings of the Holy Spirit. Your inner guidance will show you with increasing clarity what techniques to use and perhaps how to create your own methods of meditation that will best meet your individual needs. Eventually the time may come when you are able to leave behind meditation techniques and consistently experience deep contemplation, as a gift from the Father.

---

1. Georg Feuerstein, *Sacred Paths: Essays on Wisdom, Love, and Mystical Realization* (Burden, New York: published for the Paul Brunton Philosophical Foundation by Larson Publications, 1991), p. 72

2. Ibid., p. 72

3. Ibid., p. 72

4. Thomas Matus, *Yoga and the Jesus Prayer Tradition* (Mahwah, New Jersey: Paulist Press, 1984), pp. 102-103 (currently published by Asian Trading, Bangalore, India; distributed by Hermitage Books, New Camaldoli, 62475 Coast Highway One, Big Sur, CA 93920)

5. Luke 18:11, 12, *The Holy Bible, Revised Standard Version* (New York, New York: Thomas Nelson and Sons, 1952). All Old Testament and New Testament quotes hereafter in this manual are taken from this version of the Bible and will be referenced only by chapter and verse.

6. Luke 18:13

7. Luke 18:35-43

8. Luke 18:42

3

PROCEDURES IN
MEDITATION

≈ ∘ ≈

A. Options

In this chapter and subsequent chapters, a structured approach to meditation is offered for your consideration. In many places, the word "optional" is used to indicate that a particular structure is not essential and can be included or excluded according to your choice. But for the sake of clarity, it needs to be emphasized that in this book *everything is optional*.

There is only one thing that is definitely not optional and that is your true relationship with God. Your true relationship with God is that He created you as part of Himself, and He loves you. Consequently, you do not have the option of changing your relationship with God. However, you do have the option of being aware of that relationship or not.

The story of *Sleeping Beauty* is well-known as a children's fairy tale, but it can also be interpreted as a story about your relationship with God. The Princess is asleep and in time the Kingdom has been overgrown by wild vegetation. The Princess is waiting to be awakened by the Prince, and then the Kingdom will be restored. In the story, the Prince comes and kisses the sleeping Princess. She awakens and immediately all the wild vegetation recedes revealing the Kingdom.

Just as the Princess in the story is asleep and waiting to be kissed and awakened by her beloved, you are asleep and waiting to be awakened by God. In some way you have already been kissed by the Holy Spirit. Otherwise you would not be interested in learning about meditation. Perhaps you have been blessed with a sudden spiritual experience, giving you a foretaste of your true beauty as a child of God. Maybe the Spirit has simply stirred your heart in faith that the divine can be found within you.

But unlike the immediate return of the Kingdom in the fairy tale, one kiss cannot awaken you all at once. The wild forms of vegetation that have overgrown the Kingdom are the many thoughts and desires that you have woven around your true Self, thus hiding your true relationship with God. Since you exerted your free will to create these thoughts and desires, you need to participate in the work of removing the inner blocks you have created.

Your goal is freedom from these inner obstacles, and in exercising your free will, you have many options of how you want to proceed. The mind itself is undivided and uncomplicated and will return to its natural state of simplicity if given the opportunity to do so. But immersion in the world produces an *addiction to complexity*. Your inner obstacles of thoughts and desires may be thought of as inner "mental addictions," similar to outer physical addictions. These inner *addictions are additions*. They are added thoughts and desires that do not really add to your true nature, but rather detract from the simplicity of your oneness with God.

To give up these addictions, which you have created by addition, you must go by a *way of subtraction*. Meditation leading to contemplation is a path of subtraction in which you let go of all those thoughts and desires that you have added. You do not really need any of these thoughts and desires. Nevertheless, you imagine that you do need them and so you need to let go of your attachment to these additions. As with letting go of any kind of addiction, you may experience withdrawal symptoms. It may be difficult to let go, and meditation is all about letting go. The next section will describe how to deal with your thoughts during meditation in your process of letting go.

Since your goal is freedom, you need the freedom to learn how to let go in your own time and way. In addition, you need to establish a certain amount of self-discipline in order to break away from your inner obstacles. The structures provided here are meant to be options for you to consider in your process of letting go.

Sometimes Christian seekers are attracted to the option of Eastern disciplines, spirituality, and philosophy. Such seekers will learn in Eastern philosophy that there are seven spiritual centers in the body and that waking up means awakening each of these spiritual centers and removing inner blocks in each of these centers of spiritual awareness. A combination of meditation techniques called *Christian Yoga Meditation* is a means of awakening the spiritual centers in the body in coordination with the action of the Holy Spirit. A description of how to practice Christian Yoga Meditation is provided in Chapters 5 and 6, and an explanation of the philosophical basis for this practice can be found in Chapters 8 and 11. There are many different kinds of inner blocks that need to be removed as you make progress spiritually. These are elaborated upon in Chapter 12.

Christian seekers who want to pursue Eastern methods of spiritual growth within a Christian context find that literature specifically written for Christians is limited. Furthermore, literature that is available does not provide comprehensive instructions describing how to incorporate Eastern methods into the process of deepening the seeker's meditation and contemplative experience as a follower of Christ. Ideally there would be places to go for spiritual direction and instruction in Eastern methods within a Christian framework, but this option is not available.

Due to this lack of information and options, some Christian seekers may feel that they are unable to both use Eastern methods and follow Christ at the same time. Not being aware of how to integrate the spiritual understandings of the East and West, these Christian seekers may feel that their only option is to make an "either or choice" between following a traditional Christian path or an Eastern path. Faced with this choice, some seekers choose the traditional Christian path and give up Eastern methods. On the other hand, some seekers choose the Eastern path and give up the Christian path. There is certainly nothing wrong with a person finding the answers for the meaning of life within an entirely Eastern context, if that is indeed that person's calling. However, if a person is called to be a Christian, in my opinion it is unfortunate to give up that calling because that person did not know that he could pursue using Eastern techniques within a Christian context.

Some seekers may choose to join an Eastern-based religious group and adopt the rituals and rules of that organization and perhaps be taught to surrender to a spiritual leader. Some souls have indeed greatly benefited from this direction. Nevertheless, other seekers have reported being disillusioned after participating in certain specific organizations. They felt they had surrendered their will inappropriately and therefore felt that they had regressed spiritually. Spiritual growth is a surrender, but it needs to be a surrender directly to God or Ultimate Reality—not to a philosophy, not to a person, and not to a structure. You can, of course, be open to other philosophies, other people, and helpful structures as part of your spiritual growth. But the answers you are seeking can only be found within. Consequently, you will need to use your discrimination to make sure that your self-surrender is directed inwardly rather than outwardly.

Whether you are a Christian or a non-Christian, your self-surrender needs to be made to the reality of your spiritual destination, which is, of course, within you. The end of your spiritual journey is always the one unchanging Reality that is worthy of your self-surrender and that will reveal your completion and oneness. Your self-surrender must never be made to the *means* of reaching your spiritual destination. The means that you may use along the way of your journey will change over time and surrendering to the means shows that you have mistaken the means for the end. You might like your car, but you would never surrender yourself to your car because you realize that it is merely a means to get from one place to another. Instead of surrendering your will to the means, you will need to exercise your will to keep your options open in regard to making changes in the means that you use in your spiritual journey.

The structures in this manual are the means to an end, not the end itself. Thus these structures are designed as a suggested way to approach meditation, but with an understanding that everything is optional. You need to be constantly looking within and asking the Holy Spirit to guide you and confirm that you are choosing structures that are right for your spiritual development. Also, some structures that are useful in the beginning of your spiritual journey may not be needed as you make progress. Consequently, you will need to exercise your option to let go of these outgrown structures. The way you meditate and the depth of your attunement will change as you grow spiritually, and you will need to make adjustments along the way on your journey of self-discovery.

B. The Purpose of Meditation

Before meditating it is good to remind yourself of the reason why you are meditating. Meditation is simply a process of purification in which the self and the cares of the world are being emptied so there may be greater receptivity to the Spirit. It is important for you to understand that you are embarking on a purification process. Some meditators perform a physical action as a symbolic representation of the inner cleansing that takes place in meditation. For example, some meditators drink a small cup of water or take a shower as a symbolic cleansing. However, there is certainly no need to express this purification process outwardly through some form of physical cleansing.

Although meditation in general is a purification process, you need to decide upon a specific purpose for meditating to which you can make an inner commitment. To do this you need to answer the question *What is my highest spiritual ideal?* Your highest spiritual ideal is the ultimate spiritual destination toward which you would like to grow. In other words your spiritual ideal would be your way of symbolizing Ultimate Reality. It is not a goal that can be reached and then possessed, such as something that you would like to do or accomplish in the world. Your spiritual ideal needs to be your highest spiritual aspiration, which forms a direction toward which you choose to live your life.

Your spiritual ideal may be represented by a name for God or a word that reminds you of God. "Love" or "oneness" are good examples since these are attributes of God's nature. You may choose a name as your spiritual ideal, such as "God" or "Jesus," so you can grow in that direction to be like God or like Jesus. Eventually you will discover your own spiritual nature not by possessing the spiritual ideal as though it were an object of attainment, but rather through uniting with the ideal to produce a state of oneness. Your spiritual ideal is only a symbol you choose to represent a spiritual reality. Therefore, uniting with your spiritual ideal means uniting with the *reality* of your spiritual ideal and discovering your own true reality in Ultimate Reality, which your ideal represents.

When deciding upon a spiritual ideal, it is best to choose one word or a few words that represent the highest aspiration that you can have for living your life. Your spiritual ideal represented by one or more words helps keep you focused on your spiritual destination. Because of the type of meditation techniques that will be recommended, it would be helpful to limit your choice to as few words as possible, perhaps one or two, or at the most four words. The choice of your spiritual ideal is a personal decision based upon your highest level of understanding.

In choosing your ideal, you need to realize that your ideal is not merely a perfect moral code or standard toward which you are growing. Viewing your spiritual ideal as just a perfect outer standard creates impossible expectations for you from your present ego perspective. As you attempt to live up to an ideal that is a perfect outer standard, you will, of course, fail in your attempts. Since your ideal creates unrealistic expectations of perfection, you will be unable to accept yourself. Thus you may be tempted to either pridefully pretend to live up to your ideal or condemn yourself for your failure to live up to your ideal.

To avoid this pitfall, you need to remember that your ideal is a name for God or a reminder of God. God is not merely an outer moral code or standard. He is a living and loving presence that is within you as your source and substance. Therefore, your ideal most of all represents that loving, divine presence that is living within you. Because of your ego condition, you are identified with the self that feels separate from the divine presence of God. However, you choose a spiritual ideal to help you form a deeper, more conscious identification with your true Self that is united with God. For your ideal to serve this purpose, you need to choose an ideal that is personally meaningful to you.

The words "purpose" and "meaning" are often used interchangeably, but they do not mean the same thing. A purpose has to do with a goal that you set out to accomplish. Once it is accomplished, you can choose another goal. Yet the question arises *How important is the purpose to you?* In other words, what is its meaning to you? You can have a meaningful purpose or a meaningless purpose. You may choose a spiritual ideal that becomes your purpose. This happens when you decide that you want your purpose, your goal, to be to grow toward that spiritual ideal. You may never fully accomplish that goal, but even growing toward that ideal can be your purpose. The crucial question is not *What is your purpose?* The more important question is *How meaningful is your purpose to you?* If it is not a meaningful purpose, you will lose your motivation and give up on your purpose. This is especially true of a spiritual ideal, since it is such a lofty goal that you may be tempted to give up such a difficult goal to reach. Therefore, it is absolutely imperative that you make your purpose as personally meaningful as possible. Thus if your spiritual ideal is to be the reason for your purpose, it needs to be one that gives meaning to your purpose.

Christian seekers often choose the word "Jesus" as their spiritual ideal because He is personally meaningful to them. Jesus can be perceived as the person who lived two thousand years ago and who is now united with God. Of course, Jesus is a perfect outer role model to emulate, but more importantly His divine presence is within you. His divine presence helps you to recognize your own true Self made in the image and likeness of the Father. If you choose Jesus as your spiritual ideal, it would be unwise for you to view Him as only a perfect outer standard that you can never hope to fully live up to. Instead, you can choose Jesus as your ideal to increase your awareness of your own divine nature and to deepen your personal relationship with Him as your guide to the Father. In time, you can learn to call upon Him as you would call upon your closest friend and know that you are loved just as you are in your present ego condition with all of your flaws.

Just like the word "Jesus" can have a personal meaning related to the person Jesus Christ and a universal meaning related to reminding you of your own divine nature, the word "Christ" as your chosen ideal can also have a dual meaning for you. Consequently, the word "Christ" can refer to Jesus Christ, who guides you to the Father, and it can also refer to the universal awareness of your true Self, your Christ Self. However, some Christians like to use the words "Jesus" and "Christ" with a singular meaning rather than with a dual meaning. In this case, the distinction is usually made for the sake of clarity that "Jesus" refers to the person Jesus, and "Christ" refers to the Universal Christ.

The meaning of the words you choose to represent your spiritual ideal is not just a theoretical consideration because your choice can affect your inward practices. For example, some Christians feel that calling upon "Jesus" nourishes their personal devotion. Other Christians feel that affirming the word "Christ" supports their universal devotion and helps to awaken their awareness of their own divine nature. You will need to choose the specific words and assign the meaning of these words that you feel will be most beneficial for you and best represent your spiritual ideal.

Before you decide upon the exact word or words which you would like to use to represent your spiritual ideal, you may want to read the next chapter, which will provide a wide variety of specific choices for your consideration. It is necessary to choose one ideal as your primary spiritual ideal, but you may have several secondary ideals. If "love" is not chosen as your primary ideal, then you may want to consider "love" as a secondary ideal. All spiritual growth is a matter of learning how to love as will be discussed in Chapter 14.

After choosing your ideal, the question you need to ask yourself is *What is the most important mental attitude I can have that will help me to grow toward my spiritual ideal?* The spiritual ideal may be thought of as your ultimate destination, while the mental attitude is that which will help you to take each step on the path toward your destination. Although final and complete union with your spiritual ideal will always be beyond your reach until the end of your journey, the mind can be used as an instrument of the Spirit to lead you in the direction of your destination. The mental attitude is the specific way you choose to use the mind along the path toward your spiritual ideal.

To further illustrate the distinction between the ideal and the mental attitude, you can think of life as a journey on a sailboat. You can choose a destination that you would like to reach at the end of the journey, and by analogy this would be your spiritual ideal. The sailboat, which is your traveling vehicle, would be the mind (and also the body), and the sail itself would be the mental attitude. The wind would be God's Spirit. Just as the sail must be filled with the wind to reach its destination, the mental attitude is that particular way of using the mind which would allow you to be filled with the Spirit and to grow toward your spiritual ideal. If you don't have a mental attitude that turns the mind toward your spiritual ideal, you won't be able to be guided by the Spirit. Consequently, you won't make progress toward your destination, just as a sailboat, without its sail being up, cannot catch the wind and will flounder aimlessly.

If your chosen spiritual ideal is "God" or "love," then you may choose a mental attitude that would help you to maintain the direction of growing toward God or love, such as "I wish to serve and be a channel of blessings to others." The mental attitude is expressed in the form of a brief statement that would be most appropriate to you. As another example, you may choose the ideal of "Jesus." In this case, you may choose a mental attitude, such as "Thy will be done," since this was the mental attitude He chose to become one with the Father. Most Christian seekers choose doing God's Will as their primary mental attitude. The importance of this particular mental attitude is elaborated upon in the beginning of Chapter 17. If the concept of doing God's Will is unclear to you, you may want to read this section before making your choice of a mental attitude.

Of course, there are many different mental attitudes you can have, but it is best to choose just one to be your primary mental attitude. This single mental attitude can form the foundation for the way in which you choose to direct your mind toward your spiritual ideal, and any other mental attitude can be a helpful secondary influence. Choosing your mental attitude does not mean that you will always be able to direct the mind in that way. For example, if "Thy will be done" is your chosen mental attitude, it will help you to express God's Will, yet it does not mean that you will always be able to express God's Will. It does mean that it is your sincere desire to do God's Will. Having this mental attitude will serve as a way of guiding your mind in this direction, and this will help you to be open to God's grace so you will make progress toward your spiritual ideal.

As an optional practice both your spiritual ideal and your mental attitude can be stated to yourself once before meditation begins and, if desired, once after meditation. This practice serves as a reminder to you of your spiritual and mental commitment to grow toward God. Your commitment, expressed in the form of a dedication before and/or after meditation, can give you not only a direction for your meditation, but eventually it can also give a direction to your whole life.

C. The Place

Where you choose to meditate is important. You will want to choose a spot that is private and quiet. Ideally, it will be a place that is not used for any other purpose. An example may be a space in front of a window in your bedroom or in front of a wall. It is best to use the same place each time you meditate because this will help as a way of conditioning yourself to establish the habit of meditating. Most meditators who choose to meditate in the evening prefer a dimly lit room rather than either bright lights or complete darkness.

D. Timing

The best times to meditate are in the early morning before eating breakfast and at sunset before dinner. A third option is at night just before going to bed, but the drawback of evening meditation is that the mind may not be as alert as it is earlier in the day because of fatigue. Also, some meditators discover that they expand their awareness so much during evening meditation that they have trouble going to sleep.

It is important to avoid practicing meditation immediately after eating because your digestion will prevent your meditation from being effective. Your digestion will not interfere with your meditation if you wait at least one and a half hours after a light meal or two hours after a heavier meal before meditating. It is not wise to meditate if you are overly hungry or if you are extremely tired. Whatever time you choose to meditate, you need to make sure that you meditate at the same time every day. This consistency of timing serves as a conditioning device that will help your meditation practice.

If you decide to conduct the Twenty-eight Day Demonstration in meditation, which will be described in subsequent chapters, you will need to set aside at least one twenty-five minute period each day for this purpose. However, it is recommend that you set aside two twenty-five minute periods each day, preferably one in the morning just after waking and one at some time in the afternoon. You may prefer to have your second meditation period in the evening as long as you are not tired or drowsy at night. Another option is to meditate one time per day on the weekends and two times a day on Mondays through Fridays when more interior time is needed to counteract the stress of a weekday work schedule. Once you have set a schedule for yourself, it is important to stick to it. Being persistent and consistent will help your practice of meditation. The effects are cumulative, so if you start skipping days or changing times, it will not be nearly as effective.

It is recommended that you set a timer for your twenty-five minute meditation, so you won't have to be distracted by being conscious of the time element. Digital timers that are available in most stores have a fairly loud ringer. You may have to go to an electronic specialty store, such as Radio Shack, to find a digital timer with a quiet ringer. If the sound that your timer makes is a little too loud, you can put something over it to muffle the sound. If you don't want to use a timer, you may have a watch or clock within view that you can look at after you think twenty-five minutes have elapsed.

After you gain some experience in the practice of meditation, you will probably develop an intuitive sense of timing. When this happens you won't consciously think about the time while you are meditating, but you will have an inner sense of when the twenty-five minutes is completed, and your eyes will open at just about the right time. Yet this ability may eventually disappear as your meditation experience deepens and you become totally unaware of time. When you are in deep meditation, a twenty-five minute meditation may appear to you as only five or ten minutes. Obviously you will require a timer, rather than a watch or clock, when your meditation deepens.

E. The Posture

For sitting meditation, your posture is very important. Having your spine in the proper alignment allows a free flow of energy, which will rise upward to enhance your meditation practice. It is recommended that before beginning your meditation practice, you check to make sure that your spine is straight, but not rigid. The center of balance in the body is the lower abdomen. It helps your meditation to relax the abdomen and have it slightly protruded. Some meditators will gently rock the upper body backward and forward to find their center of balance and then rock the upper body from side to side to center the spine properly.

Another way to make sure the spine is in the proper alignment is to imagine that a string is attached to the very top of the head and the string is being pulled straight up. Imagining this string being pulled up can help you to mentally check to make sure the neck and head in particular are properly aligned. To align the head, the chin needs to be drawn in very slightly. The chest needs to be held slightly up and out. If the chest slumps down, the head will move forward out of alignment. If your spine is properly aligned, the side view of your body will show the tip of the nose in line with the navel and the ears in line with the shoulders. Before beginning your meditation practice, you can remind yourself to mentally check to make sure that you have a good posture in which the spine is straight, but relaxed.

Most people prefer meditating in a chair. The illustration shown on the opposite page depicts the recommended body posture for meditation practiced while sitting in a chair. You place the legs about a foot apart in line with the shoulders. You place the feet flat on the floor and have the legs relaxed. When using a chair, you sit with the spine erect so that your back does not lean against the chair. Leaning your back against the chair prevents the spine from being in the proper alignment for establishing correct body balance. Also, placing your back against the chair inhibits the subtle energy within your body that becomes activated during meditation. If you have a back problem that is relieved by leaning against a chair, then you need to sit in whatever way is most comfortable for you.

Any solid chair with a flat surface can be used. Typically this is the type of chair used for sitting at the dinner table rather than a soft chair usually found in the living room. You can place a cushion on the chair both for softness and to adjust the height so you are not sitting too high or too low. Although the cushion can be flat, you can give yourself a significant additional advantage by placing a folded towel under the back of the cushion. This is intended to raise the back portion of your

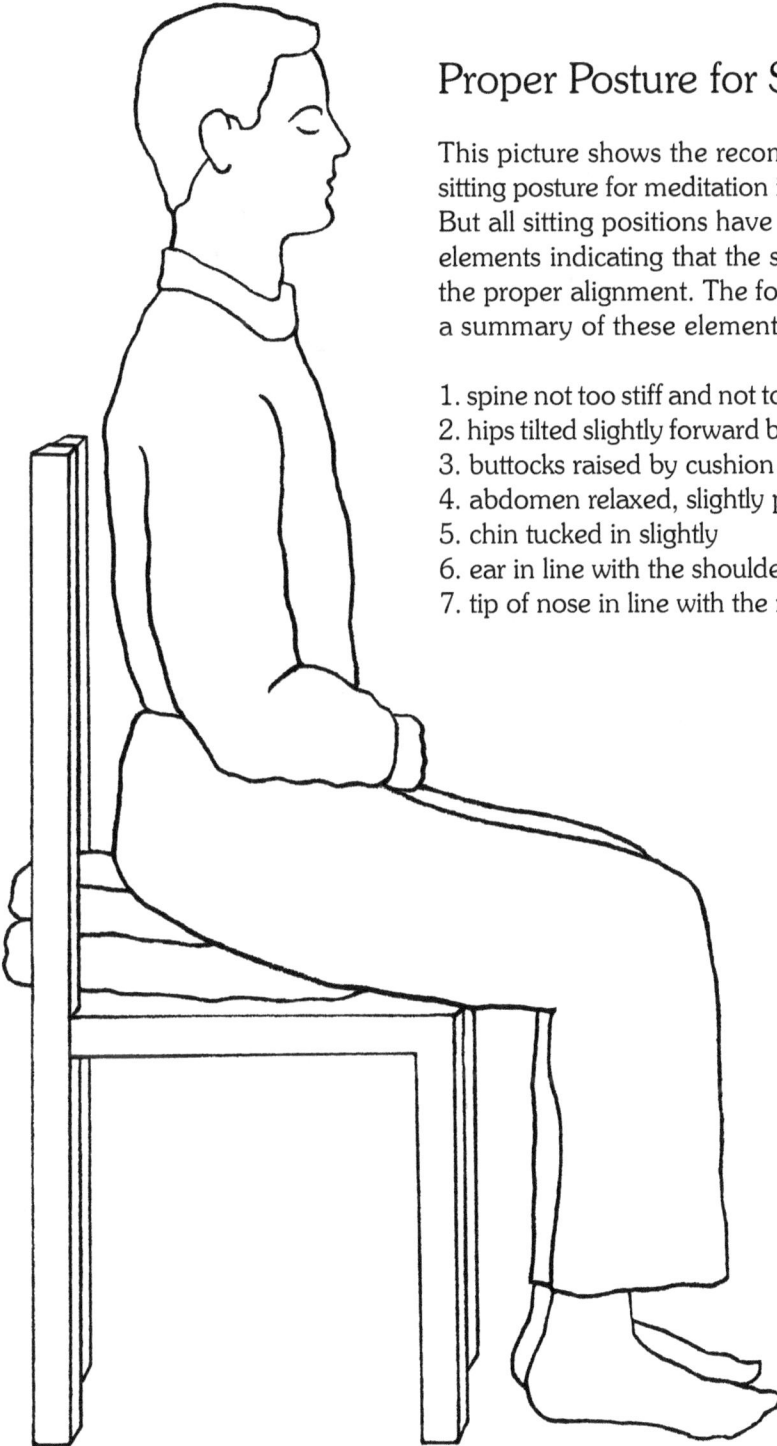

Proper Posture for Sitting

This picture shows the recommended sitting posture for meditation in a chair. But all sitting positions have the same elements indicating that the spine is in the proper alignment. The following is a summary of these elements:

1. spine not too stiff and not too relaxed
2. hips tilted slightly forward by cushion
3. buttocks raised by cushion
4. abdomen relaxed, slightly protruded
5. chin tucked in slightly
6. ear in line with the shoulder
7. tip of nose in line with the navel

Hand Positions for Meditation

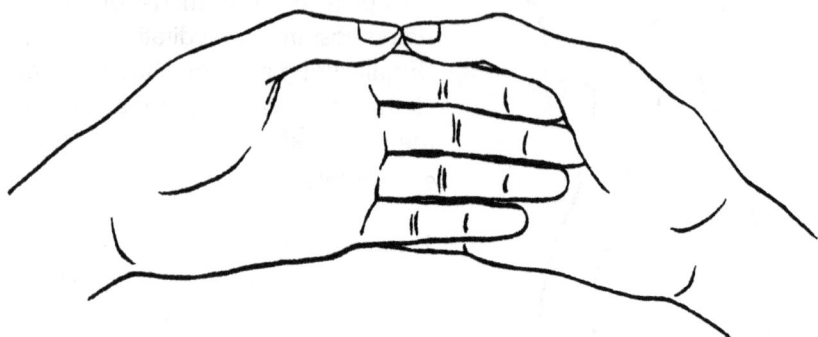

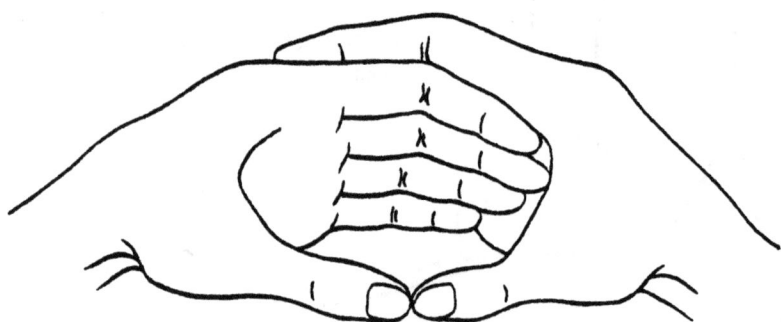

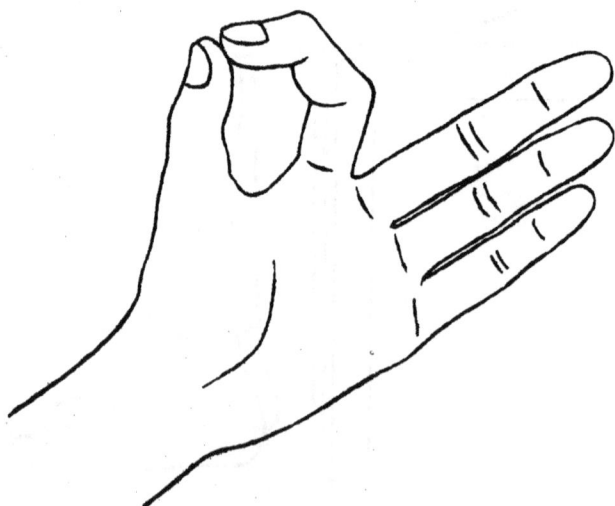

sitting surface so your hips are tilted just slightly forward. The purpose of the forward tilt is to keep the back straight and to place the hips in the ideal position for raising energy within the body. Having the back portion of the sitting surface raised helps to spread and raise the buttocks. Spreading and raising the buttocks also help to place the abdomen in a slightly protruded position that aids the posture and the body balance.

Sitting in a chair is recommended for most beginners, but some meditators prefer sitting on the floor with the legs crossed, although at first it may feel uncomfortable. One option is the full lotus position, in which each foot is placed on top of the opposite thigh with the soles of the feet turned upward. This is not a realistic sitting position for most meditators because it requires a great deal of flexibility. Others use a half lotus, which requires a moderate degree of flexibility to place just one foot on top of one thigh. Most meditators who sit on the floor just cross their legs in the usual way. If you are not used to sitting with the legs crossed, it may take a while to stretch the muscles and the ligaments of the legs and to get out the stiffness.

For sitting on the floor, you use a folded blanket or a firm cushion. Sitting on a raised seat is recommended not only because it is easier on the legs, but also because it helps to keep the spine erect and to maintain the body balance. Instead of sitting with the legs crossed, some meditators prefer the kneeling posture, in which the legs are folded underneath the body. In this posture, a blanket or cushion is placed under the buttocks to relieve the pressure of the body weight upon the legs. In addition, there are special meditation benches that are available commercially for sitting meditation.

It is best to keep the hands resting in the area just below the navel because this is the center of balance for the body. However, if this is not comfortable, you can lower the hands to the place where they feel most relaxed and where the body balance can be most easily maintained. You may want to experiment with different hand positions until you find the one that is the most comfortable for you.

In considering a hand position, it is most important to find a relaxed position for the hands. You can choose to use any relaxed and unstructured hand position. There are also specific and structured hand positions that you can use. You can see in the illustration shown on the opposite page that there are three specific hand positions that you may want to consider. The top hand position in the illustration is sometimes used by Buddhist meditators. For this hand position, you place the left hand on top of the right hand with both palms facing upward to form the lower half of a flattened circle. In this hand position, the tips of the thumbs of each hand are gently touching each other. In this case, the thumbs of each hand are placed against the index finger of the left hand. The hands rest in the lap with the little fingers touching the lowest part of abdomen.

The middle hand position shown in the illustration is a variation of the previous hand position and is used by Zen Buddhist meditators. As with the previously described hand position, the left hand is still placed over the right hand with both palms facing upward. However, by repositioning the thumbs away from the other fingers, this variation changes the lower half of the flattened circle into a full flatten circle. For this variation, the thumbs are raised upward, away from the other fingers, so the index fingers and the thumbs create an oval shape. The tips of the thumbs are placed together. The thumbs are gently touching each other and are located against the abdomen just below the navel.

Another popular hand position is to place the hands on the legs with the palms turned upward. The bottom hand position in the illustration is a structured way of placing the hands on the legs. For this hand position, you place the right hand on the right leg and the left hand on the leg. The tip of the thumb and the tip of the index finger of each hand are gently touching each other. The touching of the thumb and index finger creates a circle out of each hand. The other three fingers of each hand are separated from each other and extended away from the thumb and index finger. This is a yoga hand position called the *jnana mudra*.[1]

These structured Hindu and Buddhist hand positions may appear as only ritualistic expressions, but there is actually a functional reason for these particular hand positions. The life force that emanates from the body and gives it life is constantly flowing through the body. Much of this energy exits the body through the hands and feet. These hand positions tend to draw energy back into the body and encourage the flow of energy upward toward the head. This upward-flowing energy creates a purifying and spiritually revitalizing effect. Any one of the three structured hand positions described above may be used by Christians. On the other hand, these hand positions may be too rigid and formal for most Christians and for most beginning meditators. You are welcome to experiment with using a structured hand position, or you may want to use an unstructured hand position of your choice. But your most important consideration is to choose a hand position that is comfortable for you.

You may also wonder why many forms of Eastern spirituality place such an emphasis on sitting with the legs crossed. This sitting position, like the hand positions, tend to draw the energy inward and upward toward the head. Yoga philosophy would identify the crossing of the legs as a unifying of the male (right leg) and female (left leg) energy. The full lotus position is the most well-known posture associated with meditation. This posture is not recommended for most Westerners because it is too difficult to maintain for extended periods. Although the full lotus position is the most effective posture for focusing the mind, it is the most difficult to maintain. The half lotus position, in which only one foot is placed over the opposite thigh, is more commonly used than the full lotus. Any position that includes crossing the legs will be helpful unless there is discomfort that distracts you from your meditation. Nevertheless, using a chair is generally recommended because it is easier and more relaxing, and therefore more effective for most Westerners.

If sitting for meditation is not possible or if it is too uncomfortable, then as a last resort you can meditate lying down. Sitting meditation is more effective at raising energy in the body than lying-down meditation, which inhibits energy from rising up the spine. Although, in general, sitting meditation is more effective, lying-down meditation may be the only possible way for some people to meditate. If you normally practice sitting meditation, you may occasionally employ lying-down meditation when you require an increased degree of physical relaxation. However, if you find that you tend to fall asleep in the lying-down method, you should practice sitting meditation exclusively. A good time to practice lying-down meditation is the late afternoon before the evening dinner, because that is a time when the body may need a rest and yet the body will not be so tired that it will fall asleep.

For lying-down meditation, it is best to lie down on the floor with a blanket underneath the body. Another folded blanket or pillow can be used to raise the head an inch or two off the floor. If no other alternative is feasible, then you can simply lie in bed. In the lying-down position, you place the hands over the area just below the navel. You position one hand over the other. The tips of the thumbs are gently touching each other and are placed just below the navel. Place the legs slightly apart.

This lying-down position is designed to relax the body for meditation and yet provide just enough structure to discourage sleeping. Instead of using the structured position described above, you may spontaneously place the hands and the feet in any position that is comfortable for you while lying down.

F. Relaxation (Optional)

Relaxing the body is a good way to prepare for meditation. Perhaps the easiest way to do this is to just give the body a mental message to relax by saying the word "relax" to the body, and then consciously feeling the body relax completely. Some meditators use an expanded form of mental suggestion for relaxation. This is done by saying the word "relax" to each of the body parts individually. The usual procedure is to begin by mentally relaxing first the feet, then moving upward one part at a time all the way to the head. This form of relaxation may be done while sitting or lying down.

Many meditators prefer to use the simple *Head and Neck Exercise* for relaxing the body in preparation for meditation. For this exercise, you move the head forward three times, backward three times, to the right three times, and to the left three times. Then you roll the head in a wide circular motion three times one way and then three times the other way. The Head and Neck Exercise is recommended in the readings of Edgar Cayce.[2]

Taking a few deep breaths before meditation is another option for helping the body to relax. You may want to practice *Yoga Deep Breathing*. With the inhalation, you can expand first the abdomen, then the lower chest, and then the upper chest. With the exhalation, you can contract the upper chest, then the lower chest, and then the abdomen. Though described in parts, the breathing is actually done in one flowing motion. By inhaling from bottom to top and exhaling from top to bottom, the breath is very deep and calming.

Establishing a daily routine of hatha yoga body postures (*asanas*) and breathing practices (*pranayama*) can be very helpful to prepare the body for practicing meditation. Hopefully you will be able to attend a typical hatha yoga class given by a hatha yoga instructor, who is not affiliated with any religious group. Such a class may be an hour or an hour and a half one day per week for six to eight weeks. However, the real benefit of taking such a class is in learning methods that you can incorporate into a daily practice at home. Practicing yoga every day will not only serve as a relaxation method, but also as a means of supporting health and as a purifying practice preparing you for deepening your meditation experience.

Stretching, listening to music, and devotional chanting or singing are also helpful methods of relaxing and preparing for meditation. You may want to experiment with different methods of relaxation to find out what works best for you. While not essential to meditation, a relaxation method is recommended as a good way to prepare for your meditation experience.

G. Preparatory Prayer (Optional)

In addition to your statement of your ideal and attitude as a dedication of yourself prior to meditation, you may want to offer a preparatory prayer to place yourself in the proper frame of mind before beginning your meditation practice. There is a fundamental difference between prayer and meditation. Prayer uses the expression of thoughts or the imagination to reach out to God, In contrast to prayer, meditation uses the reduction of thoughts and setting aside of the imagination to quiet the mind in order to contact the Spirit at a deeper level.

Before offering a preparatory prayer, you can pause briefly to feel yourself becoming inwardly quiet. Then you may choose, for instance, to simply ask God in prayer to surround and protect you from distracting influences during your meditation. Some meditators choose to use a spontaneous preparatory prayer, while others prefer repeating a formal prayer, such as the Lord's Prayer. This optional preparatory prayer should only take a minute or two and serves as a way for you to prepare for shifting the mind and heart toward the direction of deepening your relationship with God. Prayers may likewise be offered after completing meditation.

There are three reasons for having a preparatory prayer. First, it prepares the mind to be quiet. Second, it is an invitation for the Holy Spirit to enter in and show you how to commune with God. Perhaps you may even want to put this invitation to the Holy Spirit into words and have it be your preparatory prayer itself. Third, it is a protection against negative influences.

In addition to the choices of preparatory prayer that use words, there is a wordless form of preparatory prayer that relies upon the imagination of white light. You simply imagine that a white light from above the head comes down over the outside of the body and surrounds it. Then you imagine a white light coming down from above the head, filling the head, and continuing downward to fill the entire inside of the body. Imagining white light can be done briefly in this manner or in another way of your choosing.

This imagination of white light is a protecting influence, and you may think of this light in either one of two ways. The white light may be considered as the light of God, since "God is light."[3] Or the white light may be considered as the light of Christ, for Jesus says of Himself, "I am the light of the world."[4]

The use of the imagination usually involves imagining something that is not real and yet the seeking of God is the seeking of Reality. Thus the imagination would not normally be used for the seeking of God. But the imagination of white light is an exception to this rule because when you are imagining white light, you are imagining something that has a reality behind it.

Saints who have experienced illumination invariably bear witness to their encounter with a supernatural light that is a reality. However, under normal circumstances, the reality of this supernatural light is hidden from conscious awareness and for most people is accessible only through the imagination. After imagining white light to be real, the reality behind that imagining begins to shine through so you become increasingly aware of the presence of that reality. In this case, white light is first imagined so you can become aware of the reality of God's light or Christ's light.

Visualization is one way of using the imagination and if you choose to do so, you can use visualization to imagine the white light. Yet you may just as easily and just as effectively imagine the white light without using any visualization. While imagining white light is an option for your preparatory prayer, the imagination and in particular visualization are generally not used during meditation itself.

H. Thoughts in Meditation

A variety of meditation techniques will be described in subsequent chapters and all of these techniques will involve the challenge of dealing with the fluctuating thoughts of the mind. Meditation is a process of inner purification in which the mind is silenced so that you can become increasingly receptive to the Spirit, which transcends rational thinking. The mind is constantly filled with many thoughts that are centered upon yourself. In order to redirect the mind from being self-centered to being God-centered, it is best to take up one thought in the mind and repeat this one thought mentally. This one thought will dominate all the other thoughts in the mind. Many thoughts may appear during meditation, especially for a beginner. However, by holding one thought, these other thoughts have no power, and they disappear as quickly as they have arisen.

When any other thoughts appear, you do not hold on to them and examine them, and you do not try to push them away. These other thoughts are like a visitor who comes to your door at a time when you are very busy doing an important project that must be done at that moment. You can hear the ringing of the doorbell by the visitor, but you do not even go to the door to talk with him. If you do open the door and talk with him, there is no telling how long your conversation will last. Before you know it, he will be inside the house, and you will have no time to do your work. Even if you open the door just to tell him to go away, he may still draw you into a lengthy conversation. It is best in such a case to not even go to open the door. The visitor will ring the doorbell a few times, and when no one comes to the door, he will go away.

Just as you do not open the door to an unwanted visitor, you do not open the door to distracting thoughts that come as visitors to the mind.

You neither invite them in nor tell them to go away. Distracting thoughts will go away if you ignore them and just continue with your project. The project, in which you have become absorbed, is the holding of just one thought firmly in the mind.

In the beginning, you may find that you can hold one thought only for a very short while, and then your mind wanders. When you realize that your mind has wandered, you can gently bring the awareness of the mind back to the one thought. This process of holding the one thought, losing it, and then returning to the one thought is called *concentration*. Through the practice of concentration, you gradually begin to practice *meditation*. From the perspective of technique, meditation may be defined as the sustaining of any one thought in the mind continuously. Through the practice of meditation, the mind is purified of self-centered thoughts, and you become increasingly aware of the divine presence within. However, inner receptivity to the Spirit is not an automatic result of holding one thought in the mind. Meditation that is reduced to merely a mental device alone would be ineffective. To be truly effective, meditation is not only a *focusing of attention*, but also a *focusing of intention* in which you express your sincere desire for God.

For the sake of clarity, a distinction needs to be made here between meditation and *contemplation*. Contemplation is a form of internal communication with God in which the soul is overshadowed by the Holy Spirit. This communion with the Spirit is a state of heightened awareness in which the normal rational thinking process is set aside. Contemplation is resting in God produced by divine grace and is not itself a technique, but techniques can lead to this experience. Meditation, on the other hand, is a method of reducing self-centered thoughts in order to increase receptivity to the Spirit. By maintaining one thought in the mind during meditation, you cannot manufacture contemplation, yet you can prepare yourself to be receptive to that gift of the Spirit.

The one thought that you choose for meditation may theoretically be any one thing that can be used as a focus for your attention. For example, some meditators focus solely on observing the breath. Others count the inhalations and/or exhalations. However, most meditators prefer choosing one thought in the form of a word or combination of words. This choice of a word or words creates a sound vibration that the body and the mind become in tune with through repetition. This one thought still remains vibrating in the mind long after the meditation period is over and gives stability to the mind even when it is employed in outward activities. Retaining any one thought in the mind will calm the mind to a certain degree. Nevertheless, there are certain words that have more power and effectiveness than others, because these words work at a deeper level of consciousness.

The best word to repeat for your meditation practice is one that will affect your total being at the deepest level. In order to find a word that will work at the deepest level within, you need to find a word that is more than just a sound vibration. It is true that repeating any one word will calm the mind. For example, even the word "tree" will work to a certain degree. Nonetheless, it is best to use a word that will draw you to the secret place within yourself where you are touched and moved most personally at the center of your being. You can find such a word in the roots of your own religion, whether you are practicing the outward form of that religion or not. This word that will enable you to go to the very center of your being is the *Divine Name*.

The Divine Name, regardless of what form it takes, is a name for God or a name that serves as a reminder or symbol of God. Therefore, you may want to choose a form of the Divine Name to represent your spiritual ideal. The practice of calling upon the Divine Name has been widely recognized as a means of invoking a greater awareness of the divine within. The use of Divine Names and choices of other words to repeat in meditation are elaborated upon in the next chapter.

The words you repeat during meditation may be called *affirmations* because you are affirming and even building within yourself the nature of those words you have chosen. Just as listening to music can create in you a vibration and feeling related to the type of music chosen, likewise this affirming is actually building within yourself the vibration and feeling of the words chosen. Therefore, the words for the affirmation need to be chosen wisely. They must be of a spiritual nature so that when repeated during meditation they will affirm the divine within and actually increase your awareness of the divine presence. For this reason, it is best to choose an affirmation that points directly (or at least indirectly) to your spiritual ideal. Consequently, a spiritual ideal, preferably in the form of the Divine Name, is recommended for your choice of an affirmation or to be used as part of your affirmation.

Nonetheless, affirmations, even those of your spiritual ideal including the Divine Name, have a built-in limitation. They are all only symbols. They are useful symbols because they represent your desire for the divine. They help to focus your intention to be one with your spiritual ideal, and meditation after all is a focused intention. But doesn't your intention itself go deeper than words? Isn't your intention a yearning that cannot be limited by words?

Learning to repeat an affirmation in order to build these words that represent your intention into your consciousness is only part of your task.

The other part is learning to let go of the affirmation and rely on your intention itself beyond words. By practicing the methods recommended in this manual, you will learn how to use an affirmation along with body awareness to help you focus on your intention to be receptive to the Holy Spirit. In addition, you will learn how to let go of repeating the affirmation and to center your mind only on body awareness in order to focus on your intention. Finally, you will learn how to let go of both the affirmation and body awareness so you can focus on your intention in silence and be led into contemplation.

Before making your choice of an affirmation, you might want to read the next chapter that elaborates upon the use of Divine Names and other affirmations. Then, after you read three additional brief chapters, you will have all the information you will need to begin your practice of meditation with the goal of becoming increasingly receptive to God's presence within.

I. Completing Meditation

After your meditation is completed, it is best not to get up quickly. You can just remain sitting quietly for a brief time. This time at the end of your meditation can be used for prayer. In your prayer, you can reaffirm your dedication to your spiritual ideal and purpose, or you can pray for others or for yourself, perhaps expressing gratitude for this time spent in divine communion.

Some meditators like to complete their sitting period with a gesture of bowing forward. If you are sitting in a chair, the hands can be located at the chest in a prayer position with the palms and fingers placed together, and you can bow forward slightly from the waist. Another option is that you can omit raising the hands to the chest and simply bend forward from the waist. After the energy has been raised up into the head during meditation, a gesture of bowing forward helps to absorb this energy into the abdomen creating an inner balance of energy stored for future use.

You can also use the expression of bowing forward described above if you had been sitting on the floor rather than in a chair. But if you are sitting on the floor, you may choose to use an alternative bowing gesture, which is actually a yoga posture, called the *Yoga Seal*. For this gesture the arms are placed behind the back with the right wrist being held by the left hand. With your hands behind the back, you bend all the way forward, relaxing and allowing gravity to exert its force over the body. During your practice of meditation, energy rises upward and into the head. After your meditation is completed, bowing forward into the Yoga Seal allows the energy that had arisen into the head to descend into the chest and heart area and then into the abdomen to be available for future use.

If you have been sitting on the floor for your meditation practice, you may discover after your meditation is finished that parts of your legs have become numb. The numbness is caused by your sitting in a body position that produces a restriction of the nerves going to the legs. Because of the numbness you may not be able to immediately move your legs as you normally would, but no physical harm has actually occurred to your legs. If the numbness does occur, you do not need to be alarmed. You can simply stretch the legs or move the feet with the hands. You will notice the legs returning to normal within seconds.

After your meditation is over, you may find that you need to urinate. This may be due to the relaxation produced by your meditation practice. Another reason is that meditation, as a purifying practice, not only cleanses the mind but also the body. Your meditation practice can throw off toxins that have previously been stored in the body, and urination helps to release these toxins. Also, meditation affects the endocrine glands, especially the pituitary gland. Your meditation can result in the pituitary gland releasing hormones, which regulate the bladder functions and result in your need to urinate.

---

1. Swami Rama, Rudolph Ballentine, M.D., Alan Hymes, M.D., *The Science of Breath* (Honesdale, Pennsylvania: The Himalayan International Institute of Yoga Science and Philosophy, 1979), pp. 126-127

2. Harold J. Reilly and Ruth Hagy Brod, *The Edgar Cayce Handbook for Health Through Drugless Therapy* (Virginia Beach, VA: A.R.E. Press, Copyright 1975), p.113 (#3549-1 of the Edgar Cayce readings)

3. First letter of John 1:5

4. John 8:12

4

DIVINE NAMES AND OTHER AFFIRMATIONS

≈ • ≈

A. Names for God used as Affirmations

Some say that there are many paths of spiritual growth, but then they refuse to follow any one of those paths. Your challenge is to allow yourself to be guided inwardly to the path that would be most helpful for you to draw closer to God and then to follow that path in your everyday life.

If you have chosen a Christian path, it is helpful to have an attitude of openness toward understanding the paths that other spiritual seekers have taken. Finding common threads in other paths helps you to better understand your own. One common practice found in most religious traditions is the use of the Divine Name of God. For example, in the Islamic approach to prayer, repeating the Divine Name of Allah is used as an affirmation, along with other prayerful words.

Likewise, Jewish mysticism employs the repeating of the Divine Name of God. The most sacred of these names is the one that was so holy that it was never to be uttered in speech. The English consonants for this sacred name for God are "YHWH," according to some scholars, while others use "JHVH." Although the vowels after each consonant were too holy to be written, they were passed down through unwritten Jewish tradition. Today, many people use the word "Yahweh" or "Jehovah," but still the true pronunciation is not known, except perhaps by Jewish mystics who wish such knowledge to remain secret. Since only the four consonants of God's name are known for certain, some Jewish meditators focus on these original four letters of the Hebrew alphabet that represent the Hebrew name for God. Other less sacred Jewish names for God that can be pronounced for meditation are "Adonai" and "Elohim."

In Hinduism the most universal Name for God is "OM," which is a *mantra* that is repeated as an affirmation during meditation. OM is considered to be the Word of God, the sound from which all of creation manifested. OM is a Sanskrit word that is often written as "AUM." Many scholars consider these two words to be interchangeable. The mouth is fully open for the first part of pronouncing OM, and the mouth is fully closed for the last part of the pronunciation. OM can be pronounced "*ooo-mmmm*" or AUM can be pronounced as either "*ah-oh-mmm*" or "*ah-uuu-mmm.*" In Hindu theology the energy of Brahman, the creator, is represented by the "A." The energy of Vishnu, the preserver of creation, is represented by the "U." And the energy of Shiva, the transformer of creation, is represented by the "M." Yoga philosophy maintains that OM contains all other sounds within it.

OM may be the root of many sacred words from different languages, such as the root of the Christian "Amen" or the Hebrew "Shalom," meaning peace. OM is associated with the feeling of peace and when listened to or chanted induces tranquility. In spite of its connection with Hinduism, OM can be used by Christians during meditation as a Name for God or a reminder of God.

However, for meditation most Christians would naturally be drawn to repeat an affirmation of a Divine Name for God that can be found within their own Christian tradition. Of course, some obvious examples are "God" or "Lord." Another example is "Father," or even "Abba," the word Jesus used to call upon His Father.

Everyone knows that God is not male or female, but in this meditation manual words like "Father," "His World," and "His Will" are used to refer to God. These male-gender words are used partially due to the fact that sometimes the English language uses male words in a gender-neutral way to indicate either male or female. The other reason for referring to God in male terms is that there is a tendency in the West to think of God in male terms. This is in contrast to the East where sometimes the term "Divine Mother" is used to describe God manifesting in the world. Of course, neutral words can be used as the only way to relate to God, but the problem with this is that for some seekers neutrality can be somewhat impersonal. Human nature wants to personalize God in order to foster a sense of approachability and intimacy with God. But the male gender applied to God is not the only way to establish this personal relationship. Some seekers prefer to relate to God in female terms rather than male terms. Consequently, you may choose to use a female-gender affirmation for God, such as "Mother." Another example is the word "Ma," which expresses greater familiarity and can be used as an affirmation. If this word is repeated for meditation, the "m" sound in particular is extended so it is repeated mentally as "*mmmmmmmmma.*"

Just like the male words for God are used with the understanding that God is not really male, the female words for God are used with the understanding that God is not really female. Nevertheless, some seekers choose to use the female gender to relate to God because of personal mental and emotional associations. For example, when you grew up, if you had a very loving mother, who was always nourishing and supportive, you are more likely to relate to God in female terms and to perceive God as a loving presence providing nourishment and support. Another factor is your own gender, which can affect your relationship with God. Specifically some female seekers can be offended by the Western bias toward referring to God in male terminology and therefore may choose to use female terms to counteract this male bias.

There is a tendency to assign male or female terms to God and perhaps assign male or female attributes as well to personalize your relationship. Yet it is necessary to set aside these kinds of associations during the practice of meditation. You do not think about the meaning of your affirmation while it is being repeated during meditation. Thus in a practical sense it does not matter if your affirmation has a male, female, or neutral connotation.

Instead of a Divine Name for God, a quality of God may be repeated as an affirmation. One such affirmation is the word "Oneness." This word can be simplified even further by using the single-syllable word "One." This simple word used as an affirmation can help you at a deep level to not only acknowledge God, but also to identify with your own oneness with Him. The word "One" may also be used as an affirmation by non-Christians who are open to God, yet not open to Jesus Christ. If you are a Christian who is not drawn to repeating the Name of Jesus Christ as an affirmation, you may want to consider using the word "One," since this simple affirmation can help you to focus upon awakening your inherent oneness with the Father. Experienced meditators who use this word exclusively report an inner peace and a feeling of inner strength and security.

However, for your affirmation, any word or words may be chosen that remind you of God or in particular remind you of your relationship to God. The sacred word or words that you choose gain their strength not from the words themselves, but rather from your willingness to allow them to summarize your intention to be open to God's presence.

B. The Jesus Prayer of the Heart

If your heart moves you to say the Name of "Jesus" as an affirmation, then stick to it. You will not find a sweeter or more powerful Divine Name than this. Repeating the Divine Name of Jesus is called the *Jesus Prayer* or the *Prayer of the Heart*. The complete form of the Jesus Prayer is "Lord Jesus Christ, Son of God, have mercy on me, a sinner." This long form may be employed. But a shortened form of the Jesus Prayer is recommended for a Christian affirmation. Here are some examples:

Lord Jesus Christ, have mercy on me
Christ, have mercy
Lord, have mercy
Jesus, mercy
Lord Jesus Christ
Jesus Christ
Christ
Jesus

The words "Jesus" and "mercy" sum up the entire message of the Prayer of the Heart. When you repeat the word "mercy," you admit your need for help. At one level this is an acknowledgment of your personal shortcomings and the need for forgiveness. At a deeper level you are recognizing that you need help because, by your very human nature, you are bound by your ego. It is true that you are made in the image and likeness of God, and you may understand intellectually that you are truly a spiritual being. But in practical, everyday life, you perceive yourself as being only a body and a mind, separate from your spiritual nature in God. This false perception of yourself is what is called the "ego," and the total of all the other thoughts built around this false perception is called the "self."

The ego, because it is a false perception, maintains its influential status by hiding the truth of your spiritual nature. Yet you know at some level that the ego does not serve you and opposes who you really are. Consequently, you begin to turn away from the ego, to seek your true nature in God. When you set out to find God, you may think to yourself "I will seek God." But who is this "I" that is setting out to find God? Is it not the ego? Since the ego can exist only in a state of separation, the ego cannot succeed in finding union with God. Realizing this dilemma, you ask for mercy as an admission that you are totally dependent on God's grace to free yourself from the ego state in order to be united with God. Even your desire to be united with God is not a sign of your initiative. Instead, it is a sign of God's initiative of grace already working within your soul and helping you realize your need for mercy.

The real meaning of mercy is often misunderstood. The Greek word for "mercy" is "eleison," which literally translated means anointment with oil—meaning the oil of God's grace. In the monasteries at Mount Athos in Greece, where the Prayer of the Heart has flourished for centuries, there is a clear recognition of this idea that mercy represents the oil of God's grace. In fact, the story is told that when you receive the merciful oil of God's grace, you become so slippery that when the devil tries to grab hold of you, you slip right out of the devil's fingers. The word "mercy," as it is used in the Jesus Prayer, is an admission of your need for the grace of the Holy Spirit, and your acknowledgment opens you to receive that gift.

While the word "mercy" admits the false nature of the ego and thus the need for grace, the word "Jesus" (or any of His other Divine Names) is a declaration that you trust that all your needs of grace will be met in that Name. These two words, mercy and Jesus, form a wonderfully balanced approach to God. They allow you to acknowledge your nothingness in regard to your ego condition and at the same time allow you to express your divine and true nature in Christ, your "Christ Self."

In so doing, you are following the advice of Jesus on how to pray:

> But when you pray, go into your room and shut the door and pray to your Father who is in secret; and your Father who is in secret will reward you. And in praying do not heap up empty phrases as the Gentiles do; for they think that they will be heard for their many words. Do not be like them, for your Father knows what you need before you ask him.[1]

After teaching His followers not to use many words in vainly repeating requests for things of this world, Jesus then gives them the Lord's Prayer, which is really a long affirmation. The Jesus Prayer is simply a condensed version of the Lord's Prayer. The words "Our Father who art in Heaven, hallowed be thy name" are summed up in the Name of Jesus Christ. While Jesus was still with His disciples, He gave them the invocation of "Father" ("Abba") to call upon. It is clear that Jesus wanted His followers to develop a relationship with God and see God as their father since He is their Creator and continuous benefactor.

However, at the last supper, He gave His own Divine Name as a new invocation. But He did not do so to replace devotion to God the Father. Jesus did not say, "Ask for anything of Me in My Name, and I will give it to you." Instead, Jesus said:

> Truly, truly, I say to you, if you ask anything of the Father, he will give it to you in my name. Hitherto you have asked nothing in my name; ask, and you will receive, that your joy may be full.[2]

When you call upon the Name of Jesus, you are not devoted to Jesus alone since Jesus is one with the Father. Therefore, your calling upon the Name of Jesus is a means of enhancing your devotion to God the Father. Some individuals are reluctant to call upon the Name of Jesus in meditation because they think that doing so will detract from devotion directly to God the Father. This is an unfortunate misunderstanding of the role of Jesus. It is in fact the role of Jesus to always be an open doorway directly to the Father, for anyone who calls upon the Name of Jesus. Instead of blocking your relationship to God, He assists in revealing your true relationship with the Father. Jesus, as the Son, reveals your own Sonship with the Father. God has one Son, Who is the Universal Christ. Jesus is the first to completely awaken to His Sonship in the one Universal Christ. But Jesus, having become the Christ, wants nothing more than for you to awaken to your Christ Self in union with God and with the Holy Spirit. Consequently, all devotion offered to God in the Name of Jesus helps you to become receptive to the Holy Spirit. Through receptivity to the Holy Spirit, you will learn to allow God's Love to flow through you, and your mind and heart will increasingly open to the awareness of your own true loving nature, your Christ Self.

The Father knows your needs even before you ask Him. Yet you are instructed to ask for your own benefit so that you might realize your greatest need, which is for His grace in your life. In the Lord's Prayer, you ask for the coming of His Kingdom, for His Will to be done, for your daily bread, and for freedom from temptation. You also ask to "forgive us our debts." Notice that this same asking for forgiveness is expressed in the second half of the Jesus Prayer with the words "have mercy on us." By using the word "mercy" in your Jesus Prayer, you are summing up all your requests into one request, which is both an acknowledgment of your total dependence on God and an asking of His grace. In the Name Jesus, you trust that all your needs of grace are met. Thus the words "Jesus, mercy" sum up both the Jesus Prayer and the Lord's Prayer.

Although there are advantages to using the affirmation "Jesus, mercy," it is best to use the Divine Name alone. The word "Jesus" alone says everything in itself, since even if the word "mercy" is not stated, it is certainly implied in the very meaning of His Name. The word "Jesus" literally means "savior." To say His Name is therefore to ask for that gracious saving power, which is, of course, the same as asking for mercy. Jesus, as the Savior, saves you from a self-centered life of separation. He has no other purpose than to increase your awareness of your own divine nature and ultimately bring you to the state of oneness with the Father.

In considering whether to use the affirmation "Jesus, mercy" or to use only the Divine Name of "Jesus," it is important to evaluate the connotation of what the word "mercy" actually means to you. If "mercy" really means only an asking for divine grace, then it may be a good word to include in your affirmation. However, the word "mercy" is not recommended in this manual as an affirmation because it has negative connotations related to unworthiness and sinfulness. As a result of these negative connotations, repeating the word "mercy" as an affirmation may only perpetuate a negative self-image about yourself that would prevent you from truly being receptive to God's Love. Whatever affirmation you choose needs to remind you that you are a child of God and as such worthy of His love. Because the word "mercy" is associated with unworthiness, it is preferable to use a form of the Divine Name of Jesus, which in itself implies receiving God's merciful love, without using the word "mercy" itself.

The focus of the Jesus Prayer, according to early Christian monks, is in the heart. For this reason, it was called by them the Prayer of the Heart. They believed that holding one's attention in the heart area cut through the rational thinking process and helped call upon that deepest core of their being far beyond the superficial self. To repeat the Name of Jesus Christ in the heart evoked their innermost faith at the ground of their being and invited the Holy Spirit to dwell therein.

It was purity of heart that these early monks sought above all else. Their focusing upon this simple prayer of faith was intended to awaken their single-minded desire for God alone. Their secret for purifying the heart was holding their awareness in the heart in order to leave behind the distracting thoughts of the mind and cleanse themselves from egotism and selfish desires. Through prayerful attention in the heart, they were able to focus upon and intensify the most important quality of their prayer life, which was devotion.

These early monks also discovered that when you repeat the *Prayer of the Heart* sincerely, you are rewarded with the wonderful quality of humility, an attribute that enables you to clearly see the reality of your condition. Humility is the recognition that you can do nothing in yourself alone and that you are totally dependent upon God. Yet humility is not weakness. On the contrary, through humility that relies totally upon God, you are strengthened and can do all things in the grace that comes from the Father through Jesus Christ.

Whether you choose the words Jesus, Jesus Christ, Christ, or another form of His Name, the most important reason for the effectiveness of the Jesus Prayer is in the divine grace that flows from Jesus Himself, whose Divine Name is being invoked. However, it is through its repetition as an affirmation that His Name gains a mastery over the mind and the ego. To understand the power of the Jesus Prayer as an affirmation, you need to properly view the mind and the ego.

Your mind is a vehicle through which your spiritual nature flows to express thought. But your rational mind cannot directly perceive its spiritual source, because thought is its only instrument of awareness and thought of the rational mind cannot penetrate Spirit. Therefore, you use your rational mind to define yourself with a thought about yourself. Since your rational mind can only perceive thoughts and bodily senses, you come to the false mental conclusion that says, "I am the rational thinking mind and the body," and this single thought is the "ego."

Since the ego is just a false thought, it would appear to be a simple matter to change the thought, but the problem is greater than that. Unfortunately, all the other thoughts you have about yourself revolve at the subconscious level around this one false thought of the ego to create a whole belief system of thoughts and habit patterns. This collection of thoughts that form a belief system is called the "self," and is the false world you create around yourself. The ego, which is at the center of this fabricated belief system of the self, is represented in the mind as the word "I." The ego represented by "I" is identified with your physical and mental nature, but not with the reality of your spiritual nature. This false perception of your yourself symbolized by the word "I" usually dominates the subconscious mental patterns of the mind. If you doubt the mental dominance of the ego, just attempt to go one day without saying the word "I."

Through repeating the Jesus Prayer the conscious mind is impregnated with the spiritual ideal of Christ. Gradually His Divine Name becomes a dominant mental pattern that sinks down into the subconscious mind where it helps to release the attachment to the "I" of the ego. Letting go of the subconscious attachment to the "I" allows your true spiritual nature in Christ to shine through and manifest not only temporarily during meditation itself, but also as an aftereffect in your daily living. The result is that instead of living a self-centered life, you live a life centered in Christ.

The affirmation of the Divine Name of Christ not only disempowers the ego so you can live in Christ, but it also affirms a deeper truth, which is hidden by the ego. That truth is that your true Identity is the Christ Self— *even now.* In your world it may not appear to be so, but in His World, you are a Son of God, made in His image and likeness. If a light bulb is turned on and then is painted black, it will outwardly appear to be black and without light, even though its light is in fact still shining. Since God turned on your light in your creation, He has never withdrawn His Life and Light from you, so you are still shining just as brightly as always, yet unaware of your true divine nature.

The ego condition of your everyday world says that you are separate from God. In reality at the core of your existence you are one with the Father, the source of your existence. It is your oneness with the Father that is your true Self, your Christ Self. But because you are not aware of your oneness with the Father, an intermediary is necessary to help you discover your true relationship with God. The Holy Spirit plays the role of being this intermediary and divine Teacher for all of God's children. However, Jesus, being already awakened Himself, serves as a personal intermediary in direct coordination with the Holy Spirit to assist you in uncovering the image and likeness of God that is your true nature, your Christ Self.

Consequently, Jesus Christ through the action of the Holy Spirit is the way to the Father, and as such you repeat His Divine Name as a reminder of your oneness with the Father. You do not repeat His Holy Name as a reminder of His miraculous earthly deeds. In your prayers you can rightly dwell upon His passion, death and resurrection. However, for your meditation upon His Name you are not focused on past events. Instead, you seek to abide in His loving presence and in the presence of the Holy Spirit. In His presence you have the assurance that you are not indulging in a form of hero worship, and you are not seeking something foreign to your own nature. Instead, as you approach Jesus, you are actually entering His World, which you discover is your own true Home as a Son of the Father.

Because you meditate to increase your awareness of your oneness with the Father, when you make your choice of an affirmation, you need to consider what words most remind you of your oneness with God. For example, as stated earlier, some people view the word "mercy," not as an invitation for divine grace, but rather as only a reminder of sin and separation from God. For such individuals, the word "mercy" would not be a good choice since it would not be an affirmation of oneness with God.

Some Christians make a distinction between the words "Jesus" and "Christ," such that the former refers to the *human* nature of Jesus Christ and the latter refers to the *divine* nature of Jesus Christ. These individuals may not be attracted to repeating the word "Jesus" since it may remind them only of a person apart from themselves. Yet these same individuals may choose "Christ" as an affirmation because this word reminds them of the divine nature that is in Jesus Christ and is likewise in everyone.

The word "Christ" as an affirmation is a wonderful choice for your meditation because it encompasses in just one syllable both a personal Divine Name for the one who is your guide to the Father and also the name for your own divine nature, the Christ Self. The term "Christ Self" is used here to convey that all God's children share the same oneness with the Father. Nevertheless, even the word "Christ" can be so identified with the personality of Jesus Christ that you may find yourself only affirming the personhood of Jesus outside of yourself and failing to affirm your own oneness with the Father. If you feel you may be strong in affirming Jesus, but weak in affirming your own inherent oneness with God, you may want to combine the Divine Name of Jesus Christ with a word that would help you to affirm your own oneness with God. For instance, you may want to use the word "One" to affirm your oneness with God. Therefore, an example of an affirmation of the Divine Name that would affirm your oneness would be "Christ, One."

Obviously, differing ideas about what the words of the Name of Jesus Christ might mean will affect your affirmation choice. Nevertheless, you can be certain that repeating His Divine Name, in whatever form you may choose, will have a profound impact upon you. The effect of letting the Jesus Prayer penetrate deep within you is summarized in the following quotation from an enjoyable book titled *The Way of a Pilgrim*:

> Many so-called enlightened people regard this frequent offering of one and the same prayer as useless and even trifling, calling it a mechanical and thoughtless occupation of simple people. But unfortunately they do not know the secret which is revealed as a result of this mechanical exercise; they do not know how this frequent service of the lips imperceptibly becomes a genuine appeal of the heart, sinks down into the inward life, becomes a delight, becomes, as it were, natural to the soul, bringing it light and nourishment and leading it on to union with God.[3]

Probably the earliest form of the Jesus Prayer sprang forth from the lips of Bartimaeus, the blind man of Jericho, who repeatedly cried out, "Jesus, Son of David, have mercy on me!"[4] Although this scriptural quote may have inspired the Jesus Prayer, no one knows when it was first used as a meditation technique. The recorded knowledge of the Jesus Prayer goes back as early as the third and fourth centuries when it was used by the early monks of the Christian church who lived in the desert. The following quotation by one of these monks, St. Macarius, will serve to summarize the merits of the Jesus Prayer:

> There is no other perfect meditation than the saving and blessed Name of our Lord Jesus Christ dwelling without interruption in you, as it is written: "I will cry out like the swallow and I will meditate like the turtledove!" This is what is done by the devout man who perseveres in invoking the saving Name of our Lord Jesus Christ.[5]

Obviously a name for something and the thing itself are two very different things. The name is a symbol for what it represents. It is not the thing itself. For example, the name "stone" is not a stone itself. It is only a symbol used to call to mind the reality of the stone itself. All names are symbols. Even a Divine Name of God is not the Reality of God, but only a symbol of that Reality. Yet a Name of God is helpful because it calls to mind the reality for which it stands. The name "stone" can only call to mind a stone, which is merely an inanimate object. However, a

Name of God calls upon awakening your awareness of the Reality of God, but more important invites God to actively interact with you.

The Divine Name, and in particular the Name of Jesus, is only a symbol, yet it can carry you beyond all symbols by helping to open your mind to Reality itself. Calling upon the Name of Jesus is not a time to ponder philosophy, theology, or dogmas. Rather, you are seeking a direct existential contact with the Ground of Being. You are seeking a personal experience of the deepest truth about your identity in God. Finding the presence of God expands your capacity to know His Will and has the aftereffect of guiding you to do His Will. This is something much more basic to your inner being than making petitions for beneficial external concerns. To rest in the ground of your being is to experience the unconditional Love that created you and keeps you in existence. To be fully aware of His Love is the deepest yearning of your heart. Nothing can completely satisfy this yearning except God Himself. Thus you call His Name in order to listen for his Word that says, "I love you. You and I are One."

While calling on the Name of Jesus seems generally accepted by most Christian groups, these groups have very definite and different ideas about the nature of Jesus. It would be impossible and unnecessary to homogenize these ideas into one universally accepted picture of Jesus. In regard to my own ideas about Christ, the only certainty is that my ideas are too small to contain Him Who is one with God, the Incomprehensible. If the ideas about Christ that are shared in this manual are different from your own, hopefully you will not let this be a stumbling block to proceeding with Christian meditation. Intellectual ideas, including both yours and mine, are only "about" Christ and cannot encompass Him and cannot enable you to feel His presence or the presence of God the Father.

Your intellectual knowledge about Christ (and about God) is very helpful at the start of your spiritual growth and is appropriately expressed in your prayers. However, when you switch from prayer to meditation, you change from thinking about Christ prayerfully to stilling the mind in order to experience the divine presence at a deeper level. The fact that Christian seekers have different theological understandings is of little importance in the practical application of meditation. It is your theological ideas, as well as all other ideas, that must be set aside during the practice of meditation. Consequently, in meditation you do not think about Christ with your ideas, but rather repeat His Divine Name and open yourself to the grace of the Holy Spirit that will enable you to experience the divine presence within. The deepest level of your relationship with Christ is not primarily based upon your theological beliefs, but rather upon His Love for you and your love for Him. Through the stillness of meditation, you are seeking to awaken your awareness of your loving relationship with God.

C. The Ideal as an Affirmation

As was stated earlier, each meditation is dedicated to your chosen ideal, which is the spiritual destination toward which you would like to grow. Similarly, each meditation is dedicated to your mental attitude because this is the specific way you are using your mind in order to grow toward your chosen ideal. You may choose to acknowledge this dedication simply by stating the ideal and mental attitude once before meditation and, if desired, once after meditation.

However, you may choose to use part or all of this dedication as an affirmation for meditation itself. You may choose to repeat the spiritual ideal as an affirmation. For example, if Christ is your ideal then, of course, the affirmation of His Divine Name would be appropriate. You may also choose to use your mental attitude as an affirmation. For instance, if Jesus is your chosen ideal, you may choose a mental attitude, such as "Thy will be done," for your affirmation. An affirmation may include both the ideal and the mental attitude. An example might be "O Lord, I wish to be a channel of blessings to others." It is recommended that affirmations be condensed into as few words as possible.

Using your ideal and/or mental attitude for an affirmation is a way of increasing your dedication to the highest within. Meditating on your ideal helps you to build within yourself the awareness of that ideal toward which you are growing and helps you to become like that ideal. Meditating upon your mental attitude helps you to focus your mind in the right way to help manifest your ideal. Meditating upon both the spiritual ideal and the mental attitude helps to create an inner harmony of spirit and mind working together to manifest through the physical. The physical body is the vehicle through which the spiritual ideal is expressed. That spiritual ideal is made manifest by the proper application of the mental attitude.

Some meditators prefer to use affirmations of not just one primary mental attitude, but a wide variety of mental attitudes that lead the mind toward their spiritual ideal. These meditators choose affirmations in the form of statements, sometimes even long sentences, that affirm their spiritual beliefs. Each statement is used as an affirmation for a short while, perhaps only a day or two, and then is replaced by a new statement. Switching affirmations repeatedly or using many varieties of statements is not the most effective way to focus the mind. Yet this approach is a necessary part for completing the one year of daily workbook lessons of *A Course in Miracles*, which are described in Chapters 20 and 21.

Of the choices of affirmations that have just been mentioned, the most highly recommended is the use of the spiritual ideal alone, especially in the form of the Divine Name. The reason is that your spiritual ideal focuses directly on what you have chosen to be the center of your spiritual life. Meditating on the spiritual ideal itself has the effect of imprinting the focus of meditation upon the very structure of the physical body so that the body itself becomes the carrier of the ideal. When this happens through meditation, then the thoughts, the feelings, the actions, and the words that manifest through the body begin to carry more and more of the divine influence. That's when the ideal is truly your ideal, not a theory or idea, but rather a living reality that is actually being applied in your life.

The application of your spiritual ideal, which is a Divine Name for God or a reminder of God, can be your purpose for living, which gives meaning to your life. With your spiritual ideal as your purpose, you can perceive God as the goal toward which you are growing, until one day you will be united with Him in Heaven. All this is certainly true from the perspective of your world, but looks very different from the perspective of His World. In your world you appear separate from God because of the ego condition, but in His World you are already united with God. His presence is within you now as your Source, even if you are unaware of His presence. In your world union with God is in the future as a possible hope; in His World union with God is a present reality and a certainty.

Consequently, your spiritual ideal as a way of defining your relationship with God needs to be understood as being more than just the final destination toward which you are growing. Your spiritual ideal is not only an *external ideal* related to how you want to navigate through the world, but also an *internal ideal*. The term "God transcendent" is used to describe the fact that God permeates all of creation and yet God transcends form, space, and time. In contrast to God as being everywhere at once, the term "God immanent" is used to describe the fact that God is within you. Your spiritual ideal as an internal ideal is a Divine Name for God immanent or a reminder of God immanent. Repeating your chosen affirmation in meditation may—and hopefully will—bear the fruit of helping you grow toward your external spiritual ideal of God by expressing love and service in the everyday world. But this is only the aftereffect of your meditation practice. Your actual meditation practice itself is an encounter with God immanent, your internal spiritual ideal. Therefore, it is vitally important to choose a word or words for your affirmation that remind you of God immanent, the divine presence within you.

You repeat your affirmation to experience His World in which you are already united with God. Your experience in His World will in no way change your reality, which has already been established by God. You are becoming aware of your ground of Being, but to do so requires your willingness to accept what already is. Your affirmation is therefore a reminder of God immanent as a belief and also an expression of your desire to be aware of His presence as an inner experience. God wants you to be aware of His presence within you, yet He does not want to impose this awareness on you. The awareness of God, although eternally present within you, comes to your conscious awareness only at your request.

The verb "affirm" means to positively assert your conviction. Repeating your affirmation affirms your conviction to make the thought of your affirmation become a dominant thought pattern in the mind to counteract negative thoughts of the ego. Yet the affirmation needs to be more than an assertion of a mental belief. Your affirmation is a "Yes" to God Himself. Your "Yes" is an affirmative assertion of your desire for and welcoming of closer intimacy with God. Your affirmation is an assertion of your willingness to become aware of God's abiding presence. You choose an affirmation that is meaningful for you, but the intellectual meaning is only a secondary concern. After all, you do not think about your affirmation during the practice of meditation, so your meditation practice is not mainly a mental activity, even though the mind participates. Your meditation practice is primarily an expression of the will.

You can continuously repeat an affirmation in meditation to express your will, but this repeating is only a symbol because words are only capable of being symbols. What is important is not the form of your affirmation, but the content of your affirmation. The form, meaning the actual word or words used, is only a symbolic reminder of the content. The meaning of your affirmation in terms of content is that it expresses your will to establish a closer relationship with God. The value of your inward seeking is that it represents an alignment of your will with God's Will. God has given himself to you totally in your creation and has never left you, but you are currently not aware of His presence. To restore your awareness of His presence requires your willingness. The content of your affirmation is your willingness. Therefore, be sure to choose an affirmation that reminds you of your willingness to become aware of God's presence.

Previously in this manual you have been encouraged to *desire God alone* in order to succeed in deepening your relationship with God in meditation and contemplation. This encouragement will be repeated in subsequent chapters. As it is used in this manual in relation to your inner attunement, the idea of desiring God alone will actually mean *wanting God above all else* at a particular moment or even an instant in time. It certainly does not mean you have made some long-term commitment to God, although some seekers may specifically decide to do so. The idea of desiring God alone in your attunement does not mean you have given up all else, but merely that you have temporarily turned away from all else and have turned to God alone. In relation to meditation, this would mean turning away from all other thoughts and holding on to only the one thought of God alone, which is your affirmation. In terms of contemplation, this would mean turning away from even the holding of the one thought of your affirmation and instead resting in the silence of God's presence alone, which transcends discursive thinking.

Since you are only being asked to desire God alone during your attunement practice and even then only for brief moments of time, it may sound theoretically like a simple and easy task. But wanting God alone, even in the sense of temporarily turning aside all other desires and thoughts, can be challenging. It would be unrealistic to expect that your desire for God alone can be anything more than very temporary and inconsistent. When you attempt to desire God alone in your very first practice of meditation, the idea that the mind is difficult to control becomes immediately apparent. Yet perhaps the underlying nature of the difficulty of desiring God alone may not be so apparent. The desire for God alone requires a certain degree of *firm willingness*, which is difficult to attain and even more difficult to sustain. You may have exerted your will in many positive ways in the past and may think of yourself as a person with a highly developed will. But true willingness is about giving your whole will without being divided. It is part of the human condition to have a divided will. Most seekers are not aware that their will is divided and therefore weakened, which presents a problem in relation to desiring God wholeheartedly and giving oneself wholeheartedly to God. Jesus is an example of complete willingness without division and even He sweat blood in saying, "Father, if thou art willing, remove this cup from me; nevertheless not my will but thine be done."[6]

Instead of the complete undivided willingness of Jesus, all you need is a somewhat firm willingness in order to desire God alone. But why is just a certain degree of firm willingness so difficult to achieve even on a momentary basis in your practice of meditation? The human mind is divided and as a result the human will is also divided. This division of the mind and subsequent division of the will is due in large part to *denial*. Your world is a world of separation, which means a world of denial. You—and everyone you know—live in an everyday world in which God is certainly present as the Ultimate Reality. Nonetheless, God is denied and therefore largely hidden from your awareness.

Just as God is denied in your outer world, He is denied in your inner world. You have a private, conscious mind that is separate from the private, conscious minds of your brothers and sisters. In addition to being separate from the minds of others, your private, conscious mind is separate from the higher awareness of God's presence. This separation from God can only be maintained by continuously denying this higher awareness. Also, you have a private, subconscious mind, which contains all the unpleasant thoughts and emotions that you have repressed and denied access to your conscious mind. The extent of your denial is extremely vast and yet denial is so much a part of your life that its operation is taken for granted and goes unnoticed. After all, denial is the *desire to not know* and therefore it is not surprising that you would not know the extent of your reliance on denial.

Meditation helps reduce denial. Your affirmation represents a change in willingness—a change from being willing to not know to being willing to know. This change in willingness does not mean a change to complete willingness, but it does mean an increase in willingness to make it more consistent and more firm. When you ask yourself the question *Do I want to know God?* the part of your mind that wants to stay private and in denial says "No." Only a part of your mind says "Yes." To respond to a question in the *affirmative* means to respond with a "Yes." But how firm is that "Yes"? Your affirmation both states and affirms your willingness to know God by symbolizing this "Yes" answer. To affirm means *to make firm*. Thus repeating your affirmation reinforces the part of your mind that says "Yes" to wanting God. This repetition and reinforcement help to make firm your willingness—to strengthen your desire for God alone, even though another part of your mind is still not willing to let go of the denial of God. The use of your affirmation in your daily meditation is a means of repeating and reinforcing your willingness. Your affirmation in words reminds you of your nonverbal willingness. This reminder of your willingness can stay with you even when you let go of the words of your affirmation and through faith enter into the silence of contemplation in which your wanting of God becomes an abiding in God.

Fortunately, during meditation when you repeat your affirmation, your complete undivided willingness is not required by the Holy Spirit. Your conscious willingness, although incomplete, is enough to welcome the Holy Spirit. Your communion with the Holy Spirit helps you to increasingly release your unwillingness. The Holy Spirit exists in a state of perfect willingness. The Holy Spirit shares this perfect willingness with you to increase your willingness and faith. Overcoming your denial and unwillingness is a gradual process. Daily application of repeating your affirmation and communion with the Holy Spirit over several years is required because of the extent of your denial and unwillingness that has been built up over many years of your life and that is part of the human condition.

Gradually your mind that has been saying "No" to God makes a transition to increasingly say "Yes" to God. This transition is symbolized by three New Testament incidents in the life of Peter. In the first incident Peter says to Jesus, "If I must die with you, I will not deny you!"[7] This statement demonstrates that because denial is the desire not to know, it is natural for every seeker to be in denial about the extent of his own denial. Thus the seeker is likely to overestimate his ability to overcome denial.

The second incident is the occurrence of Peter denying Jesus three times and then weeping. These denials by Peter shows how difficult it is to let go of denial even after having been exposed to the truth. Peter's weeping represents the unhappiness that is the fruit of remaining in denial. The third incident occurs when the resurrected Jesus asks Peter, "Do you love me?" Peter replies affirmatively. But Jesus makes a point of asking Peter the same question three times so Peter can give his "Yes"answer three times to make up for previously denying Jesus three times. Just like Jesus gave Peter the opportunity to counteract his past denials and unwillingness, the Holy Spirit through your invitation gives you the opportunity to repeatedly replace denial with acceptance and replace your unwillingness with a firm willingness.

Some beginners find it helpful to repeat the affirmation continuously, but this manual emphasizes repeating your affirmation and then letting go of it. Letting go of the affirmation means only letting go of the form of your affirmation while retaining the content. In this way your affirmation is just a form-related reminder of your deeper content-related intention. If stray thoughts distract you during meditation, you can return to repeating the affirmation only to remind you of your intention. Your intention is to give your willingness to God. Your affirmation reminds you of your intention for a deeper relationship with God. It expresses your desire that opens you to becoming aware of God's presence. Letting go of the words of your affirmation allows you to rely on your intention itself that goes deeper than words. Eventually your intention to become aware of the divine presence will allow you to rest in God during contemplation, but will also invite the divine influence and activity that will help to remove any inner obstacles to your awareness of the divine presence. Obstacles that have been denied and suppressed into the subconscious mind will be released into your conscious awareness so you can come to a place of acceptance and let go of these blocks with the aid of the Holy Spirit. It can be disconcerting at times to face the parts of yourself that you have denied so you can release them and arrive at a place of acceptance. Times of peaceful rest in God and times of less peaceful transformation in which blocks are released are both needed in order to overcome denial and to accept the divine within.

D. Other Affirmations

If you desire a Christian affirmation and none of the ones already mentioned appeals to you, then you may find a word from scripture that appeals to you personally. For example, you may want to use the word

"Amen," which is normally translated "truly" or "so be it." Another possibility is that you may choose a very brief scriptural phrase or a statement, such as "Be still, and know that I am God."[8] You may want to employ a form of the Divine Name in combination with another word or words of your choice. For example, you may want to choose "Christ Light," "O Christ," "O my Jesus," or "Come Christ Jesus." You may want to repeat the Divine Name with a virtue or quality. For instance, you may want to say "Jesus, humble" or "Jesus, peace." For your choice of a virtue or quality to combine with the Divine Name, you would want to choose an attribute that you feel you need. In so doing you can be assured that you will acquire that attribute. You may possibly want to express praise by repeating the affirmation "Jesus, thank you." Since so much of spiritual growth is based on learning to love, two of the affirmations recommended most highly are "Jesus Christ Love" and "Christ Love." You can allow your choice to be guided by the Spirit within.

E. Invoking the Holy Spirit

The role of the Holy Spirit is very important to your spiritual growth. Unlike God, Who is Reality itself, the Holy Spirit has one foot in the reality of His World and one foot in your world. Acting as a bridge between these two worlds, the Holy Spirit, with the assistance of Jesus Christ, leads you back to the Father in Heaven. You are now attached to your world of separation, and God would never force you to give up your world because He wishes to honor your free will. It is your free-will choice to direct your own life or to allow the divine influence to motivate your thoughts, words, and deeds. Like God, the Holy Spirit will not violate your free will, so if you want assistance or guidance, you must pray and ask for help from the Holy Spirit. In addition to a direct request in prayer for the Holy Spirit to come into your life, meditation is a means of inviting the Holy Spirit to come upon you and transform you.

Meditation involves letting go of self-centered thoughts and developing receptivity to the incoming of the Holy Spirit. Your spiritual growth in general, both expressed inwardly in communion with God and outwardly in relation to your brothers and sisters, is a continual opportunity to set self aside and be responsive to the prompting of the Holy Spirit. Receptivity and responsiveness to the Holy Spirit is a continuing theme that will be emphasized in later chapters. For now it is important to understand that meditation is an opportunity to focus on invoking the Holy Spirit.

This invoking can be done directly or indirectly. All the affirmations that have been suggested thus far are indirect ways of inviting the Holy Spirit. An example of a direct invocation is the asking of the Holy Spirit to enter as a part of your preparatory prayer before meditation. Another direct invocation is choosing an affirmation for meditation that includes the invoking of the Holy Spirit. A possible choice of an affirmation is "Come, Holy Spirit." Another possible affirmation is simply "Holy Spirit" repeated with the feeling of welcoming that spiritual presence.

Whether you choose to invite the Holy Spirit directly or indirectly, this invitation is central to a proper understanding of meditation. While meditating, you may repeatedly be distracted by your thoughts, but this does not make your meditation fruitless. Although your own efforts to control the mind may be weak, you need to realize that you are not relying on your own skill. Instead, you are relying on the fact that you have invited the Holy Spirit into your inmost being. It is not your technique, but rather your purity of intention that opens your heart and mind so the Holy Spirit may enter. You know by faith that your invitation is being answered each time you practice meditation with a pure intention.

Even though you may not feel the presence of the Holy Spirit as a conscious experience during meditation, your invitation allows God to have free reign in your subconscious mind. There beneath your conscious awareness, the Holy Spirit has a healing effect that removes inner obstacles to your spiritual growth. The obstacles that the Holy Spirit removes may be desires, thoughts, habit patterns, and emotions, which you have suppressed into the subconscious mind and never completely resolved and released.

Sometimes the Holy Spirit will assist you by bringing your inner obstacles to your conscious awareness so you can then give them back to the Holy Spirit for their release. At other times the Holy Spirit will spontaneously produce an inner healing without the aid of your conscious awareness of the nature of the inner obstacle that was removed. The releasing of inner blocks with the help of the Holy Spirit is described in detail in Chapter 12. Gradually the Holy Spirit can bring about an inner transformation because of your daily meditation practice that opens you to receive God's grace. As you allow the Holy Spirit to transform you at the subconscious level, you become more willing to likewise allow the Holy Spirit to affect your conscious experience of everyday living. Thus your thoughts, your conversations, and your dealings with your brothers and sisters increasingly convey the divine influence so you become a greater expression of Christ's love in the earth.

F. Counting Meditation

I have suggested choosing a word or words to represent your spiritual ideal and using this choice as an affirmation for meditation. Now a way of focusing the mind without using an affirmation will be described. This is

Counting Meditation. For this method you count mentally from one to ten and then return to the number one and repeat this process of counting for the entire meditation. If you forget the count or count past ten, simply start again by returning to number one. The counting is coordinated with the breathing. Number one and all the odd numbers are inhalations. Number two and all the even numbers are exhalations. This is an initial technique that is practiced by beginning students of Zen Buddhism.

If you regularly meditate with an affirmation of your ideal, you may choose to use Counting Meditation briefly as a way to aid your ability to reduce stray thoughts. The way you can do this is to begin your practice by first using Counting Meditation as a means of clearing away the cares and concerns of daily life. After a short while of focusing on counting, you can gain greater mental clarity and then you can switch to using an affirmation of your ideal in your regular form of meditation.

Another reason for employing the counting method is that initially meditating on an affirmation of your ideal may create unwanted mental pictures or thoughts. For example, if you meditate on the affirmation of "Jesus," you may see mental images of Jesus and think about Him. This would be very good as a form of prayer, which involves using both the imagination and thoughts to communicate with God. But in meditation you seek to set aside the imagination and thoughts—even if they are holy thoughts. Therefore, having mental pictures of Jesus or thoughts about Him during meditation would be a distraction, which would prevent the stilling of the mind. Thus you may choose to temporarily use the counting method in meditation to remove these mental pictures and thoughts. Then when the mind becomes more still, you may return to repeating the affirmation of "Jesus" without creating any mental pictures of Jesus or thoughts about Him. The purpose for using an affirmation of the Divine Name of Jesus Christ is not to mentally intellectualize about Christ, but rather to experience and feel the divine presence within as a living reality.

---

1. Matthew 6:6-8

2. John 16: 23, 24

3. *The Way of a Pilgrim and The Pilgrim Continues His Way*, translated from the Russian by R.M. French (New York: Seabury Press, 1972), p. 203. Originally published by the Seabury Press; rights owned by Winston Press Inc., Minneapolis, Minnesota.

4. Mark 10: 47

5. From Amelineau, quoted by Resch in *Doctrine Ascetique des Permiers Maltres Egyptiens*, p. 151. In turn, quoted by Thomas Merton in *Contemplative Prayer*, cited from the paperback edition (New York: Image Books, 1971), p. 21. The original, hardcover edition was titled *The Climate of Monastic Prayer* (Kalamazoo, Michigan and Spencer, Massachusetts: Cistercian Publications, 1969).

6. Luke 22:42

7. Mark 14:31

8. Psalm 46:10

5

TECHNIQUES OF
MEDITATION

≈ ● ≈

A. Body Awareness and Distraction

Many of the meditation techniques presented in this manual employ body awareness as part of the meditation practice and are intended to lead toward contemplation that does not employ body awareness. Before describing the specific techniques of inward seeking recommended in this manual, it may be helpful to discuss issues related to body awareness during meditation.

Meditation is a helpful means of becoming increasingly receptive to the Holy Spirit. Developing receptivity to the Holy Spirit is a gradual process, and body awareness can be a stumbling block to that process. When beginners attempt to meditate using the Divine Name without incorporating a technique of body awareness, they discover they are distracted from meditation by their own body awareness, which cannot be ignored.

Body awareness can be compared to a child. Anyone who has worked with children knows that children want attention. To the child getting attention is an outer demonstration of a person's love for the child. If a child cannot get a person's attention through positive behavior and if a child is ignored, he will find a wide variety of negative ways to get that person's attention. If that person is wise, he will give the child a task that will occupy his time positively and enable him to get the attention he wants in an appropriate way. In addition, the task performed by the child may prove to be very helpful to that person.

Just as a child seeks attention in this example, body awareness is constantly seeking to get your attention during meditation. If body awareness cannot get your attention positively because it is ignored as part of your meditation technique, then body awareness will become a negative attention getter. This will take the form of all sorts of body sensations and feelings that will be presented to the mind as a reminder that the body is being ignored. These reminders are sometimes gross and sometimes subtle. Their effect is to distract you from focusing on the affirmation and prevent meditation from deepening.

On the other hand, if body awareness is given a positive task by being incorporated into your meditation technique, it becomes an asset rather than a liability. This will not eliminate body awareness as a distraction altogether, but it will greatly lessen this distraction and deepen meditation.

To understand specifically how to incorporate body awareness into your communication with God, you need to understand the mechanics of the vehicle God has given to you for this communication. The body is constantly receiving stimuli and recording these in the brain. You selectively choose to become aware of only a very small portion of these. Some body stimuli present themselves to your awareness spontaneously without your seeming to have any choice in the matter. For example, you may hear an airplane fly overhead without choosing to hear it. This may be considered involuntary awareness. However, from the viewpoint of meditation, it is more important to discuss where you place your awareness voluntarily.

When you voluntarily bring your awareness to a part of the body, your entire awareness does not remain in your conscious mind. Your awareness will actually go to the part of the body where you choose to place your awareness. A certain kind of energy will accompany your awareness and therefore also go to the part of your body where you are focusing your mind, as will be explained in Chapter 8. In relation to preventing distraction, the key element to consider here is the fact that your awareness becomes localized in the part of the body where you have placed your awareness.

If you feel the big toe on your right foot, for example, and hold your awareness there, you cannot feel the thumb on your right hand unless you decide to move your awareness to that thumb. Once you move your awareness to your thumb and hold it there, you cannot feel your toe anymore. In order to feel any part of your body, you need to make a voluntary choice to bring your awareness to that body part. If you decide to hold the awareness of the mind on any one part of the body, the other parts of the body are not in your awareness consciously because you choose not to bring your awareness to them. (The exception to this is when an experienced meditator can hold the awareness simultaneously in several parts of the body or even be aware of the body as a whole.) The significance of this is that you can hold the awareness in one part of the body to prevent the distraction in meditation caused by allowing the awareness to wander from one part of the body to another.

It is important to keep in mind that during meditation you do not visualize or *think about* the part of the body in which you are holding your attention. Rather, you actually bring your awareness into the physical location of the part of the body you are focusing on. Holding the awareness in one part of the body is one example of a general ability of the mind, which can be called *selective attention*. This type of attention involves focusing on a specific aspect of something and ignoring other aspects. Selective attention can be unconscious or conscious. If you look at a green field with a single yellow rose, the rose will initially receive more attention. This is an example of unconscious selective attention. You may think that you are absorbing the whole scene all at once, when actually you have taken in only the area where you are placing your attention and merely have a general sense of the remainder of the scene. You are using a conscious type of selective attention when you make a mental decision to bring your awareness to something and ignore other aspects of that thing. Practicing meditation involves a conscious form of selective attention since you attend to holding one thought in the mind while you ignore all other thoughts. All variations of meditation rely on conscious selective attention. Focusing on one part of the body to ignore the rest of the body is one particular type of selective attention that makes meditation more effective, especially for beginners.

Usually conscious selective attention involves placing your attention on an interesting task or object rather than an uninteresting one. A very common example is watching television instead of looking at a bookshelf. I recently watched an informative television show that illustrated how we use our attention selectively. The moderator asked the audience to watch two teams of basketball players. The specific task was to count the number of passes made by the team wearing white outfits. I finished the task along with the studio audience. Afterwards the moderator asked if anyone had noticed anything unusual. Only one person in the studio audience had seen that the moderator had run onto the court, done a spin of his body, and then left the scene. The rest of the studio audience and I had been so focused on the passing of the ball that we had entirely missed seeing the moderator come onto the court. A replay of the passing scene allowed me to see the moderator come onto the court. The moderator explained that the inability to see him initially was an example of "selective inattention," which can also be called "inattentional blindness." Selective inattention explains why meditators often don't hear noises in their environment when focusing inwardly during meditation. It also explains why focusing on one part of the body (selective attention) allows you to ignore other aspects of the body (selective inattention) that might otherwise draw your attention.

When the inexperienced meditator makes a choice not to exercise the ability of selective attention, the awareness tends to move from one part of the body to another, subject to the attraction of outer stimuli that affect different parts of the body. This causes distraction and makes meditation less effective. If your mind is distracted in this way, you can literally say that you have a "wandering mind," because the awareness actually changes locations as it wanders through the body that is distracted. However, you can choose to develop your ability to hold the awareness in one part of the body and thus prevent the distraction in meditation caused by allowing the awareness to wander from one part of the body to another.

At first it may be difficult to hold the awareness in one part of the body, but gradually with daily practice this ability to maintain the awareness in one place will increase and the awareness will be less likely to wander to other parts of the body. When you have developed the ability to hold the awareness in one place, you will find that distractions occur less frequently, and when they do occur they are less intense and less likely to disrupt the meditation process.

There are other ways to include techniques related to body awareness as a part of meditation. Breathing is a body process which is important to meditation. Breathing is an involuntary process that goes deep within, but it also can be a voluntary process that can be affected by your conscious thoughts. There is a strong link between breathing and the mind. Calming the mind will automatically calm the breathing, and calming the breathing will automatically calm the mind. Hence, by simply observing the flow of the breath without manipulating the breath, you can calm the mind. In fact, some meditators use this as a meditation technique in itself without using any affirmation for meditation.

Those who choose to use an affirmation such as the Divine Name find that coordinating the affirmation with the natural flow of the breath will deepen meditation considerably. Some of these meditators choose not to focus on any single part of the body, because they are satisfied with focusing on breathing alone in coordination with the affirmation as an effective means of using body awareness to aid meditation. This manual emphasizes focusing on a part of the body in addition to awareness of breathing, because awareness of part of the body reduces distraction.

Generally speaking, when Christians are taught meditation they are not taught to include body awareness as part of their meditation technique. The concept of letting go of body awareness sounds like a simple and easy approach. However, it is actually quite difficult to put this into practice because it presupposes that the meditator can exclude body awareness from the meditation process. Generally speaking, beginning meditators do not have the ability to meditated deeply enough to allow them to leave behind body awareness altogether. Consequently, if you are a beginning meditator, you may want to first use a meditation method that includes body awareness as part of the technique. After being successful at using methods that include body awareness, you can set aside a short time at the end of your practice for using a technique that does not use body awareness. If you feel comfortable using this technique at the end of your practice, you can gradually increase the time for methods that do not use body awareness.

B. Body Awareness for Receptivity

In addition to reducing distraction, there is another more important reason for holding the awareness in particular parts of the body. By focusing on certain body parts, you can increase your receptivity to the Spirit in a variety of ways. An example that illustrates this principle is the holding of your awareness in the chest area, which can help you to become increasingly receptive to developing the spiritual quality of devotion.

Early Christians recognized this fact and indeed referred to the Jesus Prayer as the "Prayer of the Heart." This heart-centered meditation is the origin of the method that is described below, called "Heart Meditation." It is primarily based on the techniques of early Christian desert hermits, who repeated the Name of the Lord while holding the awareness in the heart. This method evolved into a very definite technique of coordinating the breathing with the heartbeat. The writings of these early Christian hermits were collected in a book called the *Philokalia*, which became a manual of spiritual discipline and meditation technique.

While the popularity of using the Name of Jesus for meditation has been growing here in the West recently, the importance of the body in meditation that was known by early Christians has been largely ignored. Generally when the Jesus Prayer is taught today as a form of meditation, meditators are instructed to repeat the prayer without focusing on any part of the body and without coordinating it with the breathing. Many seekers have been helped in this way by simply repeating the Divine Name, but it is unfortunate that so many are missing out on the benefits that nourished the spiritual life of the early Christians.

Meditation that focuses on the *heart area*, in addition to encouraging openness to devotion, also helps to develop "emotional receptivity." This kind of receptivity is an openness to both letting go of negative emotional tension and building a base of emotional stability. The heart is not the only beneficial focusing area in the body. By focusing on the *navel area* you can develop "physical receptivity." This will assist you in releasing physical tension and help to redirect sexual energy in a way that will enhance your meditation experience. Another important focusing area is the *brow area*, which may include the forehead. By focusing there you can be assisted in developing "mental receptivity," which will help you release mental tension and enable your mind to be increasingly focused. Focusing on the *crown area* at the top of the head helps to develop "integrating receptivity," which is related to releasing overall tension that affects your entire body, emotions, and mind. Holding your awareness on the whole body all at once helps to develop "intuitive receptivity," which releases inner blocks to the intuitive level of your being.

Meditation is a *focused intention*. Your focused intention in practicing meditation techniques that use body awareness is really a combination of a general intention and a specific intention. The general intention is your desire to grow toward your spiritual ideal, expressed in a word or words by your affirmation. Your general intention also includes your desire for the Holy Spirit to enter your consciousness to assist you in growing toward your spiritual ideal. However, in the practice of body awareness techniques there is a specific intention for receptivity related to the parts of the body that serve as a focus. The release of tension described above is not solely the result of focusing on parts of the body. It is a result of your intention for receptivity, which is your openness to the Holy Spirit to come into you to bring about an inner transformation. With your invitation to the Holy Spirit, you are cooperating with the Holy Spirit to release inner tension as part of your transformation process.

You always retain your general intention, but your specific intent varies depending on the method you use. When you focus on the navel area, your specific intention is your desire for physical receptivity, which is your openness to a physical transformation. When you focus on the heart area, your specific intention is your desire for emotional receptivity, which is your openness to an emotional transformation. When you hold your attention on the brow area, your specific intention is your desire for a mental transformation. When you turn your attention to the crown area, your specific intention is your desire for integrating receptivity, which is your openness to an overall transformation of the physical, emotional and mental aspects of your being so these aspects work together in coordination with one another. When you expand your awareness to encompass the entire body as a whole, your specific intention is your desire for a transformation of the intuitive level of your being.

All these kinds of receptivity represent an openness to allowing the Holy Spirit to facilitate changes in you that will help to integrate and unify the physical, emotional, mental and intuitive levels of your being as a preparation for contemplation. Meditation techniques that do not include body awareness can lead you to the experience of contemplation. But such techniques are more effective after you have already used methods that include body awareness to increase your physical, emotional, mental, integrating, and intuitive receptivity to the action of the Holy Spirit.

Incorporating body awareness into your meditation practice helps to reduce distraction and increase receptivity as described above, but there is another significant reason for employing body awareness. By focusing on a series of areas within the body, you can dramatically assist a natural process that occurs as you invite the Holy Spirit into your consciousness and open yourself to inner spiritual transformation. This natural process is explained below in the section that describes *Christian Yoga Meditation*, which includes focusing on a series of areas that follow a sequence from bottom to top within the body. Christian Yoga Meditation is a combination of the six different meditation techniques. The first five of these techniques use body awareness. Focusing on particular parts of the body helps you contact spiritual centers of awareness associated with these parts of the body. Detailed information about these spiritual centers of awareness can be found in Chapter 11, which explains why and how body awareness can be beneficial to your experience of meditation and can serve as a preparation for contemplation.

Instruction will be provided below in how to use body awareness as an aid to meditation, as well as how to gradually develop the ability to let go of body awareness techniques in order to become receptive to experiencing contemplation. Contemplation is not a technique, but rather a gift of the Spirit. The techniques described here will help to prepare you to receive this gift by aiding in producing receptivity to the Spirit within.

C. Choosing and Using your Affirmation

The first five meditation techniques described below will show you how to combine repeating an affirmation with focusing the awareness on various parts of the body in order to produce physical, emotional, mental, integrating, and intuitive receptivity to the Holy Spirit. For these kinds of meditation methods, you will need to choose a Divine Name or other affirmation that represents your spiritual ideal or reminds you of your spiritual ideal. Your affirmation represents your intention to grow toward your spiritual ideal and your desire to be open to the divine presence.

It is best to have only a short affirmation, preferably one word. But you may choose to use two, three or four words for your affirmation. After you choose one word or a very brief combination of words, it is important to remain with this one choice without making the mistake of continually changing from one affirmation to another. Using just one affirmation increases the potency of its effect. In the following explanations, however, several different affirmations will be used as examples. Five separate methods of meditation that use body awareness will be explained. Then in the next chapter there will be an explanation of a sixth method, called "Inner Silence Meditation," that does not use body awareness. Finally there will be a description of how these methods may be combined into one technique, called "Christian Yoga Meditation."

For the following techniques, the affirmation will be coordinated with the breathing so that the first half of the chosen affirmation is mentally repeated on the inhalation and the second half of the affirmation is mentally repeated on the exhalation. For example, if you have chosen the Divine Name of "Jesus" to represent your spiritual ideal and you would like to use this as your affirmation, then "Je" would be repeated on the inhalation and "sus" would be repeated on the exhalation. If a one syllable word is chosen for your affirmation, the same single syllable word can be repeated on the inhalation and then again on the exhalation. Some meditators prefer to repeat the single syllable affirmation only on the exhalation, but not on the inhalation. Other meditators prefer to repeat the one syllable affirmation only on the inhalation, but not on the exhalation. Although a specific way of coordinating the affirmation with the breathing is recommended below, you may choose to repeat the affirmation and be aware of the breathing in any way that feels comfortable to you.

There are two different ways to use an affirmation. One approach is to use the affirmation strictly as a yoga mantra that is continuously repeated throughout the entire meditation in order to build that affirmation into your consciousness. The benefits of continuous repeating of a mantra are supported by the long history in India of using Hindu mantras. The benefits can also be found in the traditional Christian usage of the Jesus Prayer, and the contemporary practice of Christian Meditation, which has been advocated by John Main and described in Chapter 10.

The other approach is to repeat the affirmation to counteract distracting thoughts, and then after the affirmation has successfully calmed your mind, you can let go of the affirmation. This manual follows this second approach because meditation is being taught here as a practice that leads you in the direction of contemplation. When your meditation has done its work of leading you into the restful state of contemplation, there is no need for an affirmation. Indeed, the activity of mentally repeating an affirmation during contemplation would itself draw you out of the silence and the rest of contemplation. Therefore, all of the techniques described below will show you how to use the affirmation and also how to let go of the affirmation. Your affirmation affirms your intention to be aware of the divine presence within, but by letting go of your affirmation you can carry forward your intention to a deeper level—a level beyond words, where you are guided by pure faith.

Although only the intermittent use of the affirmation is mentioned and recommended in each meditation technique described below, this is not intended to be a hard and fast rule without flexibility. For example, if you are a beginner, you may find yourself becoming discouraged in your meditation practice because you are constantly becoming distracted by stray thoughts. In the event that you are having a great deal of difficulty with calming the mind, there is a possibility you may find more success initially by repeating your affirmation continuously. If you choose to use the approach of continuously repeating the affirmation to help learn how to calm the mind, you can, of course, change that approach at a later date. After learning how to calm your mind, you will be better prepared to use the affirmation and then let go of it for increasing intervals of time in order to experience the inner silence of contemplation.

Yet some seekers who do better with continuous repeating of the affirmation as an ongoing practice, even after becoming an intermediate meditator. If you want to make this your permanent practice, the major benefit is the building of your affirmation into your consciousness at a deep level. The continuous repeating of your affirmation is a more active practice than the passive approach of using of the affirmation and then letting go of it. Thus the active approach of using the affirmation continuously is best suited to those who have a very active, physical, emotional, and mental disposition. As an experiment, you may want to practice using your affirmation continuously on a daily basis for an extended period of time, and then switch to using the affirmation and letting go of it for an equally long period of time. These two periods of time to experiment with each approach will give you a frame of reference based on experience to determine which approach works best for you. It is important to find a method that feels comfortable and which will best help you deepen your awareness of the divine presence within you.

The first five techniques of Christian Yoga Meditation, which will be described in detail below, can be successfully practiced with the option of continuously repeating the affirmation rather than the recommended method of letting go of the affirmation when the mind is calm. But Inner Silence Meditation, the sixth technique of Christian Yoga Meditation, can only be practiced by using the affirmation and then letting go of it in order to experience the objectless and wordless awareness of contemplation. For your sixth method of Christian Yoga Meditation, you can choose to repeat your affirmation continuously and let go of body awareness. In this case, this continuous repetition of your affirmation should actually be called Christian Meditation, as recommended by John Main, rather than Inner Silence Meditation.

What if you prefer to repeat your affirmation continuously, but would also like to experience contemplation? The fundamental drawback of continuously repeating your affirmation is that this practice prevents you from entering the inner silence of contemplation in which there is no holding on to thoughts, not even holding on to the single thought of your affirmation. Is there a way to repeat your affirmation and to still experience the resting in God of contemplation in which thoughts are silenced? Yes, you can apply the continuous repeating of the affirmation only for the first five techniques of Christian Yoga Meditation, but not for the last technique. For the final method, Inner Silence Meditation, it will be necessary to implement this practice just as it is described below in order to lead you to the experience of contemplation. Your practice of the first five techniques of Christian Yoga Meditation will allow you to hold on to your affirmation continuously for the vast majority of each meditation session. Then your practice of Inner Silence Meditation at the end will still give you the opportunity to have a short period of time to let go of your affirmation and hopefully enter the restful state of contemplation.

D. Centering Meditation

The first technique that will be described is *Centering Meditation*. This method helps you to find your center of balance and to establish a calm breathing pattern. The major benefit of this technique is that it helps develop *physical receptivity* to the Holy Spirit. Consequently, practicing Centering Meditation will enable you to let go of physical tension in the body and also free the natural physical energy of the body. This physical energy is what we normally call sexual energy, but it actually would more properly be termed "creative energy." This creative energy can become sexual energy if it is directed toward sexual purposes. Yet this same creative energy can become a purifying energy that rises upward if is dedicated to spiritual purposes. Through focusing on the navel area, Centering Meditation produces physical receptivity to the action of the Holy Spirit that allows the creative energy of the body to rise upward. The rising energy releases physical blocks in the body and produces a purifying effect. When the creative energy is rising during meditation, it is a subtle energy that normally cannot be felt as a conscious experience, especially by beginning meditators.

After having done the preparatory work of sitting, relaxing the body, and completing the preparatory prayer, you are ready to begin meditation. While sitting erect with the eyes closed, you observe the area stretching from the navel to three-finger widths below the navel. You can feel this area just below the navel as the center of balance within the body. You focus the mind on the navel area not by using visualization, but rather by actually bringing your awareness into the navel area. You can be aware of the breathing in this area, but without trying to manipulate the breath in any way. The mouth is closed during meditation, so naturally you are breathing through the nostrils.

If you observe the breathing of a baby, you will notice the pronounced expanding and contracting of the baby's abdominal area. This abdominal breathing is the most natural and relaxed means of breathing. Thus it is the best form of breathing for meditation, regardless of what technique is used. Ideally during meditation the body is as still as possible, and abdominal breathing occurs automatically with minimal expansion and contraction of the chest.

To help you focus on the area below the navel during Centering Meditation, you observe this area expand outwardly with each inhalation and contract inwardly with each exhalation. At first it may be easier to focus on the surface of the skin at the navel area, but gradually it will become natural for you to hold your awareness underneath the surface of the skin. In Zen Buddhism this navel area is called the *hara*, which is the focusing area employed in the Zen practice of sitting meditation, called *zazen*.

Your chosen affirmation is divided in half. You mentally repeat the first half of the affirmation on the inhalation and repeat the second half on the exhalation. With "Jesus" as the sample affirmation, you keep the awareness in the area below the navel and mentally repeat "Je" with each inhalation and extend the sound "jjjeeee" for the entire inhalation. Then with the awareness still just below the navel, you mentally repeat "sus" with each exhalation and extend the sound "sssuuusss" for the entire exhalation. It is important to be relaxed and for the breathing to be natural and not manipulated in any way.

This practice is very simple and effective. In fact, it is so easy that it may seem absurd to some. But by participating in this practice, you will experience the benefits for yourself. It is important to pay no attention to stray thoughts. You do not want to be attracted to any thoughts, and in particular you do not want to indulge in any form of evaluating yourself during your meditation practice. If thoughts come, your only reaction needs to be to hold more firmly to "Je" on the inhalation and "sus" on the exhalation, while continuing to focus your awareness on the area below the navel. Though the awareness is focused just below the navel, it is actually the whole abdomen that naturally expands with each inhalation and contracts with each exhalation. As meditation deepens, the breathing will naturally become slower and more relaxed. In fact, the breathing may become so slow that you cannot feel the navel area expanding and contracting at all, yet the awareness can still be focused on that area.

In addition to holding the affirmation, there is also the opportunity to let go of your affirmation. When your mind becomes calm through using your affirmation, you can release repeating the affirmation yet retain your focus on the navel area. After letting go of the affirmation, focusing on the breathing is not required. But if you find it helpful, you can temporarily focus on both the breathing and the navel area by noticing the expansion of the navel area with each inhalation and the contraction of the navel area with each exhalation. After a while you can also let go of focusing on the breathing and just hold your awareness on the navel area alone. Thoughts will probably continue to present themselves to your conscious mind during most of your meditation, but you can let go of the affirmation if these thoughts are not distracting you. Thoughts only become distracting if you allow your awareness to follow these thoughts by participating in creating a succession of new thoughts. At those times when you can allow thoughts to float by without being concerned about where these thoughts are coming from or going to, you can let go of the affirmation.

If your mind becomes calm by ignoring thoughts as they float by, you do not need your affirmation. Instead, you can focus just on the navel area alone, as long as you do not become attracted to any stray thoughts and as long as you do not push away any stray thoughts. But if you become distracted again by allowing your attention to be carried away by stray thoughts, then you can gently return to repeating your affirmation. When your mind becomes calm again, you can let go of the affirmation and return to focusing on the navel area. In this process the holding of the affirmation assists you to focus on your spiritual intention in words, and letting go of the affirmation allows you to take your intention to a deeper level beyond words.

If you are a beginner and find that initially your mind is constantly distracted, you may find it necessary to maintain your practice of repeating your affirmation for your entire meditation period. However, as you make progress and calm your mind, you will notice that your thoughts can come and go without you becoming preoccupied by them. When you find that thoughts can float by in your mind for short intervals of time without you being distracted by them, you can then learn to let go of the affirmation for increasing amounts of time. The same process of holding your affirmation at times and then letting go of it for short intervals of calmness is used for each of the next meditation techniques that will be described in the sections below. Each of these techniques has a different focusing area in the body for meditation. For the method called Inner Silence Meditation, you can let go of both the affirmation and the body awareness. This method allows you to enter inner silence, leading toward contemplation as will be described in detail in Chapter 6.

It is important not to confuse Centering Meditation with another similarly named practice called "Centering Prayer," which has been popularized by Thomas Keating and Basil Pennington. Centering Prayer, described in Chapter 10, does not advocate focusing on a part of the body as does Centering Meditation. Actually the practice of Centering Prayer is very similar to Inner Silence Meditation, which will be described in the next chapter.

E. Heart Meditation

The second method is *Heart Meditation*, in which the awareness is held in the chest area. The major benefit of Heart Meditation is the development of *emotional receptivity* to the Holy Spirit, which enables you to release emotional tension and to increase devotion. Emotional receptivity is particularly important because tension and stress can build up over time, creating emotional anxiety. This emotional anxiety can become a stumbling block that hinders your ability to learn how to be open to divine love. By focusing on the chest area, you develop the emotional receptivity that gives permission for the Holy Spirit to assist you in releasing the stored up emotional tension within you. Releasing this emotional tension produces a deeper level of emotional stability and openness to love that is necessary to make progress in your spiritual growth.

If you are a beginning meditator, you will not initially experience this release of emotional tension as a conscious and dramatic experience. Instead, you will simply feel calmer and more peaceful at an emotional level as a result of your meditation. Thus the ups and downs of daily life will have less of an effect on you. Likewise, if you have emotional moods swings during meditation itself, these too will tend to level off. As you become more experienced in your meditation practice and as your emotional receptivity increases, you will be able to open yourself at a deeper level to the action of the Holy Spirit.

For the practice of Heart Meditation, you can focus your awareness either on the left side of the chest in the location of the physical heart or in the center of the chest. If the location of the physical heart is chosen as your focus for meditation, you may find one very small area on the left side of the chest that draws your attention more readily than any other area. Then you can allow your awareness to remain focused in that area. If the center of the chest is chosen, you may find one area (higher or lower) that attracts your attention, and the awareness may be focused in that area. As with the previous method, the first half of your chosen affirmation is repeated mentally and extended for the entire inhalation, and the second half of your chosen affirmation is repeated mentally and extended for the entire exhalation. For example, if "Jesus Christ Love" is your chosen affirmation, "Jesus" would be repeated on the inhalation and "Christ Love" on the exhalation. Again the breath is observed without manipulating it in any way.

As with Centering Meditation, you follow the same process of holding and letting go of the affirmation. You repeat the affirmation to counteract stray thoughts. If your mind becomes calm so you can ignore stray thoughts, you can let go of repeating the affirmation and hold your awareness only in the heart area or in the center of the chest. After you let go of the affirmation, you no longer need to focus on the breathing. Nevertheless, if you find it helpful, you can continue for a short time to be aware of the breathing while holding your awareness on a focusing area in the chest. But after a while you can let go of being aware of the breathing and be aware of only a focusing area in the chest. If your mind wanders because of stray thoughts catching your attention, you can allow this to be a gentle reminder for you to return to repeating the affirmation in coordination with your breathing. At first most of your practice may be just repeating your affirmation. But gradually you will be able to let go of your affirmation for short intervals and then later for longer periods of time. You are led in this process by your intention to grow toward your spiritual ideal. You do so first by holding your affirmation and then by letting go of your affirmation to allow your intention to go to a level deeper than words.

While the focus of awareness remains in the chest area, you may experience a feeling of energy or a feeling of warmth. Also, you may feel a tingling sensation, or you may feel the heartbeat. Feeling the heartbeat or any of these other sensations in the heart area can be employed as a way of helping to focus the awareness. Nonetheless, these feelings do not occur to everyone, and they are not necessary for this method of meditation. If awareness of the heartbeat or some other sensation does occur, this should not draw the attention away from repeating the affirmation. More information about coordinating the heartbeat with the affirmation is explained in Chapter 9. Generally this manual does not recommend coordinating the heartbeat with the affirmation unless you feel intuitively guided to do so. Most meditators who practice Heart Meditation simply coordinate the affirmation with the breathing and maintain the awareness in the chest area without coordinating the heartbeat.

With Heart Meditation there is the possibility of side effects caused by an accumulation of too much energy in the area of the physical heart. If you feel a slight pain in the chest or if your heartbeat suddenly becomes faster while practicing Heart Meditation, you need to temporarily switch to another technique. These side effects may be caused by concentrating for too long on the heart area, resulting in excessive energy being released. Sometimes this energy is reabsorbed by the pericardium (the fibro-serous sac that surrounds the heart), causing the heart to beat faster. This may also lead to difficulty in breathing or to pain in the chest. Therefore, it is wise to temporarily use another method of meditation, such as Centering Meditation, if you begin to feel pain in the chest or a rapid heartbeat.

These symptoms are not common, but are more likely to occur when you choose to focus on the area of the physical heart for long periods of time. If such symptoms do occur, then you may find that these symptoms do not recur when the focus is held in the center of the chest instead of the location of the physical heart.

Although symptoms are less likely to occur while meditating with the awareness held in the center of the chest, there is no attempt here to discourage you from holding the awareness in the location of the physical heart. If you feel guided to focus on the physical heart, you are certainly encouraged to follow your intuition, as long as none of the previously described negative symptoms occur. Beginning meditators may not notice any significant difference between holding the awareness on the physical heart and holding the awareness in the center of the chest.

However, many intermediate meditators prefer focusing on the physical heart because they discover that doing so awakens a deeper devotional quality than focusing on the center of the chest. As meditation deepens you may have a feeling of the divine presence in the location of the physical heart or even a feeling of both love and light in the heart. After first focusing on the physical heart and feeling light and love in that area, some intermediate meditators switch to focusing on the center of the chest to facilitate the expansion of love and light into the whole chest area. More information about feeling love and light in the physical heart and in the center of the chest is provided in Chapter 14, which describes a technique called *Inner Light Meditation.*

F. Brow Meditation

The third method of meditation is *Brow Meditation*, in which the awareness is held in the *brow area* slightly above the space between the eyebrows, but within the head itself. The practice of holding the awareness in the forehead area during meditation increases your ability to focus the mind. Brow Meditation specifically encourages *mental receptivity*, which gives the Holy Spirit permission to guide your thinking process. Your openness to the Holy Spirit's mental guidance helps you to stay on track in your process of learning how to let go of stray thoughts during meditation as well as learning how to hold on to the one thought of your affirmation.

Your increased mental receptivity not only aids you in letting go of stray thoughts in meditation and focusing the mind, but also assists you in releasing mental tension. Old habitual thinking patterns are stored in the subconscious mind. These ego-based thinking patterns may have been placed there from childhood and can produce tension in your mind. Your increase in mental receptivity due to bringing your attention to the brow area gives permission to the Holy Spirit to assist you to let go of these old discordant thinking patterns that are not in harmony with your spiritual growth. The result is a release of mental tension and a reorientation of your thinking process that changes your perception of yourself and others as well as your perceptions regarding spiritual matters. Gradually this brings about a change in your basic belief system, but you will generally not be aware of any change taking place as an inner conscious experience during meditation. You will instead become aware of the effects of your increased mental receptivity in your daily life. You will notice that you will have a greater willingness to look at yourself and your life in a new light. With a clearer mental picture of yourself, you will find that your mind is calmer and you will also feel a deeper sense of dedication toward manifesting your spiritual purposes outwardly through service to others.

For practicing Brow Meditation, you may hold your awareness just above the space between the eyebrows. However, the exact location may vary depending upon finding the place along the center of the forehead that feels intuitively right for you. Some meditators prefer the space between the eyebrows, but most meditators prefer an area slightly above that in the middle of the forehead. Feel free to meditate at whatever area you feel intuitively guided to bring your awareness. Just as with the previous methods, the affirmation is coordinated with the breathing. For example, if "Christ, Light" is the chosen affirmation, then "Christ" would be repeated on the inhalation and "Light" would be repeated on the exhalation.

With each of the previously mentioned methods of meditation, it is important to not think intellectually about the meaning of your chosen affirmation during meditation. You will need to rely on repeating the words themselves, rather than on an intellectual analysis of the words. This does not mean that the affirmation should be repeated mechanically. On the contrary, you repeat the affirmation with your wholehearted attention and desire for God. Allow all of your innermost being to be summed up and expressed in just these few words you have chosen. By repeating these words without intellectualizing, you will be brought beyond the level of conceptual thinking.

Your mind will become calm by repeating your affirmation so your thoughts will pass by in your mind without attracting your attention. When you can hold your focus without being distracted, you can let go of your affirmation and focus solely on holding your awareness in the brow area. You can release being aware of the breathing when you let go of the affirmation. However, if you find it helpful, you can temporarily continue to be aware of the breathing while also focusing on the brow area. Then after a while, you can let go of being aware of the breathing and focus only on the brow area.

After letting go of the affirmation, you may notice the mind wandering because of stray thoughts. If stray thoughts grab your attention, you can then allow this to remind you to bring your focus back to repeating the affirmation again. Your meditation can be a continuous repeated process of holding your affirmation and then letting go of it. Whether you are using your affirmation or letting go of it, you can maintain your intention of growing toward your spiritual ideal.

G. Crown Meditation

The fourth method of meditation focuses on the top of the head and is called *Crown Meditation*. You focus your awareness on the *crown area*, which is a circular area that includes the very top of the head and the highest part of the back of the head.

As with the previous methods, you repeat an affirmation in coordination with the breathing. For example, if "Christ Love" is your choice for an affirmation, then "Christ" would be repeated on the inhalation and "Love" would be repeated on the exhalation. You focus on the crown area and use your affirmation in coordination with your breathing to calm the mind.

During meditation when thoughts float by in your mind without your attraction or aversion, you can let go of repeating your affirmation and focus only on holding your awareness in the crown area. When you release the repeating of your affirmation, you can also let go of being aware of the breathing. Nevertheless, if it is your preference, you can continue for a short time to be aware of the breathing while focusing on the crown area. But then after a short while, you can let go of being aware of the breathing and focus only on the crown area.

You can continue to focus on the crown area as long as you are not distracted by the thoughts that float through the mind. However, if stray thoughts attract your attention, you can let this be a gentle reminder for you to return to repeating your affirmation again. Your practice of Crown Meditation will be a process of fluctuating between the holding of your affirmation and the letting go of your affirmation. The repeating of your affirmation is an assertion in words of your intention to grow closer to the divine within, and your letting go of your affirmation is an assertion without words of this same intention.

When you first start using Crown Meditation, it may be difficult to focus on the top of the head because you may feel a little "uncentered" or "ungrounded." This may possibly happen because the top of the head is associated with universal awareness and not individual awareness. Since so much of your conscious awareness is directed toward yourself as an individual, it may be disorienting to be exposed to this universal awareness. Sometimes even experienced meditators feel disoriented when they first start using Crown Meditation. However, after continued practice the disorientation will disappear.

The illustration shown on the opposite page displays the focusing areas that are used for the four techniques that have just been described. When you hold your awareness in the heart area for Heart Meditation or in the brow area for Brow Meditation, the focusing area can be a small area, perhaps a one-inch-wide area or smaller. But for Crown Meditation the focusing area is larger and is a circular area with approximately a four-inch diameter. This area is tilted slightly downward on the back side so it covers the very top of the head and also the highest portion of the back of the head. The tilting of this circular area is interestingly similar to the way halos are tilted in the side view of the paintings of saints.

An illustration of this circular crown area is provided below. A single line is used in this drawing to indicate the circumference of the circular crown area. Just as a circle drawn in the sky is a symbolic but not an exact depiction of the sun, the line drawing below shows a representation of the circular crown area, but not an exact depiction. This is because the circular crown area is an area of energy, so the actual circumference is not really as distinct as is shown in the line drawings below.

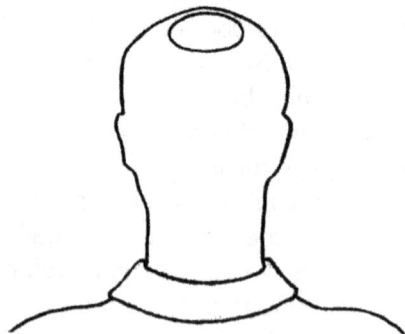

Brow Meditation

Focusing at the space between the eyebrows or at the middle of the forehead

Crown Meditation

Focusing at the crown of the head

Heart Meditation

Focusing at the heart or at the center of of the chest

Centering Meditation

Focusing at just below the navel

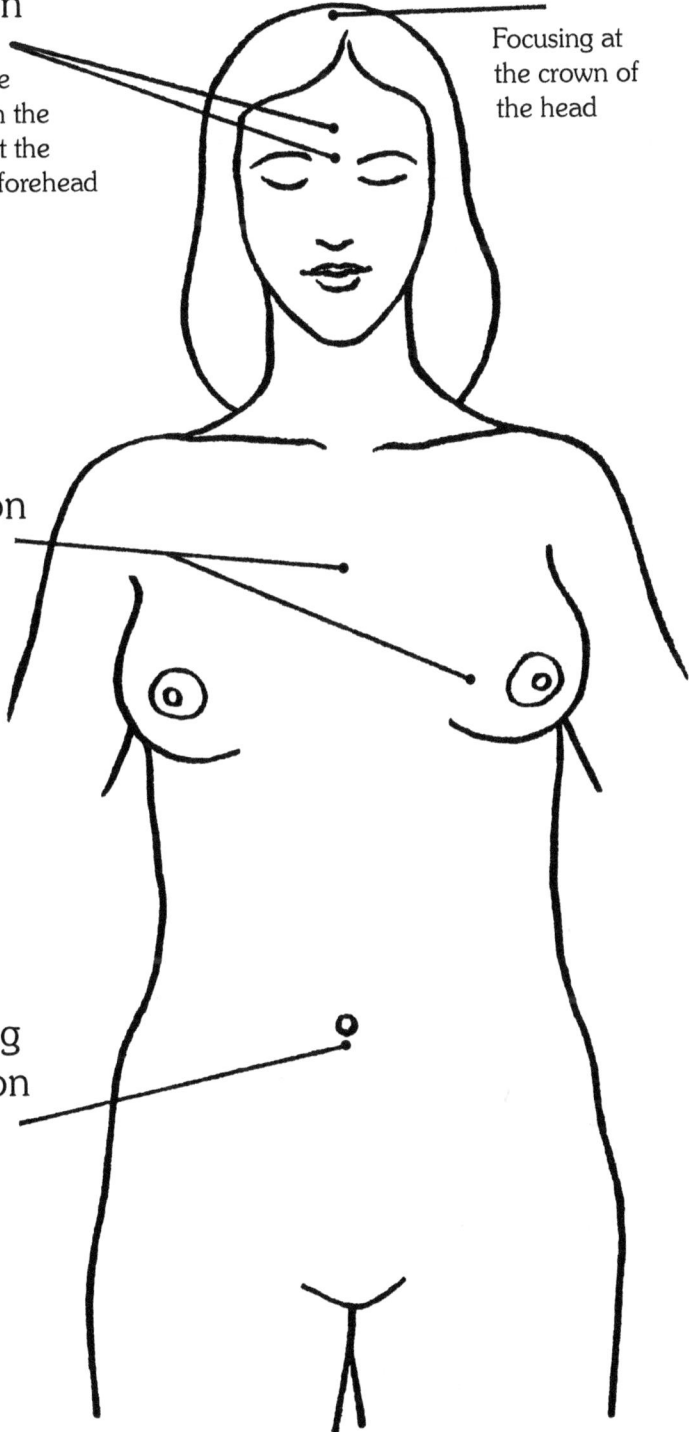

Some meditators who practice Crown Meditation feel this circular crown area on the top of the head being filled with energy. It is hard to describe how the energy of the crown area feels in terms of its shape because it is more like an energy field than like a distinct shape. Some meditators perceive it as a circular "opening," but it is more commonly perceived as an amorphous, rounded shape of energy. If you become aware of this energy in the crown area, you may consider it an outward indication of progress in your opening to the Spirit. However, the same accumulation of energy in the crown area can certainly occur without your conscious awareness, so do not give this any special significance in your mind. An outward sign of progress may not be the best indicator of overall progress. Instead, it's best to rely on pure faith that does not require any outward confirmation of progress.

The three techniques of meditation previously described produce physical receptivity, emotional receptivity, and mental receptivity. Crown Meditation produces *integrating receptivity*, which invites the Holy Spirit to positively affect your body, emotions, and mind to bring about a coordination between these three aspects of yourself. Focusing on the crown of the head helps you to contact the universal awareness, which creates an inner integration facilitated by the Holy Spirit. In spite of the disorienting effect that sometimes occurs when initially practicing Crown Meditation, the integrating effect of this method over time can lead you in the direction of gaining a greater awareness of the intuitive level of your being. Consequently, this method is a preparation for *Oneness Meditation*, which is related to your openness to your intuitions. Oneness Meditation is the next meditation method described below. In addition, the integrating effect of Crown Meditation is a preparation for the unifying effect of Inner Silence Meditation in which you enter contemplation, as will be described shortly.

H. Oneness Meditation

The techniques previously described rely on focusing your awareness on specific parts of the body. *Oneness Meditation* is a method in which you place your awareness on the whole body all at once. Placing your awareness on the entire body helps you to be aware of the wholeness and the oneness of the body. This kind of oneness related to the physical body is a rudimentary experience of oneness and is a preparation for being aware of an even deeper inner feeling of oneness. Transcending physical awareness, this deeper level of experiencing oneness is related to your spiritual connection with all other life forms and with God.

Although the deeper level of oneness is beyond body awareness, the emphasis in this meditation method is on being aware of the oneness of the body by expanding your awareness to include the entire body. If you are a beginner, you may find it difficult initially to expand your awareness to include focusing simultaneously on all parts of the body. If you discover that you cannot extend your awareness to encompass the entire body, then you may start with focusing on both the head and the chest. When you can focus on these two areas, you can expand your awareness to also include the navel area. Next you can add the awareness of your hands and then your arms. Finally you can include your feet and then your legs in your awareness. If you use this piecemeal approach to expanding your awareness, you may find that you are able to include a large portion of the body, but still cannot encompass the whole body. If you cannot focus on the entire body, just focus on as much of the body as you can.

While focusing on the whole body, or as much of the body as you can, you also focus on an affirmation and coordinate your affirmation with your breathing. For example, if your affirmation is "Christ One," you can repeat "Christ" on the inhalation and "One" on the exhalation. As with the other methods, when your mind is calm, you can let go of the affirmation and focus only on the body as a whole.

When you let go of your affirmation, it is no longer necessary to focus on the breathing. But if you do want to continue to focus on the breathing temporarily, you may do so while also focusing on the whole body. After a while you can let go of being aware of the breathing and focus solely on the entire body as long as the mind remains calm. When stray thoughts catch your attention, you can let this be a gentle reminder to return to repeating your affirmation. As with the other methods that have been described, your practice of Oneness Meditation will be a continuous process of holding your affirmation and letting go of your affirmation.

The techniques of meditation that have been described previously can be used alone at times, but Oneness Meditation is best practiced right after Crown Meditation and/or before Inner Silence Meditation, which is described below. Oneness Meditation is effective after Crown Meditation because holding your awareness at the crown area helps to produce an inner integration that prepares you to be aware of oneness within you.

When Oneness Meditation is used just before Inner Silence Meditation, it can become a helpful transition to this method that does not use body awareness. Toward the end of practicing Oneness Meditation, when you are ready to make a transition to Inner Silence Meditation, you can introduce a change in your practice to facilitate this transition. For this transition you allow your mind to become calm and let go of focusing on your affirmation and breathing. You then focus only on the whole body, or as much of the body as you can. To complete the transition, you let go of all body awareness, but retain the feeling of oneness that you felt when focusing on the whole body. If you are able to be aware of this feeling of oneness without body awareness, it will appear to you that you are the person holding this awareness. But after practicing this method over a period of time, you may be able to sense that the feeling of oneness is actually holding you, rather than you holding this feeling.

Even though you may associate your feeling of oneness with the feeling of the whole body, you are opening yourself in this transitional practice to realize that your feeling of oneness is not limited to the body. You can take this feeling of oneness into your practice of Inner Silence Meditation and use this method in the way that it is described in the next chapter. There is no need to be concerned if you can or cannot experience this feeling of oneness without body awareness when you first attempt the transition to Inner Silence Meditation. You can just make the attempt, and if you do not experience the feeling of oneness, you can simply move on to your practice of Inner Silence Meditation without looking back.

Crown Meditation produces *integrating receptivity* that helps the physical, emotional and mental parts of your being work together in coordination. This prepares you to become aware of your oneness, which may happen during Oneness Meditation. You can experience your oneness both when you are focusing on the entire body and when you let go of body awareness. This feeling of oneness is really an *intuition*. Oneness Meditation is a method that helps you to be open specifically to the feeling of oneness, but also in a general sense to be open to other intuitions. Consequently, the kind of receptivity that Oneness Meditation fosters is *intuitive receptivity*. This kind of receptivity is an openness to allowing the Holy Spirit to enter into the intuitive level of your being to produce an inner transformation. Intuitive receptivity is an openness to your *inner feelings*, meaning your intuitions, that lead you beyond the physical senses, beyond your emotions, and beyond your rational thinking.

Allowing you to go beyond your normal way of sensing, feeling, and perceiving, your intuitive receptivity can open you to experiencing many different kinds of inner feelings that come from the intuitive level of your being. If you do experience these inner feelings, they can assist your spiritual growth. But the lack of such experiences is not a drawback, since the foundation of your spiritual growth needs to rest on pure faith that does not require a felt experience to confirm your contact with the Spirit. In fact, faith itself is the highest form of intuition and is much more than just an inner feeling. A comprehensive explanation of intuitions and how to develop some specific intuitions can be found in Chapter 14.

6

TECHNIQUES LEADING TO CONTEMPLATION

≈ ○ ≈

A. Inner Silence Meditation

After learning how to use an affirmation along with focusing on body awareness, as was described in the previous chapter, you may want to consider using a technique that does not rely on body awareness. One such method is *Inner Silence Meditation*, which will assist you in learning how to let go of body awareness in order to experience the inner silence of contemplation. For this method you repeat your affirmation without focusing on any part of the body. When your mind becomes calm, you can let go of your affirmation and allow yourself to be open to the divine presence in silence. If your mind becomes distracted by stray thoughts, you then return to the stabilizing influence of repeating your affirmation. Your meditation during Inner Silence Meditation consists of alternating between times of using the affirmation and times of letting go of the affirmation in order to rest in silent receptivity to the divine presence.

The goal of meditation is to silence the mind so that the Spirit can shine through. Normally an affirmation is used for this purpose. But some beginning meditators decide to learn meditation without using any affirmation and attempt to go directly into silence. A few may succeed at this, yet most beginners fail to experience inner silence because of being assailed by numerous stray thoughts.

The problem of overcoming distracting thoughts is addressed by the use of an affirmation to help silence the mind. Initially in meditation you will have difficulty in controlling the tendency of the mind to wander. Then through repeating an affirmation, you will notice a gradual improvement in your ability to reduce stray thoughts. The affirmation calms the many thoughts of the mind by turning the awareness toward the one thought of the affirmation.

Nevertheless, that one thought of the affirmation is itself one step away from complete silence. Your affirmation is like a physical ladder that helps you to climb one step at a time to the top of a roof. Once you are on top of the roof, it would be foolish to pull the ladder up and carry it around. Similar to a ladder, the one thought of the affirmation does its work of lifting you up to a higher state of having a quiet mind. Then you can let go of this one thought so you can rest on the rooftop of your awareness, which is the inner silence of contemplation.

Using Inner Silence Meditation is an ongoing process, which alternates between two activities. The first activity is to hold the affirmation without focusing on the body and to let go of the thoughts that pass through the mind. When the mind becomes calm because you are not distracted by stray thoughts, you can practice the second activity. This second activity, which is more of a non-doing than a doing, is to let go of the affirmation and enter inner silence. There are deep states of inner silence that can potentially be reached in which there are no thoughts, but invariably thoughts will appear during your experience of inner silence. These thoughts which float by in your mind do not in themselves have the power to disturb the silence of your contemplative practice. However, if you have some sort of reaction to these passing thoughts, you give these thoughts the power to distract your mind. Your goal is to let thoughts float by without paying any particular attention to them. Your approach is to follow a path between the extremes of aversion and attraction, so you do not push any thought away and you do not attract any thought. This is a process of continually letting go and surrendering to the Holy Spirit. You rely only on pure faith without the support normally provided by your reason, memory, or imagination.

After being absorbed into inner silence briefly, you may find yourself distracted by wandering thoughts that have captured your attention. When this occurs, it would be a mistake to judge yourself adversely for having become distracted. Evaluative monitoring of yourself will only add even more distracting thoughts to an already distracted mind. Instead of evaluating yourself, you gently pick up your affirmation again and focus on your choice of a sacred word or words. You continue to hold your awareness on your affirmation, until your mind becomes calm again and you are ready to let go of your affirmation and again enter inner silence.

This process of letting go of discursive thinking, entering silence and relying on pure faith in the Christian tradition has generally been called "contemplative prayer." But the term "prayer," as it is used in this manual, refers to expressive communication with God, while meditation refers to receptive communication with God. Therefore, in this book instead of using the term contemplative prayer, the process of entering into contemplative silence is called "Inner Silence Meditation." A similar process of going into inner silence is commonly taught today under the specific name of "Centering Prayer," as it is described in Chapter 10.

The term "contemplation" by itself is the best way to describe the overshadowing of the Holy Spirit that tends to occur when practicing the technique of Inner Silence Meditation. Contemplation is both a restful and dynamic state of inner absorption, in which your mind has an inner focus that allows stray thoughts to pass by without causing distraction. This inner absorption has no object that serves as a focus.

You do not "manufacture" the state of communion with the divine in contemplation because your union with God is already a pre-existing condition of your true nature. This condition of union is hidden from your awareness, but you can assist in letting go of the blocks to your awareness that prevent you from recognizing your union with God. Since your self-centered preoccupation with your own thoughts is your major stumbling block, you can use the affirmation to help you let go of your thoughts, which will assist you in revealing deeper and deeper levels of awareness. You do not think about the meaning of your affirmation because this would only add more discursive thinking and increase your preoccupation with your thoughts, rather than reduce your self-centered preoccupation. The affirmation can help to reduce thoughts and increase your awareness of the divine presence by being used in different ways depending on the needs of the seeker.

The affirmation is a way of leading you toward union with your spiritual ideal. The affirmation consists of both the form and the content of the affirmation. The form is the actual word or words used. The content is not the literal meaning of the words, but rather your intention to awaken your awareness of the divine presence. If you are a beginner, you may initially rely on using the form of your affirmation as a means of leading you to the content of your intention. Then, as your experience deepens, you can learn to rely less on the form and more on the content itself. Relying on the content of your intention will then lead you through faith to the experience of the divine presence in contemplation.

The next pages provide a list of four phases of using the affirmation in the practice of Inner Silence Meditation. These four phases can be used one after the other in sequence during one meditation session, but usually your awareness will fluctuate back and forth between these phases. This list starts with the most structured, gross, and form-related usage of the affirmation. Then it proceeds to less structured, and more subtle and more content-related usages of the affirmation. The more structured, gross, and form-related usages are most helpful for beginners, and with progress these will be less needed and can be reduced or omitted altogether.

The goal is to *internalize* the affirmation because in doing so you are internalizing your spiritual ideal. The word or words of the affirmation that represent your intention for a closer relationship with God are first used and then are left behind and replaced by the fulfillment of your intention—your communion with the divine presence. Each individual phase is only a stepping stone to the next, culminating in the experience of contemplation.

Four Phases of Using the Affirmation in Inner Silence Meditation

1. Mentally Pronouncing the Affirmation

For the first phase, you repeat the affirmation, pronouncing it in your mind only, not with your lips as an outward verbal expression. You do not think about the literal meaning of the word or words of the affirmation. You understand that the word or words are an external form-related representation of your inner spiritual ideal of God and your intention to unite with your spiritual ideal. You mentally repeat each syllable of the affirmation in whatever way feels most natural to you, yet there is no focusing on any part of the body. You do not coordinate the repeating of the affirmation with the breathing. Nonetheless, if you find that you are having unusual difficulty with very distracting thoughts, you may occasionally coordinate your affirmation with your breathing just to overcome this temporary difficulty.

This repeating of the "word form," the mental sound of the word or words, is done only to counteract distracting thoughts. When the mind is calm enough to go to a deeper level, you can let go of repeating the affirmation in the form of a sound pronounced mentally. In addition to overcoming distracting thoughts, the repeating of the sound of the affirmation is a way of affirming your desire for God. The next phase is a more receptive and less structured way of expressing your desire. As a beginner you can learn how to use the first phase of mentally repeating the affirmation and then you can switch to the next phase. However, you have the option of omitting this first phase altogether and starting with the less structured and less form-related second phase described below.

2. Allowing the Affirmation to Deepen your Awareness

The second phase lets the thought of your affirmation bring you to deeper and deeper levels of awareness by letting that thought come to your mind in whatever way it presents itself. You allow the thought of your affirmation to be an unstructured reminder of your intention to be open to God's presence. Consequently, the thought of the form of your affirmation becomes a symbolic reminder of the thought of your intention, which is the content of your affirmation. Your affirmation serves as an expression of your desire for God, and your giving of your permission to God to come into your awareness. You let the affirmation come to your mind however it presents itself in order to lead you to your awareness to God's presence and activity within you. Since the affirmation is only a reminder of your desire, you do not have to repeat the affirmation in a structured way during the second phase. You just let your affirmation enter your awareness as a transition point to your intention for God, which your affirmation symbolizes. This phase occurs prior to actually experiencing God's presence and instead is primarily about your desire for God and your willingness to become aware of His presence.

You do not try to control how the affirmation "should" come into your awareness. You gently remind yourself of the affirmation when you are distracted by stray thoughts, but you allow the affirmation to be clear or indistinct in whatever way it may come to your awareness. Your affirmation is just a symbol of your intention, so you can allow the form of the affirmation to come to you in any way. For example, when you recall your affirmation, it may come to you spontaneously as the sound of the affirmation. Also, it may come as the thought of the word or words of the affirmation, without the accompanying sound, and, of course, without conjuring up the intellectual meaning of the word or words. It may come to you as a vague thought, an impulse of the will, or a feeling.

You allow the affirmation's form to be whatever it is and to lead you to your intention itself, which the form symbolizes. Thus the form of your affirmation can fade away as your intention itself takes over. You can allow your intention to be the focal point of your awareness, while other thoughts are passing through your mind. But if these other thoughts divert your attention away from your intention, you can then bring your awareness back to the form of your affirmation to help redirect your mind back to your intention of bringing about a deeper relationship with God. As soon as the thought of your intention is reestablished, the word form of your affirmation is not necessary because you are focused on the content of your affirmation. You can begin with the first phase and progress to this second phase, or you can skip the first phase and start your practice with this second phase. The idea is to move in the direction of experiencing the divine presence and to release distracting thoughts in the least structured manner so eventually the form of your affirmation will be less and less needed.

3. The Affirmation Leads to Faithful Awareness

In the previous phase, you let the thought of your affirmation lead you from the form of your affirmation to the content of your intention for God, which is your desire for God. In this third phase, you give your consent to His presence and His activity within you. This, of course, requires your faith that God Himself is indeed within you. By investing in your intention and your faith, you progress to this third phase, in which you have a *faithful awareness* of abiding in God's presence. In this third phase, your faith has expanded your awareness allowing you to have an inner knowing that God is right there within you in the present moment. You are not quite resting in God's presence yet, but you can sense and experience His presence in the darkness of faith, which is your faithful awareness of Him. The previous phase was more about your desire for God and giving your permission to God to come into your awareness. This third phase is less about desire, which you have already expressed, and more about consent, which is your acceptance of God's presence that has become increasingly apparent to you through your faith.

It is hard to draw a firm line between the desire of the previous phase and your consent and faithful awareness of this third phase, because your awareness may certainly fluctuate back and forth between your desire for God on the one hand and your faithful acceptance of His immanent presence on the other hand. In the second phase, you desire what it appears you do not have, but in this third phase you switch to acceptance as soon as you realize you already have what you had desired. This third phase represents a step forward since you are becoming aware that God is responding to your intention by enabling you to recognize His presence through your consent and your faith. Your faithful awareness is God's gift to you, allowing you to become aware of Him. If your mind becomes distracted by stray thoughts so you lose your faithful awareness of the divine presence, you will need to return your awareness to one of the previous phases in order to calm your mind again.

4. The Affirmation Culminates in Contemplative Resting in God

Your faithful awareness of God's presence in the previous phase leads to not just being aware of His presence, but to the fourth phase, in which you rest in His presence during contemplation. This resting in God brings about an inner absorption in God that is not due to any concentrative effort on your part. In fact, this inner absorption is brought about by letting go of your own efforts and allowing God to be God in your inmost being. Since your affirmation is an expression of your intention for union with your spiritual ideal, resting in God is the true content of your affirmation, even though the form of the affirmation in words has no expression at this deep level of pure awareness.

Contemplative resting in God is the destination toward which your affirmation is pointing. Although contemplation is the culmination of the inward journey toward which the affirmation is leading you, the journey to this contemplative destination needs to be repeated as an ongoing process. The process of interiorizing your affirmation will need to be repeated because initially you will only be able to rest in God for very short intervals of time before you are drawn out of this contemplative experience. Your brief intervals of contemplative rest will be interrupted by distracting thoughts so you will have to revert back to previous phases. You may have to go back to either the first or second phase— whichever of these phases you think would best help you let go of your distracting thoughts and reestablish your awareness of your intention for divine communion.

Inner Silence Meditation consists of two parts: one meditative and the other contemplative. Meditation is the holding of one thought in the mind, which would be the maintaining of the word or words of your affirmation in your mind. Thus the meditative part of Inner Silence Meditation is your repeating of the affirmation to calm your mind and your releasing of the affirmation when your mind becomes calm. In contrast to meditation in which you hold one thought of your affirmation as your focusing object, contemplation has no focusing object. Contemplation cannot occur until you let go of the form of the affirmation as a focusing object. Therefore, the contemplative part of Inner Silence Meditation occurs after you let go of the form of your affirmation, when your mind becomes so calm that you are drawn into a state of inner absorption that does not need a focusing object. Your awareness has left the contemplative state when you notice that your inner absorption has given way to distracting thoughts. You then let your distracting thoughts remind you to return your awareness to repeating your affirmation as a meditative practice.

Contemplation is a gift given freely by the Holy Spirit. However, to receive this gift, it is necessary to have a certain degree of receptivity. The term *unifying receptivity* may be used to describe the kind of receptivity developed by practicing Inner Silence Meditation. Unifying receptivity is an openness to being drawn increasingly into the experience of being unified at all levels. All meditation techniques develop receptivity since all methods are an invitation for the incoming of the Holy Spirit. The Holy Spirit can transform you only to the degree of permission that you allow. Unifying receptivity is an openness to all of the kinds of receptivity previously mentioned. Thus unifying receptivity is a joining together of all forms of receptivity, including physical receptivity, emotional receptivity, mental receptivity, integrating receptivity, and intuitive receptivity. This in turn becomes an invitation to the Holy Spirit to transform all aspects of yourself. Your unifying receptivity is your openness and invitation that allows you to enter into the experience of contemplation or in other words to enter into His World.

Your unifying receptivity is your consent to allow the Holy Spirit to be present in all aspects of your consciousness. Your primary means of consenting to the Holy Spirit is *pure faith*. The practice of Inner Silence Meditation is an exercise in faith. As you exercise your faith with this practice, you grow in faith, increasing your unifying receptivity. Since contemplation involves the incoming of the Holy Spirit based on pure faith, it may not be recorded in your conscious mind as an experience that can be felt by the senses. Nevertheless, in some cases your meditation or contemplation experience may bring about an observable inner feeling, which has been called a "felt experience" in Chapter 2. This experience consists of an expanded awareness of one or more inner feelings that are *intuitions*. These intuitions are signs of making progress, but they should never be considered more important than pure faith. Specific descriptions of these intuitions are provided in Chapter 14. Additional information about the practice of Inner Silence Meditation can be found in Chapter 8.

After successfully using the affirmation combined with techniques that use body awareness to calm the mind, you may want to consider using Inner Silence Meditation. However, instead of replacing body awareness techniques altogether by using Inner Silence Meditation exclusively, it is recommended to practice this technique along with body awareness methods as part of Christian Yoga Meditation, which is described below. When first practicing Inner Silence Meditation as part of Christian Yoga Meditation, you can set aside a few minutes at the end of your practice for this purpose. During these few minutes just before concluding your meditation, you can simply let go of repeating the affirmation and allow yourself to "Be still, and know that I am God."[1] After you become comfortable using Inner Silence Meditation as part of Christian Yoga Meditation, you can increase the time for this method and reduce the time for body awareness techniques. Eventually in your practice of Christian Yoga Meditation, you may want to devote most of your sitting time to Inner Silence Meditation.

B. Christian Yoga Meditation

The five body awareness techniques that have been described in the previous chapter and Inner Silence Meditation have been presented as methods that can be practiced separately. However, all six of these individual methods can be combined into one meditation practice. This practice is called *Christian Yoga Meditation*. To practice this combination of techniques, you start with Centering Meditation, in which you hold the awareness at the navel area and mentally repeat the first half of your affirmation on the inhalation and the second half of your affirmation on the exhalation. The breathing is observed, but not manipulated in any way. You can let go of the affirmation when the mind becomes calm and is not distracted as you focus only on the navel area. If your mind becomes distracted by stray thoughts, you let your awareness of the distracting stray thoughts be a reminder for you to return to repeating your affirmation again. Each of the six techniques in this sequence of methods employs this same process of holding your affirmation and releasing it when it is not needed.

When you feel ready to move on to the second technique in this sequence, you let go of Centering Meditation and begin practicing Heart Meditation. For this practice you hold your awareness in the heart area or in the center of the chest and again repeat your affirmation in coordination with your breathing. You let go of the affirmation when your mind becomes calm and focus only in the heart or center of the chest. You decide intuitively how long to practice Heart Meditation before moving on to the next technique.

The third technique that you practice is Brow Meditation, in which you observe your breathing and repeat your affirmation while your attention remains in the brow area. Again you release your affirmation when the mind becomes calm and focus only on the brow area.

For the fourth method, you practice Crown Meditation, in which you focus on your breathing and affirmation while you hold your awareness at the crown area of the head. As with the previous methods, when your mind becomes calm, you let go of the affirmation and focus only on the crown of the head.

The fifth method practiced in this sequence is Oneness Meditation, in which you focus on the whole body or as much of the body as you can hold in your awareness at one time. You repeat your affirmation in coordination with your breathing and let go of your affirmation when the mind becomes calm, as you focus only on the whole body or as much of the body as you can. When you are ready to transition to Inner Silence Meditation, you let go of all body awareness in a very specific manner. This conclusion to Oneness Meditation consists of first allowing the mind to become calm and letting go of repeating your affirmation so you can focus only on the whole body or on as much of the body as you can hold in your awareness. While focusing on the body only, you allow yourself to be aware of the oneness of the body and then let go of body awareness altogether. However, when you let go of body awareness, you see if you can retain the feeling of oneness that you had experienced previously, but without relating this feeling to the body. If you can hold on to the feeling of oneness without body awareness, you can also see if you can sense that this feeling of oneness is holding you, instead of you holding this feeling of oneness.

Then you move right into practicing Inner Silence Meditation whether you feel you are successful in experiencing the feeling of oneness without body awareness or not. Oneness Meditation is intended to be practiced only briefly as a transition meditation from Crown Meditation to Inner Silence Meditation. If you practice Oneness Meditation and find that you can be aware of the whole body or much of the body and if you find that it is helpful, continue to use it. However, some beginning meditators are unable to expand their awareness to the whole body or much of the body, and therefore may feel this method is not helpful. If you do not feel comfortable using this method, feel free to consider Oneness Meditation as an optional practice that you can omit from your practice of Christian Yoga Meditation.

For the sixth and final technique, Inner Silence Meditation, you let go of all body awareness and focus only on your affirmation. Then when your mind becomes calm, you can let go of your affirmation and enter inner silence without any object to use as a focus for your awareness. If your mind becomes distracted by stray thoughts, you return to focusing on your affirmation. When your mind becomes calm again you let go of the affirmation again in order to enter inner silence.

During these intervals of inner silence, your mind may at times enter a state of inner absorption that requires no object for focusing and a state in which you can let go of stray thoughts as they pass by in your mind. These experiences of inner absorption are intervals of contemplation, which is an overshadowing of the Holy Spirit. This contemplative experience is a gift of the Spirit, but this gift comes as a natural outcome of meeting the conditions of the gift.

There are four conditions for receiving the gift of contemplation. The first condition is a calm mind and ideally an integrated and unified mind. All of the six meditation techniques of Christian Yoga Meditation are designed to produce this peaceful state of mind that invites the Holy Spirit to enter your consciousness and transform you. Inner Silence Meditation by itself can calm the mind to prepare you for the gift of contemplation, but the entire sequence of six techniques produces an integration and unification of all aspects of your being. This integration and unification serves as a very stable and long-lasting foundation for entering contemplation, for increasing the depth of your contemplative experience, and for allowing the experience of contemplation to become a regular part of your practice. Also, this solid foundation prepares you for handling the dynamic forces that are released by contemplation. In particular, this foundation helps you face the dark side of your nature that is brought to light by contemplation as a necessary part of your inner transformation.

The second condition of the gift of contemplation is your desire for God. The third condition is your consent to His presence. Desire and consent sound very similar, yet are different. What is the distinction between these two? Desire comes first and is about *wanting*. Consent comes after desire and is about *accepting* what is wanted. Both of these two conditions of desire and consent involve using your will. You exercise your will through your intention to find God, which is your desire for Him. You offer your invitation to God through your will being used to desire His presence. In addition, you also exercise your will by consenting to the presence of the Holy Spirit in your mind. The more comprehensive and wholehearted you can make your invitation and give your consent, the more the Holy Spirit can accomplish in you to bring about an inner spiritual transformation. Your invitation and consent rests on your degree of willingness and openness.

All six methods of Christian Yoga Meditation help you to expand your invitation and consent to the Holy Spirit by your openness to physical, emotional, mental, integrating, intuitive and unifying receptivity. The Holy Spirit is sensitive to whatever parts of yourself that you wish to withhold from transformation and will not violate whatever limitations you place on your transformation. The sequence provided by Christian Yoga Meditation helps you to systematically focus on every aspect of yourself so you can surrender all parts of yourself to inner transformation.

The fourth condition for receiving the gift of contemplation is your application of your faith. The amount of your faith is not nearly as significant as your implementation of whatever faith you do have. Your faith, even with your doubts remaining, needs to be directed toward your intention of drawing closer to God. Your faith tells you that God is there within you. The implementation of your faithful knowing of His presence opens you to increasing your awareness of His presence. All of the methods in the practice of Christian Yoga Meditation represent a practical application of your faith, since you are making an investment of time and energy in these techniques as an expression of your faith. You are investing in your faith that God is present within you and in your faith that with His assistance you can expand your awareness of His presence. Your faith also opens you to allowing the Holy Spirit to bring about an inner transformation of your character and consciousness. The first five methods lead to the sixth method, Inner Silence Meditation, which helps you to increasingly rely on your faith and hopefully enter contemplation, as is explained in greater detail in Chapter 8.

Each of the six methods of Christian Yoga Meditation can be used individually and can produce beneficial effects. But combining these six techniques in sequence is like walking up the steps of a staircase with each step leading to a higher level of awareness. What makes these six methods especially effective in raising consciousness is that this specific sequence of meditation techniques follows a natural upward progression that occurs within the body. This upward progression is related to the flow of creative energy within the body. Creative energy rises from the lower parts of the body upward and helps to raise consciousness. The six techniques of Christian Yoga Meditation cooperate with and even facilitate this natural raising of creative energy, which in turn assists in raising consciousness. The relationship between meditation and the raising of creative energy is explained in detail in Chapter 11, which describes the kundalini energy and spiritual centers of awareness.

The raising of consciousness can be symbolized by the image of a ladder. There is an analogy in a previous section that compares the affirmation to a physical ladder that leads you to the rooftop of your awareness, which is the inner silence of contemplation. The most appropriate analogy of a ladder is the symbolism of Jacob's ladder, the Old Testament ladder that Jacob experienced in a dream in which he saw angels descending and ascending from earth to Heaven. Communication with God is like this ladder, which represents the different levels of awareness, from earthly awareness of the physical realm to heavenly awareness of the spiritual realm.

The rungs on Jacob's ladder rise to progressively higher levels of consciousness. Climbing these rungs is accomplished by practicing each of the six steps of Christian Yoga Meditation in sequence. The first level of consciousness is the physical awareness, the second level is emotional awareness, and the third level is mental awareness. The fourth level is an awareness of how to coordinate the physical, emotional and mental levels of your awareness to create an integration of these. The fifth level is an awareness of inner feelings, meaning your intuitions—for example, the feeling of oneness. The sixth level is unifying awareness. After integrating the various levels of your awareness and opening to your intuitions, you go beyond coordination to a certain degree of unification. This unifying awareness helps you to practice contemplation and increasingly reveals your divine oneness with God. Although there are higher rungs, higher levels of consciousness, this explanation only deals with the rungs of the ladder that lead to contemplation.

Communication with God can occur at any one of these levels. However, in order to experience your divine nature, you will need to learn to communicate on all of these levels. The lowest rung of Jacob's ladder is closest to the earth and corresponds to the physical level of your awareness. For your communication with God, this physical level is your starting point that then leads upward in a natural progression to each successive rung of the ladder that extends to Heaven.

To emphasize this point, an Eastern master gave his students a rope tied with a series of knots with no space between each knot. He asked his students to untie the rope. However, he stipulated that they must start to untie the rope in the middle and could not start at the end. The students admitted they could not untie the rope in the middle, but they could untie the rope at one end and then untie each knot in succession until all the knots would be untied. The Eastern master demonstrated to his students by this example that there is a series of steps that need to be completed in a specific sequence in order to make spiritual progress. Skipping the first step in the sequence and attempting to work on a step in the middle of the sequence is a shortcut that will not work.

Like the knot at the end of the rope and like the lowest rung of the ladder that is closest to the earth, the first level of communication with God is physical receptivity, which is learned by Centering Meditation. Then comes emotional receptivity, which is learned by Heart Meditation. This is followed by mental receptivity, which is learned by Brow Meditation. Next is integrating receptivity, which is learned by Crown Meditation.

Why is this sequence so important? It is because the rungs of the ladder and the knots of the rope are actually related to parts of your own physical body. As was well-known by the Eastern master in the above story, there are different centers of consciousness in the body that need to be opened and purified in sequence from bottom to top in order to grow spiritually. Four very important centers are related to the navel area, the chest area, the brow area and the crown area. In the practice of Christian Yoga Meditation, focusing on these four areas in succession serves as a preparation for practicing Oneness Meditation and then Inner Silence Meditation, which leads to contemplation.

Oneness Meditation is an optional method designed as a transition from Crown Meditation to Inner Silence Meditation. Through focusing on the whole body, Oneness Meditation can help you to contact your inner feeling of oneness through being aware of the oneness of the body. Then as a conclusion to this method, you can let go of body awareness so you can experience your oneness beyond form as you enter inner silence. Oneness Meditation can help you develop intuitive receptivity, meaning an openness to the intuitive level of your being.

Inner Silence Meditation can help you to open yourself to unifying receptivity, which in turn can lead to experiencing contemplation and entering His World. This form of receptivity is an openness to allow the separate parts of yourself to not only become integrated so they work together in coordination, but also join together in such a way as to raise your level of awareness of the divine. Indeed, the inner absorption that occurs during contemplation is brought about by a certain degree of unification of your inner faculties produced by divine grace. Your unifying receptivity is needed to provide the invitation to the Holy Spirit to facilitate the raising of your awareness to the contemplative level. All the previously described methods help you to calm and unify the mind. Hopefully your mind will become unified enough for the Holy Spirit to take this unification process to another level, which is the contemplative level that is beyond your control, except for requiring your consent.

What if you have not done enough preparatory work of walking one step at a time up the lower rungs of the ladder of consciousness so you are able to unify to some degree the various levels of the your being? In that case, it will probably be less likely for you to be drawn into contemplation. For example, if your first and only method of attempting meditation is Inner Silence Meditation, you may not be properly and fully prepared to be open to contemplation. Your task would be similar to the challenge presented by trying to untie the middle knot in the row of knots in the rope described in the previous analogy.

It's unfortunate that most forms of teaching Christian contemplation exclude any reference to the first knot that needs to be untied, namely the physical level of your being, and to the energy released at this first level. This form of Christian denial leaves out a very important element in preparing for entering contemplation. There are two ways to prepare for contemplation, one originating in the East and the other coming from the West. The one that is well-known in the East is the unlocking of the subtle creative energy that rises from the lower part of the body. Creative energy rises upward from the lowest end of the spine, which is the location of the "rope of knots" in your body. This rising energy unlocks seven energy centers, considered spiritual centers, in sequence within your body. This sequence of opening these centers of spiritual awareness from the bottom to the top is a natural process and natural progression. With your consent, this natural process is facilitated by the action of the Holy Spirit and can be accelerated by methods focusing on body awareness.

Yoga as a meditation practice in the East is often taught as a way of focusing on these energy centers. In this Eastern approach, meditators typically start by bringing their awareness to the lowest center first, and then progressively moving the awareness to higher energy centers. This upward succession of focusing awakens energy within the body that is purifying and prepares you to become increasingly aware of your spiritual nature. Also included in Eastern spiritual growth is the need to surrender to God, but the central focus is on practicing techniques that assist in awakening higher awareness.

In contrast to the Eastern approach of using techniques to awaken spiritual centers, the way of approaching contemplation that is usually taught in the West places the emphasis on surrendering to the Holy Spirit. Your surrender to the Holy Spirit creates a purifying effect that prepares you for contemplation, leads you into contemplation, and sustains you during contemplation. Most Christian seekers are only exposed to one approach, which in itself can succeed to draw you into deep contemplation. This surrender to the Holy Spirit is usually taught today with a focus on surrendering the mind and without any direct focusing on body awareness or the emotions as a part of this method. This approach to inward seeking, called Centering Prayer, is very similar if not identical to Inner Silence Meditation.

A comparison between Inner Silence Meditation and other methods, such as Centering Prayer, is provided in Chapter 10. Thomas Keating, who teaches Centering Prayer, maintains that in his experience he has met many members of typical contemplative monastic communities who have never actually had the consciously felt experience of mystical graces associated with contemplation.[2] Indeed, some seekers practice Centering Prayer for many years and never have the consciously felt experience of the inflowing of the divine presence into their faculties during their contemplative practice. Their persistence is a wonderful and commendable example of manifesting pure faith. Certainly such seekers are rewarded by God for their steadfast practice. The purifying action of the Holy Spirit can enter your faculties and proceed to bring about your inner transformation without your consciously felt awareness of this process occurring. Nevertheless, in my opinion, those who are seeking to have a conscious experience of contemplation would be much more successful if they started with untying the lower knots first, rather than focusing on trying to untie one of the middle knots in the rope of knots.

The Holy Spirit has the ability to unlock all your inner knots, removing all inner blockages. But the Holy Spirit can only transform you to the degree that you give your permission. If you do not give permission to the Holy Spirit to untie the lower knots of your physical and emotional faculties, then the transformation of all of your lower faculties will not occur in a holistic way that would prepare you for entering into contemplation.

The danger of the Western approach of practicing Centering Prayer (equivalent to Inner Silence Meditation) *exclusively* is that this method of surrender to the Holy Spirit may be too much of a mental approach that only indirectly allows for the transformation of your physical and emotional faculties. Because Centering Prayer does not incorporate bringing your attention directly to important focusing areas in your body, it does not fully prepare you to surrender all of your physical and emotional faculties to the Holy Spirit. The practice of Centering Prayer by itself will to some degree positively influence your physical and emotional faculties. However, meditation methods that focus on areas in the body will have a greater impact on helping you surrender the physical and emotional levels of your being.

Just as there is a danger with the Western approach, there is a danger with the Eastern approach, especially when meditation is not practiced in moderation. The Eastern method of consciously focusing on the centers of awareness in the body from the lowest to the highest has the danger of the seeker allowing his ego to be too much in control. Placing your ego in control of your spiritual growth is like letting the fox guard the chicken coop. There are ways of forcing the creative energy upward that can be caused by self-will and doing so does not produce the natural purification and integration that is a preparation for contemplation. In fact, some extreme Eastern practices can at times be harmful for your physical, emotional, and mental well-being.

However, this manual emphasizes that both the Eastern approach and the Western approach to contemplation are more effective when combined and indeed they probably occur together for anyone who is successful at entering the contemplative state of awareness. The Eastern meditator who is successful at raising his creative energy is most certainly assisted by the Spirit within in his process, even if he is not consciously aware of this assistance. Likewise, the successful Western seeker who regularly experiences contemplation through consciously and consistently surrendering to the transforming action of the Holy Spirit will probably not be consciously aware of what is happening at an energy level within his body. Through his surrender he allows the Holy Spirit to bring about the same raising of the creative energy and the same purifying effect that occurs for the Eastern meditator, but perhaps without the conscious awareness of these energy changes.

The advantage of Christian Yoga Meditation is that this approach combines the best of what the East and the West have to offer. The result is a *synergy*, meaning that the combined effect is greater than the sum of the parts. Just meditating to consciously raise the creative energy or just surrendering to the Holy Spirit are not nearly as effective when practiced alone as they are when practiced together. By combining six techniques, Christian Yoga Meditation produces a holistic effect that joins all the levels of your being and is your best preparation for entering contemplation.

The experience of contemplation itself may be considered as a state of spiritual unification brought about by the overshadowing of the Holy Spirit. Before being ready to enter this spiritual unification, you will need to make a certain degree of progress toward unifying yourself at all the levels below the spiritual level. Your request of the Holy Spirit to transform you by bringing you into the contemplative state of unification cannot be merely a mental request. Making a mental decision of the intellect alone, no matter how firm or sincere, can only carry the weight of the mental level of your being. To increase the effectiveness of your invitation to the Holy Spirit, your request will require a certain degree of experiential wholeheartedness. Since a house divided cannot stand, all the levels of your being need to be speaking with one voice, requesting the incoming of the Holy Spirit. There needs to be a certain degree of integration between the physical, emotional, and mental levels of your being in order to make a wholehearted invitation for the Holy Spirit to open you to higher consciousness.

Christian Yoga Meditation is recommended as a way to invite the Holy Spirit into the physical, emotional, mental, integrating, intuitive and unifying levels of your being. When the first five techniques of this sequence of methods are combined, a creative energy rises within the body, bringing about a purifying effect, an integration and a sense of oneness. The integration and unification of the various levels of your being serves as a solid foundation necessary for entering into the higher consciousness of contemplation. Such a foundation of stability will be necessary before proceeding into the uncertainty of the unknown, relying only on pure faith during the experience of contemplation.

Having acquired this solid foundation then prepares you to be open to revealing your true spiritual nature. The sixth method, Inner Silence Meditation, can be practiced without this foundation, but is much more effective with this foundation. For that reason the combination of six techniques in Christian Yoga Meditation is recommended as a method that would benefit anyone seeking to enter into contemplation.

The process of learning to go into inner silence during Inner Silence Meditation may not be easy to learn. Therefore, it is recommended that you only set aside a few minutes at the end of Christian Yoga Meditation in order to gradually expose yourself to experiencing the inner silence for brief periods of time. After being successful at this, you may choose to increase the amount of time for inner silence. Eventually most of your Christian Yoga Meditation practice may consist of this inner silence in which contemplation takes place.

This experience of dwelling in inner silence during contemplation opens your subconscious mind, which allows unresolved thoughts and feeling that were previously hidden to be revealed so you can release them. You will also have to deal with the ordinary ego-based thoughts and feelings that accumulate every day. The long-standing thoughts and feelings that surface from the past as well as the daily parade of thoughts need to be processed in contemplation in the same way: You need to let them pass by in your mind through practicing nonattachment— having no desire to keep these thoughts and having no desire to ward off these thoughts.

Likewise, you may experience various unusual experiences during your opening to contemplation, in which you are overshadowed by the Holy Spirit. These unusual experiences may be sensations, emotions, or other by-products of meditation and contemplation, which are described in Chapters 12, 13, and 18. These experiences are to be released just as any other stray thoughts are released. You should neither invite unusual experiences by attraction nor push them away by aversion. The idea is to let go of these experiences just like you let go of any thoughts that float by in the mind without paying any particular attention to them.

In the practice of Christian Yoga Meditation, an arbitrary decision cannot be made on how long each of the six techniques should be employed. The timing of when to switch from one technique to the next technique is an individual matter to be decided intuitively. As your experience with Christian Yoga Meditation increases, you may find that one particular technique is especially helpful and effective, so you can increase the amount of time for that technique and reduce the time for the other techniques. If Christian Yoga Meditation becomes your regular form of meditation, over time hopefully you will feel comfortable increasing the time for Inner Silence Meditation, which will lead you into contemplation.

However, Inner Silence Meditation is not the only technique during which contemplation can occur. In fact, contemplation may happen spontaneously during any meditation practice if there is an openness for this to happen. The spontaneous occurrence of contemplation that sometimes occurs during the practice of body awareness techniques is described in Chapters 8 and 14.

---

1. Psalm 46:10

2. Thomas Keating, *Open Heart, Open Mind: The Contemplative Dimension of the Gospel* (New York, New York: The Continuum International Publishing Group, 2001), Copyright 1986, 1992 by St. Benedict's Monastery, reprinted by permission of The Continuum International Publishing Group, p. 11

7

THE TWENTY-EIGHT DAY DEMONSTRATION

≈ • ≈

A. The First Three Days

The Twenty-eight Day Demonstration is recommended as a means of demonstrating your intention to increase your awareness of the divine presence within. The previous two chapters provided descriptions of six meditation techniques and how to combine these in the practice of Christian Yoga Meditation. The following sections in this chapter provide an outline of how to proceed in a systematic way that will allow you to experience these meditation techniques.

For the first three days of the Twenty-eight Day Demonstration, you practice only Centering Meditation. For this meditation method, you hold the awareness at the area just below the navel. You repeat the first half of your chosen affirmation on the inhalation and repeat the second half on the exhalation. You allow the breathing to be normal and relaxed. When the mind becomes calm, you can let go of focusing on your affirmation and breathing and just focus on the navel area. If the mind wanders because of stray thoughts, you can gently return to focusing on your affirmation in coordination with your breathing while also holding your focus on the navel area.

B. The Fourth, Fifth, and Sixth Days

For the fourth, fifth, and sixth days, you employ only Heart Meditation, in which the awareness is focused in the heart or in the center of the chest. You coordinate the affirmation with the breathing as previously described. You can let go of focusing on the affirmation and breathing if the mind becomes calm and only focus on the heart or center of the chest. If you become distracted by stray thoughts, you can return to your affirmation and breathing along with your focus in the heart or the center of the chest.

C. The Seventh, Eighth, and Ninth Days

For the seventh, eighth, and ninth days, you practice only Brow Meditation, in which the focus of awareness is in the brow area and the affirmation and breathing are coordinated in the same way as the previous methods. When your mind becomes calm, you let go of focusing on the affirmation and breathing and only focus on the brow area. If your mind becomes attracted by stray thoughts, you can return to focusing on your affirmation and breathing while continuing to focus on the brow area.

D. The Tenth, Eleventh, and Twelfth Days

For the tenth, eleventh, and twelfth days, you use Crown Meditation followed by Oneness Meditation. For Crown Meditation you focus on the crown of the head while coordinating your affirmation with your breathing. As with the other methods, you can let go of focusing on your affirmation and breathing when your mind becomes calm and then return to focusing on your affirmation and breathing if your mind wanders. You focus on the crown area during your entire meditation.

You allow most of your meditation to consist of Crown Meditation, but you save a short time at the end of your practice to use Oneness Meditation, in which you focus on the whole body or as much of the body as you can retain in your awareness at one time. You can also focus on your affirmation and breathing. However, you can let go of focusing on your affirmation and breathing when your mind becomes calm and return again to these focusing objects if your mind becomes distracted. If you find that Oneness Meditation is too difficult because you cannot focus on the whole body or much of the body, you may choose to omit this practice and only use Crown Meditation.

E. The Thirteenth, Fourteenth, and Fifteenth Days

For the thirteenth, fourteenth, and fifteenth days, you practice first Oneness Meditation and then Inner Silence Meditation. You practice Oneness Meditation just as it is described above, but if you find this method too difficult, you may omit this technique and only practice Inner Silence Meditation. If you decide to use Oneness Meditation, you practice this method only for a short time at the beginning of your practice before moving on to using Inner Silence Meditation.

When you decide to make your transition from Oneness Meditation to Inner Silence Meditation, there is a slight change in the way you conclude Oneness Meditation. For this change you first focus on the whole body or as much of the body as possible. You focus on your affirmation in coordination with your breathing. Then you allow the mind to become calm and let go of the affirmation and breathing and focus only on the whole body or on most of the body. Finally for the transition itself, you conclude your practice of Oneness Meditation by letting go of all body awareness and yet allow yourself to retain the feeling of oneness that you had when you were focusing on the whole body. Although your feeling of oneness seemed to rely on your being aware of the oneness of the whole body, you will find that eventually you will be able to retain this feeling of oneness without relating it to the oneness of the whole body. Whether you can retain this feeling of oneness without body awareness or not, you simply move on to practicing Inner Silence Meditation.

For your practice of Inner Silence Meditation, you let go of all body awareness. You can repeat your affirmation and use it to calm your mind. Once your mind is calm, you can let go of the affirmation and enter inner silence. Without having a focusing object for meditation, you allow your pure faith to carry you into inner silence. Your mind may enter a state of inner absorption in which stray thoughts pass by without distracting you. When this happens you have entered contemplation in which the Holy Spirit overshadows you to produce this state of inner absorption. If your mind wanders again because of stray thoughts, you can return to your meditative practice of repeating your affirmation without focusing on body awareness.

F. The Sixteenth Day and Thereafter

The first fifteen days are designed to familiarize you with the six basic techniques that have been described. For the remainder of the Twenty-eight Day Demonstration you practice Christian Yoga Meditation, which is the combination of all six of these methods. You incorporate body awareness while using the first five techniques in the following sequence: Centering Meditation, Heart Meditation, Brow Meditation, Crown Meditation, and Oneness Meditation. Then for your sixth and final method, you let go of body awareness to practice Inner Silence Meditation. All six techniques of Christian Yoga Meditation involve the use of an affirmation. While practicing Christian Yoga Meditation, you decide intuitively when to make the switch from one method to the next.

In your practice you may omit using Oneness Meditation if you find you cannot focus your awareness on the whole body or much of the body all at once. Another technique that may be difficult for you initially is Inner Silence Meditation, which is more advanced than methods that use body awareness. It may take time to learn how to practice letting go of the affirmation and entering into inner silence. Initially when you practice Christian Yoga Meditation, you may want to limit the amount of time you use Inner Silence Meditation. As you feel more comfortable using Inner Silence Meditation, you may increase the time for its usage and reduce the time for using the five techniques that use body awareness.

The detailed structure provided previously for the Twenty-eight Day Demonstration is designed only as a guideline. Please feel that you have the freedom to make any adjustments that will meet your individual needs. Whether you are a beginner or an experienced meditator, you need to be sensitive to the inner prompting of the Holy Spirit in how you apply what is presented here. For example, in the procedures for meditation outlined in Chapter 3, there are many optional choices to be considered, so you need to decide inwardly what feels right for you based on your guidance. Even the procedures and structures in this book that are not specifically identified as "optional" are in fact optional in the sense that you will need to exercise your free will option to use or not use any procedure or structure based on you being guided primarily by the Holy Spirit.

If you discover that a certain method or aspect of meditation is quite difficult for you, that difficulty may be a blessing in disguise. Since you are venturing into His World, where the self is losing control, the self may try to convince you to avoid areas of growth that would be difficult but very beneficial. During the Twenty-eight Day Demonstration, you will need to discern when you have a true spiritual prompting, which needs to be followed, even if it is perhaps a deviation from the precise structure provided here. You will also need to discern when the self is seeking to express some resistance to change or fear, or a desire to avoid aspects of the demonstration that are difficult challenges, but are areas where you really need to grow.

G. The Beginner's Challenge

If you are a beginner, the primary challenge you will have is developing the ability to focus the mind, which will at first be like a wild horse that has not been tamed. Every time the mind wanders, and it will countless times, you will need to gently bring it back to your chosen affirmation. You can let your wandering mind be just a reminder to return to the work before you. If you refocus your mind every time you notice it has wandered, then your meditation will deepen. But sometimes you may notice that the mind has wandered and instead of refocusing immediately, you will judge yourself for having allowed your mind to wander. The wandering mind itself is a problem for every meditator, yet it becomes a much greater problem if you focus on it as a problem rather than refocusing on the affirmation.

You are accustomed to solving problems by evaluating them, but in this case *the evaluating itself is the problem*. Of course, very little meditation can be occurring if you let yourself evaluate how well you are meditating by judging yourself in the process. Regardless of whether you are evaluating yourself positively or negatively, self-evaluating thoughts are the self's way of remaining in control. Self-evaluating thoughts that attempt to judge your meditation experience, just like any other distracting thoughts, need to simply be a reminder to return to your affirmation. It takes an effort of the will to control the mind, but it needs to be an unstrained effort that relies on the affirmation and God's grace.

During your meditation practice, thoughts cannot be considered as good or bad for that gives them power to affect you. If you think some thoughts are good, such as special insights, even spiritual insights, then you will encourage and entertain them in your mind and leave your purpose of seeking God alone. If you think some thoughts are bad, such as memories of past mistakes, you will judge yourself for having such thoughts and leave your purpose of seeking God. You need to be neutral toward your thoughts so you do not encourage them by attraction and you do not attempt to push them away by aversion. Both attraction and aversion create inner tension that prevents the mind from becoming calm.

Every mind is filled with thoughts. Normally these thoughts follow a progression so that one thought leads to another. The goal of the beginner cannot be to stop this sequence of thoughts from occurring. As thoughts float by in your mind one after another in sequence, the passing thoughts themselves do not have the power to interfere with your meditation practice. It is possible for you to be in deep meditation or contemplation and be undisturbed by this parade of thoughts.

To explain how thoughts can be passing through your mind without disturbing your practice, think of professional athletes who say that they are in a "zone" when they are at top of their game. When in this zone, they can tune everything out, except their role in the game. For example, a good hitter in professional baseball will stand at home plate with his bat cocked as he waits for the baseball to come his way. Thousands of screaming fans may be in the stands, yet because he is not paying attention to these fans their sounds recede from his awareness. These sounds register in his consciousness as background noise, but do not entirely disappear from his awareness. The hitter does not pay attention to this background noise because his mind is locked in only to the flight of the ball as it heads toward home plate. Just as the good hitter can place his whole attention on the ball and allow the sounds of the fans to recede in his mind, you can learn to place your whole attention in faith on your divine intention. As you focus on your divine intention only, you can allow the passing thoughts to recede from your conscious awareness by not paying attention to them.

Becoming a good hitter takes time, patience, and practice. Similarly, learning to have a single-minded focus in meditation takes time, patience, and practice. Therefore, if you are a beginner in meditation, you will not be able to completely tune out the passing thoughts of the mind. You will find yourself noticing a particular thought, and instead of letting it pass by, you will have *a thought about that thought*, which means you have become distracted. Then you may even judge yourself for being distracted, which causes more distraction. When you become aware of your distracting thoughts, you will need to learn to have a single response. Your single response to distracting thoughts will need to be to remind yourself to gently return to your affirmation.

If you are a beginner, you will need to accept dealing with distraction as an ongoing and necessary part of your learning experience. In fact, your whole meditation will invariably be a process of repeating your affirmation followed by distracting thoughts. It would be unrealistic for you as a beginner to expect any more than this repeated thought pattern of your affirmation followed by distracting thoughts. When you make progress at practicing Inner Silence Meditation, your repeated pattern will hopefully have three distinct parts in the following sequence: Part one would be your affirmation. Part two would be inner silence. Part three would be distracting thoughts. Your distracting thoughts would simply remind you to return to the affirmation to start the whole pattern over again.

Consequently, even as you make progress you will still find yourself in the process of refocusing the mind. Much of the benefit of this refocusing is not in what you are refocusing to, which is your affirmation, but in the act of patiently refocusing itself. If this refocusing is done properly with a light touch, it is a continuous exercise in nonattachment. You are learning to let go. Ultimately your desire for God is a desire to let go of the false self. Your refocusing is a process of letting go of the false self by letting go of your thoughts one at a time. The cumulative effect is that you are no longer held fast in the grip of the false self, which itself is simply a collection of false thoughts about who you are. While you cannot let go of all thoughts, you can let go of your attachment to them. As you develop detachment from your inner thoughts, you may discover this detachment carrying over into your daily life so you develop *equanimity* in which you are not disturbed by the highs and lows of everyday life.

Even though dealing with the wandering mind is the major challenge for the beginner, you need to remember that your meditation is not a demonstration of how well you can control the mind. It is a demonstration of your intention and commitment to seek God. Even if you can make only limited progress in controlling the mind, you have still set your heart's desire on God, and in doing so have reached beyond your world and into His World. It is the self that wants magnificent results. As you apply your will to focus the mind, you can safely place your trust in God and leave the results to Him.

If you choose to make a firm commitment to daily meditation for twenty-eight days, then your commitment needs to be based on pure faith without expectations. Your pure faith tells you He will respond to your desire to deepen your relationship with Him. Indeed, your pure faith during meditation aids you in being open to receiving His response of love. But your expectancy for His response can only remain pure if you have no expectations for Him to respond in any specific way you have chosen. The effects of meditation are often subtle and not immediately noticeable to the beginner. Thus you need to trust that He is responding to you, even when there is no apparent outward manifestation of His response.

H. Commitment

The Twenty-eight Day Demonstration is your opportunity to make a commitment to deepening your relationship with God and to put your commitment into practical application through the practice of daily meditation. For this commitment you will need to set aside a minimum of one twenty-five minute period each day. But it would be preferable to set aside two such periods, perhaps one in the morning before breakfast and another one at some time before dinner. Another option is to meditate before bedtime, if tiredness is not a problem for you in the evening.

Your world may be very busy and finding time, or rather making time, to enter into His World may seem difficult, but it is necessary if you truly want to deepen your relationship with God. You may think of it in terms of the way a relationship develops between a man and a woman. If you feel the relationship is important, you adjust your world to accommodate the needed time. At first, you only need a little time to get to know one another. Then you expand this time if you really want to know each other at a deeper, more intimate level.

As you deepen your human relationship with another person, you notice your world overlaps into the other person's world and the other person's world overlaps into your world. Your relationship with God is different, but also has some overlapping. When you enter His World, you must leave your world, because your world cannot overlap His World. As you go deeper into His World in meditation and then return to your world, you discover a curious thing—that His World completely overlaps and interpenetrates your world. Also, you realize that He, the silent One, has been quietly in your world all along, yet you had been blind to His presence. Thus, you learn to see two realities—the everyday reality you live in, which is a "physical, emotional, and mental world" and His Reality, which is a "spiritual world" that is the source and substance of your world.

This is more than merely a new intellectual viewpoint, because it has a practical application to your life. After entering His World, you come back to your world with a new awareness that allows you to bring forth His hidden presence into your world. The result is that you allow Him to be the master of your life in your world. There are many benefits to practicing meditation, both those that may come to your conscious awareness and those that you may not consciously realize. But the most significant result of your inner practice is the effect that it produces in your everyday life. Deepening your contact with the divine within allows His loving presence to flow through you into your everyday world and relationships expressed through a life of service.

I. Application

A wise old gentleman who had meditated for many years told me that there are three rules for meditation, which are as follows:

> The first rule is "sit."
> The second rule is "sit."
> The third rule is "sit."

There is a vast difference between *intellectual understanding* and *wisdom*. If you acquire intellectual understanding, but do not apply that understanding to your daily life, then your understanding is useless intellectual theory. On the other hand, if you put the understanding you receive into practical application in your life, then the result is wisdom. This is true especially about the understanding of meditation, since meditation itself is not a theory—it is a practical experience.

The purpose of this book is to supply you with understanding, yet it is up to you to decide if you want to apply that understanding and transform it into wisdom. The most important kind of wisdom worth having is the awareness of God's presence felt inwardly and expressed outwardly. The Twenty-eight Day Demonstration will enable you to put the understanding you have received into practical application.

Some of what has already been expressed here has only been explained partially and will be elaborated upon later. Consequently, in order to expand your understanding of meditation, it would be helpful for you to read this entire manual. However, right now you already have acquired in these first seven chapters all of the understanding that you need to begin the Twenty-eight Day Demonstration. In particular, if you are a beginner in meditation, this will be your opportunity to conduct this demonstration of your desire and commitment to open yourself to God's presence within. Likewise, if you already have experience with meditation, the practical experience gained through using the techniques in this demonstration will serve as a solid foundation for growing toward contemplation.

If you are considering whether or not to make a commitment to conducting the Twenty-eight Day Demonstration, you are encouraged to turn to God in prayer and ask Him if conducting this demonstration would be helpful for you. If you do decide to conduct the Twenty-eight Day Demonstration, this demonstration of your commitment to spiritual growth will help you to become more aware of God's presence in whatever way He might choose to increase your awareness.

J. Preparations for the Twenty-eight Day Demonstration

1. COMMITMENT— Before beginning, you will need to decide if you are willing to make a commitment to meditate every day for twenty-eight days.

2. TIMING — You will need to decide the exact time when you want to meditate for a minimum commitment of one twenty-five minute period at the same time each day. If you decide to make a deeper commitment, you can choose two twenty-five minute periods each day—for example, one in the morning before breakfast and one sometime before dinner.

3. PLACE — It is important to choose a quiet place to sit and to use the same place each day.

4. POSTURE — You may decide to sit in a chair. You may prefer to sit on a folded blanket or a pillow in a cross-legged position on the floor. You can choose whatever sitting posture and whatever hand position is most comfortable for you. Before beginning to meditate, you will need to check your posture to make sure that your spine is in proper alignment.

5. SETTING THE IDEAL AND THE MENTAL ATTITUDE — You will need to choose your spiritual ideal, and then choose a mental attitude that will help you grow toward your ideal. You may want to write both of these down on paper for the sake of clarity. You will need to select an affirmation, which may be a word or a brief combination of words, such as a form of the Divine Name, that will represent your spiritual ideal or remind you of your ideal.

6. SCHEDULE — Before following this schedule, make sure you have reviewed and clearly understood the detailed directions given for how to practice these techniques that are described in the previous two chapters.

a. The First Three Days —
- Centering Meditation

b. The Fourth, Fifth, and Sixth Days —
- Heart Meditation

c. The Seventh, Eighth, and Ninth Days —
- Brow Meditation

d. The Tenth, Eleventh, and Twelfth Days —
- Crown Meditation,
- Oneness Meditation (optional)

e. The Thirteenth, Fourteenth, and Fifteenth Days —
- Oneness Meditation (optional),
- Inner Silence Meditation

f. The Sixteenth Day and Thereafter — Christian Yoga Meditation, consisting of the following six techniques:

- Centering Meditation,
- Heart Meditation,
- Brow Meditation,
- Crown Meditation,
- Oneness Meditation (optional), and
- Inner Silence Meditation.

7. STARTING DATE — You will need to decide when you are going to begin the first day of the Twenty-eight Day Demonstration.

K. Daily Procedures for Each Meditation Period

1. CLEANSING (optional) — You will need to approach meditation with the understanding that this is a purification process in which the self is being emptied so there may be greater receptivity to the Spirit. Although it is not necessary, some meditators choose to perform an outward form of cleansing, such as drinking a small amount of water or taking a shower, as a symbol of this cleansing process.

2. RELAXATION (optional) — Prior to starting your meditation, you may want to employ a relaxation method of your choosing. Some examples are relaxing the body with mental suggestions, doing head and neck exercises, practicing yoga postures, or using yoga breathing practices.

3. DEDICATION (optional) — You may want to dedicate your meditation by inwardly stating your spiritual ideal and the mental attitude that will help you grow toward your ideal.

4. PREPARATORY PRAYER (optional) — You may offer a spontaneous or formal prayer to help turn the mind and heart in the direction of becoming quiet and to invite the incoming of the Holy Spirit. If desired, you can imagine the body to be surrounded and filled with white light.

5. MEDITATION — For the Twenty-eight Day Demonstration, you will use the method or methods of meditation appropriate for the day on which you are meditating. In general, for all meditation techniques, you will close the eyes and mentally repeat the affirmation of your choice. You will want to be sure that the breathing is normal and relaxed. You allow thoughts to pass by in the mind without paying any attention to them. You can let go of your affirmation when your mind becomes calm. If your mind becomes distracted by stray thoughts, you allow the distraction to be a gentle reminder to return to repeating your affirmation.

6. COMPLETION OF MEDITATION (optional) — After your meditation ends, you may want to restate your spiritual ideal and mental purpose and/or offer any spontaneous prayers for yourself or others. To complete your meditation, you may want to use a bowing forward gesture. It is best to remain seated for a minute or so, and then get up slowly and gently without disturbing your peace.

7. WITHHOLD JUDGMENT — It is very important to set aside any judgments about the depth of your meditation experience and also to release any expectations of specific results you want to see happen. You need to be willing to patiently wait the full twenty-eight days before evaluating your meditation practice and trust that, whatever happens, God is guiding you and will meet your deepest, truest needs in the way that is most appropriate for you.

PART TWO

~ • ~

GUIDELINES FOR DEEPENING MEDITATION

8

AFTER THE
TWENTY-EIGHT DAY
DEMONSTRATION

≈ ○ ≈

A. Evaluating with Faith

Twenty-eight Day Demonstration is a way to express your intention to become increasingly aware of God as a living reality within your being. However, once you have completed the demonstration, how can you be sure that you have contacted God's presence within you? There are many rational arguments to prove the existence of God's presence within you. Nevertheless, none of these intellectual proofs will convince you fully, since the mind can only have concepts about God. The rational mind cannot experience God.

I ask you to evaluate your twenty-eight days of meditation by faith. Even your rational mind will have to acknowledge that something was happening in meditation beyond the thinking mind's ability to grasp. Although you may be like most people who have difficulty controlling the wandering thoughts of the mind, your meditation experience will tell you there is still something occurring deep within that can only be experienced by faith. Your faith encourages you to start meditating, helps you to recognize the value of meditation, and inspires you to continue meditating on a daily basis.

What is faith? Faith is an inner knowing without intellectual proof of the rational mind. When you have an inner feeling and an inner knowing about something that proves to be true, you call this an "intuition." How then is intuition different than faith? They are not different except to say that faith is the highest form of intuition. Intuitions can be described as inner feelings. But faith is too exalted of an intuition to be called an inner feeling. A certain kind of intuition may tell you spontaneously to visit a friend one day, and you may discover that your friend very much needed your help at that particular time. Faith differs from this sort of inner knowing in that it is directed toward the source itself of all intuition. In other words, when your intuition is focused on God Himself, you can call that faith. The very fact of turning toward God is faith. Why would you turn to God unless somewhere inside of yourself you know that He is there? Faith is simply this inner knowing that says, "He is there." Your inner knowing of the divine presence may be called your *faithful awareness*. This awareness is elaborated upon in the section below that describes Inner Silence Meditation.

However, faith is not a matter of just saying, "I believe God is in me." Mental belief is only the result of faith. Faith is a matter of inner trusting. If you have ever trusted another person, you know that this is a matter of the heart and not the head. Yet what if you feel that you have only a little faith? Perhaps your faith is only a mental belief, which may contain some doubts about God's presence. You do not need to be discouraged or allow this to be a stumbling block for your meditation. The only way to increase your faith is to express what little faith you do have, along with your doubts, and know that God accepts you right where you are in this moment. You can follow the example of the man who was asked by Jesus about his faith, and he responded, "I believe; help my unbelief!"[1]

Faith is trusting in what is not seen, and if it is not seen, it is in doubt. In most cases for faith to be present so must doubt also be present. Therefore, usually there cannot be faith without doubt by which faith is tested. It is true that some individuals overcome their doubts and are blessed by God with a faith that is an inner knowing without doubt. But for most individuals the development of faith is a very gradual learning experience that includes doubts. Consequently, God does not require you to have a faith without doubts. He only asks you to express whatever faith you have already been given as a foundation to build upon in order to increase your faith.

Practicing meditation is a practical way of expressing your faithful awareness that God is present within you. An important characteristic of your faith that enables you to reach into His World during meditation is that it requires no experience on your part to confirm His presence. Not seeking an experience, but rather allowing God Himself to remain the object of your faith is expressed by waiting for Him in meditation and emptying yourself of any expectations of how He might respond to produce an experience in you. But there is hardly a beginning meditator who does not carry within himself a hidden fantasy of being filled with some great light and raised up to God's presence in a wave of bliss.

However, in the everyday practice of meditation, you may experience nothing happening, boredom, passing disharmonious feelings, scattered thoughts throughout, and a whole range of ordinary responses. Precisely because you seek God's presence in faith, knowing that He is there, these impressions and responses test your faith. You have to accept the fact that you still have the mask of self to deal with and its diversions that would carry you away from expressing your faith. Yet it is your faith that tells you by inner knowing that, in spite of appearances, you are reaching beyond your momentary responses and diversions in meditation to the place where you are truly one with God.

It is true that some meditators do at times feel the divine presence as a conscious experience of heightened awareness, but not the awareness of intellectual thinking. This conscious experience may come to your awareness as inner feelings, which are described in detail in Chapter 14, along with a description of ways of opening to these inner feelings. Nevertheless, whether you have a conscious experience or not, your meditation practice fosters within you an inner receptivity to the divine presence. Your meditation itself is not merely a technique of affirmation. More importantly, it is also an *invitation* for God to fully permeate your subconscious mind and allow His Will of love to be done in you and through you. Even though your meditation practice may seem to be scattered to your conscious awareness, your faith confirms that your loving Father cannot refuse to accept your invitation. At first you may have only a provisional faith, which is merely an openness to God's presence. However, through the repeated practice of meditation your faith will gradually grow as you learn to trust in His unseen presence.

Your faith may not be great, but if it is pure, it is pleasing to God. I know a woman who is a good example of faithfully seeking God with a pure intention. While meditating, she can hardly go for a few minutes without her mind wandering. Therefore, she always feels she is miles away from God. I asked how long she had been meditating, and she said she had been practicing daily meditation for over five years. Many people get discouraged when they cannot control the mind and, lacking perseverance, they stop meditating. I asked her why she has steadfastly continued when she feels so blocked in her meditation experience. She had a very simple response: "Because it's the only thing that matters!" Then she paused and added, "If I have God, I have everything."

When I told her what a wonderful example of faith she presented by persevering all these years, she responded that she didn't feel she had a deep faith. She said she lacked that inner sense of feeling God's presence, and what little faith she had was based mostly on a mental belief in God. Nonetheless, it seems to me that the depth of your faith is proven by your willingness to act on whatever amount of faith God has given to you. What greater faith or love can you express than waiting for your Beloved year after year as this woman has done? Your faith tells you He is there and that He will come, and your love is your desire for Him to come.

It is your faith that says, "Yes, You are in me and I am in You," when everything in your world says, "No." Through your faith you are able to give up expectations of what you can get out of your meditation so you can have purity of heart and seek Him alone beyond appearances.

Faith is the best way to evaluate your meditation experience, but there is another significant means of evaluating your practice. You can look at the effects that your practice produces in your daily life. You may find that you are more peaceful and your thinking is clearer. But the most important outer sign of progress is an increased ability to cooperate with others and extend love to others. A dramatic change in your expression of love may not be noticeable after the Twenty-eight Day Demonstration. Nonetheless, learning to be more loving will be the long-term effect of ongoing daily meditation practice. By focusing on improving your relationship with God in meditation, you will naturally find that your personal relationships with others will also improve. Meditation itself may appear to be a solitary experience between yourself and God alone, yet it is actually a way of joining with others, who have the same center in God as you do. Thus learning to love God automatically means learning to love your brothers and sisters in whom God is equally present. Your relationships therefore become your means of determining how much progress you are making in regard to your seeking of God.

B. Continuing Meditation

When the Twenty-eight Day Demonstration is completed, your faith will guide you in being able to judge for yourself if you want to continue to practice meditation. If you decide to continue to meditate, you will become either an intermittent meditator or a daily meditator. Those who meditate intermittently usually find it difficult to increase the depth of their meditation experience. In fact, they are often not able to maintain the stillness of mind that they achieved through daily meditation during the demonstration. An intermittent meditator is like a person who is trying to drill a well by continually moving around and drilling many holes, without ever drilling deep enough to find water. But if that person would spend the time necessary to stay in one place and drill deep enough, he would succeed.

Likewise, if you want to go deep within to reach the "living water" of your spiritual depths, it is necessary to make a commitment to meditation as a daily experience. It's like brushing your teeth. You don't debate with yourself every day over whether you should or should not brush your teeth. You just do it. It's a habit. It's part of your daily routine since you feel it's necessary, and you have made a commitment to yourself to do it.

A world-famous musician was asked if he still had to practice on a daily basis after becoming so accomplished in his art. The musician answered that when he missed even one day of practice, he noticed the difference. When he missed two days, the critics noticed the difference. When he missed three days, the audience noticed the difference.

To be really effective, growth in meditation must be a continuous process, because the effects of meditation are cumulative and produce a gradual deepening of meditation. A meditation practice of twenty-five minutes twice a day is recommended. Yet if twice a day is too much of a commitment, then one twenty-five minute meditation period per day is the minimum commitment needed to make continuous progress in deepening your meditation. Another option is to meditate twice a day on weekdays when there is more tension due to the stress of work, and meditate one time per day on the weekends. The best time to start your commitment to daily meditation is immediately after the end of the Twenty-eight Day Demonstration. This is because you already are experiencing the benefits, and you have the habit and conditioning going for you, so it's easy to just keep right on going.

After making this commitment, then you have to decide what you would like to use as your own regular form of meditation. If you want to use one consistent practice as your continuous approach to meditation, Christian Yoga Meditation is highly recommended. This combination of five body awareness techniques followed by Inner Silence Meditation has been described already, but a more detailed explanation of these techniques is provided below in case you would like to continue with Christian Yoga Meditation as your ongoing practice.

For Christian seekers the goal of all meditation techniques is to go beyond techniques in order to enter into contemplation in which you are overshadowed by the Holy Spirit. With this in mind, you need to consider what techniques will prepare you for contemplation. Since Inner Silence Meditation is the most effective means of leading you to contemplation, it is best to grow in the direction of using this technique increasingly over time. But other methods can be used to prepare you to make Inner Silence Meditation more effective. Christian Yoga Meditation is recommended as your ongoing meditation practice because the five body awareness techniques combined with Inner Silence Meditation in this method lead you to proceed one step at a time up the ladder of your awareness toward contemplation. This internal ladder of awareness is symbolized by the image of Jacob's ladder that stretches from earth to Heaven. Over time you will find yourself reducing the time for the first five methods and expanding the time for Inner Silence Meditation, which will lead you into contemplation.

However, instead of practicing Christian Yoga Meditation as an ongoing practice, you can climb the ladder of your awareness in a slightly different way. Rather than using all of these techniques together in one practice, you can use these same techniques separately for a month at a time in order to go to a deeper level with each individual method. After first going to a deeper level with individual techniques by using them exclusively for a month at a time, you can then combine them in the practice of Christian Yoga Meditation and find that your overall meditation deepens.

When using individual techniques exclusively for one month at a time and then combining them, it is important to follow a particular sequence that would best help you climb the ladder of your awareness, leading to contemplation. This particular sequence is outlined in the One Year Program, described in the next chapter for your consideration as a way of deepening your meditation experience. Toward the end of the One Year Program, you will be practicing Christian Yoga Meditation at a deeper level because of first having gone to a deeper level using each of the individual techniques separately.

After completing your Twenty-eight Day Demonstration, you may want to continue with Christian Yoga Meditation as your daily practice, or you may want to follow the One Year Program. Either direction is recommended. However, if you want to consider other possibilities, you might want to experiment for a while with different methods. There are additional methods described later in this manual for your consideration. For example, Chapter 14 explains how to practice Expanded Christian Yoga Meditation, which helps you to open to the inner feelings of light and love. Once you have found what technique feels right for you, then stay with your choice for as long as you feel guided to do so.

There are many possible ways in which you may be prompted to practice meditation. Once you have firmly established your spiritual ideal, preferably in Christ, and your mental attitude, such as doing God's Will, then the application of your ideal will become apparent. The Spirit within you knows your individual needs and will show you what methods would be most helpful for you and how to use them and when to let go of them. Each technique that you use may be seen as a bridge that leads from one area of development to another. Because the bridge is used only for crossing, it is just a means to an end and must be left behind in order to make progress. You need to be careful not to allow techniques to become ends in themselves. The single most important thing to remember about techniques it that their main purpose is to help you to be receptive to a greater awareness of the Holy Spirit and the love that the Spirit would enkindle in you. In your future growth, allow your inner guidance to draw you in the direction that would be best for your development.

C. Body Awareness Methods for Receptivity

The first five methods of Christian Yoga Meditation are body awareness methods, which work together to create inner harmony and increase your receptivity to the Spirit. You are truly a spiritual being. Your true Self is the core of your being where you are one with God, Who is the source of your existence. The nature of your true Self is love, just as God Himself is love. But your true Self, which may be called your Christ Self, is clouded over by the doing self that is identified with the body and mind, though not with your spiritual source in God. Your spiritual growth is dependent on your willingness to give over the functions of the self to the Spirit so that the self may be a servant of God's Will of love. The self has three basic aspects that need to be surrendered to the Spirit. These are the physical aspect, the emotional aspect, and the mental aspect. The self has selfish desires for using each of these aspects. You need to train the self to release these selfish desires and become receptive to allowing the Spirit to control these functions so your desires originate from your true nature of love. Even though you may consciously want to surrender the physical, emotional, and mental desires of the self to the Spirit, you may have difficulty in letting go of the inner tension that selfish desires have created within you.

The Spirit always acts on you to create integration and wholeness by filling you with God's Love and helping you to be aware of your own love nature. However, inner blocks reduce your receptivity, which limits the amount of love you can accept into your conscious awareness. Your receptivity to the Spirit is blocked by inner tension originating from selfish desires. Meditation may be considered as a method of helping you to become inwardly relaxed so you can let go of physical, emotional, and mental tension, yet the process of relaxing to let go of tension is not as easy as it may sound. As a beginner, you may be aware of only the relaxing and calming effects of meditation in your initial experiences with meditation. Later in your development, you may deepen your meditation and become more sensitive to inner tension and the process of its removal.

In your everyday life when you make unloving choices, you create disharmony within yourself. What's the result? Tension is produced within the body, emotions, and thoughts. This is where the term "disease" comes from, because it is a combination of "dis" and "ease," meaning not being at ease. Long after you may have forgotten specific unloving choices, the resulting tension remains at an inner level of which you are normally not aware. Some of this tension comes from childhood experiences that remain in the subconscious mind. Meditation increases your awareness and allows you to become aware of the inner tension you have created. To correct the effect of past unloving responses that created this inner tension, meditation allows you to experience this tension with a loving awareness produced by your receptivity to the Spirit.

In practical terms this means that as your meditation experience deepens, it is not always peaceful. Rather, it is a dynamic process that allows tension to surface so it can be faced and then released. Tension may appear to the conscious mind at the physical level as unusual body sensations, at the emotional level as unexpected emotions, or at the mental level as uncommon thought impressions. These by-products of meditation are described more fully in Chapter 11. When such symptoms of tension reach your conscious awareness as meditation deepens, you learn to let go of this tension and continue with your meditation practice that allows the Spirit to penetrate, heal, and control the physical, emotional, and mental aspects of yourself.

Tension and selfish desires that cause tension are associated with various parts of the body. Physical desires that cause physical tension are primarily, though certainly not exclusively, related to the generative functions and to the lower part of the body. Emotional desires that cause emotional tension are generally related to feelings associated with personal relationships and to the heart area. Mental desires that cause mental tension are usually related to the rational thinking process and the head.

The first three techniques of Christian Yoga Meditation, which are Centering Meditation, Heart Meditation, and Brow Meditation, are designed to systematically focus on each of these parts of the body. The purpose is to focus on the lower part to develop *physical receptivity*, to focus on the heart area to develop *emotional receptivity*, and to focus on the head to develop *mental receptivity* to the Spirit.

In order to do this in a step-by-step fashion, these first three methods of Christian Yoga Meditation include three specific focusing areas, which are the navel area (actually just below the navel), the heart area (in the heart or in the center of the chest), and the brow area (the space between the eyebrows or forehead area). Meditating at each of these focusing areas helps to produce receptivity to the action of the Holy Spirit.

Meditating at the navel area helps in particular to release inner physical tension and allows physical receptivity to calm and to beneficially affect the physical body. Through this openness the physical functioning of the body is given over to the action of the Spirit and results in a strengthening of the body to make it a better vehicle for expressing God's Will.

Focusing at the heart area fosters emotional receptivity. This kind of receptivity removes emotional tension and promotes balanced emotional responses that express God's Will. Emotional receptivity encourages and intensifies the development of devotional qualities.

Meditating at the brow area in particular alleviates mental tension and induces mental receptivity that enables the mind to be guided by the divine influence. The result is that the mind can become a loving instrument of the Spirit.

Ideally meditating on these three focusing areas of the body would not be necessary if you could wholeheartedly say, "Here I am Lord. I am yours to do as You will," and fully mean it from the bottom of your being. However, even though you may want to surrender yourself completely to God now, you may find that you are not able to do so. To give something to someone, you must first possess it as your own, and then you can give what is yours to another. You may think you possess your physical, emotional, and mental responses, but often it is truer to say that these *possess you*. You are frequently driven by your desires at each of these levels. Even if you gain control of these desires consciously, they are not cut off at the root and therefore remain deeply imbedded in the subconscious mind and motivate much of your life. Your physical drives, emotional drives, and mental drives are often on automatic pilot, so even if you say you give these to God's Will, you will most likely not be able to bring these under your control to truly give them to God. As you make the attempt to give these over to God, you will be holding back much of yourself from Him.

Generally speaking, the aspect you will hold back most frequently will be your physical functioning if you may consider this either unimportant or unspiritual. In this case, you will simply avoid that part of yourself and imagine that you can transcend the body by ignoring it. When the physical vitality of the body is not handed over to the Spirit, then your devotion may lack strength and intensity, and your ability to focus the mind may be weakened. It is important to realize the body is a spiritual vehicle, and all its functions can be used to the honor and glory of God.

When you hold back the emotional aspect, you may know mentally all about spirituality, but never quite get the feel of it. After all, you are seeking here to deepen your relationship with God and in turn allow that inner relationship to affect all of your outer relationships. Relationships, whether inner or outer ones, are a matter of feeling in the heart and so the heart must be given over to the Holy Spirit.

If you hold back the mental aspect, you may be open hearted, yet scattered and unable to focus the mind. You won't have the mental clarity to discern how to manifest your inner feelings. If the Spirit is not allowed to guide the mind, then you cannot do God's Will effectively because the mental ability to understand and discern God's Will is lacking.

Initially in your meditation experience, if you do not focus on all three of these areas, it is quite likely you will develop one area of strength and avoid the other areas. Whatever you hold back from God will remain in control of the self and will prevent the self from being a servant of God's Will. Since the self is so much in control of your life already, it will not totally give over any of these functions without resistance. Allowing the Spirit to take control of your life at the physical, emotional, and mental levels is not a quick or easy process. It is a gradual letting go of the self, which is all the more reason for repeating the affirmation of your spiritual ideal at each focusing area to make a deep inner impression of your desire and willingness to be receptive to the Spirit.

It is important for you to allow the Holy Spirit to control the physical, emotional, and mental aspects of yourself. Allowing the Holy Spirit to control each of these different aspects involves being open to an integration and coordination of all these aspects producing inner harmony. Crown Meditation, as the fourth technique of Christian Yoga Meditation, helps to produce *integrating receptivity*, which is your openness and invitation that allows the Holy Spirit to produce this integration. Focusing on the crown area of the head brings you into contact with a universal consciousness that at first may seem odd to you in contrast to your usual ego-based individual consciousness. This universal consciousness brings with it a coordinating effect on your overall makeup.

Oneness Meditation, as the fifth method of Christian Yoga Meditation, helps to develop *intuitive receptivity*. Focusing on the whole body all at once or on most of the body can enable you to open up to the intuitive level of your being. You can become aware of the feeling of oneness first by focusing on the whole body. Then by letting go of body awareness at the end of this meditation, you can become aware of the intuitive feeling of oneness that is not limited to the body.

Christian Yoga Meditation allows you to decide how long to use each of these five individual methods while progressing from one focusing area of the body to another. Therefore, if you feel you need one technique more than the others, you can choose to employ that technique for more time while allowing less time for each of the other techniques. These five methods that use body awareness lead to the sixth method, Inner Silence Meditation, which does not use body awareness.

D. Inner Silence Meditation

For Inner Silence Meditation, you use an affirmation and let go of the affirmation when the mind becomes calm. With the other five methods of Christian Yoga Meditation, you retain your awareness on some form of body awareness, but for this method you let go of body awareness altogether. You enter inner silence by allowing the mind to switch from the thought of your spiritual ideal in the words of the affirmation to an inner awareness of the spiritual ideal in silence. Even without repeating the affirmation consciously, you are still aided by the affirmation when you go into silence. This is because, besides serving as a tool to reduce stray thoughts, the thought of the affirmation remains in your subconscious mind as a dominant thought pattern that can serve to counteract the ego-based thought patterns of the mind. If your mind is dominated by ego-based thought patterns, it will be difficult to go into inner silence without being distracted by stray thoughts. But by having built a dominant thought pattern in your subconscious mind of your spiritual ideal, you are better prepared to remain in inner silence without being distracted

Although you do not take the repetition of the affirmation into inner silence, the thought pattern of your spiritual ideal remains in your mind. Of course, your affirmation in word form is only a symbol of your spiritual ideal. However, having built this symbol into your mind, it remains there as a mental representation of the reality of your spiritual ideal. Besides representing your spiritual ideal, it more importantly symbolizes your desire for God, which welcomes the Holy Spirit to come into you in order to transform your awareness. Before learning to meditate, your mind is most likely dominated by ego-based desires, to which you have previously given your invitation, but which are now running on automatic pilot. This is why you may at times have emotional reactions, which you seem to be unable to control. Many of these reaction patterns are locked away in your subconscious mind and are still affecting you without your conscious awareness. Your affirmation builds within you a thought pattern that is in direct opposition to your ego-based desires and reaction patterns.

When you go into inner silence, you will find that you can remain there only briefly, and then you will be assailed by stray thoughts of the self. You can let go of these stray thoughts by not reacting to them, expressing neither attraction nor aversion. For intervals of calmness, you can let these thoughts pass by in your mind without allowing them to distract you from resting in inner silence. But then you will find yourself reacting in some way to passing thoughts by holding on to thoughts. You may realize you are monitoring or analyzing your thoughts instead of letting go of them. You let your awareness that your mind has wandered be a gentle reminder for you to pick up your affirmation and use it as a way of calming the mind.

Each time you calm your mind with your affirmation and then let go of your affirmation, you will have an opportunity to enter inner silence. This inner silence will not be simply an empty void, but rather an opportunity to consent to the presence of your spiritual ideal at an even deeper level, the level beyond words. It is that consenting to a closer union with the presence of your spiritual ideal that then allows you to rest in inner silence during Inner Silence Meditation. Your previous experience with meditation in which you have built your affirmation within as a dominant thought pattern in your mind can serve as a foundation for being able to enter inner silence.

Assuming that your spiritual ideal is a name for God or a reminder of God, you will be consenting to the divine presence when you practice Inner Silence Meditation. As you rest in inner silence, you will only be able to rely on your pure faith to sustain you. Your pure faith will tell you that the divine presence is there with you in the inner silence. As you enter inner silence, you move away from meditation, which focuses on the thought of your affirmation. Through the letting go of concepts, you experience contemplation, which is both a restful and dynamic state of inner absorption.

Unlike meditation, which requires concentration, contemplation is not the result of focusing the mind. It is a state of openness into which you are drawn by meeting the conditions that would produce this state. There are four conditions that need to be met in order for you to be drawn into contemplation. The contemplative state of resting in God cannot occur if your mind is preoccupied with distracting ego-based thoughts, so the first condition to be met is to have a calm mind, undisturbed by passing thoughts. Contemplation cannot come to you if it is not wanted, thus the second condition is your desire for the divine presence. Another word for your desire is your *intention*, which is expressed by your affirmation. Your intention is related to your wanting of contemplative communion. But when that wanting manifests as the actual experience of the divine presence, you will need to give your consent to this presence. Consequently, your consent to the divine presence is the third condition of contemplation. Although the experience of contemplation is a very receptive state, you do assert your will to draw this divine communion to yourself. You exert your will to desire God, and you exert your will to consent to both the divine presence and the divine activity within you.

Contemplation cannot happen if you are investing in faithlessness, so the fourth condition for resting in God to occur is investing in your faith in God. If you are like most people, you are not black or white in regard to faith. You are not entirely faithless, and you are not entirely full of faith. Everyone has doubts, and the root source of doubts is fear. Everyone is aware of some degree of faith, and the root source of faith is your true nature of love, given to you by God. You do not have to determine how many doubts you have based on fear, and you do not have to evaluate how much faith you have based on love. The relevant concern you need to address is, "Where am I making my investment— in which direction am I turning my awareness?"

You can turn the awareness of your mind toward faithlessness or toward faith, similar to the way you can drive your car north or south. You cannot drive your car north and south simultaneously, so you need to choose one direction for your car and likewise you need to choose one direction for your mind. Once you choose your direction, you may go off course at times, but at least you have set your purpose on investing in one direction. You cannot invest in faithlessness and in faith simultaneously because these two are mutually exclusive, just like fear and love are mutually exclusive. Investing in the direction of faithlessness leads to fear, which is its source. Investing in the direction of faith leads to love, which is its source. If you choose to turn your awareness in the direction of faithlessness, you close the door to the contemplative experience. Even though you are not free of doubts, if you turn your awareness in the direction of your faith, you are seeking to be led by the Holy Spirit.

It is not enough to say you believe in God as an idea. You will need to implement your faith by applying whatever amount of faith you already have. Applying your faith is certainly learning to see God as your final goal, but in practical terms applying your faith is also learning to rely on God as the means to that final goal. Through relying on God to supply the means, your trust allows God to guide you to the awareness of His presence. Your implementation of your faith in God is the condition needed to allow yourself to become aware of His loving presence in contemplation and become embraced by His rest, like a child sleeping in the safe arms of his mother.

In summary, the conditions that need to be met for contemplation to occur are:

The Four Conditions of Contemplation

1. Calmness of the mind
2. Desire for God
3. Consent to the divine presence
4. Faith invested in God

Consequently, to prepare yourself to receive the gift of contemplation, it will be necessary to have a calm mind, a desire for a closer union with Spirit along with your consent to the divine presence, and the application of your faith in the direction of God. When you meet these four conditions, contemplation is a natural result.

The Spirit is always ready to enter your consciousness and draw you into the contemplative state with your consent. The contemplative state is both restful and dynamic. During contemplation a natural inner absorption takes place in which stray thoughts may come and go, without causing you to let go of this inner absorption. However, if stray thoughts cause your mind to wander, you can then practice meditation again by picking up the affirmation. When repeating the affirmation has stilled the mind sufficiently, you can let go of the affirmation again and return to the inner silence and rely on your pure faith in the divine presence.

Four phases of using your affirmation in Inner Silence Meditation, as a way of leading you in the direction of contemplation, have already been described in Chapter 5. The first, second, and third phases meet the four conditions for contemplation to happen. Therefore, these phases are a preparation for the experience of contemplation itself, which happens in the fourth phase of using the affirmation. The list below summarizes the phases of using your affirmation and how these phases meet the four conditions in order for contemplation to be the natural outcome:

Four Phases of Using the Affirmation in Inner Silence Meditation

1. Mentally Pronouncing the Affirmation
• the structured and form-related phase
• meets the first condition of a calm mind

2. Allowing the Affirmation to be as it presents itself
• the intention phase
• meets the second condition of desire for God

3. The Affirmation Leads to Faithful Awareness
• the acceptance phase
• meets the third condition of consent to the divine presence
• meets the fourth condition of investment in faith in God

4. The Affirmation Culminates in Resting in God
• the contemplation phase
• the four conditions have been met and contemplation occurs
• pure faith is essential to maintain this state
• inner feelings may or may not be experienced

The first phase, which relies on the structure and form of repeating the word or words of the affirmation, is recommended to help produce a calm mind, but this phase is optional. If you are a beginner, you will probably find it very helpful to repeat the sound of your affirmation as a means of letting go of distracting stray thoughts and affirming your intention of deepening your relationship with God. If you become very distracted by unwanted thoughts, you may want to temporarily coordinate the repeating of your affirmation with your breathing in order to overcome this difficulty. But generally you can release distracting thoughts by redirecting your mind to your affirmation without coordinating the affirmation with the breathing. Also, the affirmation does not have to be distinctly repeated as with earlier described techniques in which each syllable is repeated and extended so the sound is mentally pronounced. You may initially choose to repeat the affirmation in word form in the first phase. However, then you may choose to move on to the second phase, in which you set aside the sounding out of the word form mentally and instead allow the thought of the affirmation to come to your mind in whatever way it presents itself.

Having this thought of the affirmation come to your mind, of course, does not mean to "think about" the affirmation and what it signifies intellectually. It means to let the affirmation come to your awareness without predetermining the specific form this will take. The affirmation may come to your mind as the words of the affirmation with or without the sound of those words. In addition, the affirmation may appear as a clear thought or a vague thought, a movement of the will, or as an inner feeling. Because the second phase is less structured and less form-related than the first phase, this second phase has a greater emphasis on the desire that your affirmation symbolizes. The affirmation, however it comes to your awareness, is simply a reminder of your desire for your spiritual ideal of God.

The first phase includes your desire for God, similar to the second phase, but the first phase is primarily designed to meet the condition of having a calm mind in order to enter contemplation. The structure and form of repeating the affirmation in the first phase can calm the mind. However, this first phase is optional because you may at some point, sooner or later, to be able to calm the mind without needing to repeat the affirmation in such a structured manner. If you can meet the condition of a calm mind by implementing the less structured approach of using your affirmation in the second phase, you can skip the first phase. An affirmation of one word, perhaps a word having only one syllable, such as "Christ," may be the most effective affirmation for the second phase, which leads to the next phase of setting aside the affirmation altogether.

After the affirmation is released, you shift your focus of awareness from the thought of the word form to a *faithful awareness* of the reality of the divine presence, for which the word form is only a symbol. The desiring of the divine presence expressed in the second phase allows you to make a natural progression to the accepting of the divine presence in the third phase. Your acceptance of the divine presence is the giving of your consent, which allows the Holy Spirit to bring about an inner transformation. Of course, God is always present within you. However, in this third phase, you learn to increasingly accept His presence and His activity within you. Your acceptance of His presence requires your faith—an inner knowing, which is not based on the normal mental process of rational thinking. Your faith in the divine presence implies a faithful awareness of an inner reality, and in addition an awareness of a reality that loves you. Naturally your faith in God's presence is important for all the phases of using the affirmation during Inner Silence Meditation, but in this third phase you can let go of your affirmation and rely on your faithful awareness alone. Although the first phase and second phase also include a certain degree of investing in your faith, this third phase represents a much deeper investment. This deeper investment involves both the third condition and fourth condition of contemplation. In this third phase of using the affirmation, you give your consent to the divine presence, which is the third condition of contemplation. In addition, the third phase of using the affirmation represents a greater faithful trust in God, which is the fourth condition of contemplation. Because you are increasingly letting go of other investments and making a single-minded investment in faith above all else, you are fulfilling the final condition for contemplation to occur during Inner Silence Meditation.

To illustrate the faithful awareness expressed during Inner Silence Meditation, you can imagine that you are in a completely dark room, and you are only aware of yourself in this silent room. At some point you sense that there is—and has been all along—someone else in this room with you. You cannot see or hear this other one, but you somehow feel this one is there, even though you cannot confirm his presence by your normal senses. Although his outer appearance is hidden from you, you inwardly know that this one is of one mind and of one heart with you. Most of all, you sense this one to be a loving presence. Your faithful awareness of his loving presence creates in you a different consciousness than when you were only aware of yourself alone. You want a closer union with this loving presence, so you are open and receptive, waiting for this one to reveal himself. On the other hand, you are grateful just to know that this one is there as a loving presence. You know that it is up to this one's initiative to reveal himself or not, and so you must wait patiently.

As this analogy illustrates, your meditation experience often begins by you only being aware of yourself as alone and separate. Yet as you become quiet within, you may have a faithful awareness that you are not alone. This faithful awareness is a recognition that is not confirmed by the senses or the rational thinking of the mind, but relies on a faithful inner knowing that the divine presence is there. You cannot force the divine presence to be revealed to you at a deeper level. All you can do is to be open to whatever way this presence might be revealed to you and to be content even if this presence is not revealed to you. This requires waiting patiently.

Your faithful awareness may lead you into the fourth phase, the resting in God of contemplation. In this restful state, there is an inner absorption that allows you to disregard stray thoughts as they float by in your mind. However, after your meditation practice, you may not be able to pinpoint or describe what has occurred during your contemplative experience. Some meditators do not have a "felt" experience during their times of inner silence, and your pure faith does not require such experiences to confirm that you have encountered the divine presence.

Yet some meditators do experience inner feelings of a positive nature, such as feelings of love or peace. Having these inner feelings are signs of progress. Nonetheless, equivalent progress can be made without such experiences. Inner feelings point in the direction of God, but are not God Himself. If you are being guided to be open to experiencing these inner feelings, then accept what you are being given without attachment or aversion. But these inner feelings are not your goal. God is your goal. Thus your inner feelings can be helpful as long as they inspire you to continue to be open to God Himself. These inner feelings are discussed in Chapter 13, which also describes ways of increasing your openness to these inner feelings in your journey of awakening to God.

There are different ways in which you may encounter the divine presence. Usually, however, your awareness of the divine presence cannot be pinned down and categorized any more than God Himself can be clearly defined. A young monk said to an old monk, "I want to find God and hold on to Him. How can I do that?"

The old monk replied, "Go outside and catch the wind and bring it inside."

When the young monk returned, he said, "I grabbed at the wind, but I could not catch it."

The old monk replied, "If you can't catch the wind, what makes you think you can catch hold of God? But if you simply stand still outside, the wind will encompass you. In the same way if you allow your mind to stand still, God will encompass and possess you."

Although Inner Silence Meditation is a technique that leads beyond techniques to contemplation, the inner absorption of contemplation may occur spontaneously during any meditation method. You may be practicing any of the first five techniques of Christian Yoga Meditation when you may be overshadowed by the Holy Spirit. You may first calm your mind sufficiently using your affirmation and then let go of your affirmation so you are holding your awareness only on the focusing area appropriate to the particular method you are using. While placing your awareness on a specific focusing area of the body, you may experience the contemplative state of inner absorption. If this happens, you may let go of holding your attention on a focusing area of the body and rest in the contemplative state as long as it lasts. If your mind is attracted to stray thoughts, you can then return to your affirmation and the focusing area of the body.

Though the experience of contemplation may occur while practicing any of the techniques of Christian Yoga Meditation, it is most likely to occur during Inner Silence Meditation. It is natural for contemplation to occur during this sixth method of Christian Yoga Meditation because the sequence of techniques used prior to Inner Silence Meditation helps to open the spiritual centers from the bottom to the top. During Crown Meditation the crown center of awareness opens and can remain open to make Oneness Meditation especially effective. Ideally the crown center of awareness also remains open during Inner Silence Meditation to increase its effectiveness as well. Although you let go of body awareness during Inner Silence Meditation, the crown center of awareness continues to be activated even though you do not consciously bring your awareness to the crown area as you do in Crown Meditation. In fact, when you are practicing Inner Silence Meditation and when contemplation occurs, it is through the crown center that the Holy Spirit acts to open you to the universal consciousness and to produce a dynamic inner absorption typical of the contemplative state.

There is a description above of how the first four techniques of Christian Yoga Meditation cooperate with the Holy Spirit in a purification process that includes raising the creative energy in the body. The last two methods, Oneness Meditation and Inner Silence Meditation, as well as contemplation, cooperate in this purification process. Ideally the crown center remains actively involved during the concluding techniques of Christian Yoga Meditation. Thus the Holy Spirit works through the crown center of awareness to regulate the raising of the creative energy in a way that is most beneficial for you. In the earlier techniques of Christian Yoga Meditation, you play a somewhat more active role in cooperating with the Holy Spirit in purifying and raising the creative energy. As you reach the later techniques in Christian Yoga Meditation, you play a less active role. When you practice Inner Silence Meditation and enter contemplation, you play the least active role of all because you do not focus on any particular center of awareness in the body. While you are relying on pure faith during contemplation, you are surrendering yourself most fully to the Spirit. At this time the Holy Spirit raises the creative energy, including the kundalini energy, in the way that would be most helpful for you.

Contemplation has been described as an overshadowing of the Holy Spirit. The function of the Holy Spirit is to be a guide and communication link between your physical world, where your ego is at home, and His World, which is your true Home. The Holy Spirit coordinates and integrates all the centers of awareness, but in particular functions through the crown center of awareness. During contemplation through your consent, you allow the Holy Spirit to open the crown center enough to allow you to enter His World. During the practice of Inner Silence Meditation, you will probably not feel this opening of the crown center of awareness because you are not focused on body awareness. Another reason for not feeling this opening is that the universal consciousness itself, manifesting through this center, transcends the three-dimensional world of form, space, and time. In contemplation you are entering His World, which you can think of as another dimension that encompasses, interpenetrates, and transcends your three-dimensional world. The effect of the universal consciousness that manifests through the crown center in contemplation is a two-edged sword. One effect is a unifying energy. The other effect is a disintegrating influence on barriers to unifying. The unifying effect has already been described and emphasized. The disintegrating effect dissolves ego-based emotions and thoughts. This is elaborated upon in Chapter 11, which explains the releasing of emotional patterns that block the expression of your true nature of love.

E. Inner Listening Meditation

Another method of meditation, called *Inner Listening Meditation*, may be practiced in conjunction with Inner Silence Meditation. If a continuous humming tone presents itself while you are practicing Inner Silence Meditation, you may ignore this steady inner sound and simply continue your practice or you may want to practice Inner Listening Meditation. If you are repeating your affirmation when you hear the humming sound, you can practice Inner Listening Meditation by releasing the affirmation and listening to this humming sound as long as it lasts. When the humming cannot be heard after a while, you can return to practicing Inner Silence Meditation. If stray thoughts have distracted you, you can return to using your affirmation. If your mind is not distracted by stray thoughts, you may let go of your affirmation in order to return to inner silence.

Let's imagine that you are practicing Inner Silence Meditation and that you have already let go of your affirmation and are experiencing the inner silence and rest of contemplation. While you are in this contemplative state, how would you respond if you heard the inner sound? You can listen to the humming sound if you are guided to do so.

However, generally speaking, it is best to ignore the humming sound in this case because your contemplation experience is a deeper level of awareness than the humming sound. Nevertheless, if the inner sound grabs your attention, drawing you out of your contemplative rest in God, you can just focus directly on listening to the humming sound. When the humming sound disappears, you can then return to your affirmation if you are distracted by stray thoughts or return to the silence of contemplation if you are not distracted by stray thoughts.

Actually the humming sound may occur during any of your meditation practices that use an affirmation or that use some other way of focusing. Regardless of the method you are using, you can switch to Inner Listening Meditation, if you feel guided to do so. Without exerting an effort to try to hear the humming sound, you can just allow this sound to come of itself as a result of repeating your affirmation. If you hear the humming, you can let go of the affirmation and allow the sound to be your focus of awareness as you remain relaxed. Some meditators hear this humming and become concerned with clinging to it, rather than listening to it in a relaxed manner. Being concerned about clinging to the sound produces a tension, which makes the humming leave the awareness of the mind. As you listen without attachment, the humming sound will continue naturally, without any effort on your part to hold on to it. Through this effortless inner listening to the humming vibration, it becomes a positive spiritual force that expresses itself naturally, and occasionally may even come into your conscious mind at times outside of your meditation practice.

The word "humming" is used to describe this steady tone for lack of a better term to identify the inner sound. Actually it would be more accurate to say that the inner sound is a very clear and continuous tone that does not fluctuate. In meditation you may hear a steady tone in one ear or in the other ear, but this is not the inner sound. The inner tone is heard emanating from within the center of the head. If you want to try a simple test on yourself, you can put your thumbs in your ears. Listen within yourself to any interior sounds. What do you hear? If there is perfect silence, then either you are a soul at deep peace or you weren't listening very carefully. If you hear the continuous and steady inner tone, then you are at peace, yet not quite as peaceful as the one who is in the silent state. If you are like most people, you will hear some other sound or combination of sounds. Examples of sounds that may be heard are the roar of the ocean, the sound of running water, bells, wind blowing, the sound of a lute, a buzzing sound, or other sounds that may be less distinct. These sounds are quite normal, yet they indicate the lack of a more peaceful harmony.

The hearing of the inner sound indicates that meditation is bringing about increased harmony and peace. When the kundalini is rising in a gradual manner during meditation, this increases the ability to hear the inner sound. In yoga philosophy the inner sound is called the "*nada*" and can be considered the uncaused sound. This inner sound is the OM. This inner tone should not be thought of as something caused by the mind, since it has a spiritual origin. When the various other interior sounds that are created by the mind are silenced through the use of an affirmation, the inner sound that is not created by the mind can then be heard.

While holding the awareness within the center of the head, some meditators feel themselves becoming one with the inner sound. Even though the inner sound emanates from the center of the head, it may feel like it is penetrating into every cell in the body. This feeling of becoming in tune with a single steady tone may seem dull compared to your usual preference for sounds that have musical variations in tone. But the actual experience of listening within to this one unifying tone can be quite pleasant.

Clarity, purity, and love are at the center of your true nature in God. Because the inner sound emanates from your spiritual core, its tone carries some of these inner qualities. Consequently, the inner sound is transformative since it helps you to become in tune with your spiritual nature. This transformation that listening to the inner sound produces is so subtle and gentle that you may fail to understand or appreciate its effectiveness. Methods that use affirmations are important for building within your mind a deep impression of your commitment to your spiritual ideal. However, after your dedication to your spiritual ideal is firmly established, you may hear the inner sound and find Inner Listening Meditation to be more effective than using an affirmation.

Although the inner sound comes from a spiritual source, it should be understood that listening to this sound is not the ideal meditative state. By God's grace you may come to know the silence of the Father from which all sound originates. Listening to the inner sound in Inner Listening Meditation can lead you in the direction of that silence. Using Inner Listening Meditation in conjunction with Inner Silence Meditation is a good combination because you can alternate between the steady spiritual tone and the inner silence that leads to contemplation. But keep in mind that the silent contemplative state leads to a deeper level of consciousness than the steady humming tone. The following chapter describes the One Year Program designed to lead you in a step-by-step manner from one meditation technique to another in the direction of contemplation. If you decide to follow the One Year Program and if the humming sound presents itself during your practice, you may practice Inner Listening Meditation if you are prompted to do so by the Holy Spirit.

---

1. Mark 9:24

9

THE ONE YEAR PROGRAM

≈ • ≈

A. Why a One Year Program?

After completing the Twenty-eight Day Demonstration, you may decide to continue to practice meditation once or twice each day. For your daily practice, Christian Yoga Meditation is recommended. But, a suggested alternative is to participate in the One Year Program that will be described in this chapter. The purpose of this program is to bring you to a deeper level in meditation by following a systematic approach that works in cooperation with the Holy Spirit to bring about an inner transformation.

Ideally it's best to experience the methods of Christian Yoga Meditation in combination. However, for the One Year Program, these techniques are practiced separately for one month at a time to increase your depth of experience with each technique. Oneness Meditation is not experienced separately since it is optional and best used in combination with Crown Meditation and/or Inner Silence Meditation. As was described in detail in Chapter 8, the sequence of techniques of Christian Yoga Meditation are placed in an order that mirrors the rising of energy in the body from the bottom to the top. This sequence also opens centers of awareness in the body from the bottom up. The monthly practices for the first five months of the One Year Program follows this bottom to top sequence.

For the sixth month and thereafter, you will combine all the methods that you had previously experienced separately for one month at a time. Having had a greater depth of experience with each individual method separately will increase the effectiveness of them in combination. For this combination you will be practicing Christian Yoga Meditation. For the sixth month and thereafter, you will practice the usual sequence of six techniques that make up Christian Yoga Meditation, but each month you will have a different emphasis. The change in emphasis each month will follow the sequence from bottom to top, so Centering Meditation will be emphasized first and Inner Silence Meditation will be emphasized last.

The overall direction of the One Year Program is to address all the centers of awareness in the body in sequence to build a solid foundation for your meditation experience. In addition to this overall direction, there is a specific emphasis on leading you in a step-by-step manner toward deepening your experience of Inner Silence Meditation, which in turn leads you to contemplation.

For the One Year Program, you set aside a minimum of one twenty-five minute period each day for your regular practice time. Preferably you will be able to set aside two such periods each day, perhaps one in the morning and one in the afternoon. Some meditators prefer one meditation period on weekends and two meditation periods during weekdays to counteract the build up of tension due to stress from work.

B. Summary of the One Year Program

1. First Month — Centering Meditation

2. Second Month — Heart Meditation

3. Third Month — Brow Meditation

4. Fourth Month — Crown Meditation, Oneness Meditation

5. Fifth Month — Oneness Meditation, Inner Silence Meditation

6. Sixth Month — primarily Centering Meditation

Christian Yoga Meditation is practiced in the following sequence: Centering Meditation, Heart Meditation, Brow Meditation, Crown Meditation, Oneness Meditation (optional), and finally Inner Silence Meditation. More time is spent using Centering Meditation than any other method.

7. Seventh Month — primarily Heart Meditation

Christian Yoga Meditation is practiced in the same sequence as the previous month, but with the difference being that more time is spent using Heart Meditation than any other method.

8. Eighth Month — primarily Brow Meditation

Christian Yoga Meditation is practiced in the usual sequence, but with more time spent using Brow Meditation than any other method.

9. Ninth Month — primarily Crown Meditation

Christian Yoga Meditation is practiced as usual, but with more time spent using Crown Meditation than any other method.

10. Tenth Month — primarily Inner Silence Meditation

Christian Yoga Meditation is practiced as usual, but with more time spent using Inner Silence Meditation than any other method

11. Eleventh Month — primarily Inner Silence Meditation

Christian Yoga Meditation is practiced as usual, but with about half the time spent in Inner Silence Meditation.

12. Twelfth Month — primarily Inner Silence Meditation

Christian Yoga Meditation is practiced in as usual, but with more than half the time spent in Inner Silence Meditation.

C. First Month —

Centering Meditation Exclusively

For the first month of the One Year Program, you practice Centering Meditation exclusively just as this method is described in Chapter 5. This technique is termed "Centering Meditation" because holding the awareness in the navel area enables you to focus on your physical center of balance. Holding the awareness in the navel area has a calming effect that tends to reduce physical tension throughout the body and encourages physical receptivity. The fact that the navel area is the center of balance in the body is well known. Nonetheless, even some experienced meditators doubt that there are any benefits to holding the awareness in this part of the body. There is a simple experiment you can conduct to illustrate the value of Centering Meditation. Here are the two steps that you can use to conduct this experiment:

1. For the first step of this experiment, you stand erect. You raise both arms straight up toward the ceiling and simultaneously raise the heels of the feet. You maintain your balance on the raised feet. Then after a few seconds, you lower the arms and feet.

2. For the second step, you do exactly as before, but you have the eyes closed throughout.

If you are curious, you can conduct this brief experiment on yourself right now before you read below about what you can expect to happen.

If you are like most people, what will happen is that when you raise your body up and balance on your feet the first time with your eyes open, you will be able to hold your balance fairly well. The second time with your eyes closed, you will not be able to hold your balance. After you have practiced Centering Meditation for some time and developed your ability to hold the awareness in the navel area, you may want to conduct the experiment again. This time, when you close your eyes and raise your body up to balance on your feet, you hold your awareness in your navel area. You will discover that you can hold your balance with your eyes closed.

Inner tension is held within your physical body, but you do not even consciously feel that tension because, as this experiment shows, you are out of touch with your physical body. You compensate for your lack of awareness of your physical vehicle by using your eyesight to orient you to your physical environment. But when you close your eyes you discover a lack of attunement with your physical vehicle, which can be corrected by holding the awareness in the navel area. Consequently, during the practice of Centering Meditation, you take the time to get in touch with the center of balance in your physical body, and through that attunement you reduce physical tension and allow yourself to be physically open to the Spirit.

Your openness allows the Spirit to regulate the physical functioning of the body. In particular, there is an allowing of the Spirit to interpenetrate those physical functions that are located in close proximity to the navel area. These vital functions include digestion, assimilation, elimination, and sexual expression. Allowing these vital functions to be surrendered to the action of the Spirit produces an increased physical vitality.

Although meditating soon after eating is not recommended, if you feel on a rare occasion the necessity to do so, then Centering Meditation is recommended. Since the focus of this meditation is the navel area, it is less likely to divert energy away from the normal digestion process.

When practicing Centering Meditation, it is especially important to sit erect and not lean the spine against the back of a chair or other support. Having the spine supported will shift the normal center of balance away from the navel area and make it more difficult to focus the awareness in that area. If you want to improve your posture before beginning to meditate, you can slowly rock the upper torso from side to side until you feel centered and then gently move the upper torso back and forth until you feel your center of balance in the navel area.

Centering Meditation is used exclusively only for the first month of the One Year Program, as a way of deepening your effectiveness in using this method. However, in general this method is recommended to be used as part of Christian Yoga Meditation and as a means of developing physical receptivity. This kind of receptivity is a preparation for meditating at the higher focusing areas. Centering Meditation increases the physical vitality of the body as a result of acquiring physical receptivity to the Spirit. Then it is necessary to develop emotional receptivity to the Spirit by focusing at the heart area. Thus the increased vitality can be directed by the Spirit toward producing a greater intensity of devotion. Consequently, physical vitality must be seen not as an end in itself but rather as an aid in helping you to become more loving.

An important function of Centering Meditation is to divert the body energy upward. Normally the creative energy in the gonad center of awareness is expressed through a downward flow of energy in the body. Centering Meditation can reverse this into an upward flow and make this energy available for spiritual purposes, which deepens meditation. Maintaining a relaxed hand position, especially with the palms turned upward, tends to enhance the flow of energy upward during the practice of Centering Meditation.

D. Second Month —

Heart Meditation Exclusively

In general, society places a greater emphasis on being able to develop the mind. Therefore, most individuals would benefit by greater heart development. There are two specific types of heart development that are important: One kind of heart development is emotional receptivity to the Holy Spirit that enables you to respond appropriately with your emotions in any situation. This type of outer responsiveness helps you to let go of emotional tension caused by habitual patterns or defense mechanisms based on fear. Developing emotional responsiveness to the Holy Spirit enables you to express love and sharing with others in obvious and overt ways. In contrast to this outer receptivity and responsiveness, the other kind of heart development is a form of inner emotional receptivity. It is emotional receptivity that is related to an opening of the heart to God the Father. It is a devotional quality, which is often lacking. It is not necessary for a beginning meditator, but it is necessary if meditation is to deepen. Both emotional receptivity that helps to express love outwardly and emotional receptivity that helps to express devotional love inwardly can be developed if there is the desire for this to happen.

For meditation to deepen, it must be more than a method of thought control. It must allow for the development of inner feelings that reach out to God beyond words and thoughts. Focusing on the heart first, before focusing in the head, ensures that the mind will be used to establish a love relationship with God, rather than the mind being used merely as a sterile mechanism for mental focusing. When you choose a spiritual ideal, your choice is based on your highest understanding, and you may only have an abstract understanding at first. Nonetheless, gradually your activity of calling on your spiritual ideal in meditation needs to lead to a genuine caring about your spiritual ideal. If methods of developing the heart are not used, the deepening of the desire and inner feeling to be one with your spiritual ideal may not occur.

When methods of developing the heart are used, there may be sudden openings of the heart that occur spontaneously. Nevertheless, usually this is a step-by-step process so that as your meditation deepens there is a corresponding progress in emotional receptivity and devotional qualities. As you make progress in your devotion to God, you will notice an improvement in your ability to have a healthy (non-egotistical) love for yourself and to express that love outwardly to others in your personal relationships.

As described previously, Heart Meditation is the traditional form of meditation used by the earliest Christian hermits, who went into the desert to be alone with God. These monks repeated the Divine Name of Jesus Christ and in addition focused on the heart. This technique is recommended as a way to develop emotional receptivity to the Spirit, which leads to devotion.

Heart Meditation, as it is described in Chapter 5, is practiced for the second month of the One Year Program. But you may want to use an optional variation of this method that has not been described previously. This variation may be used if you feel the heartbeat in the chest during your meditation. The simplest form of this variation is to bring your attention to the heartbeat as a way of focusing on the heart. This placing of your attention on the heartbeat should not be considered as a more advanced method but simply a different method based on personal preference.

A more complex variation is to coordinate the affirmation with the heartbeat and with the breathing. For example, when you are able to sit calmly and breathe slowly, there may be two beats of the heart for each inhalation and two beats of the heart for each exhalation. If you are using "Jesus Christ love" as your affirmation, you can keep your attention focused in the heart area. While using this affirmation, you mentally repeat the two syllables of "Jesus" along with two heartbeats during the inhalation and mentally repeat the two words "Christ love" along with two heartbeats during the exhalation. If you find that you can coordinate your heartbeat and breathing with your affirmation in a way that is natural and relaxed, you may do so.

If you are using a variation that includes focusing on the heartbeat, and if your mind becomes calm, you can let go of the affirmation and just focus on the heart without coordinating the breathing. You have the option of focusing on the heartbeat, or you can let go of being aware of the heartbeat and just focus on the heart area. If you become distracted by stray thoughts, you can then return to repeating your affirmation.

When you use Heart Meditation exclusively, you may experience a feeling of warmth, energy, or a tingling sensation either in the heart area or in the center of the chest. This can help to focus the awareness, although these feelings are not necessary to use this method. In the event that you experience a slight pain or a rapid heartbeat in the chest, you need to switch temporarily to another method, such as Centering Meditation, until this condition disappears. The abnormal condition of pain or a rapid heartbeat should not be confused with the common feeling of energy or slight pressure (without pain) that may occur in the chest as a natural result of focusing the awareness on the heart area during meditation.

If the abnormal condition just described does not occur and your attention intuitively goes to the left side of the chest and not the center of the chest, then it is recommend that you hold your awareness at the location of the physical heart. The early Christian desert hermits meditated with their awareness held on the physical heart. They discovered that by bringing the attention of the mind into the physical heart during their practice of meditation, they could awaken a deeper sense of devotion than focusing on any other part of the body. The advantage of meditating on the center of the chest is that there is less likelihood of negative side effects. The advantage of meditating on the physical heart is that there is a greater potential for enkindling devotion.

Some beginning meditators learn to focus their awareness at the heart initially and then after gaining experience in practicing meditation, they change the focus of their awareness to the location of the center of the chest. The reason for this is that once the heart is awakened and used as a focusing area on a regular basis, the energy from the heart easily expands and fills the center of the chest, which then becomes a natural focusing point for meditation. There is a "flame" in the heart that once enkindled can eventually set the whole chest on fire with divine love. There is more information about this flame in the heart in Chapter 14 that describes *Inner Light Meditation*.

E. Third Month —

Brow Meditation Exclusively

After meditating on the heart for the second month of the One Year Program, it is appropriate to move on to Brow Meditation for the third month. If you have good mental concentration, you will feel comfortable meditating in the head, and if you have a good heart development you will feel comfortable meditating in the heart. However, the benefits of meditation are not always related to which technique feels more comfortable. In fact, if you have a good heart development, then you may benefit more by practicing Brow Meditation with the awareness at the space between the eyebrows. This will help you focus yourself single-mindedly toward God so that your love is not distracted. If you have good mental concentration, it may be more beneficial to practice a form of meditation that will help to open and purify the heart more fully, such as Heart Meditation.

Heart Meditation and Brow Meditation are both important because you need to develop a balance between the heart and the head. After practicing Heart Meditation for the second month to increase your heart development, you are then prepared to practice Brow Meditation for the third month to develop mental receptivity to the Spirit and the ability to focus the mind one-pointedly toward God without distraction. For Brow Meditation you repeat the chosen affirmation and coordinate it with the breathing, as described in Chapter 5. The awareness is held at the space between the eyebrows, not on the surface of the skin, but rather within the head itself. You may feel your awareness drawn to the area about an inch above the space between the eyebrows. In this case, feel free to meditate with your awareness at the middle of the forehead, if you feel guided to do so.

Normally with your eyes open, you project your awareness outwardly through the eyes. Therefore, when you are first learning how to meditate with the eyes closed, you may still unconsciously want to project your awareness outwardly. You may experience a feeling of fullness or energy in front of the head during meditation. Even if you feel this energy, it is important for you to maintain the awareness within the head rather than projecting it outwardly. Keeping your eyes closed and still, in one position, helps you to focus the mind and to hold the awareness within the head at the space between the eyebrows.

While using Brow Meditation, you may be able to feel energy rising upward from below. Occasionally you may feel energy accumulating at the lower portion of the back of the head, where the medulla oblongata is located. If this happens, instead of bringing your awareness to the back of the head where this energy has accumulated, it is best to continue to focus your awareness at the brow area. This energy lodged in the lower portion of the back of the head will eventually clear by moving into the upper part of the head. If energy accumulates in the lower portion of the back of the head on more than one occasion, it is recommended that before you begin your sitting period, you practice the head and neck exercise described in Chapter 3 in the section on relaxation.

Meditation in general and Brow Meditation in particular can produce expanded awareness. The most common forms of awareness are related to the mental thinking process of the mind. But during meditation you may experience a keen awareness that is not an expression of rational thinking. Awareness in its broadest expression may be thought of as simply consciousness. One attribute of God is pure consciousness. As you become more aware of your true spiritual nature, you expand the access that you have to pure consciousness. Focusing in the head that occurs in Brow Meditation increases your awareness because the head is the primary location of your access to higher consciousness.

The head may be considered the location of a gateway of awareness that leads in two directions—outwardly and inwardly. When you direct your awareness outwardly from the head, you allow your consciousness to become aware of other parts of the body or your outer environment. When your awareness is directed inwardly into the head, you become increasingly aware of your spiritual source from which your consciousness originates. In particular, by first developing the devotional qualities of the heart and then holding a loving focus of awareness within part of the head, as in Brow Meditation, you can have a direct impact on your degree of spiritual awareness.

By focusing at the head and allowing the mind to be used as a loving instrument of the Spirit, you may open a door to higher awareness. The door to higher awareness begins to open after the heart is turned to God, which produces a loving awareness. This loving awareness, first enkindled in the heart and then focused on in the head, invites the incoming of the Holy Spirit so the mind can be open to the awareness of your true nature as a child of God made in His image and likeness. Your mental awareness of your oneness with the Father is increasingly awakened. Your mental view of the world is your stumbling block to the awareness of your oneness with God. Opening the door to higher awareness means you are beginning mentally to see the world through the eyes of Christ in you. You take on more of His consciousness and bring the individual will into accord with God's Will. As the Apostle Paul might phrase it, you take on "the mind of Christ." This is not merely a following of His outer example, but rather a radical inner transformation in which you allow yourself to be increasingly imprinted with His consciousness of love and oneness with the Father. Through your openness to Christ, you increase your awareness of your own true Self, your Christ Self, that is at the core of your being, where you are (and have been all along) truly one with God.

F. Fourth Month —

Crown Meditation and Oneness Meditation

After practicing Brow Meditation for the third month, you increase your mental receptivity and open your mind to Christ consciousness. However, Brow Meditation is an opening to higher consciousness, but with an emphasis mostly on mental openness. Developing this mental openness is important as a preparation for Crown Meditation in which you open at a deeper level to Christ consciousness. This deeper level of opening is *integrating receptivity*, which allows the physical, emotional and mental levels of your human nature to be integrated.

When using Crown Meditation, you focus on the crown area, which is a circular area that covers the top and the back of the head. This circular area has about a four-inch diameter and is tilted back to intersect the head diagonally, much like the circumference of a yamaka, which is a small Jewish hat that sits on the top and back of the head. An illustration of this circular area is provided in Chapter 5.

Some meditators may consciously feel the crown area being filled with energy. Even though the crown area covers a circular area, it is difficult to describe what this area feels like. To some it may feel like a circular "opening," but more frequently it feels like a nebulous, rounded shape of energy. Most meditators would not feel this energy consciously, but the energy can be present whether it can be felt or not. When some of the inner obstacles are removed and when a certain amount of the creative energy rises up to the top of the head, the creative energy flows into this circular crown area and allows an integrating energy to descend downward into the whole body, coordinating all the centers of awareness. Some meditators can feel this integrating energy from the crown center coming down from the head and being distributed to the whole body. In some instances the energy can be experienced as descending down into the center of the chest and then being distributed to the whole body.

Although you focus only on the crown of the head during Crown Meditation, this focusing produces a coordinating effect on the whole body. Even though most meditators do not feel this coordinating effect as a consciously felt experience, the integration can still occur. Because of this effect on the whole body, it is appropriate for the fourth month to practice Crown Meditation followed by Oneness Meditation, which focuses on the whole body. These methods are practiced as they are described in Chapter 5. During your daily practice, most of the time is devoted to Crown Meditation, but you save time at the end of your meditation for Oneness Meditation. Crown Meditation opens the crown center of awareness, and this center remains open as you progress to using Oneness Meditation. The practice of Oneness Meditation produces intuitive receptivity, opening you to the intuitive level of your being. Intuitions are described in detail in Chapter 14. Oneness Meditation is optional as always, so you may choose to omit this practice altogether and practice Crown Meditation exclusively for the fourth month.

G. Fifth Month —
Oneness Meditation and Inner Silence Meditation

For the fifth month, you use Oneness Meditation followed by Inner Silence Meditation, as described in Chapter 6 and Chapter 8. In your practice, you allow only a short time for Oneness Meditation and most of the time for Inner Silence Meditation. Oneness Meditation is optional and may be omitted altogether. This month is your opportunity to focus primarily on Inner Silence Meditation in which you let go of body awareness and open yourself to contemplation. You are mostly using Inner Silence Meditation for your meditation period, but you are still being supported by the solid foundation you have built by practicing body awareness techniques for the previous four months. Inner Silence Meditation produces unifying receptivity that takes the integration of the physical, emotional, and mental levels of your being to a deeper level of unification, increasing your awareness of your oneness with God.

H. Sixth Month and thereafter —
CHRISTIAN YOGA MEDITATION

After practicing individual methods intensively for a month at a time, you then combine all these methods in the practice of Christian Yoga Meditation. Having had a greater depth of experience with each method separately will increase the effectiveness of them in combination. Each month from the sixth month onward you practice one of the techniques of Christian Yoga Meditation more than the others. The sequence of which method is emphasized follows the rising of energy and the centers of awareness from the bottom to the top, as follows:

Sixth Month — primarily Centering Meditation

Christian Yoga Meditation is practiced in the following sequence:

Centering Meditation, Heart Meditation, Brow Meditation, Crown Meditation, Oneness Meditation (optional), and finally Inner Silence Meditation. More time is spent using Centering Meditation than any other method.

Seventh Month — primarily Heart Meditation

Christian Yoga Meditation is practiced in the same sequence as the previous month, but with the only difference being that more time is devoted to using Heart Meditation than any other method.

Eighth Month — primarily Brow Meditation

Christian Yoga Meditation is practiced in the usual sequence, but with more time spent using Brow Meditation than any other method.

Ninth Month — primarily Crown Meditation

Christian Yoga Meditation is practiced as usual, but with more time spent using Crown Meditation than any other method.

Tenth Month — primarily Inner Silence Meditation

Christian Yoga Meditation is practiced as usual, but with more time spent using Inner Silence Meditation than any other method

Eleventh Month — primarily Inner Silence Meditation

Christian Yoga Meditation is practiced as usual, but with about half the time spent using Inner Silence Meditation.

Twelfth Month — primarily Inner Silence Meditation
Christian Yoga Meditation is practiced as usual, but with more than half the time spent using Inner Silence Meditation.

Oneness Meditation is part of Christian Yoga Meditation, yet it is optional and only practiced briefly as a transition from Crown Meditation to Inner Silence Meditation. For the tenth month, you practice Inner

Silence Meditation more than any of the other techniques in Christian Yoga Meditation. For the eleventh month, you practice Inner Silence Meditation for about half of the time. For the twelfth month, you use Inner Silence Meditation for more than half of your time for practicing Christian Yoga Meditation.

I. After the One Year Program

After completing the One Year Program, it is recommended that you continue to practice Christian Yoga Meditation with an emphasis on increasing the time for Inner Silence Meditation. Some people may be attracted to practicing Inner Silence Meditation exclusively without body awareness techniques. If you are prompted by the Holy Spirit to do so, by all means follow your guidance. Perhaps you can develop the ability to consistently enter into contemplative communion with the divine presence without needing body awareness techniques to help you arrive at that restful state of awareness. However, many meditators find it helpful to use body awareness techniques to lead in the direction of contemplation. Consequently, in general if you want to increase your practice of Inner Silence Meditation, it is recommended that you still practice the body awareness techniques of Christian Yoga Meditation, even if only briefly.

In addition to going to a deeper level in your practice of Inner Silence Meditation, one of the purposes of the One Year Program is to enable you to go to a deeper level in using body awareness methods. Going to a deeper level with body awareness methods means greater efficiency. Thus it will take only a brief contact with the centers of awareness in the body to raise your creative energy from the bottom to the top. Being more efficient at meditating with body awareness means an increase in the development of integration and unification. As you shift your awareness from the lower centers of awareness to the higher centers, the physical, emotional, mental, and intuitive levels of your being become integrated and unified more easily and more rapidly. This step-by-step climb up the internal ladder of your consciousness prepares you for Inner Silence Meditation that leads to contemplation.

Becoming more effective at opening the centers of awareness means you will need to devote less time to employing the first five techniques, which leaves more time for the practice of Inner Silence Meditation. Most of your meditation time can be used to practice Inner Silence Meditation, but it is still important to continue to use all the other five techniques of Christian Yoga Meditation. Even if used very briefly, the five body awareness techniques of Christian Yoga Meditation produce a stabilizing and harmonizing influence, which should not be eliminated altogether unless you feel guided by the Holy Spirit to do so.

Also, you may have times in your practice when you are releasing inner tension and emotions that are so upsetting that you cannot practice Inner Silence Meditation effectively. At such times it may be advisable to temporarily reduce the time for Inner Silence Meditation and increase the time for the body awareness techniques of Christian Yoga Meditation. In particular, the time for Centering Meditation and Heart Meditation can be increased temporarily during times of stress. Meditating during times of emotional stress will be discussed in more detail in Chapter 12.

On the other hand, as soon as you sit down to meditate, you may feel yourself being overshadowed by the Holy Spirit and immediately drawn into contemplation. At such times you can let go of using any of the five body awareness techniques of Christian Yoga Meditation, and you can practice Inner Silence Meditation exclusively. Some very experienced meditators reach a level in which their entire sitting period is a prolonged experience of contemplation, and they do not have to even practice Inner Silence Meditation because the affirmation is not needed at all.

J. Variations of the One Year Program

The One Year Program is described in a structured way to provide a helpful guideline for deepening your meditation experience. But, you are encouraged to ask for inner guidance on how to apply what has been presented here. You may be guided to make variations that would be helpful for your growth. For some variations to consider, you may want to first read Chapter 14, which describes methods for opening to light and love.

If you are attracted to employing any of the techniques described in Chapter 14, you may want to practice these techniques as part of this One Year Program. For example, you may decide that you would benefit by using *Inner Light Meditation*. If you decide to practice this technique that focuses on the heart, it can be used as a replacement for Heart Meditation in the second month of the One Year Program. Another possibility is that you may want to practice *Expanded Christian Yoga Meditation*. If you decide to use this technique, it can be a replacement for Christian Yoga Meditation, and it can be employed for all or selected parts of the One Year Program. Making this replacement would not be disruptive because, as the name implies, Expanded Christian Yoga Meditation uses most of the methods in Christian Yoga Meditation. However, it is an expanded version, which places a greater emphasis on the experience of the inner feelings of light and love.

10

DIFFERENT APPROACHES TO CONTEMPLATION

~ • ~

A. Christian Meditation Advocated by John Main

This meditation manual offers a new approach to the divine embrace of contemplation. To address why a new approach is needed, it will be helpful to first identify two alternative approaches to inward seeking that are in some ways similar to the techniques offered in this book. These two approaches are contemporary movements that represent a renewal of traditional Christian contemplative practices. One of these movements is *Centering Prayer*, which is described in the next section. The other is called *Christian Meditation*. While John Main was a British diplomat in Malaysia, he learned how to meditate from a Hindu guru. He returned to England and became a Benedictine monk and taught the practice of Christian Meditation. In 1972 John Main came to Canada and began teaching Christian Meditation at a house of prayer, which he founded in Montreal. When John Main died in the early 1980s his work was carried on by another Benedictine monk, Laurence Freeman, who promoted The World Community of Christian Meditation as the organization through which Christian Meditation has become known worldwide.[1]

Since John Main learned his method from a Hindu guru, it is not surprising that Christian Meditation relies on the repeating of a mantra, which may likewise be called a sacred word or affirmation. The outstanding distinctive feature of this method is that the mantra is repeated continuously throughout the entire meditation, which is the traditional way the mantra is used in many Hindu meditation practices. The idea is to choose just one mantra that through repetition can dominate all the other thoughts of the mind and become a spiritual anchor for one's consciousness.

An example of one widely used word advocated by John Main and in turn by his disciple, Laurence Freeman, is "Maranatha." This is an ancient Aramaic word meaning "Come, Lord." Maranatha, being an uncommon word, does not lend itself to creating mental images or mental associations that would be distracting to the meditation process. This word is pronounced "Ma-ra-na-tha" so that each syllable is mentally repeated with an equal emphasis.[2]

Once the meditator chooses a sacred word (or words), this choice is not generally changed, unless there is clear inner guidance to make a change. The whole purpose of the mantra is to interpenetrate the mind and to free the mind from being attached to self-centered thinking. The continuous repetition of the mantra from the beginning to the end of each meditation period and the consistency of this practice over many years helps to transform the mind.

There are two premises that support the use of Christian Meditation. The first premise is that choosing a sacred word directs the mind toward the presence of God and away from your self-centered thinking, which revolves around your image of yourself as a separate being. The second basic premise is that the nature of the mind is to be active and to produce a multiplication of thoughts. You cannot expect the mind to become perfectly silent because that is not the nature of the mind. The active nature of the mind creates a steady stream of unending thoughts. This ongoing stream of thoughts will be constantly fluctuating and producing instability, but by giving the mind one thought, one sacred word, the mind becomes stabilized and directed toward God.

Christian Meditation is correctly identified as an example of meditation, since by definition meditation is the holding of one thought in the mind continuously. But is Christian Meditation a form of contemplation? The answer depends on how you define contemplation. If contemplation is defined loosely as any form of inward receptivity to the divine, then Christian Meditation can be called "active contemplation" or "acquired contemplation." The activity of using concentration and continuous effort on the part of the seeker is the reason why Christian Meditation is an example of active contemplation. Acquired contemplation, synonymous with active contemplation, conveys the meaning that the seeker is exerting his own efforts to bring about an inner transformation. But Christian Meditation is not entirely active since there are many receptive elements present. For example, the repeating of the sacred word allows for a certain degree of divine receptivity because distracting thoughts, including self-analysis, the imagination, and the memory, are all set aside. It is these receptive elements that give meditation a contemplative aspect and bring about an openness to the divine influence.

Sometimes contemplation is defined as inward seeking that produces mystical awareness in which God's grace manifests in the form of a felt experience or occurs without the seeker having any conscious experience that would confirm the divine presence. Using this definition Christian Meditation can also be considered a contemplative experience in which God's work of transformation takes place in overt or less obvious ways. Christian Meditation does invite divine grace and succeeds in producing inner transformation because of the intent of the seeker for this to happen, which gives the Holy Spirit permission to bring about inner changes.

There is no question here of the effectiveness of Christian Meditation to be a beneficial means of spiritual transformation, but there is a semantic question regarding how to define contemplation. This meditation manual makes a very precise definition of contemplation in order to make a clear distinction between meditation and contemplation. In contrast to the broad definition of contemplation as any form of inward receptivity or mystical experience, this meditation manual defines contemplation more specifically as simply resting silently in the divine presence without words being used. Contemplation involves a giving up of concepts. Meditation involves a giving up of many concepts by holding on to one concept as a focusing object, which is usually in the form of a word or words. Unlike meditation, contemplation involves letting go of concepts without having one thought as a focusing object. Thus contemplation is a state of objectless awareness.

Using this definition, contemplation is not active at all, but only passive. Being passive means placing no distracting self-created thoughts between yourself and God. It is possible at times to be in a temporary state of deep contemplation without any thoughts. However, generally speaking, you can be in a contemplative state even if thoughts are present in the mind as long as the thoughts do not become distracting by drawing your attention to them. Contemplation produces an inner absorption in which thoughts come and go without your paying attention to them as they pass by in your mind. Avoiding distracting thoughts creates an empty space, which allows God to be Himself in you. Resting passively in God is a time of not doing—meaning not even doing the holding of a sacred word. Resting in God is a time of *being* only. It is a letting go that creates a nonverbal invitation for the divine to take over within to produce an inner transformation. Contemplation occurs due to an overshadowing of the Holy Spirit in which the divine within becomes the active principle precisely because the seeker withdraws all self-initiated activity.

Using the definition of contemplation as resting silently in the divine without words being used, contemplation would not be associated with concentration or active practices. From the frame of reference of perceiving contemplation as resting in God, the term "active contemplation" would be a meaningless contradiction in terms. Christian Meditation or any other kind of meditation that uses active concentration could not be called contemplation, which is entirely receptive in nature. But saying that Christian Meditation is not contemplation, as it is defined in this manual, is not intended to imply that this method is not a valuable means of spiritual transformation as a meditation method.

The strength of Christian Meditation is the positive effect produced by the continuous repetition of a single mantra used unchangingly in daily meditation. The self-centered nature of modern society creeps into every aspect of daily life, including into spiritual endeavors. Focusing the mind consistently on a sacred word can free you from this self-centeredness and redirect your mind toward being God-centered. During meditation your mind will at times become distracted by stray thoughts. However, when you notice you have inadvertently forgotten your sacred word, you simply return to repeating your mantra again. This process of holding on to your sacred word allows you to disconnect from the habitual self-concern and self-consciousness that promotes anxiety and to become receptive to the peace that comes from trusting in God.

Christian Meditation can take you very far along on the spiritual path and produce many positive changes in consciousness. Many seekers are drawn to use this method exclusively as their lifelong means of divine attunement. Although the use of Christian Meditation is a very beneficial practice, the use of this method as one's sole way of inward seeking is not recommended in this book *as a lifelong practice* because the main purpose of this manual is to lead you to the experience of contemplation. The strength of Christian Meditation lies in its ability to help stabilize and calm the mind. This strength is very helpful especially for the beginning meditator, who may find it challenging initially to focus the mind because of numerous distracting thoughts.

On the other hand, the limitation that Christian Meditation presents is an inherent result of its strength. The strength of continuously holding the sacred word means that Christian Meditation is not contemplation and cannot lead directly to contemplation because this method does not allow you to completely rest in the objectless awareness of God. It is very true that repeating the sacred word will help to bring about a certain degree and perhaps a high degree of divine peacefulness by calming the mind. But Christian Meditation will not allow the complete emptiness of thought—empty even of repeating the sacred word—which would allow the deep resting in God that occurs is contemplation, as defined in this manual. This limitation is not really a problem for beginners because most beginning meditators are very easily distracted by stray thoughts and would find it very difficult to let go of all thoughts and enter contemplation. Consequently, most beginners would benefit by practicing Christian Meditation or a similar meditation practice using continuous concentration on one word or one focusing object.

In spite of the benefits of repeating a sacred word continuously, the time may come when the practice of Christian Meditation can be replaced by other methods that lead toward wordless contemplation, if that is your goal. Using Christian Meditation cannot produce contemplation, but it can help you make progress in calming the mind and thus increase your potential for being able to let go of thoughts. When you reach the point where you feel you have a greater potential for silencing the mind and resting in God during contemplation, it would be helpful for you to ask in prayer for inner guidance. You might want to ask a question such as, "Lord, would you want me to let go of repeating my sacred word continuously during my attunement in order to learn how to reach a deeper level of being aware of Your presence in the objectless awareness of contemplation?" If the answer is "No," then you can simply continue with your current practice of holding on to your sacred word continuously as the advocates of Christian Meditation recommend. If the answer is "Yes," then you can consider options for practicing contemplation.

If you are currently using a method of meditation, such as Christian Meditation, that uses the sacred word continuously and if you decide to move in the direction of experiencing contemplation, you will not have to give up the use of the sacred word entirely. The techniques that have been presented previously in this manual describe how to hold on to an affirmation of a sacred word or words, similar to the practice of Christian Meditation. But these techniques also indicate how to exercise the option of letting go of the affirmation in order to experience contemplation. When using the techniques in this manual, if you are a beginner, you may find it necessary initially to hold on to the affirmation for all or most of your meditation period. However, the purpose of the meditation techniques presented in this manual is to serve as a stepping stone that hopefully will lead you to the letting go of your affirmation in order to experience the silence and rest of contemplation.

B. Centering Prayer

Thomas Merton, the author of *Contemplative Prayer*, was a leading figure in the renewal of ancient Christian contemplative practices. Unlike this manual's definition of prayer as inner asking, Merton used the term *contemplative prayer* to describe the contemplative practice of letting go of words and images in order to find the divine presence within the depths of one's own heart. Merton spoke of inwardly finding one's center within oneself and within God. From Merton's emphasis on finding one's center came the term "Centering Prayer" to describe a method for entering into the contemplative experience based on traditional Christian practices of inward seeking. Centering Prayer has become in recent years a popular contemporary approach to inward seeking. Trappists Basil Pennington, the author of *Centering Prayer*, and Thomas Keating, the author of *Invitation to Love* and *Open Mind, Open Heart*, are two leading advocates of the practice of Centering Prayer.

Through the efforts of Basil Pennington and William Menninger, the practice of Centering Prayer began as a monastic renewal originating at St. Joseph's Abbey in Spencer, Massachusetts, in the 1970s. This method that benefitted the monks was passed on to visiting priests and later to lay people. Workshops were offered, and Thomas Keating initiated an advanced workshop for the purpose of training others to become teachers of Centering Prayer. In the mid-1980s, Thomas Keating gave instruction in Centering Prayer to some New York parishes. From these parishes the practice of Centering Prayer reached greater numbers of religious and lay people. The Contemplative Outreach, Ltd. was created in 1984 as an outreach program to meet the needs of seekers who want to deepen their prayer life. This outreach program encourages not only individual practice of Centering Prayer, but also the formation of small mutual support groups that practice of this method as a group experience.[3]

Like the practice of Christian Meditation, Centering Prayer employs the use of a sacred word (or words) as a focusing tool, but unlike Christian Meditation, Centering Prayer does not require the holding of the sacred word for the entire contemplative practice. In Centering Prayer the thought of the sacred word is held briefly at the beginning of your practice simply as a reminder of your intention to draw closer to the divine presence. You do not think about the meaning of the sacred word during your practice. The meaning of the sacred word is not relevant to your practice, because the sacredness of the word comes from being a symbolic reminder of your intention for inviting divine communion. Your intention is your willingness and choice to deepen your relationship with God.

You let go of the sacred word, which is only a symbol of your intention, in order to more directly invest in your intention itself for union with God. Various stray thoughts may pass by in your mind, and you can still be in a contemplative state of mind as long as you let each thought come and go without allowing your attention to be diverted from your intention of union with God. If you become preoccupied with distracting thoughts, it means you have forgotten your intention. Then you return your awareness to the sacred word to accomplish the dual purpose of turning away from distracting thoughts and returning back to your pure intention for the divine presence. After the sacred word has accomplished its purpose of calming the mind and reminding you of your intention, you can again let go of the sacred word in order to rest in the silence of the divine presence.

In contrast to Christian Meditation, which requires a greater degree of self-effort to hold on to the sacred word continuously, Centering Prayer relies to a greater degree on divine grace and produces what is sometimes called *passive contemplation* or *infused contemplation*. The words "passive" and "infused" emphasize that your work as a seeker is to get out of the way and do nothing to impede the action of the Holy Spirit. It is the divine impulse within the center of your being that accomplishes the real inner work of transformation. All that is required of you is to give your invitation to the Holy Spirit and to make every minute of your daily contemplative practice a renewal of your permission to allow the divine influence to bring about your inner transformation.

Centering Prayer has a basic premise similar to Christian Meditation, which is that the sacred word can direct the mind toward the presence of God and away from self-centered thinking. However, Christian Meditation places a premium on form being just as important as content in the sense that the form of the sacred word needs to be retained and continuously used as an expression of the content of the sacred word. The content of the sacred word is not the literal meaning of the sacred word; the content of the sacred word is your intention of seeking the divine presence. Centering Prayer emphasizes content over form in that the form of the sacred word is only a symbol that can be set aside and replaced entirely by the content of the sacred word, which is your intention. The form of the sacred word is only a tool to be used to bring your attention away from distracting thoughts and to simultaneously refocus on your intention. After having brought your attention back to your intention, you can set aside this refocusing tool, the sacred word. By setting aside the sacred word you can be aware of your intention alone that goes deeper than words. Instead of your sacred word being the primary focus of your spiritual practice, Centering Prayer places your intention of a closer union with God and your faith at the center of your spiritual practice.

Centering Prayer is also unlike Christian Meditation in that it has a very different basic premise regarding the nature of the mind itself. An underlying premise of Christian Meditation is that the nature of the mind is to actively multiply thoughts producing a complex network of thoughts. Therefore, the sacred word needs to be constantly repeated to tame this tendency to multiply many thoughts. This is partially correct in that the mind guided by the ego is inclined to multiply thoughts. Yet it is incorrect to attribute this multiplication of thoughts to the mind itself. It is really the ego, the false perception of a separate self, that is the cause of the multiplication of thoughts. The multiplication of thoughts is actually an unnatural condition of the mind. Different from the view of the mind as a thought multiplier, Centering Prayer has a basic underlying premise that the mind itself is naturally simple and uncomplicated. Letting go of the sacred word allows the mind to rest in God and return to its natural state of being simple and uncomplicated, just as God Himself is simple and uncomplicated in His oneness.

The mind is naturally inclined toward rest and silence. However, if the sacred word is always repeated continuously as in Christian Meditation, how will you ever discover for yourself the simplicity of the mind that is its natural state? What is unnatural to the mind, which is the multiplication of thoughts caused by the ego, appears natural to you because of your identification with the ego. Likewise, what is natural to the mind, which is restful silence and simplicity, appears unnatural to you because silence and simplicity are unnatural to the ego, with which you are identified. Centering Prayer gives you the opportunity of becoming aware of the natural condition of the mind by learning to rest in the divine presence. This experience of objectless awareness in contemplation allows you to let go of ego identification and become increasingly identified with your true nature in God.

Your first experiences of contemplative resting in the divine presence will give you a frame of reference to distinguish between the natural simplicity of the mind and the unnatural state of the mind produced by ego identification. It would be nice if you could enter and stay in the restful state of contemplation consistently and continuously for your entire inward practice, but this usually happens only after many years of daily practice. Your practice will most likely become an experience of resting in the divine presence only for short intervals of time. Intruding on your rest will be distracting thoughts, and your sacred word can be used to redirect your mind back to your intention of divine communion. Sometimes these distracting thoughts can be very emotionally charged, and more about releasing these thoughts during Centering Prayer will be described below. In summary, Centering Prayer is a very helpful and effective method for entering into contemplation and making progress in terms of releasing inner blocks and therefore becoming a better reflection of divine love.

C. A New Approach to Contemplation

Centering Prayer is certainly beneficial as a spiritual practice that leads to contemplation. This manual advocates an equivalent spiritual practice, which is called *Inner Silence Meditation*. Centering Prayer is described with a slightly different emphasis and terminology than Inner Silence Meditation. For example, in Centering Prayer any word may be chosen as your sacred word or words, and for Inner Silence Meditation any affirmation may also be chosen, but the choice of the Divine Name of Jesus Christ is specifically emphasized and recommended.

These two methods offer slightly different recommendations for how to use the sacred word. Both methods acknowledge that the sacred word can be used as an aid in letting go of distracting thoughts and is a way of assisting you to reach deeper and deeper levels of awareness. Also, both methods say that you do not think about the meaning of the sacred word during your inward seeking practice because the idea is to let go of discursive thinking in order to deepen your relationship with God and experience the divine presence. Both methods agree that the sacred word is a symbol of your intention. Although both methods agree on the *content* of the sacred word being a symbolic representation of your intention, they disagree about how to implement the *form* of the sacred word, such as the sound of the sacred word itself or the thought of the sacred word itself.

Advocates of Centering Prayer do not consider the form of the sacred word to be significant in itself, because the content of your sacred word is what is important. Consequently, your purpose in Centering Prayer is to stay centered in your intention, of which your sacred word is only a symbolic reminder. Inner Silence Meditation maintains that the form of the sacred word is indeed primarily a reminder of the content of your intention. In addition, the form itself can play an important secondary role in your practice. The form of your sacred word can be a stepping stone to the content of your sacred word, which is your intention of deepening your relationship with God. In particular, repeating the form of the sacred word can be very helpful in setting aside distracting thoughts. Since most beginners have difficulty with mental distractions, most beginners are likely to benefit from temporarily repeating the form of the sacred word in order to divert the mind away from distracting thoughts. Hopefully you will grow out of the need to repeat the form of the sacred word as you make progress in your practice of Inner Silence Meditation. Then you can rely only on your intention itself, which is an expression of your faith in God.

Inner Silence Meditation recommends repeating your sacred word at brief intervals to counteract distracting thoughts and calm the mind before letting go of the sacred word. Thomas Keating in his book about Centering Prayer, titled *Open Mind, Open Heart,* does not specifically emphasize that you "repeat" the sacred word, but does say to "return"[4] to the sacred word and "to go back"[5] to the sacred word to remind yourself of your intention when you realize that you are thinking of something other than your intention. You do not go back to a predetermined form of your sacred word, such as the repetition of the word itself, but you do go back to the thought of the sacred word in whatever way it appears to you, as a reminder of your intention. Thomas Keating explains that Centering Prayer uses the sacred word as a symbolic reminder of your intention to fully open yourself to God. The emphasis on "returning to" the sacred word rather than "repeating" the sacred word is intended to distinguish Centering Prayer from repetitive practices. Centering Prayer is a receptive practice that does not require automatic repetition in contrast to the continuous repeating of a Hindu mantra, which is a concentrative practice.

Thomas Keating describes below the process of using the sacred word:

> To start, introduce the sacred word in your imagination as gently as if you were laying a feather on a piece of absorbent cotton. Keep thinking the sacred word in whatever form it arises. It is not meant to be repeated continuously. The word can flatten out, become vague or just an impulse of the will, or even disappear. Accept it is whatever form it arises.
>
> When you become aware that you are thinking some other thought, return to the sacred word as the expression of your intent. The effectiveness of this prayer does not depend on how distinctly you say the sacred word or how often, but rather on the gentleness with which you introduce it into your imagination in the beginning and the promptness with which you return to it when you are hooked on some other thought.[6]

Ideally seekers can allow the sacred word to be used in the unstructured manner described above by Thomas Keating in order to let go of distracting thoughts and remind them of their intention, but most beginners find that it is difficult to let go of distracting thoughts. Because of this difficulty, Inner Silence Meditation includes an initial way of using the sacred word in a more structured manner in order to help you release distracting thoughts. This initial way involves repeating the form of the sacred word at brief intervals to counteract distracting thoughts, and at these intervals the sacred word is very temporarily used as a repeated mantra in meditation. This way of repeating the sacred word, which emphasizes form initially and then leads to the content of your intention, has been elaborated upon in previous descriptions of Inner Silence Meditation.

Four phases of using your affirmation in the practice of Inner Silence Meditation have already been identified in Chapters 6 and 8:

1. Mentally Pronouncing the Affirmation
2. Allowing the Affirmation to be as it presents itself.
3. The Affirmation Leads to Faithful Awareness
4. The Affirmation Culminates in Resting in God

This list of four phases encompasses not only the outer husk of the affirmation, which is the repeating of the form in words, but also the seed contained within. That seed is your desire for God and your acceptance of His presence in the darkness of faith. Your faith in turn leads you to the nourishing kernel of that seed, which is the resting in God that occurs during contemplation. The form of your affirmation points the way to the formlessness of contemplation, yet only divine grace makes the journey from form to formlessness possible. You can resist the divine grace of God drawing you to Himself. However, your affirmation serves the purpose of reminding you that you have decided to give up your resistance and have consented to the attraction of divine grace.

The first phase of using the affirmation, which emphasizes using the form of the affirmation in a structured repetitive manner, is inconsistent with the practice of Centering Prayer, which does not encourage reliance on the repetition of the sacred word. This initial phase is recommended especially for beginners, but is optional and therefore may be omitted. The final three more advanced phases, which use your affirmation in a less structured way, emphasize reminding you of the content of your intention. This less structured approach is very similar to, if not identical to, the practice of Centering Prayer, although the terminology may be slightly different. In the practice of Inner Silence Meditation, if you choose to omit the initial optional phase of using the affirmation, your practice would actually be indistinguishable from the practice of Centering Prayer.

In spite of some terminology differences, Centering Prayer and Inner Silence Meditation can be considered as roughly equivalent practices at the functional level, because both use the sacred word as a reminder of your intention of deepening your relationship with God and both lead through faith to the experience of contemplation. Even though these two methods of inward seeking are equivalent in terms of their practice and their common goal of contemplation, there is a difference in how Inner Silence Meditation is recommended to be used in this manual and how Centering Prayer is recommended to be used by its advocates. Centering Prayer is recommended to be used alone for your entire attunement, but does not exclude the use of other methods of prayer and attunement at other times. In contrast to using Centering Prayer exclusively, the daily practice of Inner Silence Meditation is recommended to be used in coordination with other specific techniques to enhance its effectiveness.

Centering Prayer is a one-size-fits-all contemplative method that does lead to contemplation for those who learn to use it effectively. But what about those who do not seem to benefit from the practice of Centering Prayer? After encountering many seekers who have come very far along the spiritual path, Thomas Keating discovered that a large percentage of these maintain that they have never had the grace of a *felt experience* of the divine presence associated with contemplative practice. Many of these seekers have spent most of their lives in a monastery, as a place and community designed for them to be contemplatives. After practicing contemplative prayer for twenty or thirty years without having felt any inner experience of the divine presence, these seekers in their latter years wonder if they have failed in their contemplative profession. Having no outward sign to reassure them, they must rely on their faith, which after all is the centerpiece of all Christian spiritual seeking.[7]

Thomas Keating has concluded that it is inappropriate to determine the value of your experience of Centering Prayer based on whether or not you have a consciously felt experience of the divine presence sinking into your faculties and producing overt changes of a mystical nature. There is a connection between the practice of Centering Prayer and *divine graces*, which are free mystical gifts from God. Indeed, the resting in God of contemplation is a gift in itself, and there are additional divine graces that come as gifts with your openness to God's presence. Divine graces are not earned by your seeking since they are gifts. However, without your seeking providing an invitation to God, you would not be able to recognize and receive these gifts, which are so freely given. But not all gifts of divine grace, which may be called *mystical graces*, are consciously experienced. You can still be receiving mystical graces without being consciously aware of God's presence penetrating into your faculties to produce an inner transformation. Thomas Keating maintains that some seekers may have these consciously felt mystical graces, and others may have mystical graces that are not consciously felt, but in either case the seeker can be going through an inner transformation through God's grace.[8]

Even though it is true that there are many seekers who are receiving "covert" mystical graces instead of "overt" mystical graces, it is somewhat startling what Thomas Keating says about the numbers of cloistered contemplatives who are not having a felt experience of the mystical graces. According to Keating, "Less than five percent of cloistered contemplatives that I know have the mystical experiences that Teresa or John of the Cross describe."[9] He goes on to say, "Their consolations are few and far between."[10]

Many of these cloistered monks practice Centering Prayer for many years without experiencing overt mystical graces. It is remarkable that they persevere for so long, relying solely on their faith without any overt confirmation of the divine presence. Thomas Keating remarks that in his experience those who are in some form of active ministry or who are married seem to have the most fulfilling mystical life. He concludes that perhaps God gives more overt graces to those in the world because of their greater need for His help and that covert graces are sufficient to meet the needs of those who live in cloistered settings.[11]

How many seekers in the world would practice Centering Prayer for thirty years without ever having experienced overt mystical graces? Generally seekers in the world who practice Centering Prayer do so because of overt benefits, or they eventually will give up the practice. Similarly, people who practice hatha yoga or any other spiritual disciplines do so because they experience the overt benefits, and that is why they continue with their practice. Overt benefits may sometimes be outwardly apparent to others, but the word "overt" as it is used here simply means *inwardly apparent in an obvious way*. So in spite of the truth that Centering Prayer can produce covert benefits, the bottom line is that this method or any other method will typically be maintained if it produces inwardly noticeable results.

Exceptional seekers, such as some cloistered monks, will continue to practice Centering Prayer and graciously accept covert divine graces, if that is all God gives. But even those seekers, who only receive covert divine graces, will continue to want overt divine graces as a confirming sign of a closer communion with God. Obviously the covert experience of the divine presence is usually a second choice, and the overt experience of the divine presence is what is really wanted. Consequently, it seems appropriate to ask the question, "How can Centering Prayer become more effective and overtly beneficial to those who want to use it?"

To answer this question, it is necessary to define any shortcomings that could be corrected. A potential shortcoming of Centering Prayer is that this method may be too advanced for some seekers. Making the leap from being highly conceptually oriented to the nonconceptual experience of contemplation may be very difficult for Westerners who are accustomed to mental activity. There is a need for a *transition* to help bridge the gap between mental activity and passive resting in God produced by letting go of mental activity. So there is not a problem with the practice of Centering Prayer itself, but rather a need for enhanced preparation for the experience of entering into the restful divine presence.

Thomas Keating believes there are beneficial methods seekers can find within Eastern and Western spiritual disciplines to help calm the mind that would serve as a preparatory foundation for practicing Centering Prayer and entering contemplation.[12] In the Western tradition, he notes that during the Middle Ages a practice called "lectio divina" was used as a preparation for entering the restful state of contemplation. Lectio divina, which means "divine reading," consisted of four stages. The first part was "lectio," the reading or listening to scripture, which was then followed by "meditatio," discursive prayer, reflecting on the meaning of this scripture.

This led to the third stage, "oratio," which is sometimes called "affective prayer," the inward and heart-felt spontaneous expression of the will directed toward God. In turn, this affective prayer in response to God ideally progressed to the final stage, "contemplio," resting in God.

Meditation, oratio, and contemplio following the reading of scripture would often overlap, rather than being distinctly separate from each other. These overlapping inner experiences within the context of lectio divina evolved by the sixteenth century into separate spiritual disciplines. The mental approach of discursive prayerful reflection could be one's spiritual discipline apart from the other approaches. On the other hand, affective prayer could be practiced alone, or contemplation could become the seeker's means of inward seeking. There was no longer a transition framework like lectio divine in which the seeker could learn to allow expression of mental prayer to lead into the experience of contemplation.[13]

This lack of a smooth framework, which could lead one step at a time to contemplation, is still a problem today. One suggestion Thomas Keating makes is that some seekers may want to prepare for Centering Prayer by reviving the tradition of lectio divina. To do this, the seeker can read sacred scripture and then reflect on the meaning of the text. After this reflection the seeker can turn to prayer addressed to God and conclude this preparatory attunement time with the practice of Centering Prayer. The original version of lectio divina in the Middle Ages did not provide specific instructions in how to enter into the contemplio (contemplation) stage of resting in God. The modern-day contribution that Centering Prayer provides is a comprehensive "how to" emphasis that describes the attunement process in detail.

However, there is still a problem with renewing lectio divina as the only means of preparing for Centering Prayer. The reading, the reflection, and the prayer aspects of lectio divina all rely on discursive thinking. Yet there is a large gap between using the mind for conceptual thinking and the letting go of conceptual thinking required for Centering Prayer. Certainly the discursive process of divine seeking is very helpful and necessary to instill the convictions of Christian faith. These serve as a conceptual foundation for progressing to contemplation. But the problem is with the attachment to holding on to this discursive approach so strongly that you cannot let go of it in order to experience contemplation.

The sixteenth-century mystic, St. John of the Cross, advises seekers to continue to use discursive reflection to approach God as long as seekers can do so effectively. St. John cautions that the time may come when God will take away the seeker's ability to use discursive reflection and express the will satisfactorily in prayer. In this case, God is calling the seeker to a deeper level of communication and relationship. Previously

God gave His blessing to the seeker's reasoning and to his experience of the senses to help him communicate with Him in prayer. However, in this transition to a deeper relationship, God withdraws the assistance He provided to reasoning and to the senses during prayer, rendering these faculties ineffective and unsatisfactory as a means of divine communication. Seekers can become very discouraged by this state, called the "night of sense." Because of being unable to pray, they may be tempted to imagine either that they have abandoned God or perhaps God has abandoned them. St. John says that instead of resisting this condition, the seeker would be wise to embrace the situation since it is a sign that God is leading the seeker in the direction of nonconceptual contemplation.[14]

The night of sense is most likely to occur with those seekers who have practiced discursive methods of attunement for a long time, perhaps many years. Such seekers may simply run out of inspiring new thoughts and feelings so that their prayer life becomes stale. At this point, a new way of approaching God without concepts may become appealing. But it would be a mistake to think that a seeker must experience the night of sense as a necessary prerequisite to be open to a nonconceptual approach to God. Instead of experiencing the night of sense, many seekers today, unlike seekers of the past who were less informed, are willing to pursue a nonconceptual approach because of being better informed in this age of communication. Thomas Keating attributes the modern-day renewal of interest in nonconceptual contemplative practices to two factors. One is to the rediscovery of the teachings of St. John of the Cross and other early Christian mystics. The other is Western exposure to Eastern spiritual disciplines, which have become popular in recent years.

Thomas Keating acknowledges the Western bias of relying on the mental approach toward spiritual seeking and feels that the interest in the East is a sign of what is missing in the West. Thomas Keating does say some Eastern disciplines can serve as a preparation for Centering Prayer and the experience of contemplation, yet he does not elaborate on the specific Eastern methods. Being an advocate of Centering Prayer, he does not personally recommend the concentrative method of continuously repeating a mantra, but he does recognize that many Western seekers, especially beginners, who generally have an active disposition, benefit by this practice, which can serve as a preparation for Centering Prayer.

The new approach to contemplation advocated in this manual relies on looking to the East as a resource for preparing the seeker to enter Christian contemplation in a systematic manner. Why look to the East? Both the East and the West have the goal of leading seekers from conceptual awareness to a deep level of nonconceptual awareness. But the East does a better job of leading the seeker in a step-by-step manner from one technique to another technique, and then to still another technique. Also, the East does a better job of including body awareness as part of the inward seeking growth process, which will eventually bring the seeker beyond body awareness.

Zen Buddhism recognizes the need for learning meditation techniques in a sequence starting with more elementary methods and leading to more difficult methods. A Zen roshi will assign to a beginner the method of counting the inhalations and exhalations. The beginning seeker will count from one to ten, and then repeat this sequence continuously while also focusing on the navel area. The second method assigned at a later date is the counting of just the exhalations. The third method is the counting of just the inhalations.[15]

The Rinzai sect of Zen Buddhism then leads the seeker to repeat a koan. Examples of koans are "What is my face before I was born?" and "What is the sound of one hand clapping?" Another koan is "Who am I?" which is likewise found in some yoga traditions of self-inquiry. These koans are questions that cannot be answered by intellectual responses. The solution to the question can only be a direct experience of the Reality that is beyond dualism. These koans are assigned by a roshi to a student with easier koans assigned first and more difficult koans assigned later. Unlike the Rinzai sect, the Soto sect of Zen Buddhism does not advocate the use of koans. The roshi belonging to the Soto sect guides the student in a systematic manner toward the practice of a nonconceptual approach to inward seeking, called *shikan-taza*. This spiritual discipline does not rely on holding on to any word, thought, or image and is an Eastern version of the objectless awareness of contemplation.[16]

Just as Zen Buddhist students are taught meditation techniques in a sequential manner, some yoga disciplines teach a sequence of focusing that leads in a systematic manner toward deeper levels of awareness. Similar to Zen Buddhism that focuses on the body, specifically the navel area, yoga techniques also focus on the body itself as a vehicle for spiritual transformation. Mantras are assigned for specific parts of the body, and the awareness is raised from the lower part of the body in a progressive manner upward toward the head. This is in sharp contrast to the traditional approach of Christian inward seeking that does not include body awareness as part of the process. There is a great deal that the West can learn from the East in regard to body awareness used as an aid to inward seeking. The importance of body awareness in meditation has been explained in Chapters 5 and 8.

The subtitle of this manual is *Opening to Divine Love in Contemplation* in order to emphasize that the techniques presented in this manual are a means of leading you from lower levels of awareness to contemplation, which is an experience of divine love. There are *centers of awareness*, which are considered to be *spiritual centers*. These centers of awareness are like inner doors, which are normally closed. Specific meditation techniques can be used in coordination with the action of the Holy Spirit to open these inner doors to create a doorway to contemplation, which in turn leads to higher consciousness. These inner doors are associated with parts of the human body along the cerebral-spinal axis and ideally open from the bottom upward.

In Eastern philosophy these centers of awareness are called *chakras* and will be elaborated upon in the next chapter. In the West the best symbol for these centers of awareness is the story of Jacob's ladder. In the Old Testament story, Jacob had a dream of angels descending and ascending on a ladder extending from the earth to Heaven. The rungs on Jacob's ladder symbolize the different levels of awareness that lead in a step-by-step progression from earthly awareness to heavenly awareness. In this manual the image of the rungs of Jacob's ladder can symbolize different techniques used in sequence that help to awaken higher and higher levels of awareness leading to contemplation.

Using this image of the rungs of Jacob's ladder as the techniques leading to higher awareness, Centering Prayer centered on contemplation is a single high rung on this ladder, and concentrative forms of mental focusing for inward seeking are very low rungs on this same ladder. Concentrative forms of attunement involve holding on to one or more spiritual thoughts. Contemplation involves the letting go of all thoughts and resting in the Spirit. Holding on to thoughts and letting go of all thoughts are two very different processes. Thus there is a large gap between the lower conceptual rungs of Jacob's ladder and the higher nonconceptual rung of contemplation. Many seekers are not successful in being able to bridge this gap and experience contemplation. To assist seekers in bridging this gap, what is needed is a sequence of rungs that can serve as steps leading to the experience of contemplation. One of the purposes of this manual is to provide a specific series of steps to fill this gap in order to make it easier for the seeker to let go of relying on mental activity and make the transition to contemplative resting in God.

Consequently, the major method recommended in this manual is Christian Yoga Meditation, in which there is a sequence of six specific techniques that are rungs on Jacob's ladder. The first five techniques lead toward the experience of contemplation in the practice of Inner Silence Meditation, which is equivalent to the practice of Centering Prayer. This sequence of techniques in the practice of Christian Yoga Meditation is designed to serve as a systematic series of steps for learning how to enter into contemplation.

D. Divine Healing

The previous section explains how a series of less advanced techniques can provide the preparation to lead the seeker to experience the more advanced state of resting in God during contemplation. The six methods of Christian Yoga Meditation can meet this need for seekers, who have never meditated or who have tried techniques but have been unable to overtly experience mystical graces that would confirm their faith in the divine presence within. However, would the sequence of techniques in Christian Yoga Meditation be of any significant benefit to you if you are already an experienced meditator, who perhaps uses Centering Prayer? Would Christian Yoga Meditation be helpful for you if you have already experienced mystical graces and the divine presence in contemplation?

To make this determination requires a closer look at the internal process described in Chapter 2 as "divine healing," which would include spiritually guided psychotherapy. Divine healing is a process of letting go of inner blocks. These obstacles may be triggered and released by practicing meditation, and even deeper blocks can be released through experiencing contemplation. During Centering Prayer your intention to enter the divine presence is not just an invitation to be at peace and rest. More importantly, it is also an invitation for transformation. Typically your inward practice will be an alternation between times of contemplative rest and distracting thoughts. If you are a beginner in practicing meditation, your mind may be so unruly that distracting thoughts may dominate your meditation period. However, because you are a beginner, these thoughts usually are the ordinary thoughts, judgments, and concerns of everyday living. After some time you will be able to let go of these passing mundane thoughts and discover contemplative intervals of peace and increase the frequency and duration of these peaceful intervals. You will still have to deal with distracting thoughts, but there will be a balance between the peaceful intervals and the distractions. The remainder of this section will assume that you have already gone through the beginning phase of learning how to let go of everyday thoughts and that you can experience intervals of peace during your attunement practice.

As you become a more experienced meditator, you will continue to encounter ordinary distracting thoughts, but in addition you will perhaps experience stronger thoughts that have a certain force behind them and therefore present a greater potential for distraction. These distracting thoughts may carry with them tension and emotions that have been suppressed. These emotionally charged thoughts may originate from immature childhood emotions and experiences that were hidden in the subconscious mind, rather that being fully resolved and released. The movement of these distracting thoughts from the subconscious mind into the conscious mind intrudes on your restful contemplation, but needs to be understood as being part of a divine healing process.

Since your true nature is love, the divine presence within you acts as a healing influence, helping you to return to the awareness of your love nature. Your times of resting in God create an inner mental environment conducive to healing. Inner healing is produced by releasing blocks to love. But you cannot generally release inner blocks while you are still hiding these blocks from your conscious awareness. Only after bringing your inner blocks to your conscious awareness can you then give these blocks to the Holy Spirit for inner healing to occur. Sometimes seekers mistakenly think that becoming aware of unresolved and immature emotions and tensions is a step backward spiritually. In fact, this is a sign of spiritual maturity, showing that the seeker is strong enough to face inner fears with divine assistance.

Ideally when these previously hidden thoughts and emotions are released into the conscious mind, you will be able to allow these to come and go without paying attention to them. Hopefully you will be able to remain centered on your intention to be aware of the divine presence. However, if you are distracted by these emotionally charged thoughts, you can simply return to repeating your sacred word as a reminder of your intention and as a way of diverting your mind away from the distracting thoughts.

Nonetheless, the ideal way of handling emotionally charged thoughts doesn't always work in practical experience. After making some progress with your practice of Centering Prayer, you may discover that instead of reducing distracting thoughts, you spend most or even all of your attunement practice being distracted. If this happens, you may find that emotionally charged thoughts have such an increased force and effect on your mind that they dominate your inward awareness. The reasons for these thoughts, such as unresolved childhood experiences or other inner conflicts, may not come to your conscious awareness. Even though the reasons may not be apparent, the tension, anxiety, and emotions can monopolize your attunement period. You may have to repeat your sacred word continuously in order to turn your awareness away from these disturbing thoughts, and even this practice may not succeed in calming the mind. As an aftereffect, you may become depressed for short or even long periods of time. All this unloading of the subconscious mind may be seen by you as proof of going backward in your spiritual life, rather than as a necessary step in your process of divine healing.

Your practice of Centering Prayer expresses your intention of having a closer personal relationship with God. In addition, manifesting your intention involves surrendering to God's Will, allowing Him to take you by the hand and lead you through whatever it takes to form a deeper relationship. What is required is not so much your willingness to face God, but rather your willingness to face your *self*—or more specifically to face your *shadow*. What is your shadow? It is a collection of thoughts in your subconscious mind. These thoughts represent the parts of yourself that you have deemed unacceptable and so have denied. This shadow is not objectively real and not part of your true Self. However, by hiding these emotionally charged thoughts away in your subconscious mind, you have given these thoughts a subjective reality within the private world of your own mind. You can change your mind about these thoughts and let go of them by giving them to the Holy Spirit for disposal. But first you have to bring this shadow portion of your mind out into the light so the divine presence can shine away the shadow. Because the emotionally charged thoughts in the shadow portion of the mind involve raw emotions, such as fear, anger, or pain, it takes courage to face these stark emotions. It also takes faith in the strength and love of God to support you during this purification process.

Facing this shadow part of your mind may occur only intermittently as part of your daily attunement practice over several years and may not overlap into your daily life, except occasionally. On the other hand, you may go through many short periods of depression that come and go because the shadow is being confronted and released at a deeper level. In your daily life experiences, conflicts or disturbances may occur that are a reflection of your inner turmoil. The outer experiences are another way for you to participate in your purification process with the help of divine grace. It is possible that you may even experience long periods of depression as you go through facing the shadow within. There is even the potential that at some time you may experience a spiritual crisis and turning point in what St. John of the Cross calls the "dark night of the soul," which will be described in greater detail in Chapter 13. This whole purification process may sound a bit daunting to you. A consoling factor is that you will face only as much of your shadow side as you are willing to look at. You will gain the growth that you are seeking and will go as far along the path as is appropriate to meet your needs at that time.

Suppose for a moment that you are very dedicated, and you want to travel very far along the contemplative path. In this case, it will be very important for you to be willing to confront the shadow at a deep level. Yet the typical Christian approach to releasing inner blocks may not be the best way to face and release the shadow. It is helpful to realize that you have alternatives, just as there are alternative routes of climbing a mountain to reach the peak.

The West and the East take different inward seeking routes, which can be illustrated by the following analogy: A man buys a flat field with a large tree in the middle. He decides to cover the entire field with cement, which surrounds even the base of the trunk of the tree. Then he decides to cover the entire tree with a large black tarp. Next he sells the field to a second man, who decides to take the black tarp off of the tree. The tree flourishes for a while in the sunshine. But after some time passes he sees that the tree is wilting because the heat of the sun is drying up the tree, so he puts the black tarp back on the tree. Next he sells the field to a third man who decides to break up and remove all the cement on the field. After the cement is removed, the tree can receive the nourishment of rainwater coming upward through the roots. Because of the water coming upward, the previously wilting tree is revived, and there is no longer a concern about the tree withering because of the heat of the sun. Thus he takes the tarp off, and the tree flourishes because of the harmonious combination of the rainwater rising up and the sunshine descending down.

This analogy is based on the premise that, generally speaking, there are three primary levels of transformation and healing that need to occur in order to return to wholeness. The top level is associated with mental transformation and the top of the body, the head. The middle level is associated with emotional transformation and with the middle level of the body, especially the heart. The bottom level is associated with physical transformation and the lower part of the body, including the navel area, the generative organs, and the base of the spine. In the analogy, the tree as a whole symbolizes the seeker. The branches and leaves represent the top-level mental transformation. The trunk represents the middle-level emotional transformation. The roots represent the bottom-level physical transformation.

The first man in the story, who puts the black tarp over the tree and places cement on the field, symbolizes the activities of separation that oppose harmony, integration, and unity. The second man, who takes the black tarp off the tree, symbolizes the typical Christian "top-down" orientation to divine healing and transformation. Removing the tarp from the top of the tree represents uncovering the mind first and the disregard of the lower levels. Just as the tree prospers at first because of the descending sunshine, the seeker flourishes at first with this entirely mental orientation. Like the excessive heat from the sun that eventually becomes oppressive to the tree, the exclusively mental orientation can eventually cause problems for the seeker. The cause of the tree's problem is that the ground level has been covered over by cement. Therefore, the tree cannot receive water coming up from below for nourishment to balance the heat descending from above. Likewise, the seeker relying exclusively on the top-down mental approach cannot receive nourishment from the lower level energy rising up from below to create an inner balance.

Examples of the top-down orientation are both Centering Prayer and Christian Meditation, which are mental practices that focus on thoughts alone and disregard body awareness. Although Centering Prayer leads to the nonconceptual awareness of contemplation, it is included here as a mental method of transformation because it is designed to change the mind and its practice totally disregards energy rising upward from the lower part of the body awareness. The practice of Centering Prayer brings many benefits in the beginning just as the tree at first flourishes in the sunlight. Yet eventually so much of the shadow can be released during Centering Prayer that the seeker can become overwhelmed and depressed. This is similar to the tree in the analogy that wilts because it is oppressed by heat from above and not physically nourished by water coming upward through its roots. The lofty top-down orientation to transformation without adequate integration of the emotions and physical body can eventually stagnate and produce the spiritual crisis of the "dark night of the soul," described in Chapter 13. This turning point can certainly be met and overcome with faith and perseverance. However, it is very important to understand that this is certainly not the *only* route to divine healing and transformation.

The third man, who breaks up the cement first and removes it so the tree can get water for nourishment, symbolizes the typical Eastern "bottom-up" orientation to divine transformation. Breaking up the cement and removing it represents starting first by placing emphasis on the lowest and most concrete level that needs transformation, which is the physical level. For example, in Zen Buddhism the meditator focuses on the navel area and in certain kinds of yoga meditation disciplines the seeker focuses first on the base of the spine before raising his awareness to higher levels. In the analogy the breaking of the cement allows water to nourish the tree, and similarly Eastern methods encourage the raising of the nourishing energy of the *kundalini*.

Of course, the kundalini can be improperly raised by extreme spiritual disciplines and produce very traumatic results. Such negative experiences have given the kundalini a bad name in the West, but actually the kundalini can be raised through moderate meditation methods in a slow and gentle manner. The kundalini acts as a means of bringing attention to inner blocks in a systematic way as it rises and helps to remove these blocks. Instead of becoming overwhelmed with blocks as can happen in the top-down orientation, the bottom-up orientation deals with releasing blocks in a piecemeal manner that follows a natural and somewhat predictable manner, as is described in Chapter 12. This natural process helps you face your shadow in a step-by-step manner in which each step builds on the previous step in a strengthening manner. As is the case with the top-down orientation, all the emotions will have to be addressed, including depression, but there is much less potential for being overwhelmed by depression in this approach.

The sequence of six techniques combined in the practice of Christian Yoga Meditation is an effective means of implementing the bottom-up orientation to inward seeking and to address the piecemeal removal of inner blocks. If you are practicing Centering Prayer exclusively, you may run into difficulties with your practice because of forceful distracting thoughts and emotions due to the release of too many unresolved parts of your shadow all at once. In this case, because you have no alternate attunement practice, you will just have to continue with your practice of Centering Prayer, even if your practice is totally dominated by distractions. In contrast to having only one meditative practice, the six techniques of Christian Yoga Meditation provide flexibility. If you have difficulty with Inner Silence Meditation because of too many unruly distracting thoughts, you can choose to spend more time on the previous five techniques. The first five techniques of Christian Yoga Meditation focus initially on calming the body, then calming the emotions, and then calming the mind. This sequence of inner calming, which is a bottom-up orientation, provides a preparation for entering the silence of contemplation. After becoming calmer within, you will be better prepared to proceed to Inner Silence Meditation and enter the rest of contemplation. When your practice of Inner Silence Meditation improves and your intervals of resting in God increase, you can decrease the time for the preparatory first five methods and increase the time for Inner Silence Meditation.

The techniques of Christian Yoga Meditation have been described previously as a Jacob's ladder, leading the seeker one step at a time from lower levels of awareness to higher levels of awareness. In Jacob's dream image of a ladder the angels are ascending and descending between earth and Heaven, but from the perspective of the seeker his approach obviously has to be a bottom-up orientation. Even though the seeker may receive divine blessings from above, he has to start his journey in the lower level awareness of the earth where his is now and from the earth move upward.

What may not be so obvious about the dream image of Jacob's ladder is that the ladder that leads from lower levels of awareness to higher levels of awareness is within the body itself. The Kingdom of God is literally within one's self. Jacob's ladder has its base in the earth, which in the body is the base of the spine where the kundalini lies sleeping and waiting to be awakened in order to trigger higher levels of awareness as it rises. The top of Jacob's ladder is in Heaven, which in the body is the crown of the head or some would say just above the head. The raising of the awareness of the seeker is a natural process of the kundalini rising in a progressive manner from the base of the spine upward along the center of the body to the top of the head.

As has been emphasized, the typical mistake made by Christian seekers is to ignore this bottom-up natural process and to focus only on the top part of Jacob's ladder. As mentioned previously, Thomas Keating offers the theory that cloistered Christian seekers are less successful in experiencing overt mystical graces than seekers in the world due to God giving more grace to seekers in the world, who need more divine help. But if this theory that God gives more grace to seekers in the world is accurate, then it would logically follow that Eastern seekers in monastic settings would have less of a mystical life than Eastern seekers in the world. Nonetheless, it is generally believed that Eastern monks have a robust, mystical spiritual life. My own opinion is that Eastern monastic seekers take the bottom-up approach to contemplative seeking that simply produces better consciously felt results.

This Eastern bottom-up approach facilitates the rising of the kundalini, the removing of inner blocks, and the revealing of the divine presence. In contrast to this, Christian cloistered monks use the top-down contemplative approach that ignores body awareness. Their restrictive lifestyle tends to deny and suppress the creative energy, which has the potential to be used for sexual purposes or to be raised up for higher spiritual purposes. The setting aside of sexual desires for moral reasons can be an asset to spiritual growth as long as this abstinence is accompanied by a corresponding raising up of the same creative energy for spiritual purposes. However, the problem for cloistered monks occurs when the sexual energy is suppressed and also the creative energy is suppressed instead of being raised up for spiritual purposes. It is this suppression of creative energy that prevents the majority of cloistered monks from experiencing felt mystical graces.

The limitations of the cloistered lifestyle tend to deny and hide inner blocks, especially blocks related to the middle and lower part of the body. These kinds of blocks are identified in detail in Chapter 12, which explains the process of removing inner blocks, starting at the bottom and moving upward. The denial of inner blocks prevents these obstacles from being revealed, confronted, and surrendered to the Holy Spirit. Implementing a bottom-up approach to contemplation could correct this situation by helping to raise creative energy and by helping to reveal inner blocks so they can be offered to the Holy Spirit for healing.

Christian seekers in the world who likewise use a top-down approach are more successful at having consciously felt mystical experiences than cloistered monks because their lifestyle is more conducive to expressing creative energy. Not being in a structured monastic setting, Christian seekers in the world are exposed to a greater variety of relationships and life experiences that tend to prevent the seeker from being in denial about his inner blocks. The revealing of these inner blocks in life experiences force the seeker to directly confront these inner blocks and to release them with the help of the Holy Spirit.

Both Christian cloistered monks and Christian seekers in the world would benefit by a Christian bottom-up approach to contemplation. The sequence of six techniques of Christian Yoga Meditation is designed as a contemplative bottom-up approach to contemplation. The first technique in this sequence brings the awareness to the lower part of the body and invites the Holy Spirit in coordination with the gentle rising of the kundalini to release inner blocks at the physical level. The second technique brings attention to the heart and invites the Holy Spirit along with the rising of the kundalini to remove inner obstacles at the emotional level. The third method focuses within the head and invites the Holy Spirit in coordination with the rising of the kundalini to release inner blocks at the mental level. The fourth technique invites the Holy Spirit to integrate the physical, emotional, and mental levels of your being. The fifth technique invites the unifying influence of the Holy Spirit to open you to the intuitive awareness of your divine oneness. Finally this leads to the sixth technique, which is Inner Silence Meditation (equivalent to Centering Prayer) that leads to contemplation.

Like the rungs of Jacob's ladder, each method builds on the previous technique and smoothly leads to the next technique. Collectively the first five techniques form a solid foundation for entering contemplation during Inner Silence Meditation. The advanced state of resting in God during contemplation is a surrender, to the best of your ability, to God. In this surrender you give your consent to the activity and presence of God. This is not a lifelong commitment. It is only a moment to moment surrender. Nevertheless, the inner blocks of the human condition make it extremely difficult to surrender your whole self to God even for a few moments.

Temporarily surrendering all of yourself, including even your thoughts, is difficult to do because it requires a willingness to be vulnerable and naked before God. Intimacy with God, like intimacy at the human level, requires a gradual transition from friendship to intimacy. You can best learn to surrender to God by surrendering piece by piece before a deeper surrender can be made. The first five techniques of Christian Yoga Meditation are really a sequence of surrendering yourself in parts as a preparation for surrendering yourself more completely to God in contemplation. Through practicing this sequence of techniques you surrender the physical, the emotional, the mental, the integrating, and then the intuitive parts of yourself to God. These partial surrenders prepare you for the more holistic surrender that occurs in contemplation during the practice of the final technique of Inner Silence Meditation.

Each of the partial surrenders of the first five techniques of Christian Yoga Meditation involve a release of inner blocks in a natural manner corresponding to the rising of the kundalini that helps facilitate this purification process. A detailed explanation of the rising of the kundalini is provided in the next chapter. The rising of the kundalini, guided by the Holy Spirit, helps you to release inner blocks of tension, anxiety, and emotions from the subconscious mind. Also, blocks are released from all parts of the body, from the lowest to the highest in a natural process. The process of releasing blocks corresponds to the stages of death and dying, identified by Elisabeth Kubler-Ross in her book *On Death and Dying.* This natural process is elaborated upon in Chapter 12, which describes emotions in relation to meditation. The six techniques of Christian Yoga Meditation are just six rungs on Jacob's ladder to higher awareness. There are other helpful rungs below these, such as various forms of prayer and devotion, as well as hatha yoga postures and breathing practices that can assist your growth. There are also rungs of attunement above the techniques of Christian Yoga Meditation. Examples of these higher techniques are presented in Chapter 14, which emphasizes learning how to open to light and love.

---

1. Thomas Ryan, C.S.P., *Prayer of Heart and Body: Meditation and Yoga as Christian Spiritual Practice* (New York, New York/Mahwah, New Jersey: Paulist Press, 1995), pp. 41-42

2. Ibid., pp. 65-67

3. Thomas Keating, *Open Mind, Open Heart: The Contemplative Dimension of the Gospel* (New York, New York: The Continuum International Publishing Group, 2001), Copyright 1986, 1992 by St. Benedict's Monastery, reprinted by permission of The Continuum International Publishing Group, pp. 143-144

4. Ibid., p. 48

5. Ibid., p. 48

6. Ibid., p. 110

7. Ibid., p. 10

8. Ibid., pp. 10-11

9. Ibid., p. 11

10. Ibid., p.11

11. Ibid., p. 11

12. Ibid., p. 29

13. Ibid., pp. 20-21

14. Ibid., pp. 28-29

15. Philip Kapleau, *The Three Pillar of Zen* (New York, London, Toronto, Sydney, Auckland: Anchor Books, Doubleday and Company, 1965, 1980), pp. 35-41

16. Ibid., p. 49

11

CREATIVE ENERGY
AND MEDITATION

≈ • ≈

A. Creative Energy and Spiritual Centers

Used in sequence, the first five body awareness techniques of Christian Yoga Meditation systematically address all those aspects of your being that you normally attempt to keep under your control. These techniques allow you to transfer your control over the functions of your life to the Holy Spirit in order to bring about an inner transformation. This transfer of control cannot be done in one decision all at once. Your invitation for the Holy Spirit to take over the functions of your life needs to be made on a daily basis. Otherwise your daily thoughts and actions would in themselves tell the Holy Spirit that you have taken back control of these functions.

With your permission renewed on a daily basis, the Holy Spirit can be placed in charge of not only the functions that you normally attempt to control, but also the functions that are not normally in your conscious awareness. This would include allowing the Holy Spirit to take control of the subtle energy within the body. The term in yoga used to describe this subtle energy is *prana*. The Sanskrit word "prana" literally means both "breath" and "life energy." It is closely associated with the breath, but is not the same as the air in your lungs. Prana is considered to be the vital life force energy in its natural undiluted state. However, prana can be subdivided and can take the form of many different "breaths," such as *apana, samana, udana, and vyana*, in order to perform different functions in the body.[1] These different subdivisions of prana are different kinds of vital energy, but are closely associated with different types of consciousness.

Normally energy is thought of as being separate from consciousness. In yoga philosophy, prana is not considered to be exactly the same as consciousness, but is considered to be very closely associated with consciousness. In fact, prana is so closely connected with consciousness that prana always accompanies awareness. Consequently, when you consciously focus your awareness on any part of the body, you will automatically bring prana to that part of the body.

There is a correlation between the amount of prana present and the levels of consciousness. Lower levels of prana are associated with lower consciousness and higher levels of prana are associated with higher levels of consciousness. Increasing the prana in the body leads to the raising of consciousness. Prana can be increased in the body through the practice of breath control, called *pranayama*. The breathing techniques of pranayama enable the practitioner to extract and absorb prana from the air. Control of prana can be used to control the life energies in the body in order to increase vital health, but more importantly to the raise of consciousness.

This manual will often refer to "energy" that may or may not be felt within the body while practicing meditation. This energy is referring to prana. During your practice of Christian Yoga Meditation, you are most likely to experience this energy or prana in a focusing area, such as the navel area, the heart, the brow, or the crown of the head. The reason why you may feel this energy is that when you hold your awareness on a particular focal point in the body, prana actually goes to that area of the body. The focusing produces what can be called a "concentration" of prana, which can also be thought of as a "concentration" of consciousness. Focusing on a particular area in the body can produce a change in the body energy and in the level of consciousness in that part of the body.

But your purpose in Christian Yoga Meditation is not to use the force of your will to impose a change onto the body. Your purpose is to bring your awareness and the prana, which naturally follows your awareness, to focusing areas within the body in order to surrender these to the action of the Holy Spirit. In this way you are assisting the Holy Spirit in transforming the energy of the body and the levels of consciousness within you, but allowing the Holy Spirit to actually make only those changes that are really needed.

In the lowest portion of the torso there is a storehouse of prana. This prana rises from the lower part of the back and front of the body. In this manual the rising energy will be called "creative energy." By your surrender to the Holy Spirit, you can allow the creative energy stored in the lowest portion of the spine and in the generative organs to rise upward. It might be helpful here to explain a little more about this creative energy that rises in the back of the body and in the front of the body. The creative energy that rises in the back of the body makes its way upward along what can be called the "cerebral-sacral axis." Along this vertical axis the creative energy rises up the spine and extends to the five nerve plexuses, which are networks of intertwined nerves extending from the ganglia that run along the spinal column. These nerve plexuses are shown on the opposite page.

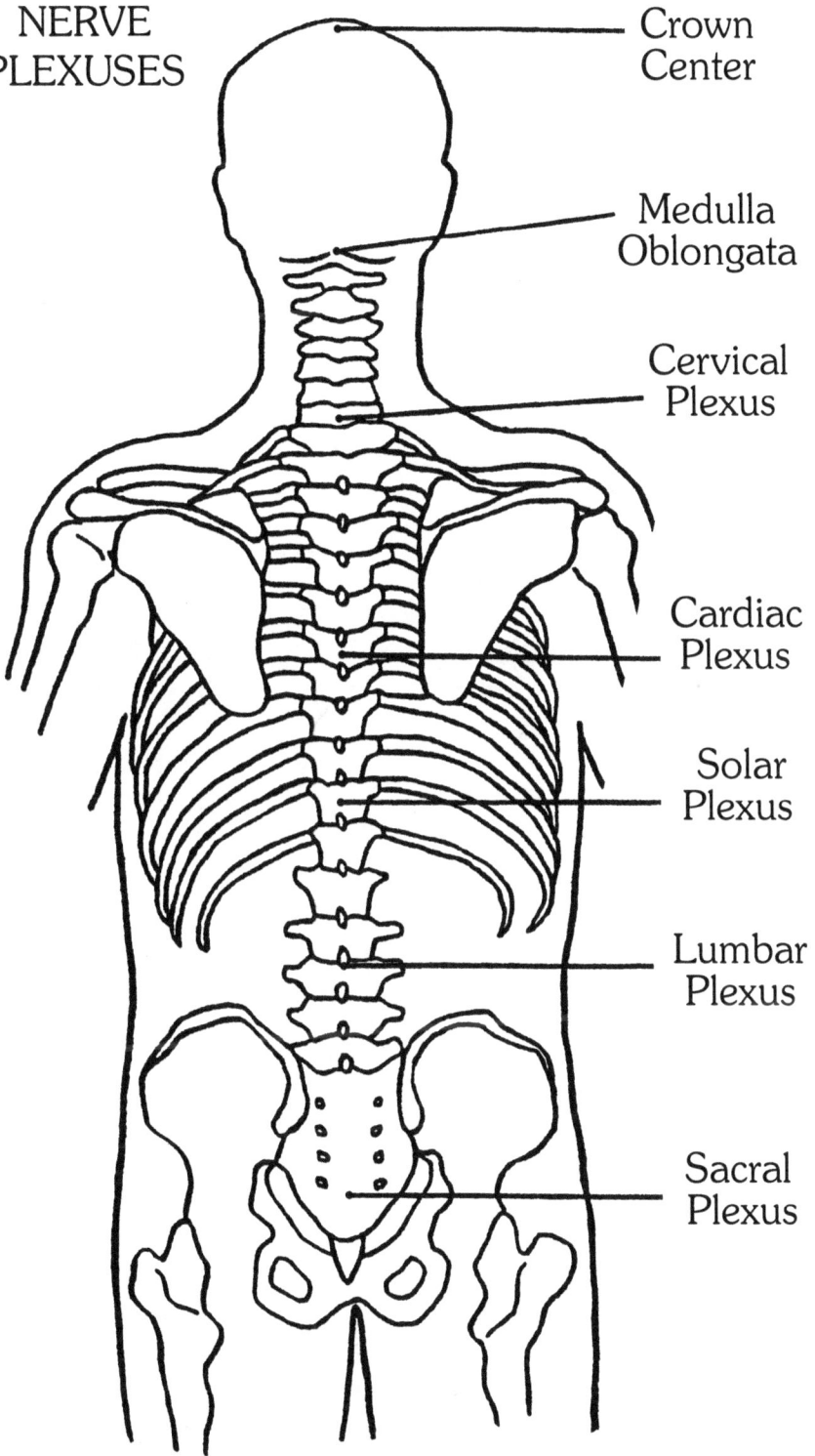

NERVE PLEXUSES

Crown Center

Medulla Oblongata

Cervical Plexus

Cardiac Plexus

Solar Plexus

Lumbar Plexus

Sacral Plexus

Pineal Gland   Pituitary Gland

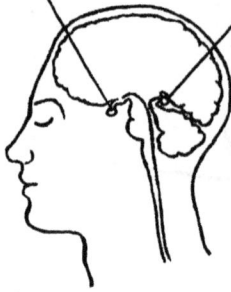

SPIRITUAL
CENTERS
AND
ENDOCRINE
GLANDS

Crown Center

Brow Center

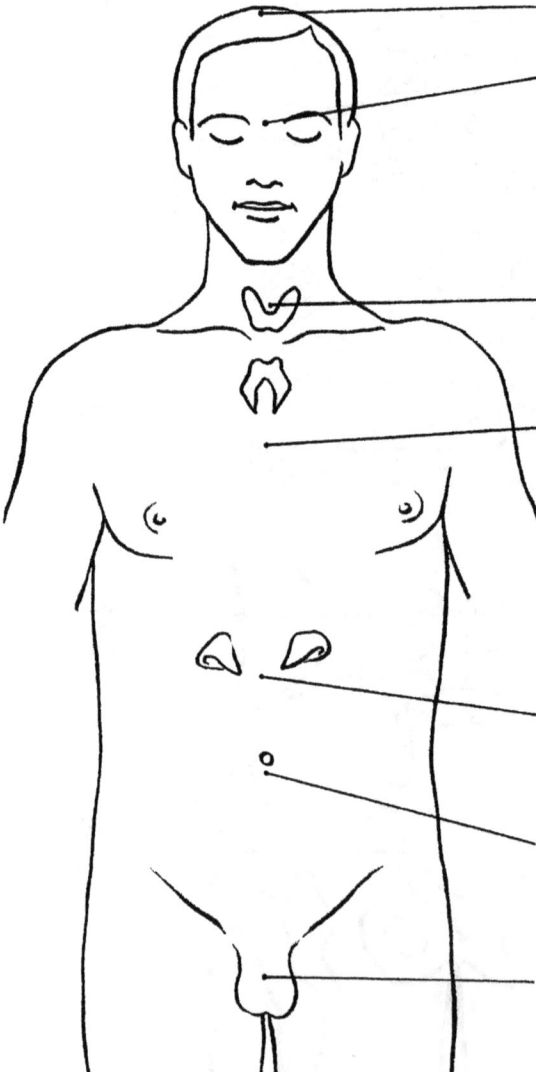

Throat Center
(Thyroid Gland)

Heart Center
(Thymus Gland)

Adrenal Center
(Adrenal Glands)

Navel Center

Gonad Center
(Gonads)

The nerve plexuses in sequence from the bottom upward are the sacral plexus, the lumbar plexus (hypogastric plexus), the solar plexus, the cardiac plexus, and the cervical plexus (pharyngeal plexus).[2] Then the rising energy goes to the medulla oblongata in the back of the head and finally goes to the crown of the head.

The creative energy that rises in the front of the body moves upward through parts of the body related to six endocrine glands. From the bottom to the top these are the gonads (sexual organs), the adrenal glands, the thymus gland, the thyroid gland, the pineal gland, and the pituitary gland. These endocrine glands regulate the whole body through the hormones that they secrete. The endocrine glands are illustrated on the opposite page along with the spiritual centers associated with each gland.

As the creative energy rises, it moves up Jacob's ladder from one level of consciousness to another. This idea of different levels of consciousness in different parts of the body is not an accepted belief in the West, where the brain is considered the physical location of consciousness. In yoga philosophy there is a relationship between different parts of the body and different levels of consciousness. Similar to the way that some parts of the body have life-sustaining functions and others do not, some parts of the body have a closer relationship with consciousness than others. Certain parts of the body have high concentrations of consciousness, and in these places the connection between the physical body and consciousness is particularly close. Because there is a close link between prana and consciousness, the various parts of the body that are closely connected to consciousness have high concentrations of prana. In addition to higher concentrations of consciousness and prana, certain parts of the body have different types of consciousness and therefore correspondingly different kinds of prana that perform different functions in the body.

In yoga philosophy there are centers of consciousness within the body called *chakras*. The number of chakras varies depending on which school of yoga philosophy is followed, but this manual will focus on seven centers of consciousness. Chakras, which literally mean "wheels," are dynamic concentrations of consciousness that contain concentric spheres of very high concentrations of prana. There are seven parts of the back of the body and seven parts of the front of the body that are parts of the physical anatomy that are related to the chakras. But the chakras themselves are nonphysical centers of consciousness. The seven parts of the back and corresponding seven parts in the front of the body have high concentrations of prana and consciousness, and they represent seven different levels of consciousness related to the chakras that are associated with these parts of the body.

The location of the chakras is usually most closely associated with seven parts of the back of the body. The first five parts are the vertebra in the spine related to each of the five nerve plexuses. The last two parts of the back of the body related to the chakras are the medulla oblongata and the crown center. Instead of emphasizing these parts of the back of the body, this book will highlight the seven parts of the front of the body that are associated with the chakras. In this manual these seven parts of the front of the body will be called, for lack of better terminology, "spiritual centers" or "centers of awareness." These spiritual centers from bottom to top are:

SPIRITUAL CENTERS OF AWARENESS

1. GONAD CENTER — related to the sacral plexus and sexual organs
   • downward-flowing creative energy

2. NAVEL CENTER — related to the lumbar plexus
   • the "physical center"
   • focusing area for Centering Meditation
   • raises creative energy up from gonad center

3. ADRENAL CENTER — related to the solar plexus and adrenal glands

4. HEART CENTER — related to the cardiac plexus, heart, and thymus
   • the "emotional center"
   • related to love, compassion, and devotion
   • focusing area for Heart Meditation
   • raises creative energy up through adrenal center

5. THROAT CENTER — related to the cervical plexus and thyroid

6. BROW CENTER — related to the medulla oblongata and pineal gland
   • the "mental center"
   • focusing area for Brow Meditation
   • raises creative energy up through throat center

7. CROWN CENTER — related to the crown of the head and pituitary gland
   • the "divine center" through which the Holy Spirit works
   • focusing area for Crown Meditation
   • activated during Oneness Meditation
   • activated during Inner Silence Meditation
   • activated during contemplation

The number of chakras is debatable depending on which yoga texts are consulted, ranging from as few as five main chakras to as many as thirteen main chakras, with numerous minor chakras. The yoga schools that advocate seven chakras usually present a slightly different sequence than the seven centers of awareness. One difference is that yoga schools advocating seven chakras indicate that the second chakra (not the first chakra) consists of the sexual organs. These yoga schools maintain that the first chakra is the "root chakra" associated with the base of the spine, rectum, and perineum. The other difference is that the third chakra is the "navel chakra" and is actually understood to be a combination of the navel center and adrenal center. Here are the chakras:

SEVEN YOGA CHAKRAS[3]

1. *Muladhara Chakra* —
    - Root Center (the base of the spine, rectum, and perineum)
    - represents earth

2. *Swadhisthana Chakra* —
    - Sexual Center (the genitals)
    - represents water

3. *Manipura Chakra* —
    - Navel Center (the navel area)
    - represents fire (often depicted in the Adrenal Center and solar plexus area)

4. *Anahata Chakra* —
    - Heart Center (the heart region, between the nipples)
    - represents air

5. *Vishuddha Chakra* —
    - Throat Center (the throat)
    - represents ether

6. *Ajna Chakra* —
    - Brow Center (the space between the eyebrows)
    - represents intuition

7. *Sahasrara Chakra* —
    - Crown Center (crown of the head, but sometimes considered to be located outside the body above the head)
    - represents the superconsciousness of universal oneness

B. Mantra Meditation

There are many different types of yoga meditation practices, but one basic approach to meditation is to focus on each of the seven chakras in a sequence, starting at the lowest chakra and proceeding one step at a time up to the crown chakra. One way to do this is to repeat a different affirmation, called a *mantra,* at each chakra.

The mantra is used as a mental tool that breaks down the ordinary link between the usage of the human language in words and the expression of consciousness. There is a connection between speech and thought that is used by the rational mind to produce conceptual awareness. The use of the mantra affects this connection producing a disintegrating effect on the usual process of conceptual thinking. Any mantra, including the affirmation of a Divine Name, can alter the process of conceptual thinking to a certain degree in order to gain access to a higher consciousness. However, the mantras that are used in conjunction with the chakras are particularly effective in breaking down the link between words and thoughts in order to reach a higher level of consciousness.

Many kinds of mantras, including the affirmations of your spiritual ideal, have a translatable meaning, but not all mantras have a translatable meaning. The kinds of mantras that are used in conjunction with the chakras do not have a translatable meaning. The fact that these mantras do not have a translatable meaning actually increases their effectiveness in breaking down the connection between words and rational thinking.

The link between words and the rational mind is maintained by the meaning of words. For instance, if you hear someone say a word, which normally has a meaning based on language, the rational mind immediately associates that word with a meaning that can be understood through conceptual thinking, which in turn brings more thoughts in the form of more words into your mind. For example, the word "chair" may bring to mind a physical structure that has perhaps four legs and a seat for sitting. But the rational mind cannot associate an untranslatable mantra into any meaning that can be understood with conceptual thinking. This is what makes untranslatable mantras so effective in breaking the link between words and rational thinking so that the meditator can be open to a higher consciousness that does not rely on conceptual thinking.

The kind of *mantra meditation* that is used in Hindu yoga to awaken the chakras involves the implementation of very specific mantras. These specific mantras that are used in conjunction with designated chakras are called *bijas*, literally meaning "seeds." Bijas are one-syllable Sanskrit words assigned to each chakra. There is no universal agreement on the correct bijas to use. One example of a sequence of bijas assigned to the chakras

from the bottom to the top is *lam, vam, ram, yam, ham, sham, and OM.*
The bijas are mentally projected onto each of the chakras from bottom
to top in order to produce certain vibrations of thought that modify
the vibration and energy of each chakra.

If looked at from a physical viewpoint, it may appear that mantras
produce their effect as audible sound vibrations mechanically projected
onto the chakras. But this is a gross interpretation of what is in fact a much
more subtle activity. Mantras actually produce their modifying effect not
as audible sound vibrations, but as *mental vibrations.* The Sanskrit word
"mantra" literally means "instrument of the mind" or "tool of thought."
Mantras, as thought vibrations, raise the vibratory rate and energy level of
the chakras and are intended to induce the rising of the creative energy
along the cerebral-sacral axis.

To assist in this process of inner spiritual purification and raising of
consciousness, some schools of yoga philosophy recommend that the
meditator consciously use the force of the will to direct the prana to move
upward along the cerebral-sacral axis. Consciously willing the prana to
ascend along the cerebral-sacral axis can become a "conditioned"
experience through the association of bijas with particular chakras. The
habitual practice of daily meditation produces an inner conditioning so
that the repeating of each bija in sequence will trigger the reexperiencing
of prana rising vertically to each corresponding chakra in the sequence.
Through this conditioning the repeating of the bijas raises the vibratory
rate of the chakras, which accelerates the upward flow of prana.

A contrast will be provided below between the use of bijas in yoga
meditation and the use of an affirmation in Christian Yoga Meditation.
Using bijas is not recommended for a Christian approach to meditation,
but the one exception is the bija for the crown center, which is "OM."
OM is more than just a bija. A description of OM has been provided in
Chapter 4, indicating that OM represents the Word of God and can serve
as a Name for God or a reminder of God. If you are attracted to this
universal word and sound, you can use OM as an affirmation and as
your choice of a spiritual ideal.

C. Kundalini

Yoga philosophy identifies the rising energy in the body as consisting
of primarily three energy currents. The best way to visually picture these
energy currents is to use the example of the *caduceus*, the symbol of
medicine, which includes a straight central rod and two snakes intertwined
rising upward along that central rod. The snakes represent the two energy
currents that rise up on both sides of the spine. These two energy currents

intersect at the chakras along the cerebral-sacral axis. These two energy currents rise in a twisting serpentine manner, each making two and a half turns around the central rod of the spine.

These subtle energy currents are called *nadis.* The energy current that affects the left side of the body is called the *ida nadi,* and the energy current that affects the right side of the body is called the *pingala nadi.* The ida tends to have a cooling effect on the body, and the pingala tends to have a warming effect on the body. To maintain a proper energy balance in the body, both energy currents need to be of about equal strength. Generally one of the two energy currents will dominate at any one time, but ideally they will alternate back and forth in this dominance to create an overall harmony with each other.

If one of these energy currents is consistently overactive and dominates all of the time and the other is consistently underactive, this could create a serious imbalance in the body. The best example of this problem of having an energy imbalance is recorded in the autobiography of Gopi Krishna, titled *Kundalini, The Evolutionary Energy in Man.* Gopi Krishna had a dramatic positive experience of inner awakening, but unfortunately as an aftereffect the pingala became very overstimulated, and he felt as though his whole body was literally burning up. This excessive overheating of the body became a persistent problem for a long time until Gopi Krishna was able to bring about a balance between the ida and pingala. An overstimulation of the ida could similarly produce an excessive cooling effect on the body. If either the ida or pingala becomes overstimulated, it is best to practice Centering Meditation exclusively. This brings the focus back down to the lower part of the body, helping you to become grounded. With the focus remaining entirely in the navel area, the two energy currents can return to their proper balance.

The third energy current is the *susumna nadi* and is the central rod of the caduceus that runs along the cerebral-sacral axis. This third energy current is normally only a *potential energy current* because it is not usually rising upward like the other two currents. This third current is the *kundalini,* which may be considered "serpentine energy," because this energy lies dormant like a coiled snake at the base of the spine. The kundalini in the coiled and dormant condition is "folded" in upon itself at the base of the spine and is considered a "downward" and "curving" energy. Even though the kundalini is dormant, in that its ability to rise upward is limited, this creative energy does express itself in the front of the body through the generative organs as a downward and curving energy.

The vital life force energy, the prana, within the body gives life to the body and has a divine origin. Consequently, this energy forms a link between human consciousness and divine consciousness. Of course, the whole body has this life force, but the prana is dispersed into many subdivisions of energy to perform various functions in the body. In the kundalini the prana is raw and undivided, containing the full force of the body's life energy in a potential condition. Since prana and consciousness are closely linked, this dormant, vital force of prana at the base of the spine is the key to unlocking the potential of human evolution toward higher consciousness.

In fact, Christopher Hills in his book *Supersensonics* describes the kundalini in this way: "...kundalini is basically *consciousness*."[4] He links the kundalini with both consciousness and light, but does not see the kundalini as being energy. As the kundalini in its nature of consciousness moves through the body, it produces energy. Therefore, the kundalini, as consciousness, is the cause, and energy is the result. Christopher Hills maintains that the kundalini, since it is consciousness itself, should not be called energy, which is only the effect of consciousness. Others speak of the kundalini and the chakras as having a multilevel reality being psychic energy or etheric energy interacting with the electromagnetic energy fields of the physical body.

However, for this manual it is enough to say that the kundalini is inseparably linked to both consciousness and energy. When the kundalini becomes activated and courses through the body, it produces both a transformation of consciousness and a transformation of energy that affects the bioenergetic system of the body. Each individual chakra, representing a unique center of consciousness and energy, is purified and transformed, and in turn produces changes in the body. Certainly the nerve plexuses and the endocrine glands play a prominent role in this transformation process. The kundalini also connects and integrates the chakras so they work together in coordination. With the natural upward movement of the kundalini into the head, a new, more powerful prana is brought into the brain, in a sense rewiring the brain to take on an apparently new consciousness. But this seemingly new consciousness is nothing more than the divine light returning to its proper place in your conscious awareness.

This transformation of consciousness will invariably produce some uncomfortable disturbances in the mind and body, but these changes can be experienced graciously or with difficulty depending on two decisive factors. One factor is the proper preparation of the body and mind through spiritual disciplines of hatha yoga body postures, breathing practices in moderation, and meditation. The other decisive factor is the maintaining of your purity of purpose in motivation. In the practice of Christian yoga, the most important aspect of raising the kundalini is to allow the Holy Spirit to initiate and regulate the entire process of inner transformation. For the majority of people, the kundalini, which is essentially a neutral and pure energy, is activated most noticeably by becoming the sexual energy expressed in a downward-moving energy. Yet this downward energy can be turned upward and applied to the purpose of spiritual transformation. In this case, the "folded," "downward," and "curving" dormant energy becomes "unfolded," "elevated," and "straightened" energy used for the purpose of raising consciousness. When this happens you will be able to unlock your spiritual potential.

There is a central channel in the body that runs upward along the cerebral-sacral axis, and the kundalini can rise upward through this channel. This central channel, associated with the central nervous system and with the center of the spinal column, is called the *susumna*. In the example of the caduceus as a visual picture of the energy currents, the susumna is the straight rod in the center of the caduceus. Running along the cerebral-sacral axis there are "knots," inner blocks, that need to be removed to allow the kundalini to rise upward. The previously mentioned story in Chapter 6 about the "rope of knots" is about the knots along the cerebral-sacral axis that need to be untied from the bottom to the top.

Because of these knots, the kundalini usually rises only partially in relation to distance and/or intensity. This partial rising in relation to distance means that the rising kundalini reaches only certain chakras, but does not go through all the chakras and reach the crown of the head. The partial rising in relation to intensity means that only a very small portion of the kundalini energy is actually being raised up. The kundalini energy may actually rise all the way to the top of the head, but due to the restricting effect of the knots, very little of the kundalini energy is raised.

During meditation a mild partial rising of the kundalini may occur that may or may not be felt consciously. If this partial rising is felt consciously, you may feel a very slow movement of energy upward or you may experience a slight jolt of energy that appears suddenly and then just as quickly is gone. These jolts can be felt as spontaneous movements of the body, such as the back quickly moving forward or the neck snapping the head forward. These slight jolts are examples of the kundalini energy rising toward the head but with only a tiny bit of the kundalini force actually being released upward. This kind of mild partial rising of the kundalini is quite common, and if it occurs while you are meditating, you can simply return to your practice of meditation. This occurrence should not be considered as being especially significant because it can happen quite frequently without having any apparent positive or negative aftereffects.

After the kundalini rises with a certain degree of intensity (but not with full intensity) to the top of the head, the result can be an opening of the crown center followed by a descending blessing that may come downward into the heart and may extend to the whole body. Although sometimes the kundalini is considered to be only a rising energy, a proper understanding of the kundalini must include an awareness of this descending blessing of energy. The kundalini produces an inner balancing effect as it rises, yet an additional balancing effect is produced by this descending blessing. This blessing of energy may be experienced as an inner feeling of light or love, or both. More about the kinds of inner feelings that may be experienced are explained in Chapters 14 and 15.

It is possible for the kundalini to rise all the way up to the crown of the head with its full force. For this to happen, the dormant coiled energy of the kundalini would have to straighten into one tremendous force rising through the susumna. This full force would pierce and untie all the knots in the cerebral-spinal axis, dissolve all the first six chakras, and completely open the crown chakra. Although this may happen, it actually occurs very rarely. There are basically two circumstances in which the kundalini rises with its full force all the way up the susumna. One circumstance is at the instant of death at the final and total release of the life force. The other is during the most profound spiritual experiences.

Yoga meditation focused on the chakras is designed to alter the chakras and in turn induce the upward flow of the kundalini. The yoga practice of projecting mantras onto the chakras is an attempt to change the vibratory rate of these centers of consciousness. Modifying the vibratory rate of the chakras in turn affects the two energy currents that intersect these centers of consciousness and encourages the kundalini to rise, creating a purifying effect. The two energy currents are considered male and female energy currents, and the perfect joining of these two currents produces the raising of the kundalini. Some yoga schools of philosophy teach that through an act of will the meditator can direct the flow of prana within the two energy currents toward the susumna to bring about the raising of the kundalini.

In addition to the use of mantras, there are also some specific yoga practices that are aimed at inducing the raising of the kundalini. For example, certain kinds of yoga breathing practices can facilitate the raising of the kundalini. These practices can be used effectively as a means of cleansing the nervous system to prepare the body to withstand the powerful energy of the kundalini. Also, these breathing practices can be used in coordination with the Holy Spirit to raise the kundalini, if they are used in moderation.

However, if these breathing practices are used excessively, they can precipitate a forceful raising of the kundalini into areas of the body that are not prepared to receive this powerful energy. These practices can release an overpowering charge of the kundalini energy that in some cases may feel like a very strong electrical charge. This tremendous charge of energy can go into areas of the body that have too many impurities or imbalances and produce a traumatic experience. This type of traumatic experience can have detrimental physical, emotional, and mental effects that can hinder spiritual growth. Since some seekers go to extremes in using breathing practices in order to bring about a spiritual experience, it is certainly important to be aware of the possible negative consequences.

D. Creative Energy Regulated by the Holy Spirit

The goal of Christian Yoga Meditation is not to induce a "kundalini spiritual experience," but rather to facilitate a gradual inner purification process guided by the Holy Spirit. This purification process includes purification related to all three of the rising energy currents, which are movements of prana within the body. The term "creative energy," as it is used in this manual, refers to the kundalini and also to the two energy currents that intersect the centers of consciousness. Thus references to Christian Yoga Meditation bringing about an upward movement of the creative energy in the body regulated by the Holy Spirit refer to all three of these energy currents. This rising creative energy would include the upward flow of energy in both the back and the front of the body.

Although all three energy currents are involved in this purification process, the upward movement of the kundalini becomes increasingly important as meditation deepens. When the kundalini is raised by the action of the Holy Spirit in coordination with a moderate application of yoga practices as a preparation for raising the kundalini, the kundalini will move upward gradually and partially. Nevertheless, the kundalini rising induced by the Holy Spirit may still trigger unusual physical, emotional, and mental symptoms. The kundalini energy is sometimes referred to as an "inner fire." As it rises it has a purifying effect in a sense "burning" away impurities. You may feel various kinds of uncomfortable tension and imbalance. Yet it would be a misunderstanding to think that the kundalini is having a negative influence.

The unusual symptoms that may be encountered as the kundalini gradually rises can be attributed to inner resistance of a conscious or subconscious nature. This resistance is an interference with a natural and beneficial process. The kundalini force itself creates a purifying and balancing effect that makes inner impurities and imbalances stand out as they are being released. As your meditation experience deepens, your challenge will be to let go of inner blocks that would interfere with the purifying and balancing effect of the kundalini rising. More about the nature and release of these inner blocks is described below in this chapter and explained in greater detail in Chapter 12.

The kundalini rises first to the lower centers of the body and in a piecemeal manner rises upward in an orderly progression from center to center. The yoga practice of using mantras to focus on the centers from bottom to top is designed to cooperate with this orderly upward progress.

Christian Yoga Meditation is a variation on this yoga practice in that you likewise awaken the centers of awareness in sequence. However, instead of the raising of creative energy by repeating specific mantras for each center of awareness, you only need one affirmation for all your focusing areas. In Christian Yoga Meditation, an affirmation is held in certain centers of awareness, similar to the way bijas are projected onto the chakras, but for a different purpose. Instead of trying to use bijas to modify the centers of consciousness with mental projections, the affirmation of your spiritual ideal is used to invite the Holy Spirit into the centers of awareness. Unlike bijas that have no translatable meaning, Christian affirmations have the meaning of your spiritual ideal. Since your spiritual ideal is a Divine Name for God or words that remind you of God, repeating your affirmation is in itself a calling on divine grace. Your affirmation in meditation is a focused intention of your invitation to the Holy Spirit to come into you to produce an inner purification and transformation.

In contrast to the yoga practice of modifying the centers of awareness through the practice of mentally repeating specific mantras, the Christian approach places a premium on pure faith. Your faith enables the Holy Spirit to control the raising of creative energy in the body. Placing the raising of creative energy in the hands of the Holy Spirit allows this energy to be raised safely in a way that is truly purifying and transforming. Letting the Holy Spirit guide the raising of the energy currents, including the raising of the kundalini, will result in a natural process, much like fruit ripening in its own time and way. Your reliance in pure faith on the Holy Spirit is your assurance that any experience due to the raising of the kundalini will be beneficial rather than harmful.

A Christian way of practicing yoga would quite naturally need to emphasize divine grace and use techniques as a means of increasing receptivity to the Holy Spirit. Eastern practices of yoga emphasize techniques in order to raise the kundalini, but there is also an important element of divine grace in Eastern philosophy. In yoga the word *shakti* is used to describe the divine energy. Consequently, the rising energy of the kundalini can be called the rising shakti. However, some schools of yoga philosophy also describe a descending energy, a descending shakti, which is a manifestation of divine grace. This descending shakti moves down from above the crown chakra through all the centers of consciousness and into the base of the spine. Like a snake charmer that raises a snake up, this descending shakti arouses the sleeping coiled energy of the kundalini to move upward, creating a purifying effect as it rises through the centers of consciousness, burning away impurities as it rises. Even though this descending shakti is considered a manifestation of divine grace, it does not usually come without the necessary preparation and purification efforts of the seeker who uses techniques to express his desire for God.

Generally techniques play a primary role in the Eastern approach of raising the kundalini, and divine grace is important, but is not the main emphasis. In contrast to the Eastern approach, a Christian seeker would primarily be focused on faith and openness to divine grace. The goal would be to surrender yourself to God, and techniques would be used to facilitate this total surrender of the self to the Spirit. Focusing on centers of consciousness in the body would not be done to project a force onto the centers but to surrender the centers of consciousness to the action of the Holy Spirit.

With your permission and preparation, the Holy Spirit can regulate and raise the creative energy in the body in a way that is similar to the way the descending shakti acts in the body as is described by yoga philosophy. However, it would be a mistake to think that the Holy Spirit is the same as the descending shakti energy. The Holy Spirit is the Spirit of Divine Love. As one third of the Holy Trinity, the Holy Spirit is much more than simply a divine energy. It would be more accurate to say that the Holy Spirit can assist spiritual growth in many different ways. One of these ways is to manifest a divine energy that can act just like the descending shakti energy, if there is an openness to the kind of transformation this energy activates.

The descending energy of the Holy Spirit enters by invitation through the crown center, reminiscent of the tongues of fire that descended on the apostles at Pentecost. This descending energy of the Holy Spirit does in fact descend down to the base of the spine and awaken the kundalini, raising it up in a partial, gradual, and safe way that produces an inner purification. It is this initial descent of divine grace that brings about the upward flow of creative energy and a transformation of consciousness. Some meditators can actually feel this descending energy of the Holy Spirit. Others cannot feel the descending energy itself but can feel the rising energy, which is the result of the descending energy. The majority of meditators cannot feel either the descending or ascending energy, but the descent of the Holy Spirit and resulting rising energy can be activated without the conscious awareness of feeling these movements of energy. With your consent the Holy Spirit will descend and raise the creative energy in the way that will be most helpful for you, with or without your consciously felt awareness.

Although the rising of creative energy comes about as a result of divine grace and is therefore a gift, this gift will normally come only after your invitation to the Holy Spirit to transform you. But what kind of invitation do you need to make to the Holy Spirit? It is certainly a step forward to make a general invitation to the Holy Spirit to bring about a transformation within you. Nonetheless, a general invitation has the drawback of giving you the option to hold back certain parts of yourself from being transformed. In order to make your invitation more effective, it is necessary to specify each of the parts of yourself that you wish to surrender to the Holy Spirit. Christian Yoga Meditation is an effective way of systematically inviting the Holy Spirit into all aspects of yourself—into your body, heart, mind, and soul to produce an integration and unification of all your faculties.

When you give your permission to the Holy Spirit to regulate your inner transformation, it does not mean that you do not have to be actively involved yourself in bringing about this transformation. In particular, you will need to renew your surrender to Spirit on a daily basis. You will need to express your faith in God and His grace by times of inner devotion in silence, as well as by outer service activity that will allow God's Love to be extended through you to others. Specifically related to inner transformation, there is a way of safely assisting the Holy Spirit in the process of controlling and raising the creative energy. Christian Yoga Meditation provides this safe way of assisting the Holy Spirit by focusing on four of the seven centers of awareness. The first four methods of Christian Yoga Meditation have an effect on all seven centers of awareness from bottom to top and produce this effect by your invitation to the Holy Spirit to enter all levels of your consciousness.

The first method, Centering Meditation, focuses on the navel center, the second center of awareness, also related to the lumbar plexus. Focusing on the navel center in the navel area and inviting the Holy Spirit into your physical body produces an uplifting effect on the first center of awareness, the gonad center, related to the sacral plexus and the sexual organs. Creative energy at the gonad center is neutral energy that can become sexual energy, if used for that purpose. This creative energy normally moves in a downward direction, although this subtle creative energy (if it is not activated into sexual energy) normally cannot be felt as a conscious experience. Focusing at the second center of awareness, the navel center, raises this creative energy upward and allows it to be used by the Holy Spirit for spiritual purposes.

The raising of creative energy within the body in coordination with the Holy Spirit creates a purifying effect, removing blockages related to where the energy is rising. Minor blockages can sometimes be removed all at once, but generally inner blockages are removed in a piecemeal manner through daily meditation. Often during daily meditation, only little bits of tension associated with specific blockages are removed piece by piece. The blockage itself that is the source of the tension may remain for a very long time. Finally when enough of the tension has been removed, the blockage itself can be eliminated altogether. Also, some blocks are released in your daily life. This is because the Holy Spirit brings opportunities into your experiences in everyday life in which you can face and overcome issues related to specific blockages. Your invitation to the Holy Spirit sets in motion an inner and outer dynamic process that will transform you first at the human level, then at a spiritual level. The first techniques of Christian Yoga Meditation help to transform your human nature, and the latter techniques are more oriented toward a deeper transformation that reveals your true spiritual nature.

The creative energy rising within the body in coordination with the Holy Spirit, removes inner blockages, producing a dismantling of the ego. This dismantling process of the ego is the only way to allow your spiritual nature to be revealed. The ego stays in control of you through *denial and repression*. Your means of dismantling it are *awareness and letting go* that counteract denial and repression. Blockages within the body are areas of denial and repression associated with specific focusing areas of the body. Your act of repeating your affirmation and bringing your awareness to specific focusing areas is your way of letting go of denial and repression associated with that focusing area.

By holding your attention in the focusing area during meditation, you bring your awareness to the inner blockages. Blockages that remain hidden in the subconscious mind often have an emotional charge to them that creates inner tension. You will not usually understand the specific nature of your inner blockages. However, at times you may feel the tension associated with these blockages. You may feel the inner tension in various ways as unusual body sensations, a generalized feeling of anxiety, or highly charged thoughts. During your meditation you just remain open to the divine as the parade of impressions pass through your conscious awareness. In regard to keeping your attention on the divine within, you need to avoid two potential ways of being distracted: First, you avoid *attraction* by not holding on to whatever presents itself to your awareness. Second, you avoid *aversion* by not pushing away anything that presents itself to your awareness. You simply let the passing sensations, feelings, and thoughts come and go of their own accord without reacting to them.

Whatever energy charge these passing sensations, feelings, and thoughts have will be dissipated by your not reacting to them.

Your focused awareness allows you to overcome your hidden inner blockages that you have denied and repressed. Your invitation to the Holy Spirit helps you to increasingly become aware of blockages and let go of these blockages. Over time you remove pieces of the tension associated with a particular blockage, and eventually with continued practice you let go of the blockage itself. With your permission, the rising creative energy is coordinated by the Holy Spirit, allowing the negative energy of the blockage to be transformed into a positive purifying force.

Christian Yoga Meditation is a systematic way of dismantling the ego by removing inner blockages from the bottom of the body upward and is a means of coordinating this dismantling with the upward flow of creative energy in the body. For the first method of Christian Yoga Meditation, Centering Meditation, you focus on the second center of awareness, which helps to purify both of the first two centers of awareness. Raising creative energy from the first center helps purify blockages related to sexual energy and has the effect of giving strength to the body, as well as strength to your meditation practice. There are also blockages related to survival and security that are addressed. By raising this energy into and through the second center of awareness, the navel area, you assist in removing blockages to meditation itself. These blockages are related to apathy and the fear of meditation itself.

The idea of meditation as a means of revealing your divine nature in union with God is an inspiring idea, easy to accept. However, when you realize that the price of revealing your true divine nature is the dismantling of the ego, you may find this idea to be challenging and fearful. The fear of meditation is related to deeper fears, which are associated with the first center of awareness. These associated fears are the fear of change, fear about your sense of inner security, and the ultimate fear, which is the fear of death. Like all fears, the fear of meditation is an ego-based reaction. The ego senses, and rightly so, that meditation is a threat to its existence. The ego is a false idea of separation that says you are only a body and mind limited to a body. Your meditation experience will loosen up the control that the ego has over your life and bring divine light into your awareness. The ego likes to remain hidden in the shadows of your awareness and to avoid the light that will bring change with the realization that God is truly at the center of your being.

The fear of meditation itself is most commonly experienced as a generalized anxiety or fear, without any specific thoughts associated with it. In fact, this nonspecific anxiety and fear is a common experience when you face most kinds of inner blockages during meditation. Your mind is full of subconscious thoughts and feeling that create inner tension. When you allow your mind to become calm, these subconscious thoughts and feelings causing tension come to your conscious awareness and can be released. It takes courage to face this inner anxiety that most often surfaces as highly charged thoughts, which do not reveal their exact source. More will be said about this divine elimination process, but for now it is only important to realize that when you sit down to meditate and feel inner anxiety or fear, you are not regressing in your practice. Instead, you have become calm enough for the psychic waste of your subconscious mind to come to your awareness so you can release it.

Your release of inner tension is brought about by not holding on to these thoughts by attraction and by not trying to push these thoughts away through aversion. You do not have to intellectually understand the specific meaning of these thoughts in order to release them. You can simply let these thoughts come and go of their own accord, and they pass away releasing inner tension. Releasing inner tension in the manner just described is a typical occurrence regardless of what method is used because of the calmness that meditation produces. Nevertheless, the six methods used in Christian Yoga Meditation are especially effective and provide a systematic means of making progress in dismantling your ego that allows you to face all aspects of your being.

When you practice the second method of Christian Yoga Meditation, which is Heart Meditation, you focus on the fourth center of awareness, the heart center. This spiritual center is related to the cardiac plexus, the heart, and the thymus gland. The heart center consists of two focusing areas, the heart and the center of the chest. When you focus on the heart or the center of the chest, you, along with the Holy Spirit, raise the creative energy upward from the navel center through the third center of awareness, the adrenal center, which is related to the solar plexus and the adrenal glands. Raising the creative energy through the adrenal center releases inner blockages related to anger and strong fears in particular. Releasing anger and/or fear from the adrenal center allows you to have this energy available at the heart center to deepen your awareness of love. Bringing the creative energy to and through the heart center in the chest area releases emotional blockages that prevent you from experiencing divine love as your true nature. This would include blocks related to depression, guilt, grievances and various kinds of selfishness. Some of the results of removing these blocks are a more loving attitude toward others, an openness to selfless service, an increased sense of devotion, and a general sense of well-being.

When you practice the third method of Christian Yoga Meditation, which is Brow Meditation, you focus your awareness on the sixth center of awareness, the brow center in the brow area. When you focus on the brow area, you, along with the Holy Spirit, raise energy from the chest area through the fifth center of awareness, the throat center, which is related to the thyroid gland and the cervical plexus. Raising the creative energy through the throat center releases inner blockages related to the will. Of course, all Christian methods require a surrender of the will to allow the Holy Spirit to guide and direct your inner transformation. Your spiritual journey will require a daily and at times even a moment-to-moment surrender of the will to the Holy Spirit. Every step of the way leading toward divine union is a continuous deepening of your ability to let go and surrender to God. Raising the creative energy through the throat center is a means of helping you in your process of surrendering by deepening your willingness to let go of the inner resistance of the ego and to accept the truth of your true divine nature.

Through the action of the Holy Spirit, your focusing at the brow area brings the creative energy through the throat center to the sixth center of awareness, the brow center, related to the pineal gland and the medulla oblongata. When the creative energy is raised to the brow center, this energy that has been raised up is not the same energy that was experienced at the navel center. One of the reasons why this sequence of focusing areas is so important is that as the creative energy rises, it is transformed by passing through each of these focusing areas. At the first focusing area, which is the navel area, the energy starts out as a neutral creative energy and here strength is added to this rising energy. Through shifting your focus to the heart area, you allow the creative energy to pass through the chest area. With the help of the Holy Spirit and with your intention to be open to divine love, the rising neutral energy will be transformed into a loving creative energy in the chest area. When you change your focus to the brow area, you will be raising the loving creative energy into your mind.

Your focusing on the brow area in coordination with the Holy Spirit allows you to release mental blockages that would prevent you from being aware of your divine nature in union with God. The blocks that may be released are pride, selfish mental patterns of thought, and false beliefs. Some results of removing these blocks may be that your mind will be calmer, your thought patterns will take on a more loving expression, and you will be better able to focus the mind.

When you practice the fourth technique of Christian Yoga Meditation, which is Crown Meditation, you bring your awareness to the seventh center of awareness, the crown center, which is related to the crown of the head. This seventh and highest center is also related to the pituitary gland, which is considered the master gland because the hormones secreted by this center regulate all of the other endocrine glands. Giving your consent to the action of the Holy Spirit and focusing at the crown of the head allows the creative energy to rise from the brow center to the crown center, creating an openness to universal awareness and receptivity to the integration of all the centers of awareness below.

The upward movement of creative energy to the crown center helps to remove blocks to the coordination of the centers of awareness. These blocks may include a fear of universal consciousness itself, which may be experienced as a fear of losing your individual consciousness or as a feeling of being disoriented, ungrounded or uncentered. Because of not being accustomed to universal consciousness, you may have difficulty initially when you attempt to focus your awareness on the crown center. If you have this difficulty, you can practice Crown Meditation only briefly and practice the other methods of Christian Yoga Meditation for longer periods of time. Gradually you can increase the time for Crown Meditation as you become accustomed to focusing on the crown of the head.

The practice of Crown Meditation helps to bring about an inner integration, so it is appropriate that the next method of Christian Yoga Meditation is Oneness Meditation. For this method you focus on the whole body or as much of the body as you can hold in your awareness. This fifth method of Christian Yoga Meditation is optional because you may not be able to focus on the whole body or much of the body all at once. Your focusing on the whole body means holding your awareness on every cell in the body, which would include all your centers of awareness. Even though your awareness is focused on the whole body and not specifically on the crown center of awareness, what makes Oneness Meditation really effective is that Crown Meditation has already opened the crown center, and it remains open. Crown Meditation opens you to an integrating energy that affects the whole body, helping to coordinate all your centers of awareness. With the crown center continuing to be open, Oneness Meditation opens you to your intuitions, your inner feelings. A description of different kinds of inner feelings is provided in Chapter 14, which also includes techniques that help you to increase your openness to your intuitions related to love and light.

At the end of your practice of Oneness Meditation, you focus on the whole body and then let go of your awareness of the whole body. Although you are no longer focusing on the body, you see if you can retain the feeling of oneness that you had when you were focusing on the whole body. In this practice you are attempting to focus on your inner feeling of oneness that is not limited to body awareness. Whether or not you are successful in experiencing this inner feeling of oneness, you move on to the practice of Inner Silence Meditation, the sixth and final method of Christian Yoga Meditation. The opening of the crown center of awareness that occurs in Crown Meditation and continues in Oneness Meditation serves as a preparation and natural transition to Inner Silence Meditation, in which the crown center of awareness is also activated.

Each of the previous five methods of Christian Yoga Meditation act like rungs on Jacob's ladder that lead you one step at a time to Inner Silence Meditation, which in turn leads you to contemplation. In this method you can learn to let go of your affirmation and let go of body awareness altogether in order to enter the silence of contemplation. The crown center is activated and open during contemplation, even though you are not consciously focusing on this area of the body. During contemplation you can find the quiet place of rest where you can relax, at least for short intervals of time, and have a fleeting, but exceedingly sweet taste of who you really are in the loving presence of God. Of course, distracting thoughts will draw you out of this holy rest, and you will have to pick up your affirmation once again to remind you of your intention of deepening your relationship with God. However, once you have tasted this sweetness, you will come back again and again to this restful place and learn to dwell for longer periods of time in His presence.

But you will not return to this restful place because of the sweetness itself. You will return because your Father, in this rest, gently whispers to you: "You are my beloved Son in whom I am well pleased." God could convey this message in words, but words are not necessary. God's presence itself *is* this message. This is the true nourishment for which your soul is longing. In this message is the promise that you are in His World, even in your worldly activities of daily life, and the promise that, when this worldly life is one day over, He will bring you back to your eternal Home.

1. Swami Vishnu-devananda, *The Complete Illustrated Book of Yoga* (New York, New York: Bell Publishing Company Inc., a division of Crown Publishing Inc.), Copyright 1960, by the Julian Press Inc., pp. 231-232

2. Swami Rama; Rudolph Ballentine, M.D.; Alan Hymes, M.D.; *Science of Breath* (Honesdale, Pennsylvania: The Himalayan International Institute of Yoga Science and Philosophy, 1979), pp. 96-98

3. The Sivananda Yoga Center, Foreword by Swami Vishnu, *The Sivananda Companion to Yoga* (New York, London, Sidney, Singapore: A Fireside Book; Simon and Schuster, 2000), p. 69

4. Christopher Hills, *Is Kundalini Real?*, article written in the book *Kundalini, Evolution and Enlightenment*, edited by John White (Garden City, New York: Anchor Press, Doubleday, Co., Inc., 1979), pp. 106-119

12

EMOTIONS
AND
MEDITATION

~ • ~

A. Full Awareness of Emotions

Some people think that spiritual advancement is related to turning off your emotions and feelings altogether. Unfortunately some individuals are led in this direction without even realizing it. Followers of one specific New Age system of growth are tested by an electrical device to see if they have any reactions to questions they are asked. In this New Age system, the highest level of achievement is considered a state in which you have absolutely no reactions to questions that you are asked. This is an example of misguided spirituality. If anything, spiritual growth ideally assists you in learning to be lovingly responsive to any situation rather than turning you into an emotional zombie with no reactions to anything.

However, learning to deal with your emotions is vitally important to your spiritual growth. Your challenge is not to repress or negate your feelings, but rather to purify and refine your feelings. The first thing to realize is that emotions and feelings are not the same thing. Negative emotions are under the control of your ego. This includes raw fear, anger, and other strong reactions that manifest outwardly and noticeably affect your body. These involve highly charged thoughts that may dominate your mind at times. Sometimes you will feel compelled to express these emotions outwardly in an uncontrollable manner.

On the other hand, feelings are a more refined expression of your feeling nature that do not dominate your psyche. Feelings can be expressed outwardly, but without the force and compulsion that often accompany emotions. Also, feelings do not involve physical expression in the way that emotions do. Feelings are a healthy expression of your feeling nature, whereas emotions often involve unhealthy expressions that in turn attract negative reactions from other people. Since emotions are so upsetting at times, you may want to repress them or act them out in an effort to get rid of them. Some therapeutic techniques teach how to overtly express your emotions as a cathartic way to discharge the energy of your emotions. It is not good to repress your emotions because then they will become lodged in your subconscious mind and produce a negative influence on your mind without you knowing it. But always expressing your emotions overtly is not the answer either. Ideally your spiritual practices will enable you to transform your emotions, resulting in letting go of their highly charged nature but without letting go of your genuine feelings that are a finer expression of your psyche.

As long as you are preoccupied with your emotions, you will neglect the development of your feelings. If you feel trapped at the emotional level of your nature, you may have to be treated by a therapist to deal with deepening your psychological understanding of why you have the emotional reactions that you have. If you are overcome by your emotions on a regular basis, it would be necessary to face your emotions and find appropriate ways of discharging your emotions through outer expression in order to bring at least temporary relief. Your emotional releases may bring increased awareness of your psychological makeup and open you to change.

Nevertheless, you will eventually need to no longer be a victim of your emotions. You will need to learn how to have emotions without being possessed by your emotions. At some point you will realize that traditional therapy or even just psychological insights can take you only so far in your progress with your emotions. You will find that attachments to old ways of repressing your emotions or of acting and reacting at the emotional level are direct obstacles to your emotional development.

There are ways of facing your emotions without either repression or overt expression. How to face your emotions as an inner meditative discipline will be addressed below, but facing your emotions can also be done as a mental discipline related to how you allow your mind to respond to emotions as they occur. This mental discipline is the practice of placing your full awareness on the emotion to avoid any suppression and yet letting go of the need to act out the emotion. If you are angry, you allow yourself to experience your anger by placing your full attention on the anger. You are fully conscious of your anger without acting it out. Your full awareness of the anger allows the anger to run its course and be dissolved like a rain cloud that runs out of rain.

When distressing emotions first appear, you will be tempted to try to push them away to avoid the uncomfortable feelings they cause. But it is only the false self that interprets your emotions as being distressing. If you turn away from your emotions with a sense of aversion, you are giving them power over you and creating a new emotion, which is the fear of your own emotions. However, instead of giving in to the temptation to turn away from your emotions, you can disempower your emotions by becoming one with them.

The first step in disempowering emotions is the obvious need to recognize that you are indeed having an emotion. It is best to bring your awareness to the emotion as soon as it appears, thinking to yourself, "I am feeling this emotion." Then if you feel an anxious, depressing, fearful, or painful emotion, you can turn your full awareness toward the emotion and sink into it. If it is an intense emotion, it may take courage to do this the first time you try it. You can invite the Holy Spirit to join with you in becoming one with your emotion. You will see that you and the divine within you are stronger than any temporary emotion. Your emotional experiences are nothing more than weather disturbances in the landscape of your psyche. In short you just endure the storms of the psyche as they come and go without identifying with them as being you. You come to realize that the alternatives of avoiding and repressing your emotions or automatically acting out your emotions only perpetuate these storms and set up the likelihood that such emotional weather patterns will be repeated on a regular basis.

As you practice the discipline of becoming fully aware of your emotions, you will increasingly realize that you are not controlled by these emotions. At first your emotions will seem like electrical thunderstorms, but by maintaining your awareness of your emotions, they will become mostly passing clouds that do not even rain down on you any more. You will reclaim the power that you had given away to uncontrolled emotions. Having freed up this power, you can direct your newly found energies toward transforming your emotions into positive channels of expression.

Your emotions carry an important message from your psyche, and therefore by placing your awareness on them you are paying attention to that message, even if you do not understand the message intellectually. The message is usually related to change and can be viewed as an invitation to let go of old, unhealthy patterns of feeling, thought, and behavior. Placing your full awareness on emotions in the moment that they occur can open the way for a transformation, bringing in new ways of responding. The stronger the emotions you face in full awareness, the greater the potential is for old structures to pass away and to be replaced by new responses. Like a powerful electrical storm that clears the air, explosive emotions that are not suppressed and not acted out can be liberating for your psyche, freeing it up for new expressions.

Your full awareness of your emotions creates a purifying effect that allows feelings, the finer level of your emotional nature, to come to the surface since they are no longer blocked by the gross nature of strong emotions. From this purifying effect, you will discover that your former tendency to act out emotions only wasted your inner energies. Every emotion carries an energy that needs to find expression in some manner, either positively or negatively. Grief, fear, anxiety, and depression can be channeled into the positive expression of your feelings. This takes not only placing your awareness on whatever you are experiencing, but also a certain degree of *disidentification* with what you are experiencing. After all, you are not your experiences, whether pleasant or painful. Your true nature is above the passing events of your psyche. Your full awareness in the moment of your emotions and also your awareness of the more refined movement of the feelings of your psyche are events occurring in your mind, yet your true nature is beyond these passing occurrences.

B. Purifying Emotions

Perhaps the single most critical aspect of your spiritual growth is how you learn to deal with your emotional nature. Initially your experience of meditation may bring spiritual consolations that encourage you to continue your spiritual discipline of setting aside time on a daily basis for deepening your relationship with God. But when God wishes to draw you closer to Himself, He may take away the sweetness of meditation in order to purify and elevate the soul. At such times, meditation will seem to create turmoil, when actually it is performing a cleansing.

For example, you may own a swimming pool that does not have a filtering system. The water in the pool may appear clean toward the top, but on the bottom of the pool there may be a great deal of mud that can only be seen if you take a deeper look. In order to clean the pool, a pump and a filter must be installed. When the water is pumped through the filter, the flow of the water stirs up the dirt on the bottom. Then the dirt that has been stirred into the water is circulated through the filter and caught in the filter. An observer who is not aware of the cleansing process may look at the pool and imagine that it is in much worse condition than before, because he sees only the dirtiness of the water. Such an uninformed observer does not understand that it is part of the cleansing process to stir up the water so that it can be purified.

In this analogy the filter is your meditation practice that includes your affirmation. As this filter is used more intensely, it creates a strong flow (like the water pump). This stirs up the waters of the mind and reveals subconscious thoughts and past emotional impressions that prevent you from being as kind and loving as you would like to be. But you should not be like the uninformed observer and imagine that when such thoughts or emotions appear, this means the condition is worsening. On the contrary, you need to realize that these are being stirred up and brought to the conscious mind so that they can be confronted and released by the power of the Holy Spirit.

Bringing your subconscious thoughts or emotions to your conscious awareness is one aspect of how meditation serves as a purification process that releases physical, emotional, and mental tension. By handing this process over to the Holy Spirit, you can be certain that tension will be released in the most appropriate and timely manner. After practicing meditation on a daily basis over a period of time, a sensitivity to tension within the body may develop. Previously the tension was present but not in your awareness. However, meditation can expand your awareness to include the conscious experience of tension as it is being released.

If you use Christian Yoga Meditation, you may discover that while holding the awareness in various parts of the body, you feel an automatic movement of energy upward from the navel area to the center of the chest. Then you may feel the energy in the chest move upward into the head. Also, if you practice other methods, you may have a similar spontaneous upward movement of energy, perhaps feeling energy rise up in the spine. Yet having such an experience is not a standard of what "should" happen. Actually most meditators do not experience energy movements nor are these conscious experiences necessary for your spiritual growth. But for those who do spontaneously experience such an energy movement, it is helpful to know that there are usually two basic reasons for these energy movements. One reason is because the energy of the body is naturally being raised up and transformed into energy to be used for spiritual purposes because of your intention to express the divine within you.

The other reason is that the energy movement may be a conscious awareness of tension being released. The tension that is released is the result of your shadow side coming to light so it can be released piece by piece. Your subconscious mind is filled with defense mechanisms, negative thoughts, emotions, and anxiety that are stored there because you simply do not want to look at them. Some of these come from traumatic childhood experiences that have left emotional scars and unresolved issues. Normally you cannot release these unhealthy elements of your subconscious, but when your mind becomes calm in meditation and contemplation, you are ready to face the hidden side of your psyche. In addition, because of your spiritual purposes and willingness to surrender to the Holy Spirit, you allow yourself to be open to bringing portions of your shadow side to the light.

Meditation on particular parts of the body, in sequence from bottom to top, helps you raise creative energy for spiritual purposes, but as part of this same process tension is released. Previous descriptions of Christian Yoga Meditation have mentioned that this sequence of methods addresses the release of inner tension, anxiety, and repressed emotions in a systematic manner. The concluding method in this sequence, Inner Silence Meditation, leads you toward contemplation. As contemplation deepens, the mind becomes so restful that the purification process can go to a deeper level by triggering the release of additional subconscious ego-based thoughts and emotions.

Just as the body has its own way of eliminating unwanted waste, this is the psyche's attempt to clean out unwanted mental and emotional waste that is stifling your inner development. At first in your meditation practice, you will perhaps only be dealing with the release of tension that is related to your emotions, but which is not as intense as raw emotions themselves. As your practice of meditation deepens, your purification process will go from releasing tension only to releasing at times the deeper underlying emotions and negative thoughts themselves that are causing the tension.

The subconscious waste from your psyche may present itself to your conscious awareness during meditation or contemplation as very highly charged thoughts and emotions that attempt to grab your attention. You can learn to let go of these highly charged thoughts and emotions by dealing with them in the same way that you would respond to any other thoughts during your practice of meditation or contemplation. Through your daily practice, you learn to relate to your thoughts in meditation as if they are garbage floating by in the river of your mind. You do not look upstream to see where the garbage is coming from nor do you look downstream to see where the garbage is going. This detachment from your thoughts is a process of *letting go and receiving.* You are letting go of thoughts and receiving the Holy Spirit to strengthen you in the process.

This letting go and receiving process for your ordinary thoughts prepares you to respond similarly when tension-filled thoughts come to your conscious mind. These tension-filled thoughts may have a certain amount of energy and emotional burst. The sudden appearance of these tension-filled thoughts and emotions may initially upon impact produce an uncomfortable feeling. If, for example, you are using Inner Silence Meditation and have let go of your affirmation, ideally you can just continue your normal practice by letting these thoughts and emotions pass by in your mind without your attraction or aversion. But because of the highly charged nature of these thoughts and emotions, it is likely that your mind will become distracted.

When this occurs, you simply hold on to your affirmation as a way of focusing your mind positively and preventing distraction. You can remain unaffected by the highly charged thoughts and emotions by placing your full awareness on your affirmation, thus ignoring these thoughts and emotions. By not paying attention to them, they fade away like any other thoughts. You have faced them by allowing them to surface in your consciousness, and you have let them go by not fighting with them. By having neither an attraction nor an aversion to these thoughts, you release the emotional charge these thoughts formerly had. Thus there is no more need to hide these thoughts in your subconscious mind. You have given up your identification with these thoughts and emotions so they are no longer your possessions. The thoughts and emotions in essence become meaningless to you and therefore you do not need these thoughts and emotions anymore, so they dissipate.

Frequently tension-filled thoughts and emotions are released from the subconscious mind and presented to the conscious mind as a generalized feeling of anxiety. However, sometimes the tension-filled emotions that surface may involve anger, pain, or some very traumatic experiences that are so strong and emotionally charged that you are unable to let these thoughts go as you would any other thoughts. You may be filled with the emotional charge of these thoughts so you are reexperiencing the trauma that caused these thoughts. Sometimes the specific source of the traumatic emotion will be presented spontaneously in the form of a psychological insight. Nevertheless, in most cases you will not have an intellectual understanding of this trauma—only the raw emotion itself. When you try to focus on your affirmation or on any other focusing object, you may be unable to do so because the emotional impact is just too strong for you to focus your mind.

If you find that your emotions are so disturbing that you cannot focus your mind even on your affirmation, you can consider another option. You can practice an inner meditative discipline just like the mental discipline described previously of placing your full attention on emotions that occur in your daily life to avoid repression and avoid acting out. During this inner meditative practice, instead of placing your awareness on an affirmation in order to divert your mind away from your emotions, you allow yourself to join with your emotions. Therefore, you become one with whatever you are experiencing by fully sinking into your feeling nature and placing your entire awareness on your emotion itself.

You join with the emotion that you are feeling. By not running from it, you absorb its emotional charge fully and defuse it by your acceptance of it. It is only by struggling with thoughts that you prolong them. Your willingness to face your emotions and experience them fully allows them to fall away since you are no longer afraid of them. There is no need to hide these thoughts in your subconscious mind because you have dealt with them and seen them in the light, finding they cannot harm you.

It is not important to try to intellectually understand the psychological nature of these emotions, and making such an attempt may actually be counterproductive. This form of release is not an intellectual process, but rather a feeling process. You are meeting your emotions at the emotional level and accepting what you find. You can dissolve intense anxiety, raw emotions, and even physical pain by accepting them in the act of becoming one with whatever you are experiencing. Your focusing object becomes your emotions until they dissolve, and then you can return to your regular meditation practice. You will be surprised to find out that often it may take only a minute or two of joining with your emotion before it is dissipated.

Yet there are deeper emotional patterns that may take longer to dissipate. These patterns are whole networks of thoughts that are highly charged with emotions. These emotional patterns may be produced by one traumatic experience, in some cases originating from childhood. But usually the emotional patterns are established as a result of repeated exposure to situations or experiences that elicit a particular emotional response from you, such as pain, fear, anger or some other emotional reaction. Through habit these emotional patterns become ingrained in your personality, so when similar situations occur, you automatically react emotionally. Releasing these kinds of habitual reaction patterns may take more time than less ingrained emotions. These habitual emotional patterns may be dissolved a little bit at a time. Emotional patterns that are being released in this piecemeal manner will reappear intermittently. Over time these emotional patterns will appear less frequently and with less intensity until, with repeated meditation practice, they will disappear altogether.

An example of an ingrained emotional pattern for some people would be the fear of pain from dental procedures. Some dental clients, because of a reaction pattern, begin to be fearful even at the anticipation of going to the dentist's office. Removing this kind of reaction pattern may be challenging since it is a habitual emotional pattern that involves intense emotions related to physical pain and the fear of physical pain. Becoming one with your emotions can be a very effective means of releasing this kind of intense emotional pattern.

One meditator I know practices Centering Meditation when he goes to the dentist and accepts no injection to numb his feelings. He diverts his attention to his affirmation and to the navel area and away from feeling the pain of dental procedures. However, when the pain becomes so intense that he can no longer focus his attention, he lets go of the affirmation and of focusing on the navel area and instead places his full awareness on the pain itself. By making the pain the object of his awareness, he disempowers the pain so it no longer has any effect on him. What he is really doing is releasing not only the pain by joining with it, but also releasing any fear of pain. Without the fear of pain, the experience of pain is just another passing experience. Also, he is releasing his aversion to pain, which is in itself a form of attachment to pain.

This is an extraordinary example of becoming one with an intense emotion in order to face and overcome that emotion. Since this process can work successfully for facing and releasing an intense emotion, such as the pain of a toothache being drilled, would it work for letting go of less intense emotions? Yes, it can work equally effectively for the less intense experience of facing the highly charged thoughts and emotions that may surface during your practice of meditation and/or contemplation. Just as in the example of overcoming dental pain, when you become one with a highly charged thought or an intense emotion during meditation, you are also releasing fear as well as any tension that may be associated with what is being released.

But sometimes you may attempt to become one with your emotions and find that the thoughts and emotions are so highly charged that you are unable even to sit still in a meditative posture. On some occasions even experienced meditators find themselves unable to calm the mind during meditation because of overwhelming emotions. If this happens to you, do not condemn yourself for this, or think that you have left your path toward God. During this difficult time, you can let go of becoming one with your emotions as a meditative practice. Although you do not practice sitting meditation at this time, you can either continue to become one with the emotions you are facing as a mental discipline in your daily life, as has been described previously, or you can simply take a time out and rest. Another option is that you can temporarily turn from meditation to prayer. If you decide to face your emotions, you can offer your prayers directly to God and ask for His guidance and help. You can give your emotions to God since He is not burdened by them. You can put all your emotions to use by turning to God with them and becoming one with the emotions you are feeling. Also, you can turn to God indirectly through seeking out a trusted friend to express your emotions, since the Holy Spirit can speak to you and assist you through your brothers and sisters.

If your emotions involve grief or pain, the most precious prayer you can offer to God is your tears. You only cry with people with whom you feel intimate. What better way to become intimate with God than to give Him your tears? At such times, you cry out from within for God's help. You can reach out to God in this way without words, or you can use whatever words may come spontaneously. You may imagine you are alone at such times, but you are not abandoned for certainly the Holy Spirit helps you in your weakness, as the Bible testifies:

Likewise the Spirit helps us in our weakness; for we do not know how to pray as ought, but the Spirit himself intercedes for us with sighs too deep for words.[5]

This prayer works when no one and nothing else can help. The aftereffect is a feeling of relief. Crying to God with tears is the dissolving of selfishness within. This is one way to release subconscious blocks and serves to renew spiritual intents and purposes, so that you can return wholeheartedly to meditation.

C. Stages of Growth

Generally speaking, the most difficult and important emotions every human being has to face are those related to death, unless death comes suddenly and unexpectedly. Research by Elisabeth Kubler-Ross has revealed that terminally ill patients seem to respond to their approaching death in a fairly consistent pattern. Her book, *On Death and Dying,* identifies five stages of awareness in anticipation of impending death:[6]

1. denial
2. anger
3. bargaining
4. depression
5. acceptance

These five stages are fairly easy to understand, except bargaining, which is less well known as a coping device used to deal with death. Bargaining is usually an attempt to make a deal with God as a way of saying, "I will change for the better and then maybe death won't happen or will be delayed." When interviewed as research for this book, many patients who were in the bargaining stage promised "a life dedicated to God" or "a life in service of the Church,"[7] in return for more time added to their life. Elisabeth Kubler-Ross suggested that such promises were motivated by guilt. She recommended that chaplains, doctors, or other hospital staff who are sensitive could provide a service by drawing the patient out to express any feelings of guilt that may be motivating the bargaining. Her hope was that pursuing this direction can be a means of relieving patients of irrational fears or the wish for punishment because of excessive guilt. She noted that specific promises that were made as bargains directed toward God or other people were almost always not kept, which in turn could only result in more guilt.

One of my past vocations was as a therapeutic recreation specialist in hospitals with chronic disease patients. Once when employed in this capacity, I worked on an emphysema ward in which patients were slowly suffocating to death. In addition to my regular recreation activities, I instituted a daily practice of visiting patients as a receptive listener, allowing them to talk freely. After a rapport had been struck, these patients very often expressed regrets in their life. They shared feelings of guilt that were surfacing in some cases for the first time as death was slowly approaching. In that youthful time of my life, I made a personal decision that I would not wait until death was around the corner before addressing the kind of issues related to guilt that were facing my patients.

Because of my own experiences with dying patients, I would make a slight adjustment in the third stage of Elisabeth Kubler-Ross's list. The third stage would essentially remain the same, but I would rename it. Instead of labeling this stage as "bargaining," I would call it "guilt," which would also include its partner, the "fear of punishment." This would be appropriate since guilt is not merely the motivating factor for indulging in bargaining. Rather, guilt is in itself a major blockage in the subconscious mind that must be addressed as death approaches.

Another reason for using the word "guilt" to rename this stage is that with this adjustment, the five stages of denial, anger, guilt, depression, and acceptance follow a pattern beyond just the facing of physical death. To a certain degree, they also follow the pattern of purifying your emotions that occurs in your practice of meditation over time. It should not be surprising that your purification process follows the same pattern as preparing for physical death because both are identical in that the goal of each is to learn how to let go of the ego. Your physical death confronts you with the false idea of the ego. You are confronted with the same false idea in your spiritual journey as you purify your emotions, so you are in a sense preparing yourself for death itself, but before deteriorating health issues force you to do so.

The ultimate goal of your spiritual journey is divine union, which can occur at the time of physical death or in rare cases while you are still alive. These are times when you can give up the ego, either permanently or temporarily. In divine union that happens in death, you permanently let go of the ego. However, some few souls experience divine union while still alive by undergoing a mystical death and transformation. This is a temporary giving up of the ego. Prior to divine union, these souls often go through a radical dismantling of the ego that occurs during what St. John of the Cross termed the "dark night of the soul."

Because of the traumatic nature of undergoing this extreme process of purification, not everyone is called to this type of radical dismantling of the ego. More information is provided later in this chapter about this radical undoing of the ego that occurs during the "dark night of the soul" as a prerequisite to mystical divine union. However, you are more likely to experience a less radical dismantling of the ego. This less radical dismantling of the ego is necessary to develop emotional maturity, which is a realistic goal for most seekers, as will be described next.

Although the ego is only a thought of separation, a thought of being a body and a mind separated from God, you cannot just let go of this thought like you would other thoughts. The reason for this is that the single thought of separation from God has a gigantic web of other ego-based thoughts surrounding and supporting it. Before the ego can be released, you need to address the ego-based thought system that makes the ego appear real to you, even though it is false. You cannot eliminate the thought system, but you can transform it by eliminating the most unhealthy thought patterns that perpetuate denial, anger, guilt, and depression. Once these are addressed you can come to a deeper place of acceptance of your true nature.

Thoreau wrote:

> If you have built castles in the air, your work need not be lost;
> that is where they should be. Now put the foundations under them.

After you have set your lofty spiritual ideal and set your heart on a divine destination, then your next step is to build a solid foundation for becoming the best human being that you can be. That means going through a process of dismantling your primary emotional blocks. The goal in this process is simply to reach a *plateau of self-acceptance* in your development where you can consistently enter the restful and dynamic state of contemplation. This plateau is reached when you have revealed to yourself much of your shadow side and let go of it in the light of your divine nature. After reaching this plateau, you are not easily distracted so you can remain in the contemplative state longer and at a deeper level.

In the stages of facing impending physical death, you hopefully make progress from denial to anger to guilt to depression in a nice, orderly sequence until you finally come to acceptance and readiness for your transition to the next life. In the purification of your emotional nature, it would be nice if you could dismantle all your ego thought patterns of denial, then all your anger patterns, then all your guilt patterns, then all your depression patterns, and finally reach a state of acceptance. But if you were to face too much of any one of these at one time, you would be overwhelmed. Your emotional purification will involve each of these steps, but you will face each aspect only a little bit at a time. This is God's mercy allowing you to face the inner blocks in your subconscious mind in a piecemeal manner, so you will not be overcome by being confronted with more emotional turmoil than you can handle at any one time.

When you meditate you will have to face and let go of whatever subconscious thoughts or emotions that rise to your awareness. These will not appear in any sequential order. You will often only experience a nervous energy or generalized anxiety that will give you no clue as to what is actually being released. Nevertheless, there is a natural sequence of purification that follows the centers of awareness within your body from bottom to top. Highly charged emotional patterns that are in the subconscious mind are also associated with the location of specific parts of the body. The placement of these emotional patterns in the body follow the sequence of the stages of facing death, as will be explained shortly. When you practice Christian Yoga Meditation, you bring your awareness to the centers of awareness from the bottom to the top. Thus you release tension that follows the sequence of these stages, yet each meditation will be different in terms of the degree of tension released.

D. The Stage of Denial

The stages of emotional growth and likewise the stages of spiritual growth may be thought of as the stages of learning to let go of the ego. Similar to the stages of facing death, these stages of both emotional and spiritual development are denial, anger, guilt and depression, and finally the plateau of self-acceptance.

In each of your individual meditation periods, you are working on all these stages of development. In addition, each year in your overall spiritual progress, you will be growing in all these areas of development. But there are times when one stage will dominate your awareness to a greater degree than the other stages. The first stage that will dominate your awareness will usually be denial because you start your journey of purification in a world of denial, where God and your own true nature are denied. When you enter the spiritual path, you probably do so naively, not knowing the true extent of your denial. Thus you will not know how long and how difficult your spiritual path will be in regard to overcoming denial.

In your first attempts at focusing the mind in meditation, you begin to realize just how much the ego is in control of your whole process of thinking. During meditation when you focus on the affirmation of your spiritual ideal, you learn to let go of passing thoughts generated by the ego. In essence you are embarking on a process of dismantling the ego one thought at a time. By being detached from your passing thoughts, you are beginning to let go of the ego's grip on controlling you, and you are learning to release the tension caused by attachment to the ego.

In this stage in which the issue of denial dominates your awareness, you begin to deal with thoughts in your meditation that previously you did not know were in your mind because they were repressed and hidden in your subconscious mind. Since these hidden thoughts come to your awareness during meditation, you start to see what you had denied. The true magnitude of your denial dawns on you as you make progress in your meditation practice. Your way through and out of this denial stage is to realize just how much you are in denial and to be willing to face what you have denied.

Centering Meditation in particular assists you in coming to grips with the issue of denial because you are bringing your awareness to the navel center, the second center of awareness. Holding the awareness in the navel area stirs up issues that have been denied and that are associated with the navel center itself. These issues are related to the various ways in which the imagination, sexual fantasy, and creative energy are used. Focusing on the affirmation of your spiritual ideal dedicates this area of the body and the creative energy that passes through this part of the body to your spiritual purposes.

Holding the awareness in the navel area affects not only the navel center itself, but also the gonad center below. Through the practice of Centering Meditation, creative energy is drawn upward to the navel area. This rising creative energy comes upward from the generative organs, where the gonad center is located. Because focusing at the navel center raises creative energy upward from the gonad center, this process involves dealing with the issues related to the gonad center. This first center of awareness is associated with sexual energy, survival issues, inner security, and the fear of death. These are gut-level emotional issues that are the most denied aspects of the ego.

In practicing Centering Meditation, you are engaging in a purification process of both the gonad center and the navel center. Holding the awareness at the navel center and raising creative energy upward from the gonad center involves facing issues that can trigger unpleasant emotions. These issues are not normally in your awareness because you have not wanted to look at them and have denied them. Bringing your awareness to these denied issues can be very challenging. In your meditation practice, you are facing specific denied issues. However, you are also coming to grips with the general issue of how your defense mechanism of denial works.

To deny something means to hide it and make it unknown to yourself. To overcome denial means to reverse this process by transforming what is hidden and unknown so it becomes revealed and known. If there is no fear of what is hidden and unknown, the process of looking within would be rather easy. Unfortunately fear is very much a factor in this process of facing and overcoming denial. Actually this process involves two fears. One fear is the fear of whatever you have hidden and made unknown to yourself. This kind of fear should not be surprising when you consider that your reason for denying something is that you are afraid of it and want to get rid of it. What you have denied may not be fearful in itself, but by your very act of denying it, you have assigned the emotion of fear to it.

Because you have assigned the emotion of fear to whatever you have denied, it follows that facing what you have denied also means facing fear. When you are facing what you have denied, you may not have an intellectual understanding of the specific issues or the specific fears that have been denied. Although facing and releasing of denied issues during meditation may not bring intellectual insights, you will know that you are facing a generalized anxiety and that you are releasing tension. It will take a certain degree of courage and determination to be willing to face the fear of what you have denied. However, you are not facing this fear alone because the Holy Spirit is right there with you. You do not have to overcome the fear yourself, but merely allow your denied emotions and/or denied thoughts to come to your awareness so you can give them to the Holy Spirit, who will release them for you.

In addition to facing your specific fears of what you have denied, there is a second fear that needs to be faced. This fear is the generalized fear of the whole process itself of looking within. Without consciously realizing it, you are afraid that if you look within, you will reveal to yourself just how awful and sinful you really are. In my opinion, everyone has an ego-based negative self-image hidden in the dark corners of the subconscious mind. This fearful negative ego-based picture of yourself that has been denied is what you are afraid to look at because you are afraid it is the truth about you. This negative self-image is in fact untrue and unreal—merely an illusion of the mind. But your fear itself perpetuates this untrue negative self-image, giving it a reality and power over you that it does not inherently possess. If you withdraw your fear, the unreality of your negative self-image will become apparent, and you will be willing to let go of it. The only way this false self-image and your fear of it can be maintained is by keeping it hidden. If you do not face this fear and bring it out in the open, you will not allow yourself to give this false picture over to the Holy Spirit for healing.

Beneath this denied false, negative self-image is a deeper denial, which is the denial of your true nature of love. You would think that there would be nothing to fear about revealing your true nature of love, but you are so identified with your ego that even revealing inner divine love can be a fearful prospect, as will be elaborated upon in the last section of this chapter.

In a practical sense, the fear of looking within specifically means the fear of meditation itself. Focusing at the navel area during Centering Meditation helps you to face and overcome the fear of meditation because this technique is directed toward overcoming the most hidden denial issues. Many seekers accept the need to overcome denial, but even so there is ironically still a tendency to deny one's own level of denial—not realizing the depth or the extent of one's own denial.

This first stage of emotional development is very critical to your spiritual growth because it represents the turning point for proceeding or retreating from your spiritual path. After a period of time, you may decide that the practice of meditation is not your cup of tea. Looking within and directly facing what you have denied may feel burdensome to you after a while. Perhaps you may not be willing or ready to go any farther because you may be sensing just how much there is hidden under the surface that you have denied, and you do not want to go there. At this point you may choose to stop your purification process because you have never really gotten out of the denial stage, and so it is not hard for you to go back to the familiar world of denial where the ego rules.

However, if you walk this purification path long enough, you get to a critical point in which you cannot go back because you know too much. At this time there is no returning to the lack of awareness found in the world of denial, because you know too much about the nature of denial. This means you have completed this phase in which the issue of denial dominates your awareness. But this does not mean you have actually overcome denial altogether. It just means you realize that you are living in an illusion that revolves around your ego and that you can no longer pretend that your illusion is real. Yet passing out of the denial stage cannot be accomplished by merely adopting a new intellectual concept. To graduate from the denial phase dominating your awareness, you will need a new understanding, which must be imprinted within your consciousness in an experiential way. This new understanding is an awareness of the truth about your own nature in contrast to the false image the ego presents. There is a part of you that knows what is true and once you have contacted that truth within you, you can no longer fully hide that truth. Some seekers are fortunate enough to get a glimpse of their true nature, but most have to rely on pure faith to awaken their consciousness of the truth. After your consciousness is awakened to a certain degree, you have reached the point where you know too much of the truth to retreat again into living a life based on denial.

E. The Stage of Anger

When denial no longer dominates your awareness, you can move on to the second stage in which your awareness is dominated by issues of anger in all its various forms. You usually think of anger as potential or overt expressions of hostility, but this is only a relatively small portion of anger in this stage of development. In its broadest expression, anger consists of all forms of attack, including subtle expressions. Thus anger includes all projection, all mental patterns of judgment of others, and especially blaming. The anger stage would also include passive-aggressive behavior. This anger stage is really any attempt to direct your energy negatively outside of yourself in any manner.

In this stage you take a closer look at your motivations for anger, including all thoughts of attack. Normally if your ego is attacked, you feel justified in attacking back. You may say you only want justice, but what you really want is revenge. In this stage you are aware of issues related to fight or flight, alternating between anger and fear. The biggest issue you face is your pervasive judgment of others, which is your way of separating yourself from them and is an attack on them. You do not overcome all the gross and subtle forms of attack in this stage, but you do face these issues, noticing just how much of your awareness is projected outwardly in negative ways.

It is important in this anger stage to notice when you are projecting negative energy outwardly toward others and to let go of your justification for doing so. You will still, of course, indulge in judgment because it is a way of life for your ego. Yet you can watch yourself in the process and begin to loosen up the grip that judgment has on your consciousness.

There is one major lesson to learn in this stage when anger issues dominate your consciousness. This lesson is to accept full responsibility for all of your actions. If you fail to accept responsibility, you will find yourself blaming fate, circumstance, bad luck, or most likely other people for your problems and emotions. Whatever you reap in your life is the result of what you have sown. Accepting responsibility for what you have sown and therefore for what you have reaped does not mean that you are just willing to pay the price for your actions. Accepting responsibility means that you realize that you are never a victim of outside circumstances and that every experience that comes into your life happens because of your invitation. Since you are not a victim, but a creator of your own experiences, you have the opportunity, freedom, and power to make different choices to bring different and better results into your life. Your acceptance of responsibility removes the need to find a scapegoat and thus removes the need for projection.

Even if you realize the need to change by accepting responsibility and by letting go of projection, you will still need to address the ingrained habit patterns of judgment and blaming that are already firmly lodged in your psyche. Projection and other anger and attack issues are associated with the adrenal center, the third center of awareness, related to the adrenal glands and solar plexus. Heart Meditation, as part of Christian Yoga Meditation, is helpful in raising energy upward from the adrenal center and into the heart center, the fourth center of awareness related to the heart. The energy that rises up to the heart helps you to develop compassion. The quality of compassion helps you to identify with the struggles of others and to gain empathy for others. Your compassion helps you to release the tendency to project negative energy outwardly toward others. Coming to grips with letting go of projection, judgments, and other forms of attack cannot be addressed only as an inner discipline. It must also be addressed outwardly in the relationships of your daily life.

Graduation from the anger stage occurs when you find that you are no longer investing in old thought patterns of anger, judgment, blame, complaining, or excessive irritation with others. Here is a description of your new state of mind: You are no longer bound by automatic projection and angry reaction patterns. When you do have an angry episode, you allow yourself to recognize the anger, so you do not repress the anger and you do not allow it to control you. You find that you can express your anger appropriately if need be, or you can choose to not express your anger depending on the circumstances. You have learned to be honest about your anger, but you find that your anger appears less frequently and less intensely. Your patience level increases so situations that once disturbed you are no longer upsetting for you. You develop an attitude of harmlessness, and you find yourself increasingly seeing the humorous side of life. You lose interest in projecting negative energy outwardly, but if it does happen you are quick to correct this mistake. This acceptance of responsibility for your own expressions of anger and judgment allows you to move on to the next stage of your emotional development.

F. The Stage of Guilt and Depression

Withdrawing projection brings about the awakening of insight that shows you that the negative flaws you saw in your judgments of others are hiding in yourself. Correcting the tendency to project outwardly then leads to the third stage, which is related to directing negative energy toward yourself. This third stage is guilt. The previous stage of anger is an attempt to shift guilt from yourself to others. Through the device of projection, you had attempted to see guilt in others so you would not see that guilt in yourself. But since you no longer invest in projection, it is natural for you to uncover within yourself the guilt that you had previously hidden from your awareness. Guilt is always attended by its companion, which is the fear of punishment. Illness seems uninvited, but is a manifestation of self-inflicted punishment caused by repressed guilt.

The fourth stage is depression, which like guilt is an attack on yourself. In fact, guilt can cause depression. In this stage you no longer turn your anger outwardly toward others. Instead, you notice that you are directing your anger and self-condemnation toward yourself. Because guilt and depression are linked as forms of self-punishment, the third and fourth stages of your emotional purification overlap each other. Therefore, they are considered here as one stage. This one stage of guilt and depression consists of all forms of attacking yourself, and it can last for a long time.

The causes of depression and in particular guilt and self-destructive impulses are so deeply submerged in the subconscious mind that it may take a long time before these negative thought patterns can be released. Aspects of depression that are closest to the surface of your conscious awareness are the first to be addressed in this stage. Thought patterns of frustration accumulate when you have ego-based desires that are unfulfilled. At those times when you blame yourself for your failure to gain what you desire, you experience unhappiness and depression. This always involves some kind of loss in the material world, such as losses related to finances, health, employment, relationships, and power. These are considered less serious forms of depression because you are aware of the cause of your depression.

One way to address this kind of depression is to withdraw the worldly desires and replace them with spiritual desires. Your meditation practice can assist in dispelling depression. It helps you to face the second stage of anger by bringing that energy from the adrenal center to the heart center, which helps you develop compassion for others. Heart Meditation, as part of Christian Yoga Meditation, also assists you to address issues of guilt and depression because these are associated with the heart. Just as you have learned to open your heart in compassion for others, you need to learn at this stage to open your heart toward yourself to become increasingly aware of the divine love that is your own true nature. Graduating into the final stage of a plateau of self-acceptance requires the establishment of a healthy non-egotistical self-love based on your having opened your heart to the all-embracing divine love that extends to everyone and everything. Your inner discipline of contacting divine love must be reinforced and expressed in your outer experience in the world. Your experience in the world will be your opportunity to test and then anchor your feelings of self-worth through your interactions in relationships.

The stage of guilt and depression may last a long time because developing self-worth takes time and maturity. This stage also becomes an extended one because you have to face not only the causes of depression that are obvious, but in addition those causes that are hidden from your awareness. Facing depression caused by ego disappointments is a mild challenge in comparison with a deeper depression that can be called *spiritual depression*. There are actually two kinds of spiritual depression. One kind of spiritual depression is a mild to moderate depression that may not be especially acute, but can be very long lasting. This sort of depression, which includes guilt, is part of the typical emotional growth of most seekers. This stage of depression attended by guilt is a challenging growth experience. However, it is also a necessary stage that leads to the plateau of self-acceptance, which is a reasonable goal for your spiritual development.

The second kind of spiritual depression is not part of the emotional growth of most seekers. This second type of spiritual depression is the very extreme spiritual depression that St. John of the Cross called the "dark night of the soul," which will be described below and explained in more detail in Chapter 13. Generally speaking, this type of deep spiritual depression is a prerequisite for divine union in this life. Nevertheless, most seekers are not called to a direct experience of divine union in this life and therefore are not called to endure this kind of very severe spiritual depression. The following description of the dark night of the soul is provided for your information without any suggestion that this should be your path. This kind of depression includes bringing to light your deepest pain, fear, guilt, and self-punishing tendencies. These are forms of self-hate that contradict your self-worth.

The onset of spiritual depression occurs when you have given up your investment in the ego's power over you to project negative energy outwardly and when you are in the process of giving up your ego-based worldly desires and replacing them with spiritual desires. Your actions tell the ego that you are serious about removing it from its place of control and power in your psyche. Just as the ego reacts to worldly losses with depression, the ego reacts even more dramatically to its loss of dominance over you. The ego becomes afraid in seeing itself being dismantled. Consequently, the ego attempts to reassert itself, causing spiritual depression in an attempt to overwhelm you with so much emotional turmoil that you will stop your dismantling process.

This emotional turmoil can be disconcerting, but is actually a good thing because the real power of the ego is in remaining hidden, and this spiritual depression is a revealing of all the loose screws in your psyche. But you have to pay the high price of facing deep pain, fear, and even hopelessness. Yet the depth of the spiritual depression that you face will depend on how far along you are on your spiritual path, not only in years, but also in your degree of commitment and how much progress you have made in dismantling the ego. If you have advanced to the point where you have already dismantled much of the ego structure and are totally committing yourself to the mystical path leading to divine union, you may experience the darkest portion of the dark night of the soul.

For this darkest level of the dark night of the soul, your ego, which always seeks self-preservation, will put up one last great effort to defend its domain. Your spiritual reserves will be depleted to the point where you are overcome by despair, meaninglessness, and mental instability. You can become engulfed by a wave of guilt telling you that you are a spiritual failure. You can feel lost in a state of confusion and become fearful that you are going insane. In the past your ego itself could provide some support, even though it was based on pride, with the false motivation of becoming a "spiritual ego." But with the ego being disintegrated, not even this questionable support is available. Spiritual consolations that had supported you in the past are no longer available, so it appears to you that God has abandoned you. You can rely only on pure faith, racked at this point with doubt. You know intellectually that this is a purification process, but even so when you are in the thick of this inner turmoil, there is no comfort in this knowledge. All your spiritual disciplines are of no use, and you can only wait out this stage until the old ego structure collapses and the new spiritual consciousness is established.

Some seekers who are in this state of depression turn to therapeutic counseling, but find traditional therapy and drugs are ineffective. It would be helpful to find a supportive friend who is a willing listener and who understands that you are going through a purification process that will produce a restructuring of your consciousness. Finding someone who can actually hear and understand you as you talk about your condition is extremely important as a stabilizing influence. However, no one can walk in your footsteps for you, and so enduring this ongoing condition that appears endless to you is your full responsibility.

When you look back to your old way of life, you see that there is no way to go back to your former mode of being in the world, and when you look forward, you see no hope for the future either. You will need to experience the depression without passively giving in to panic and total despair. When the depression is at its worst, you will have the greatest opportunity for transformative healing. A breakthrough can occur only by waiting out this condition, which will take courage. Also, it will take self-discipline to keep your mind attentive to your experience. Becoming one with what you are experiencing can dissolve an acute, emotionally charged thought pattern. This depression is much more than a passing emotional pattern, so it will not dissolve so easily. But still you can best deal with this ongoing condition by being fully present in every moment.

You are really facing two problems—one is the depression itself and the other is your fear of the depression. Your fear of the depression feeds the depression negatively, prolonging it and making it worse. Placing your full awareness on everything that you experience will not eliminate the depression, but it will at least reduce the fear of depression by facing what you are feeling with your attentiveness.

In addition to experiencing feelings of despair and desperation, you may have the symptoms of disruptive sleep patterns, loss of appetite, loss of interest in entertainment and socialization, loss of vocational motivation, and loss of planning for the future. There may be immature emotional responses because of overreacting to situations. This may be an acting out of childhood issues that were never resolved. Physcial symptoms may also appear and add to the difficulties of facing this condition. Likewise, you may experience an overall loss of self-worth. Ultimately you will have to wait out the depression itself until divine grace intercedes and a breakthrough in consciousness occurs.

During this time of waiting, you will not have much motivation for your usual pursuits. But you can help yourself by following a structured daily routine that includes physical activity, which will assist you in remaining grounded. It will be beneficial to be fully attentive to whatever you are doing. If you are walking, you can be attentive to walking. If you are eating, you can be attentive to eating. Being fully present in the moment helps you to stay focused on what you are experiencing.

Although it may appear to you that God has abandoned you because you no longer have access to His spiritual consolations, the dark night of the soul is actually an ongoing encounter with God—an extended stay in His World. Your presence in His World produces both a unifying effect and a disintegrating effect on the barriers to unification. If you were able to identify with your true nature, you would be focused on the unifying effect of His World. However, in the dark night of the soul, instead of noticing the unifying effect, you are focused only on the disintegrating effect. You feel depressed because you are identifying with your ego that is being disintegrated.

Because you are not identified with your true nature and no longer have spiritual consolations, it seems to you that you are not in His World. From your perspective, it appears that you are in the *Void*, a mystical nothingness that defies description. This odd state of nothingness is first experienced as a meaninglessness and despair. The depressive state of consciousness that occurs in the dark night of the soul is really a dwelling in the "darkness of God," in which the old personality is taken apart and divinely restructured in a distressing process that feels like death.

The dark night of the soul may be thought of as an expanded version of what happens during contemplation. Normally contemplation is a resting in the divine presence that is described as an experience of the "cloud of unknowing" because your intellect cannot perceive what is happening. There is what might be thought of as a "wall," for lack of a better term, that serves to separate the conscious mind from the subconscious mind. Yet during contemplation the divine influence allows this wall to be permeable so thoughts and emotions can move from the subconscious side of the wall to the conscious side of the wall. These emotionally charged thoughts can then be released in the meditative process, as has been previously described.

After your experience of contemplation, your mind returns to its normal condition. During the contemplative process, sometimes you are confronted with highly charged thoughts that are part of a complex emotional pattern of thoughts in the subconscious mind. You can release the highly charged thoughts, but you may not be able to release the whole emotional pattern. In this case, when you complete your practice of meditation, you may find that you are disoriented by the experience and feel a little off center for a short while because you have stirred up a subconscious emotional pattern without releasing all of it. It may take several meditation periods to finally remove the whole pattern.

To understand what happens during the dark night of the soul, you can imagine that the wall that separates the conscious mind from the subconscious mind starts to become permeable, not just during your meditation practice, but on an ongoing basis in your everyday life. In your daily life, emotional patterns that once were hidden safely in your subconscious mind begin to present themselves spontaneously to your conscious mind. Just like in contemplation, you do not get an intellectual understanding of the reason for these emotionally charged thoughts. You feel these charged thoughts as depressing thoughts that intrude on your daily life, disorienting you and throwing you off center. This is similar to what occurs to you when your contemplation produces partially released emotional patterns, except that you will not be able to so easily overcome the depressing thoughts that keep coming into your conscious mind.

This is an extremely distressing situation, which corresponds to the kinds of challenges faced by the seriously mentally ill. Some mentally disabled individuals have psychotic episodes in which they find it hard to tell the difference between their fantasy world and the world of daily appearances. They are experiencing the breaking down of the solidness of the wall that serves as a barrier between their conscious mind and their subconscious fantasy world. You have the advantage over the mentally ill in that you know, at least intellectually, that your dark night of the soul is a spiritual purification. But this does not stop you from gradually developing a fear of actually going insane. This fear can be stronger than the fear of death, and suicide may seem at times like an option to be considered. Not even your thoughts about God are spared from being dissolved, leaving you no solid belief system on which to stand. You can only rely upon pure faith that is challenged by your suffering and recurring doubts.

What you are encountering is the Ground of Being, which is a divine nothingness and darkness that disintegrates everything in its influence in order to transform it and bring about divine union. It appears frightening from an ego perspective because the very foundation of the ego is being disintegrated. This Void offers none of the spiritual consolations and supports that contemplation offers. If contemplation can be described as a "cloud of unknowing," the Void can be considered a black hole of incomprehensibility. You live in a three-dimensional world of length, width, and depth in which you are confined to form, space, and time. Standing apart from any limitations of form, space, or time, the Void defies being defined by any measures of your everyday world. Even though a complete definition is beyond the ability of the human mind, it is helpful to have theories *about* the Void, as long as you do not become too strongly invested in your theological theories.

No intellectual theories will be of any assistance to you in your encounter with the Void. Fortunately your relationship with the Void does not rest on your intellectual understanding of the Void. It is really a matter of faith that tells you that the unfathomable Void, whatever it is, is your Father. Your faith does not require an experience of the Void for confirmation, but the Void can be experienced. Your experience of this Void is your encounter with a knowledge that transcends all knowledge, but more importantly it is a personal encounter with God. The personal encounter with the Void that occurs in the dark night of the soul comes to a climax in the consciousness symbolized by the words of Jesus: "My God, my God, why hast thou forsaken me?"[8] Yet the end result is a radical transformation of consciousness producing divine union.

However, I do not recommend that anyone seek out the experience of the Void that occurs in the dark night of the soul. There are too many pitfalls involved to make such a recommendation. I personally know of one person who went temporarily insane in the process and another who committed suicide. In both these cases, the individuals were enticed by spiritual pride and had not built a strong spiritual foundation. They had not reached the more realistic goal of the plateau of self-acceptance, which could have served as a spiritual foundation for them. They were also young and did not have the maturity and wealth of life experiences that would have assisted them in their difficulties. A major factor is that neither of them had a spiritual counselor or trusted friend to turn to for guidance in their dark night of the soul.

Being drawn into the dark night of the soul is not something you decide to do as a spiritual accomplishment that would appeal to your pride. It is an experience that you allow to happen out of a mature devotion and commitment to God and because of God calling you to this path. Very few souls are called to experience mystical divine union prior to physical death. Therefore, very few seekers have to endure the extreme spiritual depression that occurs in the dark night of the soul. Yet the plateau of self-acceptance is a realistic goal that you can set for yourself. If you chose to set this goal, you will eventually experience either a mild or a moderate spiritual depression that is more in line with the level of resistance that the ego puts up as you attempt to develop emotional maturity and reach the plateau of self-acceptance.

The rest of this section will address the mild to moderate spiritual depression that is the stage of growth leading up to the plateau of self-acceptance. Although the spiritual depression that occurs prior to the plateau of self-acceptance is milder than the depression of the dark night of the soul, this milder depression will probably still be very challenging for you. Like the more extreme spiritual depression of the dark night of the soul, you may have no idea how long your milder depression will last. Perhaps the milder depression may last a long time, in some cases even years of struggling with issues of guilt and depression that fluctuate in intensity. When the depression stage becomes intense at times, you may not be able to practice your spiritual disciplines. If you cannot practice your usual disciplines, you need not add more guilt by blaming yourself for this. Yet if you can practice a discipline of daily meditation, it would be helpful for you to do so. But your inner discipline is not your only means of releasing your depression. You can find opportunities in everyday life to extend love and serve others that will help to inspire meaningfulness and self-worth to counteract guilt and depression.

There is no way to eliminate the stage of guilt and depression, but Christian Yoga Meditation is designed as a means of building a strong foundation for facing this stage. Christians have historically been taught to use only methods of meditation similar to Inner Silence Meditation that do not include body awareness. While such techniques are excellent in themselves, you run the risk of ignoring the lower centers of the body that are associated with denial, anger, guilt and depression. Meditation techniques that do not include body awareness are primarily mental practices and produce positive mental development. However, these methods do not bring your awareness to the rising of energy from the lower centers of awareness upward. They indirectly open you to love, but they do not directly focus on bringing this rising energy into the heart and awakening your awareness of divine love in the heart.

As stated previously, Heart Meditation, as part of Christian Yoga Meditation, helps to address depression by bringing your awareness to the heart area, which is associated with guilt and depression. Now let's review information about the storage of emotional patterns in the body. Emotional patterns are stored in the dark corners of the subconscious mind so there has to be a mental release of each pattern. Meditation methods that do not use body awareness can bring about a release of the thoughts of the mind that make up these emotional patterns.

Yet emotional patterns are not stored just in the mind. It is true that the mind manufactures emotional patterns, and through denial it hides these emotional patterns in the subconscious mind as a misguided attempt to get rid of these emotional patterns. In a further misguided attempt to get rid of these displeasing thought patterns, the mind projects these emotional patterns onto the body. These attempts are misguided because projecting thoughts is the way to keep them both in the mind and in the body, not the way to get rid of them. Emotional patterns are projected by the mind onto the centers of awareness in the body, and in addition these emotional patterns produce tension in other parts of the physical body. These projections can cause both mild and serious health problems. That is why it is very important for you to bring your awareness directly to the centers of awareness in the body in order to release the energy of emotional patterns that is stored there and in turn release emotional tension stored in other parts of the physical body. Bringing your awareness to the centers of awareness requires a certain amount of courage to face your emotional patterns so they can be offered to the Holy Spirit for healing.

As has been described in Chapter 6, using only methods that do not include body awareness is like trying to untie a row of knots in a rope by untying the middle knot first. Unlocking the knots from bottom to top, following the sequence of the centers of awareness, is your best way to build a strong inner foundation so when the storms of the psyche come during the guilt and depression stage of your emotional development you are prepared to weather these storms. In fact, this foundation will allow you to remove enough negative patterns along the way to reduce the intensity and duration of the guilt and depression stage. By focusing in particular on using Heart Meditation during Christian Yoga Meditation, you will be opening yourself to the divine love that will be necessary in order to develop the degree of self-worth and self-acceptance that you will need in order to progress out of the guilt and depression stage and into the concluding stage of the plateau of self-acceptance.

But if you are unable to sit still for the practice of sitting meditation during your guilt and depression stage, you can consider an alternative practice called *Inner Love Meditation*. This is a technique specifically designed for use in the stage of guilt and depression. Inner Love Meditation is a way of opening you up to divine love. It is practiced while lying down to help you relax, although it can be practiced while sitting if you prefer. This technique is recommended as a way to relieve stress and depression by helping you to gain greater self-acceptance. The description of how to practice Inner Love Meditation can be found in Chapter 14.

The stage of depression and guilt does not generally come in one continuous space of time. Instead, this stage presents itself intermittently, appearing and disappearing over a long period of time until a peaceful self-acceptance plateau is established. Throughout this stage of highs and lows in depression, you learn important lessons. Previously in the stage of anger you learned to accept responsibility and not to blame others. But when you accepted responsibility by withdrawing blame from others, you mistakenly directed blame toward yourself by turning the negative energy of guilt toward yourself. During the anger stage, you learned to overcome old reaction patterns of projecting negative energy toward others. In the guilt and depression stage, you will need to learn to overcome old reaction patterns, which involve feelings of guilt and the directing of negative energy toward yourself.

Your way out of the stage of guilt and depression will need to include opening to forgiveness. You realize that past grievances are only harming you, and you forgive all past mistakes that others have made or that you imagine others have made. If you do not forgive others, you will not be able to forgive yourself. By forgiving others you clear the way to forgive yourself for all your own real or perceived mistakes. Your forgiveness of yourself enables you to let go of guilt and grow out of the guilt and depression stage.

Learning to forgive yourself and let go of guilt requires not only your willingness to change, but also requires divine grace. You do not need God's forgiveness, because God has never condemned you. Your guilt is a self-condemning mental pattern, which you may know intellectually is not appropriate or healthy, but which you find difficult to release. To help you release your self-condemnation, divine grace intercedes on your behalf, giving you permission to forgive yourself. Divine grace lets you know that you are always loved by God just as you are, and there is no need to condemn yourself because God does not condemn you. If you condemn yourself, you are disagreeing with God's judgment of you, which is that you are His child, worthy of all His Love.

Divine grace can come to you in an intellectual insight, but more likely manifests in a breakthrough of divine love, in which you experience truly being loved by God, even if only for an instant. One of the signs of emerging from the stage of guilt and depression is an increased awareness in you of divine grace, manifesting like a light appearing in the midst of your darkness. In some significant way, you notice that the Spirit is interceding on your behalf, allowing a change in consciousness and enabling you to overcome blocks that previously seemed insurmountable.

Along with this expression of divine grace comes a profound sense of gratitude on your part for divine intervention. It dawns on you in your gratitude that if God loves you enough to come into your world and accept you, perhaps you can accept yourself without self-condemnation. Through divine grace you are being lifted up and out of your old reaction patterns and brought into a new way of responding. You are learning that divine love is real, and it is in you. This realization helps you to accept yourself as you truly are. Yet it takes a long time of struggling with issues of self-worth before you have enough maturity and life experiences to make this realization a solid foundation for future growth. Eventually you will reach the stage of the plateau of self-acceptance, and you will escape to a significant degree the overwhelming dominance of the ego.

G. The Plateau of Self-Acceptance

After releasing many emotional patterns of guilt and depression, and gaining a deeper sense of self-worth and maturity, you will arrive at the stage of the plateau of self-acceptance. When this happens you will feel a new sense of freedom from habitual reaction patterns and a detachment from the physical, emotional, and rational world that had previously monopolized your consciousness. You will encounter certain situations that would have elicited from you a particular emotional reaction pattern if they had occurred in the past. But because of your growth these same situations will no longer affect you emotionally in a negative way. You will be able to respond to situations instead of reacting. You will be able to gracefully handle circumstances that would have been difficult for you in the past. You will gain confidence in your ability to be a problem solver and will have emotional reserves to handle even stressful or emergency situations. Of course, you will have ups and downs, but not dramatic mood swings. You will still make mistakes, but you will be able to correct mistakes without condemning yourself. You will be more patient with others and yourself and quick to forgive others and yourself.

Your plateau of self-acceptance will be a consolidation period of your gains. Your consciousness has been significantly restructured so you will feel like a more whole and well-rounded person. You will know that you will still have to continue on your spiritual journey, yet you will be able to rest to a certain degree in a more peaceful overall consciousness. Your subconscious mind has become relieved of so many emotionally charged thoughts that your meditative practice of opening to His World will generally be experienced as less challenging than in the past. Since so much emotional clutter has been removed, you will notice that you are increasingly open to positive inner feelings that begin to surface, and these will be described in Chapter 14. In your meditation you will find that it will be easier for you to enter into contemplation and to remain for longer intervals of time resting in the Spirit without distraction.

Your plateau of self-acceptance means accepting to a greater degree your true divine nature of love. Yet it also means a greater acceptance of the ego. Acceptance of the ego means knowing it is a false perspective of yourself, and at the same time allowing it to be and dealing with it by neither denying its power nor surrendering to its power. You deal with your ego by following a middle path of setting reasonable limits on the ego that neither entirely suppress ego desires nor entirely give in to ego desires. You will find that the divine love in you can manifest even in your ego expressions by doing God's Will to the best of your ability and understanding. In this way, you will become a servant of God's Will, even in your ego condition.

Although the plateau of self-acceptance is a time of consolidation of your gains, it is not a time for complacency. You will still have lessons to learn in this stage, just as you have lessons to learn in the earlier stages. The first stage of denial is related to releasing blocks from the gonad center and navel center by emphasizing Centering Meditation as part of Christian Yoga Meditation. The second stage of anger is related to releasing blocks from the adrenal center by emphasizing Heart Meditation as part of Christian Yoga Meditation. The third stage of guilt and depression is related to releasing blocks in the heart by emphasizing Heart Meditation as part of Christian Yoga Meditation.

The stage of the plateau of self-acceptance does not mean that you will no longer have any blocks in the lower centers. Thus all of the six methods of Christian Yoga Meditation will still help you to release inner blocks. For example, you will still have some denial obstacles that can be released with Centering Meditation. You will also have blocks of anger, depression, and guilt that can be released with Heart Meditation.

Yet these obstacles that surface during the plateau of self-acceptance may be deeper and more subtle aspects of these blocks that come to your conscious awareness so you can release them. For instance, you may find yourself learning to let go of all forms of judgment through practicing Heart Meditation. Judgment in the form of overt negativity toward others, such as blaming, is a block of the earlier anger stage. But more subtle types of judgment are released during the plateau of self-acceptance. These more subtle kinds of judgment consist of any evaluations of others based on the ego perspective of separation. These judgments value a person based on whether the person is pleasing to the ego or not. It is a common personality trait to make negative judgments about other people and then to base decisions on these judgments. Letting go of judgment allows you to release making your own decisions based on the perspective of what is best for your ego. By not relying on ego-based judgment, you can allow the Holy Spirit to make your decisions for you based on what is best of everyone from a divine perspective.

Also, ego-based judgment is a dishonest and inaccurate appraisal of your brother, who is just as divine as you are. Judgment produces guilt, and your negative appraisal of your brother becomes your negative appraisal of yourself. Judgment consciously appears to be about judging your brother but is actually a judgment of yourself. Because the plateau of self-acceptance is about accepting yourself, this means it must be about not judging yourself. The way to escape from judging yourself is to let go of judging others, which will also allow you to let go of the guilt that comes with your judgment of others. Of course, you will still need to have some way of evaluating situations and making decisions, if you let go of your judgments. You can learn to rely on the Holy Spirit to meet this need. The Holy Spirit can give you the divine perspective of situations and show you what decisions would be most helpful.

Many of the ego-based patterns have been released prior to reaching the plateau of self-acceptance, but this releasing of blocks and undoing of the ego is a lifelong process. Besides letting go of obstacles that are still in the lower centers, there will also be the necessity for releasing blocks in the throat center, the brow center, and the crown center by emphasizing Brow Meditation, Crown Meditation, Oneness Meditation, and Inner Silence Meditation as part of Christian Yoga Meditation.

Blocks released from the throat center are related to the use of the will and require deepening your surrender of the will to the divine influence, which is divine love. However, if surrendering your will is seen as a sacrifice of something that is desirable, it will appear to you that there is a conflict between doing your will and God's Will. For example, exerting your own will apart from God seems to be a manifestation of the desirable quality of "freedom." Yet this apparent "freedom" only binds you directly to the will of your ego, which means binding you to the idea of separation that leads to alienation and then suffering. Thus surrendering your will to God's Will is not a sacrifice of something desirable. Rather, it is the release of suffering. Exerting your will apart from God cannot be your *true will* since suffering cannot be what you really want. Your surrender to God's Will involves learning that there is really no conflict between doing God's Will and doing your will. God's Will is the will of His Love, and that is your *true will* because divine love is all that you really want.

Perhaps you can see some obvious ways of how exerting the will of the ego can produce suffering. It may take longer to realize that subtle forms of following the will of the ego produce subtle forms of suffering. It may take still longer to realize that true freedom comes only in expressing your true will that can overcome all suffering. Your true will is in fact God's Will, and only God's Will leads to the finding of inner peace. This lesson can be learned gradually during the plateau of self-acceptance since this is the time to listen more closely to the Holy Spirit, Who reveals to you God's Will as your true will, as is elaborated upon in Chapter 17.

Inner blocks released at the brow center involve mental shortcomings and learning to open your mind to change in thought and action. The major mental block released at the brow center during the plateau of self-acceptance is egotism (the idea of separation) and pride (the idea of being better than others). As you make spiritual progress, obstacles of egotism and pride get more subtle. Gross materialistic kinds of pride can change into more subtle intellectual forms of pride. In turn, intellectual pride can change into a spiritual pride in spiritual accomplishment.

As egotism and pride become more refined and less obvious, you can have an attitude of acceptance about these shortcomings. This attitude of acceptance helps to reduce the power of egotism and pride to affect you. Your acceptance allows you to be aware of the tendency toward egotism and pride, and this awareness takes away the power of egotism and pride to affect you in a hidden manner through denial. But your acceptance of egotism and pride is certainly not an encouragement of egotism and pride. The goal is to avoid the two extremes of aversion and attachment. By trusting in the Holy Spirit, you can grow toward disempowering egotism and pride and allow these shortcomings to be gradually replaced by a greater awareness of union and by humility. Awareness of union can be increased through meditation, and humility can be increased through realizing that your strength lies in your reliance on the Holy Spirit rather than reliance on the ego. Deepening your Brow Meditation practice can help you to let go of mental preoccupation with your ego that is the source of egotism and pride.

Releasing blocks related to the crown center allows you to go to an even deeper level of letting go of the ego. Blocks released at the crown center have to do with letting go of the limitations of individual awareness and learning to accept universal consciousness. On the one hand, your goal is ultimately divine union with God. On the other hand, there is a fear of God, which includes fear of union with God. This fear of God is the major block associated with the crown center. The fear of God is actually the *fear of God's Love,* since God is Love. This block of the crown center, the fear of God's Love, is identical to the *fear of losing your individuality.*

Since human associations with love are so warm and welcoming, it may seem strange to think of love as something to be feared. But this block of the crown center is not about fearing human love, it is about fearing God's Love. God's Love is unlimited. Yet you think of yourself as limited, because of your ego. In fact, the ego itself is the idea of limitation and separation. God's Love calls you to become aware of your own unlimited nature. God's Love calls you to awaken to your true Self that loves God perfectly and is loved by God perfectly. What can this unlimited and perfect love mean to your ego that only allows you to see yourself as limited and imperfect? Although you want divine union, the ego perceives that God's loving embrace in divine union means the death of your individual self.

There is a death that occurs when divine union happens, but what really dies? The ego tells you that *you* die at divine union because you give up your body. When divine union occurs at physical death, or even when divine union occurs as a temporary state of illumination in this life, there is a permanent or temporary giving up of the body. This is necessary because divine union is the awakening of your true spiritual Identity, your true Self in Christ. If you were the body, as the ego tells you that you are, you would die in divine union. Fortunately you are not a body, and you are not the ego that tells you that you are a body.

Divine union is a death, but it is the death of the ego itself. When the ego dies, you do not die. However, it should be mentioned that, strictly speaking, the ego cannot really die, because the ego, being an illusion, was never alive. You give up the ego permanently at physical death or temporarily in illumination, when divine union occurs, because the ego itself, being the idea of separation, dissolves in the reality of union. Yet your ego dissolving in divine union does not mean you are giving up your individuality. You do give up the false sense of individuality based on the idea of a separate self-sufficient self. But you do not give up your true individuality, which is based on relationship, not separateness. Your true individuality can be found only where it has been established in eternity—in your relationship with God the Father, with the Holy Spirit, and with the one Christ. You and all your brothers and sisters are parts of what can be called the *Sonship*, the collection of all the parts of the one Christ. Your true nature in God is expressed in your individuality as a part of the one Christ with your unique place in the Sonship.

But ego identification based on the idea of separation hides your true individuality from your conscious awareness. Your identification with the ego creates a fear of loss. This fear is an obstacle to divine communion and needs to be faced and released at the crown center. It may appear to you that you are afraid of losing your individuality and that you are afraid of God and His Love, but ironically you are really afraid of your own all-consuming love for God. If your love for God would fully awaken completely and all at once right now, you would jump full force into Heaven out of unrestrained ecstasy. Nonetheless, fully awakening to divine love typically happens in a piecemeal manner because it is just too incredible to believe in unlimited divine love in the face of the apparent limitations that the ego constantly presents.

The fear of losing your individuality, the fear of God's Love, and the fear of your love for God are hidden deeply in the subconscious mind. These fears are so imbedded in the psyche that it is hard to bring them to your conscious awareness, making it difficult to hand these blocks over to the Holy Spirit for healing. In addition, these blocks are so deep and so large that they can only be released a little bit at a time. Sometimes the hidden fear of divine love or fear of losing your individuality presents itself spontaneously during meditation when the mind has been cleared of the more superficial and familiar mental distractions. With God's grace these blocks can be released bit by bit over a long period of time. Deepening your practice of Crown Meditation, Oneness Meditation, and Inner Silence Meditation can help to release the fear of union and to open your awareness to accepting universal consciousness.

Your acceptance of divine love, which is the acceptance of universal consciousness, allows you to enter contemplation on a consistent basis and also deepens your experience of contemplation. In the earlier stages of growth, it is important to consistently exert a sustained effort in your meditation practice to counteract the ingrained nature of your daily ego consciousness. Yet after your practice has become firmly established, it becomes necessary to learn how to let go of striving so your practice becomes more of an *effortless effort*. This means using the will to exert some effort but without straining. It requires a relaxation of the throat area in particular since the throat center controls the will. Learning how to let go of striving, which is an ego trait, will help you to relax into contemplation. Your goal in the plateau of self-acceptance is to increasingly let go of techniques and allow your practice to be a relaxed alertness that allows you to enter and remain in contemplation consistently. There is certainly still much to learn during the plateau of self-acceptance, as you continue to accept yourself as a child of God and as you grow toward awakening to your awareness of your spiritual ideal. Your growth in self-acceptance is essential because the major barrier to inward seeking is your false idea that you are not worthy of being aware of the divine presence.

As was indicated previously, you can be working on all five areas of growth at one time in your life or even in one sitting period when you raise energy through each of the centers of awareness. Nonetheless, the different stages of growth are mentioned to indicate that at times one area of growth will dominate the others. Thus during the time when the plateau of self-acceptance dominates, you will still have to occasionally face some issues related to earlier stages of growth. However, you will be better able to handle these issues, allowing them to surface and then letting go of them. The illustration on the opposite page indicates the location of the inner blocks associated with specific parts of the body and with the centers of awareness. Page 260 shows the inner blocks related to the stages of growth and reviews the primary lessons that need to be learned during each of these stages.

Identifying these stages is intended to be a helpful way to look at the range of issues and blocks that may be encountered. Yet these stages are only a general sequence of areas of growth that will not universally apply to everyone, since each individual will have his or her own unique experience. For example, instead of following this specific pattern of releasing blocks, you may have one particular major inner block that is most important to your development. Releasing this one obstacle may be the dominant area of transformation that you will have to deal with for many years before you are able to fully release this block.

Also, some individuals experience a spiritual crisis (perhaps even the deep spiritual depression of the dark night of the soul) and a profound spiritual awakening right at the beginning of their conscious spiritual journey. This is like getting a quick helicopter ride to the top of a mountain and then just as suddenly being returned to the bottom of the mountain. This gives the advantage of knowing what the top of the mountain looks like, but then the goal becomes to do the hard work of walking up the mountain one step at a time. Whether you have this kind of glimpse of the divine in advance or not, the hard work of walking up the mountain will be the progressive dismantling of the ego. With persistence anyone can release enough of the ego to reach the plateau of self-acceptance, so this is certainly a realistic goal. Additional information on letting go of the ego is provided in Chapter 18, which discusses nonattachment.

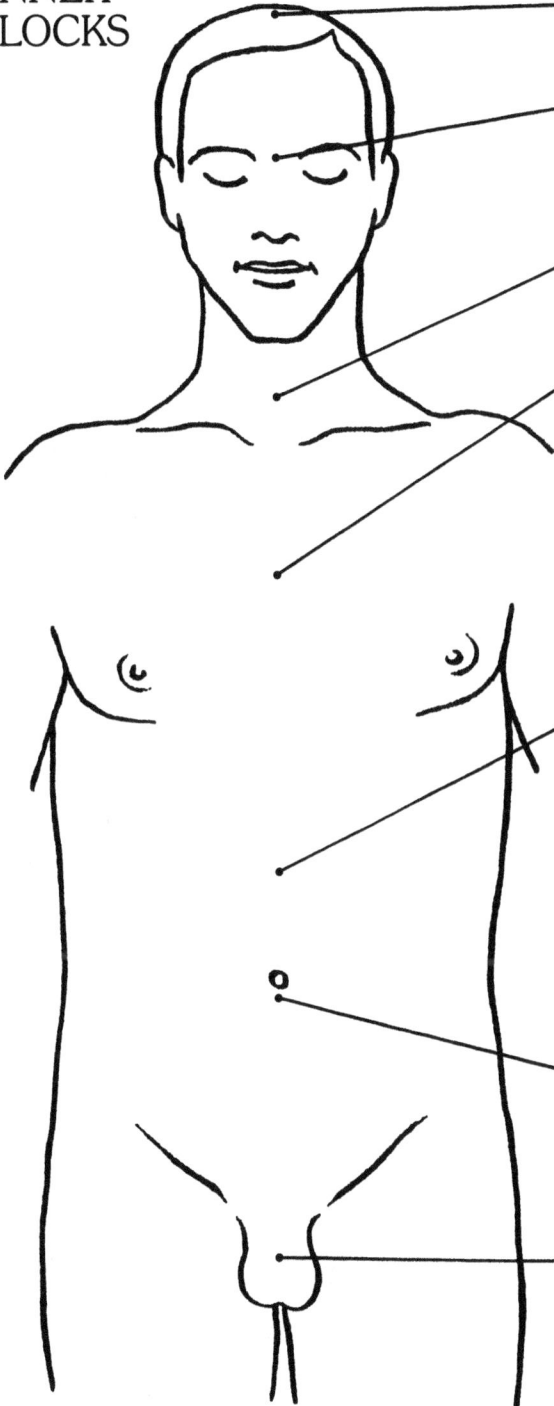

INNER BLOCKS

Crown Center
fear losing individuality

Brow Center
mental blocks,
lack of openness

Throat Center
misuse of the will

Heart Center
depression and guilt,
fear of punishment,
losses, selfishness,
lack of self-worth,
self-condemnation,
lack openness to love

Adrenal Center
inner or outer hostility,
passive aggressiveness,
judgment, blaming,
complaining, revenge,
attack thoughts,
projection

Navel Center
fear of meditation,
misusing imagination,
sexual fantasy

Gonad Center
sexual issues, laziness,
inconsistency, apathy,
insecurity, confusion,
fear of death

STAGES OF GROWTH

Crown
Center

Brow
Center

Throat
Center

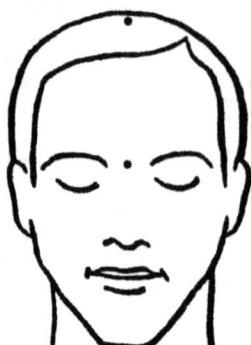

Plateau of Self-Acceptance

surrender the will, accept
yourself and divine love,
open your mind to change,
trust God with pure faith,
consolidate gains made,
continue daily disciplines

Depression / Guilt

withdraw worldly desires,
forgive others and yourself,
learn gratitude, have
non-egotistical self-love,
remove heart center blocks
by using Heart Meditation

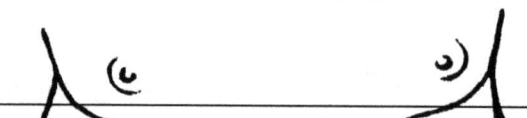

Heart
Center

Anger

accept responsibility,
let go of projection, have
compassion for others,
properly express anger, let
go of adrenal center blocks
by using Heart Meditation.

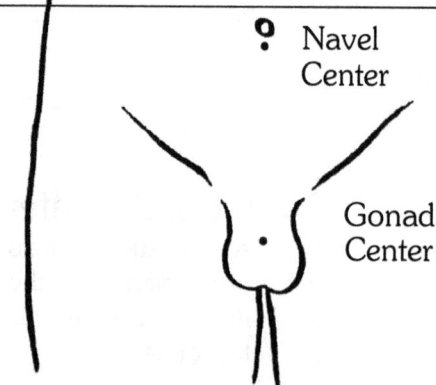

Adrenal
Center

Navel
Center

Denial

rely on faith in God, be
willing to change, look
at denial issues, perceive
false nature of the ego,
trust in your true nature,
remove gonad and navel
center blocks by using
Centering Meditation

Gonad
Center

The diagram on the opposite page shows the stages of growth from denial, to anger, to guilt and depression, and to self-acceptance. In this diagram you can also see how these growth stages correspond to the releasing of blocks in sequence, from the lowest spiritual centers to the highest centers. The raising of the kundalini in coordination with the Holy Spirit facilitates the removal of inner blocks. The correlation between the releasing of blocks and the raising of the kundalini is one of the least understood and most overlooked aspects of Christian spirituality.

The dark night of the soul in which there can be extreme inner experiences bordering on insanity is related to the activity of the raising of the kundalini. Nevertheless, the raising of the kundalini usually goes unrecognized as a factor in the dark night of the soul. Christian mystics in traditional religious organizations in the past did not have the option of using yoga terminology to explain their transformational experiences. Today, with greater openness between the West and the East, more seekers are willing to learn about the awakening of the kundalini in relation to spiritual transformation. The changes that occur as you release blocks and perhaps experience the dark night of the soul are difficult in themselves, but understanding what is really happening can make your experience of these changes much easier.

Just as there are developmental stages in the physical growth of the body from childhood to adulthood that form an identifiable growth pattern, there are likewise *developmental stages in the spiritual growth* of seekers. Some of these spiritually-oriented developmental stages are the emotional and the psychological stages of denial, anger, guilt and depression, and the plateau of self-acceptance that have been described in this chapter. These various developmental stages form a predictable sequence because of the nature of the kundalini to rise from the base of the spine upward. The rising of the kundalini facilitates a natural process of removing inner blocks, generally in the sequence from the lowest chakras to the highest chakras. Christian Yoga Meditation is designed to help facilitate this process of the raising of the kundalini, which has been described in Chapter 11. Both the body postures and breathing practices of hatha yoga used in moderation serve as a preparation for the raising of the kundalini and for the removal of inner blocks. This preparation can help make it easier for you to release inner blocks and reduce the negative effects of the dark night of the soul.

---

1. Romans 8:26
2. Elisabeth Kubler-Ross, *On Death and Dying* (New York, New York: Macmillan Publishing, 1969), pp. 263-264
3. Ibid., p. 84
4. Matthew 27:46

13

CONTEMPLATION AS A PATH OF DARKNESS

≈ • ≈

A. Contemplation as Imageless Self-Awareness

Many paths lead to God, but perhaps these can be narrowed down to two basic paths: One is the *path of darkness* and the other is the *path of light*. Both paths culminate in a transformation of consciousness that involves a transcendent experience of divine Light, but the path itself is the steps you take along the way, not the culmination. As the above title indicates, this chapter will focus on seeking God through contemplation in the darkness of pure faith. In contrast to this chapter, Chapter 15, titled "Contemplation as a Path of Light," will focus on seeking God, still with faith, but also with an emphasis on opening to divine light.

Contemplation is a wordless form of communication with God that does not involve focusing on body awareness and that comes by grace. During contemplation the Holy Spirit overshadows you as you rest in a state of *inner absorption*, which may also be called a state of *imageless self-awareness*. While in this state, there is no desire to use any of the functions of the rational mind to unite with God. Contemplation is not something that you can do, but rather something that happens to you by the action of the Holy Spirit. Contemplation occurs after using various forms of meditation for some time and is a manifestation of grace.

While in the state of contemplation, the mind is fully alert and at the same time empty of all desire for any thoughts. Thoughts themselves may appear, yet there is no desire for them. These thoughts may float through the mind, but they are not possessed. To possess a thought is to judge it, or even to recognize it, by thinking, "This is my thought." Thoughts come and go as garbage floating in a river. As the garbage floats in front of you, you do see the garbage. Nevertheless, you do not look upstream to see where the garbage is coming from, nor do you look downstream to see where the garbage is going. You let the garbage come and go without paying any attention to it.

As progress is made in contemplation, even these thoughts that float by also disappear for intervals of time. The mind is totally alert and yet empty. Your mind does not reflect on itself as to how it feels or how it thinks, but rather simply rests in the state of imageless self-awareness. This form of wordless meditation should not be confused with an idle stupor of the mind. It is really a state of keen awareness, though not intellectual thought-awareness. Neither should contemplation be considered to be a state of thought suppression. The very effort to suppress thought would stir up more thought. Some people foolishly attempt to counterfeit true contemplation by "blanking out" the mind in a state of thought negation. Manipulating the mind in a mechanical way that negates thought may actually succeed only in dulling the mind rather than bringing about the heightened awareness produced by contemplation.

The initial stage of contemplation can be facilitated by a technique, such as Inner Silence Meditation. But contemplation itself, especially in its deeper stages, should not be thought of as a method of emptying the mind, nor can it be taught. During contemplation the mind is indeed emptied, but this state should be more clearly understood as a filling of the Holy Spirit, which silences the functioning of the rational mind. Since contemplation is not a technique, but rather a gift of grace from the Holy Spirit, contemplation itself cannot be taught. Yet you can be taught how to prepare yourself to be receptive to this gift. This preparation consists of learning how to practice various preliminary spiritual activities or disciplines that form a foundation for experiencing contemplation.

If you desire the gift of contemplation, you need to prepare yourself to receive this grace first by performing good works in the active life. You cannot receive the inner peace of contemplation without first learning to live at peace by serving your brothers and sisters. In addition to purifying the heart through service to others, you need to also prepare a clean dwelling place for the Holy Spirit through prayer and meditation, which will help to overcome negative emotional factors and mental distractions. Consistency in practicing prayer and meditation is very important. The best prayer is to do God's Will in all the activities of daily life, yet in order to do that, you need to establish a daily habit of prayer and meditation, the effects of which carry over into outward activities.

Just as there are many methods of meditation, there are many ways of praying. You can practice forms of prayer that are most spiritually moving for you, including formal prayers such as the Lord's Prayer, or prayers of petition, spontaneous prayer, group prayer, worship services, and many other ways of communicating with God. These forms of prayer increase your devotion, faith, and humility, and along with meditation they prepare the soul for contemplation.

Besides attracting spiritual graces, the effect of prayer and meditation techniques that use words is that these words create and instill strong positive impressions in the mind. Through repetition practiced over a period of time, these positive word impressions have a stronger impact on the mind than the negative impressions of past memories. If you were to attempt to go directly into wordless contemplation without first having built a solid foundation of positive word impressions, you would be opening yourself to a potentially harmful situation. In your wordless meditation, you might be confronted with negative past impressions and/or suppressed emotions, which you might not know how to handle. However, with a store of positive impressions, you have a means of counterbalancing and overcoming these negative impressions.

All forms of communication with God can help to build this positive foundation. Nevertheless, techniques such as Christian Yoga Meditation that include the repeating of an affirmation of your spiritual ideal are especially effective in establishing a firm foundation of positive mental impressions. Your affirmation, perhaps in the form of the Divine Name, is your best tool for dispelling negative past impressions and at the same time attracting divine grace.

With the first five methods of Christian Yoga Meditation, you use your affirmation with body awareness methods. However, after meditating with your affirmation and with body awareness, then you may practice letting go of your affirmation and letting go of body awareness to allow yourself to be moved by the Holy Spirit at a level beyond words. This way of meditating is Inner Silence Meditation, the concluding method of Christian Yoga Meditation. As has been described previously, the purpose of Inner Silence Meditation is to lead you from a technique of stillness toward contemplation.

As you use your affirmation, without trying to use the rational mind to intellectualize about its meaning, and then let go of your affirmation, occasionally contemplation may occur. You may drift into and out of the contemplative state of self-awareness without images and at times without thoughts. For intervals when you let go of your affirmation during Inner Silence Meditation, all thought may stop. You will have an intuitive self-awareness, but you will not be able to analyze this state intellectually while you are in it. As you drift out of this state, you may attempt to use your rational mind to comprehend where you have been. Instead, let your intellectual thoughts simply be a reminder for you to return to repeating your affirmation. Where you have been can only be experienced. It cannot be explained satisfactorily in a purely intellectual way even to yourself.

Meditation, in general, attempts to lead you from a state of "doing" to a state of "being," but since Inner Silence Meditation is a technique, there is still at least some sense of "doing" something to empty the mind and to feel the divine presence. Contemplation relies to a greater degree on just "being," and allowing the Spirit to be the doer within you. It is the difference between subtly attempting to possess God and freely allowing God to possess you. Therefore, to allow contemplation to happen by divine grace, you need to be completely passive and only receptive to God's initiative of love without taking any initiative of your own.

When you practice Inner Silence Meditation, if you find that your attention is drawn toward stray thoughts of the rational mind, then return to the repetition of your affirmation. However, when your mind becomes calm, you can let go of your affirmation to enter inner silence. As you rest in inner silence, if you find yourself naturally absorbed into the state of imageless self-awareness, then continue in this way as long as stray thoughts do not divert your attention.

Inner Silence Meditation guides you toward contemplation, but it should be mentioned that contemplation can occur spontaneously at any time with any meditation method. For example, contemplation may occur when you are practicing any one of the body awareness methods of Christian Yoga Meditation. After you have let go of your affirmation and while you are still focusing only on a particular focusing area in the body, you may be drawn into the contemplative state of imageless self-awareness. If this contemplative state presents itself spontaneously, you can let go of focusing on a part of the body and rest in the inner absorption of imageless self-awareness. If you become distracted by stray thoughts, you can return to your affirmation and to the focusing area appropriate for the body awareness technique that you are using.

Although you are practicing techniques in which contemplation may occur, it is important to realize that this state of imageless self-awareness is not really caused by any technique. It is a gift. The experience itself of imageless self-awareness will not be the result of calling on the Name of God or any other method. It is because God is calling you. His calling of you has moved you to call on Him, first with words and then at a level beyond words.

Contemplation, as a gift of being overshadowed by the Holy Spirit, is not like human gifts, which are given intermittently. It is a divine gift given constantly. Like many spiritual gifts, it is a present that is always available to you, yet awaits your opening. You open this gift by meeting four necessary conditions. These four conditions were initially introduced in Chapter 6 and then described in Chapter 8. Now for emphasis this chapter will elaborate upon the nature of these four conditions.

Learning to meet the conditions of contemplation may be compared to learning to float in the ocean. The buoyancy of water is what enables you to float, and buoyancy is always present awaiting your meeting of the conditions that would allow you to float. You need to meet four conditions. The first condition is to produce a calm body and mind, which is necessary for floating to occur. Just as with your practice of meditation, you calm yourself for floating by allowing the body to be as motionless as possible, by slowing down your breathing, and by calming your mind, allowing your body to be surrounded by water. The second condition is to have the desire to float. The third condition is your consent, which expresses your free will to accept being in the water to make floating happen. The fourth condition is to have faith in your ability to float. Before you actually have the experience of floating yourself, you need to have faith that this process of placing yourself in the uncertainty of being horizontal in the water will result in you actually being able to float. After calming yourself, desiring to float, and giving your consent to accept this process that would make floating possible, the last requirement is your faith. Through implementing your faith that this process will actually work, you meet all the conditions necessary to make floating possible. Meeting all four of these conditions allows the natural buoyancy of water to create a lifting effect on your body, resulting in floating.

The lifting effect produced by the buoyancy of water is always there awaiting your meeting the conditions of calming yourself, expressing your desire, giving your consent, and offering your faith to trust that floating will occur. Similarly, the uplifting spiritual effect produced by the Holy Spirit is always there awaiting your meeting the conditions of calming yourself, expressing your desire, giving your consent, and offering your faith that contemplation will occur. The first condition for receiving the gift of contemplation is a calm mind. The calmer the mind, the more you can be open to contemplation and the deeper your experience of contemplation will be. Your meditation practice is designed to calm the mind sufficiently enough to open you to contemplation. The second condition is your desire for God expressed in words by your affirmation, which is a focusing of your intention to open to God. The third condition is your consent to accept His presence. When you let go of your affirmation, you allow your desire and consent to be expressed in inner silence at a deeper level beyond words where you are guided by your pure faith in God, which is the fourth condition for contemplation to occur.

In summary, in order to float, you calm your mind, make your body motionless, express your desire to float by sinking into the water, give your consent to accept being encompassed by the water, and finally express your faith that you will float by surrendering to the whole process.

The result is that you experience floating. Likewise, for contemplation to occur, you will need to calm your mind, make your body motionless, express your desire by sinking into the Spirit, give your consent to accept being encompassed by the divine presence, and finally allow your faith in God to allow you to surrender to the Spirit. Having met the necessary conditions, you will experience the gift of contemplation.

The result of meeting the conditions of floating is the natural state of floating, and the result of meeting the conditions of contemplation is the natural state of contemplation. But the contemplative state appears to be an unusual state, not a natural state. This is because the idea of being separate from God seems natural and the idea of being with God seems unnatural. Ironically it is your idea of separation from God that is what stands between you and your awareness of God. You are joined with God every moment, just as God is joined with every object and every form of existence. Yet your idea of separation, which is your ego, keeps you preoccupied with attachments and compulsions that appear "natural" to you because of conditioning and familiarity. Your preoccupations divert your mind from its true, natural inclination to be open to your divine nature. By learning to let go of your thoughts that pass by in your mind, you release, even if only temporarily, your attachments and compulsions. You are willing to engage in this process of letting go of thoughts, because you have faith that beyond these thoughts there is a divine presence. You desire to become more aware of this divine presence, and you give your consent to accept this presence being revealed to you and being expressed in you. Thus the combination of the four conditions listed below results in the experience of contemplation:

The Four Conditions of Contemplation

1. Calmness of the mind
2. Desire for God
3. Consent to the divine presence
4. Faith invested in God

The degree of calmness in the mind, the degree of your desire, the degree of your consent, and the degree of your investment in faith determine both the depth and the consistency of your contemplative experience. The practice of Christian Yoga Meditation is important as a means of increasing the degree of your calmness, desire, consent, and faith, so your contemplation will be experienced deeply and consistently. Using the first three techniques of Christian Yoga Meditation, you give your consent to accept the divine presence by opening to God at the physical, the emotional, and the mental levels of your being. During

Crown Meditation, you give your consent to accept the Holy Spirit, allowing the integration of these levels and allowing the crown center of awareness to become open to universal consciousness. The crown center remains open during Oneness Meditation as you give your consent to the Holy Spirit to open you to your intuitions—your inner feelings.

Having the crown center opened in the practice of Crown Meditation and Oneness Meditation prepares you for Inner Silence Meditation. Giving your consent to accept the presence of the Holy Spirit in Inner Silence Meditation allows you to be overshadowed by the Holy Spirit and enables the crown center to open increasingly. With your continued consent, the Holy Spirit acts through all your centers of awareness and in particular through the crown center. This action of the Holy Spirit opens you to His World, a dimension transcending the physical world. Entering His World brings about the dynamic inner absorption of contemplation. This contemplative experience produces what is described in greater detail below as the "cloud of unknowing," because your rational thinking (your normal way of knowing) is not at home in His World.

Your desire for God and your consent to accept the Holy Spirit are important conditions for contemplation to occur. Of course, the other conditions of achieving a deepening of calmness in your mind and implementing your faith also need to be present for contemplation to occur. Another term for a calm mind is a "unified mind." Sometimes when the word "mind" is used, it refers only to the discursive thinking portion of the mind. But the word "mind," as it will be used now, has a broader meaning that includes the ability of the mind to be aware of levels of consciousness beyond just rational thinking. The mind is naturally simple rather than complex, unified rather than divided. The mind has a divine origin, and its natural inclination toward simplicity and unity is a reflection of God, Who is Oneness, simple and undivided. One way of describing contemplation is to say it is a natural state of consciousness in which the mind is simple, unified, and open to Spirit by your consent.

Even though contemplation is a natural state of mind, at first it seems unnatural. In contemplation you enter His World, which seems unnatural, and you leave your world, which appears natural to you only out of familiarity. But the truth is that in your daily life you live in an unnatural world where the mind is divided between the worldly thoughts of the ego and the desire for union with God. The mind that is divided becomes complex as it becomes preoccupied with ego-based thoughts that produce tension. As you let go of ego-based thoughts in meditation, the mind becomes increasingly free to pursue its natural inclination toward simplicity and unification. When the mind reaches a certain degree of simplification and unification, the mind no longer presents an obstacle to the natural occurrence of contemplation.

Although any meditation technique can help you to calm the mind, Christian Yoga Meditation is especially helpful in creating a unified mind. Calmness of mind is created by a cumulative effect of systematically emptying both your conscious mind and subconscious mind of your ordinary ego-based preoccupations. Christian Yoga Meditation is a comprehensive and systematic means of addressing your attachments and compulsions at the physical, emotional, and mental levels, forming a foundation for spiritual development. In addition, Christian Yoga Meditation opens you to your intuitions and produces an integration and unification of your faculties, which in turn brings the mind to a deeper level of calmness that facilitates the deepening of contemplation.

Your first experiences of contemplation require only a momentary consent, calming of the mind, and expression of faith. Correspondingly, they produce a fleeting experience of contemplation. By practicing Christian Yoga Meditation, you extend your consent to the Holy Spirit to act on all the levels of your being, allowing a release of subconscious clutter and tension. This release of inner blocks and tension and also the integration and unification of your centers of awareness produce a deeper level of calmness and a greater investment in your faith. By expanding your consent, increasing the application of your faith, and reaching a deeper level of calmness, you are bringing about a simplification and unification of the mind. Continuing to practice Christian Yoga Meditation will increase the consistency and quality of your contemplation.

Progress in your meditation cannot be solely viewed by how calm your mind is during your practice. Every practice in which you are assailed by stray thoughts is your continuing opportunity to relieve the subconscious mind of its attachments and compulsions. The subconscious mind has its own ego-based value system that is programmed into you from your early childhood. As you attempt to let go of your thoughts in meditation, you may encounter at times highly charged thoughts and emotions, which are extremely challenging for you to face. It is these difficult encounters with your subconscious clutter that can be very helpful for your overall growth, even though it may appear to you that for the time being you have failed in calming your mind. There comes a time, and realistically it may take years, when the subconscious clutter in your mind has been largely evacuated to the point where your experience of contemplation becomes deep and consistent. Instead of contemplation being a fleeting few moments at a time, you can make progress so that you can climb up the ladder of your consciousness, enter contemplation, and stay there on the rooftop of your awareness for most or all of your daily practice.

B. Going Beyond Self-Awareness

Contemplation has been described previously as a restful and yet dynamic inner absorption, a state of imageless self-awareness. But this is not the deepest level of contemplation. The goal in contemplation is not "awareness of" but "awareness" itself. "Awareness of" means you are the possessor of the awareness of some object from which you are separate. In this case, the self is present and the object is present, and each appears to be separate from the other. The result is always self-awareness. In contemplation you want to eventually be able to transcend the self so you can experience "awareness" alone rather then "self-awareness."

Self-awareness, even though it can be experienced without thoughts or images, is still really self-centered. What remains in this self-awareness, after the thoughts and images have passed away, is a naked knowledge of your own self. This naked knowledge, just as Adam's knowledge of his nakedness, is what separates you from God. It is the first knowledge Adam experienced in separating himself from God and also the last knowledge you need to dispense with before returning to God, because this knowledge of yourself is not the knowledge of your true nature in God. It is the elemental knowledge of your ego, your separate self.

Unfortunately you can become so preoccupied with your own self (as you think of yourself, which is your ego) that, considering yourself as the subject of meditation, you mistakenly believe the experience of self-awareness to be the all-important experience. This is unfortunate because, whereas previously the self was attached to the senses of the body and the ordinary thoughts of the mind, now the self is attached to spiritual experiences as well. If there is to be spiritual progress, however, you need to drop this idea of yourself as the subject of meditation, which has in turn made God into an object of meditation. It is equally wrong for you to look on yourself as an object on which God is working, as though you are a separate object that does not already exist within the Being of God. The forms of prayer and meditation already mentioned, including imageless self-awareness, are helpful techniques of drawing closer to divine union, but such methods continue to perpetuate the ego's subject-object division between you and God.

God is nothing and He is not worthy of your belief, unless He is everything and infinitely more than your highest conception of what everything is. He is the Being that transcends your being, since He is the cause of all that exists and His Being is the being of all that exists. Thus you do not have a being distinctly separate from God. Because you have an ego, a false perspective of yourself, you do not realize that God is the being of everything, and God is therefore your own being, your own existence. Your ego tells you that you are alone, yet the truth is that God is always with you and you can never be alone. Your true relationship with God is beyond the subject-object division, which views God as something other than your own being. If you wish to experience God most intimately, you need to be willing to first admit that you, as you currently think of yourself, are only a shadow of your true Self in God.

You may acknowledge that the ego is a lie and that your soul exists in the Being of God, but this is only intellectual agreement. It is the ego that says "Yes" intellectually and yet says this from a perspective of separation. Thus this needs to be experienced, not from an intellectual viewpoint based on the ego, but rather from an inner awakening of consciousness. This awakening would be an experience of yourself as being inseparable from God and existing totally within His Being. The only thing that prevents this realization as an experience is the ego itself. The ego ultimately needs to be given up.

This does not conflict with learning to deal with and accept the ego on your spiritual journey. As long as you live on earth with a body and a mind, you will have an ego. You must not try to get rid of the ego. Ideally you will dedicate the ego to doing God's Will as a service. For most people, the opportunity to completely give up the ego will come at the moment of death. When your body is about to die, you imagine that you are dying. However, your true Self that exists within the being of God cannot die. Therefore, what is dying with the body is only what you have imagined yourself to be, which is a body and a rational mind limited to the body. If throughout your life you have trained the self to be a servant of God's Will in order to allow your true being Self of love to flow through the vehicle of the body and mind, then you will be prepared to give up the ego and be united with God when the moment of truth called death arrives.

In your spiritual journey, a realistic goal is to release inner ego-based blocks that hide your true nature of love and after many years perhaps reach the plateau of self-acceptance. This is a state in which you have learned to accept the ego, and at the same time you place limits on your ego-based desires. When you reach this plateau of self-acceptance, you will be able to calm the mind sufficiently to experience contemplation for longer periods of time on a consistent basis. In addition, you may occasionally reach a deeper level of contemplation beyond imageless self-awareness. It is a wonderful accomplishment for you to reach the plateau of self-acceptance, and this is recommended as a realistic goal for anyone who wishes to grow spiritually. The process of reaching this plateau of self-acceptance has been described in detail in Chapter 12.

Perhaps at times your experience of contemplation will go beyond imageless self-awareness. If this happens, you will be going to a deeper level of letting go of the self. This deeper letting go of the self during contemplation occurs spontaneously. If you realize it is happening, your realization itself will be enough to bring you out of this state. Obviously self-awareness has returned when you become aware that you have given up the self, so you can only reflect back on this state after it has already happened. However, realistically not everyone is called to go beyond contemplation with self-awareness to contemplation without self-awareness.

Likewise, not everyone is called to enter the deeper levels of the "dark night of the soul." Just because there are deeper levels of renunciation does not mean that you are meant to pursue these deeper levels. It is important for you to carefully evaluate yourself to determine if you have the degree of desire, renunciation, and determination to pursue deeper levels of letting go of the self. After evaluating yourself and receiving inner guidance, you may be led to pursue a deeper level of letting go of the self. If God's Will has called you to experience the deeper levels of contemplation, the ego must be given up at least for the time of the contemplation. If God's Will has called you to the deeper levels of the "dark night of the soul," you will have to undergo an even more radical giving up of the ego.

Why is it necessary for the ego to be given up for the occurrence of deep contemplation that goes beyond self-awareness and for undergoing the "dark night of the soul"? Why can't you think of the ego as an identity that is expanding and that will reach a higher state of fulfillment? It is because the ego is nothing more than a false idea of separation. As a lie, it cannot co-exist with the truth. While you are experiencing imageless self-awareness or other forms of meditation, you may feel the peaceful presence of God within you. However, there is still a division that exists between you and God by the very fact that you consider God to be working on you as an object, as though God were something other than your own being. This false idea that you are an object in separation from God and that God is not your own being is the very foundation of the ego. Since the ego is the idea of separation from God, this idea of yourself must be given up in order to go beyond self-awareness.

Man's false belief in the ego is like the false belief that the sun revolves around the earth, which mankind believed to be the truth in the times of the earthly ministry of Jesus. Gradually, a few men said that the earth revolves around the sun, but they were not believed. They met disbelief because most men were deceived by appearances since the sun appeared to revolve around the earth as it rose and set every day. Today, mankind knows that the earth revolves around the sun and that the false belief, which mankind was clinging to, is actually a lie.

The way this relates to man's belief in the ego is that mankind continues to be deceived by appearances. The body and mind appear to be separate from God, and the ego-based belief in a separate self is confirmed by the appearances of this world. A few men have directly experienced God as their own existence, as the cause and ground of their being. These men have realized that man is not a separate body and mind, but rather that man is a spiritual being made in the image and likeness of God. These men then have told other men that the ego is only a false perception, which mistakenly views man as the center of consciousness, when in reality God is the center and very being of man.

Though these few men have spoken the truth, they have likewise met with disbelief, just as the men who said the earth is not the center of the universe were disbelieved. There are different kinds of disbelief. The obvious kind of disbelief is the viewpoint of the atheist that says, "You are a body and mind imagining that you are a spirit." This is in direct opposition to those few men who have directly experienced God and have spoken the truth by saying, "You are a spirit thinking that you are only a body and a mind limited to the body."

There is another more subtle kind of disbelief that distorts the truth by compromising the truth. The truth is compromised by combining a false idea with a true idea. In this case, the compromise takes the form of the idea that says, "You are a body and a mind separate from God and also simultaneously you are a spiritual being." The truth in this statement is the words "...you are a spiritual being," but that truth is compromised by the other words in the statement. What is true and what is false are mutually exclusive. Therefore, you cannot accept both what is true and what is false simultaneously without compromising the truth.

The convenient compromise of combining the belief that you are both an ego and a spirit is created because most people find it just too hard to let go of the belief that says, "You are a body and a mind separate from God." If this is your belief, it isn't particularly harmful in a practical sense for you because it allows you to function comfortably in this world where this idea makes perfect sense. You can even hold on to this belief and make a great deal of progress spiritually by dedicating your body and mind to God's service in this world.

But what if you want to experience deep contemplation in His World? From the perspective of His World, do you think God looks on you as a body and a mind separate from Him? No, that's how you view yourself mistakenly. God looks on you as you are. He sees you as a spirit made in His image and likeness, and He sees Himself as joined with you as your source and substance. Any other viewpoint is your illusion about yourself.

Consequently, when a false statement, such as "You are a body and a mind separate from God," is combined with a true statement, such as "You are a spiritual being," the result is a compromise of the truth. You cannot combine a true statement with a false statement and have the combined statement remain true. If you are really seeking the truth, you will need to give up any false ideas that would compromise the truth. For example, could mankind believe in both the old false belief of the sun revolving around the earth and in the new truth of the earth revolving around the sun at the same time? No, of course not, since before the new truth can be accepted, the old false belief must be acknowledged as an error and be given up.

You may ask, "How can I give up the false perception of the ego in order to experience God as my own source and substance? What method should I use?" In answer to this first question, "you" cannot do that since the you that you think you are is the you that needs to be eliminated. In answer to the second question, no method can bring you directly to God. To do that, God must take you by the hand and truly empty you of all things in the darkness of faith. He will not show you His Light in its full mystical brightness because your ego could not bear it, and so He takes you into a mystical darkness and emptiness. In this manner He helps you to surrender your ego by showing you that what you think you are is absolute darkness and nothingness. He will lead you during contemplation from the state of self-awareness into the Void, referred to in Chapter 12, where the self will feel lost and afraid. Faith must be very strong to step into the Void, because the soul has nothing to call its own. The soul is surrendering the old, familiar ego-centered consciousness. The soul with faith and detachment needs to wait passively and patiently in mystical darkness and nothingness. This is what the sixteenth-century mystic St. John of the Cross refers to as the "dark night of the soul." St. John of the Cross describes the detachment necessary to pass through this dark night in order to move on toward divine union when he says:

A soul is greatly impeded from reaching this high estate of union with God when it clings to any understanding or feeling or imagination or appearance or will or manner of its own, or to any other act or to anything of its own, and cannot detach and strip itself of all these.... Wherefore, upon this road, to enter upon the road is to leave the road; or, to express it better, it is to pass on to the goal and to leave one's own way and to enter upon that which has no way, which is God. For the soul that attains to this state has no longer any ways or methods.... [1]

To further clarify this, another mystic writer, John Tauler, states:

> When we have tasted this in the very depth of our souls it makes us sink down and melt away in our nothingness and littleness. The brighter and purer the light shed on us by the greatness of God, the more clearly do we see our littleness and nothingness. In fact, this is how we may discern the genuineness of this illumination; for it is the Divine God shining into our very being, not through images, not through our faculties, but in the very depths of our souls; its effect will be to make us sink down more and more deeply into our own nothingness.[2]

Thomas Merton comments on these two previous quotations in his clear-sighted book, *Contemplative Prayer*, by saying:

> There are two simple conclusions to be drawn from this. First, that contemplation is the summit of the Christian life of prayer, for the Lord desires nothing of us so much as to become, Himself, our "way," our "truth and life." This is the whole purpose of his coming on earth to seek us, that He may take us, with Himself, to the Father. Only in and with Him can we reach the invisible Father, whom no man shall see and live. By dying to ourselves, and to all "ways," "logic" and "methods" of our own we can be numbered among those whom the mercy of the Father has called to Himself in Christ. But the other conclusion is equally important. No logic of our own can accomplish this transformation of our interior life. We cannot argue that "emptiness" equals "the presence of God" and then sit down to acquire the presence of God by emptying our souls of every image. It is not a matter of desire, of planned enterprise, or of our own spiritual technique.
>
> The whole mystery of simple contemplative prayer is a mystery of divine love, of personal vocation and of free gift. This, and this alone, makes it true "emptiness" in which there is nothing left of ourselves.[3]

Many would like to experience the illumination that Christ experienced, but how many would like to experience His cross? To follow Christ into the depths of mystical contemplation means a sacrifice of the small self, a total self-surrender to the Will of God. If you wish to follow Jesus, in the beginning you need to desire sincerely to be illuminated by the Light of Christ. Yet in the deepest mystical contemplation, you must surrender even the desire for illumination. Why? Because, who is it that wishes to express such a desire? It is the ego that wishes to make even illumination into an object that it can grasp and hold on to. The ego, which tries to manipulate all things to revolve around itself, is the first to apply as the candidate for illumination, as though it were something to be possessed. But the small self that applies for illumination is not the same Self that receives the gift of illumination. Yet the ego is allowed to see itself as it really is, which is darkness and nothingness in contrast to the true Self that is revealed in God's Light after the small self is completely surrendered.

If you are called to mystical contemplation, you may not even cling to the desire for illumination as something that you might possess. If you surrender yourself entirely to the Will of God, you will find that one desire will remain within you. That one last desire is the pure desire to love God. The pure desire to love God is not an ordinary desire that originates within the self, for such a desire can bear no fruit since its origin is in the self and therefore is not pure. Rather, this pure desire originates in God, who infuses the soul with this desire of pure love for Him. The Will of God has no other purpose than to elevate the soul to a union of love with Him. The person who is bound by the lie of the ego can be filled with the love of God by His grace. The effect of such a love is that the person who is faced with the choice of experiencing himself as he presently imagines himself to be, or experiencing God as He is, will choose not to experience himself. Thus denying himself and forgetting himself, he will wait in nothingness and emptiness until God chooses to reveal Himself.

C. The Cloud of Unknowing

An unknown Christian mystic of the fourteenth century wrote two books—*The Cloud of Unknowing* and *The Book of Privy Counseling*.[4] These two books are recommended as spiritual manuals for those called to contemplation. In *The Cloud of Unknowing*, it is explained that between the individual and God stands a barrier called the "cloud of unknowing" and to pierce that cloud with love, you need to proceed by way of a "cloud of forgetting."

Those who are called to contemplation are advised in both of these spiritual manuals to drop all conceptualization by allowing all thoughts to be absorbed by the "cloud of forgetting." To do this, *The Cloud of Unknowing* suggests using an affirmation as a tool of meditation. The idea is to take one word in which you can place all your desire for God alone and to choose a simple word, which can be retained easily by the mind and which is especially meaningful for you personally. The book explains a specific procedure to be followed after choosing your word:

Then fix it in your mind so that it will remain come what may. This word will be your defense in conflict and in peace. Use it to beat upon the cloud of darkness above you (referring to the cloud of unknowing) and to subdue all distractions, consigning them to the cloud of forgetting beneath you. Should some thought go on annoying you, demanding to know what you are doing, answer with this one word alone. If your mind begins to intellectualize over the meaning and connotations of this little word, remind yourself that its value lies in its simplicity. Do this and I assure you these thoughts will vanish. Why? Because you have refused to develop them with arguing.[4]

You may use an affirmation if you desire to do so. But whether an affirmation is used or not, *The Cloud of Unknowing* states that there is only one basic requirement for contemplation. Most of all, you need to simply raise your heart to God with a single naked desire for God alone. In this regard, *The Book of Privy Counseling* gives the following advice:

See that nothing remains in your conscious mind save a naked intent stretching out toward God. Leave it stripped of every particular idea about God (what He is like in Himself or in His works) and keep only the simple awareness that He is as He is. Let Him be thus, I pray you, and force Him not to be otherwise. Search into Him no further, but rest in this faith as on solid ground. This awareness, stripped of ideas and deliberately bound and anchored in faith, shall leave your thought and affection in emptiness except for the naked thought and blind feeling of your own being.[5]

If you are called to a deeper level of contemplation, both of these spiritual manuals advise you to go beyond the use of an affirmation and likewise to go beyond the naked feeling of your own being, which has been described previously as imageless self-awareness. *The Book of Privy Counseling* explains this as follows:

But now I want you to understand that although in the beginning I told you to forget everything save the blind awareness of your naked being, I intended all along to lead you eventually to the point where you would forget even this, so as to experience only the being of God. It was with an eye to this ultimate experience that I said in the beginning: God is your being. At that time I felt it was premature to expect you to rise suddenly to a high spiritual awareness of God's being. So I let you climb toward it by degrees, teaching you first to gnaw away on the naked blind awareness of your self until by spiritual perseverance you acquire an ease in this interior work; I knew it would prepare you to experience the sublime knowledge of God's being. And, ultimately, in this work, that must be your single abiding desire: the longing to experience only God. It is true that in the beginning I told you to cover and clothe the awareness of your God with the awareness of your self, but only because you were still spiritually awkward and crude. With perseverance in this practice, I expected you to grow increasingly refined in singleness of heart until you were ready to strip, spoil, and utterly unclothe your self-awareness of everything, even the elemental awareness of your own being, so that you might be newly clothed in the gracious stark experience of God as He is in Himself.

For this is the way of all real love. The lover will utterly despoil himself of everything, even his very self, because of the one he loves. He cannot bear to be clothed in anything save the thought of his beloved. And this is not a passing fancy. No, he desires always and forever to remain unclothed in full and final self-forgetting. This is love's labor; yet, only he who experiences it will really understand. This is the meaning of the Lord's words: "Anyone who wishes to love me let him forsake himself."[6]

Forsaking yourself, which is the giving up of the ego, is not a suicidal running away from yourself. Also, it is not a struggle between a good self and a bad self, which is the root of all forms of false asceticism. You only have one Self that is the real you. But your one true Self is obscured by a false idea you have about your true nature. There is a separation in your mind, which is divided in its allegiance between the Truth and your false perceptions of your own being. Truth is Wholeness and Oneness so can only be recognized in a whole mind that is not separated—not divided in its allegiance. You can only find the Truth by letting go of what is false. Learning to identify with your true Self cannot be accomplished directly until you learn first to "disidentify" with your false perceptions. This first requires a stripping of all thoughts of the rational mind so that you may have the most direct and elemental experience of your own naked self-awareness. Then you need to come eventually to realize as an experience that this very self-awareness is a false perception with which you are bound as a bird in a cage.

Self-awareness may be so comfortable that encountering the falseness of self-awareness can be painful. This can become an especially painful experience when you realize that self-awareness alone separates you from a union of love with God. Nevertheless, it is only by being confronted with the painful wretchedness of your false condition of ego-centered awareness that you are prepared for divine union. This is elaborated upon in *The Book of Privy Counseling* in the passage below:

> Yet do not misunderstand my words. I did not say that you must desire to un-be, for that is madness and blasphemy against God. I said that you must desire to lose the knowledge and experience of self. This is essential if you are to experience God's Love as fully as possible in this life. You must realize and experience for yourself that unless you lose self you will never reach your goal. For wherever you are, in whatever you do, or howsoever you try, that elemental sense of your own blind being will remain between you and your God. It is possible, of course, that God may intervene at times and fill you with a transient experience of Himself. Yet outside these moments this naked awareness of your blind being will continually weigh you down and be a barrier between you and your God, just as in the beginning of this work the various details of your being were like a barrier to the direct awareness of yourself. It is then that you will realize how heavy and painful is the burden of self. May Jesus help you in that hour, for you will have great need of Him.
>
> All the misery in the world taken together will seem as nothing beside this, because then you will be a cross to yourself. Yet this is the way to our Lord and the real meaning of His words: "Let a man first take up his cross" (the painful cross of self) that afterward he may "follow Me into glory," or, as we might say, "to the mount of perfection." But we listen to His promise: "There I will let him savor the delight of My love in the unspeakable experience of My divine person." See how necessary it is to bear this painful burden, the cross of self. It alone will prepare you for the transcendental experience of God as He is and for union with Him in consummate love.[7]

D. Contemplation as a Loving Interior Absorption

In the *Ascent of Mount Carmel*, St. John of the Cross describes the degree of detachment from self that is required of anyone who truly wishes to take up his cross and follow Jesus wholeheartedly. On this pathless path, only God Himself can be the guide, and the soul must be passive and open to His promptings. St. John of the Cross, in his book *Living Flame of Love*, explains how the soul is delicately anointed with the Spirit, who gradually draws the soul closer to union with God in a step-by-step process.

The first taste of contemplation may occur while a meditator is practicing Inner Silence Meditation. Likewise, this first experience may happen when using any meditation technique, as well as, surprisingly, even when not meditating. By God's grace you may find that you are spontaneously overshadowed by and filled with the Holy Spirit. If this happens during meditation, you can let go of thoughts effortlessly and feel like an object on which God is working His grace.

This initial stage of contemplation is described by St. John of the Cross as a state in which the contemplative is led into the silence of the Father and feels a *loving awareness* of God. St. John referred to this loving awareness as a "loving knowledge" or "passive loving receptivity," meaning an inner listening in which the heart opens to God.

The contemplative is advised by St. John not to be attached to any feeling or desire, but rather to be completely open to whatever way God would guide the soul. Thus, in general, the Spirit would prompt the contemplative, as just stated, to spontaneously feel this loving awareness. But then the contemplative needs to be willing to even let go of this loving awareness. St. John of the Cross referred to the letting go of this loving awareness, which he termed a "loving advertence," in the following way:

> When this comes to pass, and the soul is conscious of being led into silence, and harkens, it must forget even this loving advertence of which I have spoken, so that it may remain free for that which is then desired of it; for it must practice that advertence only when it is not conscious of being brought into solitude or rest or forgetfulness or attentiveness of the spirit, which is always accompanied by a certain interior absorption.[8]

Therefore, there is a "loving advertence," meaning "loving attention," that leads to an "interior absorption." Christian Yoga Meditation can help you to allow yourself to be drawn into this interior absorption because it is an aid in opening to love by removing the blocks to love in a systematic order. The body awareness methods form a foundation for practicing Inner Silence Meditation. The purpose of this technique is to serve as a transition from methods to no methods, and from active participation to the passive inner absorption of contemplation.

A contemporary of St. John of the Cross and another mystic, John of St. Samson, refers to the interior absorption as a simple, naked "gaze" beyond methods, as follows:

> In this state the soul is in a simple, naked and obscure condition, without even knowledge of God. The spirit is elevated above all

inferior light to the state where it is unable to act with its interior faculties, because they are all willingly drawn and fixed by the power of their unique and simple Object, God. They remain fixed in a supereminent view at highest point of the spirit. All this is accomplished in the depth of the All-incomprehensible in nakedness and obscurity. There, all that is sensible, specific and created is dissolved in unity of spirit, or rather, in simplicity of essence and spirit. Within, all powers look steadily and attentively upon God who engages them uniformly in contemplating him. They are quite simply absorbed by the action of his continual gaze which he maintains in the soul, and which the soul mutually maintains in him.[9]

The term "gaze" does not refer to the picturing of a visual mental image in your mind. It is a term to describe the drawing of your wholehearted awareness toward God and brought about by God Himself. Ideally this simple and naked gaze may become established as one's regular and consistent experience in contemplation of God, but often this is instead a momentary experience that may come and go. To make this gaze a constant practice requires a dedication to inward seeking over a long period of time. It also requires a giving up of active methods by being passively receptive and a willingness to set self aside. Like St. John of the Cross, John of St. Samson also stresses the need to die to self, which leads toward divine touches. He describes this when he writes:

> Here the condition of dying constantly is appropriate for the soul, because, by this means, it follows that which it knows not and sees not. Due to a very simple gaze that is lost in God, the soul has an active and joyful inclination which places it in a most singular and supereminent repose. One infallibly leads to the other.
> In this state the soul begins to see God simply, without forms or images. All that is annihilated along with the soul's own life in this ardent, superessential center into which it is transfused. When the soul's active desire is entirely suppressed by the strength and simplicity of love, it begins to enjoy its Spouse purely in his essence by means of simple touches. These touches dilate and enlarge it in simplicity in a way that it has never experienced.[10]

In order to die to self, you must experience spiritual darkness. But this darkness that is experienced by the soul is actually excessive light that is mistakenly perceived as darkness. This is explained by another mystic, St. Symeon the New Theologian, in the following quotation from *Writings From the Philokalia on Prayer of the Heart*:

Like a man who, standing in a dark room with all windows and doors fastened, opens a window and the light streaming in suddenly envelops him in such a brilliant glare that, unable to bear it, he closes his eyes, wraps up his head and hides; so if a soul, totally imprisoned in the sensory world, lets its mind peep out into the supersensory world, as out of a window, it becomes bathed in the radiance of betrothal with the Holy Spirit, which is within it, and unable to bear the brilliance of the uncovering of Divine light, it immediately trembles in its mind, hides within itself and flees as though into a house, seeking cover in the sensory and the human.[11]

The abundance of divine light has the effect of causing blinding darkness and blocking understanding for anyone not accustomed to such excessive light, as is confirmed by John of St. Samson, as follows:

The divine darkness is the Divinity, which thus makes itself obscure to the soul, and especially to the understanding. This faculty is surrounded by it and dazzled by the abundance of its blinding light. There, it is divinely elevated and suspended in admiration at the ravishing beauty of the Object which fills it. The soul is transported with the greatest delight as it contemplates the divine Object in a superessential manner, that is, in a completely naked, abstract and simple manner, in the superessential unity of God. Quite often it is elevated to this state without knowing what it is or where it is. God caused this darkness for his own greater glory and for the soul's perfection.[12]

The soul needs to persevere in this darkness to be purified and learn to be open to the divine light. In order to encourage the soul, God elevates the soul by means of God's divine gaze, as well as by intermittent divine "touches," mentioned above, and further described by John of St. Samson in this way:

Sometimes God knocks gently within the deepest part of the soul. Stirred by this very brief and sudden touch, it is completely renewed within and filled with strength, understanding, love and delight. By such frequent touches, God seems to be saying, "Behold me within you. Do not be afraid of losing me." This is so wonderful that the soul's faith in God and its belief in his awareness of it are continually renewed by this inspiring and exciting gaze and by his delightful and ardent touch.[13]

Then these divine touches and also even the divine gaze may be withdrawn altogether so that one is only aware of oneself again. These times of divine withdrawal are tests to see if the soul is seeking God alone and not just His pleasing gifts. But for the soul that perseveres and does not lose faith because of this time of dryness, an inner transformation happens that opens the soul to a deeper relationship with the divine. The darkness that oppressed the soul disappears with new inner experiences, as John of St. Samson writes:

> But finally, after so many sorrowful and touching aspirations, the Beloved, moved with compassion, returns suddenly in a momentary act, like a flash of lightning. In this encounter the soul feels completely renewed. Darkness vanishes and is succeeded by an infinite light. Its former multiplicity and distractions cease to exist and all is reduced to unity of spirit. Now it experiences a new attraction as it is transported and caressed by Jesus Christ, its Spouse and Lover. Profoundly dilated, it abides in his divinity in a state of complete liquefaction. All its anguished laments are completely forgotten, as if they never existed.[14]

In addition, the divine touches return to lead the soul toward deeper levels of inner transformation, as John of St. Samson explains:

> Often too, it is so deeply penetrated by a touch of love that it feels as though it were melted and completely transformed by the immense sea of fire which consumes it. It is so plunged and absorbed in this fire that it constantly becomes the same thing with it and in it, as well as one life with it.[15]

In the quotations above, John of St. Samson, like so many other mystics, refers to a consuming "fire" and to "light" as part of the spiritual transformation process. Christian mystics did not have the Eastern understanding of the term "kundalini," but their references to "fire" and to "light" are attempts to describe the experience of the activity of the kundalini, described in Chapter 11. According to John of St. Samson the divine gaze and divine touches lead the soul toward the state of divine union. John of St. Samson describes this transforming union by writing:

> When thus favored, they are filled with every kind of happiness and perfection, and seem to be entirely overwhelmed by it even to the point of pouring it out upon others. But the highest and most intimate state in this degree consists in a very simple and intimate

exchange between God and the soul. The soul contemplates God constantly and is, so to speak, imperceptibly absorbed in what it sees and feels.[16]

The state of divine union may be easier to describe by what it is not than by what it is. Of this state, John of St. Samson writes:

In short, in this condition, there is neither creature nor created object, knowledge nor ignorance, all nor nothing, word nor name, past, future nor even present; not even the eternal now. All is lost and dissolved in this obscure mist which God himself produces.[17]

To summarize much of what has been said about contemplation, there is a consistent experience of "interior absorption" in God in which the Spirit leads the soul by the hand into various states of awareness of God. The soul remains completely passive and receptive, while the soul feels like an object on which God is working, and because of this, there is still a feeling of separation. The soul is gradually purified and transformed as it is led to deeper states of contemplation. In these deeper states, there is an increased feeling of oneness that serves as a preparation for the spiritual marriage of the soul and God in divine union.

When divine union is achieved, the feeling of being an object on which God is working is entirely dissolved in oneness. In divine union the soul is in a state in which it can hardly draw distinctions between itself and God, Who is indisputably its Source. John of St. Samson says of this:

In this degree of transformation the soul says to its Spouse, "You are what I am, and I am what you are without there being any difference between us."[18]

A quotation from *Merton's Theology of Prayer*, by Father John Higgins, refers to the transformation process of divine union with God as follows:

In this transcendent experience it becomes evident that the individual subject really undergoes a radical change, an inner transformation, or what Merton refers to as a "transformation of consciousness" from an awareness of his empirical self (also called man's false self or ego-self) to an awareness of his transcendent self (also referred to as man's true self or his person). The individual is no longer conscious of himself as an isolated ego but sees himself in his inmost ground of being as dependent on Another or as being formed through relationship with God. By forgetting himself both as subject and object of reflection, man finds his real self hidden with Christ in God. And so his self-consciousness changes, the individual is transformed, his self is no longer its own center; it is now centered on God. There is death of the self-centered and self-sufficient ego and in its place there appears a new and liberated self who loves and acts in the Spirit. Man is now empty of all ego-consciousness; he is a Transcendent Self—a person who has gone beyond his individual self and has found his true self in the presence of God. Hence, it is through this dynamic process of inner transformation or transformation of consciousness that man empties himself and transcends himself, and thus ultimately becomes his true self in Christ.[19]

Deep contemplation is the highest expression of the Christian prayer life, but, as has been emphasized, it is a divine calling and is not expected of everyone. God wants everyone to be drawn to Himself in divine union, yet God is not so small in giving His grace that only contemplatives will reach such a high state of spiritual union. God brings each man closer to Himself by whatever gift of prayer He gives each individual. Prayer in its broadest and most important sense is the doing of God's Will in all the activities of daily living. You set aside special times for prayer and meditation only so that you may be strengthened inwardly by His Spirit to be able to follow His Will throughout each day.

Your prayer life is a necessary part of your life, yet you are certainly not justified by your prayers. It would be a mistake to think that anyone can practice contemplation or meditation or prayer, and thereby "earn" divine union. Divine union with God is a free gift offered to everyone. But like so many spiritual gifts, it is a gift that has already been given and continues to be given. This gift is only awaiting your acceptance. It may take a lifetime of opening the door of your heart to receive this gift with thanksgiving. Most individuals are not called to unwrap this gift and fully receive it during their lifetime. However, everyone is called at the time of physical death to let go of the ego entirely and to receive the gift of divine union at that time. If you have lived your life with the desire for the gift of divine union, your passage out of this world of appearances will not be an ending, but rather a birth, awakening, and acceptance of divine union in His World.

What is the true nature of the gift of divine union, which is the gift of salvation? You are saved only from yourself. A more accurate way of saying this is that you are saved from your illusions about yourself. Because of the ego, you think you are a body and a mind that will one day be united with God in divine union. The words "divine union" are used to describe spiritual fulfillment, but these words are misleading because they imply two are becoming one. Actually divine union is not a union, but rather a subtraction. What really happens in divine union is all the illusions you have about yourself are eliminated. You are saved from the false idea that you are a body and a limited mind. What remains is not merely the understanding of who you really are, but rather the *realization* of who you are as an *experience* of your spiritual being.

When you let go of the ego and realize your spiritual nature, you will see yourself as God has always seen you. You will see yourself as part of God and understand that at no time have you ever been separate from God. When you were in your world of apparent separation, you thought you were a body and mind separate from God. But after entering His World, you will see that your separation was only an illusion of separation. You will understand that if you really had been separate from God, you would have ceased to exist. Your existence depends on union with God because God is existence itself and everything that exists is part of God. If you were not part of God, you would not exist. The dropping of your illusions reveals that you are now and have been all along one with God.

Salvation then is a change in awareness—a change of consciousness. Prior to divine union, you are not aware of your union with God, and when divine union occurs, you become aware of your union with God. Salvation then is ironically the revealing of the divine union that has existed all along, but which was hidden from your awareness.

It may be hard to accept that you are already united with God now, but are unaware of that union. Is it really necessary for you to accept this idea? No, it is not necessary. Many of the ideas presented here about the ego and about your true spiritual nature may be extremely challenging for you. After all, you are not now seeing yourself from the perspective of His World. Everything in your world says that you are a body and a mind and that you are separate from God. So why should you accept new ideas that challenge your perception of yourself? You are not being asked to accept these theological ideas. Traditional religious organizations require their members to accept a set of specific theological ideas as a dogma. But you are not being asked to join a religious organization. If you belong to one, you are not being asked to give up your present theological thought system. Fortunately your goal in meditation is not directly related to theological ideas. In fact, it would be best for you to set aside any ideas you find in this book that would create a stumbling block for you.

This manual is designed to encourage you to communicate with God. Challenging ideas are presented in this book because as you deepen your communication with God, you cannot do so without being confronted with the question *Who am I?* The answer that you will find in your world of outer appearances will be sufficient to help you to function in your everyday world. However, as you enter His World, you will feel a need to answer this question at a deeper level. Some theological ideas here address the question at a deeper level, but a book cannot give you the answer to this question. You will have to find the answer within yourself. It is not important if your conclusions are different from those presented in this book. It is only important that you continue to seek the divine within yourself as an experience rather than as an intellectual idea. Hopefully your experience of the divine within will provide your answer to the question *Who am I?*

1. St. John of the Cross, *Ascent of Mount Carmel*, edited by E. Allison Peers (New York, New York: Image Books, a division of Doubleday and Co., Inc., 1958), pp. 174f. This book was published by arrangement with the copyright holder and original publisher, Newman Press, which has been absorbed by Paulist Press, Mahwah, New Jersey.

2. John Tauler, *Spiritual Conferences of John Tauler*, translated by Eric Coledge (St. Louis, Missouri: 1961), in Sermon 52, p. 232

3. Thomas Merton, *Contemplative Prayer*, cited from the paperback edition (New York, New York: Image Books, 1971) pp. 93-94, from the original, hardcover edition, *The Climate of Monastic Prayer* (Kalamazoo, Michigan-Spencer, Massachusetts: Cistercian Publications 1969), p. 127

4. These two books by unknown authors have been incorporated into one edition by Father William Johnston, who edited them and wrote the introduction (New York, New York: Image Books, a division of Doubleday and Co., Inc., 1973).

5. Ibid., p. 56

6. Ibid., pp. 149f

7. Ibid., pp. 171f

8. Ibid., pp. 172f

9. St. John of the Cross, *Living Flame of Love*, edited by E. Allison Peers (New York, New York: Image Books, a division of Doubleday and Co., Inc., 1962), pp 105-106. This book published by arrangement with the copyright holder and original publisher, Newman Press, which has been absorbed by Paulist Press, Mahwah, New Jersey.

10. Ibid., p. 130

11. Ibid., p. 129

12. *Writings From the Philokalia on Prayer of the Heart*, from the Russian text, "Bobrotolubiye," translated by E. Kadloubovsky and G. E. H. Palmer (London, England: Faber and Faber, eighth edition, 1975), p. 118

13. John of St. Samson, O. Carm., *Prayer, Aspiration and Contemplation*, translated and edited by Venard Poslusney, O. Carm. (Asbury, New Jersey: printed by Fr. Venard Poslusney, The 101 Foundation, 1994), p. 133

14. Ibid., p. 128

15. Ibid., p. 155

16. Ibid., p. 120

17. Ibid., p. 131

18. Ibid., p. 130

19. Ibid., p. 153

20. John J Higgins, SJ., *Merton's Theology of Prayer* (Spencer, Massachusetts and Kalamazoo, Michigan, 1971), pp. 33f

14

OPENING TO
LIGHT AND LOVE

≈ • ≈

A. Guideposts of Meditation

If you decide to continue with meditation on a daily basis, you may be asking yourself. "What will my experience be like in the future when my meditation deepens?" There are many kinds of unusual phenomena that may spontaneously occur and disappear during meditation. It is best to let these come and go without attachment or aversion. However, there are other positive experiences that may happen, and in some cases may happen consistently as meditation deepens.

Everyone's experience of deepening meditation is unique. If travelers are climbing a mountain, each may take a different route and yet arrive at the same point on the top of the mountain. But a wise traveler will take a map with various routes on it. Such a map will show guideposts to indicate where he is along the way. On your meditation journey, you may experience any of the following seven guideposts:

1. an inner feeling of love
2. an inner feeling of oneness
3. an inner feeling of heightened awareness
4. an inner feeling of light
5. an inner feeling of the divine presence
6. an inner feeling of peace
7. an inner feeling of joy

The most important guidepost is not mentioned above. That guidepost is a growth in pure faith. There are two basic ways in which meditation can deepen. One way is through pure faith that does not give you any "felt" experience related to contemplation. To practice the previous techniques of meditation that have been provided and to enter contemplation does not require any felt experience, just a willingness based on faith to be open to the hidden action of the Holy Spirit.

The second basic way that meditation can deepen also relies on pure faith, but in this case there is in addition a felt experience related to your meditation and contemplation. This felt experience has to do with the development of the intuitive level of your being. Pure faith itself is the highest form of intuition, but is too lofty of an expression of your intuition to be called an "inner feeling."

The inner feeling of the divine presence is a felt experience of being in the presence of holiness, which may be an experience of God, of Christ, or of the Holy Spirit. This kind of inner feeling of the divine presence is perhaps the inner feeling most closely associated with faith, since faith is the inner knowing of the divine being present within you. But faith is more than a sensing that you are in the presence of holiness. Faith is more than a compass that points in the right direction. It is also an indescribable inner impulse that allows you to reach out and actually contact and find the divine within you that you are seeking, even if you must do so with all your senses and faculties in darkness.

If your pure faith can be considered the ultimate expression of your intuition, the seven inner feelings identified above may be thought of as ordinary intuitions. Whereas pure faith is your most important guidepost and your indispensable form of intuition, these seven inner feelings are also guideposts that show progress yet are not necessary for your growth in meditation and contemplation.

These seven inner feelings are not mentioned to define the limits of your meditation experience, but rather to identify some of the possibilities that indicate the deepening of meditation. The term "inner feeling" refers to your intuition, meaning an inner sensing or inner knowing, which is not based on the normal, rational thinking process of the mind.

Emotions are gross expressions of your feeling nature. Emotional reaction patterns are stored in the subconscious mind and correspondingly in parts of the physical body producing tension. As you release the unconscious emotional clutter in your mind and the tension in the body, your feeling nature becomes more refined. Therefore, you are less likely to have emotional reactions. Instead of emotional reactions, you become aware of your feelings without being controlled by them. Through your practice of meditation you are able to purify your feeling nature so that you can be responsive to others with your feelings. In addition to being aware of your feelings, your meditation may deepen even further so you can become at times sensitive to your inner feelings that are intuitions. These intuitions are not a direct experience of the divine. Rather, they are only by-products of approaching your true spiritual nature.

The stages of your emotional development that lead you toward reaching the plateau of self-acceptance have been described in Chapter 12. Your inner feelings may surface at any time in your growth, but they are more likely to surface consistently and at a deeper level after you reach the plateau of self-acceptance. This is because a significant amount of your emotional garbage has been removed enabling you to reach a deeper level of meditation and contemplation in your practice of Christian Yoga Meditation. After removing so many blocks to love and reaching the plateau of self-acceptance, you will find yourself experiencing a greater openness to divine love in particular.

One of the most important inner feelings that you can encounter is the inner feeling of love. Since divine love can be defined as oneness, there may be a question about why the inner feeling of love and the inner feeling of oneness are indicated as two separate inner feelings. It is because love has many facets and can be experienced in different ways. For example, when you are meditating with a primary focus on the heart, you can experience an "inner feeling of love" that is personal, intimate and devotional in nature. On the other hand, when you are meditating with a primary focus in the head, you will not have the same kind of personal and devotional feeling. It will be more of a universal "inner feeling of oneness."

The inner feeling of heightened awareness is a feeling that your consciousness is being raised in some manner. Consciousness is closely related to prana, vital life force energy. Consequently, one possible way you may experience the feeling of heightened awareness is to experience the feeling of energy or movements of energy during your practice of meditation. Both consciousness and prana are associated with light, and the life force energy of prana may be considered *light-energy*. Thus the energy or movements of energy that you feel during meditation may be experienced not only as energy, but also as the inner feeling of light.

As your meditation experience deepens, you may experience one or more of these seven inner feelings. You may already be experiencing some of these inner feelings, but continued meditation practice will increase the depth of your experience of these inner feelings. Although these guideposts are described separately here, they may overlap so any combination of these inner feelings may be experienced simultaneously.

These inner feelings, as guideposts, reflect the reality of God's presence, yet cannot reveal His presence directly. As indirect perceptions, these inner feelings serve as signs that point to the reality of seven qualities of God. While the attributes of God are as limitless as He is, the qualities of God that are most important in relation to deepening meditation are the following seven: totally pure love, endless oneness, infinitely heightened awareness (pure consciousness), boundless light, immeasurable peace, unconditional divine love, and the divine presence that permeates all of existence. If, by divine grace, you would have a direct and complete experience of any one of these seven qualities, you would automatically be experiencing all of these qualities in union with God.

For now it is only necessary to know that meditation is an indirect perception of these qualities. It would be incorrect to think that when you meditate, you can create these qualities, because then you may deceive yourself into trying to manufacture feelings of these qualities. What actually happens during meditation is that you inwardly become aware of these qualities of God that are already within you, but which you are unable to experience directly. Thus the best you can do is to become increasingly sensitive to the feeling of the qualities that are hidden within you.

At first in meditation you may indirectly perceive the qualities of God only mentally. The significance of the seven guideposts of inner feelings is that they are signs of moving to a deeper level of experiencing the divine within. During the beginning experiences of meditation, there is the goal of controlling the stray thoughts of the mind, so the focus is on the mental process of letting go of thoughts. Therefore, you learn to hold one thought of the affirmation and to let go of the many other distracting thoughts. But as you gain the ability to hold one thought firmly, the direction of your growth may change from thought to feeling. This is because with the distracting thoughts removed, you are able to tune into inner feelings that you never knew were there. It's like adding a fine-tuning device to a radio. The tuning device blocks out static and allows you to discover channels that were not available to you before.

The question of if, when, and to what degree you may experience any of these inner feelings cannot be predetermined. You may not experience these inner feelings at all. If you do have these inner feelings, it will depend primarily on the spontaneous action of the Holy Spirit, but also requires your willingness and openness to receive the awareness of these inner feelings.

There are different theories about how to respond to these inner feelings when they occur during your meditation experience. One way to respond is to continue to hold on to your affirmation and just allow these inner feelings to come and go without attachment or aversion. Taking this approach treats these inner feelings just as you would respond to thoughts that are seeking to grab your attention, so you use the affirmation to prevent your mind from being distracted. This approach of releasing inner feelings is recommended for Inner Silence Meditation. Letting go of inner feelings can also be used for other techniques of meditation and may be most effective at times when these inner feelings present themselves as short bursts of awareness that appear and disappear suddenly.

However, letting go of inner feelings is not generally recommended in this manual because these inner feelings are not like the thoughts that are seeking to grab your attention during meditation. Instead, these inner feelings are given to you to lead you beyond thought in the direction of increasing your awareness of your divine nature. Therefore, instead of ignoring these inner feelings and holding on to your affirmation, it is recommended that you let go of your affirmation and allow yourself to focus on these inner feelings if they appear.

The recommendation to "focus" on these inner feelings does not mean to evaluate, analyze, or think about these inner feelings. Just like you can focus on the experience of breathing without intellectualizing about the breathing, you can focus on the experience of inner feelings. This focusing on the experience of inner feelings occurs in the present moment, rather than as an intellectual reflection of looking back on these inner feelings immediately after the fact. Consequently, this focusing means to direct your awareness to being open to these inner feelings as they occur. Also, focusing on inner feelings does not mean to try to hold on to them, but rather to direct your awareness by faith toward allowing these inner feelings to embrace you. This is an expression of openness to allowing the divine radiance to encompass and penetrate you.

If the inner feelings disappear and you become distracted by stray thoughts, you can return to the repeating of your affirmation. This is the approach to be taken during the first five techniques of Christian Yoga Meditation. These five techniques focus on body awareness, but focusing on inner feelings can take you to a deeper level beyond body awareness. You can let go of the affirmation and body awareness, and then you can be aware of these inner feelings as long as they last.

But focusing directly on inner feelings is definitely *not* recommended for practicing the final method of Christian Yoga Meditation. The final technique, Inner Silence Meditation, is designed to lead you toward contemplation, which will require you to let go of clinging to anything, including inner feelings. Of course, inner feelings may spontaneously present themselves during Inner Silence Meditation or contemplation. If this happens, you do not hang on to these inner feelings and you do not try to resist them. You let them come and go just as you would allow thoughts to come and go. But you do not directly focus on these inner feelings because your goal is inner silence that leads to contemplation. Any form of clinging, even to positive inner feelings would be a diversion from your goal of coming to God with an open mind and heart. By not clinging to any thought or inner feeling you can proceed in pure faith.

Christian Yoga Meditation provides the opportunity to focus on the awareness of inner feelings for the first five techniques, if these inner feelings spontaneously occur. However, focusing on inner feelings is not used for practicing Inner Silence Meditation. In addition to responding to inner feelings that spontaneously occur during meditation, there is also a proactive approach that can be taken toward these inner feelings. You can choose to practice particular techniques that are designed to focus on specific inner feelings. You can choose inner feelings that you would like to experience at a deeper level and experiment with techniques that will help you move in that direction.

Some meditation methods that focus on inner feelings are described below. These techniques emphasize using the inner feeling of love and the inner feeling of light as focal points for your meditation experience. These methods are particularly effective if you are already intermittently experiencing inner feelings spontaneously and also if you would like to experience these inner feelings on a more consistent basis.

Remember, however, that experiencing these inner feelings is not your final destination. These inner feelings, as guideposts, are only signs that point in a direction. Would you worship a sign and not move in the direction it is pointing? A wise traveler decides his destination first before setting out on a journey. This is the reason why you have chosen your spiritual ideal. It is your final destination—the top of the mountain. Your destination is a state of oneness with your ideal that is called "divine union." You need to remember that techniques of meditation cannot bring you to the final destination of divine union. These can only help prepare you to receive this gift of God's grace.

B. Growth in Divine Love

Meditation is simply a device to help you to experience God's Love. Hopefully this message has not been clouded over by the descriptions of various techniques and other aspects of meditation. This section will review parts of what has been already stated about divine love and add a few new concepts to clarify the role of divine love in relation to meditation.

Spiritual growth is a matter of learning to love. Perhaps you may not consider yourself to be a very loving person, so the idea of becoming more loving may be a bit overwhelming and even disheartening. But do not be discouraged. Your recognition that you lack love is in itself an indication that you are ready to change. Those who are justified in their own eyes do not realize their need for love. Openness to divine love comes from the awareness of your need for love. The very fact that you are reading this book and considering meditation as a step in your life is itself a sign that God's Love is motivating you to draw closer to Him. It is His Love within, which you may not even yet feel, that will guide you to the form of meditation that will help you discover God's Love for you. Or if you are already aware of His Love, it will help to deepen your awareness of that Love.

For your initial encounter with meditation, and even if you have already experienced meditation, Christian Yoga Meditation has been recommended for one reason: It is really a method that aids you to grow toward fulfilling the commandment that Jesus gave and that was also the cornerstone of the Old Testament:

> And you shall love the Lord your God with all your heart, and with all your soul, and with all your mind, and with all your strength.[1]

To understand how this relates to Christian Yoga Meditation, you may view the physical body as the temple of your worship, since that is exactly what it is. Within this temple you may consider that you have four altars. The first altar is the navel center, where you can learn how to open yourself to loving God with all of your strength. You do this in Centering Meditation, the first technique of Christian Yoga Meditation, by focusing on the navel area and allowing the body's physical functioning to be given over to the action of the Spirit. Through this receptivity to the Spirit, you are revitalized at the physical level and can offer the strength of the physical body to God's purposes.

The second altar of the temple of your body is the heart center, where you learn how to be receptive to loving God with your whole heart. You do this in the second technique, Heart Meditation, by focusing on the heart area to offer your feeling nature to the Spirit. This produces the quality of devotion. At first, this may not be felt, but gradually you begin to develop the qualities of compassion, sharing with others, and a deeper desire for union with God based on love and thanksgiving.

The third altar of the temple of your physical body is the brow center, where you learn how to open yourself to loving God with your whole mind. Through Brow Meditation you can hold your awareness at the brow area and offer the activity of the mind to the divine influence. Thus the mind becomes the loving instrument of the Spirit. The brow area, associated with the mind, may be considered the doorway to higher consciousness that leads to the fourth altar.

The fourth altar of the temple of the physical body is the crown center, where you learn to open yourself to loving God with your whole soul. The crown area is generally considered part of the physical body located at the top of the head, but some believe it is actually above the top of the head. In either case, the crown center transcends the physical body and is the location of the "Holy of Holies." It is the contact point with Spirit.

The last three methods of Christian Yoga Meditation involve opening the crown center of spiritual awareness. Of these three methods, Crown Meditation is the only one in which you focus directly on the crown area itself. Crown Meditation has an influence on the whole body, helping to integrate all functions and coordinate all seven centers of awareness.

After opening the crown center of awareness during the practice of Crown Meditation, the crown center ideally remains open as you practice Oneness Meditation and shift your awareness to the whole body, including, of course, all four of the altars of worship in your temple. This opens you to your intuitions, your inner feelings, as described above. One of the most important of these is the inner feeling of love, which is a revealing of your true nature of love in union with God.

Hopefully your crown center of awareness continues to be open as you move on to the final technique, Inner Silence Meditation. For this practice you let go of body awareness to transcend your temple and enter the Holy of Holies. As you do so, you reach into a deeper level of His World and by faith increase your awareness of His silent, loving presence. When His Spirit draws you into the state of deep contemplation, you will be able to love God with your whole strength, heart, mind, and soul.

The first awareness of love in relation to God is invariably not your love for God, but rather God's Love for you. It is for this reason that meditation may be considered inner receptivity to the Spirit that allows you to be open to receiving God's Love. Meditation, regardless of what method you choose, allows you first to accept the love that God has for you and then in turn allows you to offer this love back to God. Practicing Christian Yoga Meditation is especially beneficial in regard to increasing your awareness of receiving love from God and expressing love to God.

In addition, a method called *Inner Love Meditation* is described in the last section of this chapter for your consideration as a means of opening to divine love. This method is recommended as a temporary alternative to your regular meditation. It may be practiced while sitting, but you may also use this method in the lying-down position to help you relax and open to God's Love for you and your love for God.

After you inwardly express your love for God, you are better able to dedicate yourself to doing His Will of Love and to offer yourself as a channel of blessing to others. This will encourage you to take the next step after meditation—which is to pray for others. Through your prayers for others the love that has been enkindled within you is given back to God as a blessing to your brothers and sisters in accordance with God's Will. Of course, the real challenge then is to allow that loving feeling that has been awakened within you to carry over into your thoughts and words and activities of daily living so that you can be a blessing to all those whom you meet. In this way you can fulfill the second great commandment: "You shall love your neighbor as yourself."[2]

Meditation, when properly understood and consistently practiced, is a reminder that more important than anything else in your spiritual life is a growth in love. You have a deep-seated psychological need to love yourself and to love others in the same way, but you have an even deeper spiritual need to feel the Love that God has for you. Without that Love, all these meditation techniques would run the risk of being only an exercise in egotism and self-will. However, with that Love, techniques can be used to purify yourself so that you will be better able to know and do God's Will.

The word "love" is used in many different ways, yet have you ever asked yourself to define "love"? It might be helpful for you to take a moment right now, before reading further, to ask yourself how you would define love, with the understanding that there is no right or wrong definition. The various definitions of love could easily fill a book and still would not exhaust all the facets of what love is all about. But a definition of love will be offered now that may help to clarify and encompass much of what has been stated so far in this book.

Love can be defined as *oneness*. Consider what this means. The single most important truth about spiritual growth is this: Love is your own true nature. Love, meaning oneness with God, is the condition in which you exist. Yet this most important truth is likewise the most difficult truth for you to understand and accept. Your ego condition contradicts this truth by telling you that you are separate from God and so you must become united with Him. Since you are not yet aware of your natural state of oneness with God, the idea of love as oneness does not meet your needs for a definition of love that will help you in a practical sense in your everyday life to grow toward your spiritual aspirations. If you accept that you are already united with God, how can you possibly "grow toward becoming" united with Him? In fact, your growth does not "manufacture" divine union, but rather you are learning to let go of the ego's false perception that imagines that you are separate from God.

Although the definition of love as oneness expresses the truth of your condition theoretically, the definition does not help you in a practical sense to let go of your false ego-based perspective of separation. Thus as a concession to the ego condition, a second definition of love can be used that takes into account that you are not yet aware of your natural state of oneness with God. As a practical aid for your spiritual growth, you may define love as the desire and the manifesting of *two becoming one*. Whereas the first definition of love as oneness is an acknowledgment of the being state of love, this second definition is an expression of the principle of love in action. In your spiritual growth, love is not only the end result of union, but love as two becoming one is also the desire for union and the entire process of bringing about that union.

Using this definition, you can see why love is so important to spiritual growth. Meditation properly applied is an expression of love because it is the manifestation of the desire for the meditator and the spiritual ideal to become one. Through love, not techniques, you may reach the highest level of communication with God beyond duality. Duality is based on your self-awareness that imagines that you and God are separate. It is love that bridges this gap out of the desire for a true oneness with God.

Of course, this gap between you and God does not really exist except in your own rational thinking mind. Since you are already united with God and cannot be separate from Him, the idea of two becoming one must in fact be an illusion. Nonetheless, it is a helpful illusion because the illusory idea of joining with God is an important motivational factor in discovering the truth that you already are one with God.

Love as two becoming one can be seen in your daily life also. It is reflected in the most intimate human relationships between a man and a woman. To a lesser degree it is demonstrated in your spontaneous desire to hug your relatives or friends as an expression of oneness. But if you look carefully behind these expressions of human love in your daily life, you will see that God is showing you His Love for you. His Love is not so much shining *on* you as His Love is shining *in* you. It is His Love in you that reminds you that from His viewpoint you are already two as one. Your world is a world of only apparent separation. From your perspective it may be difficult to see that your world is overlapped by His World and that you truly draw your very existence from His World, which is a world of oneness. No definition can adequately define God by saying He is this only and no more. Yet keeping the inadequacy of defining God in mind, it may be helpful here to describe God in His unmanifested state of Being as both Love and Oneness. Since God, as Love and Oneness, is everywhere and in everything, it is impossible for Him to be separate from anyone. The challenge is to realize that you are not separate from Him. If you were apart from God, how could you exist, since His Love for you keeps you in existence? Because He is in each individual, you have the opportunity to see Him in every person you meet, if only you have "eyes to see and ears to hear."

Many years ago while I was visiting Philadelphia, I was invited to a small gathering of spiritually minded people and was asked to conclude their meeting with a meditation. I talked for a few moments about the Jesus Prayer and about Christian techniques of meditation, which we practiced together. After the meditation was completed, several people came over to talk with me, but I noticed a young man in a wheelchair who was being ignored as everyone else was socializing. I went over to him and looked in his eyes. I felt very close to him, and I hugged him. He hugged me back, almost like a drowning man would clutch a life preserver. He continued hugging, and then he started crying. Yet I could feel his tears were tears of joy, of being accepted, and of being loved.

Within myself I felt the same feelings—joy, acceptance, and love. When we separated, he pointed to a card with the letters of the alphabet written on it. He couldn't speak, so he pointed to letters in succession in order to spell—"G..O..D....L..O..V..E..S....Y..O..U." I pointed to him and said, "God loves you." He smiled broadly and pointed to letters on the card again—"G..O..D....L..O..V..E..S....U..S."

This brief encounter had a great impact on me. I felt I could see right through that crippled body, and there was a perfect child of God, perfectly Loved by his Creator. I could feel love for him, too, not the sympathy that perhaps he sometimes got. I could see he sensed what I was feeling. He could also see that I accepted his love for me and that I accepted him as my equal before God. He was teaching me, too. In case I might miss the message, it was being spelled out for me that God loves me. It's a message that everyone has to learn—and relearn daily.

The message is everywhere, just as God is everywhere in His creation. But are you able to see Him and His message? It takes so long to go from birth to the age of reason that somewhere along the way you forget that everything around you is a miracle constantly in the process of unfolding. The sun rises every day, but you fail to see the miracle because you and everyone around you have collectively taken it for granted. God is there in every breath of air you breathe, yet you have become accustomed to it, so there seems to be no miracle. Every part of creation is working together like a perfect symphony to keep you alive. Why? Because it is God's way of saying He loves you.

You may mentally believe that God is in everyone and everything, but in your daily life it is often difficult to see God in other people or to see God's Love in creation. Even if you have the perception to see God in these ways, it will never satisfy your deepest yearning, which is to recognize His presence within yourself, and ultimately to become one with God in divine union.

Techniques of meditation cannot bring about divine union. However, they can be a significant aid in becoming receptive to that gift. While techniques can aid you in your spiritual growth, in the final analysis you can not base the true value of your meditation experience on how successful you may be in your practice. The real importance of practicing meditation is that it serves as a way for you to express your *desire* to be one with God. It's not your meditation results, but rather your desire for

God's presence and His saving grace that will bring about divine union. Techniques of meditation, while not necessary for everyone, are helpful for those who are drawn to them as a means of crystallizing their desire, as a preparation for divine union. Since divine union is a spiritual marriage, it requires a desire and willingness on the part of the soul to create the bond of love, because God will not impose Himself on anyone. From this you can see that if you have developed great mental abilities through years of meditation, but do not have love, you are wasting your time. On the other hand, if you are a poor meditator or have never meditated, and yet you have love, you are richly prepared to receive the gift of divine union.

The story of the prodigal son is a good reminder of divine love. It is easy to identify with the prodigal son. He squandered all of his inheritance and experienced suffering. Then he decided to go back to his father and offered to be a lowly servant. "But while he was yet at a distance, his father saw him and had compassion, and ran and embraced him and kissed him."[3]

In this same way, God responds to you whenever you wish to change your life and make one little step toward Him. He makes ten running strides to you and touches your heart with His embrace. This is how it will be for anyone who decides to take the step of using meditation as a way of drawing closer to God. Even if you feel that you are able to make only limited progress in your meditation practice, God will still shower many spiritual blessings on you for your effort. As far a God is concerned, it is your sincerity of heart that matters.

C. Inner Light Meditation

If in meditation you experience the inner feelings described above, there are different ways of responding. Initially when these inner feelings present themselves to you in meditation, you may have an inappropriate attachment to them simply because they are pleasant, and you may be starved for spiritual sweetness. You may want to cling to these pleasant feelings, and your ego may attach a prideful significance to having these feelings. Your attachment may actually prevent these inner feelings from recurring more frequently. You may make the mistake of valuing your meditation experience based on whether these feelings occur or not. Yet the most valuable meditations you have may be the ones that appear to be a struggle for you, but in which you are facing and removing inner blocks.

When these inner feelings first begin to appear, it may be best to treat them like any other thoughts. You can focus on your affirmation and let these inner feelings come and go without attachment or aversion. Some approaches to meditation teach that this is always the way you should respond to these inner feelings. This is really a safe approach because when you are seeking God, you must rely most of all on pure faith that does not require your having a felt experience to confirm your faith. This approach prevents you from mistakenly interpreting these inner feelings as evidence of having a direct experience of God Himself, instead of correctly realizing that they are only signs that point the way to God.

Nevertheless, there comes a time in your development when you understand that these inner feelings can be used as a means of drawing you closer to God without being a distraction or attachment. Your inner feelings are not like other thoughts that grab your attention during meditation because inner feelings are guideposts reminding you of your divine nature. As long as you remain centered on your faith in God, you do not have to ignore these inner feelings and therefore disregard the message that these inner feelings have for you.

One way of accepting your inner feelings as an aid to your practice is to let go of your affirmation and focus your awareness on your inner feelings when they appear. This focusing does not mean thinking about your inner feelings, but rather placing your attention on the experience of these inner feelings as they occur in the present moment. You can focus on any one inner feeling or any combination of inner feelings that comes to your awareness. If the inner feelings disappear and your mind becomes distracted, you can return to using your affirmation. You can apply this same approach to the five techniques of Christian Yoga Meditation that focus on body awareness. You can let go of your affirmation and hold your awareness in the focusing area within the body appropriate to the technique being used. While focusing on body awareness, you can also focus on inner feelings when they present themselves. When the inner feelings leave your awareness, you can return to just focusing on body awareness, or if your mind becomes distracted, you can return to focusing on both your affirmation and body awareness. A description of how to respond to inner feelings during the practice of Inner Silence Meditation and contemplation is provided in the next section.

The approach that has just been explained relies on responding to inner feelings when they occur spontaneously without your consciously attempting to uncover these inner feelings. After you have made progress in removing subconscious emotional clutter, your mind may become calm to the degree of allowing more of these inner feelings to surface. If you notice that inner feelings are naturally surfacing more frequently, you may want to take another approach that may allow you to experience these inner feelings consistently. For your new approach, you can proactively initiate the uncovering of these inner feelings. The rest of this section focuses on initiating the opening of yourself to experiencing the inner feeling of light, the inner feeling of love, and other inner feelings.

If you want to increase your awareness of the inner feeling of light, you may be guided to create your own meditation technique related to the awareness of light. Some meditators, who imagine white light to be surrounding and filling the body as a preparation for meditation, find this process so effective that they continue to focus on white light throughout their meditation. Other meditators find it helpful to focus on a candle flame with the eyes open, and then closing the eyes, they focus on the light within. Some imagine a sphere of light like the sun within the head and imagine light radiating outward from that sphere. There are also meditators who can actually see a steady inner light and meditate on that light. The ability to see light within may occur spontaneously or may be learned. One way of learning this ability is to first close your eyes during meditation and focus on seeing blackness. Within that blackness you can look for the slightest bit of light. Then you focus on that tiny bit of light. Gradually after repeated practice, the amount of light you can see will increase until ideally you can consistently see an inner light.

There is a technique of focusing on light, which does not use the imagination and does not use the visual experience of seeing light. This method is called *Inner Light Meditation*. For this method you are aware of feeling the presence of light and allow that inner feeling to be the focus of your meditation. Sometimes you can feel this light as it moves through the body. It is quite different from imagining white light because it appears to be something happening to you in your receptive state of mind, rather than something you are actively attempting to produce through your imagination. Oftentimes this inner feeling of light seems to carry with it other feelings as well, such as an inner feeling of the divine presence, love, or peace. It may also be accompanied by a feeling of heightened awareness, which may be experienced as expanded consciousness or as energy.

Initially the presence of light may be felt as a temporary experience within the body that comes and goes of its own accord. Consequently, this inner feeling may at first be difficult to use as a consistent focus for meditation because of its spontaneous coming and going. But there is one area of the body where this feeling of inner light can be experienced most consistently. This area is the location of the physical heart. The exact location is not the whole area of the physical heart, but rather a very small area on the left side of the chest that can be felt intuitively during meditation. If you develop a sensitivity to this inner feeling, you will experience a light emanating from this area. This sensitivity cannot happen through a forceful effort of the will. In order to feel this light, you literally need to open your heart. In other words, the light in the heart can only be felt by you when you are in a loving state of mind.

When you first start your practice of Inner Light Meditation, your practice is just like Heart Meditation in that you repeat your affirmation and hold your awareness in the heart area. When your mind becomes calm, you let go of the affirmation and only focus on the heart area. For Inner Light Meditation, you specifically hold your awareness on a very small area of the heart. It may take many meditation periods before you are able to tune into the light and love that emanates from the heart. When you do experience the inner light and/or love, you focus on the heart and also on that inner feeling as long as you are able to do so. You can eventually make this a consistent focus for your meditation, rather than an intermittent focus.

In the area on the left side of the chest where the light is felt, there may also be a subtle energy or very slight pressure without pain that pinpoints the exact spot. This spot is referred to by St. John of the Cross in his book *The Living Flame of Love*, when he speaks about the presence of a divine inner flame. In fact, the phrase "living flame of love" perfectly describes this spot in the heart where divine love is waiting to be awakened. This phrase is usually interpreted as only a literary metaphor used by St. John of the Cross. However, this loving and living flame is the exact description of what can actually be experienced in meditation. It truly feels like a flame of subtle energy that is alive and actually sending out light and love. It is a really an eternal flame that is in every individual heart. The flame can be limited to only a tiny spark of light and love, but it can never be extinguished. Invariably it is covered over by the cares of the world so that you do not notice it.

As you focus on this area and perhaps can feel the presence of this flame, your meditation will deepen, and your feeling of light, love, and energy will increase. Eventually after awakening the flame in the heart on a consistent basis, it will be quite natural for the light, love, and energy to expand outward from the heart. Gradually the light, love, and energy will expand to the whole chest, especially to the center of the chest.

With continued practice, the light, love, and energy naturally rise upward through the neck and into the head. The light, love, and energy may go up the front of the head but is more likely to first go up to the lower portion of the back of the head. Finally the head may become filled with light, love, and energy.

Inner Light Meditation may be used as part of a variation of Christian Yoga Meditation, which is described in the next section. In this variation Inner Light Meditation replaces Heart Meditation. So when the light, love, and energy rise from the heart center into the head, you can shift your awareness to the brow area for Brow Meditation, as part of this variation, which is called *Expanded Christian Yoga Meditation*.

When practicing Inner Light Meditation, you may feel energy currents rising upward from the base of the spine into the head while focusing on the light and love in the chest. In addition, there may be jolts of energy that suddenly rise upward through the neck and jerk the head somewhat. Regardless of whatever occurs on a form level, you will need to remain focused on your intent of maintaining a loving state of mind and seeking the divine within.

It is important to remember that experiencing inner light is fueled only by remaining in a love state. If the mind becomes distracted by unloving thoughts, the light will literally go out and very quickly at that. If the feeling of inner light disappears, you can focus on an affirmation, such as "Christ Light" or "Jesus Christ Light," and hold the awareness in the heart area. If your mind becomes calm, you can release the affirmation and hold your awareness in the heart area, just as you would do in Heart Meditation. When the awareness of inner light returns, you can focus on the heart area and also focus on the inner feeling of light and love.

Since the cares of the world literally cover over the flame in the heart, it is necessary to have a purity of purpose if you intend to uncover this flame. The goal should not be the attainment of an experience, but the desire for God Himself. Also, once the flame is initially uncovered, there are still many inner blocks that would hinder your progress in meditation. These inner obstacles are the ego-based concerns of the world that are like a dark cloud around the flame. This dark cloud lifts as you release inner blocks by focusing on the heart, as was explained in Chapter 12.

After releasing blocks over an extended period of time, you will notice an increased sensitivity to being aware of light, love and energy within. You may find that when you attempt to hold your awareness on the flame in the heart, your awareness instead goes to the center of the chest where you feel a strong light, love, and energy emanating. If this happens, feel free to allow the center of the chest to be your ongoing focusing area for your regular practice of Inner Light Meditation.

Hopefully you will be able to open both your physical heart and the center of your chest to the divine love that is your true nature. For your practice of Inner Light Meditation, you can hold your awareness on whichever of these two locations draws your attention, as you are in the process of literally opening your heart to the divine influence.

Through practicing Inner Light Meditation, as part of Expanded Christian Yoga Meditation, you will eventually have an increased ability to be aware of light, love, and energy filling the chest, the head, and then the whole body. Eventually your increased awareness of light and love can help bring about a noticeable inner and outer transformation. The results of this transformation are not only a significant deepening of meditation, but also an enhancement of your personality that increases your outer expression of love to others. By removing many inner blocks while focusing on the inner feelings of light and love, you will experience a deep peace and an inner sense of well being. Discovering the light and love within your own heart is indeed a wonderful blessing.

For the practice of Inner Light Meditation, you may experience a combination of the feeling of inner light, the feeling of inner love, or the feeling of heightened awareness, which can be felt as an expansion of your consciousness or more tangibly as a subtle energy within the body. Also, you can focus on any one of these inner feelings.

If you are attracted to practicing Inner Light Meditation, you may incorporate this method into the One Year Program. In this case, you can use Inner Light Meditation as a replacement for Heart Meditation for all or selected parts of the One Year Program.

D. Expanded Christian Yoga Meditation

If you have been practicing Christian Yoga Meditation over a period of time and would like to increase your awareness of inner feelings, you may want to consider using a variation of your regular practice. This variation, called *Expanded Christian Yoga Meditation*, includes all the techniques of Christian Yoga Meditation except Heart Meditation, which is replaced by Inner Light Meditation that also focuses on the heart area.

The first method of Expanded Christian Yoga Meditation is Centering Meditation. This method is practiced exactly as in your regular practice of Christian Yoga Meditation. There is no particular emphasis on opening to inner feelings during Centering Meditation because first you want to establish a relaxed breathing pattern and begin your practice just as you always do when using Christian Yoga Meditation. The only adjustment in your practice may be changing your affirmation if you feel a new affirmation would help you to open up to your inner feelings. For example, you may choose an affirmation such as "Christ Light" or "Christ Love."

For your second method of Expanded Christian Yoga Meditation, you practice Inner Light Meditation, which focuses on a specific area of your physical heart and on the inner feelings emanating from this area. These inner feelings of light, love, and/or energy become your focus for meditation, as has been described previously. But if your awareness is naturally drawn to the inner feelings of light, love, and energy in the center of the chest, you may focus your awareness there instead of in the location of the physical heart. Under ideal circumstances you will experience the light, love, and/or energy from the heart expanding and filling the chest and then rising into the head, which will be the best preparation for practicing the next method, Brow Meditation.

For your practice of Brow Meditation, a change from your regular practice of this method is that when you focus on the brow area, you also focus on the inner feelings of light, love, and/or energy in the brow area. You place your focus entirely on the brow area for this practice. But without consciously intending to do so, you may feel light, love, and/or energy in the heart area or in the center of the chest as a result of previously practicing Inner Light Meditation. You continue to focus at the brow area even though you may feel the light, love, and/or energy rising up from the heart or from the center of the chest and into the head. Whether or not you can feel light, love, and/or energy rising up from below, the goal is to allow your mind to be a loving instrument of the Spirit. You can use an affirmation if you become distracted, yet as you make progress, the affirmation will be needed less and less.

For the fourth technique of Expanded Christian Yoga Meditation, you practice Crown Meditation. You focus on the crown area as you would normally, but also on the inner feelings of light, love, and/or energy in the crown area. As with the other methods, you can use an affirmation if your mind becomes distracted. For this practice you focus only on the crown area. However, without consciously intending to do so, you may also feel light, love, and/or energy in the heart area, in the center of the chest, or in the brow area. You to continue to steadfastly maintain your focus on the crown area, even though you may feel the light, love, and/or energy rising upward from below and into the crown area. The purpose is to be open to the manifestation of light, love, and energy that the Spirit would reveal to you as a way of reminding you of your true spiritual nature. Focusing on light, love, and/or energy while practicing Crown Meditation helps to increase your receptivity to allowing the Holy Spirit to coordinate all seven spiritual centers of awareness and all functions within the body.

For those meditators who specifically feel energy in the body while practicing Expanded Christian Yoga Meditation, it may be helpful here to review the ways that energy may manifest itself during the practice of the first four techniques. The energy that is being felt is prana and can be felt in many different ways. It can be felt as concentrations of energy in each focusing area in the front of the body or as the energy of tension being released in any part of the body. It may also be felt as movements of energy up the front or the back of the body that may be experienced as slow, steady movements or sudden, jerky movements.

The partial rising of the kundalini in the body can be felt as energy manifesting in various ways, which have been explained in Chapter 11. One possible specific way in which the partial rising of the kundalini can occur in Expanded Christian Yoga Meditation will be described now. This specific partial rising goes all the way up to the crown area, but is partial in terms of intensity since it is only a small portion of the full kundalini force that is being raised up. The way this may manifest is that some of the coiled prana at the base of the spine rises very slowly up the spine as the meditator is holding his awareness in the navel area, the heart area, the brow area, and the crown area during the first four methods of Expanded Christian Yoga Meditation. Some meditators can feel the prana as it rises slowly up the spine, then to the lower part of the back of the head at the medulla oblongata, and finally to the circular crown area.

Some meditators cannot feel the energy rising in the spine, yet can feel the crown area being activated by this rising energy. In some cases the crown area can be felt as a circular "opening" or simply as an increase of energy at the top of the head. In general, most meditators do not feel the energy rising in the spine or the energy in the crown area. But the rising of energy in the spine and activation of the crown area can certainly occur without the conscious awareness of the meditator. When some of the inner blocks are removed and a certain amount of the creative energy rises up to the top of the head, the creative energy flows into this circular crown area and allows an integrating energy to descend downward into the whole body, coordinating all the centers of awareness. This rising creative energy and resulting descending energy is due to the activity of the kundalini. The kundalini removes blocks as it rises and integrates the spiritual centers as it descends. This brings about the experience of the inner feelings that are described in this chapter.

Those who can feel the integrating energy from the crown center as it descends downward may first feel the energy come down into the center of the chest and then feel the entire body being filled with energy. The Twenty-third Psalm makes a reference to this overflowing energy:

> Thy rod and thy staff, they comfort me. Thou anointeth my head with oil. My cup runneth over, surely goodness and mercy shall follow me all the days of my life.

The "rod" is the endocrine glands in the front of the body. The "staff" is the nerve plexuses in the spine plus the medulla oblongata and also the crown area that creates the curve to the top of the staff. The "cup" is the crown center. The anointing with "oil" is the oil of God's grace that takes the form of the creative energy filling the crown center and overflowing, just as a cup can be filled to overflowing. This overflowing energy integrates the physical, emotional, and mental levels of your human nature, bringing them into accord with your spiritual nature.

Although during Crown Meditation the focus is on the crown of the head, this focusing produces a coordinating effect on the whole body. Even though most meditators do not feel this coordinating effect as a consciously felt experience, this integration can still occur without the conscious awareness being present. Since Crown Meditation creates an integration of the whole body, it is a natural preparation for focusing on the whole body in the next technique, which is Oneness Meditation.

For the practice of Oneness Meditation, you focus on the whole body or most of the body. This method is optional because some meditators are unable to extend their focus to this extent. While you focus on the whole body, you focus on a feeling of oneness, just as you ordinarily would. However, in addition to the feeling of oneness, you also focus on the whole body being filled with light, love, and/or energy. You use an affirmation only if your mind wanders because of stray thoughts. For the conclusion of Oneness Meditation, you let go of body awareness altogether and briefly focus only on the inner feeling of oneness, light, love, and/or energy as a transition to the next method, which is Inner Silence Meditation. After this brief transition, you let go of focusing on oneness, light, love, and or energy, and practice Inner Silence Meditation, just as you would ordinarily for Christian Yoga Meditation.

If you can feel energy in the body and if the prior example of energy rising in the spine and descending from the crown center occurs, you may feel energy throughout the whole body during Oneness Meditation, as an aftereffect of Crown Meditation. Sometimes this can present a slight problem in relation to moving on to the next method, Inner Silence Meditation. Moving from Oneness Meditation to Inner Silence Meditation requires releasing body awareness altogether, but if you feel your whole body filled with energy, it may be difficult to let go of body awareness.

If you are unable to let go of body awareness, you will need to let go of your desire in relation to feeling energy in the body. You can still rest in inner silence and contemplation while body awareness and energy awareness are present to some degree, as long as you can let go of your desire for these. You can let go of your desire by setting aside both attraction to energy awareness and aversion to energy awareness. Since the faculty of your will is not involved, you can let energy awareness come and go of its own accord without your invitation or rejection. In this way energy awareness experienced passively may still occur, but since you are not using this awareness of energy as a focusing object, you will be able to practice Inner Silence Meditation without being distracted.

For Inner Silence Meditation, the sixth and final technique, you let go of body awareness as much as possible and open yourself to resting in the divine presence. As with all six methods of Expanded Christian

Yoga Meditation, you can repeat an affirmation at those times when your mind becomes distracted. With the crown center of awareness having been opened by Crown Meditation and remaining open for Oneness Meditation, the crown center of awareness ideally will continue to be open for Inner Silence Meditation. Hopefully you will be receptive to the unifying effect of the Holy Spirit acting through the crown center of awareness. With your consent the Holy Spirit will assist you to calm and to unify the mind enough for you to enter contemplation. During contemplation you can rely on your pure faith alone, which is the highest form of intuition that goes deeper than your inner feelings. Your faith is a reliance on your inner knowing of the divine presence, which may not be felt experientially. During your contemplation you are drawn into an inner absorption that allows you to let go of mental distractions.

Your faith is essential to bring about the overshadowing of the Holy Spirit and to enter contemplation. Although your faith does not require a felt experience to confirm the divine presence, it certainly does not exclude having a felt experience of the divine presence. Thus because of your openness to your inner feelings during your practice of the previous five techniques of Expanded Christian Yoga Meditation, you may find yourself continuing to experience the inner feelings of light, love, and/or other inner feelings as you rest in inner silence. If these inner feelings, including the feeling of energy, spontaneously present themselves, you can be open to them and feel them as long as they last, without feeling as though you need to cling to them or push them away.

The previous methods of Expanded Christian Yoga Meditation focus directly on the inner feelings of light, love, and/or energy. Yet when you let go of your affirmation during Inner Silence Meditation, you do not focus specifically on these inner feelings. These inner feelings may come to you anyway, but during Inner Silence Meditation you want to be completely open to the action of the Holy Spirit so that you exert no initiative of your own directed toward what you would like to experience.

You learn to let go in order to reach a deeper level of receptivity. You will need to be willing to let go of yourself, as you think of yourself. This includes letting go of your own desires, even self-chosen spiritual desires. In order to succeed, you will need to have faith that you will be supported by the Spirit in your process of letting go. Your trust in the Spirit will be rewarded. You will be supported, but not necessarily in the way in which you expect. You will receive from the Spirit whatever you truly need to make progress spiritually, rather than what you may consciously want.

The body awareness methods of Expanded Christian Yoga Meditation allow you to proactively direct your awareness toward experiencing inner feelings. However, this proactive expression of the desire for experiencing inner feelings is counterbalanced by the nonattachment of Inner Silence Meditation, in which you do not consciously direct your awareness toward revealing your inner feelings. It would be helpful here to mention some differences between meditation and contemplation in order to explain why you do not use your inner feelings as a focusing object during the practice of Inner Silence Meditation, which leads to contemplation.

Meditation is communication with God, which always has an object as the focus for meditation, so in meditation you are the one deciding to hold on to that object. Consequently, you can have your inner feelings of light and love as your focusing object for your meditation. In contrast to meditation, contemplation is communication with God in which you do not have a focusing object. Thus during contemplation you cannot direct your mind toward your inner feelings as a focusing object. But you can experience whatever inner feelings present themselves as they come and go, but without any feeling that you must hold on to them or push them away. This approach allows you let go of your own desires and leaves you entirely open to the divine influence.

Directly focusing on inner feelings when practicing techniques that use body awareness can work for the lower rungs of the ladder to higher consciousness. Yet when you want to let go of body awareness and enter contemplation, a greater degree of nonattachment is required. The reason for emphasizing the need to let go of directly focusing on inner feelings during Inner Silence Meditation is that holding on to inner feelings represents a form of possessiveness that reinforces the false self. The ego survives by its ability to possess not only material things, but also by possessing thoughts and feelings, even spiritual thoughts and feelings.

You may be so starved for spiritual experiences that when inner feelings occur, you may want to hold on to them in a clinging fashion. But this clinging itself is a fear of loss, which will close off your openness and trust and thus shut down your experience of inner feelings. When you can let go of the clinging to these inner feelings, you will no longer be under the influence of the aspect of the ego that seeks spiritual experiences for the sake of spiritual pride. In doing so you will not close the door to spiritual sweetness, but rather you will have only given up your possessiveness that is so characteristic of the ego. Ironically it is by giving up this very possessiveness that you actually remove a hindrance to having spiritual consolations coming to you spontaneously.

God cannot be possessed in the way that the ego is accustomed to possessing objects. *But you can allow God to possess you.* By allowing the Holy Spirit to come over you in contemplation, you are allowing yourself to be embraced by the Spirit. Being embraced by the Spirit requires that you possess nothing, letting thoughts come and go. Likewise, let your inner feelings of spiritual sweetness come and go of themselves.

After you learn to let go of any sense of possession regarding inner feelings, you may discover that when inner feelings do spontaneously occur, it feels in a way that the inner feelings are possessing you. When the Holy Spirit overshadows you in contemplation, inner feelings may come as well. Generally these inner feelings come and go. Yet after you have been exposed to contemplative experiences over a long period of time, you may notice that these inner feelings stay without your exerting any initiative for this to happen. After you have released many inner blocks and reached the plateau of self-acceptance, these inner feelings that stay may last for most of your practice. When these inner feelings stay with you, it may appear to you that these inner feelings are holding on to you.

Inner feelings are from God, but they are not God, just as sunlight is from the sun but is not the sun. These inner feelings are the radiance of God. When these inner feelings persist without you exerting your will for this to happen, it appears to you that you are being possessed by God. It feels as if you are an object that God is embracing with His Light and Love, even if it is only an indirect embrace.

Earlier, when you were trying to possess these inner feelings, you viewed yourself as a subject, who is the one possessing these inner feelings, and you viewed your inner feelings as the object you were possessing. In this more advanced state you view yourself as the object who is being possessed and view God as the subject, Who is indirectly possessing you. But this view of yourself as an object upon which God is radiating is still an illusion that perpetuates the subject/object division between you and God. This illusory division is caused by the ego, which is the thought of division. In reality, it is only your lack of awareness of your true nature and your investment in the ego that prevents you from realizing that you are one with God.

Your contemplative experience of the Holy Spirit overshadowing you is a state of *imageless self-awareness*. You give up your possessiveness, but there is still the awareness of yourself as the observer of the parade of both thoughts and feelings. Your awareness is not totally unified so you may actually be experiencing different levels of awareness at the same time. For example, in what might be called the "foreground" of your awareness, you may be experiencing inner feelings, and in what might be called the "background" of your awareness, you may be dimly conscious of the stream of thoughts passing by in the mind. You are the observer placing most of your attention on your inner feelings and to a lesser degree noticing unwanted thoughts pass by, but without paying attention to them. It may happen that even the passing unwanted thoughts disappear entirely from your awareness, so you experience only inner feelings. But even in this state, you would still be aware of yourself as being the observer.

The next step on the ladder to higher consciousness is going from contemplation with self-awareness to the experience of contemplation without self-awareness. This deeper level of contemplation beyond being aware of yourself may be called *pure awareness* or *pure consciousness*. In the state of self-awareness, you are aware of yourself as the one who is seeking and who is separate from what you are seeking. In the state of pure awareness or pure consciousness, you let go of yourself, as you think of yourself. You let go of the false self, the ego, which means you let go of the illusory idea that you are separate from God.

You cannot exert the force of your will to bring yourself into the deeper contemplative state of pure awareness, because this state occurs spontaneously of itself by divine grace. Nonetheless, you can prepare yourself for this by letting go of the desire for spiritual experiences. After all, if you are seeking spiritual experiences of inner feelings as possessions for the ego, how will you be able to let go of the false self in order to be in a state of pure awareness?

If you have decided that your final destination is divine union, you need to recognize that your divine union is far beyond any temporary experience you may have in your journey toward your destination. If you have set your course on reaching a mountain top, you can stop for a few minutes to refresh yourself by drinking from a natural spring that you find along your way. However, then you need to continue on your journey in order to reach the top of the mountain. Releasing the need to hold on to the inner feelings that may come and go will give you a new freedom in which spiritual experiences are not a concern, but still can be accepted without attachment or aversion. In this way your heart can remain truly devoted to God alone, Who can meet your every need.

The final technique of Expanded Christian Yoga Meditation is not much different from your regular practice of Inner Silence Meditation, except that you may notice an increase in the number and depth of inner feelings that spontaneously occur during your practice. Your increased awareness of inner feelings will be the result of having opened yourself significantly to the Spirit during the previous methods that used body awareness. Through your increased openness to the Spirit, you may find that during your practice of Inner Silence Meditation you are able to experience contemplation more consistently and at a deeper level.

If you are attracted to practicing Expanded Christian Yoga Meditation, you may incorporate this method into the One Year Program. In this case, you can practice Expanded Christian Yoga as a replacement for Christian Yoga Meditation for all or selected parts of the One Year Program.

E. Inner Love Meditation

While all meditation methods help you to increase your awareness of God's loving inner presence, *Inner Love Meditation* in particular helps you to be receptive to God's Love. Using the imagination has not been recommended for the meditation methods in this book. However, this technique is the exception to that rule as will be explained shortly. Before attempting to use this technique that does focus on love, it is helpful to look at your own perceptions of what love means to you.

Your perception of love is influenced by your perception of yourself. The ego-based self tells you that you are a limited mind and a body that is separate from God. This false self is how you normally perceive yourself. Although this perception is what separates you from your awareness of God, you cannot reject the self as your enemy. Actually you need to accept the mask of self and indeed love that mask because in doing so you are allowing your true Self, your true nature of love, to be expressed. You are conditioned to think it is selfish to love yourself. In reality, it is *only* by accepting and loving yourself that you are able to accept and love others. In fact, Jesus said that you must love your neighbors in the same way that you love yourself. This means you must love yourself without allowing your self-love to make you think you are better than your neighbors, since this is pride. Having a healthy self-love for yourself means accepting the mask of self and loving yourself with the love that God has for you.

Loving your mask does not mean that you approve of the selfishness of the ego condition. Rather, it means that you are loving the limited form through which your true Self is now expressing itself. You accept the fact that sometimes your limited form will produce selfishness, but basically you love that limited form in the same way that you would love a child. When a child misbehaves, you neither approve of the inappropriate behavior of the child nor do you condemn the child for his inappropriate behavior. You know that the child's misbehavior is part of his normal process of growing up. Therefore, you don't love the child's misbehavior, but you do love the child. Similarly, you do not specifically love the selfishness of the ego condition, but you can in a general sense love your mask. You love the mask, not because of what it is in itself, but rather because of your true Self in union with God that stands behind that mask and gives it life.

Inner Love Meditation can be used to help you develop a healthy self-love. The first step in learning to love yourself in the right way is to realize that God loves you unconditionally. For this reason, in the beginning of Inner Love Meditation, you relax and imagine a blessing of God's Love is coming down over the top of the head and filling the entire body. Instead of feeling a descending blessing, you may choose the option of focusing on God's blessing emanating from the heart, then filling the entire body.

The manner in which you perceive the blessing occurring is not as important as your attitude of openness and willingness to receive this blessing. You focus on accepting this blessing of love for no other reason than being alive. It is essential to not put any conditions on this love, even though you may normally only allow yourself to accept love when you are "good," which trains you to condemn yourself when you are "bad."

By focusing on a feeling of being loved and nourished, you accept God's Love. To intensify this love, an affirmation is repeated, such as "God loves me," "Love," "Thank You, Lord," or "This is how God feels about me."

For most Christians, God's Love can be experienced most intimately through an openness to Jesus Christ. If you wish to develop receptivity to Christ's Love for you, then you may want to use an affirmation that includes His Holy Name, such as "Jesus loves me," "Jesus Christ Love," "Christ Love," or simply "Jesus," with a feeling of being loved.

For Inner Love Meditation, you set aside all feelings of how you feel about yourself, and think only of yourself as one who is being loved. At first, repeating the affirmation and imagining yourself accepting love will seem to be mechanical and not really felt. But slowly, the inner feeling of being loved will begin to manifest and grow. Some meditators imagine that God's Love for them is expressed through the vehicle of light, so if you are drawn to imagine yourself being filled with both love and light, feel free to do so.

As you practice Inner Love Meditation, you will learn to accept this love as God's Love for you and will experience it. After your "imagined" feeling of God's Love for you changes to an inner feeling that God really is in fact loving you, then you will find that you will genuinely be able to love God in return. Unfortunately most people, even people who are actually very loving, do not consider themselves to be very loving. Since you may be one of those people who question their ability to love, you are not being asked to imagine your love for God. If you were being asked to imagine your love for God, you might feel that you are faking your love and creating a manufactured love that is not genuine.

Consequently, instead of being asked to imagine your love for God, you are being asked to imagine God's Love for you, which by faith you know is a reality. Then when you actually do feel the presence of God loving you, you can allow His Love to affect you while you remain passive. Spontaneously and naturally His Love will come forth and eventually will draw forth a loving response from you.

First you will feel yourself as one who is being loved by God. Gradually you will feel the ability to return your love to God. Then there will seem to be two loves—an apparently external love coming from above the head and filling the body, and an inner response to that love that allows you to love God in return. However, perhaps on a rare occasion brought about purely by God's grace, the apparently external love and the internal love may at least temporarily merge into a loving state of being that just *is*.

Some people use visualization to help them use their imagination. Yet the term "imagination" as it is used here does not mean the visualization of mental pictures. To imagine something is to make believe—to make something so real to you that you can feel its presence. The key to using the imagination in meditation is that you must choose to imagine only those things that do in fact have a reality behind them—but a reality that is hidden from you and is therefore only accessible through the imagination. After you imagine something to be real, then the reality behind that something shines through so you can become aware of the presence of that reality.

Although you begin Inner Love Meditation by imagining God's Love, this is not a manufactured experience or a "power of positive thinking" experience. You are simply using the imagination to tune into the reality of love that is really there, and then the reality becomes apparent. You can accept love since love is your true nature and power. As you accept love, your love nature manifests spontaneously in a way that can be experienced directly. As an aftereffect of this experience, you can learn to love yourself in your everyday life as one who is loved by God.

Imagining God's Love is the exact opposite of the kind of "imagining" you are doing in your present ego condition. Actually right now you are "imagining" that God does not love you. Since God is Spirit, and you imagine yourself to be only a body and a mind, you imagine that you are separate from God and separate from His Love. You may have some ideas about God loving you, but these ideas are permeated with contradictory ideas of separation that restrict your openness to His Love. Because of your ego, you imagine an illusion of separation, a false reality, which seems to be confirmed by your experiences of separation in everyday life. Since you are imagining a false reality, it makes sense to also use the imagination to counteract the illusion that you have created. You can do this by giving yourself permission to imagine the true reality of God's Love for you, as is suggested in Inner Love Meditation.

All six techniques of Christian Yoga Meditation are designed to help remove blocks that prevent you from becoming aware of God's Love. Blocks are related to parts of the body, as was explained in Chapter 12. The most significant block related to the crown center is the *fear of God's*

Love. This block needs to be released in order to become completely open to God. Why is this block so important? Because of what God's Love means to your ego. God is infinite and eternal, and so His Love is infinite and eternal. The ego is finite and time limited. To the ego, the infinite and eternal Love of God means annihilation. The ego and the full force of God's Love are mutually exclusive, so you can have one or the other but not both. Practicing Inner Love Meditation is not a means of producing a full acceptance of God's Love and the complete giving up of the ego, which can only occur as a result of divine grace. The total acceptance of divine love can happen during a deep experience of illumination or at the moment of truth that comes at physical death.

The fear of God's Love and the parallel fear of your own love for God are hidden from your normal awareness by defense mechanisms of the ego. The fear of God's Love is a very large inner obstacle that can only be overcome by divine grace. Nevertheless, a portion of that grace is allowing you to release tiny bits of that block in a gradual manner. Although Inner Love Meditation is not a means of removing the entire block, the repeated practice of this method can assist you through the action of the Holy Spirit to remove little pieces of your block to God's Love. Through this piecemeal process, you can learn to accept a small amount of God's Love for you and accept a small amount of your love for God. In this gradual process of learning to accept love, you are correspondingly letting go of little bits of your ego-based thoughts of separation that had previously blocked your awareness of love.

Since releasing the fear of God's Love also involves letting go of the ego, another way of describing the fear of God's Love is to call it the fear of losing your individuality, mentioned in Chapter 12 as a major block related to the crown center. In the practice of Inner Love Meditation, the imagining of love descending from over the head downward is a way of helping to reduce this block associated with the crown of the head and freeing up divine love to manifest more fully as it descends upon the body.

This form of meditation may be practiced while sitting. Yet it may also be practiced while lying down, but only if reclining does not cause you to become drowsy. To avoid drowsiness the best time of day to use the lying-down position is in the middle of the day, rather than at the start or end of the day. Inner Love Meditation is suggested to be practiced as a lying-down alternative to your regular form of sitting meditation. This technique is especially recommended if you are going through a difficult period in which you are so unsettled that you are unable to practice your regular meditation in a sitting position.

For using the lying-down position, you place the hands one over the other at the navel area. The tips of the thumbs can be placed together so they are gently touching each other just below the navel. If placing the hands over the navel area feels uncomfortable, you can place the hands along the sides of the body with the palms turned upward.

After Inner Love Meditation is completed, you may want to pray for others to allow the love that has been received from God to be passed on as a blessing to others. Inner Love Meditation can be used as part of the kind of healing prayer that includes the laying on of hands. As you feel God's Love for you, you can allow that loving feeling to pass through your hands and into the person receiving the healing. You may want to also coordinate your breathing while doing the laying on of hands. For this option you let yourself inhale and feel yourself absorbing God's Love, and then exhale to feel God's Love flowing through your hands and into the other person. Regardless of what technique is used, the secret of healing others is in caring about them and allowing God's Love to flow through you. The source of all forms of healing is God's Love. His Love facilitates healing by awakening the divine love nature that is already within the person who is receiving the healing.

Whether Inner Love Meditation is used as a meditation method or for healing, it should be used only if it feels inwardly right to do so. For example, you may feel uncomfortable with imagining God's Love for you because of a concern about fabricating an artificial experience created by yourself. In this case, instead of using the imagination, you might want to request God's help with an affirmation, such as "Lord, help me to feel Your Love." Another approach is to focus on your mental knowledge of love, rather than your feeling of love. With this emphasis on mental awareness, you can use a statement for your meditation that affirms your knowledge of God's Love. Another option is to focus on the word "acceptance" rather than love. Thus you can choose an affirmation of God's acceptance of you, or even your own acceptance of yourself.

Any method that uses the imagination is subject to distortion. Thus Inner Love Meditation is recommended to be used only temporarily as a stepping stone to increase your awareness of love within and as a preparation for using other methods that do not use the imagination, such as Christian Yoga Meditation. While you are practicing Inner Love Meditation, you may hear the inner humming sound, and then you can let go of your affirmation and switch to practicing Inner Listening Meditation. Since the inner humming sound originates from a spiritual source, you may discover that listening to this inner tone actually helps you to feel the divine within as a loving presence.

---

1. Mark 12:30
2. Mark 12:31
3. Luke 15:20

15

CONTEMPLATION AS A PATH OF LIGHT

~ • ~

A. The Path of Light

Chapter 13 previously described contemplation as it is usually taught in the West, as a path of seeking God in the darkness of pure faith. In the East the path of darkness is best exemplified by Zen Buddhism, which speaks of the "Void." In Chapter 12 the Void was described as an expression of God experienced as divine nothingness and emptiness that transcends all things. The Buddhists do not use the word "God," but their version of the Void is a state of emptiness and pure undifferentiated consciousness that can be experienced. Some Zen Buddhist meditators do have a profound experience of Light during enlightenment, but their path to awakening requires going through the emptiness of the Void.

In Christianity the best example of the path of darkness is St. John of the Cross. Divine union, according to St. John of the Cross, is a transformation in God's Light, but the path along the way is primarily an encounter with "nada, nada, nada"—"nothing, nothing, nothing." The "dark night of the soul" is a systematic letting go of everything in complete detachment and self-surrender of all desires. In Chapter 13 contemplation has been described as a path of proceeding toward God in the darkness of faith alone. This path of darkness eventually leads to the light, as St. John of the Cross indicates in *Living Flame of Love*. However, the path of darkness is not the only way to the light. You can also proceed to the light, by a way of light. Therefore, this chapter will examine contemplation as a path of light. This approach of receptivity to divine light requires faith, as does the path of darkness and any Christian form of spiritual seeking.

The path of light is best represented in the East by yoga meditation that focuses on the currents and concentrations of prana in the body.

This prana is not just energy, but is considered an expression of the life force associated with consciousness and with light. Prana may be thought of as *light-energy*. The rising of the kundalini is a movement of prana that produces an inner fire that purifies all the centers of consciousness in the body, bringing about an inner transformation. If the proper preparations and spiritual disciplines are implemented, the rising of the kundalini will manifest as a path of light. However, if the proper preparations and disciplines are not implemented, the kundalini can still rise, but will be experienced as more of a path of darkness than a path of light.

In Christianity the path of light can be seen most clearly in life of St. Symeon the New Theologian (949 to 1022 AD). The writings of St. Symeon make many references to being transformed over a period of time by a radiant light that not only transformed his consciousness but penetrated into every part of his body. His openness to divine light was his means of awakening to Christ. The Eastern Orthodox Church from which St. Symeon came advocates his approach to contemplation as a path of light. But this approach is not generally emphasized in the West, which has traditionally followed the mystical path of St. John of the Cross in the darkness of faith alone.

Whether your path is primarily a path of darkness (with some light) or a path of light (with some darkness), it will most likely not be a matter of personal preference, as much as one of divine calling. According to St. John of the Cross, all Christians must seek God in pure faith, which is required regardless of entering the path of darkness or the path of light. So far in this book the path of darkness has been emphasized because it is the path most commonly taken. The previous chapter described the inner feelings of light, love, oneness, heightened awareness, the divine presence, peace, and joy. Those individuals who do not experience these inner feelings during meditation will follow the path of darkness in pure faith.

Those seekers who do experience inner feelings, such as the inner feeling of light, will still follow the path of darkness in their journey, but along the way may be drawn to the path of light by divine calling. The information presented in this manual has been an attempt to explain how to first use techniques and then to proceed in the darkness of faith leading to contemplation, which is generally a path of darkness. However, for those who are attracted to the path of light, additional methods have been included. Two methods that may assist individuals to follow the path of light are *Inner Light Meditation* and *Expanded Christian Yoga Meditation*, which have been described in the previous chapter. Although these methods help to open the meditator to inner light, it needs to be understood that following the path of light comes as a result of divine initiative and grace. God gives each person the gifts that they truly need to approach him.

B. The Inner Feeling Path of Light

The steps along the way to God will be different for each individual who follows the path of light, but for those who are practicing Christian Yoga Meditation this manual will describe two approaches to the path of light. The first approach is the *Inner Feeling Path of Light*. This approach has a sequence of five stages that you may choose to take on the path of light. These stages are listed below:

THE INNER FEELING PATH OF LIGHT

1. preparation
2. opening the flame in the heart
3. letting the light expand
4. allowing the light to embrace you
5. consistently resting in the light embracing you

The first stage of the Inner Feeling Path of Light is *preparation*. This stage consists of first walking the path of darkness as a preparation for walking the path of light. The practice of Christian Yoga Meditation would provide this preparation and would include learning to enter the silence of contemplation. In contemplation you are walking on the path of darkness while relying on pure faith. To enter the path of light you will need to be open to inner feelings, but first you may have to walk a long way on the path of darkness. In fact, you may have to release many of the inner blocks that were described in Chapter 12 before you have the degree of openness to inner feelings that would allow you to enter the path of light.

The second stage of the Inner Feeling Path of Light is *opening the flame in the heart.* This stage is the exploration of the path of light through the practice of Inner Light Meditation. For this meditation practice you focus on experiencing the inner light in the chest. You begin by focusing on a flame in the location of the physical heart. Then, with progress, you allow the flame to expand and feel an inner light in the center of the chest. Opening to light in this way also involves opening to love.

The third stage on the Inner Feeling Path of Light is *letting the light expand.* Expansion of the light involves allowing the light to rise upward from the heart and center of the chest to the crown and then letting the light descend down again and fill the body. This expansion of light is facilitated by the practice of Expanded Christian Yoga Meditation. At this point you are exploring the path of light, but you have not really totally left the path of darkness. It is still necessary to follow the path of darkness in regard to using Inner Silence Meditation, which is the last technique of Expanded Christian Yoga Meditation. For Inner Silence Meditation, you let go of attempting to focus on any inner feelings. During Inner Silence Meditation and contemplation, you still may experience inner feelings that come spontaneously. You do not cling to these feelings, and you do not push these away. This detachment in regard to inner feelings allows you to continue to follow the path of darkness and rely on pure faith in God, even though you are also exploring the path of light in the first five techniques of Expanded Christian Yoga Meditation.

The fourth stage of the Inner Feeling Path of Light is *allowing the light to embrace you*. Ironically when you let go of proactively focusing on inner feelings, you may discover that the inner feelings that you no longer attempt to possess will begin to possess you. In this regard when the inner feeling of light begins to hold on to you and embrace you, then you are truly entering the path of light. Just experimenting with holding on to the inner feeling of light during Inner Light Meditation and Expanded Christian Yoga Meditation is an exploration of the path of light. But you become fully established on the path of light only when the divine initiative and grace have intervened on your behalf so that divine light possesses and embraces you indicating that this is indeed your path.

Learning to allow the light to embrace you is a very important step. Previously Inner Silence Meditation has been described as a letting go of body awareness and letting go of repeating an affirmation in order to experience inner silence and be drawn into contemplation. However, the time may come in your practice when your whole body is experienced as being filled with the inner feeling of energy and light during Oneness Meditation, which is the fifth technique of Expanded Christian Yoga Meditation. At the end of your practice of Oneness Meditation, when you attempt to let go of body awareness in order to make your transition to Inner Silence Meditation, you may discover that you cannot let go of body awareness. This is not because of a lack of detachment. You can attempt to give up your possession of the inner feeling of energy and light, but the energy and light you feel in the body does not go away because the light possesses you as a result of being open to the action of the Holy Spirit.

If this happens you can just accept your body awareness being filled with energy and light. Although contemplation is normally a letting go of body awareness, in this particular case you can experience contemplation as an overshadowing of the Holy Spirit that just happens to include body awareness. Contemplation has no focusing object, and there is no focusing object in this case because you are not striving to focus on the energy and light in the body. Instead, the awareness of energy and light are present in your consciousness during contemplation without exerting effort for this to happen. Indeed, any of the inner feelings described in Chapter 14 may also be present in your awareness.

This new kind of contemplation is a surrendering of the will in which you attempt to let go of body awareness and inner feelings, but the body awareness and inner feelings remain anyway. Normally in contemplation you can let go of body awareness and allow inner feelings of light, love, and energy to come and go. To avoid confusion, it is necessary to make a distinction between the normal nonphysical contemplation and the new body awareness contemplation. The new contemplation in which divine light possesses you will be termed *Integrated Contemplation*. Yoga means both "union" and "integration." The name "Integrated Contemplation" is used to indicate that the seeker is experiencing an integration of the body, mind, and spirit, which is the goal of Christian inward seeking with yoga influences. This kind of infusion of divine light—reaching into your physical vehicle and holding on to you during Integrated Contemplation— can start as an occurrence that may happen on some occasions but not on others.

The fifth stage of the Inner Feeling Path of Light is *consistently resting in the light embracing you*. A coming and going of the inner feeling of light may occur spontaneously during Inner Silence Meditation and contemplation. However, a sure sign of being on the path of light occurs when Integrated Contemplation occurs consistently—when the inner feeling of light seems to take over your practice and stay with you for most or all of your sitting period. It may take a long time of walking the path of darkness before you are able to experience the feeling of light embracing you during contemplation for almost all of your sitting practice. You will probably have to wait until many inner blocks are released and until you reach the plateau of self-acceptance before you are able to open yourself enough to allow the feeling of light to possess you so consistently. Through the intercession of this divine grace as an experience of light, your regular practice can become a resting in the divine embrace during Integrated Contemplation.

This resting in Integrated Contemplation produced by divine grace can become your regular daily experience of contemplation. Nonetheless, this ongoing experience of the inner feeling of energy and light should be considered as just another step on your path of light. Your experience of the inner feeling of light can begin as a very subtle feeling. Depending on your receptivity, the inner feeling of light and of energy can increase in intensity as you make gradual progress.

The inner feeling of energy that is being described here that you may experience initially is a feeling that may produce a tingling or other sensation that can be experienced physiologically so that every part of the body is energized. The inner feeling of light that is most likely to be experienced initially is only an inner knowing that does not produce a physiological impression of visually seeing light. As you rest in the silence of contemplation, the experience of the inner feeling of light can increase in intensity and can be accompanied by other inner feelings. Although you may experience other stages described below that involve a visual experience, this stage in itself is a rather advanced state of receptivity to divine light. The seeker who does not experience the divine presence as a visual experience need not be concerned. After all, this experience is a matter of divine grace, and each seeker receives the gifts from God that are most helpful.

C. The Visual Path of Light

Some seekers will only experience the path of light as the experience of an inner feeling. There are other seekers who by divine grace take a different approach to the path of light. This second approach is the *Visual Path of Light*. This approach has the following aspects:

THE VISUAL PATH OF LIGHT

1. *praxis*, actions of purification[1]
2. *gnosis*, knowledge of the divine perceived externally in creation[2]
3. *theoria*, the contemplative vision of light[3]

The first aspect of the Visual Path of Light is *praxis*, the preparation of living an active life of manifesting virtues in daily living that release attachment to bodily senses.

The second aspect of the Visual Path of Light is *knowledge of the divine perceived externally*, which St. Symeon the New Theologian called *gnosis*. Gnosis literally means "knowledge," but to St. Symeon this meant knowledge of the divine manifested by seeing God in all external forms. Gnosis is the mental perception of the meaning of the divine in all people and things. Gnosis, or divine perceptual knowledge, directed toward people reveals their virtuous strengths that reflect the divine and likewise their shortcomings that do not reflect the divine. In addition, in my opinion the divine perception of gnosis goes beyond just perceiving the divine meaning of all things. It extends to also include the visual perception of seeing light. This is meditative seeing with the eyes open in which light becomes an external visual perception of the divine presence. Seeing the light externally in your surroundings and in other people is called *Light vision* in this manual, but this external visual perception is a by-product of another kind of deeper vision, called *Christ's vision*, which will be described in the next chapter. The external seeing of light visually, Light vision, depends on divine grace, yet also requires openness and effort to become receptive to divine grace.

The third aspect of the Visual Path of Light is *theoria*, which is the contemplative vision of light as an internal experience. St. Symeon's explanation of theoria will be elaborated upon later in this chapter. The various methods of experiencing light in meditation that are described in this manual will help to prepare for theoria, but a specific technique will not be provided for how to create theoria itself, because this is a matter of divine grace. This third aspect of seeing light as a contemplative vision of divine light produces an inner transformation. Theoria and the resulting inner transformation can occur in many different ways, depending on the action of divine grace. The extraordinary experience of St. Symeon is just one example of the ultimate spiritual transformation that can occur. It is helpful to be aware of this ultimate potential for transformation. However, it would be unfair to compare yourself to St. Symeon, who is considered by many to be the greatest medieval mystic of the Eastern Orthodox Church.

The seeing of divine light and the transformation that occurs in this light depends on the action of divine grace, but St. Symeon maintained this transformation will not come unless it is sought. Nevertheless, even the self-effort that is involved in seeking the light needs to be guided by reliance on receptivity to the grace of the Holy Spirit. Self-effort must take into account the acceptance of God's Plan for each individual seeker's life, which may or may not involve the manifestation of inner light. Although some seekers will be granted the visual experience of divine light in the second or third aspects of the Visual Path of Light, a more realistic goal for individuals who follow the path of light is Integrated Contemplation, the fifth stage of the Inner Feeling Path of Light. While practicing Integrated Contemplation, a typical seeker may consistently experience light as an inner feeling—usually without having any visual experience either externally or internally. This experience of an inner feeling is in itself indeed a wonderful sign of divine grace to be received with gratitude. Regardless of whether you have a visual experience or not, the most important factor is your growth in consciousness and your openness to divine love.

D. Christian Transformation in the Light

This section addresses spiritual transformation in divine light, yet for clarity this book makes a distinction between two types of spiritual light. When this book refers to "Light" with a capital "L," this is related to the ultimate Reality of God. But when the lowercase words "divine light" are used, this light refers to both God's Light itself and the lesser reflections of light that originate from His Light. A variety of different reflections of light can be experienced on the spiritual path, and these are indirect experiences of God that lead toward the direct experience of God's Reality in His Light.

For a Christian seeker the path of light can be a progressive opening to divine light over a long period of time in which there is a transformation of consciousness. The overcoming of the subject/object division between the meditator and God is an important part of the transformation of consciousness, as has been described in Chapter 13. However, regarding the path of light, the overcoming of the subject/object division needs to be explained in terms of the transforming effect of the divine light. The awareness of light that occurs as a divine grace in contemplation is not really a consciousness *of* light. The fact is that consciousness *is* light. Contemplation is an awareness that has no object of awareness, so even light is not an object of awareness. Consciousness that has no object, as is the case in contemplation, becomes a revealing of consciousness itself as light. This revealing of divine light, as consciousness revealing itself, is not only light but also union.

Inner receptivity is needed to experience consciousness itself. This receptivity requires a certain emptiness of the mind that would allow you to receive the inner light that would reveal consciousness as itself. But the highest achievement of awareness in this life is not merely a blankness of contents in the mind. Rather, it is a unification of the mind. This unification is a radical transformation of consciousness that enables you to experience yourself and everyone and everything else in the divine light. You will see God in yourself and yourself in God, yet you will still know Him as unknowable. You will have divine light originating from God as your own light, as long as you can experience it without trying to possess it. You become the light by not possessing the light, but by allowing the light to possess you and reveal itself as you in God.

This happens because you are accepting God as He is, as the giver of life and light within you. God is not an object outside of yourself. When you become conscious of divine light as a grace, you also become conscious of consciousness itself. In your nonpossessiveness of the light, you allow the light to possess you. In allowing the light to possess and embrace you, you allow God to infuse your mind with a modified way of relating to other people, to the things of this world, and to God Himself. The ego is the awareness of yourself as separate. But this new consciousness in light allows you to be aware of yourself as being assimilated into your true Self made in the likeness of God. To be conscious of God in divine light is to forget yourself as you formerly were aware of yourself and to awaken to a transformed awareness of God making you into His likeness.

Only the presence of God in your own soul could bring about this transformed consciousness that is really a revealing of your own true nature. When this transformation occurs and the soul is absorbed in divine union with God, the false "I" of the ego, based on attachment to the separate body and the separate mind, is abandoned totally. This does not mean that in such a state the soul does not have an identity anymore. It does mean that the soul's true identity is centered, not in the limitations of the separate body or the separate mind, but in God Himself. Of the state of the soul in perfect divine union of love, St. John of the Cross writes, in *Living Flame of Love*:

> So, as has been said, the understanding of this soul is now the understanding of God; and its will is the will of God; and its memory is the memory of God; and its delight is the delight of God...and is thus God by participation in God, which comes to pass in this perfect state of the spiritual life, although not so perfectly as in the next life. And in this way the soul is dead to all that was in itself, for this was death to it, and alive to that which God is in Himself; wherefore, speaking of itself the soul well says in this line: "In slaying, thou hast changed death into life." Wherefore the soul may here very well say with Saint Paul: "I live, now not I, but Christ liveth in me."[4]

The experience called the "the illumination of glory" is the highest form of divine union that can occur in this life in which the soul is withdrawn from the body, as is described in Chapter 18. In this advanced state the soul merges with Spirit and leaves behind all awareness of form, space, and time in a temporary transcendental experience of divine light. This is the most dramatic kind of vision that can occur to the mystic seeker, but it is not the culmination of mystical experience. After this kind of dramatic mystical cognition, the next step for the mystic is to retain this awareness of divine light and also bring the awareness of the divine presence into his lower faculties of the human condition. Thus mystical culmination is a transition from a nonphysical mystical cognition to a bodily mystical integration brought into everyday life. The above quotation describes this integrated state in which Christ lives fully within the soul.

The spiritual transformation that generally occurs in spiritual growth follows a particular pattern that I call the *Transformation Pattern*. This general pattern includes five steps of opening to inner light. The first step is *preparatory seeking* for the divine light, which usually involves some form or forms of spiritual exercise. At some point the second step occurs, which is the *awakening*, the opening to the awareness of God in the Light. This awakening may come after only a little seeking or after many years of seeking. The awakening occurs suddenly and disappears, without the seeker being able to retain or fully integrate the experience. The third step is *more seeking* to increase inner receptivity to the divine influence. The fourth step is *familiarity*, becoming accustomed to the awareness of divine light. The fifth step is *integration,* which involves allowing the experience of divine light to become integrated into lower faculties and the everyday experiences. This final integration of both the human and the divine is a paradoxical combination of being somehow within the body and beyond the body at the same time.

The mystic John of St. Samson generally functioned in the world appearing as an ordinary person, who happened to be blind. Normally, out of humility, he was able to successfully hide from others the inner mystical light that was welling up from within him. But sometimes he was so overshadowed by the divine presence that he glowed with a bright light clearly observable to his fellow monks. His faculties, both those that relate to the soul and those that relate to the world, were completely possessed by God. He describes how a soul can function in the world and simultaneously be in a state of union with God, as follows:

> Or they be so filled with his superabundance that it overflows into all their faculties, causing great dilation. Hence, under the influence of this active and mutual love the soul lives in a paradise of delights, as far removed from the created objects surrounding it, as if they did not even exist. For, although it performs external actions for its own needs or those of its neighbor either out of obedience or charity, its attention is fixed only upon the beatific Object which draws and ravishes it above itself, and often out of itself. It does this by means of certain simple, impetuous transports which are so strong and sweet that they at once carry away the soul and all its faculties to joyful union with the Beloved.[5]

Two other mystics who experienced this state are St. John of the Cross from western Christianity and St. Symeon the New Theologian from eastern Orthodox Christianity. Each of these saints described a mystical transformation in fire and light in which the seeker merges with God and sees himself as inseparable from God. The individual sees himself no longer as a distinct separate entity, but rather as being joined in light with God and as becoming light by fully accepting God's Light. The initial full embrace of divine union is a very dramatic and overpowering experience that draws the soul completely out of the body. There may be many partial spiritual embraces within body awareness prior to this full embrace. On the other hand, this full embrace may be an individual's very first spiritual experience, as it was in the case of St. Symeon. He was overcome with God's Light, brighter than any star. It left him in awe, but did not immediately impart perceptual knowledge of what had happened. Only later, after devoting himself to living the contemplative life, did he realize that he had seen Christ in God.

St. Symeon's mysticism culminated in the full expression of divine light permeating his everyday life. He was no longer in an altered state of ecstasy that had occurred in his first encounter with the light. In a sense he had become accustomed to the light, so it became his natural state, rather than an altered state. He experienced himself as entirely luminous, and the light in him as giving him life. As he felt his awareness go outside of himself and went into an ecstasy, the light receded from his awareness and could be seen at a distance. As he returned to his center in the heart, the light expanded again becoming like the sun. St. Symeon beheld himself as light, taking on the image and likeness of God within. Having learned to identify with divine light, his awareness was transformed in the light. As far as his spirit was concerned, this may not have been a transformation at all, but rather was a revealing of the true nature of his spirit.

What is generally thought of as the natural condition of the person with an ego attached to both the body and rational mind may from a spiritual perspective be very unnatural. Therefore, the spirit in St. Symeon could allow these lower faculties to be transformed in the light and released to perform their truly natural functions. For St. Symeon this was a concrete transformation of spirit, soul (psyche) and every faculty, including the physical body. For example, he maintained that in the divine light Christ became his hand and Christ became his foot. Thus he wrote, "I...am Christ's hand, Christ's foot!"[6] St. Symeon went a step further when he said that Christ was in his finger and in "this organ...."[7] The translation found in *Hymns of Divine Love* discretely left out the word St. Symeon actually used to identify *this organ*, which was "nut" (testicle).[8] St. Symeon used a bit of shock value here to emphasize that all things are transformed in the consciousness and even in the physical body by union with Christ in God. From St. Symeon's perspective, his transformation in divine light was always both transcendental and concrete.

In the Transformation Pattern, described above, there are five steps in regard to theoria, the vision of light. The first of these is *preparatory seeking*, which may be for a short period of time or for many years. The second step is the *awakening*. Initially the revealing of divine light from within may appear to be an unfamiliar state of altered consciousness that is experienced as a sudden awakening, which may come spontaneously at any time. St. Symeon's first encounter with the light produced only awe and wonder as an overwhelming experience, but he did not understand perceptually the nature of what was happening. This mystical initiation occurred at the very beginning of St. Symeon's spiritual journey, so his period of initial seeking was a very short period of time.

Only later did he realize that he had seen *the face of Christ* shining like the sun. After doing so little seeking prior to this mystical initiation, St. Symeon was motivated for the third step of *more seeking*. Through this seeking St. Symeon sought to open again to the vision of light that he had already seen in his awakening. In fact, his final state of permanent mystical awareness became a return to this original awakening but with the ability to integrate the illuminated consciousness that had come and gone so suddenly.

Through this additional seeking, St. Symeon started to open to the vision of light again but in a gradual manner. A baby can open his eyes and see the world yet has no understanding of what he is seeing until he becomes familiar with his surroundings. In the same way, St. Symeon experienced the fourth step of *familiarity*. Through frequent exposure to the light, he gained familiarity with the light, which then led to the fifth step of *integration*.

In the final step of integration, St. Symeon reached a level of permanent transformation. In this transformed consciousness, he was joined in the light with God and simultaneously was fully integrated into the everyday world. For St. Symeon the purification process was a bathing in the light to become divinized and fully transformed in and with the mind of Christ, becoming inseparably united with God. St. Symeon wrote that once one is illuminated by God, he would be changed in every way—meaning altered in his intelligence, heart, and soul. He would even be changed in the way he hears and sees because of the light shining in his mind.[9]

Certainly St. Symeon's descriptions of the transforming light indicated that he experienced the divine light as an inner visual experience, but also as an outer visual experience. When he looked out into the world he could see a world transformed in divine light. Thus he could see the virtue in all things through his habitual awareness of divine light within himself. He could see Christ in everyone and everything by seeing with the eyes of Christ. The ability to visually see light externally as a reflection of the inner divine light, which I call *Light vision*, in my opinion is an aspect of what St. Symeon termed gnosis. The ability to visually see divine light outwardly may manifest over time on the path of light, although it is not as important as seeing the divine light inwardly.

The inner vision of divine light can become a visual experience, but not visual in the usual sense of seeing with the physical eyes. St. Symeon, who came from the Eastern Orthodox Church, used the Greek word *theoria* to describe his experience. The usual translation of theoria is "contemplation," but the meaning of the word is "vision of light."[10] For St. Symeon the individual has a "psyche," which is the individual "soul," yet also has a "spirit." This spirit (with a small "s") is called the *nous*, and is the individual's highest point of contact with the divine Spirit. This spirit, the nous, is considered the "spiritual eye" or "lamp of the soul."[11] This spiritual eye has the faculty of mystical cognition. However, the nous is dormant until it is opened by divine grace and receives illumination from the divine light that comes from Christ.

According to St. Symeon, the process of purifying the nous and becoming transformed in Christ has three aspects—*praxis*, *gnosis*, and *theoria*. Praxis is the active life, meaning the pursuit of virtue. Seeking virtue would involve maintaining moral purity and employing ascetical practices.[12] Praxis would include every effort made to seek God through an integration of the body, soul, and spirit. Praxis is a life of faith in the active expression of virtues, such as any form of loving service. Also inner purification techniques express praxis. Some examples would be fasting, prayer, and meditation, including, for instance, focusing on the Jesus Prayer. Praxis is a purification of the bodily senses from attachment and is a preparation for awakening the ability to perceive the divine light.

Gnosis literally means knowledge. To St. Symeon gnosis meant the knowledge coming from the vision of God as seen in Creation.[13] This includes seeing other people, creatures, and objects in the light of God. Seeing in the light of God can mean perceiving the divine meaning in things without an attending visual perception of light. Yet I believe it can also include the outer visual perceiving of light—which is Light vision of the world. The ability to visually see the divine in all things in Light vision is a gift, but does not come without the necessary receptivity and desire for this new way of seeing. The seeing of divine light externally is a preparation for perceiving the divine light internally.

Theoria is contemplative vision of God inwardly seen as divine light. The capacity to see this vision of God in divine light can increase as spiritual progress is made. Eventually seeing this divine light can reveal both God and one's own self joined in the light as one. Nevertheless, this joining in light is not really a joining in essence, according to Eastern Orthodox mysticism. God has His own distinct essence as the First Cause, so the created creature cannot become the Creator. On the other hand, Eastern Orthodox mysticism believes that the seeker can aspire to *deification* ("theosis"[14]), meaning to become God by union with God in participation with the *divine energies.*[15] God in His Love gives Himself to you to the full capacity that you can receive Him in this life, which is only a fraction of the capacity for union that will be possible in the next life.

The teachings of St. Symeon on gnosis are important because he felt that seeing the world in light could purify the nous as a preparation for theoria. In his teachings, St. Symeon sought to instruct others to discern divine light in nature and to see virtues and faults in all beings and creatures.[16] He advocated using God as the mirror through which all things can be seen in the light. He advised the seeker to absorb the virtues seen in the light and to let go of the faults seen in the light. In addition, he taught that seeing the divine in nature would train the seeker to see the divine light within himself, which may also be called the image and likeness of God. Instructions on how to obtain the aspect of gnosis that I call *Light vision*—the seeing of light in others and in your surroundings—is elaborated upon in the next chapter.

Although St. Symeon attempted to describe the ultimate state that he learned to live in, he made it clear that he could not explain what he was experiencing in words. Although mysticism is sometimes mistakenly thought of as only a vertical ascent to God, St. Symeon's daily experience of being filled with transcendental divine light and being at home in both His World and this world simultaneously is an example of the highest mysticism. It is the fullest expression of the mysticism of the cross, uniting the human and the divine through the blessings of Jesus Christ.

E. Theoria as the Contemplative Vision of God

The third aspect of the visual experience of the path of light is theoria. If this contemplative vision of God occurs, it will be a matter of the Holy Spirit taking you by the hand and guiding you beyond any methods. This is a very personal journey that is likely to be different for each person who has this calling. But if theoria does occur, it will happen over a period of time in phases. The preparation for theoria would be the first two aspects of the visual experience of light, which are praxis, the active life of virtue, and gnosis, which includes visually seeing the divine light in the world.

After the first phase of preparation, there are four additional phases of the unfolding of theoria, summarized by St. Symeon in this way:

> ...it is fire, it is also ray,
> it becomes a cloud of light,
> it perfects itself as the sun.[17]

The key words are *fire*, *ray*, *cloud*, and *sun*, and St. Symeon went on to elaborate upon each of these as phases of experiencing the light of theoria. St. Symeon said the second phase, which follows the initial preparatory phase, is a *fire*. For St. Symeon the fire was an important symbol of his inner purification. In this phase of fire the soul is warmed so the heart is enkindled and becomes excited with the desire and love for God.[18] Prior to the fire there may be only a faint inner warmth or energy. The warmth or energy may be felt initially in the heart. For others the warmth or energy may be felt along the spinal column and in the head, and then flowing into the heart and from the heart to the entire body.

Theoria begins as a fire that becomes as light. The heart is where the fire burns like an altar upon which St. Symeon offered himself to the Spirit. The fire burns away impurities, creating smoke rather than light. But when the soul is purified enough, there is a flame, a shining light. The flame enlightens the mind and the heart, increasing the desire for the love of God. From the heart, the energy of the flame spreads to the whole body. The fire is a two-edged sword that produces delight and pain as the soul is inflamed by the Spirit. This symbolism is consistent with the fire produced by the rising of the kundalini in yoga philosophy. Focusing on the inner flame in the heart during Inner Light Meditation can be a preparation for this phase.

This second phase, in which a fire becomes a flame, leads to the third stage. St. Symeon described the third phase as a *ray*. When the soul becomes inflamed by the fire in the second phase, the soul then becomes like a ray that carries light.[19] Like the sun shines down its rays, God's Light shines down a ray of light into the soul, expanding the awareness of the mind. The ray comes down like a rope of light that St. Symeon tried to grasp and ascend to the greater Light, which he symbolically described as being like the sun in its brightness and immenseness. St. Symeon used the ray to ascend to the Light, but then he could not hold on to the ray and so he descended. He alternately rose and descended and recognized his spiritual progress in this ongoing process of approaching of the Light and withdrawing from the Light. As the ray of light appeared momentarily, and then it receded, St. Symeon said that it had the effect of purifying one passion of the heart, yet only one, since passions could not be extinguished all a once.[20] The light assisted St. Symeon in a gradual process of becoming passionless except for his passion for the love of God. The ray of light purified the heart. Doing all that he could to strip himself of passions, St. Symeon was assisted by the light as a ray, which was a manifestation of divine grace that came and went when it would:

> ...then, dimly, like a delicate ray, minute, having enveloped his mind suddenly, it enraptures him in ecstasy....[21]

> Gradually this light is kindled, stirred up by waiting, and it becomes a big flame, which reaches the heavens....[22]

St. Symeon explained that he often had an overflowing of tears. This experience was a gift that cooled and refreshed his soul after the fire within had burnt away impurities. In addition to the purifying of fire, the tears themselves were also purifying. Rather than the water of tears putting out the inner fire, they enkindled an even greater desire for God and opened the way to the light becoming what St. Symeon called in the above quotation *a big flame, which reaches the heavens*. The flame that started out small enlarged to what might be likened to a *pillar of fire*, the familiar biblical image of the divine fire that led the Israelites by night through their desert experience. But from the perspective of yoga this pillar of fire would stretch from the base of the spine to the crown of the head, which would correspond to the "heavens" of universal consciousness.

After the fire that becomes a flame, and after the ray comes the fourth phase. For St. Symeon the fourth phase was the *luminous cloud*. This cloud of light descended on the head, but St. Symeon was overcome by fear of the luminous cloud.[23] Clearly this shining cloud was a much more powerful experience than the cloud of unknowing, yet just as inscrutable. For St. Symeon the descending cloud was always related to the head. At times the cloud started on the head and rose upward. At other times, the cloud is seen as descending from above to rest on the head. In St. Symeon's experience, the cloud on the head facilitated the ascending of his own limited consciousness to the superconsciousness of God.

From the perspective of yoga, the shining cloud is indicative of a deeper opening of the crown center, bringing with it initially a nebulous and disorienting feeling. The cloud is a familiar symbol of the divine presence as seen in the cloud that led the Israelites by day in their desert wanderings. Coming into the presence of the luminous cloud is like coming into the presence of God, which can be an experience of awe and fear as it was for St. Symeon. Due to his fear, he was not at first able to be open to divine love. But he searched for divine love again, and the fifth and final phase was revealed. St. Symeon described this final stage by saying, "I saw it like a solar disc."[24] In the final phase of the *solar disc*, St. Symeon had to adjust to the Light that was like the sun. He fluctuated in his awareness back and forth between *ecstasy* to *enstasy*. "Ecstasy" is an expansion of human awareness beyond the individual psyche (soul) to the universal consciousness of God. "Enstasy" is a penetration of the awareness into the center of the heart to the nous (spirit).

St. Symeon experienced light shrinking to become like a star and then experienced the light expanding again to its full solar-like immenseness and brightness. At first he saw himself as entirely united to the light. His nous (spirit) was itself light, and he saw the All in the light. However, then he shifted his awareness from the nous (spirit) to the psyche (soul). He recognized that the psyche (soul) was in the light, and he went into an altered state of an ecstasy, in which his awareness expanded to universal consciousness. The psyche (soul) reflected on itself in this ecstasy and produced psychological reactions. This self-reflection was an ego-based activity that produced a contraction of the light. After the ecstasy and following the self-reflection, the light could be seen only from a distance.

But then he shifted his awareness from the psyche (soul) back again to the nous (spirit). Returning to the nous meant going into enstasy—bringing the awareness back to the center of the heart where the nous resided. Returning to the nous meant regaining the spiritual eye, the faculty of mystical cognition of the light. This enstasy in which the awareness was centered in the heart, in the nous, caused the light that had contracted to then expand and return to its fullness. Eventually the light no longer expanded and contracted as St. Symeon learned to see himself as being the light itself and beheld God in the light as joined with himself.

Thomas Matus, a Camaldolese monk, who has studied the works of St. Symeon, described the saint's mystical state in the following way:

> Categories of "within" and "without," "self" and "other" cannot be applied except paradoxically to this state. The mystic's very self seems to *be* the light, a luminous source which illumines all things; and yet the self *receives* the light and is enlivened by it.[25]

Paradoxically St. Symeon felt himself as *being* the light and *receiving* the light simultaneously. This is because God did not create your being and then leave it. God's gift of your being is an ongoing giving of Himself to you. He continuously extends the Being of His Light to you without that Light ever leaving its Source and without you ever leaving your source in Him. Thus you are God's Light. Your existence is an endless outpouring of His Love for you. Opening your awareness to God's gift of Himself to you is a profound spiritual awakening to your true nature.

Yet St. Symeon did not seek to escape the world, but rather to fully awaken to his place in the world. Of course, as every seeker, he wanted to go to Heaven. But following God's Will for him meant to do what he could to bring Heaven to this world. Once St. Symeon's nous was purified and penetrated by the light and became light, the light was able to transform what may be considered the lower human functions and lower levels of consciousness. Thomas Matus described this transformation:

> The ultimate stage, the goal of the contemplative quest, is not itself an "altered" or extraordinary state of consciousness. It is rather the "proper state" of the spirit, *nous*, totally transformed into the light which is God. When the spirit reaches this level, it then begins to free the lower faculties to assume once more their own functions, while itself remaining in the light. As Symeon says, the mystic gradually becomes accustomed to the light, which penetrates all the ordinary levels of consciousness. The soul is no longer carried out of itself but eventually lives in the habitual awareness of a luminous presence.[26]

St. Symeon reached the final phase when his contemplation became a permanent mystical condition. St. Symeon's perception of reality was completely transformed in the light. For him the light became the means through which all of life was experienced. He became one who was continually in the presence of God known to him by the light that joined them. St. Symeon went through a very gradual process of becoming familiar with the light. Eventually the alternating between ecstasy and enstasy changed into a paradoxical state of ecstasy and enstasy occurring simultaneously. At first the expansion of human consciousness to God consciousness in ecstasy caused the psyche to be in an altered state, which was also a self-reflective state that caused the light to withdraw. But then the expansion of human consciousness to divine consciousness in ecstasy became natural (without self-reflection) to the psyche (soul) and lower functions, and then the light did not withdraw. Thus ecstasy became a natural rather than altered state, and at the same time enstasy likewise became a natural condition in which the nous (spirit) became light itself. Therefore, St. Symeon was in the infinitely expansive state of universal consciousness, and he was simultaneously conscious of being centered in the nous in the center of the heart.

In this combination of ecstasy and enstasy, the divine light that had been supernatural became an entirely natural and permanent condition for St. Symeon. His new natural condition was the highest mystical state in which the consciousness of the soul, the world, and God became transformed by the nous in the mystical cognition of light. Even though St. Symeon attempted to describe this state, he indicated that he was incapable of adequately explaining his mystical awareness.

Some forms of yoga refer to a corresponding ecstasy and enstasy. In yoga there is a point of light called the *bindu* that resides in the heart. It represents the true Self or the Christ Self, which in yoga may be called the *Atman*. When the yogi realizes this indivisible point of light in the center of the heart, the light becomes an infinitely expanding circumference of blazing Light, and the soul awakens to its universal consciousness.

For St. Symeon the "heart" was very important. St. Symeon liked to refer to the scriptural line: "Blessed are the pure in heart, for they shall see God."[27] The heart is the inner altar in which the purification by fire occurs, providing the means of producing an integration of the body, soul, and spirit. The inner purification of yoga involves raising the inner fire of the kundalini from the bottom spiritual center to the top spiritual center. The full opening of the top spiritual center, the crown center, is a union with God in which the soul is completely withdrawn from the body. The nonphysical union is called in yoga "nirvikalpa samadhi." In Christianity it is called the "illumination of glory." However, this full opening of the crown center needs to be integrated into the fabric of everyday life, and for this to occur the heart center takes a central role.

The heart center is the meeting place of integration between the three higher centers and the three lower centers. The light from the crown center comes into the heart center further purifying the nous, the spiritual eye, which resides in the heart, but opens the mind. The light received from above radiates outward from the heart center like the sun and bathes all the body with this transforming light. For this reason St. Symeon said he saw love as a solar disc in the center of my heart. Over time light coming from above and radiating from the heart transforms all the lower human functions so daily life becomes a natural condition of living in the light. The purified center of the heart, the purified nous, becomes light and sees itself, the world of men, and God in that light. God-realization and Self-realization are not two events, but one awareness seen in the light.

St. Symeon went to great lengths to encourage others to be open to experiencing the divine light in this life because he wanted others to experience what he experienced. But he believed that even the highest mystical attainment in this life is not anywhere near the profound vision of God that is available in the next life. St. Symeon felt that seeking divine light in this life is a preparation for this eternal vision of divine glory.

The most advanced type of mystical experience and integration that St. Symeon attained is beyond the range of most seekers. Nonetheless, the dedicated search for the Light is what is important. Even if you do not seem to be making very much progress in actually finding the Light, your efforts will bare fruit for you when you pass on to the next life.

Having wanted God for so long, you will be inspired then to embrace the Light at the moment of Truth when the soul returns to its Source.

The three aspects of the Visual Path of Light described by St. Symeon were praxis, gnosis, and theoria. However, based on the above phases of theoria, the Visual Path can be summarized as five phases in this way:

VISUAL PATH OF LIGHT

1. preparation—praxis and gnosis
2. the fire changing into a flame
3. the ray enlarging
4. the cloud
5. love as a solar disc in the heart

This summary of five phases of Visual Path of Light will be elaborated upon in the next section.

F. A Comparison of the Two Paths of Light

A general spiritual growth process called the Transformation Pattern has been identified above as having five steps—*preparatory seeking, awakening, more seeking, familiarity,* and *integration.* As was mentioned earlier, after some seeking St. Symeon had a profound spiritual awaking early in his life. Then he lost that lofty state of awareness, and the rest of his life was about making that awareness his own—integrating that divine awareness into his everyday life. Consequently, his whole life followed this general Transformation Pattern.

In addition to the lifelong transformation pattern, this section will demonstrate how you can go through a Transformation Pattern in each of the two paths of light described above—the Inner Feeling Path and the Visual Path. Both of these paths have five parts that are related to each other and also related to the five parts of the Transformation Pattern.

Discussing the five parts in sequence helps to clarify the similarities in each part, as follows:

Part one similarities are:

Transformation Pattern: preparatory seeking
Inner Feeling Path: preparation, first following the path of darkness
Visual Path: preparation of praxis and gnosis

The obvious common theme here is preparation.

Part two similarities are:

Transformation Pattern: awakening
Inner Feeling Path: opening the flame in the heart
Visual Path: the fire changing into a flame

The common theme here is the awakening of the awareness of the light as a fire or flame in the heart. However, St. Symeon's example of opening the flame in the Visual Path was a more intense awareness of light than the similar opening of the heart in the Inner Feeling Path.

Part three similarities are:

Transformation Pattern: more seeking
Inner Feeling Path: letting the light expand
Visual Path: the ray enlarging

This theme is increasing the awareness of the light that extends outward and then upward from the heart. In the Inner Feeling Path this expansion of light can be facilitated by the practice of Expanded Christian Yoga Meditation, which includes Light Meditation. But St. Symeon's kind of experience in the Visual Path of Light was more pronounced than the usual experience of light expanding during Expanded Christian Yoga Meditation. The more seeking part of the Visual Path is a ray of light that rises and lowers and that also contracts and expands. This implies a connection between the heart and the head. St. Symeon's description of a "pillar of fire" provides a vivid image of light and energy that rises from the heart into the head and then descends down again. This implies an intense experience of the kundalini, which is felt as a rising and then descending of light and energy.

Part four similarities are:

Transformation Pattern: familiarity
Inner Feeling Path: allowing the light to embrace you
Visual Path: the cloud

Here the theme is becoming accustomed to the divine presence, which is first experienced as unfamiliar or even disorienting and then becomes familiar, like adjusting to the experience of the cloud of unknowing. This has to do with contacting universal consciousness through the opening of the crown center in the top of the head, which can be disorienting. In the

Inner Feeling Path of Light learning to allow the inner light to possess the seeker can seem unfamiliar initially. But in the Visual Path, the opening to the divine presence is described by St. Symeon as a cloud descending upon the seeker. At first the cloud is disorienting, and it is even frightful until the time comes when the seeker eventually becomes accustomed to the new consciousness. Again this implies that the experiences of the Visual Path are very similar to the Inner Feeling Path, only much more intense.

Part five similarities are:

Transformation Pattern: integration
Inner Feeling Path: consistently resting in the light embracing you
Visual Path: love as a solar disc in the heart

The common theme here is an integration centered in the heart and radiating through all parts of your being. The integration of Integrated Contemplation is consistently resting in the light embracing you, and the integration of theoria is contemplation as an inner visual experience. Both paths of light are an expression of the kundalini rising and producing integration. In both paths the light rises up the spine to the head and down from the head into the heart from which it radiates to the whole body. The final integration is a balance of the head and heart, with the divine presence descending and resting in the heart consistently. Even though both these paths involve the same inner process of rising and descending energy, the Visual Path is a much more intense and profound experience of integration, as was experienced by St. Symeon in the final phase of his visual experience of the path of light.

There is an obvious overall difference between the Inner Feeling Path and the Visual Path. The steps along the way are very similar, but the difference is one of intensity with the Visual Path being a sequence of very intense experiences. The experience of theoria, in which the vision of light becomes a deep inner visual experience like the one described by St. Symeon, is a matter of both divine calling and sincere seeking.

Even if you do not have the deep inner visual experience of theoria, Integrated Contemplation can take you very far along the path of light as you open to the inner feeling of divine light. The challenge of opening to inner feelings in the Inner Feeling Path is not related to having a few peak experiences, but rather to having a consistent daily contemplative experience of resting in the state of allowing the light to embrace you. This consistency applied over time can facilitate a gradual and subtle inner purification and transformation of character and consciousness.

G. The Transformation Pattern and the Kundalini

This section describes the relationship between the Transformation Pattern and the kundalini. The five steps of the Transformation Pattern are based on the process of how the kundalini awakens and manifests in the body in coordination with the Holy Spirit. The *preparatory seeking* step is the inviting of the Holy Spirit to activate the rising of the kundalini. In this preparatory step you dedicate your consciousness to the divine origin and welcome the divine influence in your life and specifically into your body. But would you invite an elephant into your house? Just as an elephant is too large for your house, God Himself is too big to invite into your current home. Nevertheless, the rest of your path consists of learning to expand your capacity to receive as much of the Unlimited as you can.

You have to start where you are? If you open a window in your house, you can let an elephant stick his trunk into your house. Your preparatory seeking allows the Holy Spirit to send an impulse down to the base of the spine and to initiate the slow and gentle rising of the kundalini that helps to remove inner blocks as it rises. Each step after this is a deeper invitation to the Holy Spirit and to the action of the kundalini.

The *awakening* step of the Transformation Pattern occurs because the Holy Spirit takes your invitation literally and demonstrates to you, if you did not know already, that God is a like an elephant—God is more than you can handle. The awakening step is always a rising of the kundalini energy from the base of the spine to the heart in coordination with the Holy Spirit. A great awakening, like the one experienced by St. Symeon, raises energy through the heart all the way to the crown center. But a minimal awakening goes only to the heart, because the heart is the center of love. The awakening of love can be a heart connection with your brothers and sisters and/or an opening to the love of God. Sometimes the awakening is only a subtle yet unexpected reminder that God is present. The key element of this awakening step is that it is temporary since it appears suddenly and disappears just as quickly.

The *more seeking* step is a rising of the kundalini all the way from the base of the spine through the heart to the brow center. This step invites to the Holy Spirit to help you respond to the previous awakening step. The more seeking step attempts to gain back the level of consciousness revealed to you at your awakening, but which you have been unable to retain. You have the advantage in this step of knowing from experience that this awareness is there within you ready to be awakened again. This step involves learning how to coordinate the heart and the head. Ideally this step will help you to open your heart and bring love into your mind, which can produce changes in your perceptions.

The *familiarity* step includes the rising of the kundalini from the base of the spine all the way through the other centers and to the crown center. As with each step there is an invitation to the Holy Spirit to be the activating element. The crown center is the major center through which the Holy Spirit acts. This center represents universal consciousness that is far beyond individual consciousness so it can be very disorienting. This explains the difficulty of adjusting to the opening of the crown center and the need for repeated exposure to this center in order to obtain familiarity with universal awareness. The familiarity step is intended to lead toward the integration and unification of all aspects of yourself. However, in this step the integrating and unifying effect is only intermittent and not firmly established.

The *integration* step is the natural continuation and result of becoming increasingly familiar with the universal consciousness until a certain level of integration is produced that can be maintained consistently. As was mentioned previously, this type of integration is an aspect of the kundalini that is produced in the final state of the Inner Feeling Path and the Visual Path. In both paths the Holy Spirit facilitates the rising of the kundalini to the crown center, and then the kundalini energy descends down from the crown center into the heart center in the center of the chest. From the center of the chest the descending kundalini energy radiates to all parts of the body, producing the final integration.

The final integration produced by the Transformation Pattern usually occurs only after an extended period of time. Indeed, the time period of applying spiritual practices can be very long to produce the degree of integration that occurs in Integrated Contemplation and happens in the more all-inclusive integration that occurs in theoria. Obviously the time period would be very long if the Transformation Pattern manifests as an overall life pattern, as it did in the life of St. Symeon.

But the Transformation Pattern can also occur as a smaller repeated pattern within a particular part of your growth, as it does with the Inner Feeling Path and the Visual Path. You can think of your spiritual growth as walking up a spiral staircase. You start at one point and walk in one complete circle, but are going higher with each step. When you have walked in one completer circle, you are back where you started, only at a higher lever. Thus with each small awakening you go through a mini-version of the Transformation Pattern. Each time you have an awakening in your life, whether it is a very small one or a larger one, you will initially not be able absorb all of the experience immediately. You will appear to lose what you have experienced, and then after more seeking and familiarity, you will be able to gain back what was lost and integrate it into your life.

A helpful understanding of the Transformation Pattern is to realize that the smallest mini-version of this pattern in terms of both intensity and time can be experienced during each individual sitting period of meditation practice. If you are a beginner and your mind is constantly wandering during your meditation, your practice may be an expression of only the preparatory seeking, the first step of the Transformation Pattern. However, Christian Yoga Meditation (and Expanded Christian Yoga Meditation) is specifically designed to facilitate the occurrence of a minimal experience of all five steps of the Transformation Pattern. The sequence of steps and meditation techniques are indicated below:

THE TRANSFORMATION PATTERN

1. preparatory seeking—Centering Meditation
2. awakening—Heart Meditation (and Light Meditation)
3. more seeking—Brow Meditation
4. familiarity—Crown Meditation, Oneness Meditation,
                Inner Silence Meditation (some integration)
5. integration—contemplation (a higher level of integration)

In addition to each meditation period providing an opportunity for manifesting a minimal Transformation Pattern, there are also plateaus of growth that can express the Transformation Pattern. Each plateau stands for a different period of time in your growth progression. Likewise, each chronological plateau represents a greater degree of integration being reached. Some sample plateaus of spiritual growth are presented below:

PLATEAUS OF SPIRITUAL GROWTH

The Twenty-eight Day Demonstration
The One Year Program
Daily Meditation over a long period of time
The Plateau of Self-acceptance
Integrated Contemplation
Theoria

Of course, these are the specific plateaus described in this meditation manual as possible options of growth. You may have some very different plateaus of growth in your individual spiritual path. On your journey, you will have to make your own way and find what works best for you through practical experience and more significantly through the guidance of the Holy Spirit.

1. Thomas Matus, *Yoga and the Jesus Prayer Tradition* (Mahwah, New Jersey: Paulist Press, 1984), p. 62 (currently published by Asian Trading, Bangalore, India; distributed by Hermitage Books, New Camaldoli, 62475 Coast Highway One, Big Sur, CA 93920)

2. Ibid., p. 103

3. Ibid., p. 62

4. St. John of the Cross, *Living Flame of Love*, edited by E. Allison Peers (New York, New York: Image Books, Doubleday and Co., Inc., 1962), pp. 202f. This book was published by arrangement with the copyright holder and original publisher, Newman Press, which has been absorbed by Paulist Press, Mahwah, New Jersey.

5. John of St. Samson, O. Carm., *Prayer, Aspiration and Contemplation*, translated and edited by Venard Poslusney, O. Carm. (Asbury, New Jersey: printed by Fr. Venard Poslusney, The 101 Foundation, 1994), p. 154

6. St. Symeon the New Theologian, *Hymns of Divine Love*, translated by George A. Maloney, S. J. (Denville, New Jersey: Dimension Books), Hymn 15, lines 153, p. 54

7. Ibid., p. 171

8. George A. Maloney, S.J., *The Mystic of Fire and Light: St. Symeon the New Theologian* (Denville, New Jersey: Dimension Books, 1975), Hymn 15, line 171, pp. 106-107

9. St. Symeon the New Theologian, *Hymns of Divine Love*, translated by George A. Maloney, S. J. (Denville, New Jersey: Dimension Books), Hymn 39, lines 63-77, p. 203

10. Thomas Matus, *Yoga and the Jesus Prayer Tradition* (Mahwah, New Jersey: Paulist Press, 1984), p. 62 (currently published by Asian Trading, Bangalore, India; distributed by Hermitage Books, New Camaldoli, 62475 Coast Highway One, Big Sur, CA 93920)

11. Ibid., pp. 102-103

12. Ibid., p. 62

13. Ibid., p. 103

14. Ibid., p. 118

15. Ibid., pp. 120-121

16. Ibid., p. 103

17. St. Symeon the New Theologian, *Hymns of Divine Love*, translation provided by George A. Maloney, S. J. (Denville, New Jersey: Dimension Books), Hymn 17, lines 323-325, p. 67

18. Ibid., Hymn 17, lines 326-329, p. 67

19. Ibid., Hymn 17, lines 330-338, p. 67

20. Ibid., Hymn 18, lines 50-54, p. 80

21. Ibid., Hymn 18, lines 62-63, p. 80

22. Ibid., Hymn 18, lines 88-89, p. 81

23. Ibid., Hymn 17, lines 371-377, p. 68

24. Ibid., Hymn 17, lines 385, p. 68

25. Thomas Matus, *Yoga and the Jesus Prayer Tradition* (Mahwah, New Jersey: Paulist Press, 1984), p. 105 (currently published by Asian Trading, Bangalore, India; distributed by Hermitage Books, New Camaldoli, 62475 Coast Highway One, Big Sur, CA 93920)

26. Ibid., p. 109

27. Matthew 5:8

16

LIGHT VISION
AND
CHRIST'S VISION

≈ ● ≈

A. Light Vision Meditation

This meditation manual has emphasized finding God within, but this chapter will address finding the divine externally. This first section starts with St. Symeon's means of finding the divine in the world. St. Symeon's contribution to the mystical understanding of opening to divine light is best understood in the context of those who influenced him and those have been influenced by him. Of course, he was very much influenced by the Eastern Christian mysticism of *hesychasm*, which involved the repetition of the Jesus Prayer for inner attunement. Eastern mysticism was founded on the contemplative ideal of the early Fathers, in particular the "Cappadocians" of the fourth century. These early Fathers include St. Basil the Great, St. Gregory of Nyssa, and St. Gregory of Nazianzus.[1]

These Cappadocian Fathers influenced St. Symeon, but he was also influenced by the teachings of Evagris Ponticus. The teachings of Evagris identified two kinds of theoria, which is contemplation experienced as the vision of light. The first type of theoria was contemplation as the vision of the light of God seen in the world and in created beings, which was called *theoria physike*.[2] The second was contemplation as the vision of the light of the Holy Trinity, which was called *theoria theologike*.[3]

The teachings of Evagris were studied by St. Symeon, who adopted the same understanding as Evagris. However, St. Symeon referred to theoria physike as *gnosis* and theoria theologike as simply *theoria*. The teachings of St. Symeon were passed on to the monks of Mt. Athos in Greece who practiced hesychasm, which was in its full ascendency in the eleventh century. Today, as hesychasm is enjoying a revitalization at Mt. Athos, St. Symeon's writings are still studied with enthusiasm by the hesychast monks. St. Symeon may be considered an inspirational forerunner of the hesychast movement, which focuses on the use of the Jesus Prayer.

The theoria physike of Evagris, equivalent to St. Symeon's gnosis, is the ability to perceive the light of God in the outer world or creatures. It was considered by St. Symeon to be a preparation for theoria, the inner contemplation of light. St. Symeon felt that seeing the light in created beings revealed both their virtues and faults. He advised absorbing the virtues seen and discarding the faults. He felt the act of seeing the light of God outwardly could help to purify the nous, the spirit, also called the spiritual eye. In time the nous, as the faculty of mystical cognition, could become transformed into light. The Cappadocian Fathers and Evagris affirmed along with St. Symeon that the soul in mystical awareness sees itself as light and in this same light sees God. These are not two separate awarenesses, but rather one awareness of the soul transformed in the new consciousness of itself and God as one in the light.

One way to look at gnosis is to consider it to be the perception of the meaning of God's presence seen in all people and things. In addition, I believe this seeing with a divine meaning can refer to the visual seeing of light in the forms of the world, which I call *Light vision*. Light Vision Meditation is one method that may be used by a meditator who would like to meditate on seeing divine light outwardly in the world as a way of purifying the nous, spiritual eye, and as a way of preparing to see the divine light within. It needs to be understood that Light vision as a visual experience is a reflection of an inner experience of love and divine grace. Light Vision Meditation is a technique that is best practiced after first becoming comfortable with practicing Inner Light Meditation and Expanded Christian Yoga Meditation. These methods are designed to contact the inner feelings of light and love that will help to develop the ability to see light visually. These techniques assist in awakening higher consciousness by raising energy, light, and love in the heart and then raising these up into the head. This inner opening of the heart and head as an activity of divine grace is what makes Light vision possible.

The rising energy is a manifestation of the activity of the kundalini in coordination with divine grace. An example of the kundalini activity playing an essential role in the occurrence of Light vision can be found in the autobiography of Gopi Krishna, titled *Kundalini: The Evolutionary Energy in Man*. Gopi Krishna experienced a dramatic awakening of the kundalini, which for a long time produced a series of traumatic negative aftereffects in his body. After these negative aftereffects subsided, he had the positive aftereffect of seeing a silver luster illuminating all objects. As a result of seeing this light, he correctly concluded that his experience of Light vision was actually an outward projection of an inner luminous radiance within his own mind. Seeing this light illuminate all people and objects in his vision became part of his daily life. At times this external seeing of light intensified, which Gopi Krishna explained in this way:

> The lustrous appearance of external objects as well as of thought forms and the brilliance of dream images was intensified during the worst period of the last disorder and grew in brightness to such an extent that when gazing at a beautiful sunlit landscape I always felt as if I were looking at a heavenly scene transported to the earth from a distant elysium, illuminated by dancing beams of molten silver. This astounding feature of my consciousness, purely subjective of course, never exhibited any alteration, save that it gained in transparency, brilliance, and penetrative power with the passage of time and continues to clothe me and all I perceive in inexpressible luster today.[4]

Because opening the heart and raising energy into the head facilitates Light vision, the technique of Light Vision Meditation is recommended to be practiced for a short period at the end of your regular sitting practice, preferably after practicing Expanded Christian Yoga Meditation. Ideally it is best to reach the experience of Integrated Contemplation, in which you consistently rest in the light embracing you, before practicing Light Vision Meditation. Initially you may want to practice this method of seeing light externally for only about five minutes.

The goal at the beginning will be to only see light around an object. Some seekers spontaneously may have already experienced this limited form of Light vision in everyday life, perhaps without even realizing it. In this case, the seeker may see tiny edges of light around an object or person. The object or person may be perceived as glowing, but you may then dismiss this visual perception as just your imagination. If this happens it is likely to occur when you happen to be in a particularly loving state of mind. For example, some individuals go to church and sometimes see the heads of the people there glowing with a white light around the edges, but do not have this experience anywhere else.

Light Vision Meditation is, of course, practiced with the eyes open, and in the beginning will be only a partial experience of Light vision, such as seeing the light around an object. The eyes may be kept fully opened, but it may be helpful to have the eyes half or three quarters closed. Beginners in this practice will have to place an object in the line of their sight on the floor. The object may, for example, be a small book or a photograph of a person. Sitting in your regular meditation posture, you gaze at the object without tilting your head forward. Your line of vision can be about a forty-five degree angle. If you decide to partially close your eyes, which I would recommend, you obviously make sure to still keep the object in view. If you are sitting on the floor, the object can be placed on the floor. However, if you are sitting in a chair facing a wall, the object can be attached to the wall.

When looking at the object, attempt to look at the object as a whole rather than zeroing in on parts of the object. Objects are usually looked at in parts with the eyes constantly moving from one part to another, so you will have to overcome this tendency in order to take in the object as a whole rather than in parts. At first you focus only on the object and see if you can see edges of light around the object, as though the object is glowing. You do not focus on the edges of the object because that would be seeing part of the object instead of the whole object. After you are able to see a glow around the object while looking at the whole object, then you may be able to see the whole object filled with light. When you can see entire objects filled with light, you can allow yourself to take in a larger area of vision and see that area filled with light. Eventually you may be able to allow yourself to take in the whole panorama of your entire field of vision. You can see this panorama also as a whole rather than seeing it as separate parts and allow everything in your vision to be filled with various shades of light.

The visual side of this practice is only one part of the experience. The other more important part is what is happening inside of you. You must have your heart open to love and your mind calm, without any judgment. The outer manifestation of Light vision is accomplished here internally with your loving state of mind. Your loving state of mind is reflected in an experience of seeing light visually. You cannot have the visual experience without having this inner loving state of mind. Consequently, this visual experience is an outer confirmation that your mind is indeed perceiving in a loving and nonjudgmental way.

In order for your internal experience of love to be reflected to you by your outer vision, you must open your mind to seeing outer forms differently. In practicing Light Vision Meditation, you are advised to set aside all those limiting ideas you may have about the object you have chosen. Instead of looking at the object according to your ideas about the object, you are advised to let go of all judgments and all thoughts related to form.

You allow your mind and heart to penetrate into the object's essence beyond all form. By removing all of your own ideas about the object, you can view it with an entirely open mind. Allow this ordinary object to surprise you. You may have seen this object many times, but now you will make an attempt to see it for the first time as it really is. Allow the object to reveal to you its beauty, its divine value, and its meaning. Normally you look at an object and distinguish it only by its value to your ego and how it is different from other objects. This time look for the sameness that this object shares with all other objects in the universe. See in this object the same meaning that every other object possesses. The universal meaning shared by all objects is that each one expresses the divine. When you can see the light in this one object, you will be able to see the same light in any other object, since all objects share the same light as an expression of the divine.

How is it possible to see this, when it has never occurred to you before? You did not know what you were looking for in the past. You were looking only for differences in objects. Now you know that you are looking for the divine sameness in this object. But are you really looking for something out there? No, you are looking for something within your own mind. You are looking for the divine light and love in your own mind. When you find it within yourself, you may then see it outside in this object as well.

However, if you do see the object light up, there will be a fundamental difference in your relationship with this object that will be an entirely new experience for you. The difference is that instead of keeping that object apart from you, you are actually joining with that object. You usually see objects in order to keep yourself apart from them. Therefore, keep in mind that what you are really attempting to do in Light Vision Meditation is to join with what you see.

When you are joining with an object with your Light vision, you have your eyes open, but you are not really seeing with your physical eyes. St. Symeon makes a clear distinction between seeing with physical eyes and with *spiritual eyes*. He states that obviously we can see sensible objects with our sensible eyes, illuminated by sensible lights. But if we are concerned only with the senses, we will be blind to spiritual matters. According to St. Symeon, we can see at a deeper level with our spiritual eyes that are illuminated by a spiritual light.[5]

Light vision enables you to see beyond the physical only because the divine in you, the nous, the spiritual eye, is seeing the divine in outer objects. To help you to see with the nous, the spiritual eye, which is the faculty of mystical cognition, you are encouraged to develop the ability to see with your heart. St. Symeon writes about the spiritual eyes being directly related to the heart, and thus he makes the connection between mystical vision and the heart.

The way to see with your heart in Light Vision Meditation is to feel your heart and feel the love within your heart, as you extend your vision outwardly. You can focus on your heart or the center of the chest while focusing your vision on the chosen object. A more advanced stage of seeing with the heart is to feel the light and love not only in the heart and center of the chest, but also feeling that light and love actually rising up into the head. The light and love can be felt to be rising up and filling the entire head and even coming into the eyes.

First practicing Inner Light Meditation and then practicing Expanded Christian Yoga Meditation in the way described previously helps you to open to divine light and love. In so doing you are extending the divine love within you to the object and joining with it. Christ within you will assist you in extending your love outwardly through your vision. Your Light vision will allow you to have a loving union with the object and enable you to see the divine in that object.

When you can see the divine in the object, it means you are not only joining with the object, but also that you are accepting your own divine nature just as you have accepted the divine light in the object. After all, it is the divine in you aided by Light vision that enables you to see the divine in the object. Once you can see this divine light in one object, you can learn to see the divine light wherever you look and thus continue to reinforce the awareness of its presence in yourself.

Because you keep your eyes open during Light Vision Meditation, it is important to limit time for meditation to about five minutes to prevent eyestrain. If you want to extend the time for the eyes being open, you can close your eyes for periods of time to rest the eyes. Some meditators choose to have the eyes open for extended periods. The way to do this without eyestrain is to allow your vision to be slightly unfocused. It is possible to see the light with slightly unfocused eyes, but it helps to keep the eyes focused while you are just beginning to develop this ability. Whether the eyes are focused or unfocused, it is important to keep them steady in one position. Moving the eyes will prevent Light vision from occurring.

Although at first you may only see tiny edges of light around the object, after a while you may notice that the whole object begins to glow and get brighter than normal because the experience reaches a deeper level. In this deeper experience there is an increase in the intensity of the rising love, light, or energy, and the visual experience of light also correspondingly intensifies. When light is seen around objects, it appears to be a white light. When entire objects are filled with a glowing light, it may appear as a luminous white color or silvery color, but you may notice it has a golden shine to it. As your awareness of light intensifies, the entire form of every object in your vision may appear to be filled with a shiny, whitish golden light.

After focusing on just one object, your vision may expand so that you can see the divine light all around the object. Later you may even feel the whole range of your vision filled with light. When this happens, colors fade from sight and are replaced by varying degrees of brightness of shining light. The normal three-dimensional appearances change so that solid objects appear to take on a shiny, transparent quality. Finally objects appear to flatten out to a two-dimensional appearance in which all objects become shimmering shapes of luminescent light. At first the light objects become much brighter, and the dark objects become darker. Then even the dark objects begin to glow so everything is a glowing light with some shapes brighter than others, but each filled with shining light. The glowing light appears to be radiant and shimmering rather than static. It may seem like there is a thin, flat, and transparent white, slivery, or golden veil over everything in your vision so that all forms seem unsubstantial and empty except for the light.

The experience of seeing light appears to correspond directly with the rising of love, light, or energy from the heart. This is often felt as a flame extending upward from the heart or a light rising from the center of the chest. This light continues upward through the neck to portions of the head, then expands to fill the entire head, and finally encompasses the entire body. Meditators who have this experience report that they can only experience this flow of love, light, or energy, and the corresponding visual experience of light, when their minds are in a loving state in which their judgment is suspended. If thoughts of judgment or even distracting thoughts enter their minds, then the flow of love, light, or energy ceases and the attending visual experience of light also stops.

While it is perhaps helpful to know that this kind of visual experience may occur to a lesser or greater degree, it is more helpful to realize that the seeking experiences of outer or inner phenomena can be an impediment to spiritual progress if the ego becomes attached to such experiences. However, if the meditator can keep the goal of seeking God as foremost in his mind, the experience of seeing light can be a very useful tool. Since this experience only happens when the meditator has a loving state of mind, the experience is useful as a biofeedback system for approaching God, Who is Love.

Also, God is the supernatural light in which you live and move and have your being. While this phenomenon of visual light is not a direct experience of that supernatural light, it is a reflection of that light, similar to the way moonlight is a reflection of sunlight. The ability to see this light is a blessing from Christ through the action of the Holy Spirit. Light vision requires you to have a loving state of mind that enables you to have this experience.

This loving state of mind that makes Light vision possible is called *Christ's vision.*[6] My understanding of Christ's vision is derived from my study and application of the spiritual principles of *A Course in Miracles*, which will be discussed in the last five chapters. In *A Course in Miracles* Christ's vision is also called "vision," "real vision," "spiritual vision," "true vision," "perfect vision," "forgiving vision," "the savior's vision," "His vision," and "the Holy Spirit's vision." All these terms refer to the same ability of being able to see the divine presence and meaning of holiness. This divine seeing reflects the meaning of the presence of God and His Love, which is everywhere. This ability is made possible through a spiritual faculty called the "eyes of Christ," the "eyes of love," or the "eyes of forgiveness." This spiritual faculty of divine cognition is roughly equivalent to what St. Symeon terms the "nous," the faculty of mystical cognition. Christ's vision brings about purified perception in which the awareness of light comes into the mind and which allows you to perceive the divine holiness inwardly and outwardly.

But what is this "holiness" that can be seen in others or within yourself by using Christ's vision? I used to think holiness was an attribute reserved for saints who lived completely virtuous lives, but I learned from *A Course in Miracles* that holiness is something possessed by everyone. Just as God gave you His Light and His Love when He created you, He also gave you your holiness. Even though your holiness has not been identified here as a distinctive inner feeling, it is, nevertheless, an essential part of your true nature in God and for your own growth needs to be accepted as such.

God always remains with His creations, and He brings with Him His Love, Light, and Holiness. God is life itself. You live now and forever in Him and can never be separate from Him in spite of illusions of separation perpetuated by the ego. Since you can never be separate from God, you always retain the holiness and other attributes that God gave you when you were created. Hypothetically, you can commit a terrible mistake and call it a sin or you can have some terrible thing happen to you. As a result, you can imagine that you have defiled yourself or been defiled by some abuse from others. Therefore, you can feel that you are filled with guilt or shame. You can believe that you have lost your holiness, but such a belief is simply not true. You can never lose your holiness just as you can never be apart from God, Who is the source of your holiness.

Christ's vision enables the mind to perceive holiness. Christ's vision is literally taking on the Mind of Christ, which allows seeing with Christ's eyes. When Christ's vision occurs, the gift of light and love enter the mind by divine grace and by your desire for this to happen. More specifically, Christ's vision is the ability of the mind to perceive the divine presence of holiness inwardly and outwardly. Christ's vision is the state of mind that is needed to produce the outer perception of light that makes Light vision possible.

Although Christ's vision produces Light vision, is it possible to have this loving state of mind without producing the outer visual perception of light? Yes, in fact Christ's vision occurs most often without causing Light vision. For example, you can see the divine presence and see holiness in a person or object without having any visual experience of seeing light around or in that person or object. In this case, you are simply seeing people or objects with a new meaning of love and holiness because of the light that has entered your mind due to Christ's vision occurring. This is by far the most common experience of Christ's vision. Yet the external seeing of light in Light vision can be learned, and thus the practice of Light Vision Meditation is offered here for your consideration.

It is necessary to think of Light vision in terms of not only the visual experience you have of light, but also in terms of the broader context of its underlying cause—Christ's vision, the loving state of mind that has the effect of producing a visual experience of light. So when you are seeking Light vision, you are seeking this loving state of mind instead of seeking only the outer phenomena of seeing light. The real advantage of having Christ's vision with the additional bonus of Light vision is that the seeing of light externally gives you a form-related confirmation like biofeedback that you indeed do possess a loving state of mind. This biofeedback of visually seeing light externally is what makes Light vision so valuable, being a reassurance of your changed and purified perception due to your loving mind. When you do experience this loving mind, Light vision reveals to you that everything in this physical universe that appears to be so solid in form is actually composed of energy and light and comes from a divine origin. Having this visual experience then, if viewed in the correct way, can lead you in the direction beyond form and toward the supernatural Light of God.

When practicing Light Vision Meditation, it is not necessary to actually see light—either in the edges around objects or at deeper levels in which everything is filled with light—in order to benefit from this practice. But it is necessary to have a loving attitude throughout, provided by inviting Christ's vision, the ability to see with the eyes of Christ. You can focus upon an object that is spiritually meaningful for you to help you to be more loving. But you can have a loving attitude toward any ordinary inanimate object by realizing God as the source of all that exists. Allow yourself to relax and become one with the object in a loving union.

The seeing of light externally is a reflection and a positive projection of the divine light being revealed in your own mind with the help of the Christ and the Holy Spirit. Christ's vision produces purified perception in which the awareness of light comes into the mind and which allows you to perceive divine holiness both inwardly and outwardly. Thus far the term "theoria" has described the inner contemplative vision of light, and the term "gnosis" has described the external perception of divine in the world. Christ's vision is the essential source of both theoria and gnosis, since Christ's vision provides the ability to see the divine presence and the meaning of holiness both inwardly and outwardly. This divine seeing reflects the meaning of the presence of God, permeated by His Love, which is everywhere.

B. Blessing Meditation

After first practicing Light Vision Meditation by looking at an object, you may want to learn how to perceive the divine light within people. *Blessing Meditation* is a meditation method that helps you to perceive the meaning of holiness in another person by using Christ's vision and perhaps also by using Light vision. For this technique you join with a meditation partner in the purpose of seeking God and finding His presence in each other. This technique is recommended only as an intermittent supplement to your regular private meditation practice.

Obviously the first practical step in employing this method is to find a partner who is willing to join with you in seeking the divine. Seeking the divine within is difficult enough in itself, but seeking the divine presence in another person is an additional challenge that Blessing Meditation is designed to meet. As the name of the method implies, the partners focus on blessing each other.

Partners can mutually agree to include an optional verbal blessing before beginning to practice Blessing Meditation. Employing this verbal blessing is specifically recommended for the initial time you practice this meditation method with a new partner. Thereafter you may want to omit this optional blessing. One partner sits or kneels, and the other partner stands, while both partners are facing each other. The standing partner places his hands on the head or shoulders of his partner and verbalizes a blessing.

One way for you to express this verbal blessing is to acknowledge that you see the Christ in your brother. For this purpose you may choose an affirmation such as, "The Christ in me blesses the Christ in you," or "I see Christ in you, and I bless you in the Name of Jesus." By seeing Christ in your brother, you shine a light into his mind and enable him to also see Christ in himself. By aiding in awakening your brother's awareness of Christ, you in turn awaken and reinforce a deeper awareness of Christ within yourself.

The exact words you choose for your blessing are not as important as your inner intention to bless your brother or sister and affirm his or her holiness. Of course, the partners reverse roles with each other so each is blessed by the other. After completing the verbal blessings, you sit in a comfortable position facing your partner. You look at your partner and mentally focus on blessing your partner. Unlike the optional preparation blessing, no words are spoken. However, the same content of blessing is conveyed. To assist you in seeing the divine in your partner, you may want to use a mental affirmation, such as, "Christ Light."

For Blessing Meditation you sit facing your partner and start your practice by first meditating with your eyes closed, and you use either Inner Light Meditation or Expanded Christian Yoga Meditation, just as you would normally. Prior to beginning your practice, you and your partner mutually decide how long to meditate with your eyes closed. If you agree upon a specific number of minutes for the meditation, you can use a timer to signal the end of the meditation period. If you do not use a timer, you or your partner can say, "Amen" to signal the end of the meditation with your eyes closed.

Hopefully your meditation with the eyes closed will assist you to feel the light and love in your heart and raise this light and love upward into the head. When your meditation with the eyes closed is completed, you both open your eyes and look at each other. With your eyes open and with your mind open to the divine influence, you are attempting to join with your partner, becoming of one mind in Christ. With this sense of joining, you are looking at your partner in the same way you would look at your chosen object when you practice Light Vision Meditation. In this case, however, there is the additional inner attitude of intending to bless your partner by seeing Christ in him or her.

The most important aspect of Blessing Meditation is how your mind is viewing your partner. This is the time to set aside all those limiting ideas that you may have about another person and to see with Christ's vision. Even though you are looking at a body, your challenge is to set aside all judgments and all thoughts related to form. Allow your mind and heart to penetrate into that person's spiritual essence beyond all form and acknowledge in your mind that this person you see is really a spiritual being, a sacred being with a holy origin. As you seek and catch a glimmering of the divine within your partner, you will enkindle and reinforce an awareness of your own divine spark within.

Blessing Meditation is an opportunity to send love and blessings to your partner and is certainly not a staring contest. To practice Blessing Meditation you do not see the person with your physical eyes alone. Your physical eyes can only see that which is physical. You invite the ability to see with the eyes of Christ that will allow you to see the divine and give a blessing to another person. Since you are seeking to give a blessing, you are also opening yourself to receive a spiritual blessing that enables you to see more than just the physical form of your partner.

The way to open yourself to receive this spiritual blessing is to open your heart to your partner so you will be able to see love in your partner. You could say that you are seeing with your heart in order to obtain Christ's vision. Your meditation practice of either Inner Light Meditation or Expanded Christian Yoga Meditation with the eyes closed prepares you for this extension of love. Although you have your eyes open, it is recommended that you focus on your physical heart or the center of your chest at the same time you are looking at your partner and sending a blessing to him. Since it may be initially difficult to focus on the chest area and look at your partner simultaneously, you may want to close your eyes occasionally and refocus on the love in your heart. When you open your eyes again, allow the love in your heart to extend outwardly to bless your partner.

At times there may be a strain on the eyes. If eyestrain does occur, close the eyes for the rest of the meditation period. Remember to keep the eyes open only if you are comfortable doing so, and if there is no strain on the eyes. Be cautious in regard to deciding how long to keep the eyes open and how long to keep them closed. Because of the potential for straining the eyes, you may want to limit the part of Blessing Meditation in which you are looking at your partner to about five minutes.

When you look at your partner with love, this is not sentimentalism or emotionalism. It is more of a total acceptance of the true nature of the person seen in the depths of that person's true nature. It is best not to be concerned with showing any expression on your face to the other person. Your expression is most likely to appear blank outwardly as your eyes remain motionless with your gaze held steadfastly on your partner. Your inner loving attitude of acceptance without judgment is what is necessary, even though your outer expression may not reflect your inner experience.

It is helpful to have experience in practicing Light Vision Meditation and learn to look at an object with Christ's vision and hopefully with Light vision also as a preparation for Blessing Meditation. You look at the head of your partner, and you take into your vision the entire head just as you looked at the object and took the whole object into your vision in Light Vision Meditation. You remember to see your partner's head in wholeness rather than in parts. Similar to the way you may see edges of light around an object, you may initially see edges of light around the outer form of the head of your partner.

After you see a glow of light forming an outline around your partner, you may notice the whole face filling with light with some parts of the face brighter then others. Next you can allow your vision to look at the body as a whole, instead of just focusing on the head. You may then be able to see the whole body filled with light. At first the light you see in your partner will appear to be a white light or silvery light, but as more light is seen, the light may appear to actually have a golden glow. This book will use the term "golden light" to refer to this glowing light, but please be aware that the color may actually vary from white to sliver to gold.

There is a possibility you may see your partner's whole body change so the colors fade and are replaced by various shades of shimmering golden light. If your mind shifts from loving thoughts to judgments or distracting thoughts, you will notice that the seeing of light in or around your partner immediately disappears. If you have this experience of Light vision, the wisest use of this ability would be to allow it to serve as a biofeedback system to let you know that you are extending love while experiencing Christ's vision.

The goal in Blessing Meditation is to see the divine in your partner. Hopefully this seeing of the divine can manifest as a vision of your partner in light, but this is in fact seldom the case. Realistically speaking, when I have conducted workshops in which Blessing Meditation is practiced, maybe one out of twenty participants actually experience seeing light in another person, and this is usually only seeing a glow of light outlining the other person. Yet workshop participants are universally very inspired by the experience of extending love to others and seeing love in their partners. They are seeing the divine in their partners as an expression of Christ's vision, yet without having the visual confirmation that Light vision provides. This goal of extending love by seeing love in others through Christ's vision is not reserved for only a few individuals who have some special ability. Love is your true nature as a child of the God of Love. As you give your love to others by blessing them with Christ's vision, you learn to recognize and claim your own love nature.

Practicing Blessing Meditation can be an uplifting experience for you, whether you see light in others as a visual experience or not. Christ's vision without Light vision can change your perception of others so you can see the meaning of love and holiness in them. Perhaps in your daily life you often take for granted your brothers and sisters and allow your mind to dwell only on the mundane outer forms that you see others manifesting. It can be quite startling to suddenly realize that hidden behind the outer forms that your brothers and sisters present is the holy divine presence for which you so much yearn.

Besides helping you to see the spiritual nature of others, Blessing Meditation can also be a very effective method for assisting individuals, as a means of resolving problems in their relationships. For example, before practicing Blessing Meditation, you and your partner can join in asking the Holy Spirit to help you both overcome any unresolved issues in your relationship by learning to see the divine in each other. Your path to God like the cross is both vertical and horizontal. Meditation usually emphasizes your vertical path toward direct union with God. However, equally important and necessary to your spiritual development is your horizontal path of manifesting loving relationships.

C. Light Vision in Daily Life

If you do happen to reach the point where you have experienced light as an outer visual experience on a regular basis during meditation, you may be able to see the light at times in your everyday life. This will usually be the seeing of edges of light around a person or object. These spontaneous occurrences in your daily life will occur at times when you happen to be looking steadily at a person or object and when you also have a loving state of mind. This is a good sign, not so much because of the experience itself, but because it shows that your meditation experience is being generalized into your daily life. Thus you are learning how to maintain a loving state of mind as a natural expression of your life as a whole.

In addition to these spontaneous occurrences, you can consciously decide to see the light in someone as you are having a conversation with that person. While you are listening and that person is talking, you can focus your gaze on that person and have a loving attitude toward that person. You will be able to see a glow of white light around the person, although seeing the whole person light up may require more time than a casual conversation would provide. You would not have to tell the person what you are doing. Instead, you will notice that when you see the light in another person that person will often respond in some way that shows a recognition of your love.

Another way to think of this is to focus on seeing Christ in another person, and that will help you to see the light in that person. When you see the light in another person, you are actually shining a light into that person's mind and allowing that person to accept his or her own light. It will be surprising to you just how natural it can become for you to see the light around others in your daily life once you have developed this ability from a regular practice of Light Vision Meditation.

D. Understanding Christ's vision and Light Vision

What is really happening during Light Vision Meditation? First of all, your eyes are not really physically seeing this golden (or white or silvery) light when you have your eyes open during meditation. A picture that a camera can take will show you exactly and only what your physical eyes are capable of seeing. A camera cannot take a picture of this golden light that you will see in meditation. Consequently, the light you are seeing is not out there where your vision is focused. The light is in your mind. That is why you can see the golden light not only with your eyes open but also with your eyes closed. In fact, when you can see the golden light in your full range of vision, you will notice that the golden light you see inwardly will look at times almost exactly like the golden light that you can see outwardly. That's a confirmation that the light you are seeing is really in your mind and not external to you. This awareness of light in the mind is the gift of the Holy Spirit that makes the loving state of mind called Christ's vision possible, which in turn makes Light vision possible.

This amounts to a new form of projection that is positive rather than negative. The word "projection" is a psychological term to describe a defense mechanism of the mind. Projection is what the mind does when it does not want to see that something negative is in the mind. In order to deny the presence of this negative idea in the mind, the negative idea is projected outside of the mind and is seen in another person rather than in oneself.

Vision of the golden light is a positive variation of this projection because it an attempt of the mind to project outward something positive that is in the mind. In contrast to negative projection, which is used to get rid of something in the mind, this positive projection is employed to convince yourself that something good is in your mind by seeing that same something outside of your mind. Of course, projecting negativity outside the mind does not have the desired effect because instead of producing denial it actually keeps your mind focused on negativity and keeps that negativity in your mind. However, this new kind of positive projection does work and proves to you that the light you see is really within you.

Light vision is not only about seeing divine light outwardly. It is also about Christ's vision, having an open and loving state of mind to make seeing the divine light outwardly possible. If your mind is open to the possibility, your Light vision will express itself by allowing you to see the divine outwardly and helping you to open your spiritual eye to see inwardly. Light vision is a blessing from the Holy Spirit attracted by your willingness to focus on forgiveness and union rather than separation. Light vision is a gift received by an open and unified mind.

What is a unified mind? It is an open mind and also a focused mind that is the goal of all meditation practice. The everyday mind is scattered and divided and becomes an unclean mirror that no longer provides a clear reflection of its divine source. But once the mind becomes focused and there is openness to receive Christ's vision as an expression of love, then Light vision is attracted to that mind because it can reflect the divine light. Once Christ's vision takes its rightful place in the unified mind, then inner conflicts can be resolved, apparent opposites can be reconciled, and mistaken thoughts can be corrected. Such a state can only occur when the mind is unified because it is focused and wants union with the Truth. This unified state of mind that opens itself to receive the gift of Christ's vision has unlimited potential for spiritual growth.

Christ's vision is a gift, which can in turn produce Light vision, but it comes about only by an invitation from an open and unified mind. Even if you make the invitation, your invitation must be wholehearted. When you invite an honored guest to your house, you make sure that you clean your house to make it a fit place for your meeting. Likewise, when you invite Christ's vision and Light vision, you must also clean out the distracting thoughts that would scatter your mind. By bringing your mind to a unified focus you demonstrate the wholeheartedness of your invitation to Christ's vision and Light vision.

Being in your mind now, the Holy Spirit through Christ's vision would like to enable you to look on everything you see with love. But you will have to accept this gift from the Holy Spirit, Who holds it for you and awaits your invitation. To receive this gift, you must see with Christ's eyes by accepting Christ's vision as your own. Christ sees *every* son of God as perfect and lovely. He wants only to share Christ's vision with you for He has never lost sight of you, although you have lost sight of Him.

Christ wants to give you Light vision in addition to Christ's vision. Unlike Light vision, your normal process of seeing is not real seeing. Your current way of seeing is the making of images. You are watching a movie that your mind is making. You know that movies are made by passing colored shapes on a strip of film in front of a light projector. The projected light creates an illusion of real people who are acting out parts in a story. By analogy, the making of images in films is very similar to what your ego does with the body's eyes.

By perceiving images through the eyes, the ego keeps your mind focused on outer forms, rather than on the light that is in your own mind. The images of these outer forms seem very real to you, just as the images of a movie appear real to you. Because movie images appear real to you,

you do not think about the light that is coming from the projector, even though the light is the real power that makes seeing the movie possible.

The images produced by the ego are much more convincing than the movie images seen in a theater, so you do not even consider that these everyday life images are your movie of your world. You do not even suspect that there is another way of seeing that would allow you to see with the light of your own mind instead of only images of illusion.

The movie that your physical eyes produce is convincing because you appear to be in it. Your movie shows you a drama in your everyday life in which you are one of the actors. In fact, you are the star of your own movie. Because your mind is scattered, you see a scattered world in which everything is seen as different. But if you could remove the film from the projector of your own mind, everything you see would change. You would see only the white light coming from the projector. Of course, that would end your movie drama, because the illusion that you were watching has disappeared.

But do you really want to see illusions or the truth? If you remove the film, you will no longer have your place in the drama, and so there will be no conflict or disharmony. You would see that the light from the projector comes from your own mind and that you are one with the light instead of one with the images you have made. When you have Christ's vision in your unified mind, you can learn to see everything from one frame of reference—from the frame of reference of the divine light in your own mind in which all things are seen as similar.

In contrast to Christ's vision and Light vision, the ego that sees through the body's eyes can only create a distortion of the light, which is an image of form, just as a movie film distorts the white light of a projector. Seeing through the images of the body's eyes, the ego enables you to look at every person and every object as though you are separate from that person or object. Remember that the ego is your idea of yourself as being a separate body and a separate mind contained in that body. The ego itself is this idea that you are separate, alone, and apart from everything and everyone else. The ego employs the physical eyes of the body to "prove" to yourself that the objects and people outside your body are separate from you. You accept this proof without question as a fact of everyday life, and so you never think to question the validity of the ego itself.

In this sense your normal vision is a means of producing an illusion of separation. This outer illusion of separation hides the truth that is very different from appearances. The truth is that the ego is only a false idea of separation that has no reality and only appears to be true to you because of your belief in it. The truth also is that your true nature is united with everyone and everything since you are one with God Who is united to everyone and everything. Unlike your normal vision that shows you an illusion that only appears to be the truth, Christ's vision and Light vision reveal the illusion and let you see that you are not separate and alone. Christ's vision and Light vision show you that everyone and everything can be seen in the same light and encourage you to see that this same light is in your own mind in which all things are unified.

In fact, you use Light vision not to separate yourself, but to join with everyone and everything. When you visually see an object glowing with light, it is a demonstration of your desire to join with that object and see your oneness with it. Seeing light in an object is also a reflection of the light in your mind and how unified your mind is. A partially unified mind can invite only the very beginning of Light vision in which you can only see the edges of light around objects. When your mind becomes more unified, your Light vision will show you more light. Eventually you may be able to see everything in your vision filled with light. In this case, you have reached a deeper level of your mind in which you will be able to recognize the union of all things in the one light that comes from God.

Christ's vision and Light vision bring blessings that are attracted by an open and unified state of mind. A divided mind perceives illusions of separation as reality so it accepts what is false as if it were true. A unified mind perceives the true reality of unity, and it only accepts what is true as true and what is false as false. The unified mind leads to forgiveness. Why does the unified mind bring about forgiveness and what is being forgiven? As a result of the ego, you see the world as a place of fear, anger, and attack. Because of our own personal thoughts of fear, anger, and attack that you store in your own mind, you project these thoughts outwardly onto the world. The description of the ego using the body's eyes similar to a projector that produces images that you see is more than just an analogy. The mind that is not unified and is guided by the ego uses the defense mechanism of projection to project onto the world the images it does not want to recognize within the mind itself, although that is where they are.

This projected view of the world is an illusion of negativity, so when you let go of this viewpoint of the world, you are also simultaneously forgiving yourself for having thoughts of fear, anger and attack in your own mind. Through this forgiving state of mind in which you forgive your own mind, your mind itself lets go of the ideas of fear, anger, and attack that your ego had produced in your mind. Because your forgiveness has released these ideas in your mind, you will be able to see a world without the illusions of fear, anger, and attack. Letting go of these illusions, you will be able to perceive the holiness in the world that allows you to experience Christ's vision. You may also experience Light vision by seeing a world filled with the beauty of a glowing light that actually originates in your own mind.

Light vision confirming your Christ's vision proves to you that you are banishing fear, anger, and attack from your own mind. More importantly, Light vision shows you that you are letting go of the ego perspective that produced these negative images and reveals that you are accepting your true love nature. The phenomena of seeing light means nothing in itself, but it does have importance in that it demonstrates the loving state of mind of Christ's vision. Thus if you feel guided to practice Light Vision Meditation, this method will be very helpful for your spiritual growth as a reminder to you of your loving state of mind.

Christ's vision and Light vision come to an open and unified mind and bring peace. When your mind is at peace with Christ's vision, you will be able to send your peace to other minds. Your light will shine into the minds of others and will help them to awaken to the light in their own minds. The light that you awaken within others will help to shine away the darkness in their minds. Therefore, your Christ's vision, which has healed your own mind, will bring healing to the minds of others.

When you heal another person, you see Christ in that person and are manifesting forgiveness. Your forgiveness manifests by overlooking the illusions that the other person maintains about himself. You see that the person you are forgiving is not the body that he identifies with. In addition, you see that the thoughts he has of fear, anger, and attack are not part of his true nature. You do not forgive anything that is real. To heal another person, you only forgive the illusions he has about himself. Your forgiveness shines a light into his mind that enables him to let go of these same illusions about himself. Your forgiveness of illusions is not offered as a condescending gift, but rather a just view that acknowledges only the truth about who he is. You give him only what he deserves because you are seeing him as he truly is in Christ. Seeing Christ in him not only shines a light from your mind to his mind, but also his light cannot fail to shine back on you, so you both are joined in light and love.

Once you have used Light Vision Meditation and have developed your ability to use Christ's vision and Light vision, you will find many opportunities to practice viewing others with forgiveness. You can do this within your own mind at a distance from others, yet it seems that forgiving others with Light vision is most effective when practiced in their presence. The opportunity to look directly at your partner in Blessing Meditation provides a perfect situation for putting into practice your forgiveness through the use of Christ's vision and Light vision.

Not only will you be able to shine your light into your partner's mind by seeing Christ in him, but you may also be able to open his mind to his own Christ's vision and possibly to Light vision as well. If your partner is open to this gift of the Holy Spirit, your seeing of the light in him as a visual experience may assist him in turn to see the light in you with his own Light vision. You may experience a joy that will leap from your heart when you are looking at your partner, and he says to you with his own joyful wonder that he can see the light in you. Then you will know your gift of light and love has certainly been received and returned back to you. But a greater reason for rejoicing is that your partner now has seen that he has Light vision himself and can learn to see the light in others and develop this ability. In all likelihood, you will have to remind your partner that Light vision is not merely the seeing of light. Light vision includes the loving state of mind in Christ's vision that allows the light to be seen visually.

Of course, you can have the loving state of mind in Christ's vision without seeing light outwardly in Light vision. But the seeing of light outwardly in Light vision comes to you to show you that light and love are your own true nature. When the eyes of Christ show you everything outwardly transformed by your perception of light and love, you will believe that light and love are really in you.

Naturally you can still believe light and love are within you without Light vision showing you the light externally. However, seeing the light outwardly helps you to believe that light is really within you. When you don't believe that the light is within, you won't be able to see it either inwardly or outwardly even though it is there. Also, you will be unlikely to transfer the light to others because of your lack of belief.

The reason why it is so important to see light in others is that when you do so, you are giving to others the loving light that is really within your own mind. Then you will realize that it is by giving this light and love to others that you keep the awareness of this same light and love in your own mind. You have learned in your world that if you give something away, you will lose it. Yet giving your light away teaches you that giving is the way to keep what you have. Likewise, your seeing of everyone and the world in the loving light of forgiveness shows you that you can apply this same forgiveness to your own mind and forgive yourself. Similarly, when you can look at your brother and see light in him, you prove to yourself that Christ is in your brother, and in turn you convince yourself that Christ must be within you as well.

In short, seeing the light outwardly is like a biofeedback system of light. It shows you what is already in your mind in a way that proves it to you. It also proves to you that you are worthy to receive all of the same light, love, and forgiveness that you see and give to others. In addition, this biofeedback system is particularly helpful in showing you not only when you have a loving state of mind, but also when you have left that loving state of mind. Because of the ego, your loving state of mind can be thrown off center by unloving thoughts of judgment or even by just distracting thoughts. If you are seeing light with Light vision and if your loving mind is thrown off center, your ability to see light visually will disappear. When you experience this happening, you can respond to this biofeedback by letting go of any judgments or distracting thoughts and by redirecting your mind toward loving thoughts.

Consequently, even though you can have a loving state of mind with Christ's vision without seeing light, there are many benefits to the outer seeing of light that is in reality projected from within your own mind. Perhaps you have a tendency to think that this ability is beyond your reach, but limited thinking will produce limited results. You will benefit if you put your main focus on the loving state of mind of Christ's vision that makes Light vision possible. Nonetheless, it would be very helpful if you could open your mind to invite the Holy Spirit to give you the gift of Light vision. Besides your invitation to the Holy Spirit, receiving Light vision will also require your own determination to let your loving state of mind allow you to see differently with Christ's vision. You will have to actively want to let your love pour out of you in such a way that you will see a world transformed by your willingness to see it in light.

The results of your attempts to obtain Light vision will depend upon divine grace, but your seeking itself is beneficial even if you do not see light outwardly. The benefit comes in setting your mind and will toward wanting the light. Through this expression of your mind and will, you are committing yourself to joining with God's Will, which is required in order to receive Christ's vision as the basis for Light vision. In doing so you have accepted the purpose that God has truly given you to discover your true nature in Him.

There are different levels of light that can be revealed to you as you go deeper within yourself. Even though seeing and then dwelling within the deepest level of supernatural light in union with God is the ultimate goal, it is not within the scope of meditation to produce this experience because meditation is only a technique of mental focusing. Indeed, God by His grace is the only one that can fully reveal His Light to you. If He chooses not to reveal His Light to you in this life, you can be sure that as you pass out of this world He will fully embrace you with His Light, as well as His Love. Then it will be your willingness, desire, and seeking for the light that will enable you to join with Him in divine union in His Light. Yet even in this life, the setting of your heart on seeing the light will bring you a deep inner peace.

The key to attracting Light vision is producing an open mind that is focused on light and love. Some individuals already are focused on light and love and can obtain Light vision simply by practicing Light Vision Meditation. But most meditators need to do preparatory work to open the mind and help the mind focus on light and love. For this purpose I suggest the One Year Deepening Meditation Program that is described in Chapter 9. This program shows you how to combine many different methods in a step-by-step approach designed to deepen your meditation experience and open your mind. For the One Year Program, you can replace Heart Meditation with Inner Light Meditation, and likewise you can substitute Christian Yoga Meditation with Expanded Christian Yoga Meditation in order to help you open to your inner feelings.

The previous chapter focused on contemplation as a path of light. Only some seekers will be attracted to this path of light as an opening to the inner feeling of light, and even fewer will be attracted to this path of light as a visual experience. But the inner feeling of love is just as important as the inner feeling of light, and may be even more important. Similar to the way you can allow the inner feeling of light to embrace you during your practice of Integrated Contemplation, you can also let the inner feeling of love embrace you. The intense feeling of light in the spine, head, and heart that some seekers experience can in addition be experienced as an equally intense opening to divine love. This involves a nonverbal surrender of the will to God, requires your invitation for the grace of divine love to manifest within you, and invariably includes an opening of the heart center in the center of the chest.

Because this is a meditation manual, the emphasis is on opening to the divine within. Opening to divine love within leads quite naturally to opening to divine love externally. Light Vision Meditation and Blessing Meditation are unusual means of opening to the divine externally and will not be suited to the majority of seekers. Yet there is no shortage of other means of finding the divine presence in everyday life. Therefore, the following chapters will address a series of issues that relate to both inward seeking and to the divine expression in daily living.

E. Inner Vision Experiment

If you learn to practice Light Vision Meditation with your eyes open, you may eventually be able to see the golden light externally. Perhaps occasionally you will even be able to see your whole panorama of vision as a veil of golden light. You may want to experiment to find out if you can see this same golden light within. Before starting to look within for the golden light, you would benefit by first making progress through each of the five stages of the Inner Feeling Path of Light that have been described in the previous chapter. Your prior practice of Inner Light Meditation and then Expanded Christian Yoga Meditation will help to open your heart to the inner feelings of light, love, and energy and raise these into the head. In your practice of Expanded Christian Yoga Meditation hopefully you will experience Integrated Contemplation, in which you will be filled with the inner feeling of light and allow that inner feeling of light to possess you. When you reach the fifth stage of the Inner Feeling Path of Light, your practice of Integrated Contemplation will become consistent, and this will be your most important preparation for seeing the golden light internally. Your attempts at seeing the divine light externally are a very helpful preparation for experiencing the divine light internally. Seeking to gain Light vision can be a temporary goal as long it is not perceived as an end in itself. Light vision is best understood as a stepping stone that leads to the more important vision of seeing divine light inwardly and as a confirmation and reassurance of having a loving unified state of mind, being a reflection of your true nature.

Even though theoria, the vision of divine light inwardly, comes by divine grace, St. Symeon felt it does not come without your seeking of this gift. One way to express this seeking for theoria is by practicing the *Inner Vision Experiment*. This experiment can be conducted at the end of your regular practice of Expanded Christian Yoga Meditation, when you are already consistently experiencing Integrated Contemplation by resting in the inner feeling of light possessing you. As you conclude your sitting time, you set aside a short time for looking inwardly for the same golden light that you may have seen outwardly in your prior experience practicing Light Vision Meditation. It is important to first learn how to rest in the inner feeling of the light before proceeding to attempting to see the light internally. For this reason a premature attempt to practice the Inner Vision Experiment, before you have already gained the ability to practice Integrated Contemplation, would probably not be very effective and is not recommended.

For the Inner Vision Experiment, you allow your vision with the eyes closed to lovingly be open to seeing the golden light. With your eyes closed you will see darkness, but you can allow yourself to see the light within the darkness. You do not focus on any one point of light. This is not a concentrative practice; it is a receptive practice. The light that you wish to see is not an object that you wish to focus on and possess with your mind as you would in meditation. You do not move your eyes around. You allow yourself to take in the whole panorama of your inner vision. You look at the light with the same loving attitude that you would look at an object or person in Light Vision Meditation, but without any sense of possession. You are unconcerned about the brightness of the light and just allow yourself to see any light, even if it is not bright at all. You passively observe what light you do see. The light may appear to be unstable and floating like a slightly glowing gas that keeps changing shape. If you see colors other than a white, silvery, or golden glow, you ignore them. You may notice a glowing light floating in darkness.

It is important that you are not striving to see the light because this would cause a strain or mental concern, which would be disruptive to the process. Instead, you let your mind be restful and passively receptive. You are alert to the light, but not concerned about it. You allow your mind in its sensitivity to light to be like a quality stringed instrument that is not strung too tightly or too loosely. When your eyes are open, you do not *try* to see; you simply see. When you have your eyes closed, you do not try to see the light internally; you simply see the light that is there.

In the practice of Inner Vision Experiment, you are not likely to see the blazing supernatural Light of God. Initially it would be enough to simply have just a minimal awareness of light since you are seeing only the light that is already in the darkness of your inner vision. There is no such thing as complete darkness. There will always be some light that can be seen in the darkness. You are not trying to find the light; you are simply observing whatever light is already obviously there.

The Inner Vision Experiment is intended to bring about a minimal seeing of light inwardly that is such a slight opening to divine light that it cannot be considered to be theoria. This introduction to seeing light in contemplation is only an invitation for theoria, the contemplative vision of divine light. The practice of the Inner Vision Experiment is primarily an expression of your desire to be open to the divine grace that would make theoria possible. The Inner Vision Experiment is not intended to be a regular form of meditation. That is why it is called an "experiment" and not a "meditation." The Inner Vision Experiment is ideally conducted only occasionally to express your desire for theoria. The experience of theoria itself comes by divine grace. If theoria occurs, it is more likely to occur unexpectedly during your regular meditation period rather than as a result of following a specific structured technique intended to induce the inner visual experience of divine light.

F. More about Integrated Contemplation

The Inner Vision Experiment can be a preparation for theoria, but a more highly recommended preparation is Integrated Contemplation. The Inner Vision Experiment may be used once in a while very briefly at the end of your regular daily practice of Integrated Contemplation, in which your primary focus is on the inner feeling of light rather than the inner visual experience of light. During Integrated Contemplation, you feel the inner light, and you rest in that light. In resting in the light, you allow your heart to open in love to the light. As you rest in the light, you allow the light to possess you. In this state of Integrated Contemplation there is no striving, only acceptance and appreciation. As you rest in the light and allow the light to possess you, you allow yourself to feel at one with the light. Ironically as you are resting in this light, you may feel a sudden jolt of energy, without pain, that affects the whole body all at once. You may also experience visual imagery or unusual emotions that suddenly appear and disappear. Your eyes may tear, not due to straining to see, but because inner blocks are being removed from the eyes themselves. If unusual experiences happen to interfere with your practice, you need not be concerned. Just return to your resting in the light and allow this rest to bring peace to your mind

During your practice of Integrated Contemplation, the intensity of the inner feeling of light will increase noticeably after many inner blocks have been released and after the plateau of self-acceptance has been reached. You may experience the inner feeling of light throughout your whole body. However, certain parts of the body may become more intensely filled with light than others. One way this may manifest is for intense light to fill the whole spine, for light to fill the head and radiate from the crown center, and for light to descend from the head into the heart center and then fill the whole body.

This opening to light in the whole body tends to activate the center of the chest in particular. The light that descends from above reveals a concentration of light radiating in the center of the chest, although some seekers may initially feel more light in the physical heart. During this contemplation you can be conscious of the concentration of light in the center of the chest and be aware of light filling the whole body. However, this is a receptive awareness in which you do not have to direct your mind to use the center of the chest as a focusing area, as you would in Inner Light Meditation. You just allow the light to possess you. Then the concentration of light radiating in the center of the chest spontaneously presents itself. Thus you may have a dual awareness of the concentration of light in the center of the chest and simultaneously of light in the whole body. While allowing the light to possess you, it is important to have an attitude of complete openness to the Holy Spirit.

Integrated Contemplation can facilitate an experience that is similar to theoria, though less intense. In this experience the spine is activated by light, the crown becomes filled with light, and a light radiates in the center of the chest and fills the whole body. However, theoria is different from this experience because it is a spontaneous revealing of the deep visual experience of light. The experience of seeing and uniting with this inner divine light creates a profound transforming effect on all levels of consciousness and all human faculties as well.

The experience of theoria, in which the vision of light becomes a deep inner visual experience like the one described by St. Symeon, is a matter of both divine calling and sincere seeking. Realistically very few are called to experience theoria at all, and even fewer are called to experience the degree of theoria that St. Symeon experienced in which the visual experience of divine light dominated his contemplation and even his daily life. Nevertheless, even if you do not have the deep visual experience of theoria, Integrated Contemplation can take you very far along the path of light opening you to the inner feeling of divine light. The challenge in this method is not related to having a few peak experiences. Rather, the challenge is to maintain a daily practice of contemplation in which you experience resting in the state of allowing the light to possess you. This consistency over time can facilitate a gradual and subtle inner purification and transformation of character and consciousness.

In order to describe the path of light, the inner feeling of light has been emphasized. But the experience of the inner feeling of light is amplified by simultaneously opening to the inner feeling of love. Just as you allow the inner feeling of light to possess you, you can similarly allow the inner feeling of love to possess you. Sometimes the intense feeling of light in the spine, head, and heart will lead to a deep opening to divine love. This usually involves the following three factors: your nonverbal surrender of the will to God, your invitation for the grace of divine love to manifest within you, and the opening of your heart center in the center of the chest. Opening to divine love increases the effectiveness of Integrated Contemplation and is a preparation for a more intense experience of theoria.

---

1. Thomas Matus, *Yoga and the Jesus Prayer Tradition* (Mahwah, New Jersey: Paulist Press, 1984), p. 7 (currently published by Asian Trading, Bangalore, India; distributed by Hermitage Books, New Camaldoli, 62475 Coast Highway One, Big Sur, CA 93920)
2. Ibid., p. 62
3. Ibid., p. 62
4. Gopi Krishna with commentary by James Hillman, *Kundalini: Evolutionary Energy in Man* (Boulder, Colorado and London, England: Shambhala, 1971), p. 196
5. St. Symeon the New Theologian, *Hymns of Divine Love*, translated by George A. Maloney, S. J. (Denville, New Jersey: Dimension Books), Hymn 33, lines 67-74, p. 184
6. In my previous book I took the liberty of using the term "Christ vision" to replace the Course's term "Christ's vision." Now my former alteration seems inappropriate so I have returned to using the Course's terminology, which more accurately reflects the idea that this vision is a seeing with the "eyes of Christ," not with the body's eyes.

PART THREE

~ • ~

MEDITATION AND OVERALL SPIRITUAL GROWTH

17

PRAYER AND MEDITATION TO EXPRESS GOD'S WILL

≈ ◦ ≈

A. Dedication of the Will

Your prayer and meditation practice necessarily must be considered within a larger context of your overall spiritual growth. This chapter and Chapters 18 and 19 will address a variety of significant issues related to spiritual living in general. The emphasis will be on the interrelationship between prayer and meditation and on how these both affect and are affected by your daily life.

Prayer and meditation are attempts to become aware of an inner wholeness, but in addition that inner wholeness needs to be reflected outwardly, especially in your relationships with your brothers and sisters. This chapter and the next two chapters are written for those who would like to consider making a deeper commitment to spiritual growth that includes both inner and outer wholeness. The first commitment you were asked to consider was conducting the Twenty-eight Day Demonstration. The second commitment was to consider practicing daily meditation on a continuing basis. The third commitment was to consider experiencing the One Year Program. Now the deeper commitment being suggested involves more than just manifesting your ideal and your mental attitude through a daily meditation schedule. This proposed new commitment is to increasingly allow His World of being to come forth and be manifested in your world of doing in every aspect of your life. Taking this direction requires a renewed dedication of the will.

During meditation you let go of thoughts to become inwardly still. Likewise, you need to learn to let go of self-will in your daily life and become still in regard to your own desires in order that the Holy Spirit may act through you in all that you do. Your calling as a Christian is to follow the example of Jesus by being as He would be in stillness and by doing as He would do in action. Jesus had no other purpose than to express love by doing God's Will. If you wish to make a commitment to deepening your relationship with God and let your commitment be expressed in your daily life and relationships, you need to build such a commitment on the solid foundation of the mental attitude of doing God's Will.

The relationship between a mental attitude, such as doing God's Will, and the spiritual ideal can be illustrated by the analogy of climbing a mountain. The spiritual ideal would be the top of the mountain. The paths before you as you climb toward the mountain top are varied— some are dead-end trails, some lead upward but are rocky, and other routes lead upward and are easier to climb. The traveler will wonder not only what paths to take, but also what tools may be needed along the way. Since you have never climbed to the top before, and since this is a lifetime journey, it would be helpful to have some way to determine how to proceed on the path.

Your mental attitude, then, would be the specific way you choose to use your mind throughout your journey. While the ideal itself is beyond your reach, this mental attitude is an attainable tool, similar to a compass that can be used to point you toward your destination, so you will know where to place your next step on the path. You need to ask yourself, "What mental attitude can I hold that would help me the most to grow spiritually?" For example, when you were asked previously to choose a mental attitude, you may have chosen "I wish to be of service." However, in order to express the mental attitude of service, or indeed any other mental approach toward your spiritual ideal, it is necessary to dedicate yourself to being in accord with God's Will. Otherwise, how would you know what action would be of most service to others? If you are doing God's Will, you will invariably be guided to do whatever service would be most appropriate.

Alignment with God's Will has two aspects, and both of these are related to love. The first is the *receptive* aspect of "being," which is an inner placing of yourself in a state of greater awareness of God's Love in its unmanifested natural state of being. The second is the *active* aspect of "expressing," which is the outward manifestation of God's Love. Since this is a spiritual journey, you are climbing the mountain whether you are receptive or active, as long as God is the guide in either case. You need both of these because your active aspect of expressing prompted by God needs to come forth from your receptive aspect of being in God. Regardless of whether you are more receptive or more active, you need to turn to God to find out how to proceed, because only God knows what path of climbing would be best for you. He knows you better than you know yourself. God also knows how each individual path affects every other path, including all the possible consequences and factors involved. It follows that only He would know the choice that would aid you the most to grow toward Him. God's Will, then, is the best and most loving choice you could make.

God's Will and God's Love are inseparable. God *is* love. He loves you since He is in you and is your source and substance. His Love for you draws you to a greater awareness of Him. The effect that His Love has on you, which leads you toward Him, is what can be called God's Will because it is His purpose for you to come Home to Him. God's Will is the will of love only. Your will is either self-will for selfish gain, which is a rocky path, or it is the choice to express (or be) love. When you choose to express (or be) love, you are doing God's Will. If you base your choices on trial and error, your choices may increase or decrease your awareness of God. If you choose to do God's Will, your choices will be the most effective ones you can make to increase your awareness of God.

If you misunderstand God's Will, you may imagine that God's Will implies that God will impose His desires on you. God never forces you to do anything. As perfect love, God shines His Love on and in you, and you can choose to let His Love shine through you or not. If you choose to let His Love flow through you, you are choosing to do God's Will.

Another common misunderstanding is the idea that surrendering to God's Will is a sacrifice of your will and of yourself. A sacrifice does in fact take place when you do God's Will, but what is being sacrificed? Your ego condition that produces selfishness and that wants to control your will is being sacrificed. From the perspective of your false nature identified with the self, it appears that you are giving up your free will. In reality, because your true Self is one with God, your *true* will is the same as God's Will. Since you are not yet consciously identified with your true Self and true will, it may take time for you to learn the value of doing God's Will. Doing God's Will may be difficult at times, but God is aware of your fears of letting go of your ego limitations. His Will takes into account your ego condition. Therefore, He does not require you to do anything beyond what you are able to bear. Often the wisdom of following God's Will becomes apparent only after you have faced and then let go of fearful or selfish aspects of your ego condition. As you repeatedly invest in seeking to know and do God's Will, and then see the benefits in your everyday life, you will gradually learn to trust in doing God's Will. You will understand that you are only sacrificing unhealthy choices and gaining the freedom to express your true nature of love.

Doing God's Will means setting aside your selfishness and keeping yourself open to doing or being whatever would be for the highest good of everyone. When you do God's Will and give up self-will, it is not a sign of weakness of will. You are really applying the strength of your free will toward doing or being what you would choose for yourself if you had all the wisdom and love that God has.

To make spiritual progress, God's Will cannot be a spiritual principle that is merely accepted intellectually and not applied. To incorporate the principle of God's Will into your spiritual life, it is necessary to turn to God and ask Him to show you His Will and how to apply it through receptivity or action. Even if you are able to manifest God's Will in your life, not every aspect of your life will express God's Will due to human frailty. You need to accept your tendencies toward self-will and, if there is faltering, you need to rededicate yourself to doing God's Will. In spite of occasional faltering in the application of God's Will to your life, the indispensable cornerstone of your spiritual growth will always be your consistency of desire and your commitment to manifest God's Will.

Occasionally you may want to employ the mental attitude of doing God's Will as an affirmation for meditation. This is suggested as a way to crystallize your desire to bring your will into accord with God's Will. For example, you may want to use the affirmation "Thy will be done." Another choice can be "One Will" since this affirmation acknowledges that your true Self is one with God and so your true will is actually the same as God's Will. An affirmation representing alignment with God's Will may replace your regular affirmation or be added to your regular affirmation. This affirmation of your desire to be in accord with God's Will can be used with whatever method of meditation you are using.

Using the mental attitude of doing God's Will as an affirmation is very helpful, but this desire to align the individual will with God's Will needs to be renewed on a daily basis. To do that, it is suggested that you choose alignment with God's Will as your number one mental attitude. Let any other mental attitudes that would help you grow toward your spiritual ideal be secondary mental attitudes. "Love" is not suggested as a choice of a mental attitude because love is a spiritual ideal that represents your final destination of oneness with God. Also properly understanding the desire to manifest God's Will as a mental attitude automatically includes the desire to express love since God's Will is in fact the will of love.

As your chief mental attitude, being in accord with God's Will can be stated prayerfully along with your spiritual ideal as a way to dedicate the beginning of your meditation, and conclude it as well. This prayerful statement should never be reduced to merely a ritual formula. Rather, you need to allow this to be a sincere prayer that keeps alive your desire to express God's Will, since it is your invitation to God to help you become aware of His Love being within you and acting through you. Hopefully you will feel this mental attitude as an inner bond between yourself and God. You will know that this mental attitude is finally established when that inner bond helps you to relate to every person, situation, and decision that enters your daily life. Then this mental attitude will become a living principle that is the first step in deepening your spiritual growth. In turn, this mental attitude will permeate and affect every subsequent step that you take, including your progress in prayer, which will be discussed next.

B. Praying for Yourself

With prayer, just as with meditation and spiritual growth in general, your progress depends on your desire for God and your willingness to put that desire into practical application. Thus you learn how to pray by the act of praying itself. Prayer does not require a silencing of the mind, as when meditation is practiced, but rather a directing of the mind and heart toward speaking to God. The manner in which you pray is less significant than maintaining a pure intention of seeking to communicate with God. In this regard, no matter how much spiritual progress you have made or imagine that you have made, you are a beginner in the sight of God and need to think of yourself as such. In spite of whatever methods or knowledge you may have acquired, when you sit down to face God within, you are completely naked. You can't do any pretending with God. You need to be a beginner again and say, not necessarily in words, but in feeling, "Help me to set aside my knowledge and who I think I am, so I can be a little child in Your arms. Let Your Holy Spirit come over me and show me how to reach out to You."

The importance of welcoming the Holy Spirit into your life through prayer is emphasized when Jesus says if you "…know how to give good gifts to your children, how much more will the heavenly Father give the Holy Spirit to those who ask Him?"[1]

The major message of this passage is that God answers your prayers when you ask for His help. Yet it is significant that Jesus says not only to pray, but what to pray for—namely, the Holy Spirit. While you may pray for specific concerns, Jesus is asking you to be receptive to the Holy Spirit because in that receptivity and connection to the Spirit within all other concerns will automatically be met. You pray for the help of the Holy Spirit, because although it is God's gift, it must be asked for as an expression of your free will. This prayer may be offered as part of your preparatory prayer before meditation begins and again after meditation is ended.

There are two ways in which you can invite the Holy Spirit into your life to increase your spiritual awareness: One way is to ask the Spirit to reveal the love and positive attributes of God in yourself and in turn help you to see these same attributes in others. The other way is to ask the Spirit to reveal the subconscious blocks within yourself, which consist of negative attitudes, desires, and emotions that separate you from your love nature. You cannot seek only God's presence and avoid those very blocks within yourself that prevent you from being aware of the divine presence. Meditation can reveal some of your hidden obstacles, but it primarily focuses on experiencing God's presence. Prayer may be used as a direct means of asking the Spirit to bring your inner blocks to your conscious awareness. Once these inner blocks are uncovered, some individuals find it helpful to carefully analyze their blocks. Yet such detailed mental analysis is not necessary since the task of removing these blocks does not rest with your mental capabilities. Instead, the Spirit has simply revealed these blocks to you so you can decide that you no longer want to keep these blocks that you have manufactured. Then your only responsibility is to willingly offer these blocks back to the Holy Spirit for healing.

Coming before God each day and asking for His Spirit to come in and show you the way is the single most important thing you need to know about prayer. The words that you use and the method of prayer that may be employed are not significant in themselves. Your words or methods only gain significance in that they help you express your total dependence on God and your desire to open your heart to Him. In time and patience, you will draw closer to God as each day you renew your invitation for His Spirit to enter your life. Eventually you will learn to trust wholeheartedly in God's presence within you, loving you, and meeting your every need. You will discover that by God's grace you really can live in His World and can allow your life to be a reflection of Him.

C. The Role of Mother Mary

Of course, Jesus can be called upon in prayer for divine intervention, but also divine grace can come to us through the intervention of Mother Mary. Direct contact with God the Father might be similar to contacting a gigantic electrical generator. If a man were to touch that dynamically powerful energy directly, he would be entirely overwhelmed. Electrical energy from a large generator is reduced by transformers to a lower level that you can use in your home, so that you can have sockets in the wall and tap energy from them in an amount you can handle. Likewise, the grace that comes from God is transformed to a level that you can tolerate. Although Jesus has risen to the right hand of the Father, He extends His Love to this world similar to a transformer bringing the grace of God to those in need. However, Jesus has likewise delegated this responsibility to Mary, the Divine Mother, with the words that He spoke while on the Cross. First He addressed Mary, "Woman, behold your son!"[2] Then He addressed John, the beloved disciple, "Behold your mother."[3] Speaking to John, Jesus is saying that just as His followers are His disciples, they are also Her children. If you consider yourself to be a follower of Jesus, you can likewise choose to consider Mary to be your Divine Mother. An openness to Mary can allow Her to nourish you spiritually and assist you in guiding your soul back to God.

In prayer you can call on the Divine Name of Mary. Her Name can be repeated alone as "Mary," "Maria," "Mother Mary," "O Maria," or a variation of your choosing. In calling on Her Name, you are asking for the pure seed of Christ to grow in the womb of your soul, just as Jesus grew in the womb of Her body. You are also asking to have that same degree of receptivity to the Holy Spirit that She demonstrated in Her life and to be as humble as She is.

Another alternative is that you may call on the Names of both Jesus and Mary, as for example "Jesus Christ, Mother Mary" or "Jesus, Mary." Through calling on Jesus and Mary together, you are acknowledging their joint mission of guiding souls back to Heaven. Human nature tends to compartmentalize things, and so it is easy to set Mary aside and see Her mission as fitting into its own specialized category apart from the mission of Jesus. Yet it is a mistake to think that Mary is in one part of Heaven assisting humanity and that Jesus is in another part of Heaven assisting humanity. This would not be possible because Heaven does not have separate parts. In Heaven every part contains the whole and is one with the whole. Jesus and Mary are now joined in perfect oneness with each other and in oneness with the Father. From their oneness with God, they extend their love as a joint expression of divine love.

Those who wish to develop their inner receptivity through practicing meditation would be wise to include Mother Mary in their prayer life, because She has a special role as a helper and guardian of spiritual seekers. She has a tender love for every soul and offers many blessings to those who are open to Her presence and assistance. Nonetheless, you must not allow your devotion to either Mary or Jesus to become a form of spiritual hero worship that exalts their divine nature, while at the same time denying your own divine nature. It is true that Jesus awakened to His own Christ Self, and it is just as true that Mary awakened to Her own Christ Self. You could decide that their achievements are too lofty for you because of your shortcomings, yet to do so would be to think that your awakening rests entirely upon your shoulders and not upon divine grace. Let the awakenings of Jesus and Mary be a reminder not of your weakness, but of the blessings God has in store for you as you proceed on your own path of awakening with the help of Jesus and Mary, who at your invitation are willing to walk your path with you. God's Plan and the joint purpose of Jesus and Mary are for you to also claim your own divine nature and awaken to your Christ Self.

D. Praying for Others

Praying for others is important for spiritual growth. First, it is best to meditate and then pray for yourself to be receptive to God's Spirit and His Love so that you may be a clear channel of blessings to others. After opening yourself to His Love, then you can pray for others in the way you are guided by the Holy Spirit. Generally praying for others is a matter of asking God to bless them, since He knows best what each one needs. A way of blessing another person in prayer is to simply hold in mind a loving awareness of that person. It is best not to assign a specific purpose of your own to your loving awareness of that person. Instead, you can feel that your loving awareness is an expression of the love of Christ or of God that is blessing the person for whom you are praying. With your prayer you ask only that this person be blessed according to God's Will, not according to what you think is best for another person.

Some meditators like to use the imagination as an aid to prayer, although it certainly is not necessary to do so. If the imagination is used, it is best to simply hold the thought of that person in your awareness and imagine that person being filled with light and love. Some people automatically visualize a mental picture of the person they are praying for and visualize that person being filled with light and love. But you can just as effectively use the imagination without using visualization, and in general visualization is not recommended unless it occurs spontaneously without any directed effort to see mental pictures.

In prayer it is appropriate to imagine light and love filling only those individuals who have specifically *asked* for your prayers. Praying for another person is an aid for yourself and the other person only if there is no self-will involved. It may be quite likely that a person with whom you have had difficulty has not asked for your prayers. It would not be appropriate to imagine white light and love to be filling a person who has not asked for prayer. This would be an exertion of self-will, even if the intentions are positive. In fact, the person receiving the prayer may feel a pressure being exerted upon him, and this may stir up more negativity within that person because he may be resisting the light and love.

A better way to pray for another person is for you to imagine the light and love only *surrounding* that person, but not filling him. This will not impose upon that person's free will, yet will serve as an opportunity for that person to be receptive to that light and love when that person is ready to do so of his own free will. You can be most helpful by praying only that God's Will may be done for another person since God always offers love but doesn't force Himself on anyone. This is also an important lesson to learn in daily life—to offer love without exerting self-will.

As you allow God's Will to take over more in your life, you will find it easier to do whatever needs to be done in any situation. In general, you will find it easier to accept and appreciate others just as they are, even though their attitudes or actions may be quite different from your own. Gradually you will release the desire to exert your will over others, and you will find many emotional problems disappearing. This is when your experience of prayer and meditation will blossom.

Your spiritual life needs to be dedicated inwardly to your highest ideal, but it has little value if it doesn't help you to reach out with love in your heart and touch the lives of your brothers and sisters. In general, it is best to offer prayers after meditation, since your meditation experience brings a closer contact with God and enables you to be more loving. With your increased love, you can then offer prayers to help others. In this way, for example, prayer can be offered for help or healing to go to others in accordance with God's Will. In addition to prayers for others, you may want to pray for yourself, or include any other prayers that may come spontaneously from within. A brief preparatory prayer prior to meditation has been recommended earlier, and if desired, other prayers may be offered after meditation. But during meditation itself, there is no conscious thought of prayer.

E. Prayerfulness

Prayer in its broadest context may be defined as *cooperating with God's Will* in all ways. This cooperating with God's Will may be called "prayerfulness." By this definition, prayerfulness is being in harmony with God's Will during every activity of daily living. Thus every action can become a service to God, expressed especially in service to your brothers and sisters. To dedicate the body and the mind to service is to take the gifts God has given and return them to Him, as expressions of His Holy Spirit. In this way your whole life can become a prayer.

Once while I was visiting for a few days at a Christian retreat house, I met a woman who told me that, besides her regular prayers, she has a habit of always thinking of Jesus, so whatever she does she dedicates to Him. If she is making a bed, she says within herself, "Jesus, I am making this bed for you." If she is cooking, she says, "Jesus, I am cooking this food for you." Each person has his own gift for prayer, and what a wonderful gift it is to offer all of your activities to your spiritual ideal.

Although few people have this woman's ability of inwardly making a mental dedication of each of her actions, many people manifest a nonverbal attitude of loving service that elevates their daily activities to the level of prayer. Without conscious knowledge, such people, with their warmhearted attitude, are consistently doing God's Will. For this reason, many who are thought not to be especially spiritual are actually highly praised in God's eyes because of their unselfish service.

If you want to develop prayerfulness, it will be necessary to surrender the doing self to God's Will. Unfortunately the doing self is similar to a temperamental actor who will rebel and try to write his own script. You cannot prevent the self from rebelling altogether, for that would be unrealistic, but you can surrender the self to God's Will each time it has temporarily taken control. When you rebel so that your motivations and actions originate from the doing self, you may consider yourself to be "uncentered." When you surrender yourself to God, you may consider yourself to be "centered" because you are centered in God.

The prayerfulness of being centered in God can also be described as Christian "recollection," which is the maintaining of an inward spiritual focus while simultaneously being active in the world. This is similar to what Zen Buddhism calls "mindfulness," which is the doing of all actions wholeheartedly. It is the idea of being fully conscious in every present moment without regard to the past or the future. This means that while you are involved with any daily activities, you can let yourself become fully absorbed into the activity itself and become one with it.

From the Christian perspective, your prayerfulness of being one with your activity depends upon whether or not you can consistently maintain your center in God. To develop prayerfulness you need to recognize when the doing self becomes uncentered, and each time return to your center in God to manifest a "centered doing self" that expresses God's Will. The best means of changing from an uncentered doing self into a centered doing self is your regular daily meditation practice. But usually this is not enough to produce prayerfulness throughout the day. If you consider prayerfulness to be really important for your spiritual growth, you need to return to your center in God many times during the day.

Whenever you are uncentered and not in harmony with God's Will, you can simply allow yourself to have a quiet time of perhaps a few minutes to become centered in your love nature, your being Self in God. Through this expression of your faith in God, you allow His grace to correct any uncenteredness and keep you centered on doing His Will. This quiet time may be used whenever an obvious self-willed desire has created an uncentered feeling within. However, if you want to develop prayerfulness, a quiet time may be used regularly before beginning your activities, such as prior to eating, driving, or specific activities that you know tend to get you uncentered. Also, as you change from one activity to another, you may want to have a quiet time, which will help to you make the wisest choice for your new activity and prepare you to perform that activity. These times to refocus and to become centered will allow your doing self to be guided by your being Self to do whatever really needs to be done more effectively without wasting time on unnecessary and disharmonious activities. When doing comes forth from being on a consistent basis, the result is prayerfulness.

This brief time to refocus and to become centered in God has been called a "quiet time" because this name implies a time for stillness, yet does not signify the use of any particular method. While it is generally recommended that the quiet time take the form of a mini-meditation, it need not be limited to only meditation. You can think of this quiet time as an opportunity to turn to God in an assortment of different ways as you are spontaneously moved in the moment. If your quiet time is not meditation, it may be a silent prayer, a verbal conversation with God, a period of thoughtful reflection, an unhurried walk, listening to inspiring music, appreciating nature, or some other way you are prompted to become quiet within. What you want to do is simply be responsive to the Holy Spirit by being still in order to experience God's loving presence inwardly and then express the divine influence outwardly.

F. The Jesus Prayer in Daily Living

The form of the Jesus Prayer that has been recommended previously is the repeating of the Divine Name of Jesus Christ in meditation. However, the Jesus Prayer can be repeated in your everyday life. For the beginner in meditation, it is best to repeat the Jesus Prayer in the form of the Divine Name in moderation. It is true that some books, such as *The Way of a Pilgrim* and *The Philokalia*, recommend to "pray without ceasing" by continuously employing the Jesus Prayer as an affirmation throughout the day. The repeating of the Jesus Prayer every minute of the day may be done on a temporary spiritual retreat, yet in general for everyday living, it is not recommended to continuously hold on to repeating the Jesus Prayer unceasingly. Continuous, unending repeating of the Jesus Prayer can become an obsessive practice that is not in accordance with balanced living. A more realistic, helpful, and practical goal is *unceasing responsiveness to the Holy Spirit*. By setting aside special times every day to repeat the Jesus Prayer during meditation, you will develop a positive spiritual outlook—an unceasing attitude of responsiveness to the Holy Spirit. This spiritual outlook of openness can be your unceasing prayer, so that your daily actions stem from your receptivity to the Holy Spirit. This kind of unceasing responsiveness to the guidance of the Holy Spirit enables you to remain in harmony with God's Will in the activities of life to produce prayerfulness.

In addition to using the Jesus Prayer as your affirmation in meditation, you can repeat the Jesus Prayer in moderation while engaged in the activities of daily living to produce prayerfulness. However, this should happen in a natural way with the feeling that you are being moved by God's grace, rather than by any determined effort on your part. You may, for example, want to mentally repeat the Jesus Prayer while walking, and you could coordinate the words with the stepping of each foot, and perhaps with the breathing as well. One possibility of coordinating all three of these would be to repeat "Je" with the step of the left foot and "sus" with the step of the right foot for the inhalation. Then you would repeat "Christ" with the next step of the left foot and "love" with the next step of the right foot for the exhalation. The method you choose does not have to be as structured as this example, since you need to repeat the words in the way that seems most natural and comfortable for you.

Some individuals find it helpful to use prayer beads to help keep the mind focused on the prayer. Others employ a finger-touching method. In this method the thumb is first touched to the tip of the index finger, and the prayer is repeated. Then the thumb is touched to each of the other fingers consecutively as the prayer is repeated each time, before returning the thumb to the tip of the index finger to start the sequence over again. In general, the use of the beads is a more effective technique than the finger-touching method, as far as holding the attention on the prayer is concerned. Nonetheless, the finger-touching method has the important advantage of being able to be practiced in public without others being aware that you are praying.

Occasionally, when you have the opportunity, such as when you are driving alone, you may want to chant the Jesus Prayer verbally and make up your own tune. Chanting is an excellent way of expressing your inner feelings outwardly.

The Jesus Prayer may be repeated whenever God's grace moves you to do so. Even if you are momentarily angry, feel afraid, or are worried, you can mentally repeat the Divine Name, and this will calm the mind. The repetition of the Jesus Prayer cures boredom as well. You can let the Jesus Prayer be the last words in your mind as you go to sleep at night and the first words in your mind as you wake up in the morning. You may be surprised to find out that the Jesus Prayer is being repeated automatically by you in your sleep. You can let all this be a manifestation of God's grace for you, but there is no need for you to feel that you must obsessively hold on to the prayer. Instead, let the prayer take hold of you, so it becomes established within you in such a way that it repeats itself whenever prompted by the Holy Spirit to do so without any effort on your part. In this case, it is not only the words that can be felt, but also, more importantly, the ever abiding presence of Christ Himself.

Even without reaching the state in which the Jesus Prayer repeats itself spontaneously, this invocation builds within you a subtle effect that helps you to develop prayerfulness throughout each day. This building of the Divine Name within you can be accomplished through repeating it in your daily life, but an even more effective way of establishing the Divine Name within is the practice of setting aside times for meditation on the Divine Name of Jesus. By designating specific times for meditation every day, you instill the words of the Divine Name as the dominant thought of the mind. Eventually the words of the Jesus Prayer continue unceasingly to dominate the subconscious mind, although the conscious mind may not be aware of this while it is involved in outward actions. It is the foundation of this one thought of the Divine Name that gives the mind stability and develops the outlook of continuous openness to the movement of the Holy Spirit. This openness helps you to do God's Will in your daily activities, making your whole life an unceasing prayer.

It is true that there may be faltering at times in the carrying out of God's Will. Nevertheless, the foundation of the Jesus Prayer will attract God's grace to carry you through difficult periods and to return you wholeheartedly to the Lord. Certainly remembering to repeat the Jesus Prayer during daily activities is a wonderful practice if it is a reflection of God's grace. Yet this should not replace regular daily sitting meditation, which is the best way to instill the Divine Name as a continuous inner awareness. In this way you become increasingly aware of the abiding presence of Christ within and of your own Christ-like nature as a son of the Father—made in His image and likeness.

G. Intensive Retreats

A basic principle of Eastern spirituality is the idea that you can go within yourself, calm the mind by focusing on one thought, and deepen your awareness of reality. A basic premise of Zen and yoga spiritual systems is a belief that reality is indeed there within you waiting to be experienced directly. The Zen Buddhists call this experience *satori* or *enlightenment*. There are as many as thirteen stages of enlightenment. The initial forms of enlightenment may involve a profound opening of awareness triggered by ordinary events like the chirping of a bird. The early stages of enlightenment include a division between the knower, the knowing, and the known. The deepest and most dramatic stages of enlightenment go beyond the body, beyond the universe, and beyond time. The final stage is symbolized by the enlightened sage selling fish in the fish market. This last stage of full enlightenment is a return to the world of form while still retaining transcendental consciousness.

The yoga tradition of Hinduism uses the term *samadhi* to describe the transcendental experience. *Savikalpa samadhi* is a state of oneness in which the meditator and the object of meditation are unified to a very high degree, but there is still an awareness of separation. This kind of samadhi is a spiritual experience that occurs while you are still in the body. This may be considered a profound yet an indirect experience of reality being expressed within the level of form and duality. The deepest level of samadhi is called *nirvikalpa samadhi* in which your soul is instantly drawn out of the body beyond form and the whole universe vanishes as you meet Reality face to face in an experience of Oneness.

The goal of meditation is to unify the mind in order to transcend the mind. The unified mind is like the prodigal son returning home. He gives up the distractions of the world and decides to come home, in this case to his true Home. The father in the story sees his son coming from far away and rushes to embrace his son. In the same way God the Father, in His grace will rush out to embrace any of His sons who has gone to the trouble of producing a peaceful and unified mind. There is, of course, a Christian contemplative tradition that values the practice of contemplation to produce a peaceful, unified mind. However, in general there seems to be a greater emphasis in Eastern spirituality on systematically using techniques as a means of bringing about a peaceful unified mind, not to "manufacture" divine union but to thoroughly prepare for it. Since traditional Christian spirituality is generally lacking in specific techniques that would prepare the seeker for divine union, it is very important for these techniques that have originated in the East to be transferred, or rather translated, into Christian spirituality. One of the most practical means of accelerating spiritual growth in the East has been the use of intensive meditation retreats, such as the type of retreats conducted by Zen Buddhists for the purpose of enlightenment.

A small though increasing number of open-minded Christians have taken the initiative to seek the presence of Christ within the framework of Zen Buddhism. There are a limited number of Christian groups that gather together to practice Zen sitting meditation, called *zazen*. Such groups may call their practice "Christian Zen," for lack of a better term. Yet there may be many Christians and Buddhists who would object to such a term. Traditional Buddhists and Christians take the position that it is important for Zen Buddhism to keep its identity and integrity and for Christianity to do likewise.

Like the traditionalists, I do not believe in Christianizing Zen Buddhism, because I do not think Buddhism lends itself to adaptability. Instead of Christianizing Zen Buddhism, it is much easier and more practical for Christians to come into Zen Buddhism as individuals who partake of Zen as is, with all of its practices and rituals remaining distinctly Buddhist.

I would also like to use the term "Christian Zen," yet not to indicate a merging of Zen Buddhism and Christianity. My use of Christian Zen would refer to Christians who practice zazen with Zen Buddhists and follow their Buddhist practices and rituals, but with an inner content of seeking Christ. Of course, this would have to be done with the prior approval of the Zen spiritual teacher, who is the *roshi*. In this case, a Christian seeker could benefit from such contact with Zen Buddhism and apply what he has learned toward his own private spiritual practice.

For Christians the objection to Christian Zen may be on philosophical grounds. One of the obvious barriers for Christians partaking in Zen Buddhism is that most Christians believe in *dualism*. Of course, dualism is the belief that reality consists of two or more opposing forces, such as good and evil or spirit and matter. If dualism was true, God would be divided against Himself. But God is Oneness and cannot be divided into two opposing forces, so dualism cannot provide an accurate picture of reality. Nevertheless, one dualistic idea accepted by most Christians is that the individual is separate from God and will some day become united with God. Several lofty Eastern philosophies are rooted in *nondualism*, also called *monism*, which is the idea that there is really only one reality, and anything that seems separate from that one reality is merely an illusion. If you have not yet been exposed to Eastern theology, it may have never occurred to you that this whole world is an illusion or that how you think of yourself, which is your self-image, is an illusion.

If you accept the premise that God Himself is Reality, and if you are separated from God, you must then be separated from Reality. Therefore, being separated from Reality, which is God, you must be unreal. Only what is joined with the Reality of God can be real. Therefore, the only possibility for you to be real is for you to be joined with God. So you can choose to believe you are joined to God and thus are real, or you can believe that you are not joined to God and are not real. Eastern theology teaches that you are joined with God and real, but you are not aware of your real nature. Even though you are joined with Reality, you are imagining that you are separate from God and from others, and so you imagine yourself as a separate being, living in a world of separation.

After you sleep and have a dream, you have no problem admitting that you were temporarily deceived about reality. During the dream you thought what you were seeing was real, but when you woke up you realized it was only an illusion. When you wake up in Heaven, you will look back at this world of illusions and have no problem admitting you were deceived. From the perspective of Heaven, you will be in the best position to decide what is real and what is not real. You don't have that same objectivity now that you will have when you wake up in Heaven.

Now you are still inside the illusion and part of the illusion, so how can you see beyond the limitations that your own ego presents to you? You will have to disregard the evidence that the ego uses to convince you to believe in the illusion of separation. You will have to follow the path less taken to overcome the illusion of the world of separation. A barrier to taking the path less traveled is that the Bible does not record Jesus telling His disciples that the world is an illusion. The answer to this barrier is that Jesus spoke to His people in the language they could understand and accept. Jesus did present many parables in which He spoke of investing in the Kingdom of God, rather than investing in this world. Jesus also indicated where to look for the heavenly Kingdom by speaking of the Kingdom of God being *within you*. For many years in the past the Western world was not ready to understand that this world is truly an illusion. But in recent years the Western world has evolved to the point where it is ready to consider the possibility that although Eastern theology lacks a focus on Christ, it may contain some truths that have been hidden from the Western way of thinking. In particular, the gift that the East has to offer the West is the emphasis placed on finding the divine within that Jesus advised as the place to find God's Kingdom.

In recent years there has been an increased willingness on the part of the West to be open to Eastern spirituality because many Westerners have wanted to experience meditation practices that would deepen their spiritual life. A sign of this openness is the growing number of Christians participating in Christian Zen through attending Zen Buddhist retreats in which participants meditate nine to ten hours per day to experience their true nature. Likewise, I have heard of Zen Buddhists attending Christian meditation retreats in which participants meditate just as intensely to grow spiritually. The Christians do not sacrifice their focus on Christ, and the Buddhists do not sacrifice their focus upon Buddha nature, but there is a new respect and appreciation for members of each group, who in their own way are seeking to find their true nature within. There are still traditionalists on both sides that are scandalized. Nevetheless, the universal approach of acceptance is encouraging, and I believe will become increasingly common in the future.

I know of one Christian, who went to a Zen Buddhist retreat after receiving permission from the roshi. He participated in all the Buddhist practices, even though he felt uncomfortable with some of the rituals. The day after the retreat he had an enlightenment experience. Later he called the roshi and with many tears of gratitude, he thanked the roshi. He told the roshi it should have happened to a Buddhist, and he did not deserve it. The roshi had to reassure him that it was all right for him to receive enlightenment, even though he was not a Buddhist.

This variety of intensive Buddhist retreat is called a *sesshin*, which literally means "to touch the mind." A sesshin is intended to bring about enlightenment. A roshi is required to assist in bringing about this spiritual transformation. He is qualified to do this because he has experienced enlightenment himself and has been trained by his own roshi to assist others as he had likewise been helped before he became a roshi.

A Christian retreat format very similar to that of a Buddhist sesshin might be as follows:

> 5:30 AM Wake up
> 6:00 AM Meditation
> 8:00 AM Breakfast, work, rest
> 10:00 AM Meditation/interviews
> 12:00 PM Lunch, work, rest
> 2:00 PM Meditation
> 2:30 PM Conference and/or communion
> 3:00 PM Meditation/interviews
> 5:00 PM Supper, work, rest
> 7:00 PM Meditation/interviews
> 9:00 PM Sleep

Such a Christian retreat would not properly be called a "Christian Zen retreat," since only the format is taken from Zen Buddhism. Such a retreat could be called a "Christian contemplative retreat," a "Christian meditation retreat," or a "Christian intensive retreat." This type of retreat follows the format and style established by Fr. Willigis Jaeger, OSB, a Benedictine monk, lecturer, and retreat leader at the St. Benedikt Haus in Würzburg, Germany. This format initiated by Fr. Jaeger has been adopted subsequently by others interested in an intensive experience of meditation and contemplation. Fr. Jaeger is himself a roshi, and other Christians who have become trained roshis are Jesuit Robert Kennedy, Trappist monk Kevin Hunt, and Redemptorist priest Pat Hawk.

The heart of the retreat is the two-hour blocks of time for meditation, which occur four times—in the early morning, late morning, afternoon, and evening. Each two-hour block of time is divided into four periods of twenty-five minutes each, which are devoted to sitting meditation. In between these periods of sitting, there are five-minute periods of walking meditation. For the sitting period, participants may want to sit in a chair, especially if they are not accustomed to sitting for long periods of time. Participants, who are already experienced at sitting for long periods of time, may use a cushion to sit cross-legged on the floor. Also, the retreat includes a functional daily work assignment that is not burdensome, such as helping with meal preparation or cleaning up after meals.

A slight variation in the format of the Christian contemplative retreat that I specifically recommend is to include a time for the practice of hatha yoga. For this variation, which could be called a "Christian yoga retreat," the first two-hour meditation block of time (6:00 AM to 8:00 AM) would be replaced by an hour and a half hatha yoga class. The class would include body postures, a guided deep relaxation period, and breathing practices, followed by a half-hour meditation.

A second variation of this Christian yoga retreat is outlined below. In the early morning, late morning, and evening there are blocks of time for meditation that are an hour and a half long. In addition, there are two one-hour blocks of time in the afternoon, separated by a conference and/or communion sharing. Distributed throughout the day are three separate half-hour periods devoted to hatha yoga practices, including postures, breathing practices, and deep relaxation. Since the blocks of time for meditation are at the most an hour and a half, rather than two hours, this variation is ideally suited to seekers who are experiencing an intensive retreat for the first time.

> 6:00 AM Wake up
> 6:30 AM Meditation
> 8:00 AM Basic hatha yoga postures
> 8:30 AM Breakfast, work, rest
> 10:00 AM Meditation/interviews
> 11:30 AM Alternative hatha yoga postures
> 12:00 PM Lunch, work, rest
> 2:00 PM Breathing practices
> 2:15 PM Deep relaxation
> 2:30 PM Meditation
> 3:30 PM Conference and/or communion
> 4:00 PM Meditation/interviews
> 5:00 PM Supper, work, rest
> 7:30 PM Meditation/interviews
> 9:00 PM Sleep

A retreat teacher can provide a daily conference and offer spiritual direction through personal interviews. The conference can be a lecture and/or a discussion. Brief personal interviews occur during the long blocks of time for meditation, and at these times retreatants discuss their meditation practice with the retreat teacher. Three other roles are required to facilitate the retreat. A monitor is needed to be the main coordinator of the functional aspects of the retreat. A timekeeper is needed to time the meditation periods and to be the leader for the five-minute periods for walking meditation. A work coordinator is required to facilitate the carrying out of work assignments, which would include responsibilities of meal preparation and clean up.

Retreatants remain silent throughout the entire retreat except for the private interviews, the opening and closing meals, and the very limited conversations absolutely necessary as part of daily work assignments. Participants do not greet each other or look at each other and have their eyes lowered as much as possible. The silent and introspective nature of the retreat is designed to help the retreatants to maintain an inward meditative focus during the whole experience of the retreat.

On the first day the participants arrive at 3:30 PM and have a light dinner at 5:00 PM. The orientation time occurs at 7:00 PM, followed by two half-hour meditation periods. The retreat concludes at lunchtime on the last day. The length of the retreat can be three, four, or five days for first time retreatants. It can be as long as seven or eight days for those who have already participated in shorter intensive retreats.

I recommend any kind of retreat that you feel will contribute to your spiritual life. But I have elaborated upon this particular format because most people do not have the self-discipline to practice meditation this intensively in their own homes. However, in a structure like this one, participants are inspired through the example of their fellow participants and for the sake of Christ to go beyond ordinary limitations. In addition, there is a tremendous spiritual power generated by seekers who come together for the common purpose of spiritual growth. This collective spiritual power helps each seeker to open more fully to the Holy Spirit and also raises the level of attunement of each individual and of the group as a whole. At first glance meditation may appear to be an individual effort, but group meditation experiences during this kind of intensive retreat help the seeker to recognize that meditation is actually a joint venture in which every soul is assisting every other soul in the process of coming Home.

An intensive retreat like this, even if only done once in your life, can bring about a remarkable inner transformation. While the goal of a Zen sesshin is enlightenment, the goal of a Christian intensive retreat is the awareness of your union with Christ. Obviously this recognition of your union with Christ does not have to be along the order of illumination to be meaningful. You can become aware of your union with Christ in the ordinary experiences of daily life, and this awareness can help you overcome inner obstacles to love. But certain kinds of deep inner blocks to love cannot be overcome through the everyday experiences of living, even if you practice meditation on a daily basis. Yet these deep blocks can be addressed and released during an intensive retreat. As a result of releasing inner blocks, tremendous leaps in the depth of your meditation experience can occur in such a retreat, and there can also be positive long-term aftereffects. In spite of the silence and seeming lack of personal contact with other retreatants, you may discover a deep bonding with all of your brothers and sisters on the retreat, as you make a deeper contact with Christ within.

After such a retreat you may discover that old thought patterns, emotional concerns, and unwanted behaviors that you have struggled with in the past suddenly and effortlessly fall away. You may reach a breakthrough in your meditation experience, and may be able to maintain a deeper level of meditation following your retreat. On the other hand, your experience of an intensive retreat may not produce any dramatic change in you. All a retreat such as this can do for you is provide an opportunity for possible transformation. First you would have to have the willingness and determination to participate in such a retreat and then you would have to be open to the transforming power of the Holy Spirit to bring about whatever inner changes would be most helpful for you. Perhaps with the help of the Holy Spirit, you will be able to go deep enough within to open your heart inwardly and outwardly. With an open heart and with a focused mind, you will more closely reflect the Christ that is within you.

---

1. Luke 11.13
2. John 19:26
3. John 19:27

18

GUIDANCE AND NONATTACHMENT

~ ◦ ~

A. Receiving Guidance

Prayer has previously been identified as expressive communication with God, and through this communication you can ask God to dedicate your meditation to helping you to know and to do His Will. In prayer you actively relate to God by expressing many different thoughts and feelings. In contrast to prayer, meditation has been defined as receptive communication with God in which you focus on using one thought, such as an affirmation, to calm your mind so you can experience God's presence. Through this inner receptivity produced in meditation, you increase your awareness of God's presence, and you also align your individual will with God's Will. This alignment of wills is manifested by allowing the Holy Spirit to enter into both your stillness in meditation and your activity in daily life. The communion you have with God in meditation that invites His presence carries over into your everyday life so you can let go of controlling your own life and allow the Holy Spirit to increasingly motivate your thoughts, words, and deeds.

But in this process you need to choose to consciously open yourself to the inner guidance of the Holy Spirit. In addition, you can use prayer to ask for inner guidance. God never imposes Himself on you. You invite Him to communicate with you so that you will know His Will. To receive clear guidance, you need to be as objective as possible, so that any prejudice within yourself does not distort your ability to know and do God's Will. One way to gain that clarity and objectivity is to ask for His guidance after completing your meditation. This is a good time because meditation brings a closer contact with God. It is good to ask for guidance in the form of a clear question. Beginning meditators formulate their questions so that the answer can be either a "yes" or a "no." This helps them to receive clearer answers.

For most people the answer is simply an intuition that is prompted by the Holy Spirit. At times there may be no answer, especially when this is first tried, but gradually you will be surprised to discover an inner knowing of what would be most helpful. If there is no immediate answer, then you can stop questioning for the time being. Often the answer will come to you later in a very clear and definite way at a time when you are not directly asking for guidance.

One way of asking for inner guidance is to evaluate your concern from a mental viewpoint and then come to a mental decision. If this is a major decision, allow your decision to incubate for a time. For some individuals a few hours is enough time for this incubation, and for others one or two days is necessary. After this waiting period, you can ask at the conclusion of your next meditation if this mental decision is the best choice for you to make. If the answer is "no," then evaluate other options from a mental viewpoint and make an alternative choice. Continue to ask inwardly until there is an inner confirmation of your choice.

A challenge in receiving any guidance is always how to maintain objectivity so the guidance will be accurate. In order to gain greater objectivity, you may not want to come to a decision first and then ask for a confirmation from the Holy Spirit. Instead, you may just ask the Holy Spirit to let you know His answer. Although it might be more expedient to make your own decision first, it can be a positive learning experience to restrain this impulse to make a decision. By delaying your decision, you can keep your mind neutral and fully open to the Spirit.

Even if you receive no answer after repeated attempts at getting guidance, you do not need to be discouraged. God honors the fact that you are looking to Him for guidance in making your decisions. When no answer is given, it may mean that this is a time for patient waiting. When you are relaxed physically, emotionally, and mentally, it is easier for you to receive guidance. But if you are tense, you may not receive clear guidance. Consequently, if you are overly concerned with getting an answer to guidance when you want it, your concern may produce an inner tension that may prevent you from receiving clear guidance.

Another possible cause of not receiving guidance is that the type of guidance you seek may be the expression of a selfish desire. Perhaps you are seeking to know something that would not be good for you to know. Thus you need to place yourself in God's hands. If no answer is given, you can then trust that He knows your true needs better than you do. Therefore, He will give you the knowledge you seek at the precise time when and if you really need to have that knowledge.

One of the problems with seeking guidance in the form of asking questions is that you may not know what to ask for or how to phrase your questions. Your questions may show a lack of openness on your part and may be "unanswerable" from God's viewpoint. For example, you may ask God, "Should I buy a new Chevrolet or a new Ford?" when perhaps neither car would be good. It would be better to ask a more open question, such as, "Do I really need a new car?" If you are not truly open and have already set a course of action in motion in your life that is not good for yourself, it is very difficult to receive clear guidance. To guard against your own prejudices and preconceived ideas, you may want to occasionally ask God to help you to be aware of any way in which you may unknowingly be blocking His Will. For example, it may be helpful to ask an open-ended question, such as, "Lord, what would you have me be aware of that would help me to do your will better?"

As you seek guidance on any outer situation in your life, you need to be aware of your ego attachments that may distort your ability to receive clear guidance. In particular, you need to examine yourself to see if you have a true willingness and openness to God. You know that you have a problem in this regard if you feel an inner resistance to surrendering the situation to God and waiting for His answer to come in His own manner and in His own time. When you notice any inner resistance to His Will, you need to redirect your focus away from the outer situation itself and toward uncovering your inner resistance and ego attachments, which may be largely hidden from your conscious awareness.

In regard to seeking guidance, one of the most beneficial directions you can take is to look at your ego condition. Whatever problems or concerns you face in your life are a direct result of attitudes, desires, and emotions of which you may be only partially aware. As long as these factors remain mostly hidden in the subconscious mind, they will continue to negatively affect your life and the lives of others. Meditation can increase your awareness and can bring some of these subconscious factors to your conscious awareness. However, you need to also make a conscious choice to direct your prayers toward uncovering the hidden aspects of your ego condition that motivate much of your behavior. It is by bringing these hidden attitudes, desires, and emotions to light that you can see your ego condition as it really is and learn to let go of your false perceptions.

It is important to understand the role that the mind has to play in the process of revealing and removing your subconscious blocks. Although mental concepts are not consciously sought during meditation, there is no attempt here to advocate "holy ignorance." Your mental understanding is extremely important. In contrast to prayer, which looks for mental understanding directly and primarily, meditation brings about mental understanding indirectly and secondarily. In meditation you temporarily set aside your mental concepts and allow the mind to be calm. During meditation when your mind becomes calm, subconscious blocks may surface. These inner blocks may be experienced as anxiety or nervous tension and usually can be released without the mental understanding of what is being released, as was elaborated upon in Chapter 12.

However, some inner blocks cannot be released without your mental understanding assisting you in the process. Even though you do not consciously seek mental understanding during meditation, the Holy Spirit will spontaneously give you whatever mental understanding you need. You will receive sudden insights and understandings of the heart that will come as a result of becoming inwardly still and receptive. Your new mental understanding will help you to uncover and understand your subconscious blocks. In fact, your inner blocks are created by yourself through improper mental viewpoints. Consequently, such new mental insights are a helpful part of your learning experience, not only to release inner blocks, but also to insure that you will not continue to create the same mistakes in the future.

Although helpful insights may come to you spontaneously during your practice of meditation and contemplation, you must allow these to come and go just as you would let any other thoughts pass through your mind. Because these insights are so new and stimulating, there is a temptation to focus on these thoughts and let your mind leave your pure intention of opening yourself to the divine presence. Once you begin to mentally analyze your spontaneous insights, they are no longer spontaneous and you are no longer meditating. By realizing that this is a temptation, you will not give into it by letting your mind wander and leave your true purpose. Following your meditation you can return your mind to your earlier spontaneous insights and ponder the meaning of these thoughts. Also, after your meditation you can use prayer to focus on these insights and ask for more understanding to be revealed.

Meditation can increase your awareness of inner blocks, but only if there is a true openness on your part to uncovering these inner blocks. Some meditators make the mistake of focusing only on experiencing divine communion and avoid looking at their ego structure. The result can be a person who on the one hand can experience deep meditative states and on the other hand allows major parts of his personality to remain defective. This creates a very unbalanced situation in which the person may have difficulty, especially in personal relationships. In other words, you need to not simply set aside the ego structure, but rather allow the light of Christ to shine on the darkest parts of the self so the physical, emotional, and mental aspects of the self can be transformed into reflections of God's Will. Of course, the major task before you is to contact the divine presence within, as has been described in discussing meditation. However, you can also set aside times for prayer in which you can allow your intuition to guide you to temporarily focus your awareness directly at those hidden blocks within you that prevent you from expressing your love nature to your brothers and sisters.

At those times when you direct yourself in prayer toward uncovering hidden blocks, you need to do so with the understanding that you need divine assistance to clearly perceive the flaws in your ego condition. You may use prayer to ask God for guidance on your inner blocks that are normally hidden from your awareness. Another way to uncover your hidden blocks is through observing all of your thoughts, emotions, repeated behavior patterns, and interactions with other people in your daily life. For example, whenever you find yourself blaming another person for something, you can redirect your focus from seeking flaws in others to looking for any flaws in your own ego condition. There are various different ways of bringing your blocks to your conscious awareness, and you need to find the ways that work best for you.

But once you become aware of an inner block, it is not necessary to mentally understand every single facet of the block. Only two mental recognitions need to be made. The first mental recognition is that you created this block by yourself as an expression of your ego condition. The second mental recognition is that you no longer want to have this block, and therefore you choose to give this block to the Holy Spirit for healing. These two recognitions are expressions of your willingness to have your blocks removed. Without your willingness, not even God can remove your blocks. The method you may use to uncover your blocks is less important than your awareness of the value of facing these blocks and your sincere desire and willingness to do so with God's help.

It is important to clarify the relationship between guidance and meditation. Guidance is only a by-product of meditation. It is not the purpose of meditation. You meditate to experience the presence of God, who in turn will give you whatever guidance you may need. When you forget this, you can become so concerned about guidance that your concern can actually separate you from experiencing God's presence. Consequently, you need to remind yourself to seek God's presence first and trust that His guidance will follow.

Some well-intentioned seekers get off track in their spiritual growth because of mixing up their priorities in regard to prayer and meditation. Meditation has been described previously as a method of gaining inner receptivity that usually involves the holding of one thought in the mind to increase the awareness of God's presence. Following meditation many thoughts may be expressed in prayer to ask God for guidance. This process of asking for guidance after meditation may be applied correctly by the beginning meditator. After becoming experienced at meditation, there is a noticeable increase in mental clarity. With their increased clarity, some meditators decide that they can ask themselves spiritual questions and reduce the amount of time for meditation. This is unfortunate since the purpose of answering questions and receiving guidance gradually becomes more important than experiencing the divine presence.

When this happens, the distinction between prayer and meditation becomes blurred. Some individuals actually forget this distinction, or rationalize it away, and settle for using most or all of their meditation time for investing in a deeper prayer guidance than they had before learning to meditate. They allow the mind to focus on their questions or problems instead of on their spiritual ideal. This process is quite justifiable in the minds of these individuals, but the result is that such individuals are no longer meditating and have abandoned the purer motive of drawing closer to their spiritual ideal. Ironically, the guidance, which initially may be clear, will become less clear because the source of the clarity and openness to the divine within has been cut off. The secret to guidance is to seek God first and foremost, and guidance will come as a natural result of seeking God's presence. But to desire guidance first and God's presence second means that neither desire may be fully realized. Therefore, it is best to seek guidance through prayer after meditation, and allow meditation itself to remain as a way of drawing closer to experiencing the divine presence within.

Seeking of guidance does not have to be reserved for only major decisions. You can also benefit by seeking guidance for lesser decisions, even everyday decisions that need to be made throughout the day. It is not necessary or even appropriate to save these decisions for your prayer time after your regular meditation, since these lesser decisions need to be made throughout the day. The best way to deal with these decisions is to have a mini-meditation by simply closing your eyes when a concern arises and becoming quiet for a moment or two to become aware of God's presence within. Next formulate the decision into a question, such as, "Lord, what would you have me do about this concern?" Then the last step is to set aside trying to analyze possible answers and just see if you can be still and feel what is right to do intuitively. This whole process takes only a few minutes and is a practical way of increasing your awareness of both God's presence and God's Will for you in the activities of your everyday life. After practicing this method consistently each day, you will be surprised to discover that you will be using your time more wisely and bringing greater harmony into your life and into the lives of others.

The approach to seeking guidance through inward asking that has been described is only for those who are drawn to it. Some individuals do not have to ask questions inwardly to receive guidance. They just go by their intuition and do whatever feels right from deep within. For such individuals meditation helps develop their intuition because it enables them to go deep within and contact their spiritual roots. Also, there are other individuals who neither ask for guidance nor are concerned with intuition. These individuals simply move through their life experiences doing what seems right to them and, most importantly, carry love in their hearts. The Holy Spirit moves such souls naturally without any need for asking. You need to find the way that works best for you.

Guidance may also come through other people and events in your life. While the foundation of your guidance needs to be based on direct communication with God within, the Holy Spirit works in the world to direct not only you, but others as well. If you go to a trusted friend, who has the ability to listen, you may discover in your sharing that the Holy Spirit is speaking through both of you. Thus both you and your friend are being nourished and guided in a way that perhaps could not have happened in solitude.

Although guidance may come to you indirectly through other people or events in your life, ultimately your choices need to be based on your direct relationship with God rather than other people or outside circumstances. Abraham Lincoln had many advisors, and yet his wisest decisions were based on his intuition, which he described in this way:

> I have had so many evidences of His direction, so many instances when I have been controlled by some other power than my own will, that I cannot doubt that this power comes from above. I frequently see my way clear to a decision when I am conscious that I have no sufficient facts upon which to found it. But I cannot recall one instance in which I have followed my own judgment, founded upon such a decision, when the results were unsatisfactory; whereas, in almost every instance when I have yielded to the views of others, I have had occasion to regret it. I am satisfied that, when the Almighty wants me to do, or not to do, a particular thing, He finds a way of letting me know it.[1]

Consequently, the means or the method that you choose to employ to receive guidance is not nearly as important as your sincere desire for God to guide you. Even if you temporarily wander from Him, He will find a way to redirect your steps toward Him, if you truly want Him to be your guide. However, your guidance may still not be effective if you are not completely open to God's Will, but seek guidance only in one area of your life. For example, a man may seek guidance in his business affairs, yet want to control his personal life. These areas where you want to remain in control are your "comfort zones"—areas where your ego feels comfortable and is resistant to change. These comfort zones test your true willingness to do God's Will. When you are willing to give up control, not just of parts of your life, but of your total self, then you can be sure that your guidance will be much clearer.

Making the decision to surrender yourself entirely to God's Will also enables you to put your guidance into practical application in your life. A challenging question you might want to ask yourself is, "Am I doing all the things right now in my life that God has already prompted me to do?" You may have habits in your life that you feel are harmful for yourself. Maybe you smoke, watch too much television, overeat, or eat foods that you know aren't good for you. There is an intuitive feeling inside that tells you that this behavior is not in your own best interests. Likewise, your intuition will also show you other activities that you could be doing, such as getting more fresh air and exercise, volunteering to perform a service for someone else, going to bed earlier, or turning to God at certain times each day. If you have an openness to change, your intuition will persistently encourage you to make a change that would be in your own best interests. Perhaps sometimes you may have a tendency to dismiss these feelings as unacceptable guilt, when they may in fact be God's Spirit guiding and inviting you to do His Will.

God is not so demanding that He expects you to follow His every prompting, yet He doesn't expect you to be deaf to His promptings, either. There may be many things that you know inwardly to do but haven't applied your will toward doing. It would be unwise to try to do everything all at once. Instead, you can apply one new thing to your life that you have already been prompted to do and that you really *want* to do. You must not make any change grudgingly because that would undermine your effort. You need to perceive the prompting you have chosen as an expression of God's Love for you and let your response of following that prompting be a manifestation of your love for God. When you have succeeded in applying this new thing so it becomes integrated with your life, then you can do the next thing that you know would be good for your growth. To succeed you need to invite the Holy Spirit to help you. You will find that the changes may not be easy, but they will give your life a new sense of purpose since you are responding to the call of grace that is lovingly prompting you to do His Will.

B. The Importance of Nonattachment

To make progress in your spiritual journey, you will need to develop increasing faith along the way and also detachment from all that is not God Himself. If you are sometimes given spiritual sweetness, you may enjoy it, but must realize this sweetness is only a sign of approaching God. You may experience inner feelings, which can serve as stepping stones for deepening your meditation experience, as was explained in Chapter 14. You will have many passing experiences during meditation, and in general it is best to let these come and go without attachment and as you continue on your path to greater divine awareness.

Some specific examples of unusual phenomena, which may occur as by-products of meditation, are unusual sounds, flashing colors, or odd smells. Even words or unusual images may appear in the mind. The body may be pulled in a jerky motion to the side, forward, or backward. Also, a whirling sensation may come over the body. You do not need to be concerned. If any of these experiences happen during meditation, make sure to ignore them and return to the meditation itself. Do not invite such experiences through desire for them. If they spontaneously come, do not try to cling to them or push them away.

Sometimes while meditating, you may hear words or sounds. In some cases these experiences may have a spiritual origin. However, it would be unwise to automatically assume that God must be sending you messages. In reality, these may be only impressions raised up from the subconscious mind and brought into conscious awareness, or these could be temptations presented by negative spirits to test your purity of heart. The by-products of meditation usually include symptoms of physical, emotional, and mental tension. These symptoms are coming to your awareness so that you can let go of them and instead learn to rely on the Spirit to restore inner harmony. It is true that God may occasionally bring about some unusual experiences during meditation, but you should not pay too much attention to them or desire them. A faith that has no concern or desire for such things is most pleasing to God, for even these experiences that come from God are only signs of approaching Him. If you continually stop to examine the signs along the path, how are you going to reach your destination, which is God Himself?

Even though meditators can become sidetracked by overestimating the value of the by-products of meditation, scientists have discovered some very interesting information by studying these by-products. This is a relatively new scientific endeavor, since meditation has in the past centuries been considered a mystical, religious experience, outside the boundaries of serious scientific research. But as scientists have been studying the functioning of the brain, their research has led them toward studies related to meditation. During the 1960s, scientists discovered that the brain hemispheres function independently. In other words, normally your awareness shifts back and forth from one hemisphere to another, so you only use half of the brain at a time. Scientists wanted to know what would happen if you used both halves of the brain simultaneously. This inquiry eventually led scientists in the 1970s to discover the answer through conducting experiments on experienced meditators. Neurologists attached electroencephalograph (EEG) machines to meditators to track their brain wave patterns. The results showed that when experienced meditators entered into deep meditation, the electrical waves in each hemisphere, which are normally different and unrelated, changed into a single rhythm. Meditation from a purely mental viewpoint can be described as taking up one thought in the mind and holding that one thought continuously. What these scientists proved is that the steady holding of one thought produces a unification of the hemispheres into one rhythm. Scientists used new terms, such as "hypersynchrony" or "whole brain synchronization," to describe the unification of the brain.

Scientists have known for a long time that only a tiny fraction of the capacity of the brain's potential is used. Normally the hemispheres do not work together, but scientists have theorized that by unifying both hemispheres you can increase the functioning capabilities of the brain. This theory seems to be supported by other scientific research that has been done on the effects of meditation. Many scientific studies have shown a wide range of beneficial effects produced by meditation. These benefits include increases in intelligence, memory, sensory perception, and creativity, as well as noticeable reductions in stress and anxiety. Findings such as these have shown that meditation is a proven process for self-improvement. However, meditation is not merely a process for expanding mental capabilities and improving physical health. These are only by-products of meditation. The real purpose of meditation is seeking the Kingdom of God above all else. This purpose must not be forgotten in considering other scientific research related to meditation.

Nonattachment is a matter of being attached to God and detached from anything that does not lead to God. Nonattachment can be the detachment from things or desires related to the outer world, or it can be detachment from unusual inner experiences like those described above. Also, nonattachment can be detachment from thought itself, which is exactly what happens during meditation. Your meditation is a letting go of thoughts so you become nonattached to your normal, rational thinking process. You allow thoughts to come and go without any attachment, without any mental or emotional reaction. Scientists have discovered a relationship between this nonattachment to your thoughts in meditation and your specific brain wave patterns. Scientists have found that as you increase your nonattachment by letting go of your thoughts in meditation, you can lower your brain waves correspondingly.

At times when you are not meditating, you experience *beta brain waves*, which are 13 to 28 cycles per second. These beta brain waves dominate the brain during your normal experiences in the world. When you close your eyes and relax in meditation, you can lower the brain waves to predominantly *alpha brain waves*, which are approximately 8 to 12 cycles per second. While practicing meditation, the brain wave patterns may lower to between 4 and 7 cycles per second, which are called *theta brain waves*. Theta waves dominate in the mind during the sleep state when you are actively dreaming and exhibiting rapid eye movements. Similarly, during meditation, when the brain waves lower to the theta range, you may see visions. These are different from mental images that can be consciously created. Such theta visions are seen in another state of awareness. But these are no more or less meaningful than dreams. Just as dreams, these visions may come from your higher spiritual nature, or they may come from your subconscious mind.

How you respond to experiencing visions is crucial to your spiritual development. These experiences of visions are tests of your intuition and your desire for God and detachment from all else. Occasionally you may feel that these visions give guidance or are psychic messages. Indeed, particular visions or inner experiences can be very helpful to you in your search for God, if you can develop your intuition to discern the true nature and significance of such experiences. One way to do this is to focus your intuition on feeling the strength and type of impact an inner experience may leave upon you.

For example, scientists maintain that, whether you remember your dreams or not, you experience many dreams every night. Although you may forget most dreams, occasionally a dream may have a strong impact upon you because it is especially clear or emotionally charged. Such a dream leaves a vivid impression. Even if you do not mentally understand the meaning of this dream, you sense that it is important to you. Similar to dreams in sleep, you can have visions when you are fully awake during meditation. You may see many mental pictures in your mind and allow them to come and go without making any deep impression. Then on a rare occasion you may see a vision that suddenly appears and is clearly seen. Typically, immediately after this vision is seen, it suddenly disappears, but leaves behind a distinct impression in your mind.

All of these visions, dreams, or other spontaneous inner experiences that are suddenly revealed to you and leave an impact upon you need to be directed toward your intuition. Your intuition will let you know if this is a symptom of releasing tension, if this is a counterfeit experience produced through spiritual suggestion by negative spirits, or if this is a message prompted by the Holy Spirit. On the one hand, you need to develop your intuition to discern the origin and meaning of your visions and other inner experiences. On the other hand, you need to have a healthy detachment from such experiences, or you will remain stuck at this level and slow your progress.

For instance, if you should develop psychic abilities as a by-product of meditation, these can prevent the deepening of meditation if you are preoccupied with them. Notice that I do not say psychic experiences are bad, for even Jesus demonstrated psychic ability when it was necessary and helpful to others. But it is attachment to such abilities that makes them turn sour. These experiences on the spiritual path are tests to see if you seek to exalt yourself or do God's Will in the darkness of faith.

How can letting go of these visions help your meditation practice? By not being attached to these visions and going deeper within, the meditator can then successfully lower the brain wave patterns to below 4 cycles per second. These are the *delta brain waves* that are within the range of 0 to 3 cycles per second and correspond to the state of both deep (dreamless) sleep and deep meditation. The difference, of course, between deep (dreamless) sleep and meditation is that sleep is a state in which the conscious mind does not function, and meditation is a state of expanded consciousness (awareness). One is a state of blankness; the other is a state of aliveness to the Spirit. However, this aliveness is realized only through an emptying of those thoughts that create the more active brain wave patterns.

Unfortunately, many souls never go beyond the alpha state since they become self-satisfied with this new state of relaxation. Others go beyond self-relaxation, but then get caught up in the egotism of visions. Therefore, they are not able to empty themselves sufficiently enough to pass beyond the theta state in order to experience the delta state.

The scientific research of the 1950s, 1960s, and 1970s showed that brain waves changed as meditation deepened, but could not explain the portions of the brain that were affected. In recent years technological advances have made brain imaging possible and have opened up the field of "neurotheology"[2] to a whole new generation of scientists. This technology allows neurotheology scientists to identify the specific circuits of the mind that are affected by encounters with the divine.

One notable neurotheologist, Dr. James Austin, had his own personal experience of the fear and self-consciousness of the ego disappearing and being replaced by the reality of eternity beyond time and space. His personal experience of the true nature of reality spurred him to research the effect of spiritual experiences on the neurological nature of the brain. He published his theories in 1998 in "Zen and the Brain." Dr. Austin maintained that certain brain circuits need to be interrupted in order to produce a mystical experience that is devoid of fear and that alters one's sense of time, space, and self-consciousness. In order for fear to be dissolved, the *amygdala*, which evaluates threats in the environment and which responds to fear, would have to be quieted. In order for the awareness of time to be suspended, the circuits of the *frontal lobe and temporal lobe*, which register time and self-awareness, would have to be disconnected. In order for space awareness and self-consciousness to be set aside, the *parietal lobe*, which provides orientation in space and draws the distinction between the self and the world, would have to be deactivated.[3]

Another neurotheologist, Dr. Andrew Newberg of the University of Pennsylvania, along with his late associate, Eugene d'Aquili, published the book *Why God Won't Go Away* based on brain imaging used to map the circuits of the working mind during the process of meditation. Brain imaging tracks blood flow to the brain, and increased blood flow indicates an increase in neural activity. Data was collected from Tibetan Buddhists and Franciscan nuns, who used forms of inner attunement. The brain imaging showed a marked increase in the activity of the *prefrontal cortex*, located near the brow center in the middle of the forehead. This increased activity was expected because the prefrontal cortex is the seat of attention in the brain and because prayer and meditation are activities that require the focusing of attention.[4]

Yet an interesting result of the data was that the superior parietal lobe became deactivated during meditation. The superior parietal lobe is located in the top and back of the brain in the area of the crown center. The superior parietal lobe is the seat of orientation and so provides information about time and space and the distinction of the self from the rest of the world. It delineates the boundaries between the body and the world. When the superior parietal lobe is functioning as it usually does, it receives sensory input to provide the physical sensation of the body and creates the sense of physical space in which the body functions. But with the deactivation of the superior parietal lobe that occurs during meditation, there is a cessation of sensory input into this neural region, resulting in the brain being unable to formulate a distinction between the self as the body and the world as the space in which the body exists.[5]

To be more specific, the *left side* of the superior parietal lobe creates the sensory awareness of the limitations of the physical body. Meditation blocks sensory information from reaching the left side of the superior parietal lobe and thus causes the elimination of the boundary between the individual self and the world. Consequently, the meditator perceives himself as having no boundaries, and so he perceives himself as being connected to everyone and everything without limit. The *right side* of the superior parietal lobe provides the sense of space required by the body to function in the physical world. The blocking of sensory input to the right side of the parietal lobe that occurs in meditation eliminates the sense of space in which the body functions. As a result of this, the meditator perceives himself as existing in infinite space.[6]

Apparently mystical experiences are attended by decreased activity of the neurons in the superior parietal lobe, which is associated with the crown center, and increased activity of the neurons in the prefrontal cortex associated with the brow center. It seems significant that mystical experiences are attended by actual scientifically measurable biological reactions in the physical brain. Before having this kind of brain imaging to prove these biological occurrences in the brain, psychologists and neuroscientists have typically denied that there were such physiological events occurring in the brain during mystical experiences. However, the interpretation of this brain imaging information is a subjective matter. An agnostic, who believes only what can be proved scientifically, might say that the biological events occurring in the brain could be *creating* imagined mystical experiences. From this agnostic outlook the biological events could be causing the individual to perceive an apparent divine reality that is in fact nonexistent. On the other hand, seekers, who base their beliefs on their faith in the divine, will interpret the occurrence of specific biological events in the brain to be the *result* of a valid mystical experience, not the cause of an imagined mystical experience.[7]

A similar controversy centers around *temporal lobe epilepsy*, which consists of abnormal surges of electrical energy on the right or left side of the brain. Some scientists maintain there is a correlation between these electrical bursts of energy and mystical visions.[8] If there is such a correlation between temporal lobe epilepsy and mystical visions, again the question can be raised of whether such electrical bursts are causing the individual to perceive imagined visions that have no basis in reality or whether the electrical bursts are the resulting by-product of some form of divine intervention creating visions. The agnostic and the seeker with faith in the divine will invariably draw very different conclusions. In spite of the fact that interpreting scientific information will continue to produce controversy, it is important to note that neuroscience has largely ignored spirituality in the past. Therefore, the new emphasis on neurotheology represents a welcome shift in regard to the scientific community being more open to exploring all aspects of consciousness.[9]

While recent scientific discoveries are certainly interesting, perhaps the best resource for understanding mystical experiences is the great sixteenth-century mystic, St. John of the Cross, who systematically defined all the various forms of revelations and spiritual experiences in his classic book, *Ascent of Mount Carmel*. The experiences, which may occur during meditation, such as unusual sounds, odd smells, flashing colors, spontaneous body movements, theta visions, or other mental impressions, are experienced through the bodily functions of the five senses. However, St. John of the Cross writes that it is possible to have two kinds of visions that are spiritual in nature and are not experienced through the bodily senses. The first is a spiritual illumination while one remains in the body and sees images of bodily substances. St. John of the Cross describes this first kind of vision as follows:

> And it is at times as though a door were opened before it into a great brightness, through which the soul sees a light, after the manner of a lightning flash, which, on a dark night, reveals things suddenly, and causes them to be clearly and distinctly seen, and then leaves them in darkness, although the forms and figures of them remain in the fancy.[10]

Concerning the visions of bodily substances referred to here that can be seen by the soul when it is in the body, St. John warns that the negative spirits can bring about a counterfeit vision through spiritual suggestion whereby he presents clear images to the mind. The mystic author describes in *Ascent of Mount Carmel* how true spiritual visions can be distinguished from counterfeit visions that come from negative spirits. More importantly, this time-tested book of spiritual guidance advises that even the true spiritual visions of bodily substances should not be desired, but rather you should proceed to God in the darkness of faith with humility and detachment.

Besides telling of the spiritual visions of bodily substances, St. John of the Cross also states that there is a second and higher kind of spiritual vision that negative spirits cannot counterfeit. This spiritual vision is a vision of nonphysical substances. It is brought about by the aid of a certain supernatural illumination that comes from God and is of a higher order than the supernatural light seen when experiencing visions of bodily substances. To illustrate this, St. John of the Cross refers to the time when Moses desired to see God as He is in Himself, and in response God told Moses: "Man shall not see Me and be able to remain alive."[11] The mystic writer comments:

> And thus these visions occur not in this life, save occasionally and fleetingly, when, making an exception to the conditions which govern our natural life, God so allows it. At such times He totally withdraws the spirit from this life, and the natural functions of the body are supplied by His favor.[12]

This form of illumination is further illustrated by the way St. Paul describes his vision on the road to Damascus, when he says of himself, "And I know that this man was caught up into Paradise—whether in the body or out of the body I do not know, God knows...."[13]

From this quote you can see that in this vision God elevated St. Paul beyond the normal boundaries of body awareness to a supernatural level. This type of vision is very unusual because the soul is entirely withdrawn from the body. St. John of the Cross calls this kind of vision the "illumination of glory."[14] It is the highest form of vision that can be experienced in this life since it is a direct union of the soul with God.

At the moment of physical death of the body, the soul leaves the body and potentially may unite with God in permanent divine union. When physical death occurs, the kundalini rises fully up the susumna, and the life force of the soul exits the body through the crown of the head. During the experience of the illumination of glory, called in yoga philosophy *nirvikalpa samadhi*, the kundalini also rises entirely up the susumna, and the life force exits the body through the crown center.

When this happens, all breathing ceases, just as it does with physical death, but the life sustaining bodily functions, except for breathing, are maintained through a supernatural divine intervention. St. John of the Cross refers to this divine intervention in the above quotation with the words, "the natural functions of the body are supplied by His favor."[15] This temporary divine suspension of breathing in yoga philosophy is called *kevela kumbhaka*.[16] This suspension of the ingoing and outgoing breaths is considered also a suspension of time, being the indivisible instant of eternal duration. This divine intervention allows the soul to return to a healthy body when the illumination of glory is over. The illumination of glory is a temporary state of divine union that is also a foretaste of the experience after death of permanent divine union, which is the ultimate destination of all spiritual seeking.

Visions such as those just described are quite rare, and they come to individuals only as a manifestation of God's grace. No vision should be desired and sought after as an end in itself. Desiring and seeking to have spiritual experiences is a sure way to separate yourself from the darkness of faith that God wishes you to use as an approach to Him.

Your desires can either reduce your awareness of God or increase your awareness of God. Desire is related to the will. You use the will to satisfy your desires. The choice of whether to satisfy a desire or not must be based on your recognition of that desire being selfish or unselfish. Selfish desires are motivated by the self and produce fear. They weaken you and separate you from being aware of God's presence. Unselfish desires are motivated by your true nature in God and express love. They strengthen you and help you to become more aware of God's presence.

Meditation produces an increased amount of energy in the body. If you are able to develop nonattachment to the desires for using this increased energy selfishly, then you will be strengthened and you will receive many spiritual blessings. If you would use this expanded energy gained in meditation to satisfy selfish desires, you would actually be separating yourself further from being aware of God. For example, after practicing daily meditation for one or two years, you may produce an expansion of energy in the body. This may be felt initially as a sudden increase of sexual energy. If you experience this kind of rapid increase of sexual energy, you may be confused and wonder if you have left your path to God. It is helpful to know that your condition is temporary and you have reached a crucial stage in your spiritual development.

If the increased sexual energy is offered prayerfully to the Holy Spirit, then that energy begins to be channeled in the direction of your spiritual purposes, and at the same time the feeling of increased sexual energy gradually disappears. But if the temporarily increased sexual energy is expressed impulsively and outwardly through desire and choice, you would slow your spiritual progress. No moral judgment is being offered here about how to you use your sexual energy. Instead, this example illustrates the reason why it is necessary to develop a greater degree of nonattachment to sexual desires as your meditation experience deepens.

The proper outlook toward the sexual desire is not suppression, which is making believe that such desires do not exist. Rather, it is acceptance and nonattachment, which allows the sexual energy to be, yet does not seek to encourage it beyond acceptance. With this outlook, you can be receptive to the action of the Holy Spirit and thus allow the energy to be used for spiritual purposes. Knowing how to deal with sexual energy is a difficult problem for everyone. Thus you need to offer any concerns you may have about this issue to God and ask for His help and guidance.

Sometimes people choose to think of themselves as being victims of uncontrollable urges. This is simply not true and is a common form of self-deception. Because of your free will, you are in control of your perceptions. The body is neutral and does not think and is not capable of making any decisions. You can think of the body as a computer that merely acts upon the programming placed in it. Your mind is entirely in charge of that programming that affects the body, and so your mind tells your body what to do or what not to do. If you make the mental choice to entertain perceptions of sexual fantasy, the result will be an increased challenge in regard to sexual energy. The energy that you call sexual energy is actually neutral energy, until you give it a purpose. If you direct it toward sexual purposes, only then does it become sexual energy. On the other hand, if you direct your mind toward spiritual purposes, the energy of the body will follow your direction. Meditation is an important way to direct the body energy toward spiritual purposes. The relationship between meditation and the raising of creative energy, including the raising of the kundalini, has already been elaborated upon in Chapter 11.

Your desires do not create your perceptions; your perceptions create your desires. Because you choose your perceptions and the desires that your perceptions produce, you are responsible for what you experience. This means that you cannot be a victim of your desires that are a result of your own choice of perceptions. Because you are totally responsible for your experiences does not mean you should feel guilty for your behavior. Guilt only keeps you locked into repeating negative behavior. No guilt is needed, even if you consider your behavior to be a mistake. If you think you are a victim and are not responsible for your behavior, then you are incapable of changing and correcting your mistakes. Therefore, accepting responsibility for creating your behavior brings with it a great freedom. By accepting total responsibility for your choices, you are free to make different and better choices. It means that if you are not happy with what you are experiencing now in the way of your desires, you can make changes. You can change your perceptions by more deeply focusing on your spiritual purposes. As a result, your desires will change accordingly, and you will have different and better experiences.

To make progress spiritually, you need to develop nonattachment toward your own perceptions, which create desires that would separate you from being aware of God. You can develop nonattachment by applying spiritual discernment in which you examine your perceptions and your desires as these arise. When a desire arises, you may look at your perceptions and ask yourself: "Is this desire selfish? Am I seeking physical gratification, fame, wealth, power, or praise? Do I really need this desire, or is it only a restlessness of the mind? If I pursue and satisfy this desire now, will my future desire be lesser or greater? Is this desire motivated by fear?"

You may also ask: "Is this desire unselfish? Am I seeking to express patience, kindness and gentleness? Will this desire be in harmony with my spiritual ideal? Is this desire motivated by love?" Actually all these questions aren't necessary to ask. Usually you can simply allow your discernment to combine with your heart to tell you if a desire is motivated by a perception that comes from the self or from your true nature of love in God. This usually isn't an elaborate mental process, but rather an intuitive inner feeling.

Nonattachment does not mean not having possessions, position, or pleasure. Nonattachment means letting these things come into your life without yearning for them and letting these things go out of your life without clinging to them. It means seeking first the Kingdom of God, and then whatever else you really need will be provided. Nonattachment is a change in outlook that places God first in your life. It is a responsiveness to God's Will that would enable you to have those things that would be most helpful for your spiritual growth and to release those things that are no longer needed.

Nonattachment should never be a self-willed effort to forcefully rid yourself of everything you consider to be an imperfection. A stern effort to be "good" and not have "bad" desires will divide the individual into a "good" self and a "bad" self. The "good" self will suppress the "bad" self, perhaps even for a long time. But eventually the "bad" self will surface and take revenge—much like the person who goes on a crash diet to lose weight and then eats twice as much as before when the diet is over. This is the problem with false asceticism that is based on self-willed effort to develop spiritually.

Nonattachment can begin with relying on your intuition to tell you if your desires lead to self-glorification or to unselfish purposes. In the practice of nonattachment, it is a mistake to make the focus a negative one of avoiding what is "bad." Rather, the emphasis needs to be on investing in your spiritual ideal and becoming increasingly dedicated to manifesting the purposes that lead to your ideal. Gaining nonattachment is aided through a balance of inward development of meditation and outward development of loving service to others. As you become a channel of blessings to others, and as you place God first in your life, nonattachment will develop gradually. Old desires will not have to be forced out; they will fall away by themselves. Even in the beginning, nonattachment will bring a new feeling of freedom and inner peace. Not only do the desires fall away, but also the specific desire for self-will itself will decrease and will be replaced more and more by the desire to do God's Will. With progress, you will see that you are releasing only imaginary needs and desires. You discover that these imaginary needs did not produce the satisfaction you desired. Ironically, freeing yourself from imaginary needs brings about the very peace and inner harmony that you were really seeking. Through practicing nonattachment great inner strength is developed in a step-by-step process, and you are better able to be a channel of blessings to others. Through this development, you come to trust in the words of the Twenty-third Psalm, "The Lord is my Shepherd, I shall not want."

For more information on nonattachment, as well as practical advice on all aspects of spiritual growth, *Ascent of Mount Carmel* is suggested, along with other works written by St. John of the Cross. His message was one of pure love for God along with systematic detachment from all other desires. He felt that by the combination of love and detachment a dedicated spiritual seeker could, God willing, experience divine union, not only in the next life, but in this life.

---

1. Abraham Lincoln, "Words to Grow On," compiled quotations, *Guidepost* (Carmel, New York: magazine published by Norman Vincent Peale), February 1987, p. 38

2. Sharon Begley with Ann Underwood, "Religion and the Brain," an article in the magazine *Newsweek* (New York, New York: Newsweek, Inc.), May 7, 2001, Volume CXXXVII, No. 19, p. 53

3. Ibid., p. 52

4. Ibid., p. 53

5. Ibid., p. 53

6. Ibid., p. 53

7. Ibid., p. 55

8. Ibid., p. 55

9. Ibid., p. 57

10. St. John of the Cross, *Ascent of Mount Carmel*, edited by E. Allison Peers (New York, New York: Image Books, Doubleday and Co., Inc., 1958), p. 304. This book was published by arrangement with the copyright holder and original publisher, Newman Press, which has been absorbed by Paulist Press, Mahwah, New Jersey.

11. Exodus 33:20, as quoted in the *Ascent of Mount Carmel*, ibid., p. 305

12. St. John of the Cross, *Ascent of Mount Carmel*, edited by E. Allison Peers (New York, New York: Image Books, Doubleday and Co., Inc., 1958), pp. 305-306. This book was published by arrangement with the copyright holder and original publisher, Newman Press, which has been absorbed by Paulist Press, Mahwah, New Jersey.

13. II Corinthians 12:3-4

14. Ibid., p. 304

15. Ibid., p. 306

16. Thomas Matus, *Yoga and the Jesus Prayer Tradition* (Mahwah, New Jersey: Paulist Press, 1984), p. 27 (currently published by Asian Trading, Bangalore, India; distributed by Hermitage Books, New Camaldoli, 62475 Coast Highway One, Big Sur, CA 93920)

19

RELATIONSHIPS
AND
MEDITATION

≈ ◦ ≈

A. Changing Obstacles into Stepping Stones

This chapter is about relationships, which may seem like an unusual topic for a meditation manual. On the one hand, meditation is basically an inward activity directed toward communication with God. On the other hand, your relationships with other people are mainly outwardly directed. Thus at first glance it may appear that meditation and relationships have little in common, but in terms of your overall spiritual growth there is a direct correlation between meditation and relationships.

Both meditation and relationships are ways of finding meaning in your life. Your relationship with God and your relationship with your brothers and sisters are what give your life meaning. These two relationships *are* your meaning. You cannot discover the true value of one of these two relationships without discovering the true value of the other relationship because these two relationships are interdependent. You do not have an identity apart from either of these two relationships. Since this manual is about finding your true identity, both your relationship with God and your relationship with your brothers and sisters need to be addressed.

You meditate to deepen your personal relationship with God. But deepening your relationship to God is not only a vertical extension to the divine within, but also a horizontal extension to the divine within your brothers and sisters. Therefore, hopefully the fruit of your meditation experience will be an inner transformation that brings about the outer development of loving relationships. This chapter will stress resolving problems in relation to other people, as well as overcoming negative attitudes that you may impose upon yourself, because these issues have a direct impact on your ability to deepen your personal relationship with God.

If you dedicate yourself to doing God's Will, meditate regularly, and pray for guidance, this obviously doesn't mean you will avoid expressing your self-will at times. You may use the word "sin" to describe these expressions of self-will that create blocks to your true nature of love. When you fail in some of your attempts to do God's Will, as you surely will in your human frailty, the way you respond is important for your spiritual growth. How you define sin may affect your response to your failure to do God's Will. I will define sin here not from a theological outlook of what is the nature of sin, but rather from a practical outlook that would help you to respond to sin in the most appropriate way.

If you go back to the original version of the New Testament, you will find that the Greek language in which it was written did not have a word for "sin." Consequently, the word that most closely approximated the word sin was used, and that word was "hamartia." Hamartia is translated as "missing the mark," with the connotation of an arrow that has been aimed at a target, but is wide of the mark. If you can think of sin in this way, you can respond in the most appropriate way to your failure by admitting that you have missed the mark. Then you can turn your full attention toward taking a better aim at the bull's eye of doing God's Will. You can correct your sin by opening your heart and mind to God in prayer to ask for His forgiveness and to receive His Love for you. Then you can forgive yourself by accepting your mistakes and loving yourself with God's Love for you. Therefore, you allow this to be a learning experience, so the same deviation from God's Will might not happen again. In this way your sins are changed from obstacles into learning experiences that serve as stepping stones for your growth.

One inappropriate way of responding to failure to do God's Will is to blame yourself. When you dwell on blaming yourself, you focus your awareness in the past, on the mistake itself, and on your fault in making the mistake. This prevents you from simply accepting the mistake and accepting yourself, which would allow you to perceive the mistake as a valuable learning experience that will make you into a better person. If you continue to blame yourself, instead of improve yourself by correcting the mistake, you may generalize your bad feeling about your mistakes into a negative self-image about yourself. When you see yourself negatively, you will act negatively again and form a repeated pattern of behavior that is not in accord with God's Will.

In a misguided way, you may think that God wants you to feel guilty for your sins. Actually the only purpose of becoming aware of your sins is to remind you that you have missed the mark, so that next time you may take a better aim at the bull's eye. God does not want your guilt; He wants your love. If you blame yourself to the point of self-condemnation, you have created another sin, since it is your own self-willed choice to continue to separate yourself from God's Love.

Humility is needed to admit your mistakes appropriately without indulging in self-condemnation. Unfortunately, humility may be seen by some as a form of self-depreciation, but that is not humility. Humility is the ability to know and acknowledge the truth that you are dependent upon God for all that you are and do. Humility allows you to rely upon God for all your strengths and to realize that when you make mistakes, it is because you have temporarily lost sight of your dependence upon God. Every good deed you do is done with the aid of God's Love acting in and through you to strengthen you and perhaps others. Every sin that you do is done entirely on your own, by the separate self, apart from God's Love—and it weakens you. Humility allows you to acknowledge and correct your sins because it enables you to see the cause of each sin in your separation from God and to see the remedy in returning to your awareness of God's Love for you. A humble person views himself clearly, and so when he fails to do God's Will, he is not surprised. He realizes the condition of the self and his human tendency toward willfulness. However, he is equally aware of his strengths in his connection with God, and so he turns in prayer to God. He asks for His grace and keeps asking each time he falls short of doing God's Will.

In contrast to a humble person, a prideful person imagines his strength to be in himself rather than in his contact with God. Since he exalts himself, he is surprised when he encounters failure. Perhaps he may be crushed by it to the point of wallowing in self-condemnation. If your self-willed pride leads you from exalting yourself to self-condemnation, you may be tempted to give up your prayer and meditation practices. You may even be tempted to no longer dedicate yourself to doing God's Will. You must not give up these spiritual expressions, because these will lead you back to feeling God's Love for you. Instead, you need to be thankful that your self-willed pride has been revealed to you and see this as your opportunity to develop humility. Then you can proceed to overcome your self-condemnation, in the way that has already been described, by correcting your mistakes without blaming yourself and by turning to God in humility and asking for His help in prayer.

Self-condemnation shows you your lack of trust in God's Love for you. Consequently, to overcome self-condemnation, you will need to understand that behind every failure and every suffering that you may experience in life, God's Love for you is hidden and is mysteriously inviting you to draw closer to Him. You cannot avoid suffering in this life, but you can make suffering meaningful by allowing it to be part of a learning experience that will bring you closer to God.

B. Resolving Problems in Relation to Others

Problems will inevitably occur in your life, but how you choose to respond determines your growth. You may not be able to appropriately accept the problems in your life, to see where you have missed the mark, and to correct yourself by prayerfully turning to God in humility. Also, you may not want to blame yourself for these problems or mistakes either, as in the case of those who dwell on self-condemnation. Often in viewing your problems you exercise a third option, which is to justify yourself and blame others. In this way you project the bad feelings you have about your own shortcomings onto others, so you won't have to blame yourself. When you do this, pride is at work because you have exalted yourself and do not see your own mistakes, which humility would make clear to you. Out of pride you justify yourself by creating a lie that covers up your own shortcomings. You add to that lie by blaming others to further shift responsibility away from yourself.

This is a bigger problem for you than self-condemnation. Whereas self-condemnation creates an obstacle between yourself and God only, justifying yourself and blaming others separates you from both God and your brothers. Consequently, you will experience suffering caused by your separation from God and also suffering caused by your separation from others. In addition, others may respond to your blaming of them in a negative way that would bring suffering into their lives as well as your own.

To eliminate this suffering, you must remove the self-willed desire to hold on to any grievance toward anyone. For this reason Jesus says in the Bible that if you have any negative feeling against a brother, you must go and settle matters with him before entering the temple and approaching the altar. To hold a bad feeling against another is really to build a bad feeling within yourself. Approaching the altar is going within to God. Yet God is the whole. If you reject any part of Him by holding any grievance toward a brother, then how can you expect to experience His wholeness?

This applies directly to meditation. Even an experienced meditator will find that if he holds any grievance toward another person, it will prevent him from going deep within during meditation. That grievance will nag at him and prevent him from feeling the divine presence unless he decides to resolve it. In some cases, old grievances that were never resolved in the past may also surface as meditation deepens, and these, too, must be resolved in order to make further progress in deepening meditation. If you find you are justifying yourself and blaming someone else for anything in the recent or distant past, you may be sure that you are holding on to a grievance that will be an obstacle to your meditation experience.

But reconciling yourself with another person does not always mean going directly to that person and discussing your relationship. It may involve this, but more importantly it means being resolved inwardly. It means seeing that person without any negativity that would make you feel separate from that person and would encourage you to falsely imagine that you are separate from God. There are two approaches to becoming resolved inwardly that will be described. The first approach is "Expressive Problem Solving," which uses the mind and prayer to understand the problem at a mental level and then resolve it.

The primary mental understanding in problem solving is to realize that your problem is *your* problem. If others act inappropriately, you must avoid the temptation to blame them for your own reactions or emotions. Perhaps you have heard the saying, "Two wrongs don't make a right." If you respond with your own inappropriate behavior, then that is your problem. No one can make you respond inappropriately. Your responses are always an expression of your own free will and your own desires. This is important to remember, because when you take responsibility for your own responses, you no longer imagine that you are a victim of other people's behavior. You can then look at your own behavior and choose to change your responses, and you can look to God for help.

It is hard to accept responsibility for your own actions in a situation if you think you are a victim of someone else. It is much easier to accept responsibility if you have the understanding that becoming a victim— meaning thinking of yourself as being a victim—is a choice that you make, not something imposed upon you. Furthermore, this choice often involves self-deception produced by the ego. There is a *victim pattern* that facilitates self-deception.

The victim pattern starts with the fact that the ego, the self-concept of separation, is reinforced by guilt, the idea of culpability for wrongdoing. Guilt is generally already present within you as a self-assessment based your belief that you are in a state of separation from God. However, God does not want you to feel guilty; it is your own choice to feel guilty. You can let go of guilt by recognizing your oneness with God, but you keep guilt strong by using the ego's method of getting rid of guilt. The ego's method is to project guilt onto others in order to not see it within yourself.

All experiences, even those that appear to be outside your control and choice, do in fact come to you by your invitation from your free will. Your actions express your choices to exercise your free will, but the universe brings back to you the consequences of these choices in experiences that allow you to receive as you have sown. But when unexpected consequences appear in your life you may not remember what you had done to bring these consequences to yourself. Thus you do not accept responsibility for this experience, and instead you claim to be a victim, receiving what you do not deserve.

When your ego claims to be a victim, you deny your true nature and accept a false idea about yourself. This acceptance of a false idea about yourself—the idea that you are a victim—is an *attack on yourself*. Disregarding this attack on yourself, the ego chooses to only perceive that it is being attacked by someone else. The ego's goal is to gain innocence by giving guilt to someone else. Claiming that you are a victim means you can see someone else as being guilty, which allows you to project guilt off of yourself and onto another person. This claim of being a victim is in itself an attack on another person, but in addition your claim allows you to feel justified in retaliating with your own attack in words or actions directed toward that person. But the ego's method of getting rid of guilt does not work because you will end up feeling guilty for attacking another person by claiming to be a victim and by retaliating, even if your way of retaliating is only the holding of a hard feeling or grievance toward this person.

This victim pattern, which is an attempt to project guilt, ironically ends up only strengthening the ego and reinforcing guilt. The bottom line is that whenever you claim to be a victim, you are unknowingly deceiving yourself. Your unknowing self-deception involves a denial of the attack you have made on yourself, which consists of you disregarding your true nature and thinking of yourself as a victim. You add to this initial deception by unknowingly being dishonest—making a false accusation that another person has victimized you. This is a convenient way to avoid accepting responsibility for your own choices and to make another person responsible for how you feel about yourself. It is important to realize that how you feel about yourself and your state of mind is your own choice and not contingent upon another person's choices.

When you do not realize that your problem is *your* problem, you attempt to make it into another person's problem. Then you may imagine that since you have become a victim of someone, you have the right to justifiably exert your will over someone else. It is always inappropriate to impose your will on others. If you make the mistake of trying to impose your will upon another person as a retaliation, the other person may then be tempted to imagine that he is now a victim of you. When each person thinks that he is a victim of the other person, it becomes more difficult to resolve the situation since neither side is accepting responsibility.

The self-destructive victim pattern can be corrected by realizing that you are never a victim and by accepting responsibility. It is simply not possible for another person to be responsible for how you feel about yourself unless you make the mistake of giving that person that power to affect your perception of yourself. To let go of the idea of being a victim, you will have to withdraw any power that you have mistakenly assigned to another person to determine how you feel about yourself. Correcting yourself always involves accepting responsibility for your own actions and understanding that all events that happen to you are the results of your choices. Of course, you are always responsible for your reactions to any situation regardless of what another person does. If you find yourself feeling that you are a victim, you can correct this by realizing that you have denied your true nature and have attacked yourself to bring about this feeling. You can then again identify with your true nature and decide to no longer attack yourself with the false idea of you being a victim.

Unfortunately some people do not understand the victim pattern. They do not realize that the person who claims to be a victim has in fact been victimizing himself. Some individuals spend their whole lives in the illusion of thinking that they are always a victim of someone else or outer circumstances. These individuals will seek out "opportunities" to be victims and will find what they are looking for. For such a person, the slightest inadvertent comment by a friend will be an opportunity to be offended. This person will claim to be a victim of what another person said and will want the other person to apologize, thus admitting guilt. This is an example of "victim consciousness"—the consciousness of a person who believes that others have the power to make them unhappy and to determine their self-worth. A victim does not realize he is disempowering himself by giving others the power to determine his happiness and self-worth.

The opposite of victim consciousness is "responsibility consciousness." The person with responsibility consciousness acknowledges that he is responsible for his own happiness and self-worth. Therefore, he does not disempower himself by giving someone else the power to determine his happiness and self-worth. To maintain responsibility consciousness, you will need to have a strong inner relationship with God. Knowing inwardly that God loves you and values you allows you to realize that your happiness and true worth come from God who created you as an extension of Himself. This knowledge allows you to resist the temptation to think that the opinions of others can determine your happiness and self-worth. Your meditation practice assists you in learning to trust in God's Love and His valuing of you, which in turn empowers you to manifest responsibility consciousness.

At times it may be difficult to maintain responsibility consciousness and to avoid the temptation to believe that you have become a victim. Even if you intellectually accept the premise that victim consciousness is always an illusion, there will be temptations to make exceptions to this premise. If you find yourself in a situation that seems by outer indications to be undeserved, it takes inner strength to respond with graciousness, neither blaming anyone nor blaming yourself. You may, for example, be overtly and publicly insulted by a friend. It will be challenging for you to give no outer response and to have an inner response of loving concern for your friend. You will only be able to respond in this loving manner if you rely on the guidance of the Holy Spirit. You will not give your friend's comments the power to affect your self-worth since your guidance will help you avoid the temptation to perceive yourself as being a victim.

Besides letting go of the temptation to claim to be a victim, it is also important to let go of the temptation to impose your will on another person for any reason. To accept responsibility for how you use your will, it is helpful to notice whenever you feel yourself wanting to exert your will to make someone else change. Attempting to exert your will over others is usually disguised and justified by good intentions. When your self-will is rejected, you may react emotionally. By removing your desire to exert your will over others, you can remove the cause of many of your emotional reactions. You have removed your self-will when you no longer have any desire to make another person think, do, or be anything but what that person himself chooses to think, do, or be. Then you can accept that person just as he is. Thus you can shift your focus to yourself and how you can change to improve your own responses with God's help.

In addition to resolving specific problems, you might want to ask yourself in general what causes problems in personal relationships. Most problems involve an attempt to impose your will upon others, so you need to be aware of why you would want to misuse your will in this way. Such behavior contradicts who you really are. As was stated earlier, the single most important truth about spiritual growth is that love is your own true nature, not something you have to manufacture. But by creating a perspective of separation, your ego blocks the natural expression of your love. The primary way in which your ego blocks your love of others is by judging them. Your judgments consist of mentally viewing others from your own world and desiring others to meet your expectations or your standards of right and wrong. From your judgments you may then make the mistake of directly or indirectly imposing your will in an attempt to make others think, do, or be something that they haven't chosen for themselves. Your challenge is to be able to set aside your judgments and willful desires so you can truly accept others just as they are.

Being able to set aside your judgments of another person requires an understanding of your world, the other person's world, and His World. First, you need to understand that your world revolves around your ego-based perspective that has its own standards, which are not centered on God's Will. Thus you need to realize just how biased and incomplete your views really are. Second, you need to be willing to enter the other person's world to see that his judgments are also biased and incomplete, but seem to him to be very valid from his ego-based perspective—just as your own judgments appear to be valid from your perspective. This will give you empathy for the other person and enable you to respect that he is viewing from his own standards of right and wrong, which seem to be valid within his world, even if they do not appear to be valid in your world.

Lastly you need to be aware of His World, which encompasses your world of separation. To enter His World in relation to understanding a problem, you need to set aside your biased judgments and ask directly for God, Jesus, or the Holy Spirit to help you. In particular you need to ask for the truth to be revealed, which means you must sincerely want to know the truth. This requires an "I don't know" attitude. By admitting that you don't really know, you open yourself to the truth of His World.

Truth is not a judgment because it is not based on an ego-centered standard or perspective. Truth is simply an expression of reality. If you are faced with a problem and ask for God's Truth, you will be faced with reality. God is Reality just as God is Love. Love, being the nature of God and your own true nature, is Reality. Saying that God's Love is Reality means that everything that is real needs to be understood from the perspective of love. Problems are caused by losing sight of the reality of love. Problems are only a lack of awareness of love. But love is not absent; it is merely unseen, like the sun hiding behind clouds. Thus refocusing on the reality of love is the way to resolve problems. You can ask in prayer for the truth of a specific problem to be revealed so you can see the reality of love as the means of resolving the problem. But it is helpful to understand a general principle of truth regarding all behavior. This truth is that your behavior or your brother's behavior can only be an *expression of love or a request for love.*

Why is it important to see all behavior as an expression of love or a request for love? Your perception of your brother's behavior will affect how you will respond to your brother. If you see your brother's behavior as an expression of love, you will naturally be drawn to respond similarly with your own expression of love. If your see your brother's behavior as a request for love, you will recognize what your brother truly wants, which is love that expresses his true nature. Seeing your brother as one who is requesting love will encourage you to respond by giving him the love that he is requesting. Giving your brother love will assist your brother to heal, because he has forgotten that love is his own true nature.

Your response of love reminds him of his own true nature and assists him to heal, but consider how you will be affected by your choice to respond with love to your brother. Your response of love reminds you of your own true nature. You cannot give love, unless you have love. When you affirm your own love nature by giving love, you not only assist your brother to heal, but also assist your own healing. Healing always comes from within as an acceptance of the love that is already within you.

But what if you do not respond to your brother with the love that he is requesting? To not respond with love is a contradiction of your true nature of love and will inevitably cause problems in relationships. It is also a contradiction of reality. You cannot change the nature of objective reality, but what you choose to perceive as real becomes "subjectively real" for you. Your subjective reality is a false perception that is not based on God or love and therefore is actually not real. Nevertheless, you will respond to your false perceptions as though they are real, even though they are not real. When you perceive lovelessly, you believe you have the right to attack reality by perceiving what is not there.

Your false perceptions give the illusion that your brother is attacking you and obscure the truth that your brother is only requesting love from you. Since you falsely perceive that your brother is attacking you with inappropriate behavior, you will respond with your own inappropriate behavior. You will also falsely perceive that you are attacking your brother and will not perceive that your response like your brother's is a request for love. Your false perceptions of your brother attacking you offer a means of justifying your attacking your brother in response.

If you perceive your brother's apparent errors as real, you will make them subjectively real for you, and you will respond to them accordingly. Ideally you can overcome errors by seeing them as unreal in the very beginning. If you see errors as requests for love right away, you will see them as unreal and not respond to them as if they were real. Yet if you fail to correctly perceive errors as unreal, these errors will appear real to you and will result in you having problems in your relationships.

To make progress spiritually, it is necessary to know how to resolve problems in relationships. You will have to realize that the truth about your problems is hidden from your awareness. Next you will have to ask God, Jesus, or the Holy Spirit to reveal the truth to you. What is revealed to you may at first be disconcerting. You may see that the truth is that you have been projecting your own faults onto others by blaming others. You may see how your judgments are inappropriate. You may see how you have been willful. You may see just how selfish you have been and how much fear, anger, or pain the other person is experiencing. You may see your own fear, anger, or pain and have to go through internally feeling the true intensity of your emotions rather than hiding them.

In short, the truth will force you to look at yourself honestly and accept that your problems are created by yourself.

If you sincerely ask in prayer for God, Jesus, or the Holy Spirit to reveal the truth, you will uncover not only the facts about the specific problem but also reveal the mask of self that perpetuates such problems. Although unmasking the self can be temporarily painful, the end result is that more of your true nature of love can shine through and manifest in your life and in the lives of your brothers and sisters. Your increased love will enable you to forgive yourself for your mistakes and forgive others for their mistakes. Your prayers that restore your awareness of love and focus on forgiveness will enable you to come to an inner resolution.

C. Expressive Problem Solving

Expressive Problem Solving is one approach to revealing the truth and coming to an inner resolution of a problem. This form of problem solving places the responsibility on you to turn to God in prayer for the correct mental understanding of the problem and then to act on that understanding. For example, if you have had a negative reaction to something that someone else did, you would ask God, Jesus, or the Holy Spirit to help you use your mental ability to analyze the problem. After gaining mental clarity, then you would ask the divine within for help in prayer so you could come to an inner resolution. The procedure for dealing with such a problem is outlined below in a five-step method. [Note that his method is not compatible with the spiritual principles of *A Course in Miracles*, as will be explained in Chapter 21.]

EXPRESSIVE PROBLEM SOLVING

1. Observation: What Happened?

Conduct a mental review by playing a video in your mind of the sequence of events. Remember exactly what the other person did and what you did. Recall your past thoughts and emotional reactions. Make a comprehensive list of your perceptions of the other person's apparent mistakes, but the purpose is not to prove to yourself you are right and the other person is wrong. It is simply to show you how your mind is thinking in relation to another person. This is the time to look at all of your thoughts in your mind and feel all of your feelings in your heart without yet evaluating the appropriateness of your thoughts and feelings. Your observations are designed to prevent denial and bring everything out in the open.

2. Pray for Help: Ask for the Truth

Make a list of all your perceptions of your own mistakes. Your mistakes would include your judgments, willfulness, inappropriate behavior, and any unloving thoughts or actions on your part. After making this initial list, ask in prayer for God, Jesus, or the Holy Spirit to help you and reveal the truth of the situation. Ask to be shown what you had consciously or unconsciously thought or done to create the problem. Make a prayer request to be shown if you mentally judged the other person by requiring him to meet your standards of right and wrong. Ask in prayer if you even slightly wanted to exert your will over this person to make him think, do, or be anything that he had not chosen for himself? Allow your prayer to reveal to you any of your thoughts, feelings, or actions that were unloving. Ask to be shown how the other person's inappropriate behavior and your own inappropriate behavior were actually only requests for love. After your prayer, make additions or adjustments to the list of your mistakes that have been revealed to you.

3. Evaluate your Judgments: Withdraw Projections

This is a re-examination of the problem in the light of what has been revealed to you by your prayerful asking for the truth. Your goal is to change your thinking by withdrawing any tendency toward blaming the other person. You withdraw blaming in order to help you accept responsibility for your thoughts, feelings, and behavior. Begin this reexamination by looking now at the list you made earlier of your perceptions of the other person's mistakes. Consider that your perceptions of another person's mistakes (even if objectively accurate) are a hindrance and temptation for you. The temptation is to allow these perceptions to become projections of your own guilt onto another person. The other person must judge his own mistakes, as you must judge your own mistakes, with the projection of guilt being one of your possible mistakes. You may have some ideas about why or how the other person responded, but these are only projections and assumptions on your part. Regardless of how the other person responded, can you blame the other person for your choice of emotional response? Can another person's mistakes justify your mistakes? Does it appear to you that the other person is really an ego? Can you see this person as an ego without also passing judgment on yourself that you are an ego? What do you gain and what do you lose by holding on to your judgments of this other person? Do your judgments cause you to be angry or afraid of that person? Why? Consider in what ways you have used projection in an attempt to get rid of your own guilt by blaming others. But has this blaming really gotten rid of your guilt or only made you feel more guilty? Make a decision to withdraw all your projections.

4. Accept Responsibility and Decide How to Change

After withdrawing your projections, you are then ready to accept responsibility. Regardless of the other person's judgments, willfulness, or inappropriate behavior, you cannot justify your own judgments, willfulness, or inappropriate behavior. Consider that the other person is not "your" problem. You are not responsible for how the other person responds to you. Rather, you are fully responsible for how you respond to others. Accepting total responsibility does not mean accepting full guilt that would produce self-condemnation. Instead, it means accepting that you have made mistakes that you now want to correct. Write down a statement in which you accept responsibility for making judgments, being willful, and not being as loving as you could have been. In your statement include your willingness and commitment to change. You can write down the following statement or a similar one in your own words: "I accept full responsibility for all my actions and my choices of emotional response. My problem rests in changing myself, not in the other person changing. No matter what the other person has done or will do, nothing prevents me from looking with love on that person, except me. I choose to change and extend love to this person." Next, consider how to implement your willingness to change. What can you do or avoid doing to improve the relationship? How can you learn to see this person, not as an ego, but as a divine being? Can you think of ways to extend love to the other person or increase your appreciation of the other person? For example, you can make a list of the other person's strengths that will help you see them in a better light. You can also make a list of your strengths that you can draw upon to help you heal your relationship.

5. Correct your Mistakes: Prayer and Forgiveness

Resolving your problem is an inner transformation that involves not merely a change in thinking but also a change of heart. Divine assistance through prayer and forgiveness is necessary to facilitate this inner transformation. The following are recommendations for prayer, which can be addressed to God, Jesus, or the Holy Spirit:

a. In prayer, ask for God's assistance to enable you to let go of your willfulness, your mental judgments, and your negative emotions.

b. In prayer, open yourself to receiving the unconditional Love of God so you can accept and love yourself now with His Love for you.

c. Ask God to help you forgive the other person for any imagined or actual mistakes he has made, and ask God to bless this person as He sees fit.

d. Ask God to help you remove any desire to project judgments onto this person and refrain from wanting to imposing your will upon this person in the future.

e. Ask God to enable you to see this person differently, not as an ego, but as a holy spiritual being, and ask for yourself to be filled with a loving attitude toward this person.

f. Ask for God to help you place your trust in Him and to assist you in correcting your mistakes.

As part of resolving a problem related to another person, it may be necessary to go to the other person and discuss how to resolve the relationship. However, it can be willfulness on your part to feel that you have to do something to resolve the relationship. If you feel you have to make someone understand something, you have not yet let go of your willfulness. If the other person is not ready to resolve the relationship, you do not need to feel obligated to do something to create an outer resolution with that person. Some relationship problems can only be resolved by yourself inwardly. In these cases you will have to trust that God, Jesus, or the Holy Spirit will guide that person to come to their own resolution.

If you feel prompted by the Holy Spirit to go to another person to resolve a problem, it is most important to be honest. You would need to say exactly what you feel, yet without exerting your will over the other person. Indeed, it is good to even tell him (or her) that you don't want to exert your will to force him to change. You can also tell him you do want him to know how you feel so that when he is making choices related to you, he can consider your feelings and concerns.

If you know that this person is comfortable with the practice of prayer and/or meditation, you can offer to participate with him in a time of prayer and/or meditation. Also, you can offer to participate with him as partners in Blessing Meditation described in Chapter 16, if you think he would be open to this possibility. Practicing Blessing Meditation together will help you both to see Christ in each other as part of your healing process. Actually any form of prayer or meditation that you practice together will assist your joint healing. Your inner guidance will help you to know if it is necessary to go to the other person to resolve the problem and will show you how to proceed and even what to say.

D. Receptive Problem Solving

Another method of resolving problems is *Receptive Problem Solving*, which involves three easy steps: The first step is meditation. The second step is prayer. The third step is the solution. The five-step approach of Expressive Problem Solving uses the mind to understand the problem from a mental perspective and then prayer to overcome the problem, and this is effective. The three-step approach of Receptive Problem Solving is also effective, but has the advantage of greater simplicity.

I have heard it said (although I don't know the source), "If you *think* you've got a problem, then you've got a problem." Problems are really only negative thoughts that you have decided to hold on to through self-will. These thoughts keep circling around in the mind like a record that keeps playing the same tune over and over again. These repeated negative thoughts bring about negative emotions. Expressive Problem Solving described above focuses first on prayerfully using the mind to mentally understand these negative thoughts. But sometimes focusing on the thoughts only stimulates more negative thoughts and more of the negative emotions that they produce. Some individuals find it difficult to get through the mental stages of Expressive Problem Solving because they are so focused on the problem that they cannot leave the problem.

Simply stated, the problem is the problem. Leaving the problem is the solution. Nothing needs to be figured out with the mind. In fact, the thought that you have to figure something out creates only more of a problem. This is like having muddy water in a bowl and trying to clear it up by stirring it with your hand. This only makes it muddier. The best thing to do is to let it be. As you leave it alone, the particles of dirt will fall to the bottom naturally, and the clear water will remain.

The particles of dirt are your thoughts. You have problems because you use self-will to stir these thoughts around. The three-step approach uses meditation to stop the self-willed thoughts simply by ignoring them and instead focusing on the one thought of your affirmation, such as the Divine Name. When the dirt (self-willed thought) has settled, the water is clear—the natural, inner harmony is restored.

Your problems, which you invariably create for yourself, are caused by self-will, which brings about negative thoughts, leading to negative emotions. The predominant negative emotion you experience is fear, which in turn can produce anger and/or pain. So if you are experiencing fear, anger, or pain, it is because you have made a self-willed choice against your true nature. The whole self-will process that brings about negative emotions is unnatural and takes a constant effort on the part of the doing self to maintain. Through meditation, self-willed thoughts fall away because there is no effort to maintain them. The result is that the natural qualities of the soul shine through. These qualities may be summed up in one word—LOVE. God's Will may more appropriately be called the will of love. You can read in the Bible, "God is love."[1] He wishes only to express the love, which He is and which you are as a part of Him. Meditation has no other purpose than to help you to express love, which is your own true nature. Meditation is a purification process that removes the blocks that prevent the natural outpouring of love.

For Receptive Problem Solving to work, you will need to have only one simple intellectual understanding that will apply to any problem. Using your will is always a choice for love or against love. If you are experiencing fear, anger, or pain, you have chosen against love. Indeed, if you have any problem, it is because you have chosen against love. Since all problems are caused by a lack of love, the remedy for all problems is to make a new choice to restore the love that was lacking. Any further intellectualizing about the problem itself may only serve to extend the problem by delaying your decision to restore the love that was lacking. In summary, the single intellectual understanding you will need to have is to realize that there is a problem because you have rejected love and thus immediate acceptance of love is needed to correct the problem.

Meditation is the first and most important step in Receptive Problem Solving because it allows you to accept love. Meditation enables you to switch from expressive doing to receptive being and helps you contact your love nature, which is your being Self in the Being of God. In the practice of meditation, you leave behind the self-willed thoughts of the doing self, and thus you leave the problem. You do not allow the doing self to figure out the problem because the doing self is actually the cause of your self-willed desires. Instead, you silence the doing self and let the being Self create an inner spiritual resolution based on returning to love and to wholeness in God.

In this three-step method of overcoming problems, prayer is the second step. Again the solution is to leave the problem, so for prayer you ask God to take the problem and resolve it. Once you have given the problem to God, let it be. Leave off from any thought about the problem or how you can resolve it. Rather, turn to prayer and ask for love to manifest through God.

Meditation, the first step of this method, *allows love* to be expressed by ignoring thoughts that would block its natural expression. Prayer, the second step, *invites love* to manifest by asking for this to happen. No analysis of the problem is necessary, except for the simple recognition that whatever problem you encounter has been caused by your choice to withhold love and that in order to resolve the problem, you need to make a new choice to manifest love. Therefore, without analyzing the problem, you ask God in prayer to help you change from withholding love to manifesting love, which corrects the problem.

Specifically to make this change from lovelessness to love, you ask God to help you release any negative judgments or willfulness that you may knowingly or unknowingly harbor against any person related to the problem. In prayer you ask for God to help you be receptive to His Love. You dedicate yourself to doing His Will of love, which is your own true will. You ask God to bless anyone related to the problem with His Love, according to His Will. One way to express this blessing is to contact God's Love for you and allow His Love to flow through you to others. In your prayer of blessing, there is no mental consideration of the problem itself and no desire on your part to exert your will over anyone.

After your prayer of blessing, you offer the problem to God for Him to resolve as He sees fit. In doing so, you take the problem out of your hands and place the problem in His Hands. Your leaving of the problem means that you do not have to figure out how to resolve the problem. Setting aside the problem demonstrates your trust in God to resolve the problem with His Love.

The third step in Receptive Problem Solving is the solution, which is the *result of love.* The solution comes as a natural outcome of applying the first two steps, which are expressions of love. With meditation and prayer, you can leave the problem and go directly to the solution— which is turning to God. Of course, God doesn't have any problems. If you find Him, then you do not have any problems either. Thus the solution may simply be an inner experience of resolution so that you feel connected with God who is the source of love within yourself. However, this solution may also involve an outer resolution that must be manifested by going to the person involved. As an outcome of your meditation and prayer, you will have an inner knowing of what is the most appropriate course of action. In this case, your *doing* will flow forth from and be an outer expression of your *being.* Ironically, even though the mental concepts are not sought consciously in meditation, these come later as sudden insights and understandings of the heart as a result of meditation. Receptive Problem Solving has been described as a way to resolve problems in relation to other people, but it may also be used to resolve any internal problems that do not involve other people. It is a way of transforming the doing self into a servant of God's Will so that your doing is an expression of your being in God.

When you use this approach, you can give your problems to God, or you can choose to give your problems to Jesus or the Holy Spirit. When you give your problems to the divine within, the Holy Spirit goes to work within your life and within the lives of others. The results can be very surprising. I was having difficulty relating to a particular man because I felt he was holding on to a negative attitude about me. I followed the three-step method of problem solving. First, I meditated to feel the divine presence. Second, after meditation, I prayed for myself to release any negative judgment or desire to impose my will that I might be unknowingly harboring toward him. Also, I prayed that God would help him in whatever way would be for his own highest good. Next, I asked God to show me if I needed to do anything to improve my relationship with this man. Then I left the problem with God for Him to come up with the third step, which is the solution.

The very next day, I went into a print shop, and this person was there. After we greeted each other, he told me he needed to wait fifteen minutes to pick up his order, but he also needed to go somewhere else for an important meeting with another person. He somewhat awkwardly asked if I would be willing to wait at the print shop for his order. I gladly agreed and offered to bring it to him a little later in the day. He thanked me and rushed off to his appointment.

I was delighted about our interaction, because I knew it was a setup that God had given me so I could be of service to this man. As a result of this incident, he changed his attitude toward me, from cool and distant to warm and friendly.

Perhaps you have heard the saying, "It is better to light one candle than to curse the darkness." It is marvelous to discover how easily problems resolve themselves if you look to the light. An added benefit of this approach is that as it is applied over a period of time, gradually there will be fewer and fewer problems occurring in your life. This is true because as meditation is used more, you become more loving and peaceful. As the desire to do God's Will of love grows, there are fewer self-willed thoughts and fewer of the emotional reactions and problems that are caused by self-willed thoughts.

The approach of Receptive Problem Solving, which consists of the three steps of meditation, prayer, and the solution, is summarized on the next page:

RECEPTIVE PROBLEM SOLVING

1. Meditation — Allowing Love

a. You recognize that you have a problem because you have made a choice to reject love, and now you need to correct the problem by accepting love. Instead of analyzing the problem intellectually, you leave the problem.

b. You meditate with whatever method helps you to increase your awareness of the divine love that is within you.

c. By ignoring self-willed thoughts and emotions, these obstacles to the awareness of love fall away of themselves.

d. As these blocks fall away, you allow yourself to accept God's Love for you and to accept your own true nature of love.

2. Prayer — Inviting Love

a. In prayer you ask for help from God, Jesus, or the Holy Spirit.

b. Without analyzing the problem, you ask God to help you release any negative judgments or willfulness that you may knowingly or unknowingly harbor against any person related to the problem.

c. In prayer you ask for God to help you be receptive to His Love and dedicate yourself to doing His Will of love.

d. You ask God to bless everyone related to the problem, according to His Will.

e. Finally you leave the problem altogether by asking God to take the problem and to resolve it. Giving the problem to God demonstrates your trust in God to resolve the problem with His Love.

3. The Solution — The Result of Love

a. The result of meditation and prayer is the solution, which is turning to God, Who is Love.

b. This may be simply an inner restoration of love and harmony.

c. This may also involve an outer resolution.

d. There will be inner understandings that will help you to know and do exactly what needs to be done, if anything.

e. Future problems occur less frequently as meditation and prayer enable your inner love to shine forth.

You may make many attempts to come to an inner and an outer resolution of a problem and yet fail to do so. If this happens, you may be trying too hard to resolve the problem yourself and thus have not truly allowed the Holy Spirit to help you. In this case, you need to give up your usual methods of solving problems by yourself so your doing self can get out of the way and so God can do as much as possible. But you need faith to give your problems wholeheartedly to God and trust that He will solve them. Otherwise, you will be like the man who gets on a train and stands holding his luggage in his hand, instead of sitting down and resting his luggage on the floor of the train. Without faith you will hold on to your luggage, which is your problems, and so you will not be able to relax. Your doing self will want to remain in control and will motivate you to figure out your solution, and so God, Who does not want to interfere with your free will, will step back until you let go of your solution and are willing to accept His solution.

The poem below by Lauretta Burns is titled "Broken Dreams":

> As children bring their broken toys,
> with tears for us to mend,
> I brought my broken dreams to God,
> because He is my friend.
> But then, instead of leaving Him
> in peace to work alone,
> I hung around and tried to help,
> with ways that were my own.
> At last, I snatched them back and cried,
> "How can you be so slow?"
> "My child," He said, "What could I do?
> You never did let go."[2]

If you find that your problems remain unresolved, you may decide that you need to blame yourself or blame God. Such loss of confidence in yourself or loss of faith in God can only further delay the resolution to your problem. Any problem that is truly given away to God is in fact resolved. You need to accept His solution, not cling to your solution. For example, as your solution to a problem, you may want some heavy burden in your life to be lifted. Instead of lifting that burden, God may respond by giving you the inner strength to bear that burden in order to make you into a better person, more fit for His World. If you ask God for one thing, and He doesn't give it, or He gives something else, you must trust that whatever way He responds is the highest and best gift that you would have chosen for yourself if you had His Wisdom and Love.

You will need to wait patiently for Him to help in His own time and in His own way. If you are unwilling to wait patiently without preconceived ideas about what "should" happen, then you have not truly given the problem to Him. In this case, you can temporarily shift your focus away from the outer problem itself and take a closer look at your own ego attachments that are creating blocks within yourself. You can ask the Holy Spirit to reveal how you are resisting God's Will. You may discover, for example, that you do not have faith that God will help, or that you do not feel you deserve God's help, or that you are afraid or unwilling to change in some way. Then when you uncover your inner resistance, you can offer your blocks back to the Holy Spirit for healing.

As a concession to the doing self, you may find that a combination of first Expressive Problem Solving and then Receptive Problem Solving will best meet your needs. Because of the human nature, the doing self likes to use the mind to mentally understand a problem. After gaining mental clarity, it is easier then to turn to God in prayer. In some cases, if you attempt to use Receptive Problem Solving immediately, you may find that you cannot let go of the problem because you are either too upset, or you need to mentally understand the problem. If you choose to use Expressive Problem Solving first, then even though the problem may not be entirely resolved, at least the intensity of upset feelings may have subsided in the process of gaining mental clarity and praying to God. As a result, you will be better able to let go of the problem through using Receptive Problem Solving. Expressive Problem Solving followed by Receptive Problem Solving may be used in general by anyone who feels both ways of problem solving would benefit them.

After practicing either one of these techniques for problem solving or using both of them, you may want to also use Blessing Meditation, which was described in Chapter 16. This meditation technique is so strongly based on seeing the divine in your brother that it assists in letting go of the judgments that often cause problems in relationships. In addition to the structured methods of problem solving that are described in this manual, feel free to create your own individual approach that perhaps employs some of the principles outlined here.

While structured methods may help you, ideally you want to grow beyond using any system or method so you can become increasingly receptive and responsive to the guidance of the Holy Spirit.

E. Responsiveness to Others

There are primarily two functional ways of interacting with the Spirit: *receptivity* and *responsiveness*. Through receptivity you allow yourself to be penetrated by the Holy Spirit. Once you have become inwardly receptive and filled with the Spirit, then hopefully you will develop responsiveness to the Spirit that enables you to respond appropriately to any outer circumstance. By your responsiveness to the Spirit you will be guided to love others as God would have you love them—whether it is with kind words or stern words, whether it is with laughter or tears, or whether it is with heart-felt expression or intellectual insight. If you place no blockage of judgment, attachment, or willfulness between yourself and the Spirit, then your responsiveness to the Spirit will allow your own true nature of love to manifest in the way that would be of the highest service to your brothers and sisters and to yourself.

Your responsiveness to the Spirit is reflected in your relationships with others because other people in your life are the means through which God works to present a mirror before you of your true nature of love. When your love nature and connection with God is shining forth through you, it is reflected back to you by your brothers and sisters. Similarly, when you are inwardly blocked so love is not flowing through you, your lack of love is mirrored by conflicts in personal relationships. Such mirroring is vital to your growth, and without it, you cannot grow in love of God. In fact, you are here together precisely to be teachers of love for one another. While every single person you meet is such a teacher for you, you need to have at least one significant person, and preferably several significant others, who can help you see and work through your blocks to love and whom you can similarly help. Superficial relationships will address and help remove superficial blocks. However, your deepest blocks to love are blind spots that you either cannot see or do not know how to deal with. For these blind spots, you need an intimate friend or friends to aid you in seeing and releasing your inner resistance to love.

There are two very different ways in which your close friends can provide a mirror for you to see yourself. The first is the ego mirror. Here you can see fear in your brother and see through your own eyes of fear. Or you can look for anger in your brother and find anger in yourself. Or you can seek any weakness in your brother and discover that same weakness in yourself. Of course, you attempt to project your faults onto others, so you won't have to see them in yourself. But close relationships eventually reveal that what you have projected is really in yourself. It may take years to learn just how destructive this projection really is. This is obviously a negative mirror, and it teaches you what you do not want to do, but does not tell you how to view yourself as you really are.

The second mirror is the true mirror of who you really are. You can look at your closest friends and love them. To do so, you need to look past the ego mirror and not reflect it back. When you become a true mirror of love, you can see love in your brother through the eyes of love in yourself. Only love can mirror love. To see love in another is to tell him, by your seeing and not your words, that you know him as he truly is. It is also to tell yourself that you know yourself as you truly are.

At one time many years ago I presumptuously thought that the best way I could help others was to tell them with their permission about how I saw their ego condition so they could change. Then one day a woman came to me who was very distraught. Every attempt of mine to understand and analyze her problem had no effect at all. In fact, my explanations made things worse. Finally I hugged her and nonverbally told her I loved her. Immediately she was relieved. In the years since then, I have come to realize that whenever anyone is emotionally upset they are saying internally, "I am not this emotion you are seeing. I am really love. Please disregard my emotion and love me. If you love me, it will help me to remember my true nature of love." At those times when you are able to see through another's mask and validate that person's true nature, you also are able to see through your own mask to claim your own true nature of love.

The word that best describes your ability to see through your brother's mask is *forgiveness*. There are some people whom you encounter in your life who present masks that are particularly ugly to you, and so you may find it difficult to forgive them. Many times you may have failed miserably to forgive and instead have just allowed time to help you forget. But forgiveness and forgetfulness are worlds apart. Forgiveness is the seeing of God in your brothers, which helps them to heal and also helps you to heal. Forgetfulness only buries unresolved issues, and these unresolved emotional reactions keep resurfacing either in the old relationship itself or in disguise in new relationships.

To resolve old instances of unforgiveness, I suggest making your own personal *forgiveness list*. On the top of a piece of paper you can write, "Father, through the love of Jesus Christ, help me to forgive and love myself, and help me to forgive and love all my brothers and sisters." Then list on the paper your name and the names of all the people whom you have had difficulty truly loving and forgiving. After making the list, use it as a daily prayer list to resolve any lingering past resentments so that you can truly love all these people and likewise deepen your love and receptivity in relation to God.

By this recommendation I am not encouraging you to dwell on past memories and build guilt. Rather, I am suggesting that you offer these people in prayer to God so that there is an invitation to the Holy Spirit to enter each relationship inwardly and heal any unresolved issues or feelings. This does not mean mentally bringing forth a debate in your mind about what you did and what they did. That is irrelevant. It is just a matter of offering your mind and heart to God to ask Him to remove any negative feelings and allow the natural inner love to come forth. Remember the goal here is not intellectual understanding, it is love— love of God, your neighbor, and yourself. In front of each name on the list write the word "Bless" to remind yourself to stay focused on blessing each one as God would have each one be blessed.

The forgiveness list may be used as long as you find it helpful. If you are not attracted to this approach, the Holy Spirit may inspire you to address the expression of forgiveness in another form. Whatever the means, the issue of forgiveness is unavoidable. If you harbor the least little bit of unforgiveness, it says, "I am separate from that other person who did evil." But the price you pay for that thought is, "I am separate from God." Both thoughts negate oneness. Forgiveness heals both these false thoughts by saying, "God loves both me and this other person, and in His Love we are one with each other and one with Him Who is Oneness itself." Forgiveness unmasks the appearances of separation that you identify as your self and the self of others, and reveals the oneness you share with each other as children of one Father.

The idea of seeing through your brother's mask is especially helpful in regard to forgiveness of people whom you find especially difficult. Yet there is nothing stopping you from looking at every one of your brothers and sisters in your everyday life and seeing through their commonplace superficial ego masks to discover their true Self and your own true Self. Unfortunately the ideal of seeing love, or God, or Christ in one another has become somewhat of a spiritual cliché. It has become something that preachers talk about in their sermons, but no one actually does it in the "real" world. However, it is not just a nice, impractical idea. It is something you can do, and the Holy Spirit will enable you to do it. The only question is, "Do you really *want* to see love in your brothers?" Everywhere you look at outer appearances you can see the fake and separate worlds your brothers have created, but if you really want to, you can see His World of love that is inside of your brothers. When you can see His World in your brothers, you can see His World in yourself. It is this wanting for His World that is so important.

Your desire for God has been stressed in regard to meditation, yet your desire to find God within yourself must be balanced by an equal desire to find God in your brothers. When you truly want to see God in your brothers, you will feel the presence of God within you. Everyone *has* an ego, but no one *is* an ego. Your temptation in everyday life is to believe that your brother is an ego because of the forms he presents to you in this world. Seeing your brother as an ego can become such a habit of daily living that you may not realize that your perception that your brother is an ego is only an *interpretation* and not a fact. When you make the interpretation that determines your brother is an ego, this interpretation is your judgment that says he is not a divine being. This does not merely affect your attitude toward your brother. The affect on you is that you will not be able to avoid perceiving yourself as an ego. Seeing yourself as an ego is a judgment against yourself that you are not a divine being. If you want to identify with your true nature as a divine being in order to grow spiritually, you will have to begin by withdrawing your view of your brother as an ego and instead see him as a spiritual being. Once you see your brother as a spiritual being, you will see yourself as a divine being also.

You may want to start with seeing the divine presence in children, who naturally have more love shining through themselves than most adults. An excellent way to begin the process of seeing the divine within adults is to pray for them and in particular to focus in your prayers on seeing them as they truly are, as divine beings made in the image and likeness of God. Then later, with the assistance of the Holy Spirit, you can learn to extend that seeing into your daily life. Another very good way to facilitate this process of being a true mirror of the divine for your brothers is to practice prayer and meditation with others. Joining with others for communion with God is certainly a distinctly different and more powerful experience than individual prayer and meditation. Even a beginning meditator will notice that his meditation is better in a group of meditators than when he is alone. Jesus has said, "For where two or three are gathered in my name, there am I in the midst of them."[3]

Obviously there is a special benefit to gathering in His Divine Name for united prayer. Two thousand years ago during the first Pentecost, the Holy Spirit descended upon a group of disciples after they had spent time together and had "...with one accord devoted themselves to prayer."[4] Your path back to God is not intended to be a solitary one. Thus if you know others who would be interested, feel free to invite them to join you in your inner communion with God. Ideally a husband and wife can gather together in His Name for divine communion. Of course, group prayer and meditation is not necessary, and often it may be difficult to find others who are willing to make a commitment to prayer and meditation practice. Yet just finding even one other person with a similar interest and commitment can be a significant source of spiritual nourishment and inspiration.

Some meditators practice daily meditation alone and then once a week join with others for group meditation or group prayer. Often such group gatherings not only enhance your communication with God but also bring about personal sharing and spiritual companionship, which might otherwise not occur. Spiritual companionship here on earth is a foreshadowing of the spiritual companionship you will experience when you enter His World completely and permanently after this life is over. Then you will find not only your true relationship with God, but your true relationship with each other and with Christ. When you come to the core of who you really are within the Being of God, you come face to face with the souls of your brothers and sisters for their center is your center. Since that single center is love as oneness with God, you are linked with every other soul in a bond that is deeper and more personal than you can possibly imagine from your present earthly perspective of separation. It is Christ who already has the perspective of love for each individual that you will one day have for everyone. Christ's Love is not content to wait in the hereafter until you are ready to recognize your true nature of love. His Love penetrates even now into your darkest corners of separation and serves as a light leading you out of your darkness.

Christ is helping to carry out the Father's Plan, which is designed for each person individually and which at the same time is being fulfilled for humanity collectively. God's Plan may be thought of as an exquisite tapestry that He is weaving, and each person's life is a strand of thread. As a single strand from your individual perspective you cannot see the beautiful picture depicted on the whole tapestry. However, by faith you know that you are part of a great and wonderful work that will one day be revealed to you. On that day you will be able to let go of your role of who you imagine yourself to be. Then you will rejoice to find out who you really are in God, and you will rejoice with all your brothers and sisters, who by God's grace have made that same discovery.

It seems appropriate to conclude this chapter with Thomas Merton's words, which sum up your true relationship with others and with Christ:

> When you and I become what we are really meant to be, we will discover not only that we love one another perfectly but that we are both living in Christ and Christ in us, and we are all one Christ. We will see that it is He who loves in us.[5]

1. First letter of John 4:16
2. Lauretta P. Burns, "Broken Dreams," in *Stories of the Heart,* compiled by Alice Gray (Sisters, Oregon: Multnomah Books), 1996, p. 229. Also cited as Author Unknown, titled "Let Go and Let God," *Guideposts* (Carmel, New York: magazine published by Norman Vincent Peale), May, 1987, p. 45
3. Matthew 18:20
4. Acts 1:14
5. Thomas Merton, *New Seeds of Contemplation* (New York, New York: New Directions, 1972), p. 65

PART FOUR

≈ • ≈

MEDITATION
IN
A COURSE
IN MIRACLES

20

ATTUNEMENT IN
A COURSE IN MIRACLES

~ • ~

A. What is *A Course in Miracles*?

This meditation book is designed for any Christian seekers who are open to Eastern influences. My thought system in my early spiritual life was a buffet-style synthesis of the West and East, and the majority of this book was written with that as my background. But later in my spiritual development, I incorporated the principles of *A Course in Miracles* into my personal life, and that philosophy is certainly part of this meditation book. For example, one term I have used in this book is "Christ's vision," which is a concept taken from *A Course in Miracles*, and it means the seeing of holiness in others by opening to the direct influence of the Holy Spirit. Nevertheless, all of the techniques described in this book can be practiced by anyone with any Christian philosophy.

Now in these last five chapters, I would like to talk to those who may want to know more about *A Course in Miracles*, which I will refer to as the Course. If you are not familiar with this philosophy, you can think of it as a course in mind training. It is set forth in three books for personal study and application. The *Text* is the first book, and it presents the theological and philosophical thought system that is the basis for this course of study. The *Workbook for Students* is the second book, and it is a one-year course of daily practices to provide practical application of the thought system. The *Manual for Teachers* is the third book, and it is for those who have learned the Course principles and would like to share their learning with others. The Course is not a religion and not affiliated with any church, but many Course students do come together for local grass roots study groups.

The Course integrates the ideas of Eastern philosophy into a Western context that can be applied by Christians of any denomination or even by followers of Christ who are not associated with any church. However, in addition to being inclusive of Eastern philosophy, the Course also mixes in a profound understanding of psychology from a spiritual perspective. This unique synthesis of Eastern and Western philosophy and theology with psychology has attracted many spiritual seekers and from its inception in the seventies has had an amazing growth spurt with no initial advertising. The Course presents many familiar spiritual concepts but explains them in a very systematic and complete way. For example, concepts of the ego as the false self and your true nature as the true Self can be found in Eastern philosophy, but the Course offers these concepts in a Western context that expands the psychological meaning of these concepts.

I have not discussed my personal life very much in this meditation manual, but have reserved that sharing for my autobiography, *Memory Walk in the Light: My Christian Yoga Life as "A Course in Miracles."* In that book I explain how for many years I resisted accepting the Course. I was drawn to many concepts in the Course, but I was initially very skeptical about this material because the Course was psychically channeled. The "scribe" of the Course was Helen Schucman, a Jewish psychologist, yet the inner source that dictated to her consistently claimed to be Jesus Himself. Speaking of Jesus, the Course states, "This course has come from him because his words have reached you in a language you can love and understand."[1] I had researched channeled material many times in the past and each time discovered internal inconsistencies in the information that revealed its inaccuracies. Yet I did not find these inconsistencies in the Course. I finally became convinced of the truth I found in this material.

Before accepting the Course, I had focused entirely on practicing Christian yoga in which I used Eastern disciplines as a way of following the example of Christ. But, after adopting the thought system of the Course, I began the practice of what I call *Miracle Yoga*, which is Christian yoga with the Course as its philosophical basis. At first glance it may appear that the Course has nothing to do with yoga. After all, the Course says nothing about exercise, breathing practices, or health activities in general. The emphasis in the Course is on one's intention and the usage of the mind being more important than form-related issues. However, this silence should not be interpreted as a rejection of employing various self-help methods. The fact that no form-related methods are included means that such choices are up to the seeker and the guidance of the Holy Spirit. Those who are guided to practice Miracle Yoga will find that this blending of yoga and the Course is—at the risk of a bit of exaggeration—"a match made in Heaven." Yoga is a very malleable form of spiritual growth that, like water, can mold its shape to any container. The principles of the Course are the perfect container for practicing the full spectrum of yoga disciplines, which encompass much more than just the postures and breathing practices of hatha yoga.

There are five components to Miracle Yoga, which are love, service, meditation, understanding, and forgiveness. *Miracle Bhakti Yoga* is the expression of Love. *Miracle Karma Yoga* has to do with selfless service dedicated to God. *Miracle Raja Yoga* is the practice of meditation, but also includes hatha yoga with its breathing practices and postures that improve health and serve as a preparation for attunement. *Miracle Jnana Yoga* is the understanding aspect of spiritual growth, which in this case is the study of *A Course in Miracles* as the philosophical basis for all of the expressions of Miracle Yoga. These four forms of Miracle Yoga are modifications of four corresponding paths in Hindu yoga. The fifth expression of Miracle Yoga is *Miracle Relationship Yoga*, which has no counterpart in Hindu Yoga. Miracle Relationship Yoga has to do with manifesting forgiveness and seeing holiness in everyone, which is the central message of the Course.

All five forms of Miracle Yoga are intended to help you become an empty vessel for the Holy Spirit. The intention of being an empty vessel is to become filled with love and allow that love to be extended through you to your brothers and sisters. This extension of love is what the Course calls a *miracle*. The miracle is facilitated by the action of the Holy Spirit and includes a change of mind. This change involves replacing false, unloving perceptions with true, loving perceptions. A miracle always produces an increase in love for both the giver of the miracle and the receiver.

I initially introduced Miracle Yoga as a distinctive spiritual path in my autobiography. To explain this spiritual path more extensively, I have written but not yet published, *Christian Yoga Inspired by "A Course in Miracles": Miracle Yoga for Forgiveness and Awakening*. This chapter and the next four will focus on the attunement practices of the Course, along with some general spiritual principles.

B. Meditation Lessons in the Course

The Course is a complete thought system encompassing the major aspects of spiritual growth with a consistent emphasis on forgiveness. For the purpose of this meditation manual, it's appropriate to focus on how attunement practices are described in the Course. The word "meditation" is not used in the Course to describe its various inward practices of mind training. However, the Course does obviously advocate inward focusing of the mind consistent with meditation techniques.

There is no one method of meditation recommended consistently throughout the Course. The Course starts with easier methods first and gradually introduces various options leading in the direction of wordless contemplation, which is the most advanced form of attunement.

The Workbook includes 365 lessons, one for each day of the year. It introduces the first specific practice of meditation in Lesson 41, "God goes with me wherever I go." The premise of this lesson is that God is always within you hiding behind your superficial thoughts. It is the same premise of all attunement practices in the Course. This particular lesson refers to your thoughts as a dark "cloud" that you can travel past to find God in the light that lies behind it:

> Today we will make our first real attempt to get past this dark and heavy cloud, and to go through it to the light beyond.
>
> There will be only one long practice period today. In the morning, as soon as you get up if possible, sit quietly for some three to five minutes, with your eyes closed. At the beginning of the practice period, repeat today's idea very slowly. Then make no effort to think of anything. Try, instead, to get a sense of turning inward, past all the idle thoughts of the world. Try to enter very deeply into your own mind, keeping it clear of any thoughts that might divert your attention.
>
> From time to time, you may repeat the idea if you find it helpful. But most of all, try to sink down and inward, away from the world and all the foolish thoughts of the world. You are trying to reach past all these things. You are trying to leave appearances and approach reality.
>
> It is quite possible to reach God. In fact it is very easy, because it is the most natural thing in the world. You might even say it is the only natural thing in the world. The way will open, if you believe that it is possible. This exercise can bring very startling results even the first time it is attempted, and sooner or later it is always successful. We will go into more detail about this kind of practice as we go along. But it will never fail completely, and instant success is possible.[2]

Some of same themes of how to practice meditation can be found in the next Course practice of meditation described in Lesson 44, "God is the light in which I see."

> Begin the practice period by repeating today's idea with your eyes open, and close them slowly, repeating the idea several times more. Then try to sink into your mind, letting go every kind of interference and intrusion by quietly sinking past them. Your mind cannot be stopped in this unless you choose to stop it. It is merely

taking its natural course. Try to observe your passing thoughts without involvement, and slip quietly by them....

If resistance rises in any form, pause long enough to repeat today's idea, keeping your eyes closed unless you are aware of fear. In that case, you will probably find it more reassuring to open your eyes briefly. Try, however, to return to the exercises with eyes closed as soon as possible.

If you are doing the exercises correctly, you should experience some sense of relaxation, and even a feeling that you are approaching, if not actually entering into light. Try to think of light, formless and without limit, as you pass by the thoughts of this world. And do not forget that they cannot hold you to the world unless you give them the power to do so.[3]

Now let's look at Lesson 41 and Lesson 44 to point out the common elements that can also be found in subsequent Course meditation practices. The Course answers six questions about the nature of attunement in the process of mind training for spiritual development.

1. *What are the obstacles of your meditation?*

The obstacles are your "idle thoughts of the world" and any "passing thoughts" that would divert your attention. In some lessons the Course uses visualization, such as the images of clouds or smoke, to identify and symbolize your thoughts that interfere with meditation. You are told "to get a sense of turning inward" and to practice "sinking down and inward." You are also instructed "to observe your passing thoughts without involvement, and slip quietly by them" and "to enter very deeply into your own mind." The idea is that your typical thoughts are only on the surface of the mind, and you can circumvent these by gently slipping past them.

2. *What is the goal of your meditation?*

The goal is always the same. It is always God or something else that represents God or one of His attributes, such as light, love, reality, or peace. Under ordinary circumstances you think that you are alone and do not possess the goal. Yet the truth is you are not seeking something that you may or may not possess. The Course constantly reminds you that you are never alone and that you are seeking what you already have eternally. The goal is always hidden in the deeper part of your mind waiting to be discovered.

3. *What is the basic meditation method in regard to word usage?*

The method described most consistently in the Course is the mental repeating of words that represent an uplifting idea. Lessons 41 and 44 point out that you do not repeat the idea for the whole meditation session. Rather, the words are only used as a response to any kind of distraction. Once the interfering distraction subsides, you can let go of repeating the focusing idea to reach a deeper level of the mind that can sense the divine presence without employing words or intellectual ideas.

4. *What is the best attitude to have toward meditation?*

Your attitude is the single most important factor in determining how effective your meditation will be. For this reason the Course goes to great lengths to fully articulate the best attitude for meditation. Any meditation method always has two components. One is attention and the other is intention. Of these two the Course places the greatest emphasis on your intention. Yes, you need a method that will help you focus your attention, but you need to place most of your attention on your intention. In order to focus on your intention, you need to know clearly what your intention is, and the Course provides this clarity repeatedly. Your intention is to find the goal mentioned previously, namely the goal of finding God's hidden presence. The Course is about mind training, but the purpose of that mind training is paramount and must be foremost in your mind while you meditate. Lessons 41 and 44 point out the significance of reminding yourself of the holiness and importance of what you are doing:

> Think of what you are saying; what the words mean. Concentrate on the holiness that they imply about you; on the unfailing companionship that is yours; on the complete protection that surrounds you.[4]

> While no particular approach is advocated for this form of exercise, what is needful is a sense of the importance of what you are doing; its inestimable value to you, and an awareness that you are attempting something very holy.[5]

5. *What are the prospects of succeeding in meditation?*

By going deep within, you're not doing something unnatural. Rather, your mind "is merely taking its natural course." You are reassured by the Course that it "is quite possible to reach God. In fact, it is very easy, because it is the most natural thing in the world." The Course asserts that success in practicing meditation can be found by anyone through persistence: "This exercise can bring very startling results even the first time it is attempted, and sooner or later it is always successful."

6. *How do I bring my meditation experience into my daily life?*

Often attunement practices are thought of as only a way of focusing the mind at specific times set aside for that purpose. But the Course emphasizes that the same kind of inner awareness fostered in a quiet time while alone can be generalized to the activities of daily living.

> Throughout the day use today's idea often, repeating it very slowly, preferably with eyes closed.[6]

> Throughout the day repeat the idea often, with eyes open or closed as seems better to you at the time. But do not forget. Above all, be determined not to forget today.[7]

The most common method found in the Course is mentally repeating the words for the Workbook lesson of the day. Yet for your meditation practice, you don't repeat the uplifting idea for each lesson constantly for the whole session. The words are only used as a response to any kind of distraction. Once the interfering distraction subsides, you can let go of repeating the focusing idea. After your meditation time is over, the cares of the world can fill your mind with thoughts that divert you from your desire to express the divine influence. Thus the Course makes a point of recommending that at various times during the day you can recall the uplifting words for the day as a way of refocusing the mind to overcome worldly distractions and to stay focused on your spiritual ideals.

C. The Name of God in the Course

The Course provides a variety of different approaches to inner attunement. The one that will be discussed now is meditation that uses Name of God. This practice has already been discussed in Chapter 4, "Divine Names and other Affirmations." In the Course this form of attunement is introduced in Workbook Lesson 183, "I call upon God's Name and on my own." In the traditional approach to repeating God's Name, the whole idea is that God is different from you and apart from you in His divinity. In contrast to this, the Course says that calling on the Name of God is calling upon your own true Identity:

God's Name is holy, but no holier than yours. To call upon His Name is but to call upon your own. A father gives his son his name, and thus identifies the son with him. His brothers share his name, and thus are they united in a bond to which they turn for their identity. Your Father's Name reminds you who you are, even within a world that does not know; even though you have not remembered it.[8]

Repeat the Name of God, and call upon your Self, Whose Name is His. Repeat His Name, and all the tiny, nameless things on earth slip into right perspective. Those who call upon the Name of God can not mistake the nameless for the Name, nor sin for grace, nor bodies for the holy Son of God. And should you join a brother as you sit with him in silence, and repeat God's Name along with him within your quiet mind, you have established there an altar which reaches to God Himself and to His Son.[9]

What makes this practice unique in the Course is that the Name of God is repeated continuously, instead of intermittently as other affirmations are used in the Course. This repetition is like a Hindu mantra intended to be one word that swallows up all other words, one thought that engulfs all other thoughts. But more than just a simple sound structure, this word carries the force of divinity and the oneness of reality with it because that is its meaning. Thus the Course reiterates in paragraph after paragraph the great significance of this meaning so when you meditate, you will not just be repeating a word without being convinced of its meaning. The Course wants you to know you will be directly calling upon your own Source and Substance. What makes this method effective is not your faith in the method itself, but your faith in the One Whom you call upon. Your conviction that God is in you, or rather that you are within God, is necessary. Or at least you will need a sincere openness to the presence of God being directly available to you at all times. The repeating of the Name of God is described in this way:

Practice but this today; repeat God's Name slowly again and still again. Become oblivious to every name but His. Hear nothing else. Let all your thoughts become anchored on this. No other word we use except at the beginning, when we say today's idea but once. And then God's Name becomes our only thought, our only word, the only thing that occupies our minds, the only wish we have, the only sound with any meaning, and the only Name of everything that we desire to see; of everything that we would call our own.

Thus do we give an invitation which can never be refused. And God will come, and answer it Himself. Think not He hears the little prayers of those who call on Him with names of idols cherished by the world. They cannot reach Him thus. He cannot hear requests that He be not Himself, or that His Son receive another name than His.

Repeat God's Name, and you acknowledge Him as sole Creator of reality. And you acknowledge also that His Son is part of Him, creating in His Name. Sit silently, and let His Name become the all-encompassing idea that holds your mind completely. Let all thoughts be still except this one. And to all other thoughts respond with this, and see God's Name replace the thousand little names you gave your thoughts, not realizing that there is one Name for all there is, and all that there will be.[10]

The Course is a course in mind training designed to shift the focus of your thought system from being ego-centered to being God-centered. All the lessons in the Workbook lead in this direction, but calling on the Name of God is a direct route to this goal because it silences all the other thoughts of the mind that would distract your attention. The Course promises peace of mind to those who seek God in His single name.

All little things are silent. Little sounds are soundless now. The little things of earth have disappeared. The universe consists of nothing but the Son of God, who calls upon his Father. And his Father's Voice gives answer in his Father's holy Name. In this eternal, still relationship, in which communication far transcends all words, and yet exceeds in depth and height whatever words could possibly convey, is peace eternal. In our Father's Name, we would experience this peace today. And in His Name, it shall be given us.[11]

The same practice that is the basis of Lesson 183 is likewise advocated in Lesson 184, "The Name of God is my inheritance." This lesson recommends setting aside times each day to repeat the Name of God.

Thus what you need are intervals each day in which the learning of the world becomes a transitory phase; a prison house from which you go into the sunlight and forget the darkness. Here you understand the Word, the Name which God has given you; the one Identity which all things share; the one acknowledgment of what is true. And then step back to darkness, not because you think it real, but only to proclaim its unreality in terms which still have meaning in the world that darkness rules.

Use all the little names and symbols which delineate the world of darkness. Yet accept them not as your reality. The Holy Spirit uses all of them, but He does not forget creation has one Name, one meaning, and a single Source which unifies all things within Itself. Use all the names the world bestows on them but for convenience, yet do not forget they share the Name of God along with you.[12]

But the obvious question is, "What is the Name of God?" After all, the Course admits, "God has no name."[13] Since God has in fact no name, you can choose any one name for Him and that is what you must do for this practice. It must be just one name that you designate as the Name of God for you—a name that will have the most meaning for you. I would recommend a single name that is short, preferably one or two syllables. It needs to be a word that triggers both your motivation for God and your love for God. It can be what you literally feel is a name for God or just a reminder of God or of one of His attributes that can symbolize Him. The many words we use in the world to describe the one God can distort our thinking to make us confused. Therefore, choosing just one word reminds us that there is only one Word, which represents the nameless reality of God and which transcends and includes all the little divisions our minds have made. This one word you choose has the power to unify your scattered mind in meditation. According to the Course, you cannot fail because God Himself will answer your call and help you see that you are awakening your awareness of your own true nature. Be sure to ask within for guidance to choose the sacred word that will be the most inspiring for you. The sacred word itself is not a magic formula. Rather, it gains its meaning and feeling from you because you are opening both your mind and heart to the divine within.

And yet His Name becomes the final lesson that all things are one, and at this lesson does all learning end. All names are unified; all space is filled with truth's reflection. Every gap is closed, and separation healed. The Name of God is the inheritance He gave to those who chose the teaching of the world to take the place of Heaven. In our practicing, our purpose is to let our minds accept what God has given as the answer to the pitiful inheritance you made as fitting tribute to the Son He loves.

No one can fail who seeks the meaning of the Name of God. Experience must come to supplement the Word. But first you must accept the Name for all reality, and realize the many names you gave its aspects have distorted what you see, but have not interfered with truth at all. One Name we bring into our practicing. One Name we use to unify our sight.

And though we use a different name for each awareness of an aspect of God's Son, we understand that they have but one Name, which He has given them. It is this Name we use in practicing. And through Its use, all foolish separations disappear which kept us blind. And we are given strength to see beyond them. Now our sight is blessed with blessings we can give as we receive.[14]

There is some flexibility in how you repeat the Name of God. Sitting comfortably with your eyes closed, you want to repeat the sacred word in a gentle unhurried manner so you can impregnate it with your intention to open to the divine presence. You can repeat the Name of God over and over again constantly or at regular intervals. As an alternative, it can be repeated only when you feel moved to repeat it. It can be coordinated with your breathing if you like, but the Course leaves this decision up to you since it makes no mention of breathing. The sacred word is your response to every stray thought that would take your attention away from opening to God's presence. Of course, your mind will wander so this is no cause for concern. Make no attempt to evaluate the various thoughts that grab your attention because all of them are equally meaningless, carrying no reality. The sacred word you have chosen for this practice is the only symbol for you of the one reality that you seek. Just gently remind yourself of the sacred word and your intention to go beyond your superficial thoughts. It is all right if your whole attunement is nothing more than an intermittent holding of the Name of God and having it slip away due to distractions. Rest assured that such efforts express your longing for the presence of God and are the small steps necessary to make your way Home.

The important thing is that your practice is a heartfelt expression of what you truly desire more than anything else. After all, God is in fact the only thing that you truly want and the only thing in this world or the next that truly has the power to satisfy you. This is because God loves you more than you love yourself. This is also because, according to the Course, you have a burning love for God already at your core that can be hidden by the cares of the world, but can never be extinguished. It is this burning love that is the eternal fire that attracts you to God like a magnet, even if you are not at all conscious of this love. Fortunately you are not seeking something that is not yours. Instead, in your meditation you are merely seeking to become aware of what is already yours forever.

D. The Name of Jesus in the Course

Workbook Lessons 183 and 184 are the only ones that recommend repeating the Name of God, but neither one gives a specific example of what name might be chosen for this purpose. That means you can choose any name that inspires you to think of God, as was already mentioned. But, wait a minute. There is one name that deserves special attention in our consideration of what name to choose to represent the Name of God. That name is the Name of Jesus Christ. The Manual for Teachers has a section titled, "Does Jesus have a special place in healing?" This section describes what it means to call upon the Name of Jesus Christ.

> He has become the risen Son of God. He has overcome death because he has accepted life. He has recognized himself as God created him, and in so doing he has recognized all living things as part of him. There is now no limit on his power, because it is the power of God. So has his name become the Name of God, for he no longer sees himself as separate from Him.[15]

What strikes me most about the above quotation regarding Jesus is the line that states, "So has his name become the Name of God...." Obviously the Course is hinting here that it specifically recommends using the Name of Jesus Christ as your sacred word in your practice of repeating the Name of God. This quotation goes on to indicate what remembering the Name of Jesus Christ means for you.

> What does this mean for you? It means that in remembering Jesus you are remembering God. The whole relationship of the Son to the Father lies in him. His part in the Sonship is also yours, and his completed learning guarantees your own success. Is he still available for help? What did he say about this? Remember his promises, and ask yourself honestly whether it is likely that he will fail to keep them. Can God fail His Son? And can one who is one with God be unlike Him? Who transcends the body has transcended limitation. Would the greatest teacher be unavailable to those who follow him?[16]

The Course asserts that some people think that some words can have a magical quality or have the power in themselves to produce a special power. The Course discourages such beliefs in magic and emphasizes that words are only symbols. Nonetheless, some symbols, such as the Name of Jesus Christ, carry a meaning that is very important.

The name of Jesus Christ as such is but a symbol. But it stands for love that is not of this world. It is a symbol that is safely used as a replacement for the many names of all the gods to which you pray. It becomes the shining symbol for the Word of God, so close to what it stands for that the little space between the two is lost, the moment that the name is called to mind. Remembering the name of Jesus Christ is to give thanks for all the gifts that God has given you. And gratitude to God becomes the way in which He is remembered, for love cannot be far behind a grateful heart and thankful mind. God enters easily, for these are the true conditions for your homecoming.[17]

The Course suggests calling upon the Name of Jesus, especially in regard to healing, as a recognition of God, rather than as a recalling of the historical man who walked the earth two thousand years ago. The Course sees all names, even Divine Names, as only symbols, and the Name of Jesus is no exception. But this symbol of God's Word is so close in meaning to what it symbolizes that calling upon the Name of Jesus Christ has the same effect as calling upon God Himself.

At the end of the Course there is a part called the *Clarification of Terms*. Here there is a section titled, "Jesus—Christ," which is devoted to clarifying these two terms. This section addresses the Name of Jesus, saying:

> The name of *Jesus* is the name of one who was a man but saw the face of Christ in all his brothers and remembered God. So he became identified with *Christ*, a man no longer, but at one with God. The man was an illusion, for he seemed to be a separate being, walking by himself, within a body that appeared to hold his self from Self, as all illusions do. Yet who can save unless he sees illusions and then identifies them as what they are? Jesus remains a Savior because he saw the false without accepting it as true. And Christ needed his form that He might appear to men and save them from their own illusions.[18]

Calling on the Name of Jesus is not calling on God *or* Jesus; it is calling upon *both God and Jesus* because They are One, although God is, of course, the Father and Creator and Jesus is the Christ. As was mentioned before, calling on the Name of God is calling on your own name as well. Similarly calling upon the Name of Christ is calling upon your own true name since the Course maintains that Christ is your own true nature.

In his complete identification with the Christ—the perfect Son of God, His one creation and His happiness, forever like Himself and One with Him—Jesus became what all of you must be. He led the way for you to follow him. He leads you back to God because he saw the road before him, and he followed it. He made a clear distinction, still obscure to you, between the false and true. He offered you a final demonstration that it is impossible to kill God's Son; nor can his life in any way be changed by sin and evil, malice, fear or death.

And therefore all your sins have been forgiven because they carried no effects at all. And so they were but dreams. Arise with him who showed you this because you owe him this who shared your dreams that they might be dispelled. And shares them still, to be at one with you.[19]

The quotation above maintains that this world is a dream of separation, and that the death and resurrection of Jesus proves this world of dreams has no power to separate you from your divine Source. The ultimate goal of Jesus in your regard is that He wants you to one day wake up from this dream as He did and to recognize your true nature in Christ, becoming what He is now.

Is he the Christ? O yes, along with you. His little life on earth was not enough to teach the mighty lesson that he learned for all of you. He will remain with you to lead you from the hell you made to God. And when you join your will with his, your sight will be his vision, for the eyes of Christ are shared. Walking with him is just as natural as walking with a brother whom you knew since you were born, for such indeed he is.[20]

Jesus remains with you and walks with you on your journey Home. The Course encourages you to "…share your pains and joys with him [Jesus], and leave them both to find the peace of God."[21] If you join your will with the will of Jesus, you are joining with the Will of God. In so doing, Jesus will give you Christ's vision. This vision allows you to see the world with forgiving eyes—allowing you to let go of judgments and enabling you to look past them to the divine in everyone you meet. The Name of Jesus can safely be used for meditation, as well as for healing, guidance, or help, since Jesus is available to those who call upon Him. Yet if you want to be in charge of your life and retain your current thought system based on the ego, then you will be limiting the role Jesus could play in your life.

Spirit need not be taught, but the ego must be. Learning is ultimately perceived as frightening because it leads to the relinquishment, not the destruction, of the ego to the light of spirit. This is the change the ego must fear, because it does not share my charity. My lesson was like yours, and because I learned it I can teach it. I will never attack your ego, but I am trying to teach you how its thought system arose. When I remind you of your true creation, your ego cannot but respond with fear.

Teaching and learning are your greatest strengths now, because they enable you to change your mind and help others to change theirs. Refusing to change your mind will not prove that the separation has not occurred. The dreamer who doubts the reality of his dream while he is still dreaming is not really healing his split mind. You dream of a separated ego and believe in a world that rests upon it. This is very real to you. You cannot undo it by not changing your mind about it. If you are willing to renounce the role of guardian of your thought system and open it to me, I will correct it very gently and lead you back to God.[22]

Jesus wants you to join your mind with His because together you have greater strength to allow God's Love to flow through you allowing miracles to bring blessings into the lives of others.

I do not attack your ego. I do work with your higher mind, the home of the Holy Spirit, whether you are asleep or awake, just as your ego does with your lower mind, which is its home. I am your vigilance in this, because you are too confused to recognize your own hope. I am not mistaken. Your mind will elect to join with mine, and together we are invincible. You and your brother will yet come together in my name, and your sanity will be restored. I raised the dead by knowing that life is an eternal attribute of everything that the living God created. Why do you believe it is harder for me to inspire the dis-spirited or to stabilize the unstable? I do not believe that there is an order of difficulty in miracles; you do. I have called and you will answer. I understand that miracles are natural, because they are expressions of love. My calling you is as natural as your answer, and as inevitable.[23]

The term *Atonement* is used in the Course to describe God's Plan for all mankind to return Home. Jesus is the central figure bringing about this awakening. His role is to help you heal your mind. Your mind is now split. Your current ego condition is based on perception, consisting of false perception and true perceptions. Jesus aids you in healing your mind by guiding you to practice right-mindedness and to experience miracles in which you replace false perceptions with true perceptions.

> Then let the Holy One shine on you in peace, knowing that this and only this must be. His Mind shone on you in your creation and brought your mind into being. His Mind still shines on you and must shine through you. Your ego cannot prevent Him from shining on you, but it can prevent you from letting Him shine through you.
>
> The First Coming of Christ is merely another name for the creation, for Christ is the Son of God. The Second Coming of Christ means nothing more than the end of the ego's rule and the healing of the mind. I was created like you in the First, and I have called you to join with me in the Second. I am in charge of the Second Coming, and my judgment, which is used only for protection, cannot be wrong because it never attacks. Yours may be so distorted that you believe I was mistaken in choosing you. I assure you this is a mistake of your ego. Do not mistake it for humility. Your ego is trying to convince you that it is real and I am not, because if I am real, I am no more real than you are. That knowledge, and I assure you that it *is* knowledge, means that Christ has come into your mind and healed it.[24]

When the mind is focusing only on true perceptions, these loving ideas open the mind to total awareness, called *knowledge*, and to the direct experience of God, which the Course calls *revelation*. Through the guidance of Jesus, "miracles lead to the highly personal experience of revelation."[25] Jesus works closely with the Holy Spirit to undo the ego and bring back your awareness of the Father. The Course refers to the Holy Spirit as "the Christ Mind which is aware of the knowledge that lies beyond perception."[26] Normally knowledge and perception are so different that they are mutually exclusive, but, metaphorically speaking, the Holy Spirit has one foot in knowledge and one foot in perception. The dual nature of the Holy Spirit is needed to lead you from perception to knowledge, which restores the split mind to wholeness.

> The Holy Spirit is the Mind of the Atonement. He represents a state of mind close enough to One-mindedness that transfer to it is at last possible. Perception is not knowledge, but it can be transferred to knowledge, or cross over into it. It might even be more helpful here to use the literal meaning of transferred or "carried over," since the last step is taken by God.[27]

Jesus is perfectly identified with the Father and the Holy Spirit so He possesses the Christ Mind and in the Course says of Himself, "I am the Atonement."[28] What is usually called a "sin," the Course calls a *mistake* or *error*. The Atonement undoes all mistakes. The sole responsibility of the miracle worker is to accept the Atonement, even if only temporarily.

> *The sole responsibility of the miracle worker is to accept the Atonement for himself.* This means you recognize that mind is the only creative level, and that its errors are healed by the Atonement. Once you accept this, your mind can only heal.[29]

This temporary acceptance of the Atonement opens the mind, even if only for an instant, and allows the miracle worker to become an empty vessel through which miracles of love can be extended to others. Jesus actively helps in the manifestation of miracles and can help you participate in the Atonement, which removes the negative effects of all errors and heals your mind while at the same time healing the minds of others.

> I am in charge of the process of Atonement, which I undertook to begin. When you offer a miracle to any of my brothers, you do it to *yourself* and me. The reason you come before me is that I do not need miracles for my own Atonement, but I stand at the end in case you fail temporarily. My part in the Atonement is the cancelling out of all errors that you could not otherwise correct. When you have been restored to the recognition of your original state, you naturally become part of the Atonement yourself. As you share my unwillingness to accept error in yourself and others, you must join the great crusade to correct it; listen to my voice, learn to undo error and act to correct it. The power to work miracles belongs to you. I will provide the opportunities to do them, but you must be ready and willing. Doing them will bring conviction in the ability, because conviction comes through accomplishment. The ability is the potential, the achievement is its expression, and the Atonement, which is the natural profession of the children of God, is the purpose.[30]

Jesus can play a very active role in your life helping you to perform miracles that bring blessings to you and to others. The role Jesus can play depends on your openness to Him. Jesus describes Himself in the Course as your "elder brother" and your equal, and He does not want you to confuse Him with your heavenly Father:

Equals should not be in awe of one another because awe implies inequality. It is therefore an inappropriate reaction to me. An elder brother is entitled to respect for his greater experience, and obedience for his greater wisdom. He is also entitled to love because he is a brother, and to devotion if he is devoted. It is only my devotion that entitles me to yours. There is nothing about me that you cannot attain. I have nothing that does not come from God. The difference between us now is that I have nothing else. This leaves me in a state which is only potential in you.[31]

I will substitute for your ego if you wish, but never for your spirit. A father can safely leave a child with an elder brother who has shown himself responsible, but this involves no confusion about the child's origin. The brother can protect the child's body and his ego, but he does not confuse himself with the father because he does this. I can be entrusted with your body and your ego only because this enables you not to be concerned with them, and lets me teach you their unimportance. I could not understand their importance to you if I had not once been tempted to believe in them myself. Let us undertake to learn this lesson together so we can be free of them together. I need devoted teachers who share my aim of healing the mind.[32]

In the Course Jesus says, "I will teach with you and live with you if you will think with me, but my goal will always be to absolve you finally from the need for a teacher."[33] Jesus wants you to learn right-minded thinking to heal your own mind with miracles and to help heal your brothers and sisters. Through performing miracles you become a teacher of how to let go of false perceptions and replace them with true perceptions. You do not have to call yourself a teacher to teach others. The example of how you live your life can be your teaching since your thoughts and actions bear witness to your learning.

Jesus will help you as much as you allow him to. However, He wants you to likewise help your brothers and sisters. Your salvation is not entirely in your hands alone because you are never alone. This must be true because you have a shared Identity. Your brothers and sisters are part of you, and you are part of them because you share your true nature in God. The Father created you and all of your brothers and sisters as extensions of Himself, making up what the Course calls the *Sonship*. This Sonship is the One Christ. You and everyone are each equal parts of this One Christ, Who is the Son of God. The Father gave all of His children His own holiness, and the appearances of sin have never taken this holiness away. Jesus inspires miracles and wants you to perform miracles to affirm your oneness with your brothers and sisters.

The Course describes miracles in many different ways, as is expressed in the following quotation:

> Miracles should inspire gratitude, not awe. You should thank God for what you really are. The children of God are holy and the miracle honors their holiness, which can be hidden but never lost.
>
> I inspire all miracles, which are really intercessions. They intercede for your holiness and make your perceptions holy. By placing you beyond the physical laws they raise you into the sphere of celestial order. In this order you *are* perfect.
>
> Miracles honor you because you are lovable. They dispel illusions about yourself and perceive the light in you. They thus atone for your errors by freeing you from your nightmares. By releasing your mind from the imprisonment of your illusions, they restore your sanity.
>
> Miracles restore the mind to its fullness. By atoning for lack they establish perfect protection. The spirit's strength leaves no room for intrusions.
>
> Miracles are expressions of love, but they may not always have observable effects.
>
> Miracles are examples of right thinking, aligning your perceptions with truth as God created it.
>
> A miracle is a correction introduced into false thinking by me. It acts as a catalyst, breaking up erroneous perception and reorganizing it properly. This places you under the Atonement principle, where perception is healed. Until this has occurred, knowledge of the Divine Order is impossible.
>
> The Holy Spirit is the mechanism of miracles. He recognizes both God's creations and your illusions. He separates the true from the false by His ability to perceive totally rather than selectively.
>
> The miracle dissolves error because the Holy Spirit identifies error as false or unreal. This is the same as saying that by perceiving light, darkness automatically disappears.
>
> The miracle acknowledges everyone as your brother and mine. It is a way of perceiving the universal mark of God.[34]

As you see the divine in your brothers and sisters, you reinforce your awareness of your own holiness. When you join with your brothers and sisters, you draw closer to Jesus and allow Him to help you expand your awareness of your true nature in God. In the Course Jesus says:

My trust in you is greater than yours in me at the moment, but it will not always be that way. Your mission is very simple. You are asked to live so as to demonstrate that you are not an ego, and I do not choose God's channels wrongly. The Holy One shares my trust, and accepts my Atonement decisions because my will is never out of accord with His. I have said before that I am in charge of the Atonement. This is only because I completed my part in it as a man, and can now complete it through others. My chosen channels cannot fail, because I will lend them my strength as long as theirs is wanting.

I will go with you to the Holy One, and through my perception He can bridge the little gap. Your gratitude to your brother is the only gift I want. I will bring it to God for you, knowing that to know your brother *is* to know God. If you are grateful to your brother, you are grateful to God for what He created. Through your gratitude you come to know your brother, and one moment of real recognition makes everyone your brother because each of them is of your Father. Love does not conquer all things, but it does set all things right. Because you are the Kingdom of God I can lead you back to your own creations. You do not recognize them now, but what has been dissociated is still there.

As you come closer to a brother you approach me, and as you withdraw from him I become distant to you.[35]

E. Meditation as a Way of Accepting God's Will

Meditation is a means of focusing on rejoining your awareness with God and with your brothers and sisters. This means of opening to your true Identity is also an acceptance of God's Will for you, since God's Will *is* your Identity. Because of the ego, God's Will seems to be a fearful idea.

Fear of the Will of God is one of the strangest beliefs the human mind has ever made. It could not possibly have occurred unless the mind were already profoundly split, making it possible for it to be afraid of what it really is. Reality cannot "threaten" anything except illusions, since reality can only uphold truth. The very fact that the Will of God, which is what you are, is perceived as fearful, demonstrates that you *are* afraid of what you are. It is not, then, the Will of God of which you are afraid, but yours.

Your will is not the ego's, and that is why the ego is against you. What seems to be the fear of God is really the fear of your own reality. It is impossible to learn anything consistently in a state of panic. If the purpose of this course is to help you remember what you are, and if you believe that what you are is fearful, then it must follow that you will not learn this course. Yet the reason for the course is that you do not know what you are....

You have set up this strange situation so that it is impossible to escape from it without a Guide Who *does* know what your reality is. The purpose of this Guide is merely to remind you of what you want. He is not attempting to force an alien will upon you. He is merely making every possible effort, within the limits you impose on Him, to re-establish your own will in your awareness.

You have imprisoned your will beyond your own awareness, where it remains, but cannot help you. When I said that the Holy Spirit's function is to sort out the true from the false in your mind, I meant that He has the power to look into what you have hidden and recognize the Will of God there. His recognition of this Will can make it real to you because He is in your mind, and therefore He is your reality. If, then, His perception of your mind brings its reality to you, He *is* helping you to remember what you are....

There is no difference between your will and God's.[36]

Many spiritual teachings advocate accepting God's Will as a way of navigating through the world. Yet the Course repeatedly emphasizes the additional teaching that in accepting His Will, you are accepting your true Identity that transcends the world. Joining your will with Jesus is one way of opening yourself to God's Will that you both share. Allowing yourself to be guided by the Holy Spirit is another way to awaken your awareness of God's Will as your true Identity.

I [Jesus] said before that you are the Will of God. His Will is not an idle wish, and your identification with His Will is not optional, since it is what you are. Sharing His Will with me [Jesus] is not really open to choice, though it may seem to be. The whole separation lies in this error. The only way out of the error is to decide that you do not have to decide anything. Everything has been given you by God's decision. That is His Will, and you cannot undo it.

Even the relinquishment of your false decision-making prerogative, which the ego guards so jealously, is not accomplished by your wish. It was accomplished for you by the Will of God, Who has not left you comfortless. His Voice [the Holy Spirit] will teach you how to distinguish between pain and joy, and will lead you out of the confusion you have made. There is no confusion in the mind of a Son of God, whose will must be the Will of the Father, because the Father's Will *is* His Son.

Miracles are in accord with the Will of God, Whose Will you do not know because you are confused about what *you* will. This means that you are confused about what you are. If you are God's Will and do not accept His Will, you are denying joy. The miracle is therefore a lesson in what joy is. Being a lesson in sharing it is a lesson in love, which *is* joy. Every miracle is thus a lesson in truth, and by offering truth you are learning the difference between pain and joy.[37]

One of the major reasons why we think we may not want God's Will is that we think we know what we want. However, the next quotation reminds us that the ego makes us think that God's Will and God Himself is apart from you. Consequently, you must learn to ask what God's Will is to learn what your own will is.

God's Will is that you are His Son. By denying this you deny your own will, and therefore do not know what it is. You must ask what God's Will is in everything, because it is yours. You do not know what it is, but the Holy Spirit remembers it for you. Ask Him, therefore, what God's Will is for you, and He will tell you yours. It cannot be too often repeated that you do not know it. Whenever what the Holy Spirit tells you appears to be coercive, it is only because you have not recognized your will.

The projection of the ego makes it appear as if God's Will is outside yourself, and therefore not yours. In this interpretation it seems possible for God's Will and yours to conflict. God, then, may seem to demand of you what you do not want to give, and thus deprive you of what you want. Would God, Who wants only your will, be capable of this? Your will is His life, which He has given to you. Even in time you cannot live apart from Him. Sleep is not death. What He created can sleep, but cannot die. Immortality is His Will for His Son, and His Son's will for himself. God's Son cannot will death for himself because his Father is life, and His Son is like Him.[38]

The ego guards your prerogative to make decisions that contradict God's Will of Love, which makes you think you actually possess a will separate from God's Will. Your ego illusions of a separate will need to be healed before you can accept that *you are God's Will*. Remembering Jesus helps you to accept God's Will as your own true will, which is the basis of your Identity.

The remembrance of me is the remembrance of yourself, and of Him Who sent me to you.

You were in darkness until God's Will was done completely by any part of the Sonship. When this was done, it was perfectly accomplished by all. How else could it be perfectly accomplished? My mission was simply to unite the will of the Sonship with the Will of the Father by being aware of the Father's Will myself. This is the awareness I came to give you, and your problem in accepting it is the problem of this world. Dispelling it is salvation, and in this sense I *am* the salvation of the world. The world must therefore despise and reject me, because the world *is* the belief that love is impossible. If you will accept the fact that I am with you, you are denying the world and accepting God. My will is His, and your decision to hear me is the decision to hear His Voice and abide in His Will.[39]

It is God's Will for you to wake up from your dreams of separation and to accept your true home in Heaven. This is your true will as well and the will of all your brothers and sisters. According to the Course, the most important lesson Jesus wants you to learn is this:

> *There is no death because the Son of God is like his Father. Nothing you can do can change Eternal Love. Forget your dreams of sin and guilt, and come with me instead to share the resurrection of God's Son. And bring with you all those whom He has sent to you to care for as I care for you.*[40]

Will you learn this lesson that Jesus wants to teach you? Of course, you will. One of the aspects of the Course that I like the most is that it is always affirmative of the inevitability of waking up—not just for some seekers, but for everyone. Why? Because that is indeed what everyone knowingly or unknowingly wants? When you go to sleep at night, you do not question whether or not you will wake up in the morning? Likewise, there is no need to question whether or not you will eventually wake up in the Arms of your loving Father?

Ultimately everyone must remember the Will of God, because ultimately everyone must recognize himself. This recognition is the recognition that his will and God's are one. In the presence of truth, there are no unbelievers and no sacrifices. In the security of reality, fear is totally meaningless. To deny what is can only *seem* to be fearful. Fear cannot be real without a cause, and God is the only

Cause. God is Love and you do want Him. This *is* your will. Ask for this and you will be answered, because you will be asking only for what belongs to you.[41]

---

1. M-23.7:1, p. 59. This is the first reference from the *Manual for Teachers* portion of *A Course in Miracles.*
2. W-41.5:3, 6:1-6, 7:1-4, 8:1-7, pp. 63-64
3. W-44.7:1-5, 9:1-3, 10:1-3, p. 70
4. W-41.9:2-3, p. 64
5. W-44.8:1-3, p. 70
6. W-41.9:1, p. 64
7. W-44.11:1:1-3, p. 70
8. W-183.1:1-5, p. 342
9. W-183.5:1-4, p. 342
10. W-183.6:1-6, 7:1-5, 8:1-5, p. 343
11. W-183.11:1-8, pp. 343-344
12. W-184.10:1-3, 11:1-4, pp. 346-347
13. W-184.12:1, p. 347
14. W-184.12:2-6, 13:1-5, 14:1-5, p. 347
15. M-23.2:4-8, p. 58
16. M-23.3:1-11, p. 58
17. M-23.4:1-7, p. 58
18. C-5.2:1-6, p. 87. This is the first reference from the *Clarification of Terms* portion of *A Course in Miracles.*
19. C-5.3:1-5, 4:1-4, p. 87
20. C-5.5:1-6, pp. 87-88
21. C-5.6:7, p. 88
22. 29. T-4.I.3:1-6, 4:1-7, pp. 53-54
23. T-4.IV.11:1-12, p. 65
24. T-4.IV.9:3-6. 10:1-9, pp. 63-64
25. T-1.III.4:5, p. 8
26. T-5.I.5:1, p. 72
27. T-5.I.6:3-6, p. 72
28. T-1.III.4:1, p. 8
29. T-2.V.5:1-3, pp. 25-26
30. T-1.III.1:1-10, p. 7-8
31. T-1.II.3:5-13, p. 7
32. T-4.I.13:1-7, p. 56
33. T-4.I.6:3, p. 54
34. T-1.I.31:1-3, 32:1-4, 33:1-4, 34:1-3, 35:1, 36:1, 37:1-4, 38:1-3, 39:1-1, 40:1-2, pp. 5-6
35. T-4.VI.6:1-7, 7:1-8, 8:1-6, pp. 68-69
36. T-9.I.1:1-6, 2:1-5, 3:5-8, 4:1-4, 5:3, pp. 160-161
37. T-7.X.6:1-10, 7:1-4, 8:1-6, p. 135
38. T-11.I.8:3-9, 9:1-10, p. 196
39. T-8.IV.2:13, 3:1-9, p. 144
40. C-5.6:9-12, p. 88
41. T-9.I.9:1-9, p. 162

21

MIRACLE LOOKING
AND
OVERLOOKING

≈ ● ≈

A. Holiness and Meditation

A Course in Miracles maintains, "...this course will teach you how to remember what you are, restoring you to your Identity."[1] But there is an obvious problem: You have already come up with your own answer to your identity, and you are wrong. Unless you are willing to let go of your answer, you will not be able to accept the new answer presented to you by the Holy Spirit.

> Would you deny the truth of God's decision, and place your pitiful appraisal of yourself in place of His calm and unswerving value of His Son? Nothing can shake God's conviction of the perfect purity of everything that He created, for it *is* wholly pure. Do not decide against it, for being of Him it must be true.[2]

The Workbook is divided into two aspects: The first aspect primarily deals with helping you to unlearn everything you have taught yourself about who you are. The second aspect is focused on helping you to accept the new truth about yourself, which is a return to what you have always been, but had forgotten.

One of the most harmful false ideas you have systematically taught yourself is that you are not holy. The new thought that you are holy is introduced in the headings of the Workbook Lessons 35 through 39:

> 35. My mind is part of God's. I am very holy.
> 36. My holiness envelops everything I see.
> 37. My holiness blesses the world.
> 38. There is nothing my holiness cannot do.
> 39. My holiness is my salvation.

These five lessons remind you that you are holy and the next lesson, Lesson 40, makes the first direct statement of your Identity, asking you to affirm, "I am blessed as a Son of God." Perhaps you already think of yourself as a Son of God so this would not be a new idea for you. But the Course offers many new ideas about the ramifications of being a Son of God. The most astounding new idea is that because you are a Son of God, you have never lost your holiness. All the thoughts of guilt that you store in your mind are merely fantasies. Here we have the foundation of the Course's message: "God's Son is guiltless."[3]

> Decide that God is right and you are wrong about yourself. He created you out of Himself, but still within Him. He knows what you are. Remember that there is no second to Him. There cannot, therefore, be anyone without His Holiness, nor anyone unworthy of His perfect Love.[4]

The Course affirms that you were created by God, Who gave you all of His Love and all of His Holiness. There is nothing you can do to take away the love and holiness He has given you, in spite of the fact that you have acquired the false belief that you are a sinner. The Course affirms, "Your only calling here is to devote yourself, with active willingness, to the denial of guilt in all its forms."[5] This is what the Course considers the *positive use of denial*. You have already denied your holiness, so the correction is to deny the guilt you have let into your mind.

All of what you have taught yourself is based on the past, including the false lessons you have taught yourself about your guilt. But what can your past learning show you about what you are now? If I ask you to tell me right now if you are convinced that you are sinless, can you answer with conviction, saying, "Yes, I am holy, forever sinless without any stain of guilt." If you cannot answer with this conviction, it is because of what you have taught yourself in the past, which tells you nothing about the present.

> *Your* learning gives the present no meaning at all. Nothing you have ever learned can help you understand the present, or teach you how to undo the past. Your past is what you have taught yourself. *Let* it all go. Do not attempt to understand any event or anything or anyone in its "light," for the darkness in which you try to see can only obscure.[6]

But the question is: "How do I let go of what I have taught myself?" To find the answer, you must understand that your mind is now split into two parts: One is darkness, the home of the ego. The other is light, the home of the Holy Spirit and your own true nature. You are always, indeed every minute and second, choosing either the ego or the Holy Spirit.

> The ego is the choice for guilt; the Holy Spirit the choice for guiltlessness. The power of decision is all that is yours. What you can decide between is fixed, because there are no alternatives except truth and illusion. And there is no overlap between them, because they are opposites which cannot be reconciled and cannot both be true. You are guilty or guiltless, bound or free, unhappy or happy.[7]

Understanding your split mind is the key to letting go of guilt and accepting the truth about your holiness. Psychology uses the specific term "dissociation" to describe the nature of a split mind. The Course gives this definition: "Dissociation is a distorted process of thinking whereby two systems of belief which cannot coexist are both maintained. If they are brought together, their joint acceptance becomes impossible."[8] As long as the ego's thought system of darkness and the Holy Spirit's thought system of light are kept apart, they both can appear real to you. But if you bring these two thought systems together, the fact that they are totally contradictory will become immediately clear. One must be given up because both cannot be accepted as true. Bringing your two thought systems together provides the means of healing your mind of all your beliefs in guilt that are hidden in the dark corners of your mind. Yet you cannot accomplish your own healing through your own efforts. You have already taught yourself to believe in darkness, so you are not qualified to teach yourself how to undo the false image of guilt you have made of yourself. You need the help of the Holy Spirit.

> The Holy Spirit asks of you but this; bring to Him every secret you have locked away from Him. Open every door to Him, and bid Him enter the darkness and lighten it away. At your request He enters gladly. He brings the light to darkness if you make the darkness open to Him. But what you hide He cannot look upon. He sees for you, and unless you look with Him He cannot see. The vision of Christ is not for Him alone, but for Him with you. Bring, therefore, all your dark and secret thoughts to Him, and look upon them with Him. He holds the light, and you the darkness. They cannot coexist when both of You together look on them. His judgment must prevail, and He will give it to you as you join your perception to His.[9]

Joining your mind with the Holy Spirit is your way of out of darkness and into the light. This is true of healing your perceptions in this world of form, just as it is equally true of your destiny to one day fully wake up in His World. You can choose each day to make no decisions alone, asking the Holy Spirit to decide for you. In this process you are joining your will with God's Will that is your own true will. By sharing your view of the world with the Holy Spirit, you will be reminding yourself that you have a shared Identity in which you are forever one with God and with all your brothers and sisters. There is a "holy meeting place" within your mind where God is still in direct communication with His Son. The Holy Spirit provides the communication link between you and the oneness of God.

> Communication between what cannot be divided cannot cease. The holy meeting place of the unseparated Father and His Son lies in the Holy Spirit and in you. All interference in the communication that God Himself wills with His Son is quite impossible here. Unbroken and uninterrupted love flows constantly between the Father and the Son, as Both would have it be. And so it is.... You and your brother may choose to lead yourselves astray, but you can be brought together only by the Guide appointed for you. He will surely lead you to where God and His Son await your recognition. They are joined in giving you the gift of oneness, before which all separation vanishes. Unite with what you are. You cannot join with anything except reality. [10]

Oneness with God Himself is in your mind now, but it is clouded over by what you have taught yourself. This is why the heading of Workbook Lesson 3 says, "I do not understand anything I see...."

Your ego tells you that you do understand what you see, but the ego is the reason why you do not understand. The Course helps the mind to let go of the ego's perspective, which is what you have taught yourself. For example, the Course reminds you to let go of all the thoughts of guilt you have accumulated and to give these false ideas to the Holy Spirit so He can help restore your awareness of holiness. Yet even if you are willing to discard the teachings of the ego, how will you know if you have been successful in replacing the ego's false learning with true learning?

> You have one test, as sure as God, by which to recognize if what you learned is true. If you are wholly free of fear of any kind, and if all those who meet or even think of you share in your perfect peace, then you can be sure that you have learned God's lesson, and not your own. Unless all this is true, there are dark lessons in your mind

that hurt and hinder you, and everyone around you. The absence of perfect peace means but one thing: You think you do not will for God's Son what his Father wills for him. Every dark lesson teaches this, in one form or another. And each bright lesson with which the Holy Spirit will replace the dark ones you do not accept, teaches you that you will with the Father and His Son.

Do not be concerned about how you can learn a lesson so completely different from everything that you have taught yourself. How would you know? Your part is very simple. You need only recognize that everything you learned you do not want. Ask to be taught, and do not use your experiences to confirm what you have learned.[11]

The Course is saying that if you are able to replace the ego's thought system with a new thought system taught by the Holy Spirit, the result is that you will find peace of mind and others will even perceive this peace in you. But what does all this have to do meditation, since that is the topic of this book? Meditation, as recommended in the Course, is one of the tools you can use to change your mind about yourself and to find peace of mind. Just as the Course itself is generally a two-part process of undoing what you have taught yourself and accepting the oneness within you that is forever true, meditation follows this same two-part process. The undoing portion of meditation is the letting go of all the stray thoughts that you have taught your mind. The acceptance portion is symbolized by your affirmation in which you accept words, such as the Divine Name, that represent the truth. During meditation when you let go of your affirmation, you are accepting the truth itself beyond the words. Your affirmation reminds you of your holiness and then releasing your affirmation lets you experience the holiness forever within you. In this experience you have communion with God, Who is the source of your holiness. Thus meditation is the undoing of guilt and the acceptance of holiness, which in turn brings peace of mind.

Meditation, as a purifying of the mind, is often compared with the idea of cleansing a mirror so that the mirror can provide the clearest divine reflection. The quotation below does not speak directly of meditation, yet it appears to be indirectly talking about the meditation process.

The Presence of Holiness lives in everything that lives, for Holiness created life, and leaves not what It created holy as Itself.

In this world you can become a spotless mirror, in which the Holiness of your Creator shines forth from you to all around you. You can reflect Heaven here. Yet no reflections of the images of other gods must dim the mirror that would hold God's reflection in it. Earth can reflect Heaven or hell; God or the ego. You need but leave the mirror clean and clear of all the images of hidden darkness [meaning guilt] you have drawn upon it. God will shine upon it of Himself. Only the clear reflection of Himself can be perceived upon it.

Reflections are seen in light. In darkness they are obscure, and their meaning seems to lie only in shifting interpretations, rather than in themselves. The reflection of God needs no interpretation. It is clear. Clean but the mirror, and the message that shines forth from what the mirror holds out for everyone to see, no one can fail to understand.[12]

I have previously quoted the Course idea that you are always choosing between the ego and the Holy Spirit and that this means you are also choosing between your imagined guilt and your true holiness. The quotation below and the next section discuss the *miracle*, which tells you if you have chosen wisely:

The miracle teaches you that you have chosen guiltlessness, freedom and joy. It is not a cause, but an effect. It is the natural result of choosing right, attesting to your happiness that comes from choosing to be free of guilt.[13]

B. Meditation Related to Miracles

Typically miracles are thought of as extraordinary and rare events because that is how they are presented in the Bible. But according to the Course, "Miracles are natural. When they do not occur something has gone wrong."[14] The first chapter of the Course gives fifty descriptions of a miracle, which are reminders that anyone can perform miracles. For example, the third description states, "Miracles occur naturally as expressions of love. The real miracle is the love that inspires them. In this sense everything that comes from love is a miracle."[15] The fiftieth description states, "The miracle compares what you have made with creation, accepting what is in accord with it as true, and rejecting what is out of accord as false."[16] In the Course false perceptions represent your thoughts that reflect your ego; true perceptions are reflections of your true divine nature in God. A miracle is considered a change in your perception in which a false perception is replaced by a true perception.

The Course encourages you to perform miracles of love with the aid of the Holy Spirit. The idea is to replace your ego orientation with a new awareness based on the fact that you are like your Father, Who created you like Himself. To help you change your perception of yourself based on the ego, the Course teaches you how to calm your mind and welcome the miracle, since: "The miracle comes quietly into the mind that stops an instant and is still."[17] To help you learn how to calm your mind, often a Workbook lesson will ask you to repeat the title of the lesson as your affirmation for the day. Sometimes a lesson will ask you to ponder thoughts related to the affirmation for the day. For instance, Lesson 67, "Love created me like Itself," has the following instructions:

> In the longer practice period, we will think about your reality and its wholly unchanged and unchangeable nature. We will begin by repeating this truth about you, and then spend a few minutes adding some relevant thoughts, such as:
>
> > *Holiness created me holy.*
> > *Kindness created me kind.*
> > *Helpfulness created me helpful.*
> > *Perfection created me perfect.*
>
> Any attribute which is in accord with God as He defines Himself is appropriate for use. We are trying today to undo your definition of God and replace it with His Own. We are also trying to emphasize that you are part of His definition of Himself.[18]

Following this review of thoughts associated with the idea that "Love created you like Itself," this lesson advises you to practice meditation by letting go of all your thoughts about yourself so you can approach experiencing the reality of the divine within.

> After you have gone over several such related thoughts, try to let all thoughts drop away for a brief preparatory interval, and then try to reach past all your images and preconceptions about yourself to the truth in you. If love created you like itself, this Self must be in you. And somewhere in your mind It is there for you to find.
> You may find it necessary to repeat the idea for today from time to time to replace distracting thoughts. You may also find that this is not sufficient, and that you need to continue adding other thoughts related to the truth about yourself. Yet perhaps you will succeed in going past that, and through the interval of thoughtlessness to the awareness of a blazing light in which you recognize yourself as love

created you. Be confident that you will do much today to bring that awareness nearer, whether you feel you have succeeded or not. [19]

In addition to setting aside a time for meditation only, the Course often asks you to repeat the main idea of the lesson throughout the day. This repetition brings the Workbook lesson into your daily life and is necessary because our negative programming about yourself is so persistent that you need constant reminders of our true divine nature that is hidden within you. This remembering of the inner truth is only partially up to you because you have help within. The Holy Spirit, called the "Voice for God" in the Course, is constantly whispering to you that you are God's Son and like your Father Who created you.

> It will be particularly helpful today to practice the idea for the day as often as you can. You need to hear the truth about yourself as frequently as possible, because your mind is so preoccupied with false self-images. Four or five times an hour, and perhaps even more, it would be most beneficial to remind yourself that love created you like itself. Hear the truth about yourself in this.
>
> Try to realize in the shorter practice periods that this is not your tiny, solitary voice that tells you this. This is the Voice for God, reminding you of your Father and of your Self. This is the Voice of truth, replacing everything that the ego tells you about yourself with the simple truth about the Son of God. You were created by love like itself.[20]

C. Meditation and Forgiveness are Interrelated

One of the distinctive features of the Course is how it uses familiar words but then gives them new meanings, different from the traditional understanding. The best example of this giving of words a new meaning is the word "forgiveness." The main message of the Course is forgiveness, identified as "true forgiveness," in contrast to the generally accepted idea of forgiveness. If you forgive your brother while still resenting him, you are not truly forgiving him. In the Course forgiveness applies not only to a situation in which it appears you have been wronged. Forgiveness is a practice that can be applied to all your interactions. When you see your brother, he appears to be a body, and you judge his appearance. You also make judgments on his personality and ego characteristics. These judgments are actually your grievances because they separate you from your brother. Forgiveness is defined in the Course as "the healing of the perception of separation."[21] Through forgiveness you join with your brother and realize he and you are equals in Christ. The added benefit is that by seeing the divine in your brother, you will increase your belief that the divine is in you too.

Forgiveness is the practice of letting go of your grievances, which are your judgments of your brother, by looking past them and seeing the divine in him. You are replacing false perceptions of your brother with true perceptions that reflect the Christ in him. Since a miracle is a change from false perceptions to true perceptions, forgiveness is the manifestation of miracles that replace your grievances. In the miracle of forgiveness a loving exchange occurs, which you may not fully comprehend at the time. In this exchange you send light and love to your brother and in gratitude your brother sends light and love to you. This miracle of forgiveness is an inner spiritual celebration in which you each acquire a loving awareness of your brother and loving awareness of yourself.

Besides giving new meanings to familiar words, the Course also has the unique characteristic of demonstrating that spiritual concepts are not defined by showing how different they are. Instead, spiritual ideas are identified by their interrelationships and by how they consistently lead in the same direction toward oneness. This interrelating of concepts with a common purpose is elaborated upon in the final chapter, but here let's look at the unusual interrelationship between the concepts of forgiveness and meditation.

Forgiveness and meditation are normally considered to be separate and very different ideas. Forgiveness seems to be about giving others a gift of your mercy, rather than being a means of internal healing of your own mind. Yet the Course sees forgiveness as a way of turning your mind toward oneness. Meditation appears to be a solitary activity of seeking God. A section below is titled "Meditation is a Collaborative Venture" to explain how meditation is not in fact a solitary practice. Meditation in the Course is a way of training your mind to join with your brothers and sisters and to move together in the direction of oneness.

Thus both forgiveness and meditation help you grow toward the common goal of oneness, but are they really distinctly different ways of seeking oneness? No, they seek oneness in the same way. *Forgiveness is meditation applied outwardly toward others.* Meditation is the mental holding of one thought of the divine in the mind and the letting go all other distracting thoughts. In practicing forgiveness, just as in practicing meditation, you are letting go of distracting thoughts by overlooking all your judgments against the person you are forgiving. Likewise, you are holding the one thought of looking for the divine in the person you are forgiving, similar to the way you hold on to the one thought of seeing the divine within yourself in practicing meditation.

Forgiveness and meditation have a reciprocal relationship. Since forgiveness is meditation applied outwardly, the inverse is equally true: *Meditation is forgiveness applied inwardly toward yourself.* When you forgive your brother by letting go of your grievances, you are helping your brother to heal his mind and simultaneously helping to heal your own mind. Your forgiveness of others is really a means of forgiving yourself. Yet this process of forgiving yourself can also be done directly by the inner practices of meditation. After all, when you go within you are letting go of distracting thoughts and judgments. You are attempting to go past these distractions, which are inner grievances that you are holding against yourself. These grievances hide your true nature. Just as you can see the divine in your brother by letting go of grievances, you can apply forgiveness toward yourself by looking past your inner grievances to find the divine within.

Let's consider Workbook Lesson 69, "My grievances hide the light of the world in me." Here the grievances of your mind are symbolized by dark clouds that you can visualize. The clouds seem to be the only reality, but you focus on moving past them to the light that is the true reality that you seek. You remind yourself how significant what you are doing is as you are motivated to find the light beyond the clouds. You can be confident that the clouds can have no power to stop you. Like practicing forgiveness, you meditate by looking past grievances to the light.

> From where you stand, you can see no reason to believe there is a brilliant light hidden by the clouds. The clouds seem to be the only reality. They seem to be all there is to see. Therefore, you do not attempt to go through them and past them, which is the only way in which you would be really convinced of their lack of substance. We will make this attempt today.
>
> After you have thought about the importance of what you are trying to do for yourself and the world, try to settle down in perfect stillness, remembering only how much you want to reach the light in you today,—now! Determine to go past the clouds. Reach out and touch them in your mind. Brush them aside with your hand; feel them resting on your cheeks and forehead and eyelids as you go through them. Go on; clouds cannot stop you.[22]

In this practice you are putting forward a conscious effort, but you are not relying entirely on your own ability. Rather, you can rest assured through faith that God has the power to help you succeed and He will surely guide you to find the light as long as your will is joined with His.

If you are doing the exercises properly, you will begin to feel a sense of being lifted up and carried ahead. Your little effort and small determination call on the power of the universe to help you, and God Himself will raise you from darkness into light. You are in accord with His Will. You cannot fail because your will is His.

Have confidence in your Father today, and be certain that He has heard you and answered you. You may not recognize His answer yet, but you can indeed be sure that it is given you and you will yet receive it. Try, as you attempt to go through the clouds to the light, to hold this confidence in your mind. Try to remember that you are at last joining your will to God's. Try to keep the thought clearly in mind that what you undertake with God must succeed. Then let the power of God work in you and through you, that His Will and yours be done.[23]

D. The Practice of Looking and Overlooking

When I first practiced the Workbook lessons for my own growth, I had to set aside more advanced meditation techniques I had learned in order to follow the instructions of the Course. I felt it was important to do *every* lesson in sequence for the 365 days of the year to complete the Workbook. I assumed that visualization methods were included in the first half of the Workbook because these would be easy for beginning meditators to practice. Yet I still wondered why an image of mental distractions, such as dark clouds, was necessary. I was relieved to see these mental images were eliminated in the later Workbook lessons.

Later I realized that there is a symbol of clouds because the Course does not want the meditator to focus on the many different distracting thoughts themselves because this would make those distractions seem real, when they are just illusions of the mind. Therefore, the clouds serve as a neutral symbol to represent in one image all those illusions that are obstacles to finding the light. Then eventually even that one image, which stands for all illusions, can be dispensed with as is the case in later Workbook lessons. From this I understood that there is one particular approach to meditation that can be found in *every* Workbook lesson on inner seeking. It's what I call *looking and overlooking*, which is another way of describing forgiveness, as well as meditation. "Looking" is the end and "overlooking" is the means to that end. The "looking" aspect is your *intention* to find what you are seeking. Your intention is to find the divine called by many different names—light, peace, God, Christ, or some other goal that represents the one reality. In contrast to "looking" that requires your total involvement in what you want, "overlooking" requires you to

have no involvement in what you do not want. "Overlooking" allows
you to look *past* your illusions, instead of looking *at* your illusions.

> Then try to sink into your mind, letting go every kind of interference
> and intrusion by quietly sinking past them. Your mind cannot be
> stopped in this unless you choose to stop it. It is merely taking
> its natural course. Try to observe your passing thoughts without
> involvement, and slip quietly by them.... [24]

If you think the clouds are real, "...you do not attempt to go through
them and past them, which is the only way in which you would really be
convinced of their lack of substance." Workbook Lesson 69 reassures
you that the clouds are indeed unreal and have no power to stop
you. But you must be determined with your overlooking to go past the
clouds and be equally determined with your intention of looking to find
the light beyond them, with the confidence that God Himself is actively
helping you.

This pattern of looking and overlooking is applicable to meditation
methods that use visualization. But it applies equally to methods in the
Course without visualization since there will always be distracting and
illusory thoughts present in the mind and there will always be the divine
reality within that is hidden by these illusions. You can give illusions a
reality they do not have by paying attention to them. Your preoccupation
with illusions gives them a meaning they do not possess, since illusions
are essentially meaningless. Instead of being concerned with illusions,
you can simply practice overlooking them with detachment.

The practice of looking and overlooking applies to inwardly forgiving
your own mind in meditation, but applies equally to outwardly forgiving
others and thus indirectly forgiving yourself. When you forgive, your
practice of looking consists of your intention to correctly perceive and
accept the reality of the divine in your brother. Your practice of overlooking
in forgiveness is the dispelling of your judgments that are the false
perceptions you have laid upon your brother. Dispelling your judgments
cannot be accomplished by pondering them, but rather by letting your
mind slip quietly past them just as you let go of distracting thoughts in
meditation. If you become preoccupied with your judgments, they will seem
real to you and you will not be able to slip past them.

> To forgive is to overlook. Look, then, beyond error and do not
> let your perception rest upon it, for you will believe what your
> perception holds. Accept as true only what your brother is, if you
> would know yourself. Perceive what he is not and you cannot know

what you are, because you see him falsely. Remember always that your Identity is shared, and that Its sharing is Its reality.[25]

E. The Fear of Looking Within

The previous section emphasized that forgiveness is accomplished through looking and overlooking outwardly and meditation is facilitated by looking and overlooking inwardly. The application of looking and overlooking depends upon the use of Christ's vision in which the seeker receives the grace of Christ and of the Holy Spirit to replace physical vision with spiritual vision. *Forgiveness uses Christ's vision applied outwardly. Meditation uses Christ's vision applied inwardly.*

Meditation is defined in yoga as the holding of one thought in the mind continuously. Using the viewpoint of the Course, meditation may be considered as any form of inward seeking that involves focusing of the mind on the divine and only on the divine and ignoring everything else. One way the Course advocates this inner focusing is related to accepting the Atonement by placing it on the nonphysical altar of God within, where it belongs. "The Atonement is the only gift that is worthy of being offered at the altar of God, because of the value of the altar itself."[26] The altar of God is the "holy of holies" within you where you regain the awareness of your own holiness in God.

> The Atonement offers you God. The gift that you refused is held by Him in you. The Holy Spirit holds it there for you. God has not left His altar, though His worshippers placed other gods upon it. The temple still is holy, for the Presence that dwells within it *is* Holiness.
>
> In the temple, Holiness waits quietly for the return of them that love it. The Presence knows they will return to purity and to grace. The graciousness of God will take them gently in, and cover all their sense of pain and loss with the immortal assurance of their Father's Love. There, fear of death will be replaced with joy of life. For God is life, and they abide in life. Life is as holy as the Holiness by which it was created. The Presence of Holiness lives in everything that lives, for Holiness created life, and leaves not what It created holy as Itself.[27]

Accepting the Atonement at the inner altar, even for only an instant, enables you to perform miracles of love that extend to your brothers and sisters. This acceptance of Atonement overcomes fear.

For perfect effectiveness the Atonement belongs at the center of the inner altar, where it undoes the separation and restores the wholeness of the mind. Before the separation the mind was invulnerable to fear, because fear did not exist. Both the separation and the fear are miscreations that must be undone for the restoration of the temple, and for the opening of the altar to receive the Atonement. This heals the separation by placing within you the one effective defense against all separation thoughts and making you perfectly invulnerable.[28]

Placing the Atonement at the center of the altar of God is achieved by meditation employing Christ's vision that overlooks past errors and looks within at the inner altar. "If you would look within you would see only the Atonement, shining in quiet and in peace upon the altar to your Father."[29] The quotation below states that Christ's vision reveals the inner "altar has been defiled and needs repair." The altar is not defiled by sin, but it is defiled by your belief in sin, and this belief needs to be released along with the fear it brings.

Spiritual vision literally cannot see error, and merely looks for Atonement. All solutions the physical eye seeks dissolve. Spiritual vision looks within and recognizes immediately that the altar has been defiled and needs to be repaired and protected. Perfectly aware of the right defense it passes over all others, looking past error to truth. Because of the strength of its vision, it brings the mind into its service. This re-establishes the power of the mind and makes it increasingly unable to tolerate delay, realizing that it only adds unnecessary pain.[30]

The looking within of meditation sounds like an easy process, but it is very difficult for beginners. Even beginners may have very advanced skills of focusing the mind in all kinds of outer activities, but often this ability does not immediately transfer to the inner process of meditation. According to the Course, the problem is related to the fear to look within. "The Holy Spirit will never teach you that you are sinful. Errors He will correct, but this makes no one fearful. You are indeed afraid to look within and see the sin you think is there.[31]

If you are afraid to look within, it is because you are listening to the ego. "Loudly the ego tells you not to look inward, for if you do your eyes will light on sin, and God will strike you blind. This you believe, and so you do not look."[32] But below this fear is a deeper fear the ego does not want you to uncover because it would call to question your belief in the ego itself. This deeper fear is expressed in the Course in this way:

> What if you looked within and saw no sin? This "fearful" question is one the ego never asks. And you who ask it now are threatening the ego's whole defensive system too seriously for it to bother to pretend it is your friend. Those who have joined their brothers have detached themselves from their belief that their identity lies in the ego.[33]

To overcome the fear to look within requires releasing the belief in guilt that is the companion of the belief in sin. "As long as you believe that guilt is justified in any way, in anyone, whatever he may do, you will not look within, where you would always find Atonement."[34] When you release the seeing of guilt in your brother, you will also release your fear of looking within, and you will be able to accept the light, love, and holiness within that are aspects of your true nature in God.

> Release from guilt as you would be released. There is no other way to look within and see the light of love, shining as steadily and as surely as God Himself has always loved His Son. *And as His Son loves Him.* There is no fear in love, for love is guiltless. You who have always loved your Father can have no fear, for any reason, to look within and see your holiness. You cannot be as you believed you were. Your guilt is without reason because it is not in the Mind of God, where you are.[35]

Due to the emphasis in the Course on forgiveness, many students mistakenly think that there is no real need to look within. Yet Jesus, as the true Author dictating the Course, wants you to overcome your fear to look within and to see Him. The altar within is the "holy meeting place" where you can meet and have communion with God, Christ, Jesus, and all your other brothers in the Sonship.

> When you look within and see me [Jesus], it will be because you have decided to manifest truth. And as you manifest it you will see it both without and within. You will see it without *because* you saw it first within. Everything you behold without is a judgment of what you beheld within.[36]

Seeing Jesus does not mean using any physical sight. It does mean perceiving the divine presence, which can be experienced as an inner feeling. But you will not be able to perceive the divine presence within if you allow your fear to get in the way. Whatever you see outside of yourself will be the result of what you see within. Perceiving the divine within will help you in your practice of forgiveness, enabling you to see holiness outwardly in your brother.

> You are afraid of me [Jesus] because you looked within and are afraid of what you saw. Yet you could not have seen reality, for the reality of your mind is the loveliest of God's creations. Coming only from God, its power and grandeur could only bring you peace *if you really looked upon it*. If you are afraid, it is because you saw something that is not there. Yet in that same place you could have looked upon me and all your brothers, in the perfect safety of the Mind which created us. For we are there in the peace of the Father, Who wills to extend His peace through you.[37]

You must decide that you want to perceive the divine within, and this decision can be part of your dedication in prayer before meditating. Then when you look within in your meditation, you can hold on to the one thought of seeking the divine, which is your intention.

> The power of decision is your one remaining freedom as a prisoner of this world. You can decide to see it right. What you made of it is not its reality, for its reality is only what you give it. You cannot really give anything but love to anyone or anything, nor can you really receive anything but love from them. If you think you have received anything else, it is because you have looked within and thought you saw the power to give something else within yourself. It was only this decision that determined what you found, for it was the decision for what you sought.[38]

In addition to deciding that you want to see the divine within, you must also decide to let go of fear. You made your fear, so your fear must be self-controlled. "Fear cannot be controlled by me [Jesus], but it can be self-controlled. Fear prevents me from giving you my control."[39] You can control your fear through your decision and by exerting your will. Workbook Lesson 309 encourages you to express this decision by affirming, "I will not fear to look within today." As you control your fear and practice meditation, you will discover that the sin and guilt you feared is gone. "Look, then, upon the light He [God] placed within you, and learn that what you feared was there has been replaced with love."[40] You are responsible for controlling your own fear, but you are not alone in your practice of looking within because you can rely on the vision that Christ and the Holy Spirit give to you. Once you overcome the fear to look within, your practice of meditation using Christ's vision will not be difficult for you. "It is not difficult to look within, for there all vision starts."[41]

Certainly forgiveness, in which you see the divine outside yourself, is the primary spiritual practice advocated in the Course. Nevertheless, the Course wants you to look within as a compliment to forgiveness. This is because what you see outside yourself in practicing forgiveness will depend upon your decision about what you want to see when you look within. It will also depend upon what you do in fact see within when you practice meditation, thus overcoming your fear to look within. The Course obviously encourages the practice of meditation, yet the following section explains why many Course students unfortunately do not appreciate the value of meditation.

F. The Kind of Meditation Not Recommended

The section above mentions that because the main message of the Course is forgiveness, some seekers believe that the looking within of meditation is unnecessary. Now let's take a much closer look at this misinterpretation of the Course. In addition to many Workbook lessons that describe specific meditation techniques, the *Manual for Teachers*, the third part of the Course, emphasizes the importance of meditation. Teachers of God are students who have read the Text and Manual and have also completed the one year of doing the Workbook lessons. The Manual advises having a "quiet time" devoted to God every morning and evening, as follows:

> It may be that the teacher of God is not in a situation that fosters quiet thought as he awakes. If this is so, let him but remember that he chooses to spend time with God as soon as possible, and let him do so. Duration is not the major concern. One can easily sit still an hour with closed eyes and accomplish nothing. One can as easily give God only an instant, and in that instant join with Him completely. Perhaps the one generalization that can be made is this; as soon as possible after waking take your quiet time, continuing a minute or two after you begin to find it difficult. You may find that the difficulty will diminish and drop away. If not, that is the time to stop.
>
> The same procedures should be followed at night. Perhaps your quiet time should be fairly early in the evening, if it is not feasible for

you to take it just before going to sleep. It is not wise to lie down for it. It is better to sit up, in whatever position you prefer. Having gone through the workbook, you must have come to some conclusions in this respect. If possible, however, just before going to sleep is a desirable time to devote to God. It sets your mind into a pattern of rest, and orients you away from fear. If it is expedient to spend this time earlier, at least be sure that you do not forget a brief period,—not more than a moment will do,—in which you close your eyes and think of God.[42]

No one specific meditation method is recommended for the daily quiet times. It is obvious that the Workbook lessons offer a variety of techniques that lead in the direction of experiencing the divine presence. The Course seems to be saying that any technique will be sufficient. But there is a type of meditation that is not recommended in the Course. The kind of meditation that reinforces a sense of sinfulness is an attempt to reach God while simultaneously feeling you are unworthy of Him. This approach is difficult because it does not affirm your true nature and worthiness. It is an attempt to make yourself holy while thinking you are basically unholy. This way of seeking God can succeed eventually because of your sincerity and determination over many years, but the Course instead recommends methods that affirm your worthiness. You do not need to do anything to make yourself worthy of God, since He has already created you holy. This is explained in the Text in the section titled, "I need do nothing."

> It is extremely difficult to reach Atonement [God's Plan for your Salvation] by fighting against sin. Enormous effort is expended in the attempt to make holy what is hated and despised. Nor is a lifetime of contemplation and long periods of meditation aimed at detachment from the body necessary. All such attempts will ultimately succeed because of their purpose. Yet the means are tedious and very time consuming, for all of them look to the future for release from a state of present unworthiness and inadequacy.[43]

This section is misunderstood by some Course students because they assume it means that any form of meditation is not helpful. Yet it is only referring to forms of meditation that affirm sinfulness rather than holiness. An example of this type of meditation focused on sin is the long form of the Jesus Prayer, "Lord Jesus Christ, have mercy on me a sinner." The Course has no problem with the short form of the Jesus Prayer that consists of the Name of Jesus Christ alone, but this longer version is too much of a reinforcement of sin and unworthiness to accelerate spiritual growth.

The Son of God can be mistaken; he can deceive himself; he can even turn the power of his mind against himself. But he *cannot* sin. There is nothing he can do that would really change his reality in any way, nor make him really guilty. That is what sin would do, for such is its purpose. Yet for all the wild insanity inherent in the whole idea of sin, it is impossible. For the wages of sin *is* death, and how can the immortal die?[44]

The Course statement "I need do nothing" does not mean you do not have to do any meditation as part of your mind training. It merely means that you do not have to do anything to make yourself worthy of God, especially considering that right now you are already part of God and His holiness is the Source of your holiness. Also, it is clear from the context of this section that the Course is offering an alternative to the tediousness of methods that remind you of sinfulness that has no basis in reality.

To do anything involves the body. And if you recognize you need do nothing, you have withdrawn the body's value from your mind. Here is the quick and open door through which you slip past centuries of effort, and escape from time. This is the way in which sin loses all attraction *right now.* For here is time denied, and past and future gone. Who needs do nothing has no need for time. To do nothing is to rest, and make a place within you where the activity of the body ceases to demand attention. Into this place the Holy Spirit comes, and there abides. He will remain when you forget, and the body's activities return to occupy your conscious mind.
Yet there will always be this place of rest to which you can return. And you will be more aware of this quiet center of the storm than all its raging activity. This quiet center, in which you do nothing, will remain with you, giving you rest in the midst of every busy doing on which you are sent. For from this center will you be directed how to use the body sinlessly. It is this center, from which the body is absent, that will keep it so in your awareness of it.[45]

Since all doing involves the body, when you do nothing, you can find the place of rest within you where the Holy Spirit abides. To do nothing means finding this "quiet center, in which you do nothing." This quiet center of rest can be found now instead of using long and tedious methods that involve years of seeking future release from present unworthiness. In fact, this quiet center can be found in an instant, so finding it is called the *holy instant,* which is described in Chapter 22.

Some early lessons of the Workbook obviously teach the practice of meditation, although the word "meditation" is not specifically stated. Then Lesson 124 does use the word "meditation" and explains how valuable this practice is by saying, "no time was ever better spent." Early lessons focus on specific techniques. Later lessons are less about the form of the method and more about simply holding your intention to awaken your awareness of divine oneness without using words, except to counteract distracting thoughts.

> Sometime today, whenever it seems best, devote a half an hour to the thought that you are one with God. This is our first attempt at an extended period for which we give no rules nor special words to guide your meditation. We will trust God's Voice to speak as He sees fit today, certain He will not fail. Abide with Him this half an hour. He will do the rest....
>
> Perhaps today, perhaps tomorrow, you will see your own transfiguration in the glass this holy half an hour will hold out to you, to look upon yourself. When you are ready you will find it there, within your mind and waiting to be found. You will remember then the thought to which you gave this half an hour, thankfully aware no time was ever better spent.[46]

G. Meditation is a Collaborative Venture

No path to God can be complete if it is a solitary path that excludes your brothers. Meditation is not the solitary practice that it appears to be and the goal of meditation is not an individual goal. I was not able to fully appreciate the significance of this awareness until I had studied the Course and practiced its principles in my daily life. One of the main reasons why the Course is emphasized in this manual is because it presents meditation and spiritual growth in general as a *joint venture*, in which God and the entire Sonship are collaborating.

When Helen Schucman was recording the Course as it was dictated to her by Jesus, she was assisted by her friend, Bill Thetford, so the Course itself was the result of a joint venture. Both Helen and Bill practiced meditation in the early dictation of the Course, and Jesus cautioned them regarding viewing meditation as a solitary spiritual activity. The following quotation from *Absence From Felicity* was part of this early dictation received by Helen. In this quotation Jesus commented to Bill regarding his practice of traditional meditation in which each day at a specific time he emptied his mind of all thoughts to become inwardly silent:

Your [Bill's] giant step forward was to *insist* on a collaborative venture. This does not go against the true spirit of meditation at all. It is inherent *in* it. Meditation is a collaborative venture with God. It *cannot* be undertaken successfully by those who disengage themselves from the Sonship....[47]

Some early parts of the dictation, in which Helen and Bill were addressed directly by Jesus, were altered so that the Course as a whole would be addressed to all seekers. The above quotation made its way into the Course in an altered manner in which the first usage of the word "meditation" was omitted altogether and the second reference to the word "meditation" was changed to the word "salvation," stated as follows:

Salvation is a collaborative venture. It cannot be undertaken successfully by those who disengage themselves from the Sonship....[48]

In fact, salvation does have a collaborative nature as is stated in the current version of this quotation, but the original version referred to the collaborative nature of meditation. The editing process of the Course resulted in taking out the names of Helen and Bill so that the reader would be able to generalize the teachings to all people. That editing direction seems warranted. But deleting the word "meditation" and replacing it with the word "salvation" was unwarranted and a mistake. The fact that salvation is a joint venture of the Sonship is mentioned elsewhere in the Course, so there was no need to insert that idea here. Yet there was a need to faithfully document the word "meditation" that was intended by Jesus. It is unfortunate the meaning of Jesus's dictation was distorted in this way. The original words of Jesus included a new definition of the "true spirit of meditation" as inherently a joining with God and the Sonship. The idea that true meditation "cannot be undertaken successfully by those who disengage themselves from the Sonship" was dictated by Jesus as a correction of the idea of isolation that is inherent in the old concept of meditation. If the original version of the new definition of the "true spirit of meditation" had been included in the Course, it may have prevented some misinterpretations of the value of meditation. Including the new definition from Jesus would have alerted Course students to the fact that meditation is helpful as a means of joining with others, as long as it is practiced without reinforcing the belief in sin and separation.

The original meaning of the quotation directed by Jesus to Bill indicated that meditation is a good practice if its purpose is properly understood as a way of joining with God *and* joining with your brothers. Combining meditation with relationships is not an alteration of meditation but rather its true purpose. Meditating with a sense of being isolated from the rest of the Sonship defeats its purpose and will not succeed. If you separate yourself from the Sonship, you separate yourself from God. If you draw closer to the Sonship, you draw closer to God. As was mentioned above, meditation is a looking within to the holy meeting place, the altar of God. However, consider this: "No altar stands to God without His Son."[49] Consequently, you cannot seek and find God without seeking and finding all of His creations, which are a part of Him located at His altar.

> In the holy meeting place are joined the Father and His creations, and the creations of His Son with Them together. There is one link that joins Them all together, holding Them in the oneness out of which creation happens.
>   The link with which the Father joins Himself to those He gives the power to create can never be dissolved. Heaven itself is union with all of creation, and with its one Creator. And Heaven remains the Will of God for you. Lay no gifts other than this upon your altars, for nothing can coexist with it. Here your little offerings are brought together with the gift of God, and only what is worthy of the Father will be accepted by the Son, for whom it is intended. To whom God gives Himself, He *is* given. Your little gifts will vanish on the altar, where He has placed His Own.[50]

The purpose of meditation is union with God *and* with the Sonship, of which you are a part. The ultimate goal of meditation is for you to find your true place in the Sonship, which is united with God. It is your relationship in the Sonship that *is* your union with God. This idea that Jesus expressed to Bill directly about the value of balancing meditation and relationships is an important concept in regard to spiritual growth.

H. Faith and Solving Problems

Chapter 2 describes the importance of having faith in God to practice meditation successfully. But the Course maintains there is another kind of faith that is just as significant as trusting that God is within you as the source of your true Identity. This other faith is your trust in the divine within your brothers and sisters. Obviously this type of faith is necessary to practice forgiveness in which you look for the divine in others and you overlook the outer appearances and errors of others. Faith enables you to accept God's Plan called the Atonement and to heal others with your forgiving eyes.

To have faith is to heal. It is the sign that you have accepted the Atonement for yourself, and would therefore share it. By faith, you offer the gift of freedom from the past, which you received. You do not use anything your brother has done before to condemn him now. You freely choose to overlook his errors, looking past all barriers between yourself and him, and seeing them as one. And in that one you see your faith is fully justified. There is no justification for faithlessness, but faith is always justified.

Faith is the opposite of fear, as much a part of love as fear is of attack. Faith is the acknowledgment of union. It is the gracious acknowledgment of everyone as a Son of your most loving Father, loved by Him like you, and therefore loved by you as yourself. It is His Love that joins you and your brother, and for His Love you would keep no one separate from yours. Each one appears just as he is perceived in the holy instant, united in your purpose to be released from guilt. You see the Christ in him, and he is healed because you look on what makes faith forever justified in everyone.

Faith is the gift of God, through Him Whom God has given you. Faithlessness looks upon the Son of God, and judges him unworthy of forgiveness. But through the eyes of faith, the Son of God is seen already forgiven, free of all the guilt he laid upon himself. Faith sees him only *now* because it looks not to the past to judge him, but would see in him only what it would see in you. It sees not through the body's eyes, nor looks to bodies for its justification.[51]

Faith in your brothers and sisters enables you to solve problems since you are investing in true forgiveness rather than letting the ego be your guide to solving problems. Chapter 19 explains two methods of problem solving. One of these is Expressive Problem Solving, which involves a careful analysis of your problem, including examining the errors of others and your own errors. This method recommends forgiveness, but would not be compatible with the Course because a detailed observation of errors makes them appear to be real. Once you have given reality to errors, you cannot overlook them. Some people who have an analytical nature will find Expressive Problem Solving to be helpful, but the Course would describe this method as the "ego's plan for forgiveness" in this way:

The ego's plan, of course, makes no sense and will not work. By following its plan you will merely place yourself in an impossible situation, to which the ego always leads you. The ego's plan is to have you see error clearly first, and then overlook it. Yet how can you overlook what you have made real? By seeing it clearly, you have made it real and *cannot* overlook it.[52]

The other approach to problem solving described in Chapter 19 is Receptive Problem Solving. This method only requires acknowledging that there is a problem, but does not include analyzing that problem. The three steps of this technique are meditation, prayer, and the solution as the result. The idea is to let go of the problem and let God's Love solve it. After all, God has no problems and so He can resolve your problems. This method is compatible with the Course because you are looking to divine love for the solution and the errors involved in the problem are overlooked thus true forgiveness can take place.

However, the Course goes a step deeper in regard to problem solving by affirming that the many problems you seem to have are really only one problem and that single problem has already been solved for you.

> The problem of separation, which is really the only problem, has already been solved. Yet the solution is not recognized because the problem is not recognized.
>
> Everyone in this world seems to have his own special problems. Yet they are all the same, and must be recognized as one if the one solution that solves them all is to be accepted.[53]

The ego tempts you to believe you have numerous special problems that you will encounter on an ongoing basis, but the Course maintains this is the nature of illusions. The complexity of the illusions you see in the world of form convince you that your problems are endless, but all illusions are really the same single illusion. This single illusion is the false belief in separation—the idea that you are separate from God and separate from your brothers and sisters. This single problem of the apparent separation has already been solved for you by God, by the Holy Spirit, and by Jesus. Although you do not have to solve this problem yourself, you do have to recognize that your single problem has already been resolved for you.

> If you are willing to recognize your problems, you will recognize that you have no problems. Your one central problem has been answered, and you have no other. Therefore, you must be at peace. Salvation thus depends on recognizing this one problem, and understanding that it has been solved. One problem, one solution. Salvation is accomplished. Freedom from conflict has been given you. Accept that fact, and you are ready to take your rightful place in God's plan for salvation. [54]

The Course maintains that the problem of separation—your only problem—was solved immediately by God Who created the Holy Spirit as the Answer to all separation by placing Him in every mind that imagined it had separated from the divine Source in God. With your recognition that your only problem has been solved, you will find the peace that you seek in your meditation. The peace you experience in the holy instant, which will be described below, will remind you that the problem of separation has indeed been solved, along with all the other problems you imagine you have. The Course encourages you to claim the peace that comes to you by accepting that your only problem has indeed been solved:

> You have recognized your only problem, opening the way for the Holy Spirit to give you God's answer. You have laid deception aside, and seen the light of truth. You have accepted salvation for yourself by bringing the problem to the answer. And you can recognize the answer, because the problem has been identified.
>
> You are entitled to peace today. A problem that has been resolved cannot trouble you. Only be certain you do not forget that all problems are the same. Their many forms will not deceive you while you remember this. One problem, one solution. Accept the peace this simple statement brings.[55]

> Now let the peace that your acceptance brings be given you. Close your eyes, and receive your reward. Recognize that your problems have been solved. Recognize that you are out of conflict; free and at peace. Above all, remember that you have one problem, and that the problem has one solution. It is in this that the simplicity of salvation lies.[56]

---

1. T-14.X.12.4, p. 296
2. T-14.III.12:1-3, p. 277
3. T-13.I.11:7, p. 239
4. T-14.IV.4:5-9, p. 280
5. T-14.V.3:5, p. 282
6. T-14.XI.3:4-8, pp. 296-297
7. T-14.III.4:2-6, p. 275
8. T-14.VII.4:3-4, p. 287
9. T-14.VII.6.1-11, p. 288
10. T-14.VIII.2:12-16, 3:2-6, p. 289-290
11. T-14.XI.5:1-6, 6:1-5, p. 297
12. T-14.IX.4:7, 5:1-7, 6:1-5, pp. 291-292
13. T-14.III.5:1-3, p. 275
14. T-1.I.6:1-2, p. 3

15. T-1.I.3:1-3, p. 3
16. T-1.I.50:1, p. 6
17. T-28.I.11:1, p. 591
18. W-67.2:1-9, p. 113
19. W-67.3:1-3, 4:1-4, p. 113
20. W-67.5:1-4, 6:1-4, pp. 113-114
21. T-3.V.9:1, p. 45
22. W-69.5:1-5, 6:1-5, pp. 117-118
23. W-69.7:1-4, 8:1-6, p. 118
24. W-44.7:2-5, p. 70
25. T-9.IV.1:2-6, p. 168
26. T-2.III.5:1, p. 22
27. T-14.IX.3:5-9,4:1-7, p. 291-292
28. T-2.III.2:1-4, p. 21
29. T-13.IX.7:6, p. 262
30. T-2.III.4:1-6, p. 22
31. T-21.IV.1:1-2, p. 454
32. T-21.IV.2:3-4, p. 454
33. T-21.IV.3:1-4, p. 454
34. T-13.X.6:1, p. 264
35. T-13.X.10:1-7, p. 265
36. T-12.VII.12:1-4, p. 232
37. T-12.VII.10:1-6, p. 232
38. T-12.VII.9:1-6, p. 231
39. T-2.VI.1:4-5, p. 28
40. T-13.IX.8:13, p. 262
41. W-188.2:5, p. 357
42. M-16.4:2-9, 5:1-8, pp. 40-41
43. T-18.VII.4:7-11, p. 389
44. T-19.II.3:1-6, p. 402
45. T-18.VII.7:1-9, 8:1-5, p. 390
46. W-124.8:3-7, 10:1-3, p. 223
47. Kenneth Wapnick, *Absence From Felicity*, Copyright 1991 by the Foundation for *A Course In Miracles*, R.R. Box 71, Roscoe, N.Y. 12776-9506, p. 287
48. T-4.VI.8:2-3, p. 69
49. T-14.VIII.2:3, p. 289
50. T-14.VIII.4:9-10, 5:1-7, p. 290
51. T-19.I.9:1-7, 10:1-6, 11:1-5, p. 400
52. T-9.IV.1.4:4-6, p. 169
53. W-79.1:4-5, 2:1-2, p. 141
54. W-80.1:1-8, p. 143
55. W-80.2.3-6, 3:1-6, p. 143
56. W-80.5:1-6, p. 143

22

INNER COMMUNION
AND DIVINE UNION

≈ • ≈

A. The Holy Instant

The Course encourages you to open yourself to the divine within and experience the holy instant right now, saying, "You can practice the mechanics of the holy instant, and will learn much from doing so."[1] What are these "mechanics"? The quotation below from the Text promises that you will receive "specific instructions." These are the instructions given for the daily Workbook lessons, including meditation practices.

> Start now to practice your little part in separating out the holy instant. You will receive very specific instructions as you go along. To learn to separate out this single second, and to experience it as timeless, is to begin to experience yourself as not separate. Fear not that you will not be given help in this. God's Teacher and His lesson will support your strength. It is only your weakness that will depart from you in this practice, for it is the practice of the power of God in you. Use it but for one instant, and you will never deny it again. Who can deny the Presence of what the universe bows to, in appreciation and gladness?[2]

The entire Workbook is designed as a means of encouraging the experience of the holy instant so it eventually becomes a daily opening to the divine influence. The holy instant is a window left open by God—a window through which you can have a glimpse of the divine:

> The holy instant is a miniature of Heaven, sent you *from* Heaven.... The holy instant is a miniature of eternity. It is a picture of timelessness, set in a frame of time.... For as the whole thought system of the ego lies in its gifts, so the whole of Heaven lies in this instant, borrowed from eternity and set in time for you.[3]

The holy instant is always an experience of the divine in the here and now. But the divine can be experienced in different ways. It can be a moment of resting in the divine—a time to be still in the heart of God Himself. This stillness allows you to temporarily let go of your identification with the body and with the world of form that you imagine to be your home. This quiet rest allows you to learn to identify with your true nature in God. "His Love is everything you are and that He is; the same as you, and you the same as He."[4] In stillness you recognize that love is your true nature in God. Your experience of God and His Love is frequently thought to be the primary purpose of meditation. But the Course consistently places a much greater emphasis on contacting the divine indirectly by finding the divine in your brothers and sisters in Christ.

Perhaps the best way to understand spirituality is to realize that in your true nature you are intimately connected with God and with your brothers and sisters. If you make conscious contact with either one, you will naturally be connecting with the other. However, you are not really technically *becoming* connected to either one. Rather, you are actually awakening your awareness of your preexisting and eternal connection to both. The holy instant provides you with the opportunity to awaken this eternal connection. The holy instant seems to happen within the context of time, but actually it is an encounter with eternity allowing you to step outside of time. The Holy Spirit uses the holy instant to show you how to transcend time, if you allow Him to do so.

> Time is your friend, if you leave it to the Holy Spirit to use. He needs but very little to restore God's whole power to you. He Who transcends time for you understands what time is for. Holiness lies not in time, but in eternity. There never was an instant in which God's Son could lose his purity. His changeless state is beyond time, for his purity remains forever beyond attack and without variability. Time stands still in his holiness, and changes not. And so it is no longer time at all. For caught in the single instant of the eternal sanctity of God's creation, it is transformed into forever. Give the eternal instant, that eternity may be remembered for you, in that shining instant of perfect release. Offer the miracle of the holy instant through the Holy Spirit, and leave His giving it to you to Him.[5]

Being eternal, the holy instant is always available to you in time and only requires you to set aside the obstacles to experiencing it. These obstacles are your own judgments and ego perspective. When you can set aside your judgments of others and yourself, you can open yourself to performing miracles and encountering the holy instant. You are, of course, responsible for your own decisions and judgments, and the best way to accept responsibility is to allow the Holy Spirit to be in charge of your decision making and judgments. You can offer the holy instant to the Holy Spirit as the Course recommends in the last five Workbook lessons: "This holy instant would I give to You. Be You in charge."[6]

When you can hand over control of your mind to the Holy Spirit, you will experience the giving and receiving of a miracle in the holy instant. The miracle and holy instant are inseparable, occurring simultaneously. Because the Holy Spirit is allowed to be in charge, He ensures that the miracle is extended through you as a blessing to your brothers and sisters. The Holy Spirit also ensures that you will receive the same blessing you have allowed to flow through you to others. Thus both you and your brothers and sisters receive an increase in the awareness of love, and there is no loss by anyone of any kind.

The holy instant brings peace of mind and is the answer to every problem because it elevates the mind to a consciousness that transcends problems. The holy instant elevates you to your right mind in Christ in which you are at peace and all your problems have been solved:

> Thus it must be that time is not involved and every problem can be answered *now*. Yet it must also be that, in your state of mind, solution is impossible. Therefore, God must have given you a way of reaching to another state of mind in which the answer is already there. Such is the holy instant. It is here that all your problems should be brought and left. Here they belong, for here their answer is. And where its answer is, a problem must be simple and be easily resolved. It must be pointless to attempt to solve a problem where the answer cannot be. Yet just as surely it must be resolved, if it is brought to where the answer is.[7]

In your right mind in Christ you are at peace and have no problems because you are aware of dwelling in God's everlasting Love. The holy instant is your avenue to this state of mind. Peace of mind is always available to you because God gave you His Love as your true nature when you were created as part of the One Son, the One Christ.

> Only the Love of God will protect you in all circumstances. It will lift you out of every trial, and raise you high above all the perceived dangers of this world into a climate of perfect peace and safety. It will transport you into a state of mind that nothing can threaten, nothing can disturb, and where nothing can intrude upon the eternal calm of the Son of God.

Put not your faith in illusions. They will fail you. Put all your faith in the Love of God within you; eternal, changeless and forever unfailing. This is the answer to whatever confronts you today. Through the Love of God within you, you can resolve all seeming difficulties without effort and in sure confidence.[8]

The holy instant is especially helpful since it is always an interpersonal experience of your eternal relationship with all the other parts of the One Sonship—your brothers and sisters who share the Love of God with you. It is your sharing of love with your brothers and sisters in the holy instant and the attending miracle that remind you of your own true nature of love given to you by God.

The ego condition of the mind tells you that you are separate and that your mind is locked within your body where it can have private thoughts. Your investment in private thoughts keeps you from suspecting that all minds, including your own, are in communication with all other minds. The holy instant teaches you that your mind is not locked within your own private thought system by showing you what it means to have perfect communication:

The holy instant is a time in which you receive and give perfect communication. This means, however, that it is a time in which your mind is open, both to receive and give. It is the recognition that all minds are in communication. It therefore seeks to change nothing, but merely to accept everything.

How can you do this when you would prefer to have private thoughts and keep them? The only way you could do that would be to deny the perfect communication that makes the holy instant what it is. You believe you can harbor thoughts you would not share, and that salvation lies in keeping thoughts to yourself alone. For in private thoughts, known only to yourself, you think you find a way to keep what you would have alone, and share what *you* would share. And then you wonder why it is that you are not in full communication with those around you, and with God Who surrounds all of you together.[9]

You are conditioned to believe you have a private mind with private thoughts. Consequently, it is a strange idea to believe your mind is in fact your means of joining in communication with all of your brothers and sisters. In Heaven your fully awakened mind will have the ability to communicate perfectly with God and all your brothers and sisters. The holy instant can give you a taste of this perfect communication now in this world. But do you want this kind of unlimited communication?

Every thought you would keep hidden shuts communication off, because you would have it so. It is impossible to recognize perfect communication while breaking communication holds value to you. Ask yourself honestly, "Would I want to have perfect communication, and am I wholly willing to let everything that interferes with it go forever?" If the answer is no, then the Holy Spirit's readiness to give it to you is not enough to make it yours, for you are not ready to share it with Him. And it cannot come into a mind that has decided to oppose it. For the holy instant is given and received with equal willingness, being the acceptance of the single Will that governs all thought.

The necessary condition for the holy instant does not require that you have no thoughts that are not pure. But it does require that you have none that you would keep. Innocence is not of your making. It is given you the instant you would have it. Atonement would not be if there were no need for it. You will not be able to accept perfect communication as long as you would hide it from yourself. For what you would hide *is* hidden from you. In your practice, then, try only to be vigilant against deception, and seek not to protect the thoughts you would keep to yourself. Let the Holy Spirit's purity shine them away, and bring all your awareness to the readiness for purity He offers you. Thus will He make you ready to acknowledge that you are host to God, and hostage to no one and to nothing.[10]

The holy instant can be experienced at any time, but meditation is your best means of uncovering the holy instant. Your meditation helps you let go of the past and brings your mind to the present moment. The ego teaches you to believe the past is the best way to determine who you are and who your brothers and sisters are. The Holy Spirit teaches you to release the past. Meditation helps you to let go of past judgments you placed upon yourself and others. It opens your mind to accept your true nature, which you share with all your brothers and sisters. You replace your frame of reference for the Holy Spirit's frame of reference.

God knows you *now*. He remembers nothing, having always known you exactly as He knows you now. The holy instant reflects His knowing by bringing all perception out of the past, thus removing the frame of reference you have built by which to judge your brothers. Once this is gone, the Holy Spirit substitutes His frame of reference for it. His frame of reference is simply God. The Holy Spirit's timelessness lies only here. For in the holy instant, free of the past, you see that love is in you, and you have no need to look without and snatch love guiltily from where you thought it was.

All your relationships are blessed in the holy instant, because the blessing is not limited. In the holy instant the Sonship gains as one, and united in your blessing it becomes one to you. The meaning of love is the meaning God gave to it. Give to it any meaning apart from His, and it is impossible to understand it. God loves every brother as He loves you; neither less nor more. He needs them all equally, and so do you. In time, you have been told to offer miracles as I direct, and let the Holy Spirit bring to you those who are seeking you. Yet in the holy instant you unite directly with God, and all your brothers join in Christ. Those who are joined in Christ are in no way separate. For Christ is the Self the Sonship shares, as God shares His Self with Christ.

Think you that you can judge the Self of God? God has created It beyond judgment, out of His need to extend His Love. With love in you, you have no need except to extend it. In the holy instant there is no conflict of needs, for there is only one. For the holy instant reaches to eternity, and to the Mind of God. And it is only there love has meaning, and only there can it be understood.[11]

The Course explains, "The minds *are* joined, but you do not identify with them."[12] You do not identify with the connection between all minds because body awareness limits your mind's ability to communicate:

The body is a limit imposed on the universal communication that is an eternal property of mind. But the communication is internal. Mind reaches to itself. It is *not* made up of different parts, which reach each other. It does not go out. Within itself it has no limits, and there is nothing outside it. It encompasses everything. It encompasses you entirely; you within it and it within you. There is nothing else, anywhere or ever.

The body is outside you, and but seems to surround you, shutting you off from others and keeping you apart from them, and them from you. It is not there. There is no barrier between God and His Son, nor can His Son be separated from Himself except in illusions. This is not his reality, though he believes it is.[13]

The relationship between the mind and the body is not immediately obvious. Chapter 12 explains how various blocks are associated with specific parts of the body. The Course explains that the body itself is neutral and cannot make decisions, so the body cannot assign inner blocks to specific body parts. The mind fabricates psychological blocks consisting of negative thoughts such as fear, guilt, anger, and depression. Then in a misguided effort to get rid of the uncomfortable feelings of these negative thoughts, the mind projects these blocks onto the body. When the ego-based mind projects guilt onto the body, this may eventually cause sickness in the body, since guilt implies the need for punishment.

> You have displaced your guilt to your body from your mind. Yet a body cannot be guilty, for it can do nothing of itself. You who think you hate your body deceive yourself. You hate your mind, for guilt has entered into it, and it would remain separate from your brother's, which it cannot do.
>
> Minds are joined; bodies are not. Only by assigning to the mind the properties of the body does separation seem to be possible. And it is mind that seems to be fragmented and private and alone. Its guilt, which keeps it separate, is projected to the body, which suffers and dies because it is attacked to hold the separation in the mind, and let it not know its Identity. Mind cannot attack, but it can make fantasies and direct the body to act them out.[14]

Projecting guilt onto the body or even onto others is a delusional activity of the mind. The ego-based mind is in denial about the nature of its projections and thinks that projecting guilt is the way to get rid of it. Yet guilt that is projected never leaves the mind projecting it.

> In this, the mind is clearly delusional. It cannot attack, but it maintains it can, and uses what it does to hurt the body to prove it can. The mind cannot attack, but it can deceive itself. And this is all it does when it believes it has attacked the body. It can project its guilt, but it will not lose it through projection. And though it clearly can misperceive the function of the body, it cannot change its function from what the Holy Spirit establishes it to be. The body was not made by love. Yet love does not condemn it and can use it lovingly, respecting what the Son of God has made and using it to save him from illusions.[15]

The body generally limits the communication of the mind, yet the Holy Spirit can use the body as a communication device to help you overcome your illusions. Though the presence of the body normally convinces you minds are not joined, there are times when body awareness is set aside.

At such times the true nature of the mind is revealed through a holy instant in which mind is released from the apparent confines of the body.

> In these instants of release from physical restrictions, you experience much of what happens in the holy instant; the lifting of the barriers of time and space, the sudden experience of peace and joy, and, above all, the lack of awareness of the body, and of the questioning whether or not all this is possible.
>
> It is possible because you want it. The sudden expansion of awareness that takes place with your desire for it is the irresistible appeal the holy instant holds. It calls to you to be yourself, within its safe embrace. There are the laws of limit lifted for you, to welcome you to openness of mind and freedom. Come to this place of refuge, where you can be yourself in peace. Not through destruction, not through a breaking out, but merely by a quiet melting in. For peace will join you there, simply because you have been willing to let go the limits you have placed upon love, and joined it where it is and where it led you, in answer to its gentle call to be at peace.[16]

Such releases from body awareness can occur at any time, perhaps quite unexpectedly and dramatically. If you experience a feeling of being transported beyond yourself, you may feel at first like you are losing yourself. In fact, you are gaining a greater awareness of your true Self. This experience of "transportation" is described in this way:

> It is a sense of actual escape from limitations. If you will consider what this "transportation" really entails, you will realize that it is a sudden unawareness of the body, and a joining of yourself and something else in which your mind enlarges to encompass it. It becomes part of you, as you unite with it. And both become whole, as neither is perceived as separate. What really happens is that you have given up the illusion of a limited awareness, and lost your fear of union. The love that instantly replaces it extends to what has freed you, and unites with it. And while this lasts you are not uncertain of your Identity, and would not limit It. You have escaped from fear to peace, asking no questions of reality, but merely accepting it. You have accepted this instead of the body, and have let yourself be one with something beyond it, simply by not letting your mind be limited by it.[17]

This description of being transported beyond yourself reminds me of the Buddhist descriptions of the lesser forms of enlightenment in which a seeker joins with something that appears to be outside himself. This sense of joining is elaborated upon in the Course as follows:

> This [transportation] can occur regardless of the physical distance that seems to be between you and what you join; of your respective positions in space; and of your differences in size and seeming quality. Time is not relevant; it can occur with something past, present or anticipated. The "something" can be anything and anywhere; a sound, a sight, a thought, a memory, and even a general idea without specific reference. Yet in every case, you join it without reservation because you love it, and would be with it. And so you rush to meet it, letting your limits melt away, suspending all the "laws" your body obeys and gently setting them aside.[18]

B. Revelation and the Face of Christ

The holy instant of joining with something that appears apart from you is not the most profound level of awakening emphasized in the Course. The Course uses the word "revelation" to identify an experience that transcends the interpersonal nature of the holy instant that includes a joining with the minds of your brothers and sisters. Revelation is the extraordinary experience of the soul awakening directly to God. The following Course quotation compares miracles with revelation:

> Revelation induces complete but temporary suspension of doubt and fear. It reflects the original form of communication between God and His creations, involving the extremely personal sense of creation sometimes sought in physical relationships. Physical closeness cannot achieve it. Miracles, however, are genuinely interpersonal, and result in true closeness to others. Revelation unites you directly with God. Miracles unite you directly with your brother. Neither emanates from consciousness, but both are experienced there. Consciousness is the state that induces action, though it does not inspire it. You are free to believe what you choose, and what you do attests to what you believe.
>
> Revelation is intensely personal and cannot be meaningfully translated. That is why any attempt to describe it in words is impossible. Revelation induces only experience. Miracles, on the other hand, induce action. They are more useful now because of their interpersonal nature. In this phase of learning, working miracles is important because freedom from fear cannot be thrust

upon you. Revelation is literally unspeakable because it is an experience of unspeakable love.

Awe should be reserved for revelation, to which it is perfectly and correctly applicable. It is not appropriate for miracles because a state of awe is worshipful, implying that one of a lesser order stands before his Creator. You are a perfect creation, and should experience awe only in the Presence of the Creator of perfection. The miracle is therefore a sign of love among equals.[19]

Revelation is equivalent to the "illumination of glory," the deepest form of spiritual experience, which is described in Chapter 18. St. John of the Cross calls this the highest form of vision, which involves divine union beyond any awareness of the physical body. However, the Course would not use the word "vision" to describe revelation. Revelation is an experience of "knowing" God, meaning the awareness of perfect union with God. The perfect oneness of "knowledge" that occurs in revelation is beyond any form of perception, which always implies a separation between the perceiver (yourself) and whatever is perceived.

True vision is the natural perception of spiritual sight, but it is still a correction rather than a fact. Spiritual sight is symbolic, and therefore not a device for knowing. It is, however, a means of right perception, which brings it into the proper domain of the miracle. A "vision of God" would be a miracle [indirect experience of the divine] rather than a revelation [direct experience of God]. The fact that perception is involved at all removes the experience from the realm of knowledge. That is why visions, however holy, do not last.[20]

Although revelation is not a vision, which always involves perception, there is a vision described in the Course that can lead to direct union with God in the experience of revelation.

Beyond the body, beyond the sun and stars, past everything you see and yet somehow familiar, is an arc of golden light that stretches as you look into a great and shining circle. And all the circle fills with light before your eyes. The edges of the circle disappear, and what is in it is no longer contained at all. The light expands and covers everything, extending to infinity forever shining and with no break or limit anywhere. Within it everything is joined in perfect continuity. Nor is it possible to imagine that anything could be outside, for there is nowhere that this light is not.

This is the vision of the Son of God, whom you know well. Here is the sight of him who knows his Father. Here is the memory of what you are; a part of this, with all of it within, and joined to all as surely as all is joined in you. Accept the vision that can show you this, and not the body. You know the ancient song, and know it well. Nothing will ever be as dear to you as is this ancient hymn of love the Son of God sings to his Father still.[21]

In my opinion, this "vision of the Son of God" is the highest experience of what the Course calls the "face of Christ," which is not Christ Himself, but rather the most holy perceptual image of Christ. A poem I wrote titled "Awaken now! Christ shows you how!" is about the face of Christ:

> What bell rings
> saying nothing?
> What candle lit
> flickers a bit
> and lights not bright
> the dark of night
> without leaving
> a song to sing?
> What sunrise East
> inspires not least
> of men to raise
> their eyes in praise?
> Why do men say
> there are today
> no miracles,
> just icicles,
> who play the parts
> of frozen hearts?
> Open your eyes
> to see the prize!
> In Christ you live!
> As you forgive,
> your brother is
> released from his
> deep sleep—awake
> at last to make
> his way back to
> his Home with you.
> Behold Christ's face
> in God's Embrace!

The face of Christ—the image of a circle of blazing light expanding infinitely—can be seen in a spiritual experience by anyone, whenever the seeker is ready for such an experience. More importantly, I believe this image of blazing light can be seen at the moment of death. In fact, the Course maintains that this image *must* be seen before God can take the "final step" of lifting you to Heaven. The previous Course quotation describing the "vision of the Son of God" and the quotation below describing the "face of Christ" are particularly inspiring because together they tell me what to expect at the crucial time of death.

> *The face of Christ* has to be seen before the [full] memory of God can return. The reason is obvious. Seeing the face of Christ involves perception. No one can look on knowledge. But the face of Christ is the great symbol of forgiveness. It is salvation. It is the symbol of the real world. Whoever looks on this no longer sees the world. He is as near to Heaven as is possible outside the gate. Yet from this gate it is no more than just a step inside. It is the final step. And this we leave to God.[22]

Not everyone sees this blazing light, but only those souls who are open to the awareness of this light. The Course neither affirms nor denies the controversial idea of reincarnation, but personally I believe souls who do not see the blazing light will be reincarnated. If the soul can open to this perceptual vision at the time of death, the soul will be fully open to the Love of God. Then God will initiate the experience of revelation. This will not be a temporary revelation that can come and go in everyday life. If revelation happens at the time of death, it is a permanent union with God in Heaven. This is "salvation's final step" described below:

> This the gift by which God leans to us and lifts us up, taking salvation's final step Himself. All steps but this we learn, instructed by His Voice. But finally He comes Himself, and takes us in His Arms and sweeps away the cobwebs of our sleep. His gift of grace is more than just an answer. It restores all memories the sleeping mind forgot; all certainty of what Love's meaning is.
>
> God loves His Son. Request Him now to give the means by which this world will disappear, and vision first will come, with knowledge but an instant later. For in grace you see a light that covers all the world in love, and watch fear disappear from every face as hearts rise up and claim the light as theirs. What now remains that Heaven be delayed an instant longer? What is still undone when your forgiveness rests on everything?[23]

This final step may sound like a new condition, but instead it is a full awakening of the soul's true Self, the Christ, Who has always existed in God. In Christ's face you see your own face reflecting your true nature. "In this vision of the Son, so brief that not an instant stands between this single sight and timelessness itself, you see the vision of yourself, and then you disappear forever into God."[24] Words are used here to describe divine union, but these words cannot provide an accurate description of the transcendental knowledge that is beyond perceptual awareness.

> Oneness is simply the idea God is. And in His Being, He encompasses all things. No mind holds anything but Him. We say "God is," and then we cease to speak, for in that knowledge words are meaningless. There are no lips to speak them, and no part of mind sufficiently distinct to feel that it is now aware of something not itself. It has united with its Source. And like its Source Itself, it merely is.
> We cannot speak nor write nor even think of this at all. It comes to every mind when total recognition that its will is God's has been completely given and received completely. It returns the mind into the endless present, where the past and future cannot be conceived. It lies beyond salvation; past all thought of time, forgiveness and the holy face of Christ. The Son of God has merely disappeared into his Father, as his Father has in him. The world has never been at all. Eternity remains a constant state.[25]

According to the Course you have never really left Heaven. You are merely asleep in Heaven, and dreaming of a world of separation. When the final step is taken by God, He helps you let go of the perception of separation and brings back your knowledge of the Oneness of Heaven. You never actually lost this oneness. It was merely hidden from your awareness. Thus the restoration of Heaven is the awakening of an eternal condition of divine union, reaffirming you are now, and have been all along, the holy Son of God, just as God created you as part of Himself.

> There is nothing outside you. That is what you must ultimately learn, for it is the realization that the Kingdom of Heaven is restored to you. For God created only this, and He did not depart from it nor leave it separate from Himself. The Kingdom of Heaven is the dwelling place of the Son of God, who left not his Father and dwells not apart from Him. Heaven is not a place nor a condition. It is merely an awareness of perfect Oneness,

and the knowledge hat there is nothing else; nothing outside this Oneness, and nothing else within.

What could God give but knowledge of Himself?[26]

You cannot exert your will and force yourself to experience revelation, which is a gracious gift of God that restores the awareness of your true Identity. But you can prepare yourself to receive such a gift, if not during this lifetime, then at the end of your life. Jesus plays a part in helping you prepare for revelation.

> "No man cometh unto the Father but by me" does not mean that I am in any way separate or different from you except in time, and time does not really exist. The statement is more meaningful in terms of a vertical rather than a horizontal axis. You stand below me and I stand below God. In the process of "rising up," I am higher because without me the distance between God and man would be too great for you to encompass. I bridge the distance as an elder brother to you on the one hand, and as a Son of God on the other. My devotion to my brothers has placed me in charge of the Sonship, which I render complete because I share it. This may appear to contradict the statement "I and my Father are one," but there are two parts to the statement in recognition that the Father is greater.
>
> Revelations are indirectly inspired by me because I am close to the Holy Spirit, and alert to the revelation-readiness of my brothers. I can thus bring down to them more than they can draw down to themselves. The Holy Spirit mediates higher to lower communication, keeping the direct channel from God to you open for revelation. Revelation is not reciprocal. It proceeds from God to you, but not from you to God.[27]

Whatever spiritual path you choose, the final step of divine union in revelation at death is always the ultimate end. Even if revelation happens while you are still alive, it can only temporarily show you the end as an encouragement for continuing your spiritual path. The Holy Spirit is your primary Teacher, Who shows you how to prepare for the final step—the one holy instant that reveals the full memory of God described below:

> The Holy Spirit has no need of time when it has served His purpose. Now He waits but that one instant more for God to take His final step, and time has disappeared, taking perception with it as it goes, and leaving but the truth to be itself. That instant

is our goal, for it contains the memory of God. And as we look upon a world forgiven, it is He Who calls to us and comes to take us home, reminding us of our Identity which our forgiveness has restored to us.[28]

C. Overcoming the Obstacles to Peace

I hope reading the various quotations in the prior section will help open your mind to the possibility of seeing the vision of a circle of light expanding infinitely, which comes just before God's final step. The full memory of God returns when the final step happens, but how can you prepare for awakening the memory of God? First let's address how the memory of God was lost before discussing how to bring it back. Most Christians take it for granted that God created this world of time and space and placed man on the earth. But the Course provides a different and quite unique explanation. According to the Course, God extended His Spirit to create one Son, one Christ, with many parts forming the Sonship. Some of these parts asked for "special love" from God, yet God could only love all parts of the Sonship equally.

> You were at peace until you asked for special favor. And God did not give it for the request was alien to Him, and you could not ask this of a Father Who truly loved His Son. Therefore you made of Him an unloving father, demanding of Him what only such a father could give. And the peace of God's Son was shattered, for he no longer understood his Father. He feared what he had made, but still more did he fear his real Father, having attacked his own glorious equality with Him.[29]

The parts of the Sonship who were refused special love decided to collectively rebel by closing off communication with God. They fell asleep in Heaven by making a collective dream. They manufactured egos for themselves while discarding knowledge of oneness and replacing it with the perception of separation. Although they were lost in illusions of separation, the memory of God was still within them, but through denial was hidden from conscious awareness and remains hidden to this day.

How can you prepare yourself to let go of denial and bring the memory of God out of hiding? Your ultimate goal is God Himself, but He can only be found by a mind that first allows peace to come and then makes way for the ultimate peace that surpasses all understanding. To find peace it is necessary to first understand the obstacles to peace and then overcome them. The Course identifies four obstacles to peace:

1. *The Desire to Get Rid of It*
2. *The Belief the Body is Valuable for What It Offers*
3. *The Attraction of Death*
4. *The Fear of God*[30]

You may consciously think you want peace and do not want to get rid of it, but your ego is threatened by peace and so wants to discard it. If you really do want peace, you must be firmly resolved in your desire for it. The body is the source of your belief in sin and guilt. The body cannot offer you peace or anything of genuine value. Nevertheless, if you believe the body can be valuable in itself, you will be moving away from your goal of peace. You may not think you are attracted to pain and death, but the ego, believing in the ideas of sin and guilt, is indeed attracted to pain and death as reinforcements of the ego's thought system of separation.

It is impossible to seek for pleasure through the body and not find pain. It is essential that this relationship be understood, for it is one the ego sees as proof of sin. It is not really punitive at all. It is but the inevitable result of equating yourself with the body, which is the invitation to pain. For it invites fear to enter and become your purpose. The attraction of guilt *must* enter with it, and whatever fear directs the body to do is therefore painful. It will share the pain of all illusions, and the illusion of pleasure will be the same as pain.

Is not this inevitable? Under fear's orders the body will pursue guilt, serving its master whose attraction to guilt maintains the whole illusion of its existence. This, then, is the attraction of pain. Ruled by this perception the body becomes the servant of pain, seeking it dutifully and obeying the idea that pain is pleasure. It is this idea that underlies all of the ego's heavy investment in the body. And it is this insane relationship that it keeps hidden, and yet feeds upon. To you it teaches that the body's pleasure is happiness. Yet to itself it whispers, "It is death."[31]

Like a computer that expresses the programming put into it, the body is itself neutral and can only expresses the purpose given to it. The ego invites fear to enter the mind to become the body's purpose. Thus the ego brings in its programming of sin, guilt, pain, and death in opposition to the Will of God, which brings peace and happiness. As you let go of the first three obstacles to peace, including releasing the fear of death, the memory of God begins to return. Yet peace must still overcome the fourth obstacle—the fear of God.

And as this memory [of God] rises in your mind, peace must still surmount a final obstacle, after which is salvation completed, and the Son of God entirely restored to sanity. For here your world *does* end.

The fourth obstacle to be surmounted hangs like a heavy veil before the face of Christ. Yet as His face rises beyond it, shining with joy because He is in His Father's Love, peace will lightly brush the veil aside and run to meet Him, and to join with Him at last. For this dark veil, which seems to make the face of Christ Himself like to a leper's, and the bright Rays of His Father's Love that light His face with glory appear as streams of blood, fades in the blazing light beyond it when the fear of death is gone.

This is the darkest veil, upheld by the belief in death and protected by its attraction. The dedication to death and to its sovereignty is but the solemn vow, the promise made in secret to the ego never to lift this veil, not to approach it, nor even to suspect that it is there. This is the secret bargain made with the ego to keep what lies beyond the veil forever blotted out and unremembered. Here is your promise never to allow union to call you out of separation; the great amnesia in which the memory of God seems quite forgotten; the cleavage of your Self from you;— *the fear of God*, the final step in your dissociation.[32]

These first three obstacles to peace are held in place by the fourth obstacle, the fear of God, which is the most difficult barrier to overcome. The quotation below mentions all four obstacles and shows how each one is overcome in the same way by God's call of Love.

For in your secret alliance with them you have agreed never to let the fear of God be lifted, so you could look upon the face of Christ and join Him in His Father.

Every obstacle that peace must flow across is surmounted in just the same way; the fear that raised it yields to the love beyond, and so the fear is gone. And so it is with this. The desire to get rid of peace and drive the Holy Spirit from you fades in the presence of the quiet recognition that you love Him. The exaltation of the body is given up in favor of the spirit, which you love as you could never love the body. And the appeal of death is lost forever as love's attraction stirs and calls to you. From beyond each of the obstacles to love, Love Itself has called. And each has been surmounted by the power of the attraction of what lies beyond. Your wanting fear seemed to be holding them in place. Yet when you heard the Voice of Love beyond them, you answered and they disappeared.[33]

The Voice of Love, beyond the dark veil covering the face of Christ, calls you, and one day you will respond by lifting the veil. But lifting the veil is not easily accomplished. The fear of God is an idea you may easily understand. Yet you know that God is Love, so the fear of God must be the fear of Love. Indeed, you do fear His Love, and likewise you fear redemption that His Love will bring when you let go of fear. The quotation below describes the fear of God's Love and of redemption:

Your real terror is of redemption.

Under the ego's dark foundation is the memory of God, and it is of this that you are really afraid. For this memory would instantly restore you to your proper place, and it is this place that you have sought to leave. Your fear of attack is nothing compared to your fear of love. You would be willing to look even upon your savage wish to kill God's Son, if you did not believe that it saves you from love. For this wish caused the separation, and you have protected it because you do not want the separation healed. You realize that, by removing the dark cloud that obscures it, your love for your Father would impel you to answer His Call and leap into Heaven. You believe that attack is salvation because it would prevent you from this. For still deeper than the ego's foundation, and much stronger than it will ever be, is your intense and burning love of God, and His for you. This is what you really want to hide.

In honesty, is it not harder for you to say "I love" than "I hate"? You associate love with weakness and hatred with strength, and your own real power seems to you as your real weakness. For you could not control your joyous response to the call of love if you heard it, and the whole world you thought you made would vanish. The Holy Spirit, then, seems to be attacking your fortress, for you would shut out God, and He does not will to be excluded.

You have built your whole insane belief system because you think you would be helpless in God's Presence, and you would save yourself from His Love because you think it would crush you into nothingness. You are afraid it would sweep you away from yourself and make you little, because you believe that magnitude lies in defiance, and that attack is grandeur. You think you have made a world God would destroy; and by loving Him, which you do, you would throw this world away, which you *would*. Therefore, you have used the world to cover your love, and the deeper you go into the blackness of the ego's foundation, the closer you come to the Love that is hidden there. *And it is this that frightens you.*[34]

The Course maintains, "You are more afraid of God than of the ego, and love cannot enter where it is not welcome."[35] If this is true, as I believe it is, you must learn how to let go of your fear of God and fear of Love. You must learn how to welcome Love. Imagine you are standing before the veil that represents the fear of God and hides the face of Christ. What would it take for you to lift this veil and raise your eyes to see the blazing light of the face of Christ? Yes, you may be afraid to lift the veil because you know the world, along with guilt, will disappear forever. Yet the Holy Spirit whispers to you that lifting the veil and looking upon the blazing light is what you want because it is your true will:

> It seems to you the world will utterly abandon you if you but raise your eyes. Yet all that will occur is you will leave the world forever. This is the re-establishment of *your* will. Look upon it, open-eyed, and you will nevermore believe that you are at the mercy of things beyond you, forces you cannot control, and thoughts that come to you against your will. It *is* your will to look on this.[36]

Although it is your will to lift the veil and reach the love beyond the blazing light, you cannot do so while you carry fear with you. Yes, you are afraid of God, but your brother holds the key for your freedom from fear.

> Before complete forgiveness you still stand unforgiving. You are afraid of God *because* you fear your brother. Those you do not forgive you fear. And no one reaches love with fear beside him.[37]

You must forgive your brother to let go of your fear of him, and to help you release the fear of God within you. You can offer him your forgiveness and love and receive as you have given.

> No one can look upon the fear of God unterrified, unless he has accepted the Atonement [God's Plan] and learned illusions are not real. No one can stand before this obstacle alone, for he could not have reached this far unless his brother walked beside him. And no one would dare to look on it without complete forgiveness of his brother in his heart.[38]

Your forgiveness of your brother must be complete for you to be redeemed. You must see your brother without projecting any stain of sin or guilt upon him. "For the redeemed son of man is the guiltless Son of God, and to recognize him *is* your redemption."[39] Forgiveness is your means of recognizing that the holy Son of God is both your brother and savior, who reminds you of your holiness and who offers you redemption.

> Brother, you need forgiveness of your brother, for you will share in madness or in Heaven together. And you and he will raise your eyes in faith together, or not at all.
>
> Beside you is one who offers you the chalice of Atonement, for the Holy Spirit is in him. Would you hold his sins against him, or accept his gift to you? Is this giver of salvation your friend or enemy? Choose which he is, remembering that you will receive of him according to your choice. He has in him the power to forgive your sin, as you for him. Neither can give it to himself alone. And yet your savior stands beside each one. Let him be what he is, and seek not to make of love an enemy.
>
> Behold your Friend, the Christ Who stands beside you. How holy and how beautiful He is! You thought He sinned because you cast the veil of sin upon Him to hide His loveliness. Yet still He holds forgiveness out to you, to share His Holiness.[40]

According to the Course, Jesus is with you always. This may seem like a fantasy, like Santa Claus giving presents to all the children in the world. Yet Jesus being everywhere is no fantasy. Jesus is awake in the Mind of Christ. You are asleep in the Mind of Christ. Since you are both in the Mind of Christ, you are joined there along with all your brothers—those who are asleep like you and those who are awake like Jesus. Your redemption means simply making the transition from sleeping to waking up in the Mind of Christ. Jesus sees you as guiltless and wants you to free your brother so you can be redeemed along with him. You free your brother by seeing his guiltlessness, and simultaneously you free yourself.

> Free your brother here, as I [Jesus] freed you. Give him the selfsame gift, nor look upon him with condemnation of any kind. See him as guiltless as I look on you, and overlook the sins he thinks he sees within himself. Offer your brother freedom and complete release from sin, here in the garden of seeming agony and death. So will we prepare together the way unto the resurrection of God's Son, and let him rise again to glad remembrance of his Father, Who knows no sin, no death, but only life eternal.
>
> Together we will disappear into the Presence beyond the veil, not to be lost but found; not to be seen but known. And knowing,

nothing in the plan God has established for salvation will be left undone. This is the journey's purpose, without which is the journey meaningless. Here is the peace of God, given to you eternally by Him. Here is the rest and quiet that you seek, the reason for the journey from its beginning. Heaven is the gift you owe your brother, the debt of gratitude you offer to the Son of God in thanks for what he is, and what his Father created him to be.[41]

It is not enough to see one brother as guiltless, or even to see most others as guiltless. Your redemption requires seeing guiltlessness in *every* brother without exception. Only this will convince you of your own guiltlessness. Only this will allow you to accept God's Love and the total healing of your mind that comes in your redemption.

But exempt no one from your love, or you will be hiding a dark place in your mind where the Holy Spirit is not welcome. And thus you will exempt yourself from His healing power, for by not offering total love you will not be healed completely. Healing must be as complete as fear, for love cannot enter where there is one spot of fear to mar its welcome.[42]

To let go of seeing guilt within yourself, you must let go of seeing guilt in anyone else. It's hard enough to see one person as guiltless, but to see *every* brother as guiltless sounds daunting, maybe even impossible, at least at first glance. But consider that exempting anyone from your love means you are returning to the original error of the separation— the mistake of thinking God could give "special favor," special love, to some of His children and not give the same love to all of them.

Release from guilt as you would be released. There is no other way to look within and see the light of love, shining as steadily and as surely as God Himself has always loved His Son. *And as His Son loves Him.* There is no fear in love, for love is guiltless. You who have always loved your Father can have no fear, for any reason, to look within and see your holiness. You cannot be as you believed you were. Your guilt is without reason because it is not in the Mind of God, where you are. And this *is* reason, which the Holy Spirit would restore to you. He would remove only illusions. All else He would have you see. And in Christ's vision He would show you the perfect purity that is forever within God's Son.

You cannot enter into real relationships with any of God's Sons unless you love them all and equally. Love is not special. If you single out part of the Sonship for your love, you are imposing guilt on all your relationships and making them unreal. You can love only as God loves. Seek not to love unlike Him, for there is no love apart from His. Until you recognize that this is true, you will have no idea what love is like. No one who condemns a brother can see himself as guiltless and in the peace of God. If he is guiltless and in peace and sees it not, he is delusional, and has not looked upon himself. To him I say:

> *Behold the Son of God, and look upon his purity and be still. In quiet look upon his holiness, and offer thanks unto his Father that no guilt has ever touched him.*[43]

It takes preparation to learn how to apply forgiveness and love to everyone equally. Likewise, it takes preparation to let go of the fear of God and fully accept His Love. "To look upon the fear of God does need preparation."[44] How do you prepare to lift the veil of the fear of God and look upon the face of Christ? How do you open to the Love of God calling you Home? Guided by the Holy Spirit, what can you do to prepare for the one instant of the final step, which will transport you to Heaven and God's Embrace. This preparation cannot be accomplished quickly or easily. It requires daily spiritual practice and the self-discipline to live your life looking to the Holy Spirit for guidance in your journey.

Your preparation involves joining with your brothers and sisters in holy relationships with a common purpose that includes seeing holiness in everyone. Your means of preparation are forgiveness, right-minded thinking, and the use of Christ's vision. As was described in Chapter 16, Christ's vision is the seeing of the divine presence of holiness in others.

> Christ's eyes are open, and He will look upon whatever you see with love if you accept His vision as yours. The Holy Spirit keeps the vision of Christ for every Son of God who sleeps. In His sight the Son of God is perfect, and He longs to share His vision with you. He will show you the real world because God gave you Heaven. Through Him your Father calls His Son to remember. The awakening of His Son begins with his investment in the real world, and by this he will learn to re-invest in himself.[45]

Although the world is a dream of sin and guilt, through your Christ's vision you learn to see a forgiven world, which the Course calls the "happy dream" of the "real world." The happy dream is still a dream and thus an illusion, yet it reflects the reality of Heaven by revealing a world blessed with forgiveness. This happy dream prepares you to transcend this world and wake up in Heaven. After all, when you have forgiven everyone and forgiven the world itself by looking for the divine and overlooking everything else, there will be nothing left to hold you to this world of time and space.

> The mind can be right or wrong, depending on the voice to which it listens. *Right-mindedness* listens to the Holy Spirit, forgives the world, and through Christ's vision sees the real world in its place. This is the final vision, the last perception, the condition in which God takes the final step Himself. Here time and illusions end together.
> *Wrong-mindedness* listens to the ego and makes illusions; perceiving sin and justifying anger, and seeing guilt, disease and death as real. Both this world and the real world are illusions because right-mindedness merely overlooks, or forgives, what never happened. Therefore it is not the *One-mindedness* of the Christ Mind, Whose Will is One with God's.[46]

When forgiveness, right-minded thinking, and Christ's vision are applied consistently, they serve as a preparation for the final step of divine union. Yet what is the role of the inward seeking of meditation and contemplation? Seeking the divine in others and in the world must be balanced by inner communion with God and with your brothers and sisters. The next section will address this inner communion.

D. Contemplation in the Course

The most common method of attunement recommended in the Course is mentally focusing upon the divine presence. This involves mentally repeating an affirmation of inspiring words only if thoughts temporarily distract you from feeling the divine presence. The beginning Workbook lessons all include affirmations to repeat as part of the practice. Workbook Lesson 124 states: "This is our first attempt at an extended period for which we give no rules or special words to guide your meditation."[47] Later Workbook lessons lead in the direction of relying less on words and more on dwelling in the divine presence. "Instead of words, we need but feel His Love."[48] In the end of the yearlong cycle of lessons there is this summary: "Our final lessons will be left as free of words as possible. We use them but at the beginning of our practicing, and only to remind us that we seek to go beyond them."[49] The Course is systematically leading the seeker toward wordless contemplation described in this way:

Simply do this: Be still, and lay aside all thoughts of what you are and what God is; all concepts you have learned about the world; all images you hold about yourself. Empty your mind of everything it thinks is either true or false, or good or bad, of every thought it judges worthy, and all the ideas of which it is ashamed. Hold onto nothing. Do not bring with you one thought the past has taught, nor one belief you ever learned before from anything. Forget this world, forget this course, and come with wholly empty hands unto your God.

Is it not He Who knows the way to you? You need not know the way to Him. Your part is simply to allow all obstacles that you have interposed between the Son and God the Father to be quietly removed forever. God will do His part in joyful and immediate response. Ask and receive. But do not make demands, nor point the road to God by which He should appear to you. The way to reach Him is merely to let Him be. For in that way is your reality proclaimed as well.

And so today we do not choose the way in which we go to Him. But we do choose to let Him come. And with this choice we rest. And in our quiet hearts and open minds, His Love will blaze its pathway of itself. What has not been denied is surely there, if it be true and can be surely reached. God knows His Son, and knows the way to him. He does not need His Son to show Him how to find His way. Through every opened door His Love shines outward from its home within, and lightens up the world in innocence.[50]

Contemplation is a simple practice of opening to the divine presence beyond words. Some seekers have a natural ability to go beyond words. Most seekers, especially beginners, find this silence difficult to achieve, even after doing all of the Workbook lessons. After completing the one year of Workbook lessons, what's next in regard to inner attunement? The Manual advises having a "quiet time" of attunement in the morning and another one in the evening. If you have been successful in dwelling in the divine presence, continue your wordless practice of contemplation.

However, if you are not satisfied with your progress, then you might want to consider alternatives not specifically recommended in the Course. The Course does not offer any form-related aids to meditation. For example, there are no instructions provided for breathing, posture, or concentrating on parts of the body. The whole message in the Course is to simply allow your mind to move past any interfering thoughts and enter into the awareness of the divine presence. Yet the omission of form-related aids does not mean they cannot be used if you find them helpful. Indeed, I feel these aids are very helpful as a transition to wordless contemplation. When you attain the ability to dwell in the divine presence, these aids can be set aside altogether. I recommend using the six practices included in Christian Yoga Meditation. These six techniques lead the seeker to become increasingly comfortable with the practice of wordless contemplation. The description of Christian Yoga Meditation, described previously in this book, can be used successfully by any Course student. As you become proficient in this combination of methods, you can reduce the time for the first five techniques and increase the time for the sixth technique, Inner Silence Meditation. This last method leads directly to contemplation. It is very close to the basic Course approach of repeating words to let go of interference and then letting go of words to dwell in the divine presence. Hopefully you will learn how to open your mind, as the Course instructs:

> Listen in deep silence. Be very still and open your mind. Go past all the raucous shrieks and sick imaginings that cover your real thoughts and obscure your eternal link with God. Sink deep into the peace that waits for you beyond the frantic, riotous thoughts and sights and sounds of this insane world. You do not live here. We are trying to reach your real home. We are trying to reach the place where you are truly welcome. We are trying to reach God.[51]

> Open your mind and rest. The world that seems to hold you prisoner can be escaped by anyone who does not hold it dear. Withdraw all value you have placed upon its meager offerings and senseless gifts, and let the gift of God replace them all.[52]

> Open your mind to Him. Be still and rest.[53]

The first five methods of Christian Yoga Meditation can be dispensed with altogether once you can consistently rest in the silence of wordless contemplation by opening your mind as instructed above. Contemplation is about opening your mind to the divine presence, but is not about opening your mind to new perceptions. A major goal of this meditation manual is to help you understand the value of practicing daily meditation and to provide instructions in how to experience contemplation in which you let go of all perception. Although the Course affirms the benefits of wordless attunement, it primarily addresses how to use your perceptions positively. The next chapter and then the final chapter will explain the Course perspective that changing your perceptions—changing your thought system—is your primary work in regard to spiritual growth.

1. T-15.II.5:4, p. 306
2. T-15.II.6:1-8, p. 306
3. T-17.IV.11:1, 4, 5, 8, p. 360
4. W-125.7:4, p. 226
5. T-15.I.15:1-11, p. 304
6. W-361-365, p. 486
7. T-27.IV.2.1-9, pp. 574-575
8. W-50. 3:1-3, 4:1-5, p. 79
9. T-15.IV.6:5-8, 7:1-5, pp. 310-311
10. T-15.IV.8:1-6, 9:1-10, p. 311
11. T-15.V.9: 1-7, 10:1-10, 11:1-6, pp. 313-314
12. T-18.VI.7:4, p. 386
13. T-18.VI:8:3-11, 9:1-4. p. 386
14. T-18.VI.2:5-8, 3:1-5, p. 385
15. T-18,VI.4:1-8, p. 385
16. T-18.VI.13:6, 14:1-7, pp. 388-389
17. T-18.VI.11:3-11, p. 387
18. T-18.VI.12:1-5, p. 387
19. T-1.II.1:1-9, 2:1-7, 3:1-4, p. 7
20. T-3.III.4:1-6, p. 40
21. T-21.I.8:1-6, 9:1-6, p. 447
22. C-3.4:1-12, p. 83
23. W-168.3:2-6, 4:1-5, p. 321
24. W-198.12:6, p. 381
25. W-169.5:1-6, 6:1-7, pp. 323-324
26. T-18.VI.1:1-6, 2:1, p. 384
27. T-1.II.4:1-7, 5:1-5, pp. 7-8
28. W-pII.8.5:1-4, p. 443
29. T-13.III.10:2-6, p. 244
30. T-19.IV.A-D, pp. 407-424
31. T-19.IV.B.12:2-7, 13:1-8, p. 415
32. T-19.IV.D.1:5-6, 2:1-3, 3:1-4, p. 420
33. T-19.IV.D.4:6, 5:1-9, pp. 420-421
34. T-13.III.1:11, 2:1-9, 3:1-4. 4:1-5, pp. 242-243
35. T-13.III.5:4, p. 243
36. T-19.IV.D.7:1-5, p. 421
37. T-19.IV.D.11:4-7, p. 422
38. T-19.IV.D.9:1-3, p. 422
39. T-13.II.9:7, p. 241
40. T-19.IV.D.12:7-8, 13:1-8, 14:1-4, pp. 422-423
41. T-19.IV.D.18:1-5, 19:1-6, p. 424
42. T-13.III.9:2-4, p. 244
43. T-13.X.10:1-11, 11:1-11, p. 265
44. T-19.IV.D.11:1, p. 422
45. T-12.VI.4:4-9, 3, p. 228
46. C-1.5:1-4, 6:1-3, p. 79
47. W-124.8:4-5, p. 223
48. W-pII.In.10:3, p. 399
49. W-Fl.In.1:1-2, p. 485
50. W-189.7:1-5, 8:1-8, 9:1-8, p. 360
51. W-49.4:1-8, p. 78
52. W-127.8:2-4, p. 231
53. W-128.7:7-8, p. 234

23

WHY CHANGE YOUR THOUGHT SYSTEM?

≈ • ≈

A. Defining Perception and Knowledge

These final two chapters are mostly about *perception* and *knowledge*. The meaning of these two words needs to be clarified. Perception and knowledge are forms of awareness. According to the Course, knowledge is total awareness, and perception is partial awareness. God gave you "...knowledge that you are a mind, in Mind and purely mind, sinless forever, wholly unafraid, because you were created out of love."[1] God created you by extending His knowledge into you so you were, are now, and forever will be part of Him.

The very real difference between perception and knowledge becomes quite apparent if you consider this: There is nothing partial about knowledge. Every aspect is whole, and therefore no aspect is separate. You are an aspect of knowledge, being in the Mind of God, Who knows you. All knowledge must be yours, for in you is all knowledge. Perception, at its loftiest, is never complete. Even the perception of the Holy Spirit, as perfect as perception can be, is without meaning in Heaven. Perception can reach everywhere under His guidance, for the vision of Christ beholds everything in light. Yet no perception, however holy, will last forever.[2]

Because God created you as part of Himself, your knowledge cannot be obliterated, yet you have lost your awareness of it. You lost the awareness of your knowledge during the separation, which was explained in the previous chapter. "The separation is merely another term for a split mind."[3] During the separation you introduced a split in your mind, which you can think of as a partition that separated your mind into one vast part containing knowledge and one very tiny part containing perception. That tiny part of your mind is your current *consciousness*, which contains only the partial awareness of perceptions. Thus you have lost your access to the total awareness of knowledge, which allows you to be fully aware of yourself as part of God.

The abilities you now possess are only shadows of your real strength. All of your present functions are divided and open to question and doubt. This is because you are not certain how you will use them, and are therefore incapable of knowledge. You are also incapable of knowledge because you can still perceive lovelessly. Perception did not exist until the separation introduced degrees, aspects and intervals. Spirit has no levels, and all conflict arises from the concept of levels. Only the Levels of the Trinity are capable of unity. The levels created by the separation cannot but conflict. This is because they are meaningless to each other.

Consciousness, the level of perception, was the first split introduced into the mind after the separation, making the mind a perceiver rather than a creator. Consciousness is correctly identified as the domain of the ego. The ego is a wrong-minded attempt to perceive yourself as you wish to be, rather than as you are. Yet you can know yourself only as you are, because that is all you can be sure of. Everything else *is* open to question.[4]

When you were aware of the knowledge within you before the separation, you were certain because you clearly knew the true nature of yourself, of God, and of the Sonship. After the separation, uncertainty entered you mind.

To know is to be certain. Uncertainty means that you do not know. Knowledge is power because it is certain, and certainty is strength. Perception is temporary. As an attribute of the belief in space and time, it is subject to either fear or love. Misperceptions produce fear and true perceptions foster love, but neither brings certainty because all perception varies. That is why it is not knowledge. True perception is the basis for knowledge, but knowing is the affirmation of truth and beyond all perceptions.

All your difficulties stem from the fact that you do not recognize yourself, your brother or God. To recognize means to "know again," implying that you knew before. You can see in many ways because perception involves interpretation, and this means that it is not whole or consistent.[5]

When uncertainty entered your mind, you questioned everything having lost the all-inclusive awareness of knowledge. Hypothetically, it could be assumed that knowing who you are would be self-evident, yet even this elemental awareness of your own nature is lost in the confusion that perception has brought to your mind.

> The ego is the questioning aspect of the post-separation self, which was made rather than created. It is capable of asking questions but not of perceiving meaningful answers, because these would involve knowledge and cannot be perceived. The mind is therefore confused, because only One-mindedness can be without confusion. A separated or divided mind *must* be confused. It is necessarily uncertain about what it is. It has to be in conflict because it is out of accord with itself. This makes its aspects strangers to each other, and this is the essence of the fear-prone condition, in which attack is always possible. You have *every* reason to feel afraid as you perceive yourself. This is why you cannot escape from fear until you realize that you did not and could not create yourself. You can never make your misperceptions true, and your creation is beyond your own error. That is why you must eventually choose to heal the separation.
>
> Right-mindedness is not to be confused with the knowing mind, because it is applicable only to right perception. You can be right-minded or wrong-minded, and even this is subject to degrees, clearly demonstrating that knowledge is not involved. The term "right-mindedness" is properly used as the correction for "wrong-mindedness," and applies to the state of mind that induces accurate perception. It is miracle-minded because it heals misperception, and this is indeed a miracle in view of how you perceive yourself.
>
> Perception always involves some misuse of mind, because it brings the mind into areas of uncertainty.[6]

The uncertainty of mind relying on perception prevents you from identifying with your true nature or even knowing what your true nature is. As a result, you become very unstable and extremely confused.

The confusion between your real creation and what you have made of yourself is so profound that it has become literally impossible for you to know anything. Knowledge is always stable, and it is quite evident that you are not. Nevertheless, you are perfectly stable as God created you. In this sense, when your behavior is unstable, you are disagreeing with God's idea of your creation. You can do this if you choose, but you would hardly want to do it if you were in your right mind.

The fundamental question you continually ask yourself cannot properly be directed to yourself at all. You keep asking what it is you are. This implies that the answer is not only one you know, but is also one that is up to you to supply. Yet you cannot perceive yourself correctly. You have no image to be perceived. The word "image" is always perception-related, and not a part of knowledge. Images are symbolic and stand for something else. The idea of "changing your image" recognizes the power of perception, but also implies that there is nothing stable to know.

Knowing is not open to interpretation.[7]

The confusion in the mind allows the ego to come up with answers that have no basis in the truth. The ego does not know who you are, so the ego tells you that you are alone since the ego is the idea of separation. The ego reinforces the idea of your separate being by telling you that you are locked into a separate body that is your true home. Ironically the ego perceives spirit as a threat, and therefore discovering your true nature in spirit is also perceived by the ego as a threat.

The ability to perceive made the body possible, because you must perceive *something* and *with* something. That is why perception involves an exchange or translation, which knowledge does not need. The interpretative function of perception, a distorted form of creation, then permits you to interpret the body as yourself in an attempt to escape from the conflict you have induced. Spirit, which knows, could not be reconciled with this loss of power, because it is incapable of darkness. This makes spirit almost inaccessible to the mind and entirely inaccessible to the body. Thereafter, spirit is perceived as a threat, because light abolishes darkness merely by showing you it is not there. Truth will always overcome error in this way. This cannot be an active process of correction because, as I have already emphasized, knowledge does not do anything. It can be perceived as an attacker, but it cannot attack. What you perceive as its attack is your own vague recognition that knowledge can always be remembered, never having been destroyed.

God and His creations remain in surety, and therefore know that no miscreation exists. Truth cannot deal with errors that you want.[8]

Having accepted perception into your mind, your ego establishes a whole thought system in your mind to justify its existence—a thought system that is a contradiction to your true nature as a creation of God. God is your Author, the First Cause, and you are His effect, being part of Him. Nevertheless, because of the ego, you have your doubts about God being your Father, and this is called the "authority problem."

> The problem everyone must decide is the fundamental question of authorship. All fear comes ultimately, and sometimes by way of very devious routes, from the denial of Authorship. The offense is never to God, but only to those who deny Him. To deny His Authorship is to deny yourself the reason for your peace, so that you see yourself only in segments. This strange perception *is* the authority problem.[9]

You may actually currently believe that God created you. However, the ego does not and cannot share your belief. "The ego believes it is completely on its own, which is merely another way of describing how it thinks it originated."[10] If the ego allowed you to fully understand the meaning of your creation by God, you would realize that the ego does not exist and you would give it up. Thus the ego uses every means at its disposal to deny your creation by God or at least deny your understanding of the true ramifications of what your creation by God really means. The ramifications of your creation by God are that He loves you and as part of Him and part of the Sonship, you are never alone, except in your imaginings of the ego that do not exist in reality. Since the "ego is the mind's belief that it is completely on its own,"[11] the ego tells you that you are also completely on your own and that you do not have a Father Who created you. The foundation of the ego's thought system is that since you are alone and Fatherless, you must have created yourself. This belief that you created yourself is not a sane idea, but the Course maintains the ego itself represents an insane thought system. Obviously you couldn't possibly have created yourself, yet through the ego, you can deceive yourself.

> Eating of the fruit of the tree of knowledge is a symbolic expression for usurping the ability for self-creating. This is the only sense in which God and His creations are not co-creators. The belief that they are is implicit in the "self-concept," or the tendency of the self to make an image of itself. Images are perceived, not known. Knowledge cannot deceive, but perception can. You can perceive yourself as self-creating, but you cannot do more than believe it. You cannot make it true. And, as I said before, when you

finally perceive correctly you can only be glad that you cannot. Until then, however, the belief that you can is the foundation stone in your thought system, and all your defenses are used to attack ideas that might bring it to light. You still believe you are an image of your own making. Your mind is split with the Holy Spirit on this point, and there is no resolution while you believe the one thing that is literally inconceivable.[12]

The ego does not understand creation but actively presents to you its interpretation, which is merely an attempt to justify its continued existence. The ego was not created by God, and so it cannot tell you that you were created by God. Whenever you agree with the ego that you are alone, vulnerable, or afraid, you are also agreeing that God did not create you and so you must have created yourself. Here is what thinking that you are the ego encourages you to believe about your creation:

First, you believe that what God created can be changed by your own mind.

Second, you believe that what is perfect can be rendered imperfect or lacking.

Third, you believe that you can distort the creations of God, including yourself.

Fourth, you believe that you can create yourself, and that the direction of your own creation is up to you.[13]

These four beliefs encouraged by the ego "represent a picture of what actually occurred in the separation."[14] The changeable nature of perception encourages you to think you can make changes in who and what you are. These beliefs are ways of saying that you think you can change reality. Yet God is Reality, and as part of God's Reality you are unchangeable.

The ego tries to exploit all situations into forms of praise for itself in order to overcome its doubts. It will remain doubtful as long as you believe in its existence. You who made it cannot trust it, because in your right mind you realize it is not real. The only sane solution is not to try to change reality, which is indeed a fearful attempt, but to accept it as it is. You are part of reality, which stands unchanged beyond the reach of your ego but within easy reach of spirit. When you are afraid, be still and know that God is real, and you are His beloved Son in whom He is well pleased. Do not let your ego dispute this, because the ego cannot know what is as far beyond its reach as you are.[15]

Accepting reality means accepting the full awareness of knowledge to replace the partial awareness of illusory perceptions. You can only accept reality, not change it. But you can and must change illusions if you want to learn how to fully accept reality. And you can only change illusions with the help of the Holy Spirit. The ego questions everything because of its uncertainty, but you can use your questioning mind in a positive way: "Questioning illusions is the first step in undoing them."[16] You need healing: "Perception is based on a separated state, so that anyone who perceives at all needs healing."[17] You need salvation, which the Course defines in this way: "Salvation is nothing more than 'right-mindedness,' which is not the One-mindedness of the Holy Spirit, but which must be achieved before One-mindedness is restored."[18] Salvation is merely a return to knowledge by changing false perceptions into true perceptions, which produces right-mindedness. Attaining right-mindedness prepares for the transfer to knowledge that is your redemption. The remainder of this chapter emphasizes the process of shifting from false perceptions to true perceptions and finally to knowledge, summarized as follows:

> Perception, at its loftiest, is never complete. Even the perception of the Holy Spirit, as perfect as perception can be, is without meaning in Heaven. Perception can reach everywhere under His guidance, for the vision of Christ beholds everything in light. Yet no perception, however holy, will last forever.
>
> Perfect perception, then, has many elements in common with knowledge, making transfer to it possible. Yet the last step must be taken by God, because the last step in your redemption, which seems to be in the future, was accomplished by God in your creation. The separation has not interrupted it.[19]

B. Motivation for Changing Your Thought System

For the sake of an analogy, let's imagine that you buy a toaster, yet later discover that it always burns your toast. You would like to return it, but there is a no return policy at the store where you bought it. Consequently, you learn to live with burnt toast, which you get used to, although you still don't like it. Then one day you see a sign in the store that says, "All items can be returned for a full refund." You bring the toaster with your receipt back to the customer service department of the store and ask, "Can I return this toaster?"

The customer service agent says, "Yes, of course."

"Are you sure?" you ask. "I feel guilty about bringing it back because I have used it for a very long time."

"How long you have had it doesn't matter to us," the agent replies, "There's no need for you to feel guilty because returning your toaster does no harm to anyone. In fact, we are happy to have the toaster back if you don't want it."

"Well, there still is one problem. This toaster always burns my toast, but I've gotten so used to burnt toast that I've become accustomed to this old toaster. It's hard for me to let go of my attachment to this old toaster, and I am worried about what will happen to it. If I do give you back this toaster, will you completely destroy it?"

"No, we don't destroy anything," the agent says reassuringly. "We recycle everything. It's not a good toaster because it burns your toast, so we will take it apart and use its parts for a better use. As far as your return, you need to decide what you want. You bought this toaster for yourself because you wanted it. Now you have to decide if you still want it based on whether you have gained or lost by your purchase. Were you happier before you bought this toaster or are you happier with having burnt toast?"

"I was happier before I bought this toaster. Since you are going to recycle the toaster for a better purpose, I think I will give it back to you for a refund." Having released any sense of guilt or regret, you hand over the toaster and happily get the full refund of your purchase price.

This is an analogy of the dilemma of what to do with the ego, which is represented by the toaster. At the separation you made the ego because you wanted it, but then later you learned that having an ego is like having burnt toast that can be eaten, yet is not tasty and does not feel nourishing. The problem with the ego is that you made it thinking it would be irreversible and wanting it to be irreversible. You did not realize that it was refundable. Since you could not be anything but what God created, your ego could only be a temporary illusion that will eventually give way to your true eternal and changeless nature in God. You did not realize that you could get a refund for the ego from the Holy Spirit, represented by the customer service agent. It is not difficult for the Holy Spirit to relieve you of your ego, but it is difficult for you to let go of the ego. You can be a great meditator who can let go of perceptions and even experience wordless contemplation, but if you do not change your perceptions, you will not be able to release the ego. You imagine you are a separated ego attached to a body in a world of form. This dream seems very real so consider this: "You cannot undo it by not changing your mind about it."[20]

The conversation with the customer service agent in the analogy brings up five questions about your refund of the ego and shows what perceptions need to be changed.

1. The first question: *Can I get a refund for the ego?*

If God had made the ego, it would be as eternal and changeless as He is and as you are in Him. But since you made the ego with your own thoughts apart from God, it can be undone. Any thoughts that you make apart from God are illusory and not real thoughts. Your illusory thoughts have only the temporary power you give them by believing in them.

> Only what God creates is irreversible and unchangeable. What you made can always be changed because, when you do not think like God, you are not really thinking at all. Delusional ideas are not real thoughts, although you can believe in them. But you are wrong. The function of thought comes from God and is in God. As part of His Thought, you *cannot* think apart from Him.[21]

The belief that the ego cannot be refunded needs to give way to the understanding that it is indeed possible to release the ego. In fact, the refund is inevitable since the ego is merely a temporary illusion that must give way to the awareness of your eternal nature that is changeless. "The word 'inevitable' is fearful to the ego, but joyous to the spirit. God is inevitable, and you cannot avoid Him any more than He can avoid you."[22] When you refund the ego, you will get back your awareness of your place in the Sonship. This is an exchange of time for timelessness.

> All the Sons of God are waiting for your return, just as you are waiting for theirs. Delay does not matter in eternity, but it is tragic in time. You have elected to be in time rather than eternity, and therefore believe you *are* in time. Yet your election is both free and alterable. You do not belong in time. Your place is only in eternity, where God Himself placed you forever.
>   Guilt feelings are the preservers of time. They induce fears of retaliation or abandonment, and thus ensure that the future will be like the past. This is the ego's continuity. It gives the ego a false sense of security by believing that you cannot escape from it. But you can and must. God offers you the continuity of eternity in exchange. When you choose to make this exchange, you will simultaneously exchange guilt for joy, viciousness for love, and pain for peace.[23]

Refunding the ego is both possible and inevitable, but it does require you to make changes that open your mind to the changelessness of your true nature, which you will have to accept as you release the changing nature of the ego. Your ego is afraid of change, yet the ego can learn.

Many stand guard over their ideas because they want to protect their thought systems as they are, and learning means change. Change is always fearful to the separated, because they cannot conceive of it as a move towards healing the separation. They always perceive it as a move toward further separation, because the separation was their first experience of change. You believe that if you allow no change to enter into your ego you will find peace. This profound confusion is possible only if you maintain that the same thought system can stand on two foundations. Nothing can reach spirit from the ego, and nothing can reach the ego from spirit. Spirit can neither strengthen the ego nor reduce the conflict within it. The ego *is* a contradiction. Your self and God's Self *are* in opposition. They are opposed in source, in direction and in outcome. They are fundamentally irreconcilable, because spirit cannot perceive and the ego cannot know. They are therefore not in communication and can never be in communication. Nevertheless, the ego can learn, even though its maker can be misguided.[24]

2. The second question: *What do I do with my guilt?*

As you begin to realize that the ego can be refunded, thoughts of guilt surface that are all tied to the ego and even go back to the separation itself.

If the ego is the symbol of the separation, it is also the symbol of guilt. Guilt is more than merely not of God. It is the symbol of attack on God. This is a totally meaningless concept except to the ego, but do not underestimate the power of the ego's belief in it. This is the belief from which all guilt really stems.

The ego is the part of the mind that believes in division. How could part of God detach itself without believing it is attacking Him? We spoke before of the authority problem as based on the concept of usurping God's power. The ego believes that this is what you did because it believes that it *is* you. If you identify with the ego, you must perceive yourself as guilty. Whenever you respond to your ego you will experience guilt, and you will fear punishment. The ego is quite literally a fearful thought. However ridiculous the idea of attacking God may be to the sane mind, never forget that the ego is not sane. It represents a delusional system, and speaks for it. Listening to the ego's voice means that you believe it is possible to attack God, and that a part of Him has been torn away by you. Fear of retaliation from without follows, because the severity of the guilt is so acute that it must be projected.

Whatever you accept into your mind has reality for you. It is your acceptance of it that makes it real. If you enthrone the ego in your mind, your allowing it to enter makes it your reality. This is because the mind is capable of creating reality or making illusions.[25]

If you want to let go of the ego, you will have to learn how to let go of guilt. "Release from guilt is the ego's whole undoing."[26] The belief in guilt must be released by understanding that all the burnt toast of the ego has done no real harm. The customer service agent in the analogy expressed the Holy Spirit's viewpoint that God sees no cause for guilt and no real harm that can be done in a world of illusions where the ego seems real. If you have a dream of you robbing a bank, you don't wake up expecting to be arrested for your dream crime. In the same way, all guilt is "dream guilt." There are no consequences for guilt that never happened in reality. Sin is the belief that reality can be violated, but since reality cannot be violated, sin does not exist. Thus guilt and punishment are not warranted.

When you feel guilty, remember that the ego has indeed violated the laws of God, but *you* have not. Leave the "sins" of the ego to me. That is what Atonement is for. But until you change your mind about those whom your ego has hurt, the Atonement cannot release you. While you feel guilty your ego is in command, because only the ego can experience guilt. *This need not be.*

Watch your mind for the temptations of the ego, and do not be deceived by it. It offers you nothing. When you have given up this voluntary dis-spiriting, you will see how your mind can focus and rise above fatigue and heal. Yet you are not sufficiently vigilant against the demands of the ego to disengage yourself. *This need not be.*

The habit of engaging with God and His creations is easily made if you actively refuse to let your mind slip away. The problem is not one of concentration; it is the belief that no one, including yourself, is worth consistent effort.[27]

You do feel responsible and guilty for all the ways you have used your mind in opposition to God's Will, but it is God's Will for you to let go of that feeling of responsibility and of that guilt. The purpose of the Atonement is to correct all errors in the mind and to remove all the effects of those errors. That is why accepting the Atonement is so important. The Atonement is the gift from God that frees you from the past and allows you to see yourself as guiltless now. Only a choice to continue to separate now can perpetuate the belief in guilt, and this choice would be a refusal to accept the Atonement.

Irrational thought is disordered thought. God Himself orders your thought because your thought was created by Him. Guilt feelings are always a sign that you do not know this. They also show that you believe you can think apart from God, and want to. Every disordered thought is attended by guilt at its inception, and maintained by guilt in its continuance. Guilt is inescapable by those who believe they order their own thoughts, and must therefore obey their dictates. This makes them feel responsible for their errors without recognizing that, by accepting this responsibility, they are reacting irresponsibly. If the sole responsibility of the miracle worker is to accept the Atonement for himself, and I assure you that it is, then the responsibility for *what* is atoned for cannot be yours. The dilemma cannot be resolved except by accepting the solution of undoing. You *would* be responsible for the effects of all your wrong thinking if it could not be undone. The purpose of the Atonement is to save the past in purified form only. If you accept the remedy for disordered thought, a remedy whose efficacy is beyond doubt, how can its symptoms remain?"

The continuing decision to remain separated is the only possible reason for continuing guilt feelings.[28]

Chapter 21 explained that the benefits of forgiveness come from your overlooking of past errors and seeing the truth of holiness. But undoing errors and the effects of errors is not your sole responsibility. Instead of relying on yourself alone, you must rely on the Holy Spirit's action. "I do not feel guilty, because the Holy Spirit will undo all the consequences of my wrong decision if I will let Him."[29] The Holy Spirit is the "Mind of the Atonement"[30] and corrects all your mistakes and their effects. You merely have to accept the Atonement and trust that the Holy Spirit has performed His function of eliminating all your mistakes and their effects.

Forgiveness through the Holy Spirit lies simply in looking beyond error from the beginning, and thus keeping it unreal for you. Do not let any belief in its realness enter your mind, or you will also believe that you must undo what you have made in order to be forgiven. What has no effect does not exist, and to the Holy Spirit the effects of error are nonexistent. By steadily and consistently cancelling out all its effects, everywhere and in all respects, He teaches that the ego does not exist and proves it.[31]

3. The third question: *Will the ego be destroyed?*

When you untie your shoelaces and take off your shoes, you are merely taking a covering off of your feet. When you let go of the ego, you are not destroying it. Rather, you are *undoing* it and uncovering what it is hiding, which is your true Self. The ego cannot die, because it never lived. Only your Self has life, which comes directly from God and has no other source, except in illusions. In the analogy, the toaster is not destroyed; it is recycled. Similarly, the Course explains the undoing of the ego as a form of recycling the ego part of your mind in this way:

> Every loveless thought must be undone, a word the ego cannot even understand. To the ego, to be undone means to be destroyed. The ego will not be destroyed because it is part of your thought, but because it is uncreative and therefore unsharing, it will be reinterpreted to release you from fear. The part of your mind that you have given to the ego will merely return to the Kingdom, where your whole mind belongs. You can delay the completion of the Kingdom, but you cannot introduce the concept of fear into it.[32]

There is a small part of your mind that you imagine is your whole mind and that you think is your whole identity. This small part of your mind is, of course, your ego. When the ego is undone by giving way to the Truth, the ego disappears because you have withdrawn your belief in it. The small part of your mind that was ruled by the ego is simply reunited with the rest of the mind so your true mind is no longer split. When this happens, the mind is whole and so perception has given way to knowledge, which restores the full awareness of your true Home in Heaven. The return of wholeness to the mind can only be accomplished by listening to the Holy Spirit, Who accomplishes the undoing of the ego.

> I have said before that the Holy Spirit is God's Answer to the ego. Everything of which the Holy Spirit reminds you is in direct opposition to the ego's notions, because true and false perceptions are themselves opposed. The Holy Spirit has the task of undoing what the ego has made. He undoes it at the same level on which the ego operates, or the mind would be unable to understand the change.
>
> I have repeatedly emphasized that one level of the mind is not understandable to another....

The Holy Spirit is the Mediator between the interpretations of the ego and the knowledge of the spirit. His ability to deal with symbols enables Him to work with the ego's beliefs in its own language. His ability to look beyond symbols into eternity enables Him to understand the laws of God, for which He speaks. He can therefore perform the function of reinterpreting what the ego makes, not by destruction but by understanding. Understanding is light, and light leads to knowledge. The Holy Spirit is in light because He is in you who are light, but you yourself do not know this. It is therefore the task of the Holy Spirit to reinterpret you on behalf of God.

You cannot understand yourself alone. This is because you have no meaning apart from your rightful place in the Sonship, and the rightful place of the Sonship is God. This is your life, your eternity and your Self. It is of this that the Holy Spirit reminds you.[33]

The undoing of the ego is accomplished by accepting the Atonement, which is the Plan that God has given you as your means of correcting the mind through the actions and blessings of the Holy Spirit.

What fear has hidden still is part of you. Joining the Atonement is the way out of fear. The Holy Spirit will help you reinterpret everything that you perceive as fearful, and teach you that only what is loving is true. Truth is beyond your ability to destroy, but entirely within your ability to accept. It belongs to you because, as an extension of God, you created it with Him. It is yours because it is part of you, just as you are part of God because He created you. Nothing that is good can be lost because it comes from the Holy Spirit, the Voice for creation. Nothing that is not good was ever created, and therefore cannot be protected. The Atonement is the guarantee of the safety of the Kingdom, and the union of the Sonship is its protection. The ego cannot prevail against the Kingdom because the Sonship is united. In the presence of those who hear the Holy Spirit's Call to be as one, the ego fades away and is undone.

What the ego makes it keeps to itself, and so it is without strength. Its existence is unshared. It does not die; it was merely never born. Physical birth is not a beginning; it is a continuing. Everything that continues has already been born. It will increase as you are willing to return the unhealed part of your mind to the higher part, returning it undivided to creation.[34]

4. The fourth question: *What do I do about the feelings of familiarity I have acquired by making adjustments to the ego?*

Like familiarity with the toaster in the analogy, growing accustomed to the ego and its thought system has indeed given you a sense of familiarity, but carefully consider if this familiarity has brought you happiness.

> The blind become accustomed to their world by their adjustments to it. They think they know their way about in it. They learned it, not through joyous lessons, but through the stern necessity of limits they believed they could not overcome. And still believing this, they hold those lessons dear, and cling to them because they cannot see. They do not understand the lessons *keep* them blind. This they do not believe. And so they keep the world they learned to "see" in their imagination, believing that their choice is that or nothing. They hate the world they learned through pain. And everything they think is in it serves to remind them that they are incomplete and bitterly deprived.
>
> Thus they define their life and where they live, adjusting to it as they think they must, afraid to lose the little that they have. And so it is with all who see the body as all they have and all their brothers have. They try to reach each other, and they fail, and fail again. And they adjust to loneliness, believing that to keep the body is to save the little that they have.[35]

The ego uses your familiarity with it to tell you it is your friend. Yet consider this: "You made the ego without love, and so it does not love you."[36] You can replace the familiarity with the ego by developing familiarity with your true friends. "Within yourself you love your brother with a perfect love."[37] Your brothers are your friends though their egos have blinded their love as it has blinded your love. "You are being blessed by every beneficent thought of any of your brothers anywhere. You should want to bless them in return, out of gratitude. You need not know them individually, or they you."[38] Jesus is your elder brother. "When you unite with me [Jesus] you are uniting without the ego, because I have renounced the ego in myself and therefore cannot unite with yours. Our union is therefore the way to renounce the ego in you.... On this journey you have chosen me as your companion *instead* of the ego. Do not attempt to hold on to both, or you will try to go in different directions and will lose the way."[39] You can become familiar with holding His hand: "I will awaken you as surely as I awakened myself, for I awoke for you.... Trust in my help...and I will walk with you as our Father walked with me."[40]

The Holy Spirit is your faithful Friend Who loves you, and you can learn to become familiar with His Voice for God that reminds you of who you are.

> The Holy Spirit is your strength because He knows nothing but the spirit as you. He is perfectly aware that you do not know yourself, and perfectly aware of how to teach you to remember what you are. Because He loves you, He will gladly teach you what He loves, for He wills to share it. Remembering you always, He cannot let you forget your worth. For the Father never ceases to remind Him of His Son, and He never ceases to remind His Son of the Father. God is in your memory because of Him. You chose to forget your Father but you do not really want to do so, and therefore you can decide otherwise. As it was my decision, so is it yours.[41]

5. The fifth question: *Is giving up the ego what I want and will I be happier without it?*

In the analogy, the customer service agent asks you to decide if you want to keep or return the toaster based on whether you would be happier with or without your familiar burnt toast. You cannot return the toaster while you still want to keep it. Likewise, you cannot return the ego to have it undone by the Holy Spirit, while you still want to keep it. "And from what you want God does not save you."[42]

You may think you know what you want, but you can hardly know what you want as long as your perception is guided by the ego, which makes you uncertain about who you are. The Holy Spirit possesses both perfect perception and the certainty of knowledge, so He knows who you are. Thus the Holy Spirit is your Guide, Who knows that what you truly want is the awareness of your own reality in God. What you want is your will, but what does that really mean? You may think you are afraid of God's Will, but that's because you are afraid of yourself due to your belief in the ego. The truth is your will is one with God's Will, as was stated in Chapter 20. "You *are* the Will of God. Do not accept anything else as your will, or you are denying what you are. Deny this and you will attack, believing you have been attacked. But see the Love of God in you, and you will see it everywhere because it *is* everywhere."[43]

The ego contradicts God's Will that is your own will so releasing the ego is what you really want. To address whether or not you will be happier without the ego, you will need to compare the kind of love the ego offers to God's Love and decide which love will make you happier. This can only be a difficult decision if you do not know how much love God has for you in comparison with the meager offering of the ego.

The ego arose from the separation, and its continued existence depends on your continuing belief in the separation. The ego must offer you some sort of reward for maintaining this belief. All it can offer is a sense of temporary existence, which begins with its own beginning and ends with its own ending. It tells you this life is your existence because it is its own. Against this sense of temporary existence spirit offers you the knowledge of permanence and unshakable being. No one who has experienced the revelation of this can ever fully believe in the ego again. How can its meager offering to you prevail against the glorious gift of God?

You who identify with your ego cannot believe God loves you. You do not love what you made, and what you made does not love you. Being made out of the denial of the Father, the ego has no allegiance to its maker. You cannot conceive of the real relationship that exists between God and His creations because of your hatred for the self you made. You project onto the ego the decision to separate, and this conflicts with the love you feel for the ego because you made it. No love in this world is without this ambivalence, and since no ego has experienced love without ambivalence the concept is beyond its understanding. Love will enter immediately into any mind that truly wants it, but it must want it truly. This means that it wants it without ambivalence, and this kind of wanting is wholly without the ego's "drive to get."[44]

Another way to describe your choice between keeping the ego or replacing it is to say it is a choice between nothing and everything. Your ego is only an illusion of yourself and all illusions, big or small, amount to the same nothingness. The awareness of your true nature is in God, Who is Ultimate Reality itself. "Reality is everything, and you have everything because you are real."[45] There is no such thing as partial Ultimate Reality because God is Wholeness itself and must contain everything.

In your own mind, though denied by the ego, is the declaration of your release. *God has given you everything.* This one fact means the ego does not exist, and this makes it profoundly afraid. In the ego's language, "to have" and "to be" are different, but they are identical to the Holy Spirit. The Holy Spirit knows that you both *have* everything and *are* everything. Any distinction in this respect is meaningful only when the idea of "getting," which implies a lack, has already been accepted. That is why we make no distinction between *having* the Kingdom of God and *being* the Kingdom of God.

The calm being of God's Kingdom, which in your sane mind is perfectly conscious, is ruthlessly banished from the part of the mind the ego rules. The ego is desperate because it opposes literally invincible odds, whether you are asleep or awake. Consider how much vigilance you have been willing to exert to protect your ego, and how little to protect your right mind. Who but the insane would undertake to believe what is not true, and then protect this belief at the cost of truth?[46]

Perhaps after addressing the five questions above, you will conclude that the familiarity of the ego is not satisfying and that you want the true happiness that the Holy Spirit holds out to you. "Eventually everyone begins to recognize, however dimly, that there *must* be a better way. As this recognition becomes more firmly established, it becomes a turning point."[47] Instead of clinging to your ego's thought system, you may be interested in the Course's proposal that offers you a "better way," a better thought system that will eventually lead you to replace the ego itself. "The first step toward freedom involves a sorting out of the false from the true."[48] This "sorting out" will require time for you to become familiar with true perceptions by studying them in the Course. The rest of this chapter addresses making perceptual changes that help you to replace the ego.

The way to correct distortions is to withdraw your faith in them and invest it only in what is true. You cannot make untruth true. If you are willing to accept what is true in everything you perceive, you let it be true for you. Truth overcomes all error, and those who live in error and emptiness can never find lasting solace. If you perceive truly you are cancelling out misperceptions in yourself and in others simultaneously. Because you see them as they are, you offer them your acceptance of their truth so they can accept it for themselves. This is the healing that the miracle induces.[49]

All of the changes in perception recommended in the Course involve a seeking of the truth that leads to accepting Truth itself. In this world of illusions, truth is very commendable as a character trait, but it is hardly considered indispensible. Truth is undervalued in a world of illusions, but if you want to correct illusions, the truth is mandatory.

What can correct illusions but the truth? And what are errors but illusions that remain unrecognized for what they are? Where truth has entered errors disappear. They are gone because, without belief, they have no life....for only truth remains.[50]

Workbook Lesson 107 asks you to remind yourself of this idea: "Truth will correct all errors in my mind." If all your errors are corrected with the necessary help of the Holy Spirit, the ego itself will disappear along with every other illusion. When all illusions are gone, you will see that "...the reality of your mind is the loveliest of God's creations. Coming only from God, its power and grandeur could only bring you peace *if you really looked upon it*."[51] When only truth remains in your mind, you will have true peace of mind, which knowledge of reality brings. This knowledge is a return to the awareness that you had before the separation. Your knowledge will bring certainty to the mind and will end your questioning of who and what you are, which is so characteristic of the confusion of the ego. What will it feel like to have the peace that knowledge brings when illusions are gone?

Can you imagine what a state of mind without illusions is? How it would feel? Try to remember when there was a time,—perhaps a minute, maybe even less—when nothing came to interrupt your peace; when you were certain you were loved and safe. Then try to picture what it would be like to have that moment be extended to the end of time and to eternity. Then let the sense of quiet that you felt be multiplied a hundred times, and then be multiplied another hundred more.

And now you have a hint, not more than just the faintest intimation of the state your mind will rest in when the truth has come. Without illusions there could be no fear, no doubt and no attack. When truth has come all pain is over, for there is no room for transitory thoughts and dead ideas to linger in your mind. Truth occupies your mind completely, liberating you from all beliefs in the ephemeral. They have no place because the truth has come, and they are nowhere. They can not be found, for truth is everywhere forever, now.

When truth has come it does not stay a while, to disappear or change to something else. It does not shift and alter in its form, nor come and go and go and come again. It stays exactly as it always was, to be depended on in every need, and trusted with a perfect trust in all the seeming difficulties and the doubts that the appearances the world presents engender. They will merely blow away, when truth corrects the errors in your mind.[52]

1. W-158.1:2, p. 298
2. T-13.VIII.2:1-8, p. 258
3. T-13.VIII.2:1-8, p. 258
4. T-3.IV.1:1-9, 2:1-5, pp. 41-42

5. T-3.III.1:3-10, 2:1-3, p. 40
6. T-3.IV.3:1-11, 4:1-4, 5:1, pp. 42-43
7. T-3.V.3:2-5, 4:1-8, 5:1, pp. 44-45
8. T-3.IV.6:1-10, 7:1-2, p. 43
9. T-3.VI.10:3-7, p. 49
10. T-4.II.8.1, p. 58
11. T-4.II.8:4, p. 58
12. T-3.VII.4:1-11, p. 50
13. T-2.I.1:9-12, p. 17
14. T-2.I.2:1, p. 17
15. T-4.I.8:1-7, pp. 54-55
16. T-3.III.2:6, p. 40
17. T-3.V.10:3, p. 46
18. T-4.II.10:1, p. 59
19. T-13.VIII.2:5-8, 3:1-3, p. 258
20. T-4.I.4:6, p. 54
21. T-5.V.6:11-16, p. 85
22. T-4.I.9:10-11, p. 55
23. T-5.VI.1:2-7, 2:1-7, p. 86
24. T-4.I.2:1-13, p. 53
25. T-5.V.2:8-12, 3:1-11, 4:1-4, p. 84
26. T-13.IX.2:1, p. 261
27. T-4.IV.5:1-6, 6:1-5, 7:1-2, pp. 63-64
28. T-5.V.7:1-12, 8:1, pp. 85-86
29. T-5.VII.6:10, p. 90
30. T-5.I.6:3, p. 74
31. T-9.IV.5:3-6, p. 169
32. T-5.VI.9:2-6, pp. 87-88
33. T-5.III.5:3-6, 6:1, 7:1-7, 8:1-4, p. 79
34. T-5.IV.1:1-11, 2:1-6, p. 81
35. T-21.I.4:1-9, 5:1-4, p. 446
36. T-6.IV.2:3, p. 100
37. T-18.I.9:3, p. 374
38. T-5.In.3:1-2, p. 72
39. T-8.V.4:1-2, 5:8-9, p. 147
40. T-12.II.7:2,5, p. 219
41. T-12.VI.2:1-8, pp. 227-228
42. T-12.VII.14:6, p. 233
43. T-7.VII.10:1-4, p. 129
44. T-4.III.3:2-8, 4:1-8, pp. 60-61
45. T-9.I.13:3, p. 163
46. T-4.III.9:1-7, 10:1-4, p. 62
47. T-2.III.3:6-7, p. 22
48. T-2.VIII.4:1, p. 34
49. T-3.II.6:1-7, p. 39
50. W-107.1:1-3, 5, 7, p. 192
51. T-12.VII.10:2-3, p. 232
52. W-107.2:1-5, 3:1-6, 4:1-4, p. 192

24

HOW TO AWAKEN

~ ◦ ~

A. From False Perceptions to True Perceptions

The Course emphasizes that if your thought system is based on the ego, you are using wrong-minded thinking. Your experience of meditation and contemplation will not correct wrong-minded thinking. You must learn to listen to the Holy Spirit in your daily life and learn how to change your false perceptions into true perceptions so your thought system is based on right-minded thinking. You cannot make the jump from wrong-minded thinking directly to the knowledge of reality. First, you must change your wrong-minded thinking into right-minded thinking, as a preparation for eventually letting go of all perceptions in order to awaken to knowledge.

If you are a Course student, I suggest you place a high value on the dedication of your meditation practice prior to your attunement itself. This dedication is a time to consolidate your commitment to God based on Course principles that express right-minded thinking. To give you an example of a Course-based dedication, I will describe how I dedicate myself before starting my contemplative practice. First, I focus on sending forgiveness and blessings to a memorized list of over a hundred people who have been meaningful in my life. I do this for each of my daily meditation periods. But for the last session, I have a longer dedication in which I slowly, and with full attention, repeat the following words:

Father, bless all my brothers and sisters. They are each the holy Son of God, who deserves to wake up in Heaven. They are the Christ, They are the Light. They are the Love. Father, bless me. I am the holy Son of God, who deserves to awake up in Heaven. I am the Christ. I am the Light. I am the Love.

I forgive all my brothers and sisters for falling asleep in Heaven. I forgive all my brothers and sisters for all their past life and their present life mis-Identifications. I forgive myself for falling asleep in Heaven. I forgive myself for all my past life and present life mis-Identifications.

I accept the Atonement as God's remedy [His Plan], removing all the effects of my mis-Identifications and proclaiming that I am God's sinless Son. Father, I know you created me with your own Love and Holiness so I am free of guilt forever. Thus I let go of my former fantasies of guilt and accept your Plan for the freedom and salvation of all my brothers and sisters and of me. Holy Spirit, please guide my mind, decide for God for me, and be in charge of my meditation experience of the holy instant. Jesus, I join my mind with Your Mind in the Mind of Christ that we share, and so I release private thoughts. Jesus, I join my will with Your Will that is God's Will that we share, so I let go of a separate will. Father, open my heart and mind to receive your Love. Let your Love pass through me to bless all my brothers and sisters. Thank you, Father.

I conclude this dedication with a note of gratitude, because the most effective meditation is always a song of gratitude offered by the created to the Creator. I am not suggesting that you repeat a long dedication such as mine. Rather, if you are a Course student, I encourage you to use your own words to come up a brief dedication that reminds you of your commitment to God based on Course principles. I make this suggestion because the Course encourages you to change your entire thought system, replacing unloving, false perceptions with loving, true perceptions. This focus on the dedication has a dual purpose. Naturally it prepares you for meditation, as it would be for any seeker. In addition, it helps you to build a strong foundation for adopting a new thought system based on Course principles. Each day as you repeat your dedication, you will become more solidly rooted in your understanding of the Course, which in turn will help you apply your understanding to your daily life experiences.

If you would like to practice Course-based Miracle Yoga, as described previously, I recommend that you choose words for your dedication that emphasize four specific intentions: The first intention is forgiveness. The second intention is your desire to accept the Atonement, which removes all your errors and the effects of your errors on others and on yourself and which enables you to perform miracles that are extensions of love. The third intention is to receive God's Love yourself and allow His Love to flow through you to bless others. This is the offering of yourself as an empty vessel to be filled with love by the Holy Spirit, Who accepts your experience of the holy instant on behalf of your brothers and sisters. In this way, miracles of love are extended through you to many others without requiring your conscious awareness of who receives them.

For your Miracle Yoga dedication, the fourth intention I recommend is choosing words that remind you of your true Identity in God and in

Christ. In regard to affirming my own true Identity, I would like to explain why I choose to use the word "mis-Identificatation," which is not a Course term. When I first started to study the Course, I was fascinated by the section in Chapter 9 called "The Correction of Error." I felt strongly drawn to read and reread this entire section. Here is part of that section:

> To perceive errors in anyone, and to react to them as if they were real, is to make them real to you. You will not escape paying the price for this, not because you are being punished for it, but because you are following the wrong guide and will therefore lose your way.
>
> Your brother's errors are not of him, any more than yours are of you. Accept his errors as real, and you have attacked yourself.[1]

Strangely enough, I was not repeatedly reading this section because I believed it so strongly. Rather, I was reading it because I really could not understand it. Yes, I did understand it intellectually, but not in a meaningful way that would allow me to apply it. For example, I knew that every time I focused on my brother's errors, I made them real to me and in so doing made my own errors appear just as real. Thus I was mentally attacking my brother and myself with my judgments. Yet my intellectual awareness did not stop me from sitting in judgment of errors. I felt like a drug addict who could not stop taking drugs while knowing full well the self-destructive nature of this behavior. How to address errors in others and myself had always been a mystery to me. I did not know how to address them in just the right way, without giving too much or too little attention to them. I knew I needed a change of mind to help me to perceive errors differently. The Course helped me learn that sins are mistakes that can be corrected, but I still had trouble dealing with the shortcomings of others and myself.

After reading "The Correction of Error" section hundreds of times, I was finally able to internalize the message contained in it. As part of my internalization, I decided that even the words "error" or "mistake" are not the best way for me to think of lack of love in others or me. Instead, I decided to think of errors as "mis-Identifications." This word is comforting for me. It reminds me of Jesus saying, "Father, forgive them; for they know not what they do."[2] He could have just as easily said, "Father, forgive them *for they know not who they are*." I like the word "mis-Identification" because it helps me see not what I have done wrong, but what I have to do to make things right. All I must do is change my mind from a mis-Identification to an Identification of who another person is in Christ and an Identification of who I am in Christ. All of my brothers' shortcomings are overcome in this one correction and likewise all of my shortcomings are overcome in this same correction. All of forgiveness and all of the 1249 pages of the Course are summarized in this simple idea of changing mis-Identifications into Identifications.

There are two evaluations of yourself in your mind: one is the Holy Spirit's and the other is the ego's. Each evaluation tells you something different about yourself since they define you in opposite ways. The ego is the part of your mind that does not love you, so it cannot tell you that love is your true nature in God. The ego believes it is up to you to decide who you are. The Holy Spirit knows the God of Love decided who you are when He created you as part of Himself. He will never change His Mind about you. The Holy Spirit sees who you really are and evaluates you accordingly. Because the ego is incapable of telling you who you really are, it encourages you to believe in all sorts of mis-Identifications.

> It is perfectly obvious that if the Holy Spirit looks with love on all He perceives, He looks with love on you. His evaluation of you is based on His knowledge of what you are, and so He evaluates you truly. And this evaluation must be in your mind, because He is. The ego is also in your mind, because you have accepted it there. Its evaluation of you, however, is the exact opposite of the Holy Spirit's, because the ego does not love you. It is unaware of what you are, and wholly mistrustful of everything it perceives because its perceptions are so shifting. The ego is therefore capable of suspiciousness at best and viciousness at worst. That is its range. It cannot exceed it because of its uncertainty. And it can never go beyond it because it can never *be* certain.
>
> You, then, have two conflicting evaluations of yourself in your mind, and they cannot both be true. You do not yet realize how completely different these evaluations are, because you do not understand how lofty the Holy Spirit's perception of you really is. He is not deceived by anything you do, because He never forgets what you are. The ego is deceived by everything you do, especially when you respond to the Holy Spirit, because at such times its confusion increases....
>
> If you choose to see yourself as unloving you will not be happy. You are condemning yourself and must therefore regard yourself as inadequate. Would you look to the ego to help you escape from a sense of inadequacy it has produced, and must maintain for its existence?[3]

You have to decide which evaluation you want to pay attention to and to believe. Your everyday thought system is permeated by the ego's idea of separation, but that thought system of separation is not capable of telling you who you are because of its limiting ideas. Standing outside your ego-based thought system, the Holy Spirit is in a position to remind you of who you are. However, you have to do your part by accepting the Holy Spirit as your Teacher and by listening to what He tells you about yourself since He is not confused about who you are.

Because the world seems so real, it bears repeating and pondering that you are asleep in Heaven. In your sleep you are merely dreaming of living in the world of form while actually still remaining in Heaven.

> "You are at home in God, dreaming of exile but perfectly capable of awakening to reality…. You recognize from your own experience that what you see in dreams you think is real while you are asleep. Yet the instant you waken you realize that everything that seemed to happen in the dream did not happen at all. You do not think this strange, even though all the laws of what you awaken to were violated while you slept. Is it not possible that you merely shifted from one dream to another, without really waking?"[4]

God is the only true Reality, which we call Heaven. Although I do believe I am real, I do not seem by outer appearances to be living in the Reality of Heaven. Nevertheless, since I am real, I must still be living in the one and only Reality of Heaven, as the Course affirms. "Heaven is your home, and being in God it must also be in you."[5] The only thing that is keeping me from waking up in the one everlasting Reality is my ongoing mis-Identifications. Thus I feel I need to do all that I can every day to learn to change my mis-Identifications into Identifications. Prior to studying the Course, I thought my task was to learn to accept my Identity in God within myself alone. Yet the Course taught me this: "Your identification is with the Father *and* with the Son. It cannot be with one and not the other."[6] The goal of the Course is for you to know who you are, but knowing yourself involves more than just looking within yourself alone.

> The goal of the curriculum, regardless of the teacher you choose, is "Know thyself." There is nothing else to seek. Everyone is looking for himself and for the power and glory he thinks he has lost. Whenever you are with anyone, you have another opportunity to find them. Your power and glory are in him because they are yours. The ego tries to find them in yourself alone, because it does not know where to look. The Holy Spirit teaches you that if you look only at yourself you cannot find yourself, because that is not what you are. Whenever you are with a brother, you are learning what you are because you are teaching what you are. He will

respond either with pain or with joy, depending on which teacher you are following. He will be imprisoned or released according to your decision, and so will you. Never forget your responsibility to him, because it is your responsibility to yourself. Give him his place in the Kingdom and you will have yours.

The Kingdom cannot be found alone, and you who are the Kingdom cannot find yourself alone.[7]

In daily activities it is easy to forget about your true Identity as part of God and as part of the Sonship that you share with your brothers and sisters. But each meditation is a time to refocus on the truth—a time to let go of your illusions and to accept your true Identity. However, this time of inward acceptance of your true nature must bear fruit by being expressed in your everyday relationships and in your way of navigating through the world. Your challenge is to learn to rely on the Holy Spirit as much in your outer world as you do in your inner spiritual world.

B. The Unification of the Mind

My approach to spirituality before studying the Course was a blending of yoga and seeking Christ within, which included a heavy emphasis on practicing meditation. Yoga means "union." I thought meditation was my best means of joining with the Holy Spirit to bring about unification. But what does the Course say about joining with the Holy Spirit?

Joining with Him in seeing is the way in which you learn to share with Him the interpretation of perception that leads to knowledge. You cannot see alone. Sharing perception with Him Whom God has given you teaches you how to recognize what you see. It is the recognition that nothing you see means anything alone. Seeing with Him will show you that all meaning, including yours, comes not from double vision, but from the gentle fusing of everything into *one* meaning, *one* emotion and *one* purpose. God has one purpose which He shares with you. The single vision which the Holy Spirit offers you will bring this oneness to your mind with clarity and brightness so intense you could not wish, for all the world, not to accept what God would have you have. Behold your will, accepting it as His, with all His Love as yours. All honor to you through Him, and through Him unto God.[8]

Yes, union with the Holy Spirit happens in meditation, but prior to studying the Course, I did not appreciate the value of perception and did not know how to best use it for my spiritual growth. I know that in meditation I could reduced my scattered perceptions by focusing on one perception. Also, I knew that I could let go of even that single perception and enter the restful state of contemplation. But I thought that the limit to perception was its unification into one perception during meditation, and I was convinced that the best use of perception was to let go of it altogether. It did not occur to me that what I had learned about perception in meditation could be generalized into my daily life. I thought that my outer experience of the world was so filled with scattered perceptions that I could not possibly unify them as I could in meditation. Yet from the Course, I would learn how to focus on what the quotation above describes as the "*one* meaning, *one* emotion, *one* purpose," which is the one purpose God shares with me. It is the purpose of oneness itself, which in a practical sense means the unification of perceptions that seem to be separate. The oneness of my meaning, emotion, and purpose, and, indeed my oneness with God Himself, is in my mind now. I realized that to find the oneness in my mind, I needed to learn how to unify my thought system, meaning to unify what appeared to be totally disorganized perceptions.

When I first started to read the Course, I learned about many ways of using perceptions to grow spiritually. Here is a list of some specific Course recommendations for changing perceptions:

THE SHIFT FROM FALSE PERCEPTIONS TO TRUE PERCEPTIONS

From self-will to God's Will
From illusions of the past to the awareness of now
From private thoughts to thinking with the Holy Spirit
From perceiving separation to perceiving oneness
From unloving perceptions to loving perceptions
From illusions of nightmares to happy dreams
From projecting guilt to accepting innocence
From holding grievances to giving forgiveness
From attack thoughts to miracles
From illusions of special love to extending love to everyone
From mistakes to corrected perception
From seeing with the body's eyes to seeing with Christ's eyes

It seems at first glance that all these approaches to changing perceptions are different, but they have the common element of unifying perceptions by directing new perceptions toward the one goal of God. Because my background was in Christian yoga, I decided to use the term "Miracle Yoga" to describe my understanding of the Course. The goal of the Course is to unify perceptions. The five aspects of Miracle Yoga emphasize a single approach to unifying perceptions. Miracle Raja Yoga arrives at the unification of perception by focusing inwardly in meditation on *one thought*, which has already been emphasized. Miracle Bhakti Yoga brings about the unification of perception by centering on *one emotion*, which is love. Miracle Karma Yoga relies on maintaining *one function* to accomplish the unification of perception. Miracle Relationship Yoga produces the unification of perception through *one relationship*. Miracle Jnana Yoga achieves the unification of perception by seeking *one truth*.

The five methods of Miracle Yoga lead to five places. In the practice of meditation used in Miracle Raja Yoga, you use one thought to bring stillness to the mind. "And turn you to the stately calm within, where in holy stillness dwells the living God you never left, and Who never left you."[9] Meditation is a process of moving the mind from many distracting thoughts to one thought. The objective is to unify the mind. "One thought, completely unified, will serve to unify all thought."[10] In meditation moving the mind in the direction of unification based on one thought leads to the "circle of your peace." This place has many other names: "inner altar," "changeless dwelling place," and "holy sanctuary."

> In Him you have no cares and no concerns, no burdens, no anxiety, no pain, no fear of future and no past regrets. In timelessness you rest, while time goes by without its touch upon you, for your rest can never change in any way at all. You rest today. And as you close your eyes, sink into stillness. Let these periods of rest and respite reassure your mind that all its frantic fantasies were but the dreams of fever that has passed away. Let it be still and thankfully accept its healing. No more fearful dreams will come, now that you rest in God. Take time today to slip away from dreams and into peace....
>
> You rest within the peace of God today, and call upon your brothers from your rest to draw them to their rest, along with you. You will be faithful to your trust today, forgetting no one, bringing everyone into the boundless circle of your peace, the holy sanctuary where you rest. Open the temple doors and let them come from far across the world, and near as well; your distant brothers and your closest friends; bid them all enter here and rest with you.[11]

Miracle Bhakti Yoga emphasizes love. The focus on this one emotion of love unifies the mind because love itself is unifying, described in this way: "...the attraction of love for love remains irresistible. For it is the function of love to unite all things unto itself, and to hold all things together by extending its wholeness."[12] Focusing on love brings you to the "real world," which is also called the "circle of brightness" and the "happy dream," and which consists of only loving perceptions.

> This world of light, this circle of brightness is the real world, where guilt meets with forgiveness. Here the world outside is seen anew, without the shadow of guilt upon it. Here are you forgiven, for here you have forgiven everyone. Here is the new perception, where everything is bright and shining with innocence, washed in the waters of forgiveness, and cleansed of every evil thought you laid upon it. Here there is no attack upon the Son of God, and you are welcome. Here is your innocence, waiting to clothe you and protect you, and make you ready for the final step in the journey inward. Here are the dark and heavy garments of guilt laid by, and gently replaced by purity and love.
>
> Yet even forgiveness is not the end. Forgiveness does make lovely, but it does not create. It is the source of healing, but it is the messenger of love and not its Source. Here you are led, that God Himself can take the final step unhindered, for here does nothing interfere with love, letting it be itself. A step beyond this holy place of forgiveness, a step still further inward but the one *you* cannot take, transports you to something completely different. Here is the Source of light; nothing perceived, forgiven nor transformed. But merely known.[13]

Miracle Karma Yoga involves taking selfless action and expressing your function. Applying the one function of following God's Will and God's Plan leads to the "Circle of Atonement." Your special function is always a form of forgiving others, which enables you to forgive yourself.

> Everyone has a special part to play in the Atonement, but the message given to each one is always the same; *God's Son is guiltless.* Each one teaches the message differently, and learns it differently. Yet until he teaches it and learns it, he will suffer the pain of dim awareness that his true function remains unfulfilled in him. The burden of guilt is heavy, but God would not have you bound by it. His plan for your awaking is as perfect as yours is fallible. You know not what you do, but He Who knows is with you. His gentleness is yours, and all the love you share with God He holds in trust for you. He would teach you nothing except how to be happy....

Each one you see you place within the holy circle of Atonement or leave outside, judging him fit for crucifixion or for redemption. If you bring him into the circle of purity, you will rest there with him. If you leave him without, you join him there. Judge not except in quietness which is not of you. Refuse to accept anyone as without the blessing of Atonement, and bring him into it by blessing him. Holiness must be shared, for therein lies everything that makes it holy. Come gladly to the holy circle, and look out in peace on all who think they are outside. Cast no one out, for here is what he seeks along with you. Come, let us join him in the holy place of peace which is for all of us, united as one within the Cause of peace.[14]

Miracle Relationship Yoga is focused on holy relationships based on partners having a common purpose and seeing holiness in everyone. Maintaining a relationship of holiness allows you to see the "face of Christ," which is the "vision of the Son of God." In the holy relationship, you have the opportunity to see the light behind your brother's body and see his guiltlessness. Looking past your brother's mask, you can even perceive the face of Christ. "The face of Christ is looked upon before the Father is remembered."[15] The face of Christ reminds you of your true relationship with God and with all your brothers and sisters in Christ.

You have a *real* relationship, and it has meaning. It is as like your real relationship with God as equal things are like unto each other. Idolatry is past and meaningless. Perhaps you fear your brother a little yet; perhaps a shadow of the fear of God remains with you. Yet what is that to those who have been given one true relationship beyond the body? Can they be long held back from looking on the face of Christ? And can they long withhold the memory of their relationship with their Father from themselves, and keep remembrance of His Love apart from their awareness?[16]

Miracle Jnana Yoga is concerned with finding truth and gaining understanding. This seeking of one truth leads you to the "borderland" where all false perceptions are replaced by true perceptions. Here you choose between illusions and truth by bringing them together and seeing that illusions are meaningless and so can be easily released.

There is a borderland of thought that stands between this world and Heaven. It is not a [physical] place, and when you reach it is apart from time. Here is the meeting place where thoughts are brought together; where conflicting values meet and all illusions are laid down beside the truth, where they are judged to be untrue. This borderland is just beyond the gate of Heaven. Here is every thought made pure and wholly simple. Here is sin denied, and everything that *is* received instead.

This is the journey's end. We have referred to it as the real world. And yet there is a contradiction here, in that the words imply a limited reality, a partial truth, a segment of the universe made true. This is because knowledge makes no attack upon perception. They are brought together, and only one continues past the gate where oneness is. Salvation is a borderland where place and time and choice have meaning still, and yet it can be seen that they are temporary, out of place, and every choice has been already made.

Nothing the Son of God believes can be destroyed. But what is truth to him must be brought to the last comparison that he will ever make; the last evaluation that will be possible, the final judgment upon this world. It is the judgment of the truth upon illusion, of knowledge on perception: "It has no meaning, and does not exist." This is not your decision. It is but a simple statement of a simple fact. But in this world there are no simple facts, because what is the same and what is different remain unclear. The one essential thing to make a choice at all is this distinction. And herein lies the difference between the worlds. In this one, choice is made impossible. In the real world is choosing simplified.[17]

Perhaps you have noticed these five places are all circles—the circle of peace, the real world that is "the circle of brightness," the Circle of Atonement, the face of Christ that is an infinitely expanding circle of light, and the borderland (another name for the real world's circle of brightness). These five terms may appear to signify different places, but they are actually the same place. This makes sense since the Course is leading you to one destination in God and so would bring you to one place where oneness can be awakened. This single place is located in the seventh chakra, which is at the top of the head, but is often considered to be located just above the head. It is the place in the body where the soul exits this world at death. Here you will also have the opportunity to accept eternal life that is always present. Yet this place is not Heaven itself. Rather, it is often referred to in the Course as a "bridge." It is the gateway to Heaven. This bridge allows you to make the transition to the acceptance of the divine Embrace, which occurs in the final step initiated by God.

In this book I have discussed climbing up a ladder of awareness toward oneness with God. Before studying the Course, I assumed that perception was relegated to the lower rungs of the ladder and that meditation and contemplation were higher rungs. I had no clue about the real value of perceptions. I did not realize that true perceptions could become so holy that they could lead directly to knowledge—the transcendental awareness of Heaven in which the mind returns to wholeness in God.

> And then the real world will spring to your sight, for Christ has never slept. He [Christ] is waiting to be seen, for He has never lost sight of you. He looks quietly on the real world, which He would share with you because He knows of the Father's Love for Him. And knowing this, He would give you what is yours. In perfect peace He waits for you at His Father's altar, holding out the Father's Love to you in the quiet light of the Holy Spirit's blessing. For the Holy Spirit will lead everyone home to his Father, where Christ waits as his Self.
>
> Every child of God is one in Christ, for his being is in Christ as Christ's is in God. Christ's Love for you is His Love for His Father, which He knows because He knows His Father's Love for Him. When the Holy Spirit has at last led you to Christ at the altar to His Father, perception fuses into knowledge because perception has become so holy that its transfer to holiness is merely its natural extension. Love transfers to love without any interference, for the two are one.[18]

It was a surprise to me that perception could become so holy and so loving that it could fuse into knowledge. The Course quotation below encourages you to *generalize learning.* After you learn a new Course principle in a limited context, the Holy Spirit guides you to generalize your learning by applying your true and loving perceptions to all people and all situations without exception. True and loving perceptions have no meaning unless they apply universally, since God's laws are universal.

> As you perceive more and more common elements in all situations, the transfer of training under the Holy Spirit's guidance increases and becomes generalized. Gradually you learn to apply it to everyone and everything, for its applicability is universal. When this has been accomplished, perception and knowledge have become so similar that they share the unification of the laws of God.
>
> What is one cannot be perceived as separate, and the denial of the separation is the reinstatement of knowledge. At the altar of God, the holy perception of God's Son becomes so enlightened that light streams into it, and the spirit of God's Son shines in the

Mind of the Father and becomes one with it. Very gently does God shine upon Himself, loving the extension of Himself that is His Son. The world has no purpose as it blends into the purpose of God. For the real world has slipped quietly into Heaven, where everything eternal in it has always been. There the Redeemer and the redeemed join in perfect love of God and of each other. Heaven is your home, and being in God it must also be in you.[19]

The Course shares with you how to shift your awareness from false perceptions to true perceptions. But the Holy Spirit's grand Plan for you is to unify your perception. "The transfer value of one true idea has no end or limit. The final outcome of this lesson is the remembrance of God."[20] In the quotation below, notice the term "total perception," which is perfect perception that is so entirely filled with love that it transcends perception itself. Total perception is reached by seeing the real world with Christ's vision through the "eyes of Christ," as a gift of grace from the Holy Spirit.

> The real world was given you by God in loving exchange for the world you made and the world you see. Only take it from the hand of Christ and look upon it. Its reality will make everything else invisible, for beholding it is total perception. And as you look upon it you will remember that it was always so. Nothingness will become invisible, for you will at last have seen truly. Redeemed perception is easily translated into knowledge, for only perception is capable of error and perception has never been. Being corrected it gives place to knowledge, which is forever the only reality. The Atonement is but the way back to what was never lost. Your Father could not cease to love His Son.[21]

Christ's vision, even before it produces total perception, is still a very powerful means of viewing the world with forgiving eyes that see true perceptions. Using the Holy Spirit's sight is a very practical means of perceiving for this reason: "There is no problem, no event or situation, no perplexity that vision will not solve. All is redeemed when looked upon with vision. For this is not *your* sight, and brings with it the laws beloved of Him Whose sight it is."[22] When Christ's vision finally produces total perception, this seeing of the entire real world—a world of all loving thoughts—is the same as seeing the face of Christ, the infinitely expanding circle of light. The fact that seeing the real world is the same as seeing the face of Christ is just one example of how the Course uses different terms to mean the same thing. Another example is the use of the term "true perception" that is a "remedy that has many names" identified below:

Knowledge is not the remedy for false perception since, being another level, they can never meet. The one correction possible for false perception must be *true perception*. It will not endure. But for the time it lasts it comes to heal. For true perception is a remedy with many names. Forgiveness, salvation, Atonement, true perception, all are one. They are the one beginning, with the end to lead to oneness far beyond themselves. True perception is the means by which the world is saved from sin, for sin does not exist. And it is this that true perception sees.

The world stands like a block before Christ's face. But true perception looks on it as nothing more than just a fragile veil, so easily dispelled that it can last no longer than an instant. It is seen at last for only what it is. And now it cannot fail to disappear, for now there is an empty place made clean and ready. Where destruction was perceived the face of Christ appears, and in that instant is the world forgot, with time forever ended as the world spins into nothingness from where it came.[23]

The Course may seem complex because of the many terms it uses, but it's really very simple. In fact, the seeming complexity of the Course can be simplified to the expression of two "shifts." The first is the shift from false perception to true perception:

This is the shift that true perception brings: What was projected out is seen within, and there forgiveness lets it disappear. For there the altar to the Son is set, and there his Father is remembered. Here are all illusions brought to truth and laid upon the altar. What is seen outside must lie beyond forgiveness, for it seems to be forever sinful. Where is hope while sin is seen as outside? What remedy can guilt expect? But seen within your mind, guilt and forgiveness for an instant lie together, side by side, upon one altar. There at last are sickness and its single remedy joined in one healing brightness. God has come to claim His Own. Forgiveness is complete.[24]

If you deny guilt within and send guilt to others, you will preserve the belief in your own guilt that you have denied. You will have to withdraw all projections of guilt toward others, before you can let go of your own belief in your guilt. Yet withdrawing projection by itself is not enough. There is still the danger that you will hold on to the guilt that was formerly denied and projected because, "…as blame is withdrawn from without, there is a strong tendency to harbor it within."[25] However, seeing guilt within can be a wonderful opportunity to let "guilt and forgiveness for an instant lie together, side by side, upon one altar," as is described in the quotation above. This comparison of the two seen together allows the false perception of guilt to be replaced by the true perception of forgiveness.

The first shift that reveals the simplicity of the Course is the shift from false perceptions to true perceptions, from unloving thoughts to loving thoughts, from guilt to forgiveness that reveals holiness. This first shift must occur before you are ready for the second shift. The second shift that reveals the Course's simplicity is the shift from true perception to knowledge, which is facilitated by seeing the face of Christ. In seeing the vision of your own true nature, you allow God to take the final step. "Yet the last step must be taken by God, because the last step in your redemption, which seems to be in the future, was accomplished by God in your creation."[26] In the final step by God, He gives Himself to you as He did in your creation, and this brings about the complete unification of your mind, which you had hidden, but not lost.

> And what He [God] gives is always like Himself. This is the purpose of the face of Christ. It is the gift of God to save His Son. But look on this and you have been forgiven.
>
> How lovely does the world become in just that single instant when you see the truth about yourself reflected there. Now you are sinless and behold your sinlessness. Now you are holy and perceive it so. And now the mind returns to its Creator; the joining of the Father and the Son, the Unity of unities that stands behind all joining but beyond them all. God is not seen but only understood. His Son is not attacked but recognized.[27]

In seeing of the face of Christ, you accept your reality in God. You see no separation between God and yourself and likewise see no separation between your brothers in the One Christ of which you are a part. Thus you accept the knowledge of Heaven and take your place in the Sonship.

> And now God's *knowledge*, changeless, certain, pure and wholly understandable, enters its kingdom. Gone is perception, false and true alike. Gone is forgiveness, for its task is done. And gone are bodies in the blazing light upon the altar to the Son of God. God knows it is His Own, as it is his. And here They join, for here the face of Christ has shone away time's final instant, and now is the last perception of the world without a purpose and without a cause. For where God's memory has come at last there is no journey, no belief in sin, no walls, no bodies, and the grim appeal of guilt and death is there snuffed out forever.

O my brothers, if you only knew the peace that will envelop you and hold you safe and pure and lovely in the Mind of God, you could but rush to meet Him where His altar is. Hallowed your Name and His, for they are joined here in this holy place. Here He leans down to lift you up to Him, out of illusions into holiness; out of the world and to eternity; out of all fear and given back to love.[28]

There may be some uncertainty in your mind about whether you will ever manage to let go of all illusions and accept your place in Heaven. But the Course maintains that there is no uncertainty in God, and so, you can trust in His Will being accomplished. "Have faith in only this one thing, and it will be sufficient: God wills you be in Heaven, and nothing can keep you from it, or it from you."[29] Your going Home is only a matter of time, and time itself is just another illusion.

C. How much does God Love you?

Before the separation, you were aware of your oneness with God in Heaven, and your knowledge gave you certainty about the meaning of love. "In Heaven, where the meaning of love is known, love is the same as union."[30] But when you made your ego, you lost your awareness of love.

Remember that the Holy Spirit is the Answer, not the question. The ego always speaks first. It is capricious and does not mean its maker well. It believes, and correctly, that its maker may withdraw his support from it at any moment. If it meant you well it would be glad, as the Holy Spirit will be glad when He has brought you home and you no longer need His guidance. The ego does not regard itself as part of you. Herein lies its primary error, the foundation of its whole thought system.

When God created you He made you part of Him....You made the ego without love, and so it does not love you. You could not remain within the Kingdom without love, and since the Kingdom *is* love, you believe that you are without it. This enables the ego to regard itself as separate and outside its maker, thus speaking for the part of your mind that believes *you* are separate and outside the Mind of God. The ego, then, raised the first question that was ever asked, but one it can never answer. That question, "What are you?" was the beginning of doubt.[31]

The Course maintains that the separation is only an illusion that never happened at all since it was not created by God in His Reality. You have not lost your "whole mind," which contains your knowledge of God. But you have temporarily lost your awareness of your true nature in Him.

> The Holy Spirit...speaks for God. He tells you to return your whole mind to God, because it has never left Him. If it has never left Him, you need only perceive it as it is to be returned. The full awareness of the Atonement, then, is the recognition that *the separation never occurred.* The ego cannot prevail against this because it is an explicit statement that the ego never occurred.
>
> The ego can accept the idea that return is necessary because it can so easily make the idea seem difficult. Yet the Holy Spirit tells you that even return is unnecessary, because what never happened cannot be difficult.[32]

The fact that the separation never happened will only be fully realized *after* you wake up in Heaven to the knowledge that your perfect union with God has never been interrupted. Until that time, you will have to take the necessary steps to help you wake up from your dream of separation.

You will only prolong your dream if you listen to the ego, because it will encourage you to think like this: "You think you are the home of evil, darkness and sin. You think if anyone could see the truth about you he would be repelled, recoiling from you as if from a poisonous snake."[33] Yet you will have to let go of thoughts of sin to welcome back the memory of God. "The holy place on which you stand is but the space that sin has left. And here you see the face of Christ, arising in its place. Who could behold the face of Christ and not recall His Father as He really is?"[34]

For you to wake up, you will have to listen to the Holy Spirit, Who will tell you this: "You cannot be anywhere God did not put you, and God created you as part of Him."[35] The Holy Spirit calls you to awaken in God.

> The Holy Spirit is the spirit of joy. He is the Call to return with which God blessed the minds of His separated Sons. This is the vocation of the mind. The mind had no calling until the separation, because before that it had only being, and would not have understood the Call to right thinking. The Holy Spirit is God's Answer to the separation; the means by which the Atonement heals until the whole mind returns to creating.
>
> The principle of Atonement and the separation began at the same time. When the ego was made, God placed in the mind the Call to joy. This Call is so strong that the ego always dissolves at Its sound. That is why you must choose to hear one of two voices within you. One you made yourself, and that one is not of God. But the other is given you by God, Who asks you only to listen to it. [36]

To wake up you will need to overcome a paradox: Love is our true nature, yet you do not currently know what love is. "You do not know the meaning of love, and that is your handicap."[37] Yet God's Love will awaken you because of "…the powerful attraction of the Father for His Son. There is no other love that can satisfy you, because there *is* no other love. This is the only love that is fully given and fully returned. Being complete, it asks nothing. Being wholly pure, everyone joined in it has everything."[38]

There is a temptation to define love, even God's Love, by limiting its meaning. In this changing world of form, it seems there are many types of love. But the Course refutes the idea there are different kinds of love.

> Perhaps you think that different kinds of love are possible. Perhaps you think there is a kind of love for this, a kind for that; a way of loving one, another way of loving still another. Love is one. It has no separate parts and no degrees; no kinds nor levels, no divergencies and no distinctions. It is like itself, unchanged throughout. It never alters with a person or a circumstance. It is the Heart of God, and also of His Son.
>
> Love's meaning is obscure to anyone who thinks that love can change. He does not see that changing love must be impossible. And thus he thinks that he can love at times, and hate at other times. He also thinks that love can be bestowed on one, and yet remain itself although it is withheld from others. To believe these things of love is not to understand it. If it could make such distinctions, it would have to judge between the righteous and the sinner, and perceive the Son of God in separate parts.
>
> Love cannot judge. As it is one itself, it looks on all as one. Its meaning lies in oneness. And it must elude the mind that thinks of it as partial or in part. There is no love but God's, and all of love is His. There is no other principle that rules where love is not. Love is a law without an opposite. Its wholeness is the power holding everything as one, the link between the Father and the Son which holds Them both forever as the same.
>
> No course whose purpose is to teach you to remember what you really are could fail to emphasize that there can never be a difference in what you really are and what love is. Love's meaning is your own, and shared by God Himself. For what you are is what He is. There is no love but His, and what He is, is everything there is. There is no limit placed upon Himself, and so are you unlimited as well.[39]

Of all the ideas I have shared in this meditation manual, the most important one is that God's Love for you is the source of your true nature:

"...you *are* love. Love is your power, which the ego must deny."[40] When the ego is successful in denying the love within you, you will not have faith in yourself. "You have so little faith in yourself because you are unwilling to accept the fact that perfect love is in you."[41] Since the ego denies the love God gives to you, you need to find ways to remind yourself of the truth that His Love is within you as your true nature.

Your meditation time can be a helpful reminder of God's Love within you. Your brothers can also remind you of God's Love. "When you meet anyone, remember it is a holy encounter."[42] You can send God's Love to your brothers and receive love from them in miracles of love. To perform miracles of love requires that you accept the Atonement for yourself, which is the same as accepting perfect love. "Perfect love is the Atonement."[43]

Every morning, when my alarm clock rings, the first words out of my mouth are: "Father, thank you for loving me. Let your love flow through me to bless all my brothers and sisters." This is one way I remind myself of God's Love. In addition, before my afternoon sitting meditation, I spend about twenty minutes lying down and listening to instrumental music while feeling God's Love. The vast majority of people all over the world spend their lives searching for love and not finding it without ever realizing that God's Love permeates them from within and is their own true nature. Nevertheless, I can in no way be self-satisfied about my own understanding since there is a natural limit to human understanding in regard to answering the question: "How much does God love you?"

> You cannot understand how much your Father loves you, for there is no parallel in your experience of the world to help you understand it. There is nothing on earth with which it can compare, and nothing you have ever felt apart from Him resembles it ever so faintly.[44]

You and I will truly understanding the depth of God's Love only after we wake up in our true Home in Heaven. Although our worldly perception and human understanding are limited now, we can still open ourselves to the experience of divine love. At this point in my own life, I live mostly as a hermit. Although I do not have much of an outer social life, the Course repeatedly reminds me that I am never alone. Meditation is normally thought of as a solitary practice, but it is in reality always a communion. I practice meditation four times every day, yet I do not perceive this as a self-imposed discipline. Instead, these times of apparent aloneness are actually my true social life and my joy. In these periods of silence, I find my true connection with all my brothers and sisters in Christ and with my Father, Who loves me. I hope this book will serve to help you to meditate at a deeper level and to find spiritual nourishment by joining in communion with God and with your brothers and sisters in Christ. This time of rest in the Arms of the Father is the best gift you can give to others and to yourself.

1. T-9.III.6:7-8, 7:1-2, p. 167
2. Luke 23:34
3. T-9.VII.3:1-10, 4:1-4, 5:1-3, pp. 175-176
4. T-10.I.2:1, 3-6, p. 182
5. T-12.VI.7:7, p. 229
6. T-8.IV.8:6-7, p. 146
7. T-8.III.5:1-12, 6:1, pp. 142-143
8. T-14.VII.7.1-9, pp. 288-289
9. T-18.I.8:2, pp. 373-374
10. W-108.5:1, p. 195
11. W-109.5:1-8, 8:1-3, pp. 197-198
12. T-12.VIII.7:10-11, p. 235
13. T-18.IX.9:1-7, 10:1-7, pp. 395-396
14. T-14.V.2:1-8, 11:1-9, pp. 282, 284
15. T-30.V.7:5, p. 637
16. T-20.VI.12.5-11, p. 439
17. T-26.III.2:1-14,3:1-6, 4:1-10, pp. 546-547
18. T-12.VI.5:4-9, 6:1-4, pp. 228-229
19. T-12.VI.6:5-7, 7:1-7, p. 229
20. M-5.II.4:5-6, p. 18
21. T-12.VIII.7:9-11, 8:1-9, p. 235
22. T-20.VIII.5:7-9.pp. 442-443
23. C-4.3:1-9, 4:1-5, 5:1-11, pp. 85-86
24. C-4.6:1-10, p. 86
25. T-11.IV.4:5, p. 201
26. T-13.VIII.3:2, p. 258
27. C-3.7:5-8, 8:1-6, p. 84
28. C-4.7:1-7, 8:1-3, p. 84
29. T-13.XI.7:1, p. 268
30. T-16.V.3:7, p. 341
31. T-6.IV.1:1-7, 2:1, 3-7, pp. 100-101
32. T-6.II.10:4-8, 11:1-2, p. 98
33. W-93.1:1-2, p. 161
34. T-26.IV.3:1-3, p. 548
35. T-6.II.6:2, p. 92
36. T-5.II.2:1-5, 3:1-6, p. 75
37. T-12.V.6:1, p. 226
38. T-15.VII.1:1-5, p. 317
39. W-50.1:1-7, 2:1-6, 3:1-8, 4:1-5, p. 230
40. T-7.VI.4:6-7, p. 174
41. T-15.VI.2:1, p. 314
42. T-8.III.4:1, p. 142
43. T-2.VI.7:8, p. 30
44. T-14.IV.8:4-5, p. 281

EPILOGUE

After completing this manuscript and before having it published, I had determined that there was no need for an epilogue, but the following dream changed my mind:

I was sitting at a table and meeting many new friends, in addition to becoming reacquainted with old friends. It was a celebration of some kind with prizes being awarded, not just to some of the participants, but to everyone. (Looking back on this now, my interpretation is that this meeting was symbolic of a heavenly celebration.)

One man pointed to a woman and said that she had great spiritual potential, but she had turned out to be only "average" because she was just a speech therapist. I told him that in my opinion this speech therapist was actually fulfilling her spiritual potential *by being average*. I do not remember the exact words I used in the dream, but the idea was that the word "average" means not superior and not inferior. Being average means being equal. God wants us to realize our equality with all our brothers and sisters and also wants us to express our equality with others by serving them in whatever vocation we are called to express ourselves. Since this woman was called to be a speech therapist, her work was certainly a service to others and pleasing to God.

Suddenly I woke up from the dream and began writing an epilogue to my just completed meditation book. In the epilogue I noted that it is important to have an inner prayer life, such as the kind recommended in my book. But I also wrote in the epilogue that the ideas of equality and service, as highlighted in the dream, are universally important for everyone to learn and apply to daily life.

Then a strange thing happened—I "really" woke up! When I previously woke up, I was actually still dreaming. My waking up in the dream and the writing of my epilogue seemed real to me in the dream, but these were only dream events. After truly waking up from my dream of writing an epilogue, I wrote this epilogue that you are reading now.

The dreaming of waking up and then really waking up is a reminder that life is a series of waking-up experiences in which what seems to be real at one time is proven to be unreal by a greater awakening. One day in the future, after an average life of equality and service, you and I will "really, really, really" wake up in the Reality of Heaven and find out that we had only been dreaming of this world of appearances.

www.ingramcontent.com/pod-product-compliance
Lightning Source LLC
Chambersburg PA
CBHW060447090426
42735CB00011B/1937